C++
ALL-IN-ONE
FOR
DUMMIES®
2ND EDITION

by John Paul Mueller and Jeff Cogswell

WILEY

Wiley Publishing, Inc.

D0117030

C++ All-in-One For Dummies, 2nd Edition

Published by
Wiley Publishing, Inc.
111 River Street
Hoboken, NJ 07030-5774

www.wiley.com

Copyright © 2009 by Wiley Publishing, Inc., Indianapolis, Indiana

Published by Wiley Publishing, Inc., Indianapolis, Indiana

Published simultaneously in Canada

WILEY

About the Authors

John Paul Mueller is a freelance author and technical editor. He has writing in his blood, having produced 83 books and over 300 articles to date. The topics range from networking to artificial intelligence and from database management to heads-down programming. Some of his current books include a C# design and development guide and a complete reference for LINQ. John also writes about areas other than programming, such as Exchange Server. His technical editing skills have helped more than 63 authors refine the content of their manuscripts. John has provided technical editing services to both *Data Based Advisor* and *Coast Compute* magazines. He's also contributed articles to the following magazines: *CIO.com*, *DevSource*, *InformIT*, *Informant*, *DevX*, *SQL Server Professional*, *Visual C++ Developer*, *Hard Core Visual Basic*, *asp.netPRO*, *Software Test and Performance*, and *Visual Basic Developer*.

When John isn't working at the computer, he enjoys spending time in his workshop crafting wood projects or making candles. On any given afternoon, you can find him working at a lathe or putting the finishing touches on a bookcase. He also likes making glycerin soap, which comes in handy for gift baskets. You can reach John on the Internet at JMueller@mwt.net. John is also setting up a Web site and blog at http://www.johnmuellerbooks.com/. Feel free to look and make suggestions on how he can improve it.

Jeff Cogswell is an experienced teacher, writer, and software engineer. He worked 15 years as a professional programmer and software engineer before leaving that field to write and edit full time. He is currently a senior editor with Ziff Davis Enterprise, writing and editing for DevSource.com and eWEEK.com. His skills include C++ as well as several other languages and platforms, such as C# and ASP.NET. In his spare time he enjoys traveling, playing the guitar, and photography.

Dedication

This book is dedicated to Dr. Michael Shonfeld and Nurse Barb McPherson, two special people who may not always get the thanks they deserve. Thank you so much for your help in returning my beautiful wife to me!

— John Paul Mueller

To my wife Angie, and my son Dylan, with love.

— Jeff Cogswell

Authors' Acknowledgments

I really appreciate Jeff having the confidence to work with me on this book. We've known each other for quite some time now and I always enjoy working with him.

Russ Mullen deserves thanks for his technical edit of this book. He added greatly to the accuracy and depth of the material that you see here. I appreciated the time he devoted to checking my code for accuracy. As I wrote this book, I also spent a good deal of time bouncing ideas off Russ, who is a valuable aid to any author.

Matt Wagner, my agent, deserves credit for helping me get the contract in the first place and taking care of all the details that most authors don't consider. I always appreciate his assistance. It's good to know that someone wants to help. Matt also helped me through an extremely difficult time in my life — this book is a tribute to the perseverance of us both.

A number of people read all or part of this book to help me refine the approach, test the examples, and generally provide input that every reader wishes they could have. These unpaid volunteers helped in ways too numerous to mention here. I especially appreciate the efforts of Eva Beattie, Osvaldo Téllez Almirall, and all the others who provided input on C++. I'd like to thank each person who wrote me with an idea by name, but there are simply too many.

Finally, I would like to thank Katie Feltman, Susan Pink, Blair Pottenger, and the rest of the editorial and production staff for their assistance in bringing this book to print. It's always nice to work with such a great group of professionals.

— John Paul Mueller

I first want to thank John Mueller for taking up such a difficult task and writing the second edition of this book, as well as his wife, Rebecca, for staying strong. Also, another book brings another big thanks to my agent and friend, Margot Hutchison, for the usual great work. And special thanks to Katie Feltman and editors Susan Pink and Blair Pottenger for their meticulous work in making this project reality. Finally, thanks to my wife Angie and my son Dylan for supporting me in all my projects.

— Jeff Cogswell

Publisher's Acknowledgments

We're proud of this book; please send us your comments through our online registration form located at http://dummies.custhelp.com. For other comments, please contact our Customer Care Department within the U.S. at 877-762-2974, outside the U.S. at 317-572-3993, or fax 317-572-4002.

Some of the people who helped bring this book to market include the following:

Acquisitions, Editorial, and Media Development

Project Editor: Susan Pink
  (Previous Edition: Pat O'Brien)

Acquisitions Editor: Katie Feltman

Copy Editor: Susan Pink
  (Previous Edition: Diana Conover, Barry Childs-Helton)

Technical Editor: Russ Mullen

Editorial Manager: Jodi Jensen

Media Development Project Manager: Laura Moss-Hollister

Media Development Assistant Project Manager: Jenny Swisher

Media Development Associate Producer: Shawn Patrick

Sr. Editorial Assistant: Cherie Case

Cartoons: Rich Tennant
  (www.the5thwave.com)

Composition Services

Project Coordinator: Kristie Rees

Layout and Graphics: Carl Byers, Ronald Terry

Proofreaders: David Faust, Amanda Graham, John Greenough, Christine Sabooni

Indexer: Broccoli Information Management

Special Help: Marilyn Hummel

Publishing and Editorial for Technology Dummies

  Richard Swadley, Vice President and Executive Group Publisher

  Andy Cummings, Vice President and Publisher

  Mary Bednarek, Executive Acquisitions Director

  Mary C. Corder, Editorial Director

Publishing for Consumer Dummies

  Diane Graves Steele, Vice President and Publisher

Composition Services

  Debbie Stailey, Director of Composition Services

Contents at a Glance

Table of Contents

Introduction

C++ is the language of the millennium. Why is C++ so popular?

+ It's powerful. You can write almost any program in it.

+ It's fast, and it's fully *compiled*. That's a good thing.

+ It's easy to use — if you have this book.

+ It's object-oriented. If you're not sure what that is, don't worry. You can find out about it by reading this very book you're holding.

+ It's portable. Versions are available for nearly every computer.

+ It's standardized. The American National Standards Institute and the International Standards Organization both approve an official version.

+ It's popular. More people are using C++ because so many other people use it.

Sure, some people criticize C++. But most of these people don't truly understand C++ or are just having a bad day. Or both.

No Experience Necessary

This book is not a big rant about C++. Rather, it's a hands-on, roll-up-your-sleeves book, where you will truly *learn* C++.

At the very beginning, we start you out from square one. We don't assume *any* programming experience whatsoever. Everybody has to start somewhere. You can start *here*. Not to brag, but you are in the hands of highly successful C++ users who have shown thousands of people how to program, many of whom started out from square one.

Great for Advanced Folks, Too!

You already know C++? This book is great for you, too, because although we start discussing C++ from the beginning, we go *all the way through it*.

Want to know how to derive a nontemplatized class from a class template? Check out Minibook IV, Chapter 5.

Want to see how to create an observer pattern in C++? See Minibook II, Chapter 6.

Want to find out the difference between deque and vector in the C++ Standard Library? Look at Minibook IV, Chapter 6.

Want to know how to make a class persistent? Minibook V, Chapter 5.

Want to know about the Boost library, the library that has added more to the Standard Template Library (STL) than just about any other source? Check out Minibook VI, Chapters 3 and 4. If you use C++ and don't use Boost, you're really missing out!

For All Computers

Although one of the minibooks in *C++ All-in-For Dummies,* 2nd Edition is devoted to Microsoft-specific topics (Minibook VII on Visual Studio 6.0 and MFC), the rest of the book is for C++ *in general.* C++ is now standardized, and you can use the information in this book for many different platforms. We wrote the samples on Microsoft Windows. But for most samples, we used a compiler called *CodeBlocks* that runs on almost every computer (Windows, Linux, and Macintosh). It doesn't matter which computer you're using!

All the code in this book, except that in Minibook VII, has been tested on both Windows and Linux. (Don't let the Windows screenshots fool you; CodeBlocks works great on just about any platform.) Even though we didn't have a Macintosh available for testing at the time of writing, we're sure that the examples will also work fine in the Macintosh environment if you use the CodeBlocks compiler as described in the book.

Conventions

As a guy who is about to head off to a convention, we thought it would be appropriate to share with you some tidbits about the conventions in this book. However, this time we're talking about the text format.

✦ When you see something in monofont, it's a computer word that you *type into the computer or read on a computer screen.* If we discuss a computer term but it's not a word that you *type* into the computer, it is in the usual font. You also see monofont for URLs and e-mail addresses.

✦ When you see something in **bold**, you can type it into the computer.

✦ When you see a word in *italics*, it's new and we explain its meaning.

✦ When code is on a single line, it looks like this:

```
MyClass.IsCool();
```

✦ When code appears on multiple lines, it looks like this:

```
MyClass.IsCool();
AndSo.IsYours();
```

✦ Lengthy program listings have a header and a listing number. These are entire programs you can type, and they should run as-is. However, you save time and effort by using the code supplied as part of the book's CD. The CD also contains a full copy of the Windows version of CodeBlocks.

Organization

This book is divided into seven minibooks. Each one covers a separate, broad topic, with chapters devoted to individual subtopics.

You can either read this book cover to cover or you can look topics up and treat the book as a reference guide — whichever works best for you. Keep it on your shelf and have it ready to grab when you need to look something up. Here are the seven minibooks and what they cover:

✦ **Minibook I, Introducing C++:** Here, we start at the very beginning, showing you all you need to know to get up and running with C++. This is also the minibook that gets you started with CodeBlocks. If you don't have a copy of CodeBlocks installed on your system, you definitely want to start by reviewing Chapter 1.

✦ **Minibook II, Understanding Objects and Classes:** In this minibook, we present all the latest information about object-oriented programming and how to use various diagrams to design your programs. Advanced readers should especially appreciate this minibook because we cover such topics as UML and design patterns. But beginners should be able to understand it, too, and find out how to get up to speed with the best software engineering ideas around.

✦ **Minibook III, Fixing Problems:** Here, we show you how to debug your programs by using a special program called a debugger. If you're a beginner, this minibook gets you started on fixing the problems in your code. If you're advanced, you can appreciate how we use the debugger supplied with CodeBlocks to locate any problems your application might have.

✦ **Minibook IV, Advanced Programming:** In this minibook, we move through advanced C++ topics. After reading Minibook IV, the beginners become intermediate or advanced programmers, and the intermediate and advanced programmers can master the C++ language.

✦ **Minibook V, Reading and Writing Files:** Yes, this entire minibook is devoted to the issues of reading and writing files. In this book, we cover stream programming, which is a special way C++ treats files.

✦ **Minibook VI, Advanced C++:** This advanced minibook includes two chapters each on STL (Standard Template Library) and Boost. The STL chapters describe some of the advanced classes not used in other areas of the book and help you create your own templates. The Boost library chapters describe all the tools found in Boost, show how to build a full set of libraries for your own use, and then provide an overview of some interesting Boost capabilities. You really miss out on a lot if you don't at least visit this minibook after you build your programming skills.

✦ **Minibook VII, Building Applications with Microsoft MFC:** Many, many people use the native code capabilities of Microsoft Visual C++. In this minibook, we show you how to create workspaces and projects in Visual Studio 2008. We then show you how to write software for Windows by using Microsoft Foundation Classes. This minibook doesn't include any discussion of Microsoft's latest offering for C++ developers, the .NET Framework.

Icons Galore

Hey, what would a *For Dummies* book be without all the great icons? These are the second best part, next to the cartoons. Here's what they mean:

We have lots of experience as both C++ programmers and instructors, and so we pass on tidbits here and there to help you along.

This icon identifies things you may want to remember to do when you're programming.

These icons can save you a lot of headaches. They're suggestions to help keep you from really messing up — the way that we probably already did. You won't cause the computer to explode if you skip these, but you'll sleep better knowing you won't accidentally lose all your code or overwrite a file.

Computer people often search for extra knowledge, even when it may not be necessary. These Technical Stuff paragraphs are fascinating information, primarily to cover your serious curiosity.

What's Next?

If you want to e-mail us, please do! We have special e-mail addresses for you:

```
readers@jeffcogswell.com
jmueller@mwt.net
```

We both get a lot of e-mail from readers, so we can't always reply, nor can we promise to have a quick-and-easy answer. Please don't be offended if you don't hear back. You can check out our Web sites, `www.jeffcogswell.com` and `http://www.johnmuellerbooks.com/`.

Jeff has a newsletter that dishes out tips and tricks for C++ programmers. Send an e-mail to `newsletter@jeffcogswell.com`, and you'll get back an e-mail on how to subscribe. We think that you'll be pleased with the information. Oh yes, and it's free.

In the pages that follow you will see just how easy it is to program in C++. When you finish this book you will have a full mastery of the language!

Book I

Introducing C++

The 5th Wave · By Rich Tennant

Okay—you were right, I was wrong. F5 opens the garage door, and F6 backs the car out.

Contents at a Glance

Chapter 1: Creating a First C++ Program

In This Chapter

✔ Organizing your programs into projects

✔ Typing code into the code editor

✔ Writing a program that writes to the screen

✔ Doing basic math

✔ Running your program

*I*t's your lucky day. You have decided to learn the most popular programming language on the planet. From the biggest skyscrapers housing huge Fortune-500 companies all the way down to the garages with the self-starting kids grinding out the next generation of software, people are using C++. Yes, there are other languages, but more programmers use C++ than any other language. In this chapter, you start right out writing a C++ program.

For this chapter we use *CodeBlocks,* a full-featured system for easily creating C++ code — and it's free! You don't need to spend hundreds of dollars to get up and running. Instead, you can install it right from the CD-ROM that came with this book. However, you're not limited to using CodeBlocks. Several other tools are available to you, but in this chapter we suggest working with CodeBlocks because it's easy to use. In fact, you may find you like it so well that you wind up almost neglecting the other tools.

We assume that you have already installed CodeBlocks. If you have not, you can find instructions in Appendix B.

Creating a Project

Creating a computer program is usually a bigger job than you'd want to organize in your head. Program code is saved in files much like the documents in a word processor. But programs often have more than one source-code file. At big companies in big buildings in big cities, some programs are *really big* — hundreds of source-code files for just one program.

Understanding projects

Projects can contain a lot of source code. To keep all that source code together, programmers use a file that manages it all called a *project*. Projects have a few key elements:

✦ A set of source-code files

✦ (Optionally) Resource information such as icons and sound files

✦ A description of how to compile (build) the application

✦ Integrated Development Environment (IDE) settings that tell how to set up the editor you use to write the application

✦ Some general descriptions of the program being built, such as its name and what type of program it is

By *type of program*, we don't mean "word processor" or "really cool earth-shattering software," even if that's what your program is. We use *type* to mean your program's overall relationship with other programs:

✦ Does this program run by itself?

✦ Does this program add to or extend the functionalities of another program (such as Microsoft Excel)?

✦ Does this program serve as a *library* (a bunch of code that you make available to another program)?

All this information, along with your source-code files, represents a project.

In the CodeBlocks tool, you create a new project each time you start work on a new program. You provide a little information about the program you're working on, and then you begin writing your code. All the code for your program goes in one place — stored in the project.

This book presents a lot of sample programs, so you may want to create a directory (or folder) on your hard drive to house all the programs you create as you work through this book. Call it MyProjects, or something specific like CPPAllInOne, or whatever you prefer.

Defining your first project

To create a new project in CodeBlocks, start CodeBlocks and choose File⇨New⇨Project or click Create a New Project on the Start Here page that appears when you start the program. A dialog box appears, as shown in Figure 1-1.

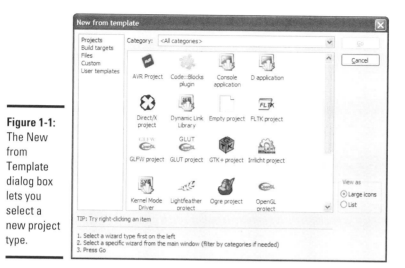

Figure 1-1:
The New
from
Template
dialog box
lets you
select a
new project
type.

When you create a project in CodeBlocks, you choose from a list of several types of programs. They're shown as icons in the New from Template dialog box. The following list shows some program types:

✦ **Win32 GUI Project:** This is a standard Windows program that includes, well, a window. You know the kind; it usually has a menu across the top and something inside it that you can either click or type into.

✦ **Console Application:** This is a program that gets a paltry Console window instead of a regular Windows window. *Console* refers to a window with a command prompt (folks who recall the old days before Windows call it a *DOS box*). You can remember this because you may have to "console it" for being just a boring DOS-type text window with a prompt.

✦ **Static library:** A *static library* is a set of C++ code that you use later in another project. It's like making a really great marinade that you won't use up today. You'll use some of it tomorrow and some of it after that. Same with a C++ library.

✦ **Dynamic Link Library:** A Dynamic Link Library (DLL) is kind of like a static library except it stays separated from the main program and gets its own file with a `.DLL` extension.

Programmers have a bad habit of dropping DLLs in your `c:\windows\system` or `c:\windows\system32` directory when you probably don't really want them there. That's why you've likely heard of DLLs before.

✦ **Empty project:** A blank project that's as clean as a blank sheet of white typing paper, ready for you to fill 'er up.

What about all of those other projects?

CodeBlocks supports a host of other application types. This book doesn't discuss them because they won't add to your initial understanding of C++ programming. However, these other projects are valuable in the right environment. For example, the GIMP Tool Kit Plus (GTK+) Project relies on a graphical user interface designed for the X Windowing system (see more at `http://www.gtk.org/`).

You'll find that CodeBlocks uses a considerable number of acronyms and abbreviations for project and resource names without defining any of them. We define all the acronyms that we employ on first use in the book. However, some of these acronyms and abbreviations go on and on. For example, you might wonder about the GIMP part of the GTK+ definition. GIMP stands for GNU Image Manipulation Program. Of course, now you need to know GNU, which stands for Gnu's Not Unix. Okay, now that we've exhausted that bit of fun, if you ever do run across an interesting acronym or abbreviation, you can always get it defined for you on the Acronym Finder Web site (`http://www.acronymfinder.com/`). The bottom line is that you need to research both projects and resources before you use them.

Frankly, it's kind of a pain to use an empty project, because you have to tweak and set a bunch of things. So we never use this option.

For the samples in this chapter, create a Console Application. Follow these steps:

1. **In the New from Template dialog box, click the Console Application icon found in the Projects tab. Click Go.**

   You see the Welcome page of the Console Application wizard.

2. **Click Next.**

   The wizard asks which language you want to use.

3. **Highlight C++ and click Next.**

   You see a list of project-related questions, as shown in Figure 1-2. These questions define project basics, such as the project name.

4. **Type a name for your project in the Project Title field.**

   The example uses `SayHello` as the project title. Notice that the wizard automatically starts creating an entry for you in the Project Filename field.

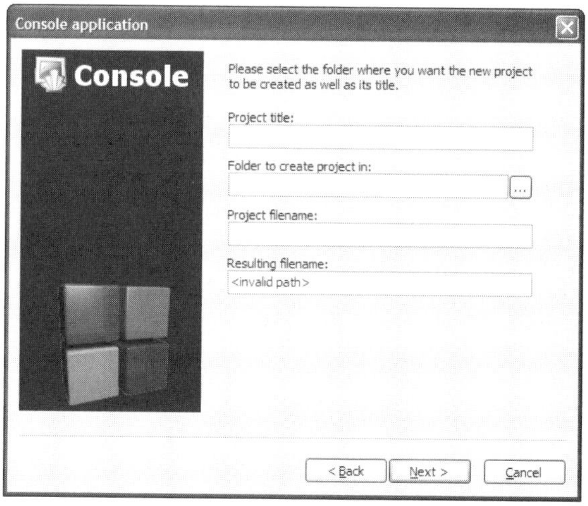

Figure 1-2:
Provide
the name
of your
project for
CodeBlocks.

5. **Type a location for your project in the Folder to Create Project In field.**

The example uses `FirstProject` as the folder name. You can also click
the ellipses button next to the Folder to Create Project In field to use the
Browse for Folder dialog box to locate the folder you want to use. Notice
that the wizard completes the entry in the Project Filename field.

If you made a folder to house all the programs for this book (as suggested in the "Understanding projects" section of the chapter), put your
`FirstProject` folder in the folder for the book. Make sure you're inside
the folder you just created.

6. **(Optional) Type a project filename in the Project Filename field.**

7. **Click Next.**

You see the compiler settings shown in Figure 1-3. Most of the projects
in this book use the default compiler settings. However, if you look
at the Compiler drop-down list, you see that CodeBlocks supports a
number of compilers and you can add more to it. The other settings control the creation and location of a Debug version (the version you use
for finding problems in your code) and a Release version (the version
that you send to a customer) of the application.

8. **Change any required compiler settings and click Finish.**

The wizard creates the application for you. It then displays the
CodeBlocks IDE shown in Figure 1-4 with the project loaded.

Figure 1-3:
Tell
CodeBlocks
where to
place the
Debug and
Release
versions
of your
application.

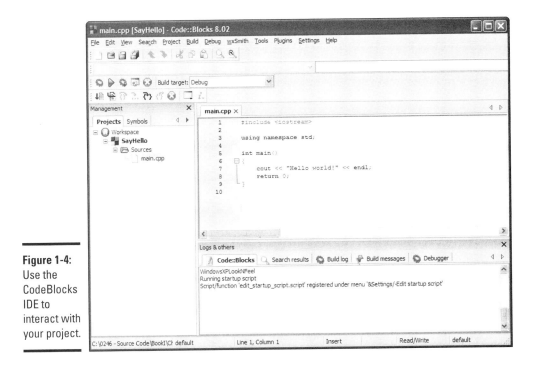

Figure 1-4:
Use the
CodeBlocks
IDE to
interact with
your project.

The project window is organized side by side:

✦ The left side is an Explorer view (called a *tree view*), which represents your project. At the top of the tree view is a workspace — the essential unit of a project. Below the workspace is the name of your project.

Underneath that are the components of your project. In this case, only one component exists so far: the source-code file whose filename is `main.cpp`. Remember that to program in C++, you enter code into a source-code file; this file, called `main.cpp`, is such a file for your `SayHello` project.

✦ The right side (which actually takes up about three-quarters of the screen) is the source-code file itself.

This part works much like a word processor or an e-mail editor, and you can type the code into the window. You notice that you already have some code there — a sort of starter code that came into being when you chose Console Application and created the project.

✦ At the bottom of the display are a number of status windows. The Code::Blocks window tells you how the wizard created your application. Don't worry about these windows for right now. You see them in action as the book progresses.

Building and executing your first application

Okay, it's time to work with your first application. Use the following steps to save the file, build the program (make it into an executable that Windows can use), and execute the program.

1. **Save the code file by choosing File⇨Save Everything.**

Saving the files ensures you have a good copy on disk should something go wrong. For example, you could completely crash the IDE if your application does the wrong thing.

2. **Choose Build⇨Build or press Ctrl+F9.**

This action creates the executable file. Building the code converts words you understand into code that Windows understands. Notice that CodeBlocks automatically selects the Build Log window for you and you see the steps that CodeBlocks takes to create your application. At the end of the process, you should see 0 Errors, 0 Warnings as the output.

3. **Choose Build⇨Run or press Ctrl+F10.**

An output window like the one shown in Figure 1-5 opens and you see your first program execute.

4. **Press Enter to stop program execution.**

The program window disappears and you see the CodeBlocks IDE again.

Well that wasn't interesting, was it? But that's okay! The program starts out in a basic situation: We have a console window, and then when the program is finished doing whatever it must do, it shows the message `Press any key to continue` — and when you do so, the program ends.

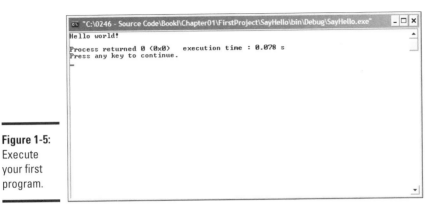

Figure 1-5:
Execute
your first
program.

Typing the Code

The right-hand 75 percent or so of the CodeBlocks window is called the *code editor;* it's where you type and change your code. Of all the tasks we just mentioned, the nearest equivalent to using the CodeBlocks code editor is composing an e-mail message.

Word movement and selection actions look a bit strange on the screen. They ignore some characters, such as *braces* — the curly characters { and }. (We recently added this to our "Mysteries of Life" on the refrigerator.)

The code editor works like the editor in an e-mail message. You can

✦ Type code.

✦ Move the *cursor* with the arrow keys (up, down, left, right) to the position where you want to type. The *cursor* is the little blinking vertical bar that shows where your text goes when you type. Some folks call it a *caret* or an *insertion point.*

✦ Click where you want to type. Use the mouse to point where you want to type, then click the mouse button. The cursor jumps to the spot where you click.

✦ Select text to delete or change. You can select text in either of two ways:

   • Point with the mouse at the first or last character you want to select; then hold down the mouse button while you drag the mouse.

   • Move the cursor to the first or last character you want to select; then hold down the Shift key while you press the arrow keys.

✦ Scroll the text up and down (vertically) or left and right (horizontally) with the scrollbars. The scrollbars work only when there is more text than you can see in the window, just like most other places in the Windows and Macintosh worlds. You can scroll up and down (if there's enough text in the editor) by using Ctrl+↑ and Ctrl+↓ key combinations.

✦ Scrolling changes only what you *see.* You must use the mouse or the arrow keys to *select* what you see.

After you play around a bit with the editor, you can use Table 1-1 to do a few of your favorite tasks. (Of course, if you're new to programming, you may not know yet whether these are your favorites — but they will be soon. Trust me.)

Table 1-1	Navigation and Edit Commands
Command	*Keystroke or Action*
Cursor movement	↑, ↓, ←, or →, Home, End
Moving from word to word	Ctrl+← or Ctrl+→
Selecting with the mouse	Click the mouse in the text, and while the mouse button is down, drag the mouse
Selecting with the cursor	Shift+↑, Shift+↓, Shift+←, or Shift+→
Selecting the next word	Shift+Ctrl+→
Selecting the previous word	Shift+Ctrl+←
Selecting everything	Ctrl+A
Going to the top	Ctrl+Home
Going to the bottom	Ctrl+End

Starting with Main

When a computer runs code, it does so in a step-by-step, line-by-line manner. But your code is organized into pieces, and one of these pieces is called the `main` *function,* or simply `main`. `main` is the part that runs *first.* `main` tells the computer which *other* parts of the program you want to use. `main` is the head honcho, the big boss.

How does the computer know what is `main`? You type lines of code between the *brace* characters, { and }. Here is the default program that CodeBlocks produces when you create a Console Application project.

```
int main()
{
    cout << "Hello world!" << endl;
    return 0;
}
```

The word main is required, and it tells the computer where main is. You might also see main shown as:

```
int main(int argc, char *argv[])
```

Don't worry about the words around main for now. You discover what these words mean later in the chapter. For now, all you need to know is that every C++ program has a main function.

The computer performs the code line by line. If a line is blank, the computer just goes to the next line. When you write lines of code, you are instructing the computer to do something (which is why some people refer to lines of code as *instructions*).

Showing Information

Ready to type some code and try it out? Let's do it! This code will open the famous console window and write some words to it.

First, make sure that you still have the CodeBlocks tool open and the SayHello project open, as in this chapter's preceding examples. *If not, follow these steps:*

1. Start CodeBlocks if it's not already running.

You see a Start page for the CodeBlocks IDE.

2. Click the SayHello.cbp project found in the Recent Projects list.

CodeBlocks opens the project for you.

If the main.cpp code isn't showing in the right 75 percent of the window, click main.cpp in the tree view on the left. It will immediately open. (If you don't see the tree view, click the little tab at the top that says Projects; it's next to a tab that says Symbols.)

Follow these steps carefully. Make sure that you type everything exactly as given here:

1. Position the cursor on the line with the opening brace.

In this case, that's line 6. You can see the line number on the left side of the code editor.

2. Press the Enter key.

The cursor should be in the fifth column. If it isn't — if it stays in the first column — then press the spacebar four times.

3. **Type the following line of code exactly as it appears here.**

   Put no spaces between the two less-than (<) symbols. Make sure that you remember the final semicolon at the end. Here's the line:

   ```
   cout << "Hello, I am your computer talking." << endl;
   ```

4. **Delete the line of code that looks like this:**

   ```
   cout << "Hello world!" << endl;
   ```

In the end, your code will look like the following example (the new line that you typed is shown here in bold):

```
#include <iostream>

using namespace std;

int main()
{
    cout << "Hello, I am your computer talking." << endl;
    return 0;
}
```

If you don't type your code correctly, the computer can tell you. This step *compiles* the program: the computer makes sure that what you wrote is okay and then translates it into a *runnable* program. (Don't worry too much about what that means. For now just think of it as making sure that your program is okay. Appendix A gives you the whole story about compiling.)

To find out whether your program is good to go, choose Build⇨Build.

If all is well, you see a window in the lower-left of the main CodeBlocks window with the really happy message, 0 errors, 0 warnings. A message like You rock! might be nicer, but 0 errors, 0 warnings ain't all that bad, we guess.

If you didn't type the line correctly, all is not lost because the computer will tell you what you did wrong. In this case, you will see something like what is shown in Figure 1-6. A list with columns appears at the bottom of your screen.

Figure 1-6: CodeBlocks tells you about errors in your program.

```
Logs & others                                                                    ☒
  Code::Blocks   Search results   Build log   Build messages   Debugger      ◁ ▷
File                     Line   Message
                                === SayHello, Debug ===
C:\0246 - Source Code\B...       In function 'int main()':
C:\0246 - Source Code\B...  7    error: 'couts' was not declared in this scope
C:\0246 - Source Code\B...  7    warning: unused variable 'couts'
                                === Build finished: 1 errors, 1 warnings ===
```

✦ The leftmost column shows the name of the file where the error was. In this case the error was in `main.cpp`, the only file we were working on.

✦ The second column shows the *line number* of the problem (in this case, 7).

✦ The third column of the list makes a basic attempt to tell us what we did wrong, like this:

```
error: 'couts' was not declared in this scope
```

When the compiler doesn't recognize a word, it says that the word is `not declared`. In other words, the compiler doesn't know what `couts` is. (The word should be `cout`.)

If we want to see the problem, we can point at the error report line and double-click. The bad line appears in the code editor, with a little red box next to the line. The line is also highlighted. As soon as we press an arrow key, the highlight vanishes.

Thus, if we press the → key a few times and get to the word `couts` and then delete the letter `s`, we can try again. If we choose Build⇨Build, this time we see the happy message `0 errors, 0 warnings`. Excellent!

No errors means that the program is good enough to run. So run it!

Choose Build⇨Run. A console appears with text that looks like this:

```
Hello, I am your computer talking.

Process returned 0 (0x0)   execution time : 0.015 s
Press any key to continue.
```

See what happened? There is now a message that says, `Hello, I am your computer talking`. Apparently the thing you typed caused that message to appear. (Go ahead and press Enter to close the console.)

And in fact, that's exactly what happened. That's how you make a message appear on the console screen. The steps look like this:

1. Type `cout`.

   Although `cout` looks like it's pronounced "cowt," most programmers say "see-out." Think of it as shorthand for *console output*. (But don't type *console output* in its place, because the compiler won't accept that.)

2. After the word `cout`, type a space and then type two less-than signs (make sure to leave that one space before them).

   These less-than signs just mean, *the thing that follows is going to appear on the console*. The thing that follows, you will notice, is in double quotes. That's the way the computer knows where it starts and ends. The words and stuff inside these double quotes is called a *string* because it's a bunch of letters strung together. (I'm not making this up.) The computer knows where the string starts because there's a double quote, and it knows where the string ends because there's a double quote. The computer doesn't display these two sets of double quotes when the program runs.

Then some weirdness follows. There's another set of less-than signs, which means you want to write more to the console. But what follows? It's endl. Notice this is not in quotes. Therefore we are not saying that we want the strange barely pronounceable word "endl" to appear on the screen. Instead, we're using a special notation that tells the computer that we want to start fresh on the next line. And if you look at the output, you'll notice that the words that follow (the message about pressing the any key) are, indeed, on the next line. Note that endl is pronounced "end-el."

So that's not so bad after all. Let us recap:

✦ The word cout means you want to write to the console.

✦ The << symbols together (with no space between them!) mean the thing that follows is what you want to write.

✦ After the << symbol, you tell the computer what you want to write. It can either be a string of letters, symbols, and other characters (all inside quotes), or it can be the word endl.

✦ You can put multiple items in a row and have them appear on the console that way, provided you start the line with cout and precede each item with the << symbols.

Oh, and if you have a sharp eye, you may notice one more thing we haven't mentioned yet: we included a semicolon at the end of the line. In C++, every line must end with a semicolon. That's just the way it's done.

Statements in C++ end with a semicolon.

It's not quite accurate to say that *every* line must end with a semicolon. You can break any line into multiple lines. The computer doesn't mind. We could just as easily have written our line as the following two lines:

```
cout << "Hello, I am your computer talking."
<< endl;
```

This is fine, provided that you don't split any individual word (such as cout and endl), or the << symbols, or the string. In effect, anyplace you have a space occurring "naturally" in the code (for example, between I and am), you can start a new line if you want. Then, when the whole *statement* is finished, you end with a semicolon. Think of the semicolon as a signal to the computer that the old statement is finished.

Doing some math

You can get the computer to do some math for you; you can use the same `cout` approach we described in the preceding section, and you throw in some numbers and arithmetic symbols.

Although addition uses the familiar plus sign (+) and subtraction uses the familiar minus (–) sign, multiplication and division use symbols you might not be familiar with. To multiply, you use the asterisk (*); to divide, you use the forward-slash (/).

Table 1-2 shows the math symbols.

Table 1-2	Math Symbols
Symbol	*Function*
+	Addition (plus)
–	Subtraction (minus)
*	Multiplication (times)
/	Division (divided by)

Yep, it's now math-with-weird-symbols time. Continue with the source code you already have. Click somewhere on the line you typed — you know, the one that looks like this:

```
cout << "Hello, I am your computer talking." << endl;
```

Press End so the cursor moves to the end of the line. Then press Enter so you can start a new line in between the `cout` line and the line that starts with the word `return`.

Whenever you want to insert a line between two other lines, the easiest way to get it right is to go to the first of those two lines, press End, and then press Enter. This will insert a new blank line in the right place.

After you press Enter, you will notice that something happened: The cursor is not at the start of the newly inserted line; instead, there are four spaces and it's indented flush with the other lines. That's not a mistake. Believe it or not, it's a serious lifesaver. Well, okay, maybe not a lifesaver, but it's almost as good as those little candies that everybody loves. The reason is that often you indent your code (this particular code is indented four spaces); if you're typing lots of code, it's a bummer to have to type four spaces (or press the Tab key) every time you start a new line. So CodeBlocks considerately (and automatically) does the indentation for you.

If, for some reason, your code didn't automatically indent and the cursor is loitering at the beginning of the line, the auto-indent feature is not turned on. It *should* be on by default, but if it isn't, here's how to turn it on:

1. **Choose Settings⇨Editor Options.**

The Configure Editor dialog box appears.

2. **Make sure that the Tab Indents check box is selected, then click OK.**

3. **Once back in the code, press Backspace to delete your new line, then try pressing Enter again.**

Behold! The code automatically indents.

4. **After your new blank line appears and indents itself, type the following:**

```
cout << 5 + 10 << endl;
```

The beginning and the end of this line are just like those of the line you typed earlier. The difference is the middle — instead of typing a string, you type a math problem: 5 plus 10. Note that we put spaces around the 5, around the +, and around the 10 — but not between the 1 and 0. If you put a space there, the computer gets confused (it doesn't know that you meant to write a single two-digit number). When you're finished, your code should look like the following code snippet (here the new line you typed is shown in bold):

```
#include <iostream>

using namespace std;

int main()
{
    cout << "Hello, I am your computer talking." << endl;
    cout << 5 + 10 << endl;
    return 0;
}
```

5. **Save your work by choosing File⇨Save Everything.**

Instead of choosing File⇨Save Everything, you can recognize that the only thing that changed is the source-code file you're currently working on. If you see the blinking cursor in the code editor, you know that the code editor is active. If not, click somewhere in your code to activate the editor. When you see the blinking cursor, press Ctrl+S. This saves your file.

In the computer world, there's an adage that goes something like this: "Save early, save often." Get in the habit of pressing Ctrl+S every so often. You won't wear out your hard drive, and the keyboard is pretty durable. Every time we type a few lines of code, we press Ctrl+S. Before we compile, we press Ctrl+S. When we're feeling paranoid that the last Ctrl+S didn't stick, we press Ctrl+S. When we're stuck at a traffic light, we press Ctrl+S.

Now you can tell the computer to compile your code. If you haven't saved it, do so now by pressing Ctrl+S. Then choose Build⟹Build. If you typed everything correctly, you should see the magical message 0 errors, 0 warnings appear in the Build Log window. But if not, don't worry; you can easily fix it. Look at your code and find the difference between the line we wrote earlier and your code. Here it is again, just for safe measure:

```
cout << 5 + 10 << endl;
```

There is a space after cout, a space after <<, a space after 5, a space after +, a space after 10, and a space after <<. And there is a semicolon at the end. Make sure that these are all correct.

Then when you successfully compile and see the happy message 0 errors, 0 warnings, you are ready to run your program. Choose Build⟹Run.

A console window opens, and you should see the following:

```
Hello, I am your computer talking.
15

Process returned 0 (0x0)   execution time : 0.000 s
Press any key to continue.
```

Notice the second line is the answer to the math problem 10 + 5. That means the computer knows how to do math, more or less correctly. (Okay, it had *better be* correct, or we're going to demand a refund from our teachers.)

Ordering the operations

If you want, you can play around with some more complicated problems. For example, you can try something like this:

```
cout << 5 + 10 / 2 * 3 + 25 << endl;
```

What do you think the answer will be? The answer depends on computer rules for the *order* in which it performs math problems. These are called *orders of operation.* Multiplication and division take precedence over addition and subtraction. Therefore, the computer does all the multiplication and division first from left to right; then it does the addition and subtraction from left to right. Figure 1-7 shows the order in which the computer does this particular math problem.

Going overboard

The computer actually has various limits, including when it comes to math. If you try something like this

```
cout << 8762547892451 * 10 / 2 * 3 + 25 << endl;
```

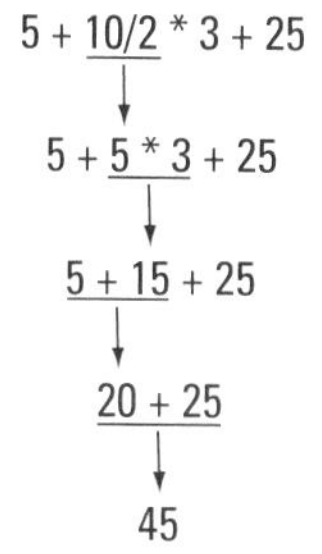

$$5 + \underline{10/2} * 3 + 25$$
$$\downarrow$$
$$5 + \underline{5 * 3} + 25$$
$$\downarrow$$
$$\underline{5 + 15} + 25$$
$$\downarrow$$
$$\underline{20 + 25}$$
$$\downarrow$$
$$45$$

Figure 1-7:
The computer likes to use orders of operation.

an error message shows up in the error window when you try to compile:

```
error: integer constant is too large for "long" type
```

This message is bad. The reason is that you've gone beyond the limits of what this style of math enables you to do. So be careful.

You can also go too big when you run your program — and (unfortunately) you won't know it. For example, the line

```
cout << 12345 * 12345 * 12345 * 12345 * 12345 << endl;
```

will *compile* correctly — but (aieee!) shows the following result:

```
253233049
```

Nope, it's not correct. Not even a good guess. So the moral here is mainly to use the approach to coding shown in this section only when you're using basic math and don't have to juggle really big numbers. If you're getting over five or six digits, you're getting into too-big territory.

The greatest positive number you can use is 2,147,483,647. The greatest negative number is –2,147,483,647. However, if you're willing to stick to only positive numbers and 0, the computer can make some adjustments inside and handle a higher positive number. In that case, your numbers can range from 0 to 4,294,967,295.

Pairing the parentheses

If you want to get around the order in which the computer does its math, you can add parentheses. For example, if you use the following line, the computer does the final operation (+) before it does the others:

```
cout << 5 + 10 / 2 * (3 + 25) << endl;
```

Whereas previously, without the parentheses, this thing came out to be 45, now it comes out to be 145. First the computer does the 3 + 25 to get 28. Then it begins with the multiplication and division, from left to right. So it takes 10 / 2 to get 5, then multiples that by (3 + 25), or 28, to get 140. Then it starts with the addition and subtraction from left to right. So it adds 5 to this to get the final number, 145.

Tabbing your output

Just as you can write a string of letters and numbers to the console, you can also write a tab. For example, take the following line from your program

```
cout << "Hello, I am your computer talking." << endl;
```

and change it to the line shown in bold in the following code:

```
#include <iostream>

using namespace std;

int main()
{
    cout << "Hello\tI am your computer talking." << endl;
    return 0;
}
```

In the preceding code, we replaced the comma and space with a backslash and then a lowercase t. (We also removed the extra line about math, just in case you tried the math things from the preceding section.) But when you compile and run this program (remember to *compile it first!*), it won't print exactly what's in the double quotes. Here's what you see:

```
Hello   I am your computer talking.
```

The extra space in the displayed line is a *tab space,* just as if you had pressed the Tab key while typing this. (Is that slick, or what?)

There's a complication to using the backslash: You can't just type a backslash or a double quote and expect to see it on the screen. A couple of workarounds will show the actual characters:

✦ Really want to display a backslash, not a special character? Use a backslash followed by another backslash. (Yes, it's bizarre.) The compiler treats only the *first* backslash as special. When a string has two backslashes in a row, the compiler treats the second backslash as, well, a backslash.

For example, the following line of code has *two* backslashes:

```
cout << "\\tabc" << endl;
```

The following text shows up at the console:

```
\tabc
```

✦ If a string starts with a double quote and ends with a double quote, how in the world would you actually *print* a double quote? Type a backslash, then a double quote, as in the following code:

```
cout << "Backslash and double quote equal \" in C++." << endl;
```

When that code runs in a program, you see this on the screen:

```
Backslash and double quote equal " in C++.
```

C++ programmers use the term *escape-sequence* to refer to any special character in a string that starts with a backslash. This is an outdated bit of vocabulary — maybe not as old as "methinks," but it does date back to the original C language of the 1970s. Back then, you made special characters appear on console screens by first pressing the Esc key.

Let Your Program Run Away

The word *execute* refers to running your program, but you need to compile (or *build* using the CodeBlocks terminology) the program before you run it. The compilation process transforms your program into an *executable file.* An executable file is a special type of file that contains a program that you can run on your computer. When you run your word processor program, you run an executable file containing the word processor program.

After the computer compiles (builds) your program, it performs a step called *linking.* People often refer to these two steps together as simply *compiling.* Indeed, in this book, we often use the term to mean both steps together. If you're curious about what goes on here, take a look at Appendix A. It has a section devoted to the compiling and linking processes.

Whenever you want to run your program, you first compile it, and then you run it. If you make more changes to your program, you must compile it again before running it. Otherwise, the executable file won't have your changes.

Because you almost always use Build and Run in sequence, the kind people who built CodeBlocks included a special menu item called Build and Run on the Build menu. The computer first compiles your code, then it immediately runs the program if there are no errors. If there are errors, the compiler doesn't run the program, and the errors are reported as usual.

We almost always use the Build and Run option, rather than clicking Build and then Run separately.

Sometimes the old-fashioned approach is more efficient: When we compile and run our programs, we use shortcut keys. It takes a bit of extra time to grab the mouse, move the pointer to a menu, and so on. Instead, we press F9 to compile.

Table 1-3 lists keyboard shortcuts for compiling.

Table 1-3	Keyboard Shortcuts for Compiling and Running
Action	*Keyboard Shortcut*
Build	Ctrl+F9
Run	Ctrl+F10
Build and run	F9

Chapter 2: Storing Data in C++

In This Chapter

- ✔ Using storage bins called variables
- ✔ Working with integer variables
- ✔ Using character variables
- ✔ Manipulating strings
- ✔ Using Boolean variables
- ✔ Using conditional operators
- ✔ Reading from the console

*W*e all love to store things away. Our closets are a perfect example of a place to store things. We have boxes in there that we have not opened in years. Perhaps we inadvertently created a time capsule. Or just a fire hazard. When you program a computer, you can also store things away. Most people know that computers have two kinds of memory: memory inside the chips and memory in the hard drive. But most people use the term *memory* in reference to the memory chips; the other is just referred to as the hard drive. When you type a business letter in a word processor, the letter is stored in the memory. After you choose File⇨Save, the letter gets stored to the hard drive, but as long as you still have it open in the word processor, it's generally still in memory.

The best way to think of memory is as a set of storage bins, much like the ones in the closet that we are afraid of. When you write a computer program, you reserve some storage bins, and you give each storage bin a name. You also say what type of thing can go inside the storage bin. The technical term for such a storage bin is a *variable*.

In this chapter, we show you how you can use these storage bins in your programs.

The programs in this and the remaining chapters work with the free compiler included on this book's CD-ROM. You can also use any other compiler, such as the C++ compiler supplied with Visual Studio. In this chapter, we're assuming that (by now) you know how to use the compiler of your choice. Chapter 1 shows you how to use CodeBlocks; to find out more about CodeBlocks see Appendix B.

Putting Your Data Places: Variables

When you write a program, you specify that you want to make use of one or more storage bins called *variables*. You can put different kinds of things in these storage bins. The difference with these computer storage bins and those in your closet, however, is that each computer storage bin can hold only *one thing at a time*.

You can put many different types of things into your variables, too. For example, you can put numbers in a storage bin, or you can put a string in a storage bin. Minibook I, Chapter 1 advises that a *string* is simply a bunch of letters, numbers, or other characters all strung together. As for numbers, they can either be *integers* (which are positive whole numbers, negative whole numbers, and 0) or they can be numbers with a decimal point, such as 3.11 or 10.0, which (for various reasons) are called *floating-point numbers*.

The term *floating-point number* means a number that has a decimal point and something to the right of the decimal point (even if it's just a 0). When you see the term *floating point*, you can remember what it means by the word *point* in its name. Think of *decimal point*.

If you are already familiar with the term *variable* from other fields, be careful that you do not apply their definitions here. Although similar, some significant differences are involved. For example, in algebra, a variable represents an unknown quantity, and you can solve for a variable. But in programming, it's simpler than that: A *variable* is simply a storage bin with an associated name.

Creating an integer variable

In your C++ program, you can easily write a line of code that creates a variable. Although what you're doing at that point is just writing code (and the variable won't actually get created until you run the program), people often refer to this process as *creating a variable*. When we are working with another programmer that we like, we will often say, "*We'll* go ahead and make a variable." What we're really doing is writing code that tells *the computer* to go ahead and make the variable. And of course, the computer won't actually make the variable until the program runs. If, on the other hand, we're working with a programmer we don't like, we probably won't say anything at all.

A variable has three aspects, as shown in Table 2-1.

Table 2-1	**A Variable Has Three Aspects**
Aspect	*What It Means*
Name	The name you use in your program to refer to the variable
Type	The type of information that the variable can hold
Value	The actual thing that the storage bin holds

The following list describes the items in Table 2-1 in more detail.

✦ **Name:** Each variable must have a name. In your program, you refer to the variable by this name. For example, you may have a variable called `count`, and you may have a variable called `LastName`. Or you could have a variable called `MisterGates`.

✦ **Type:** When you create a variable, you must specify the type of information the variable can hold. For example, one variable may hold an integer, and another variable may hold a single character. After you pick a type for the variable in your program, you can put only things of that type into the variable.

✦ **Value:** At any given moment, a variable holds a single value. For example, an integer variable might hold the number `10`, and a character variable might hold the character `a`. In your program, you can store something in a variable, and later you can store something else in the variable. When you store something else, the variable forgets what was previously inside it. So in this sense, you can think of a computer as having a one-track mind.

The code in Listing 2-1 demonstrates how to create a variable. This is a full program that you can run.

Listing 2-1:   Creating a Variable

```
#include <iostream>

using namespace std;

int main()
{
    int mynumber;
    mynumber = 10;
    cout << mynumber << endl;
    return 0;
}
```

Take a careful look at Listing 2-1. Remember that the computer starts with the code inside the braces that follow the word `main`, and it performs the code line-by-line.

The first line inside `main` looks like this:

```
int mynumber;
```

When you declare a variable, the first thing you specify is the type of thing the variable can hold. Here, we used the word `int`. This word is the C++ word for *integer*. Thus, the variable that we're declaring can hold an integer. Next is the name of the variable. This variable is called `mynumber`. Then a semicolon ends the variable declaration.

Notice that, in this line, we have covered two of the three aspects of variables; we have given the variable a name, and we have told the computer what type of thing we want the variable to hold. The order seems a little odd; in C++, we first say the type and then the name. That's just the way it's done in C++, and a good reason stands behind it, which you can read about in "Declaring multiple variables," later in this chapter.

The next line looks like this:

```
mynumber = 10;
```

This puts something in the variable. It puts the number `10` in it. Because we already said that the variable can hold an integer, we're allowed to put in a `10`, because it is an integer. If we had tried to put something other than an integer in it, the compiler would have given us an error. The compiler makes sure that we put into a variable only the type of thing that we said we would. It's good at keeping us in line. And of course, you noticed that the statement ends with a semicolon. In C++, every statement ends with a semicolon.

To put something in a variable, you type the variable's name, an equals sign (surrounded by optional spaces), and the value. You then end the line with a semicolon. This line of code is called an *assignment*. Or you can say that you are *setting* the variable to the value.

The next line is this:

```
cout << mynumber << endl;
```

Minibook I, Chapter 1 describes what this line does. It's a `cout` statement, which means that it writes something on the console. As you can probably guess, this code tells the computer to write the *value* of `mynumber` on the console. It does not write the string *mynumber*. Rather, it writes whatever happens to be stored in the storage bin. The previous line of code put a `10` in the storage bin, and so this line will print a *10* on the console. When you run the program, you see this:

```
10
```

Think of it like this: When you type the variable's name, you are accessing the variable. The exception to this is when the variable's name appears to the left of an equals sign. In that case, you are setting the variable.

You can do two things with a variable:

✦ **Set the variable:** You can set a variable, which means that you can put something inside the storage bin.

✦ **Retrieve the value:** You can get back the value that is inside the variable. When you do so, the value stays inside it; you are not, so to speak, *taking it out.*

When you retrieve the value that is in a variable, you are not *removing* it from the variable. The value is still inside the variable.

Declaring multiple variables

Many years ago, when we first learned the original C programming language (which was the language that served as the predecessor to C++), we thought it odd that we had to first say the type of the variable and then the name. But this actually works out well, because it makes declaring multiple variables of the same type easy. If we want to declare three integer variables in a row, we can do it all in one shot, like this:

```
int tom, dick, harry;
```

This statement declares three separate variables. The first is called `tom`; the second is called `dick`; and the third is called `harry`. Each of these three variables holds an integer. We have not put anything in any of them, so we may follow that with some code to stuff each of them full with a number. For example, this code puts the number 10 in `tom`, the number 20 in `dick`, and the number 3254 in `harry`.

```
tom = 10;
dick = 20;
harry = 3254;
```

When you run your programs, the computer executes the statements in the order that they appear in your code. Therefore, in the preceding code, the computer first creates the three storage bins. Then it puts a 10 inside `tom`. (Now doesn't that sound yummy.) Next, `dick` will get a 20. And finally, `harry` will consume a 3254.

Changing values

Although a variable can only hold one thing at a time, you can still change what the variable holds. After you put something else in a variable, it forgets what it originally had. So when people accuse us of being forgetful, we can just say, "Yes, but you should see that computer we work with all day long!"

You put something new in the variable in the same way you originally put something in it.

Look closely at Listing 2-2. Notice that the first part of the program is just like Listing 2-1. But then we added two more lines (shown in bold) that look pretty much like the previous two: The first one sticks something (20) in the same variable as before, and the next one writes it out to the console.

Listing 2-2:   Changing a Variable

```
#include <iostream>

using namespace std;

int main()
{
    int mynumber;
    mynumber = 10;
    cout << mynumber << endl;
    mynumber = 20;
    cout << mynumber << endl;
    return 0;
}
```

As before, the line where we put something new in the variable follows the same format: There's an equals sign, with the variable on the left and the new value on the right. As described earlier in this chapter, this statement is an *assignment* statement.

When you see a single equals sign by itself, the item on the left side is the variable or item that receives the information that is on the right side.

Setting one variable equal to another

Because you can do only two direct things with variables — put something in and retrieve the value — setting one variable equal to another is a simple process of retrieving the value of one variable and putting it in the other. This process is often referred to as *copying* the variable from one to another.

For example, if you have two integer variables, say start and finish, and you want to copy the value of start into finish, you would use a line of code like the following.

```
finish = start;
```

Although we said *copy the value of* start *into* finish, notice that the first thing we typed was finish, and then the equals sign, and then start. Don't let the language confuse you. The left side of the equals sign is what *receives* the value; it is an *assignment* statement.

When you copy the value of one variable to another the two variables must be the same type. You cannot, for instance, copy the value from a string variable into an integer variable. If you try, the compiler issues an error message and stops.

After the computer runs this copy statement, the two variables hold the same thing. Listing 2-3 is an example of copying one variable to another.

Listing 2-3: Copying a Value from One Variable to Another

```
#include <iostream>

using namespace std;

int main()
{
    int start = 50;
    int finish;
    finish = start;
    cout << finish << endl;
    return 0;
}
```

Initializing a variable

When you create a variable, it starts out as an empty storage bin. Before it can be of much use, you need to put something in it.

If you try to retrieve the contents of a variable before you actually put anything in it, you end up with what computer people fondly call *unpredictable results*. What they really mean to say is, *don't do this because who knows what's in it.* It's kind of like if you go in the attic and you discover the former owners left a big, ominous box. Do you *really* want to look inside it? With variables, the problem you run into is that the computer memory has something stored in that particular place where the variable now sits, and that stored item is probably just some number left over from something else. But you can't know in advance what it is. So always make sure that you place a value inside a variable before you try to retrieve its contents, a process called initializing the variable.

You can initialize a variable in two ways. The first way is by declaring the variable and then assigning something into it, which takes two lines of code:

```
int mynumber;
mynumber = 153;
```

MyThis and MyThat

As you progress through your computer programming life (which is, we hope, in addition to your life as a millionaire), you are likely to notice that, for some reason, some computer programmers seem to favor variable names that start with the word *My*. Other computer programmers despise this practice and completely distance themselves from it. We have seen such computer identifiers as `MyClass`, `MyNumber`, `MyHeight`, `MyName`, `MyCar`, `MyWhatASurprise`, `MyLar`, `MyStro`, and `MyOpic`. Personally, we have no problem using names that start with *My*, especially in training exercises.

But the other way is a bit quicker. It looks like this:

```
int mynumber = 153;
```

This method combines both worlds into one neat little package that is available for you to use whenever you want. You see us initializing variables both ways in this book, depending on how we feel at the moment.

Creating a great name for yourself

Every variable needs to have a name. But what names can you use? Although you are free to use names such as Fred or Zanzibar or Supercount1000M, there are limits to what you are allowed to use.

Although most C++ code is in lowercase, you are free to use uppercase letters in your variable names. However, C++ distinguishes between the two. Therefore, if you have a variable called `count`, you cannot access it later in your program by calling it `Count` with a capital C. The compiler treats the two names as two different variables, which makes C++ *case sensitive*. But on the other hand, please don't use two separate variables in the same program, one called `count` and one called `Count`. Although the compiler doesn't mind, the mere humans that may have to read your code or work on it later might get confused.

Here are the rules you need to follow when creating a variable name:

✦ **Characters:** You can use any uppercase letter, lowercase letter, number, or underscore in your variable names. Other symbols (such as spaces or the ones above the number keys on your keyboard) are not allowed in variable names. The only catches are that

- The first character *cannot* be a number.

- The variable name *cannot* consist of only numbers.

✦ **Length:** Most compilers these days allow you to have as many characters in the variable name as you want. Just to be sure, and to prove we're easily amused, in CodeBlocks we successfully created a variable with a name that was over 1000 characters in length. However, we wouldn't want to have to type that thing over and over. Instead, we recommend keeping your variable names long enough to make sense but short enough that you can type them easily. Most people prefer anywhere from five to ten characters or so.

Examples of acceptable variable names include `Count`, `current_name`, `address_1000`, and `LookupAmount`. Table 2-2 lists some variable names that are not allowed.

Table 2-2	Examples of Bad Variable Names
Bad Variable Name	*Why It's Not Allowed*
12345	It has only numbers (plus it starts with a number, which is wrong as well).
A&B	The only special character allowed is the underscore, _. The & (ampersand) is not allowed.
1abc	A variable name cannot start with a number.

Manipulating Integer Variables

Just like your friends, integer variables can be manipulated. But in this case, manipulation means simply that you can do arithmetic. You can easily do the usual addition, subtraction, multiplication, and division.

In Minibook I, Chapter 1, we introduced the characters that you use for the arithmetic operations. They are

+ + for addition
+ - for subtraction
+ * for multiplication
+ / for division

You can, however, perform another operation with integers, and it has to do with remainders and division. The idea is that if you divide, for example, 16 by 3, the answer in whole numbers is *5 remainder 1.* Another way of saying this is that 16 doesn't divide by 3 evenly, but 3 goes into 16 five times, leaving a remainder of 1. This remainder is sometimes called a *modulus.* Computer people actually have an important reason for calling it *modulus* rather than *remainder,* and that's because people in the computer field like to use confusing terms.

When working with integer variables, remember the two basic things that you can do with variables: You can put something in a variable, and you can retrieve it from a variable. Therefore, when working with an integer variable, the idea is that you can retrieve the contents, do some arithmetic on it, and then print the answer or store it back into the same variable or another variable.

Adding integer variables

If you want to add two integer variables, use the + symbol. You can take the result and either print it or put it back into a variable.

The following example adds two variables (start and time) and then prints the answer to the console. The addition operation is shown in bold.

```cpp
#include <iostream>

using namespace std;

int main()
{
  int start;
  int time;
  start = 37;
  time = 22;
  cout << start + time  << endl;
  return 0;
}
```

This code starts with two integer variables called start and time. It then sets start to 37, and time to 22. Finally, it adds the two variables (to get 59) and prints the results.

In this example, however, the computer doesn't actually do anything with the final sum, 59, except print it. If you want to use this value later, you can save it in its own variable. The following code demonstrates this; the storage operation is shown in bold:

```cpp
#include <iostream>

using namespace std;

int main()
{
  int start;
  int time;
  int total;
  start = 37;
  time = 22;
  total =  start + time;
  cout << total << endl;
  return 0;
}
```

In this code, we declared the integer variable `total` along with the others. Then, after we stored 37 in `start` and 22 in `time`, we added the two and saved the total in the variable called `total`. Then we finally printed the value stored in `total`.

You can also add numbers themselves to variables. The following line adds 5 to `start` and prints the result.

```
cout << start + 5 << endl;
```

Or, you can save the value back in another variable, as in the following fragment:

```
total = start + 5;
cout << total << endl;
```

This adds 5 to `start` and saves the new value in `total`.

When you use such code as `total = start + 5;`, although you are adding 5 to `start`, you are not actually changing the value stored in `start`. The `start` variable itself remains the same as it was before this statement runs. Rather, the computer figures out the result of `start + 5` and saves that value inside `total`. Thus, `total` is the only variable that changes here.

Now here's where things get a little tricky in the logical arena. This might seem a strange at first, but you can actually do something like this:

```
total = total + 5;
```

If you have taken some math courses, you might find this statement a little bizarre, just like the math courses themselves. But remember, `total` is a variable *in computer programming*, and that definition is a bit different from in the math world.

This statement really just means we're going to add 5 to the value stored in `total`, and we'll take the value we get back and store it *back in `total`*. In other words, total will now be 5 greater than it was to begin with.

The following code shows this in action:

```
#include <iostream>

using namespace std;

int main()
{
  int total;
  total = 12;
  cout << total << endl;
  total = total + 5;
  cout << total << endl;
  return 0;
}
```

When you run this program, you see the following output on the console:

```
12
17
```

Notice what took place. First, we put the value 12 inside total and printed the value to the console. Then we added 5 to total, stored that back in total, and printed the new value of total to the console.

Now it's no big secret that we computer people are lazy. After all, why would we own computers if we weren't? And so the great makers of the C++ language gave us a bit of a shortcut for adding a value to a variable and storing it back in the variable. The line

```
total = total + 5;
```

is the same as

```
total += 5;
```

We computer folks also have a special way of pronouncing +=. We say *plus equal*. So for this line, we would say, *total plus equal five.*

Think of the total += 5 notation as simply a shortcut for total = total + 5;.

You can also use the += notation with other variables. For example, if you want to add the value in time to the value in total and store it back in total, you can either do this

```
total = total + time;
```

or you can use this shortcut:

```
total += time;
```

If you are adding just 1 to a variable, you can use an even shorter shortcut. It looks like this:

```
total++;
```

This is the same as total = total + 1;.

Table 2-3 summarizes the different things that you can do that involve the addition of variables.

Table 2-3	Doing Things with Addition
What You Can Do	*Sample Statement*
Add two variables	`cout << start + time << endl;`
Add a variable and a number	`cout << start + 5 << endl;`
Add two variables and save the result in a variable	`total = start + time;`
Add a variable and a number and save the result in a variable	`total = start + 5;`
Add a number to what's already in a variable	`total = total + 5;`
Add a number to what's already in a variable by using a shortcut	`total += 5;`
Add a variable to what's already in a variable	`total = total + time;`
Add a variable to what's already in a variable by using a shortcut	`total += time;`
Add 1 to a variable	`total++;`

Subtracting integer variables

Everything you can do involving addition of integer variables you can also do with subtraction. For example, you can subtract two variables, as shown in Listing 2-4.

And now the answer to The Great Question

In C++, as well as in the original C language upon which C++ is based, the operator ++ adds 1 to a variable. So this finally brings us to a point where we can answer The Great Question: Where did the name C++ come from? When the guy who originally designed C++, Bjarne Stroustrup, needed a name for his language, he decided to look into its roots for the answer. He had based the language on C; and in C, to add 1 to something, you use the ++ operator. And because he felt that he added only 1 thing to the language, he decided to call the new language C++. Okay, that's not quite true; he actually added a great deal to the language. But that entire great deal can be thought of as just one thing made of lots of smaller things. What did he add? The main thing of those smaller things is the capability to do object-oriented programming. That's something we cover in the next chapter. And by the way, the originator of C++, Mr. Stroustrup, is still alive and still doing work for the language at AT&T. You can see his Web page at www.research.att.com/~bs/.

Listing 2-4:   Subtracting Two Variables

```
#include <iostream>

using namespace std;

int main()
{
  int final;
  int time;
  final = 28;
  time = 18;
  cout << final - time << endl;
  return 0;
}
```

When this program runs, the console shows the number 10, which is 28 – 18. Remember that, as with addition, the value of neither `final` nor `time` actually changed. The computer just figured out the difference and printed the answer on the console without modifying either variable.

You can also subtract a number from a variable, and (as before) you still aren't actually changing the value of the variable, as in the following example:

```
cout << final - 5 << endl;
```

You can subtract one variable from another and save the result in a third variable:

```
start = final - time;
```

And you can change the value in a variable by using subtraction, as in the following four sample lines of code. This first subtracts `time` from `start` and saves it back in `start`:

```
final = final - time;
```

Or you can do the same thing by using the shortcut notation:

```
final -= time;
```

Or you can do the same thing with a number:

```
final = final - 12;
```

And (as before) you can alternatively do the same thing with a shortcut:

```
final -= 12;
```

Finally, as with addition, you have a shortcut to a shortcut. If you want to just subtract one, you can simply use two minus signs, as in

```
final--;
```

This is pronounced, *minus minus.*

Multiplying integer variables

To do multiplication in C++, you use the asterisk (*) symbol. Like addition and subtraction, you can multiply two variables, or you can multiply a variable by a number. You can take the result and either print it or save it in a variable.

For example, you can multiply two variables and print the results to the console with the following:

```
cout << length * width << endl;
```

Or you can multiply a variable by a number as in this:

```
cout << length * 5 << endl;
```

And as with addition and subtraction, you can multiply two variables and save the result in a third variable:

```
area = length * width;
```

And you can use multiplication to modify a variable's value, as in the following:

```
total = total * multiplier;
```

or to use the shortcut

```
total *= multiplier;
```

And (as before) you can do the same with just a number

```
total = total * 25;
```

or

```
total *= 25;
```

Dividing integer variables

Although addition, subtraction, and multiplication are pretty straightforward with integer variables, division is a bit trickier. The chief reason is that, with whole numbers, sometimes you just can't divide evenly. It's like trying to divide 21 tortilla chips *evenly* between 5 people. You just can't do it. Either somebody will feel cheated, or everyone will get 4, and 1 chip will be left over for everyone to fight over. Of course, you could break every chip into 5 pieces, and then each person gets $\frac{1}{5}$ of each chip, but then you're no longer working with whole numbers — just a bunch of crumbs.

If we use a calculator and type 21 divided by 5, we get 4.2, which is not a whole number. If we want to stick to whole numbers, we have to use the notion of a remainder. In the case of 21 divided by 5, the remainder is 1, as we figured out with the tortilla chips. The reason is that the highest multiple of 5 in 21 is 20 (since 5 times 4 is 20), and 1 is left over. That lonely 1 is the remainder.

So in terms of strictly whole numbers, the answer to 21 divided by 5 is *4 remainder 1*. And that's how the computer does arithmetic with integers: It gets two different answers: The *quotient* and the *remainder*. In math terms, the main answer (in our example, 4) is called the *quotient*. And what's left over is the *remainder*.

Because two different answers to a division problem may occur, C++ uses two different operators for figuring these two different answers.

To find the quotient, use the slash (/). Think of this as the usual division operator, because when you deal with numbers that divide evenly, this operator gives you the correct answer. Thus, 10 / 2 gives you 5 as you would expect. Further, most people just call this the division operator, anyway.

To find the remainder, use the percent sign (%). This is often called the *modulus operator*.

The sample program in Listing 2-5 takes two numbers and prints their quotient and remainder. Then it does it again for another pair of numbers. The first pair has no remainder, but the second pair does.

Listing 2-5:   Finding Quotients and Remainders

```
#include <iostream>

using namespace std;

int main()
{
  int first, second;
  cout << "Dividing 28 by 14." << endl;
  first = 28;
  second = 14;
  cout << "Quotient  " << first / second << endl;
  cout << "Remainder " << first % second << endl;
  cout << "Dividing 32 by 6." << endl;
  first = 32;
```

```
    second = 6;
    cout << "Quotient  " << first / second << endl;
    cout << "Remainder " << first % second << endl;
    return 0;
}
```

When you run this program, you see the following output:

```
Dividing 28 by 14.
2
0
Dividing 32 by 6.
5
2
```

 Notice, in Listing 2-5, that we used a couple new tricks in addition to (or divided by?) the division tricks. For one, we combined our variable declarations of `first` and `second` variables into one statement. A comma separates the variable names, and we wrote the type (`int`) only once. Next, we combined the output of strings and numbers into a single `cout` statement. We did this for four of the `cout` statements. That's acceptable, as long as you string them together with the `<<` signs between each of them.

You can do all the usual goodies with both the division (/) and remainder (%) operators. For example, you can store the quotient in another variable, as you can with the remainder:

```
myQuotient = first / second;
myRemainder = first % second;
```

And you have shortcuts available, as well:

```
int first = 30;
first /= 5;
cout << first << endl;
```

In this case, `first` becomes 6, because 30 / 5 is 6.

```
int first = 33;
first %= 5;
cout << first << endl;
```

And in this case, `first` becomes 3, because the remainder of 33 divided by 6 is 3.

Characters

Another type of variable you can have is a character variable. A character variable can hold a single — *just one* — character. A *character* is anything that can be typed, such as the letters of the alphabet, the digits, and the other symbols you see on the computer keyboard.

To use a character variable, you use the type name `char`. To initialize a character variable, you put your character inside *single* quotes. (If you use double quotes, the compiler issues an error message.) The following is an example of a character:

```
char ch;
ch = 'a';
cout << ch << endl;
```

The character variable here is called `ch`. We initialized it to the character a, which, you notice, is surrounded by single quotes. We then printed it by using `cout`.

Null character

One important character in the programming world is the *null* character. Deep down inside the computer's memory, the computer stores each character by using a number, and the null character's number is 0. There's nothing to actually see with the null character; we can't draw a picture of it in this book for you to hang on your wall. (Bummer.) All we can do is describe it. Yes, every once in a while computer people have to become philosophers. But the null character is important because it is often used to signify the end of something. Not the end of the world or anything big like that, but the end of some data.

To notate the null character in C++, use \0, as in

```
char mychar = '\0';
```

Nonprintable and other cool characters

In addition to the null character, several other cool characters are available, some that have a look to them and can be printed and some that do not and cannot. The null character is an example of a *nonprintable* character. You can try to print one, but you will get either a blank space or nothing at all, depending on the compiler.

But some characters are special in that they do something when you print, but you can't type them directly. One example is the *newline* character. A newline character symbolizes the start of a new line of text. In all cases, the computer places the *insertion point*, the place where it adds new characters, on the next line. If you are printing some text to the console and then you print a newline character, any text that follows will be on the next line. Most compilers these days start the text at the far left of the next line (column 1), but some compilers start the text in the next column on the next line, as in the following output. In this case, the text appears on the next line, but it starts at column 4, rather than at the far left (column 1).

```
abc
   def
```

What is that symbol?

Never known to turn down the chance to invent a new word, computer people have come up with names for characters that may not always match the names you know. You've already heard the use of the word *dot* for a period when surfing the Internet. And for some characters that already have multiple names, computer folks may use one name and not the other. And sometimes, just to throw you off, they use the usual name for something. The following are some of the names of symbols that computer people like to use:

.   dot (but not period or decimal point)

@   at

&   ampersand (but not and)

pound (but not number sign)

!   bang, but most people still say exclamation point

~   tilde

%   percent

*   star (not asterisk)

(left paren or left parenthesis

)   right paren or right parenthesis

[left square bracket or left bracket

]   right square bracket or right bracket

==   equal-equal (not double equal)

++   plus-plus (not double plus)

−−   minus-minus (not double minus)

/   forward slash

\   backslash

{   left brace or left curly brace or open brace

}   right brace or right curly brace or close brace

^   caret, but a few people say hat (for real — no joke here!)

"   double quote

Here, we printed `abc`, then a newline, and then `def`. Notice that the `def` continued in the same position it would have been had it been on the first line. For the compilers that we use in this book, however, printing `abc`, then a newline, and finally `def` results in this output:

```
abc
def
```

But to accommodate the fact that some other compilers sometimes treat a newline as just that (start a new line but don't go anywhere else), the creators of the computers gave us another special character: *the carriage return*. (Can you hear the crowd say, "ooooh!"?)

The carriage return places the insertion point at the start of the line, but not on a new line. (Which means that if you use just a carriage return on a computer expecting both a carriage return and a newline, you'll overwrite what's already on the line.) That's true with pretty much every C++ compiler.

In Minibook I, Chapter 1, we describe the tab character and other characters that start with a backslash. These are individual characters, and you can have them inside a character variable, as in the following, which prints the letter *a,* then a tab, and then the letter *b.* Notice that, to get the tab character to go into the character variable, we had to use the \ then a t .

```
char ch = '\t';
cout << "a" << ch << "b" << endl;
```

In Minibook II, Chapter 1, we mention that to put a double quote inside a string, you needed to precede the double quote with a backslash so the computer won't think that the double quote is the end of the string. But because a character is surrounded by single quotes, you don't need to do this: You can just put a double quote inside the character, as in the following.

```
char ch = '"';
```

Of course, now that raises an important question: What about single quotes? This time you *do* have to use the backslash:

```
char ch = '\'';
```

And finally, to put a backslash inside a character, you use two backslashes:

```
char ch = '\\';
```

When the compiler sees a backslash inside a string or a character, it treats the backslash as special and looks at whatever follows it. If you have something like '\' with no other character inside the single quotes following it, the compiler thinks the final quote is to be combined with the backslash. And then it moves forward, expecting a single quote to follow, representing the end. Because a single quote doesn't appear, the compiler gets confused and issues an error. Compilers are easily confused. Kind of gives you more respect for the human brain.

Strings

If any single computer word has become so common in programming that most computer people forget that it's a computer word, it would be *string.* Minibook I, Chapter 1 introduces strings and what they are, and it gives examples of them. In short, a *string* is simply a set of characters strung together. The compiler knows the start and end of a string in your code based on the location of the double quotes.

You can create a variable that can hold a string. The type you use is string. The example program in Listing 2-6 shows you how to use a string variable.

Delimiters limit de tokens

When you read an English sentence, you can tell where one word starts and one word ends by looking at the spaces and the punctuation. The same is true in a computer program. Words are normally separated by spaces, but other characters also denote the beginning and end of a word. With a string, this character is the double quote. Such word dividers are called *delimiters* (pronounced dee-LIM-it-ers). And just to make sure we stay confused, computer people use the word *token* to mean the individual words in a program that are set apart by delimiters. However, you won't hear us use that term again in this book, as we prefer the word *word*.

Listing 2-6:   Using the string Type to Create a String Variable

```
#include <iostream>

using namespace std;

int main()
{
  string mystring;
  mystring = "Hello there";
  cout << mystring << endl;
  return 0;
}
```

When you run this program, the string `Hello there` appears on the console. The first line inside `main` creates a string variable called `mystring`. The second line initializes it to `"Hello there"`. The third line prints the string to the console.

Getting a part of a string

Accessing the individual characters within a string is easy. Take a look at Listing 2-7.

Listing 2-7:   Using Brackets to Access Individual Characters in a String

```
#include <iostream>

using namespace std;

int main()
{
  string mystring;
  mystring = "abcdef";
  cout << mystring[2] << endl;
  return 0;
}
```

Those strange # lines

Now for those strange-looking lines that start with a # symbol. In Minibook I, Chapter 5, we talk about how you can divide your code into multiple pieces, each in its own source file. That is a powerful way to create large software programs, because different people can work on the different parts at the same time. But to do so, somehow each file must know what the other files can do. And the way you tell the files about the other files is by putting a line toward the top of your file that looks like this:

```
#include <string>
```

This line means that your program is making use of another file somewhere, and that file has a filename of string. Inside that other file is a bunch of C++ code that essentially gives your program the ability to understand strings.

To see this file in CodeBlocks, right-click the filename and choose Open Include File: <filename> from the context menu. The line

```
#include <iostream>
```

gives your program the ability to write to the console, among other things. And finally, the line

```
#include <stdlib.h>
```

provides some general C++ features that you aren't yet using. As you progress through C++, you discover more lines that you can include at the top of your program, each starting with `#include` and each giving your program more features and capabilities. We use many of these throughout this book. Now how is that for a teaser?

Notice that the seventh line, the cout line, has the word mystring followed by a 2 inside brackets. When you run this program, here's what you see:

```
c
```

That's it, just a letter c, hanging out all by itself. The 2 inside brackets means that you want to take the second character of the string and only that character. But wait! Is c the second character? Our eyes may deceive us, but it looks to us like that's the third character. What gives?

Turns out, C++ starts numbering the positions inside the string at 0. So for this string, mystring[0] is the first character, which happens to be a. And so really mystring[2] gets the *third* character. Yes, life gets confusing when trying to hold conversations with programmers, because sometimes they use the phrase *the third character* to really mean the third position; but sometimes they use it to mean what's really the fourth position. But to those people, the fourth position is actually the fifth position, which is actually the sixth position. Life among computer programmers can be confusing. In general, in this book, we use *fourth position* to really mean the fourth position, which you access through mystring[3]. (The number inside brackets is called an *index*.)

A string is made of characters. Thus, a single character within a string has the type `char`. This means that you can do something like this:

```
string mystring;
mystring = "abcdef";
char mychar = mystring[2];
cout << mychar << endl;
```

In the preceding example, `mychar` is a variable of type `char`. The `mystring[2]` expression *returns* an item of type `char`. Thus, the assignment is valid. When you run this, you once again see the single character in the third position:

```
c
```

Changing part of a string

Using the bracket notation, you can also change a character inside a string. The following code, for example, changes the second character in the string (that is, the one with index 1) from a *c* to a *q:*

```
string x = "abcdef";
x[1] = 'q';
cout << x << endl;
```

This code writes the string `aqcdef` to the console.

Adding onto a string

Any good writer can keep adding more and more letters to a page. And the same is true with the `string` type: You can easily add to it. The following lines of code use the += operator, which was also used in adding numbers. What do you think this code will do?

```
string mystring;
mystring = "Hi ";
mystring += "there";
cout << mystring << endl;
```

The first line declares the string `mystring`. The second line initializes it to `"Hi "`. But what does the third line do? The third line uses the += operator, which appends something to the string, in this case `"there"`. Thus, after this line runs, the string called `mystring` contains the string `"Hi there"`, and that's what appears on the console when the `cout` line runs. The fancy programmer term for adding something to a string is *concatenation.*

You can also do something similar with characters. The following code snippet takes a string and adds a single character onto it:

```
string mystring;
mystring = "abcdef";
mystring += 'g';
cout << mystring << endl;
```

This code creates a string with `"abcdef"`, and then adds a `'g'` character on to the end to get `"abcdefg"`. Then it writes the full `"abcdefg"` to the console.

Adding two strings

You can take two strings and add them together by using a + sign just as you can do with integers. The final result is a string that is simply the two strings pushed together side by side. For example, the following code adds `first` to `second` to get a string called `third`.

```
string first = "hello ";
string second = "there";
string third = first + second;
cout << third << endl;
```

This code prints the value of `third`, which is simply the two strings pushed together, in other words, `"hello there"`. (Notice the string called `first` has a space at its end, which is inside quotes and, therefore, part of the string.)

You can also add a *string constant* (that is, an actual string in your program surrounded by quotes) to an existing string variable, as in the following.

```
string first = "hello ";
string third = first + "there";
cout << third << endl;
```

You may be tempted to try to add two string constants together, like so:

```
string bigstring = "hello " + "there";
cout << bigstring << endl;
```

Unfortunately, this won't work. The reason is that (deep down inside its heart) the compiler just wants to believe that a string constant and a string are fundamentally different. But really, you don't have a good reason to do this, because you could accomplish the same thing with this code:

```
string bigstring = "hello there";
cout << bigstring << endl;
```

You can do a lot more with strings. But first, you need to understand something called a *function*. If you're curious about functions, read Minibook I, Chapter 4, where we cover all the nitty-gritty details.

Deciding between Conditional Operators

One of the most important features of computers, besides allowing you to surf the Web and allowing telemarketers to dial your telephone automatically while you're eating, is the capability to make comparisons. Although this topic may not seem like a big deal, computer technology did not start to take off until the engineers realized that computers could become much more powerful if they could test a situation and do one task or another task, depending on the situation.

You can use many ways to write a C++ program that can make decisions; see Minibook I, Chapter 3, for a discussion about this topic. But one way that is quite handy is through the use of the *conditional operator.*

Think about this process: If two integer variables are equal, set a string variable to the string "equal". Otherwise, set it to the string "not equal".

In other words, suppose we have two `integer` variables, called `first` and `second`. `first` has the value 10 in it, and `second` has the value 20 in it. We also have a `string` variable called `result`. Now, to follow the little process that we just described: Are the two variables equal? No, they are not, so we set `result` to the string `"not equal"`.

Now we do this in C++. Look carefully at the following code. First, we are going to declare our variables `first`, `second`, and `result`:

```
int first = 10;
int second = 20;
string result;
```

So far, so good. Notice that we didn't yet initialize the string variable `result`. But now, we're going to write a single line of code that performs the process we just described. First, look the following over, and see whether you can figure out what it is doing. Look carefully at the variables and what they may do, based on the process we described earlier. Then we explain what the code does.

```
result = (first == second) ? "equal" : "not equal";
```

This is probably one of the more bizarre looking lines of C++ code you'll see in this book. First, we'll tell you what it means. Then we'll break it into parts to show you why it means what it does.

In English, this means `result` will get `"equal"` if `first` is equal to `second`; otherwise it will get `"not equal"`.

So now, break it into two parts. A single equals sign indicates that the left side, `result`, receives what is on the right side. So we need to figure out that crazy business on the right side:

```
(first == second) ? "equal" : "not equal"
```

When you see this strange setup, consider the question mark to be the divider. The stuff on the left of the question mark is usually put in parentheses, as shown in the following:

```
(first == second)
```

This actually compares `first` to `second` and determines whether they are equal. Yes, the code shows *two* equals signs. In C++, that's how you test whether two things are equal.

Now the part on the right of the question mark:

```
"equal" : "not equal"
```

This is, itself, two pieces divided by a colon. This means that if first is indeed equal to second, `result` gets the string `"equal"`. Otherwise, it gets the string `"not equal"`.

So take a look at the whole thing one more time:

```
result = (first == second) ? "equal" : "not equal";
```

And once again, consider what it means: If `first` is equal to `second`, `result` gets `"equal"`; otherwise, it gets `"not equal"`.

Remember that the storage bin on the left side of the single equals sign receives what is on the right side. The right side is an *expression,* which comes out to be a string of either `"equal"` or `"not equal"`.

Now here's the whole program in Listing 2-8.

Listing 2-8:   Using the Conditional Operator to Do Comparisons

```cpp
#include <iostream>

using namespace std;

int main()
{
  int first = 10;
  int second = 20;
  string result;
  result = first == second ? "equal" : "not equal";
  cout << result << endl;
  return 0;
}
```

Boolean variables and conditional operators

You can use Boolean variables with conditional operators. In a conditional operator such as

```
result = (first == second) ?
    "equal" : "not equal";
```

the item (`first == second`) actually works out to be a Boolean value, either `true` or `false`. Therefore, you can break this code up into several lines. We know: Breaking something into several lines seems a little backwards. The reason for breaking code into lines is that sometimes, when you are programming, you may have an expression that is extremely complex, much more complex than `first == second`. As you grow in your C++ programming ability, you start to build more complex expressions, and then you start to realize just how complex they can become. And often, breaking expressions into multiple smaller pieces is more manageable.

To break this example into multiple lines, you can do the following:

```
bool isequal;
isequal = (first == second);
result = isequal ? "equal" :
    "not equal";
```

The first line declares a Boolean variable called `isequal`. The second line sets this to the value `first == second`. In other words, if `first` *is* equal to `second`, then `isequal` gets the value `true`. Otherwise, `isequal` gets the value `false`. In the third line, `result` gets the value `"equal"` if `isequal` is `true`; or `result` gets the value `"not equal"` if `isequal` is `false`.

The reason that this code works is that the item on the left side of the question mark is a *Boolean expression*, which is just a fancy way of saying that the code requires a Boolean value. Therefore, you can throw in a Boolean variable if you prefer, because a Boolean *variable* holds a Boolean *value*.

Telling the Truth with Boolean Variables

In addition to integers and strings, another type in C++ can be pretty useful. This type is called a Boolean variable. Whereas an integer variable is a storage bin that can hold any integer value, a Boolean variable can hold only one of two different values, a `true` or a `false`. Boolean values take their name from George Boole, the father of Boolean logic (you can read about him at `http://en.wikipedia.org/wiki/George_Boole`).

The type name for a Boolean variable is `bool`. Therefore, to declare a Boolean variable, you use a statement like this:

```
bool finished;
```

This declares a Boolean variable called `finished`. Then, you can either put a `true` or a `false` in this variable, as in the following:

```
finished = true;
```

or

```
finished = false;
```

When you print the value of a Boolean variable by using code like the following

```
cout << finished << endl;
```

you see either a `1` for `true` or a `0` for `false`. The reason is that, deep down inside, the computer stores a `1` to represent `true` and a `0` to represent `false`.

Reading from the Console

Throughout this chapter and the preceding chapter, we have given many examples of how to write information to the console. But just writing information is sort of like holding a conversation where one person does all the talking and no listening. Getting some feedback from the users of your programs would be nice. Fortunately, getting feedback is easy in C++.

Writing to the console involves the use of `cout` in a form like this:

```
cout << "hi there" << endl;
```

Reading from the console (that is, getting a response from the user of your program) uses the `cin` (pronounced *see-in,* as in, "When I see out the door, I'm a-seein' the mountain from here") object. Next, instead of using the goofy looking << operator, you use the equally but backwardly goofy > operator.

The << operator is often called an *insertion operator* because you are writing to (or *inserting into*) a *stream,* which is nothing more than a bunch of characters going out somewhere. In the case of `cout`, those characters are going out to the console. The >> operator, on the other hand, is often called the *extraction operator*. The idea here is that you are extracting stuff from the stream. In the case of `cin`, you are pulling letters from the stream that the user is, in a sense, sending into your program through the console.

Listing 2-9 shows how you can read a string from the console.

Listing 2-9: Using the Conditional Operator to Make Comparisons

```
#include <iostream>

using namespace std;

int main()
{
  string name;
  cout << "Type your name: ";
  cin >> name;
  cout << "Your name is " << name << endl;
  return 0;
}
```

When you run this code, you see the console ask you to type your name, then it stops. That's because it's waiting for your input. Notice that the insertion point appears immediately after "Type your name:". That's because the first `cout` statement lacks the usual `endl`. It's normal to leave the insertion point, the cursor, on the same line as the question to avoid confusing the user. Type a name, such as Fred, without spaces and press Enter. The console then looks like this:

```
Type your name: Fred
Your name is Fred
```

The first line is the line you typed (or whatever name you chose to go by), and the second line is what appears after you press Enter.

Notice what happened: When you typed a word and pressed Enter, the computer placed that word in the `name` variable, which is a string. Then you were able to print it to the console by using `cout`.

You can also read integers, as in the following code:

```
int x;
cin >> x;
cout << "Your favorite number is " << x << endl;
```

This sample code reads a single integer into the variable `x` and then prints it to the console.

By default, `cin` reads in characters from the console based on spaces. If you put spaces in your entry, only the first word gets read. `cin` reads the second word the next time the program encounters a `cin >>`.

Chapter 3: Directing Your C++ Program Flow

In This Chapter

✔ Comparing numbers and evaluating other conditions

✔ Doing things based on a comparison

✔ Repeating code a certain number of times

✔ Repeating code while certain things are true

✔ Repeating code that repeats code that . . . well, you get the idea

*A*s you program in C++, many times you need to present the computer with a choice, allowing it to do one thing for one situation and something else in another situation. For example, you may have a program that asks for a user's password. If the password is correct, the program continues; but if the password is incorrect, the program asks the user to reenter the password. After some number of times, usually three, the program performs yet another task when the user enters the incorrect password. Such situations are called *conditions.* In the case of the password, the condition is whether the password matches.

You may also encounter situations where you want several lines of code to run over and over. These are called *loops,* and you can specify conditions under which the loop runs. For example, you may want to check the password only three times; and if the user fails to enter it correctly on the third time you may bar access to the system. This would be a loop, and the loop would run under the condition that a counter has not exceeded the value of 3.

In this chapter, we take you through different ways to evaluate conditions within your programs and cause different sections of code to run based on those conditions. We talk about how you can use C++ commands called *if statements,* which are very similar to what-if situations in real life. And we show you how to use other C++ statements (such as do-while) to performs *loops* (repeating the same program sections a number of times).

To make the explanations clear, this chapter gives you real-world examples that you can feel free to incorporate into your life. The examples usually refer to groups of friends and how you can get money from them. So, you see, the benefits of this chapter are twofold: you find out how to program by using conditions and loops, and you find out how to make money off your unsuspecting friends.

Doing This or Doing That

As you go through life, you're always faced with decisions. For example, when you bought this book, you faced the following decision: Should I buy this really great *For Dummies* book where I'm sure to find out just what I need to know, or should I buy some other book?

When you are faced with a decision, you usually have options that offer different results — say plan A and plan B. Making a decision really means making a choice that results in the execution of either plan A or plan B. For example, if you approach a stoplight that just turned yellow, you must either slam on the brakes or nail the accelerator. If you slam on the brakes, the car will stop just in time (you hope). If you nail the accelerator, the car will speed up, and you'll go sailing through the intersection just before the stop-light turns red (right?). The choice is this: Should I press the brake or the accelerator? And the plan looks like this:

If I press the brake, I will stop just in time.

If I press the accelerator, I will speed through the intersection.

Computers are faced with making decisions too, although their decisions are usually a little less exciting and, we hope, don't yield the possibility of police interaction. And computer decisions are usually simpler in nature. That is, a computer's decisions usually focus around such issues as comparing numbers and strings of characters. For example, you may be writing a computer program for a bank where the user of your program (that is, the bank customer) has a choice of plan A: Making a Deposit or plan B: Receiving a Cash Withdrawal. If the user chooses to make a deposit your program adds to the balance the amount of the deposit. If the user chooses to make a withdrawal, your program instead subtracts the withdrawal amount from the balance.

In C++, decisions usually take the form of an if statement, which is code that starts with the `if` keyword followed by a condition, which is often a numerical condition wherein two numbers are compared, and then two blocks of code appear: one that runs if the condition is satisfied and one that runs if it is not.

Evaluating Conditions in C++

Most decisions that the computer makes are based on conditions evaluated by comparing either two numbers or two characters. For numerical comparisons, you may compare a variable to a number, as in the following statement:

```
x > 10
```

This comparison evaluates whether the variable x is greater than the number 10. If x is indeed greater than 10, the computer sees this condition as true. If x is not greater than 10, the computer sees the condition as not true.

We often use the word *satisfied* with conditions. For the condition x > 10, if x really is greater than 10, we say that the condition is satisfied. It's kind of like, "We're satisfied if our IRS tax refund is five figures." For this, if the condition is x > 9999, and if we really did get that much money back from Uncle Sam, the condition is satisfied (and so are we).

For character comparisons, you may compare if two characters are equal or not, as in the following statement:

```
mychar == 'A'
```

This comparison evaluates whether mychar contains the letter A. Notice that you use two equals signs, not just one. Using just one equals sign would assign the value A to mychar.

To test whether the character is not equal to something, you use the some-what cryptic-looking != operator. Think of the ! as meaning *not,* as in:

```
mychar != 'X'
```

Finding the right C++ operators

Each statement in the previous section uses an *operator* to specify what comparison to make between the numbers or the strings. Table 3-1 shows you the types of operators available in C++ and the comparisons that they help you make in your programs.

Table 3-1	Evaluating Numerical Conditions
Operator	*What It Means*
<	Less than
<=	Less than or equal to
>	Greater than
>=	Greater than or equal to
==	Equal to
!=	Not equal to

Some operators in this table — and how you use them — can be a bit annoying or downright frightening. The following list gives examples:

✦ The operator that tests for equality is *two* equals signs. It looks like this:

```
x == 10
```

When the computer finds this statement, it checks whether x equals 10.

If you put just one equals sign in your statements, most C++ compilers will not give you an error — though a statement like x = 10 is not really a condition! Instead, x = 10 is an *assignment,* setting the variable x to 10. When code contains such a statement, the result of the evaluation is always the same, regardless of what value x has.

✦ The operator that tests for inequality is an exclamation mark followed by an equals sign. For the condition x != 10, the condition evaluates as true only if x is not equal to 10 (x is equal to something other than 10).

✦ When you're testing for greater than or less than conditions, the condition x > 10 is not true if x is 10. The condition x > 10 is true only if x is actually greater than, but not equal to, 10. To also test for x being equal to 10, you have two choices:

• If you're working with integers, you can test whether x > 9. In that case, the condition is true if x is 10, or 11, or 12, and so on.

• You can use the greater-than-or-equal-to operator to x >= 10. This condition also is true if x is 10, 11, and so on.

To test for all numbers greater than or equal to 10, the condition x > 9 works only if you're working with integers. If you're working with floating-point numbers (refer to Minibook I, Chapter 2, for information on the types of numbers you can work with in C++), the statement x > 9 won't work like you want. The number 9.1 is greater than 9, and it's not greater than or equal to 10. So if you really want greater than or equal to and you're not working with integers, use the >= operator.

Combining multiple evaluations

When you make evaluations for program decisions, you may have more than one condition to evaluate. For example, you might say, "If I get a million dollars, or if I decide to go into debt up to my eyeballs, then I will buy that Lamborghini." In this case, you would buy the car under two conditions, and *either* can be true. Combining conditions like this is called an *or situation*: If this is true *or* if that is true, something happens.

To evaluate two conditions together in C++, you write them in the same statement and separate them with the *or* symbol (||), which looks like two vertical bars. Other programming languages get to use the actual word *or,* but C++ uses the strange, unpronounceable symbol that we call *The Operator Previously Known as Or*. The following statement shows it performing live:

```
(i < 10 || i > 100)
```

This condition is not of much use. If you use the *or* operator (||), accidentally ending up with a condition that is *always* true is easy. For example, the condition (x < 100 || x > 0) is always going to be true. When x is -50, it's less than 100, so the condition is true. When x is 500, it's greater than 0, so it's true.

In addition to an *or* situation, you can have something like this: "If I get a million dollars and I really feel bold, then I will buy a Lamborghini." Notice that we're using the word *and*: In this case, you will do it only if both situations are true. (Remember that with *or,* you will do it if either situation is true.) In C++, the *and* operator is *two* ampersands, &&. This makes more sense than the *or* operator, because the & symbol is often associated with the word *and.* The *and* comparison in C++ looks like the following:

```
(i > 10 && i < 100)
```

This example checks whether a number is both more than 10 and less than 100. That would mean the number is in the range 11 through 99.

Combining conditions by using the && and || operators is a use of *logical operators.*

To determine if a number is within a certain range, you can use the *and* operator (&&), as we did earlier in this chapter.

With the *and* operator, accidentally creating a condition that is never true is easy. For example, the condition (x < 10 && x > 100) will never be true. No single number can be both less than 10 and simultaneously greater than 100.

Including Evaluations in C++ Conditional Statements

Computers, like humans, evaluate conditions and use the results of the evaluations as input for making a decision. For humans, the decision usually involves alternative plans of action, and the same is true for computers. The computer needs to know what to do if a condition is true and what to do if a condition is not true. To decide a plan of action based on a condition that your program evaluates, you use an if statement, which looks like this:

```
if (x > 10)
{
    cout << "Yuppers, it's greater than 10!" << endl;
}
```

This translates into English as: If x is greater than 10, write the message "Yuppers, it's greater than 10!"

In an if statement, the part inside the parentheses is called either the *test* or the *condition*. We usually apply *condition* to this part of the if statement and use the word *test* as a verb, as in "I will test whether *x* is greater than 10."

In C++, the condition for an if statement always goes inside parentheses. If you forget the parentheses, you get a compile error.

You can also have multiple plans of action. The idea is simply that if a condition is true, you will do plan A. Otherwise, you will do plan B. This is called an *if-else block*, which we discuss in the next section.

Deciding what if and also what else

When you are writing the code for a comparison, usually you want to tell the computer to do something if the condition is true and to do something else if the condition is not true. For example, you may say, "If I'm really hungry I will buy the Biggiesupersizemondohungryperson french fries with my meal for an extra nickel; otherwise, I'll go with the small." In the English language, you will often see this kind of logic with the *otherwise* word: If such-and-such is true, I will do this; otherwise, I will do that.

In C++, you use the else keyword for the *otherwise* situation. It looks like the following:

```
#include <iostream>

using namespace std;

int main()
{
    int i;

    cout << "Type any number: ";
    cin >> i;

    if (i > 10)
    {
        cout << "It's greater than 10." << endl;
    }
    else
    {
        cout << "It's not greater than 10." << endl;
    }

    return 0;
}
```

In this code, you test whether a number is greater than 10. If it is, you print one message. If it is not, you print a different message. Notice how the two blocks of code are distinct. The first block immediately follows the if statement; it's the code that runs if the condition is true. The next block is preceded by an `else` keyword, and it runs if the condition is not true.

Think carefully about your `else` situation when dealing with numbers. If you are testing whether a number is greater than 10, for instance, and it turns out that the number is not greater than 10, the tendency of most people is to assume it must, therefore, be *less than 10*. But that's not true. The number 10 itself is not greater than 10, but it's not less than 10 either. So the opposite of *greater than 10* is simply *not greater than 10*. If you need to test the full range of numbers using a simple `if` statement, create an `if` statement that uses either >= or <= (see Table 3-1 for a listing of operators).

Going further with the else and if

When you are working with comparisons, you often have multiple comparisons going on. For example, you may say, "If I go to Mars, I will look for a cool red rock; otherwise, if I go to the moon, I will jump up really high; otherwise, I will just look around wherever I end up, but I hope there will be air."

This type of sentence has several *ifs* in it; and in C++, the sentence looks like the following:

```
#include <iostream>

using namespace std;

int main()
{
    int i;

    cout << "Type any number: ";
    cin >> i;

    if (i > 10)
    {
        cout << "It's greater than 10." << endl;
    }
    else if (i == 10)
    {
        cout << "It's equal to 10" << endl;
    }
    else
    {
        cout << "It's less than 10." << endl;
    }

    return 0;
}
```

Here you can see how we have several different conditions, and only one can be true. The computer first checks to see if `i` is greater than `10`. If `i` is greater, the computer prints a message saying that `i` is greater than `10`. But if not, the computer checks to see whether `i` equals `10`. If so, the computer prints a message saying that `i` is equal to `10`. Finally, the computer assumes that i must be less than 10, and it prints a message accordingly. Notice, for the final else statement, we didn't put a condition (and, in fact, you cannot have a condition with else statements). But because the other conditions failed, we know that i must be less than 10 by our careful logic.

Be careful when you are thinking through such if statements. You could have a situation where more than one condition could occur. For example, you may have something like this:

```cpp
#include <iostream>

using namespace std;

int main()
{
    int i;

    cout << "Type any number: ";
    cin >> i;

    if (i > 100)
    {
        cout << "It's greater than 100." << endl;
    }
    else if (i > 10)
    {
        cout << "It's greater than 10" << endl;
    }
    else
    {
        cout <<
            "It's neither greater than 100 nor greater than 10."
            << endl;
    }

    return 0;
}
```

Think about what would happen if i is the number 150. The first condition, i > 100, is true. But so is the second condition, i > 10. 150 is greater than 100, and 150 is also greater than 10. So which block will the computer do? Or will it do both blocks?

The computer only does the first condition that is satisfied. Thus, when i is 150, the computer prints the message "It's greater than 100." It does not print the other messages. In fact, the computer doesn't even bother checking the other conditions at that point. It just continues with the program.

Repeating Actions with Statements That Loop

Suppose that you're writing a program that needs to add all the numbers from 1 to 100. For example, you may want to know how much money you will get if you tell 100 people, "give me one dollar more than the person to your left." With a mastery of copy and paste, you could do something like this

```
int x = 1;
x = x + 2;
x = x + 3;
x = x + 4;
```

and so on until you get to `x = x + 100`. As you can see, this code could take a long time to type, and you would probably find it a tad frustrating, too, no matter how quickly you can choose the Edit⇨Paste command (or press Ctrl+V). Fortunately, the great founders of the computer world recognized that not every programmer is a virtuoso at the piano with flying fingers and that programs often need to do the same thing over and over. Thus, they gave us a really great tool called a `for` loop. A *for loop* does the same piece of code over and over for a certain number of times. And that's just what you wanted to do in this example.

Looping situations

Several types of loops are available, and next you'll see how they work. Which type of loop you use depends on the situation. We've already mentioned the first type, called a `for` loop. The idea behind a `for` loop is to have a counter variable that either increases or decreases, and the loop runs as long as the counter variable satisfies a particular condition. For example, the counter variable might start at 0, and the loop runs as long as the counter is less than 10. The counter variable increments each time the loop runs, and after the counter variable is not less than 10, the loop stops.

But another way to loop is to simplify the logic a bit and say, "I want this loop to run as long as some condition is true." This is called a *while loop*, and you simply specify a condition under which the loop continues to run. When the condition is true, the loop keeps running. After the condition is no longer true, the loop stops.

Finally, there's a slight modification to the `while` loop called a *do-while loop*. The `do-while` loop is used to handle one particular situation that could arise. When you have a `while` loop, if the condition is not true when everything starts, the computer will skip over the code in the `while` loop and not even bother executing it. But sometimes you may have a situation where you would want the code to always execute at least once. In that case, you can use a `do-while` loop.

Table 3-2 shows the types of loops. In the sections that follow, we show you how to use these types of loops.

Table 3-2	Choosing Your Loops
Type of Loop	*Appearance*
for	for (x=0; x<10; x++) { }
while	while (x < 10) { }
do-while	do { } while (x < 10)

The following list describes the situations under which you may want these loops.

✦ **for loop:** Use the for loop when you have a counter variable and you want to loop while the counter variable increases or decreases over a range.

✦ **while loop:** Use the while loop when you have a condition under which you want your code to run.

✦ **do-while loop:** Use the do-while loop when you have a condition under which you want your code to run, and you want to ensure that the loop always runs at least once, even if the condition is not satisfied.

Looping for

To use a for loop, you use the for keyword and follow it with a set of parentheses that contains information regarding the number of times the for loop executes.

For example, when adding the numbers from 1 to 100, you would want a variable that starts with the number 1; then you would add 1 to x, increase the variable to 2, and add the next number to x again over and over. The common part here that doesn't change each time is the "add it to x" part, and the part that changes is the variable, called *a counter variable*.

The counter variable, therefore, starts at 1 and goes through 100. Does it include 100? Yes. And with each iteration, you would add 1 to the counter variable. Your for statement would look like this:

```
for (i = 1; i <=100; i++)
```

This statement means that the counter variable, i, starts at 1, and the loop runs over and over while i is less than or equal to 100. After each iteration, the counter variable increments by 1 due to the i++ statement.

The following list shows the different portions inside the parentheses of the `for` loop:

✦ The first portion is the *initializer.* You use it to set up the counter variable.

✦ The second portion is the *condition* under which the loop continues to run.

✦ The third portion is the *finalizer.* In it, you specify what happens after each cycle of the loop.

REMEMBER

Three items are inside the `for` loop, and you separate them with semicolons. If you try to use commas, your code will not compile.

Now this code we just showed you doesn't do anything for each iteration other than add one to `i`. To tell the computer the work to do with each iteration, follow the `for` statement with a set of braces containing the statements you want to execute with each iteration. Thus, to add the counter variable to `x`, you would do this:

```
for (i = 1; i <=100; i++)
{
    x += i;
}
```

This would add `i` to `x` with each loop. Of course, we didn't start `x` out with anything in particular, so we should probably include that, too. Here's the final thing, complete with the way to write the final value of `x` to the console after the loop is finished:

```
#include <iostream>

using namespace std;

int main()
{
    int x = 0;
    int i;

    for (i = 1; i <= 100; i++)
    {
        x += i;
    }

    cout << x << endl;
    return 0;
}
```

Notice a few things about this block of code. First, we declared both variables that we're working with, `x` and `i`. Second, the `for` statement initializes the counter variable, specifies the condition under which it continues running, and tells what to do after each iteration. In this example, the `for` loop starts with i = 1, and it runs as long as i is less than or equal to 100. For each iteration, the computer adds the value of the counter to x; the process that adds the value to x is the code inside the braces. Finally, the computer adds 1 to x, which we specified as the third item inside the parentheses. The computer does this part, adding 1 to x, only after it finishes the stuff inside the braces.

Meddling with the middle condition

The middle portion of the for statement specifies a condition under which to continue doing the stuff inside the for loop. In the case of the preceding example, the condition is i <= 100, which means the stuff inside the braces continues to run as long as i is less than or equal to 100.

If you're familiar with other computer languages, the middle condition specifies a condition under which to continue the loop, not a condition under which to terminate the loop. Other languages will say *do this until such-and-such is true,* but that is not the case in C++.

In our example, we want the loop to iterate for the special case where i is 100, which still satisfies the condition i <= 100. If we had instead said i < 100, the loop would not have executed for the case where i is 100. The loop would have stopped short of the final iteration. In other words, the computer would only add the numbers 1 through 99. And if our friends are gathering money for us, we would be cheated out of that final $100. And, by golly, that could make the difference between whether we pay rent this month or not.

The question of when the loop stops can get kind of confusing. If we had gone crazy (but can we really *go* crazy since we're crazy to begin with?) and said that we wanted to add the numbers 1 *up to but not including* 100, we would have wanted a condition such as i < 100. If we had just said *up to* 100, it would not have been clear exactly which we wanted to do, include the 100 or not. If that had been the case and you were writing the program for us, you would want to ask us for clarification. (Unless we're the 100th friend, in which case we may get out of paying our dues.)

In the example we've been using, the condition i <= 100 and the condition i < 101 have essentially the same meaning. If our condition were i < 101, the program would operate the same. But the only reason that's true is because we're working with integers counting up to and including 100. If we were instead adding, for instance, floating-point numbers, and we incremented the counter by 0.1 after each iteration, these two conditions (i <= 100 and i < 101) wouldn't be the same. With i <=100, we would get up to 99.5, 99.6, 99.7, 99.8, 99.9, and finally 100, after which we would stop. But i < 101 would also include 100.1, 100.2, up to and including 100.9. You can see they are not the same.

Going backwards

If you need to count backwards, you can do that with a `for` loop as well. For example, you may be counting down the number of days left before you get to quit your job because you learned C++ programming and are moving on to an awesome new job. Or you may be writing a program that can manipulate that cool countdown timer they show when the Space Shuttle launches. Counting up just isn't always the right action. It would be a bummer if every day were one day longer before you get to quit your job and move to an island. Sometimes counting backwards is best.

To count backwards, you set up the three portions of the `for` loop. The first is the initial setup, the second is the condition under which it continues to run, and the third is the action after each iteration. For the first portion, you set the counter to the starting value, the top number. For the condition, you check whether the number continues to be greater than or equal to the final number. And for the third portion, you decrement the counter instead of increment it. Thus, you would have this:

```
for (i=10; i>=5; i--)
```

This starts the counter variable `i` at `10`. After each iteration, `i` becomes 1 less, and thus it moves to 9, then 8, then 7, and so on. And this process continues as long as `i` is at least 5. Thus, `i` will count 10, 9, 8, 7, 6, 5. The whole program might look like this:

```
#include <iostream>

using namespace std;

int main()
{
    int i;

    for (i=10; i>=5; i--)
    {
        cout << i << endl;
    }

    return 0;
}
```

When you run this code, you see the following output.

```
10
9
8
7
6
5
```

Incrementing one step at a time

In our example, we declared the counter variable before the `for` loop. However, you can actually declare the counter variable inside the loop, as in `for (int i = 0; i <= 100; i++)`. The end result is identical to declaring the counter variable beforehand. You must declare the variable each time you use it in a loop, as shown in the following example:

```
int x = 0;

for (int i = 0; i <= 100; i++)
{
    x += i;
}

for (int i = 200; i <= 300; i++)
{
    x += i;
}
```

In our earlier example under "Going backwards," we were working with integers, and after each iteration we added 1 to the counter variable. But we can do other things with each iteration. We already hinted that we could work with floating-point numbers and add 0.1 with each iteration. To do this, we can use a program like the following:

```
#include <iostream>

using namespace std;

int main()
{
    double x = 0.0;
    double i;

    for (i = 0.0; i <= 100.0; i+=0.1)
    {
        x += i;
    }

    cout << x << endl;

    return 0;
}
```

Now notice the third item in the `for` statement, `i += 0.1`. Remember that this item is the same as `i = i + 0.1`. Therefore, this third item is a complete statement. A common mistake is to instead include just a partial statement, as in `i + 0.1`. Unfortunately, some compilers allow that to get through with only a warning. C++ is notorious for letting you do things that really don't make a whole lot of sense, but newer compilers tend to fix these errors.

Yes, it's true: The entire statement `i = i + 1` is considered to have a *side effect*. In medicine, a side effect is some extra little goodie you get when you take a pill the doctor prescribes. For example, to cure your headache with a medicine, one side effect may be that you get severe abdominal pains — not something you really want. But in computers, a side effect can be something that you may want. In this case, we want the counter to get incremented. The partial statement `i + 0.1` just returns a value and doesn't put it anywhere; that is, the partial statement doesn't change the value of `i` — it has no side effects. (If you try this at home by replacing one of the `for` loops in the earlier examples with just `i + 0.1`, your loop will run forever until you manually stop the program. The reason for this action is that the counter always stays put right where it started, and it never increments. Thus the condition `i <= 100` will always be satisfied.)

The final portion of the `for` statement must be a complete statement in itself. If the statement simply evaluates to something, it will not be used in your `for` loop. In that case, your `for` loop can run forever unless you stop it.

Getting sneaky (and too complicated)

If you need multiple counter variables, the `for` loop can handle it. Each portion of the `for` statement can have multiple items in it, separated by commas. For example, the following line of code uses two counter variables. Look carefully at it because it's a bit confusing. In fact, we're going to say a little something about that shortly.

```
for (i = 0, j=10; i <= 5, j <=20; i++, j=j+2)
{
    cout << i << " " << j << endl;
    x += i + j;
}
```

To understand this, look at each portion separately. The first portion starts the loop. Here, the code creates two counters, `i` and `j` — `i` starts at `0`, and `j` starts at `10`.

So far, easy enough. The second portion says that the loop will run as long as the following two conditions are true: `i` must be less than or equal to `5`, and `j` must be less than or equal to `20`.

Again, not too bad. The final portion says what must happen at the end of each iteration: `i` is incremented by `1`, and `j` is incremented by `2`.

And thus you have two counter variables. And it's not too bad, except . . . imagine if we did something like this instead:

```
for (i = 0, j=20; i <= 5, j >= 10 ; i++, j=j-2)
{
    cout << i << " " << j << endl;
    x += i + j;
}
```

If you look carefully, you'll notice that aside from i, j starts out at 20, the loop runs as long as j is at least 10, and that with each iteration, 2 is subtracted from j. In other words, j is counting down by 2s from 20 to 10.

But i is counting up from 0 to 5. Thus, we have two loops: one counting up and one counting down. (Does it seem to you that just maybe we're starting to make this a little confusing?)

But wait, there's more. If you think *this* is confusing, take a look at the following gem, which we took great pride in putting together:

```
for (i=0, j=10; i<=5, j <=20 ; i++, j=j+2, cout<<i+j, x+=i+j)
{
}
```

If you type this, you can see that it does do something. But can you tell what it does just by looking at it? Probably not. (If you can, that's probably not a good thing either.) The truth is, this kind of code is just too complicated. Best to stick to simpler code. Although you may know what this code means, your coworkers will only get frustrated trying to decode it. And if you just write code for fun at home, six months from now — when you go back and look at this code — you might have trouble figuring it out yourself!

Putting too much inside the for statement itself is easy to do. In fact, if you're really clever, you can put almost everything inside the for loop and leave nothing but an empty pair of braces, as we did in our preceding example. But remember, just because your code is clever doesn't mean that what you did was the best way to do it. Instead, sticking to the common practice of using only one variable in the for statement is a good idea (as is not using multiple statements within each portion).

Keeping your programs clear so that other people can figure out what you were trying to do when you wrote the code is always a good idea. Some people seem to think that if they keep their programs complicated, they're guaranteeing themselves job security. Oddly, all the people we know like that tend to leave their jobs and have trouble getting good references. (Imagine that!)

You may recall that with the ++, you can have both i++ and ++i. The first is called a *post-increment* and the second is called a *pre-increment*. You may be tempted to try something like this: for (int i = 0; i <= 5; ++i). Although that looks cool and some people actually prefer it, the truth is that it doesn't change anything. The ++i still takes place at the end of the loop, not at the beginning as you might hope. To me, that setup just makes code confusing, so we use i++ in our for loops, and we avoid ++i.

Looping while

Often, you find that for loops only work so well. Sometimes, you don't want a counter variable; you just want to run a loop over and over as long as a certain situation is true. Then, after that situation is no longer the case, you want to stop the loop.

For example, instead of saying that you'll have 100 people line up and each will give you one more dollar than the person to his or her left, you may say that you will continue accepting money like this as long as they're willing to give it.

In this case, you can see that the *condition* under which the thing continues to operate is the "as long as they're willing to give it."

To do this in C++, you use a while statement. The while keyword is followed by a set of parentheses containing the condition under which the program is to continue running the loop. Whereas the for statement's parentheses include three portions that show how to change the counter variable, the while statement's parentheses contain only a condition.

For example, you may have

```
#include <iostream>

using namespace std;

int main()
{
    int i = 0;

    while (i <= 10)
    {
        cout << i << endl;
        i++;
    }

    cout << "All Finished!" << endl;

    return 0;
}
```

This code runs while i is less than or equal to 10. Thus, the output of this program is

```
0
1
2
3
4
5
6
7
8
9
10
All Finished!
```

The while loop is handy if you don't have a particular number of times you need the loop to run. For example, let's consider a situation where your application is reading data from the Internet. Unless you control the Internet data source, you won't know how much data it can provide. (There are many other situations where you don't know how much data to read, but Internet applications commonly experience this problem.) Using a while loop, the code can continue reading data until your application has read it all. The Internet data source can simply *stream* the data to your application until the data transfer is complete.

Often, for this kind of situation, we make a Boolean variable called done, and we start it out as false. My while statement is simply

```
while (!done)
```

This translates easily to English as *while not done do the following.* Then, inside the while loop, when the situation happens that we know the loop must finish (such as the Internet data source has no more data to read), we set

```
done = true;
```

For example, the following would do this sort of process:

```
#include <iostream>

using namespace std;

int main()
{
    int i = 0;
    bool done = false;

    while (!done)
    {
        cout << i << endl;
        i++;
        if (i == 10)
            done = true;
    }

    cout << "All Finished!" << endl;
    return 0;
}
```

In the case of the Internet data example, after you encounter no more data, you would set done to true. In the case of your friends giving you money, after one of them refuses, you would set done to true.

TIP

If you have worked in other languages, you may have come across the notion of while loops always executing at least once. This is not the case in C++. If the condition in the while statement evaluates to false, the while loop will not execute at all.

Doing while

The `while` statement has a cousin in the family called the `do-while` statement. A loop of this form is very similar to the `while` loop, but with an interesting little catch: The `while` statement goes at the end. It looks like this:

```
#include <iostream>

using namespace std;

int main()
{
    int i = 0;

    do
    {
        cout << i << endl;
        i++;
    }
    while (i <= 10);

    cout << "All Finished!" << endl;

    return 0;
}
```

Notice here that the loop starts with the `do` keyword, then the material for the loop follows inside braces, and finally the `while` statement comes at the end. The idea is that you're telling the computer *do this while such-and-such is true,* where *this* is the stuff inside braces and the *such-and-such* is the condition inside parentheses.

The `do-while` loop has one important caveat: Unlike the `while` loop, the `do-while` loop always runs at least once. In other words, even if the condition isn't satisfied the first time you run the loop, it runs anyway. That can be a problem sometimes, and if you don't want that behavior, you should consider using a `while` loop instead of a `do-while` loop.

Breaking and continuing

Sometimes, you may write a program that includes a loop that does more than just add numbers. You may find that you want the loop to end under a certain condition that's separate. Or you may want the loop to suddenly skip out of the current loop and continue with the next item in the loop. When you stop a loop and continue with the code after the loop, you use a `break` statement. When you quit the current cycle of the loop and continue with the next cycle, you use a `continue` statement. The next sections show you how to do this.

Breaking

For example, you may be writing a program that reads data over the Internet, and the loop runs for the amount of data that's supposed to come.

But midway through the process, you may encounter some data that has an error in it, and you may want to get out of the `for` loop immediately.

C++ includes a handy little statement that can rescue you in such a situation. The statement is called `break`. Now nothing actually breaks, and it seems a bit frightening to write a program that instructs the computer to break. But this use of the term *break* is more like in *break out of prison* than *break the computer*. But instead of breaking out of prison, it breaks you out the loop. This can be any kind of loop — a `for` loop, a `while` loop, or a `do-while` loop.

The following code demonstrates this. This sample actually just checks for the special case of `i` being 5. We could have accomplished the same thing by simply changing the end condition of our `for` loop, but at least it shows you how the `break` statement works.

```
#include <iostream>

using namespace std;

int main()
{
    int i;

    for (i=0; i<10; i++)
    {
        cout << i << " ";
        if (i == 5)
        {
            break;
        }
        cout << i * 2 << endl;
    }

    cout << "All Finished!" << endl;

    return 0;
}
```

In the preceding code, the first line inside the `for` loop, `cout << i << " ";`, runs when `i` is 5. But the final line in the `for` loop, `cout << i * 2 << endl;`, does not run when `i` is 5 because we told it to break out of the loop between the two `cout` statements.

Also notice that when you break out of the loop, the program does not quit. It continues with the statements that follow the loop. In this case, it still prints the message, `"All Finished!"`.

You can actually leave the second portion of the `for` statement (the condition) empty by just putting a blank between the spaces. Then, to get out of the loop, you can use a `break` statement. However, doing this makes for messy code. And treat messy code like a messy house: Although sometimes we don't mind, the truth is that most people really don't care for a messy

house. And you really don't want other people to see your messy house —
or your messy code. Yes, as a programmer, sometimes being a little self-
conscious is a good thing.

Continuing

In addition to the times when you may need to break out of your loop for a
special situation, you can also cause the loop to end its current iteration; but
instead of breaking out of it, the loop resumes with the next iteration.

For example, you may be, again, reading data from over the Internet, and
you are doing this by looping a specified number of times. In the middle of
the loop, you may encounter some bad data. But instead of quitting out of
the loop, you may want to just ignore the current piece of bad data and then
continue reading more data.

To do this trick, you use a C++ statement called `continue`. The `continue`
statement means *end the current iteration but continue running the loop with
the next iteration.*

The following code is a slightly modified version of the previous example
in the section called "Breaking." When the loop gets to 5, it doesn't do the
second `cout` line. But instead of breaking out of the loop, it continues with
6, then 7, and so on until the loop finishes on its own.

```cpp
#include <iostream>

using namespace std;

int main()
{
    int i;

    for (i=0; i<10; i++)
    {
        cout << i << " ";
        if (i == 5)
        {
            cout << endl;
            continue;
        }
        cout << i * 2 << endl;
    }

    cout << "All Finished!" << endl;

    return 0;
}
```

Nesting loops

Many times, you need to work with more than one loop. For example, you
may have several groups of friends, and you want to bilk the individual

friends of each group for all you can get. You may host a party for the first group of friends and make them each give you as much money as they have. Then, the next week, you may hold another party with a different group of friends. You would do this for each group of friends. Oh wait, we just said the word *for,* so that's probably what we're onto with this.

We could draw out the logic like this:

```
For each group of friends,
    for each person in that group
        bilk the friend for all he or she is worth
```

This is called a nested loop. But if you do this, don't be surprised if this is the last time your friends visit your nest.

A *nested loop* simply means a loop inside a loop. Because computers aren't good at making friends, although they can be used to bilk people, we'll use an example that's a bit nicer: Suppose you want to multiply each of the numbers 1 through 10 by 1 and print the answer of each multiplication, and then you want to multiply each of the numbers 1 through 10 by 2 and print the answer of each multiplication, and so on, up to a multiplier of 10. Your C++ code would look like the following.

```cpp
#include <iostream>

using namespace std;

int main()
{
    int x,y;

    for (x = 1; x <= 10; x++)
    {
        cout << "Products of " << x <<endl;
        for (y = 1; y <= 10; y++)
        {
            cout << x * y << endl;
        }
        cout << endl;
    }

    return 0;
}
```

In this example, we simply have a loop inside a loop. The inner loop can make use of the counter variable from the outer loop. Beyond that, nothing is magical or bizarre about this kind of thing. It's just a loop inside a loop. And yes, you can have a loop inside a loop inside a loop inside a loop. You can also have any loop inside any other loop, like a while loop inside a for loop.

And notice that we have stuff going on outside the inner loop, but inside the outer loop. That is, we have a `cout` calls before and after the inner loop. You can do this; your inner loop need not be the only thing inside the outer loop.

Although you can certainly have a loop inside a loop inside a loop inside a loop, the deeper you get, the more potentially confusing your code can become. It's like the dozens of big cities in America that are promising to build an *outer loop*. Eventually, that outer loop won't be big enough, so the cities have to build yet another and another. That's kind of a frightening prospect, so try not to get carried away with nesting.

If you put a `break` statement or a `continue` statement inside a nested loop, the statement applies to the innermost loop it sits in. For example, the following code contains three loops: an outer loop, a middle loop, and an inner loop. The `break` statement applies to the middle loop.

```cpp
#include <iostream>

using namespace std;

int main()
{
    int x,y,z;

    for (x = 1; x <= 3; x++)
    {
        for (y = 1; y < 3; y++)
        {
            if (y == 2)
                break;
            for (z = 1; z < 3; z++)
            {
                cout << x << " " << y;
                cout << " " << z << endl;
            }
        }
    }

    return 0;
}
```

You can see that when `y` is 2, the `for` loop with the `y` in it breaks. But the outer loop continues to run with the next iteration.

Chapter 4: Dividing Your Work with Functions

In This Chapter

- ✓ Calling a function
- ✓ Passing things, such as variables
- ✓ Writing your own great functions
- ✓ Fun with strings
- ✓ Manipulating `main`

*P*eople generally agree that most projects throughout life are easier when you divide them into smaller, more manageable tasks. That's also the case with computer programming. If you break your code into smaller pieces, it becomes more manageable.

C++ provides many ways to divide code into smaller portions. One way is through the use of what are called functions. A *function* is a set of lines of code that performs a particular job.

In this chapter, we show you what functions are and how you can use them to make your programming job easier.

Dividing Your Work

If you have a big job to do that doesn't involve a computer, you can divide your work in many ways. Over the years of studying process management, people have pretty much narrowed division of a job down to two ways: using nouns and using verbs.

Yes, that's right. Back to good old English class, where we all learned about nouns and verbs. The idea is this: Suppose that we're going to go out back and build a flying saucer. We can approach the designing of the flying saucer in two ways.

First, we could just draw up a plan of attack, listing all the steps to build the flying saucer from start to finish. That would, of course, be a lot of steps. But to simplify it, we could instead list all the major tasks without getting into the details. It might go something like this:

1.   Build the outer shell.

2.   Build and attach the engine.

That's it. Only two steps. But when you hire a couple dozen people to do the grunt work for you while you focus on your daytrading, would that be enough for them to go on? No, probably not. Instead, you could take these two tasks and divide them into smaller tasks. For example, Step 2 might look like this:

2a.   Build the antigravity lifter.

2b.   Build the thruster.

2c.   Connect the lifter to the thruster to form the final engine.

2d.   Attach the engine to the outer shell.

That's a little better; it has more detail. But, it still needs more. How do we do the *Build the antigravity lifter* part? That's easy, but it requires more detail, as in the following:

2aa.   Unearth the antigravity particles from the ground.

2ab.   Compress them tightly into a superatomizing conductor.

2ac.   Surround with coils.

2ad.   Connect 9-volt battery clip to the coils.

And, of course, each of these requires even more detail. Eventually, after you have planned the whole thing, you will have many, many steps, but they will be organized into a hierarchy of sorts, as shown in Figure 4-1. In this drawing, the three dots represent places where other steps go, but we chose to leave them off so the diagram could fit on the page.

This type of design is called a *top-down* design. The idea is that you start at the uppermost step of your design (in this case, *Build flying saucer*) and continue to break the steps into more and more detailed steps until you have something manageable. For many years, this was how computer programming was taught.

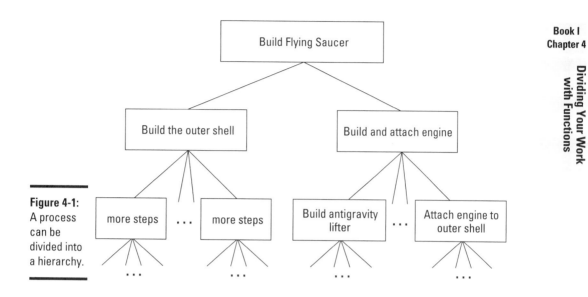

Figure 4-1:
A process
can be
divided into
a hierarchy.

Although this process works, people have found a slightly better way. First, before breaking the steps (which are the verbs), you divide the thing you're building into parts (the nouns). In this case, we kind of did that already in the first two steps. But instead of calling them steps, we call them objects: One object is the outer shell, and one object is the engine. This way, two different factories can work on these in sort of a division of labor. Of course, the factories would have to coordinate their activities; otherwise, the two parts may not fit together when they're ready to go. And before figuring out exactly how to build each of these objects, it would be a good idea to describe each object: What it does, its features, its dimensions, and so on. Then, when we finally have all that done, we can list the exact features and their details. And finally, we can divide the work with each person designing or building a different part.

As you can see, this second approach makes more sense. And that's the way programmers divide their computer programs. But at the bottom of each method is something in common: The methods are made of several little processes. These processes are called *functions*. When you write a computer program, after you divide your job into smaller things called objects, you eventually start giving these objects behaviors. And to code these behaviors, you do just as we did in the *first* approach: You break them into manageable parts, again, called functions. In computer programming terms, a *function* is simply a small set of code that performs a specific task. But it's more than that: Think of a function as a machine. You can put one or more things into the machine; it processes them, and then it spits out a single answer, if anything at all. One of the most valuable diagrams we have seen draws a function in this manner, like a machine, as shown in Figure 4-2.

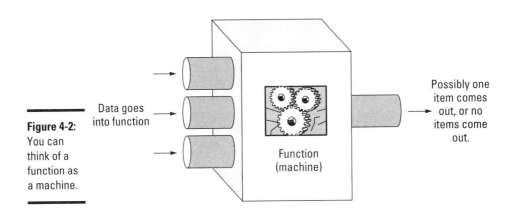

Figure 4-2:
You can
think of a
function as
a machine.

This machine (or function) has three main parts:

✦ **Inputs:** The function can receive data through its inputs. These data elements can be numbers, strings, or any other type. When you create such a machine, you can have as many inputs as you want (or even zero if necessary).

✦ **Processor:** The processor is the function itself. In terms of C++, this is actually a set of code lines.

✦ **Output:** A function can *return* something when it has finished doing its thing. In C++, this is in the form of numbers, strings, or any other type.

To make all this clear, try out the code in Listing 4-1. (Don't forget the second line, #include <math.h>, which gives you some math capabilities.)

Listing 4-1:   Seeing a Function in Action

```
#include <iostream>
#include <math.h>

using namespace std;

int main()
{
  cout << fabs(-10.5) << endl;
  cout << fabs(10.5) << endl;
  return 0;
}
```

When you run this program, you see the following output:

```
10.5
10.5
```

In this code, you used a function or machine called `fabs` (usually pro-nounced *ef-abs* for floating-point absolute). This function takes a number as input and returns as output the absolute value of the number. Remember that the absolute value of a number is simply the positive version of the number. The absolute value, for example, of –5 is simply 5. The absolute value of 12 is still 12. An absolute value is always positive. And the absolute value of 0 is 0. (The reason for the `f` before the name `abs` is that it uses float-ing-point numbers, which are simply numbers with decimal points.)

So the first line inside `main` *calls* `fabs` for the value –10.5. The `cout` then takes the output of this function (that is, the *result*) and prints it to the console.

Then the second line does the same thing again, except it takes the absolute value of the number 10.5.

And where is the processor for this function? It's not in your code; it's in another file, and the following line ensures that your program can use this function:

```
#include <math.h>
```

You have seen functions in many places. If you use a calculator and enter a number and press the square root button, the calculator runs a function that calculates the square root.

But functions can be more sophisticated than just working with numbers. Consider this carefully: When you are using a word processor and you high-light a word and do a spelling check on the word, the program calls a func-tion that handles the spelling check. This function does something like the following:

```
This is a function to check the spelling of a single word.
Inputs: A single word.
Look up the word
If the word is not found
    Find some suggestions.
    Open a dialog box through which you (the user)
        can change the word by either typing a new word
        or picking one of the selections, or just leaving
        it the same.
    If you made a change,
        Return the new spelling.
    Otherwise
        Return nothing.
Otherwise
    Return nothing
```

Notice how we grouped the `if` statements with indentations. The final `oth-erwise` goes with the first `if` statement because its indentation matches that of the `if` statement.

So that's a function that performs a spelling check. But consider this: When you do not highlight a word but run the spelling checker, the spelling checker runs for the whole document. That's another function. Here it is.

```
This is a function to check the spelling of the entire document
For each word in the document
    Check the spelling of the single word
```

How does the computer do the step inside the `for` loop, *Check the spelling of the single word*? It calls the function we described earlier. This process is called *code reuse*. We have no reason to rewrite the entire function again if we already have it somewhere else. And that's the beauty of functions.

Calling a Function

When you run the code in a function, computer people say you are *calling* the function. And just like every good person, a good function has a name. When you call a function, you do so by name.

Often, when we're writing a program and write code to call a function, we will say that *We are calling a function.* This is just partly computerspeak, and partly a strange disorder in which we computer programmers start to relate just a little *too* much with the computer.

To call a function, you type its name and then a set of parentheses. Inside the parentheses, you list the items you want to send to the inputs of the function. The term we use here is *pass*, as in you *pass the values to the function*.

For example, if you want to call the `fabs` function, you type the name, `fabs`, an open parenthesis, the number you want to pass to it, and then a close parenthesis, as in the following:

```
fabs(-10.5)
```

But by itself, this does not do anything. The `fabs` function returns a value — the absolute value of –10.5, which comes out to be 10.5 — and you probably want to do something with that value. You could, for example, print it to the console:

```
cout << fabs(-10.5) << endl;
```

Or you could store it away in another variable. But there's a catch. Before you can do that, you need to know the *type* the function returns. Just as with variables, function return values have a type. In this case, the type is a special type called `double`. The `double` type is a floating-point type that can hold many digits in a single number. To save the result of `fabs`, you need to have a variable of type `double`. The code in Listing 4-2 does this.

Listing 4-2: Seeing Another Function in Action

```
#include <iostream>
#include <math.h>

using namespace std;

int main()
{
  double mynumber;
  mynumber = fabs(-23.87);
  cout << mynumber << endl;
  return 0;
}
```

This code declares a `double` variable called `mynumber`. Then it calls `fabs`, passing it –23.87, and returning the value into `mynumber`. Next it prints the value in `mynumber` out to the console.

When you run this program you see the following, which is the absolute value of –23.87.

```
23.87
```

Passing a variable

You can also pass the value of a variable into a function. The code in Listing 4-3 creates two variables; one is passed into the function, and the other receives the results of the function.

Listing 4-3: Seeing Yet Another Function in Action

```
#include <iostream>
#include <math.h>

using namespace std;

int main()
{
  double start;
  double finish;

  start = -253.895;
  finish = fabs(start);

  cout << finish << endl;
  return 0;
}
```

(We separated the parts of the code with blank lines to make it a little easier to follow.) This code first creates two variables; the first is called `start`, and the second is called `finish`. It then initializes `start` with a value of –253.895. Next, it calls `fabs`, passing it the value of `start`. It saves the return value in the `finish` variable, and it finally prints the value in `finish`. When it runs, you see the following appear on the console:

```
253.895
```

Saving a function result to a variable is useful if you need to use the result several times over. For example, if you need the absolute value of –253.895 for whatever reason and then a few lines later you need it again, you have a choice: You can either call `fabs(-253.895)` each time or you can call it once, save it in a variable, and then use the variable each time you need it. The advantage to saving it in a variable is that if you later, for example, say, "Oh wait! I didn't just want the absolute value! I wanted the negative of the absolute value!" you only have to change one line of code — the line where it calls `fabs`. If, instead, you had called `fabs` several times, you would have had to change it every time you called it. And by the way, in case you're curious about how to take the negative of the absolute value and store it in a variable, you just throw a minus sign in front of it, like so:

```
finish = -fabs(start);
```

Passing multiple variables

Some functions like to have all sorts of goodies thrown their way, such as multiple parameters. As with functions that take a single value, you put the values inside a single set of parentheses. Because you have multiple values, you separate them with commas. Listing 4-4 uses a function called `pow` to calculate the third power of 10. (That is, it calculates 10 times 10 times 10. Yes, *POW!*). Make sure that you include the `math.h` line in the includes section so that you can use the `pow` function.

Listing 4-4:   Seeing Yet One More Function in Action

```
#include <iostream>
#include <math.h>

using namespace std;

int main()
{
  double number = 10.0;
  double exponent = 3.0;
  cout << pow(number, exponent) << endl;
  return 0;
}
```

When you run the program, you see 10 to the third power, which is 1,000:

```
1000
```

You can also pass a mixture of variables and numbers, or just numbers. The following code snippet also calculates the third power of 10 but passes an actual number, 3.0, for the power.

```
double number = 10.0;
cout << pow(number, 3.0) << endl;
```

Or you can pass only numbers:

```
cout << pow(10.0, 3.0) << endl;
```

Writing Your Own Functions

And now the fun begins! Calling functions is great, but you get real power (ooh!) when you write your own specialized functions. Before writing a function, remember the parts: the inputs, the main code or processor, and the single output (or no output). The inputs, however, are actually called *parameters,* and the output is called a *return value.*

Listing 4-5 shows both a custom function and code in `main` that calls the custom function. (The function goes outside `main` — before it, in fact.)

Listing 4-5:   Writing Your Very Own Function

```
#include <iostream>

using namespace std;

int AddOne(int start)
{
    int newnumber;
    newnumber = start + 1;
    return newnumber;
}

int main()
{
    int testnumber;
    int result;

    testnumber = 20;
    result = AddOne(testnumber);

    cout << result << endl;
    return 0;
}
```

After you get all this typed in and your fingers are feeling nice and exercised, go ahead and run it. Because there's a good bit of code, you may get some compiler errors at first; look carefully at the lines with the errors and find the difference between your code and what's here in the book.

After you run it, you see

```
21
```

Now before we explain the code for the function, we'll save the fun for last. Take a look at these three lines of `main`:

```
testnumber = 20;
result = AddOne(testnumber);
cout << result << endl;
```

You can probably put together some facts and determine what the function does. First, we called it `AddOne`, which is a pretty good indication in itself. Second, when you ran the program, the number `21` appear on the console, which is one more than the value in `testnumber`; it added one. And that, in fact, is what the function does. It's amazing what computers can do these days.

When you write your own functions, try to choose a name that makes sense and describes what the function does. Writing a function and calling it something like `process` or `TheFunction` is easy, but those names do not accurately describe the function.

So now take a look at the function itself. First, here are a few high-level observations about it:

+ **Position:** The function appears *before* `main`. Because of the way the compiler works, it must know about a function before you call it. And thus, we put it before `main`. (You can do this in another way, which we discuss in "Forward references and function prototypes," later in this chapter.)

+ **Format:** The function starts with a line that seems to describe the function (which we explain later in this section), and then it has an open brace and, later, a closing brace.

+ **Code:** The function has code in it that is just like the type of code you could put inside a `main`.

After noting these high-level things, take a look at the code inside the function. The first part of it looks like this:

```
int newnumber;
newnumber = start + 1;
```

So far, this is pretty straightforward. It declares an integer variable called `newnumber`. Then it initializes it to `start` plus one. But what is `start`? That's one of the inputs.

Finally, this line is at the end of the function, before the closing brace:

```
return newnumber;
```

This is the output of the function, or the return value. When you want to return something from a function, you just put the word `return` and then indicate what you want to return. From the preceding two lines, you can see that `newnumber` is one more than the number passed into the function. So this line returns the `newnumber`. Thus, we have covered all three parts: We have taken the input or parameter; we have processed it by creating a variable and adding one to the parameter; and we have returned the output, which is one more than the parameter.

But what is the parameter? It's called `start`. And where did that come from? Here's the very first line of the function:

```
int AddOne(int start)
```

The stuff in parentheses is the list of parameters. Notice that it looks just like a variable declaration; it's the word `int` (the type, or integer) followed by a variable name, `start`. That's the parameter — the input — to the function, and you can access this parameter throughout the function by simply using a variable called `start`.

We think that's rather ingenious, if we do say so ourselves. Okay, so we didn't invent it, but nevertheless, we think it's ingenious: *You can use the input to the function as a variable itself.*

And so, if down in `main` we had written

```
result = AddOne(25);
```

then throughout the function, the value of `start` would be `25`.

But if we had written

```
result = AddOne(152);
```

then throughout the function, the value of `start` would be `152`.

But here's the really great thing about functions. Or, at least, one of the loads of really great things about functions! We can call the function several times over. In the same `main`, we can have the following lines

```
cout << AddOne(100) << endl;
cout << AddOne(200) << endl;
cout << AddOne(300) << endl;
```

which would result in this output:

```
101
201
301
```

Arguing over parameters

Technically, the term *parameter* refers strictly to the inputs to the function, from the function's perspective. When you call the function, the things you place in parentheses in the call line are not called parameters; rather, they are called *arguments*. Thus, in the following function header the variables `first` and `last` are parameters. But in the following call to this function

```
ConnectNames("Bill", "Murray")
```

the strings `"Bill"` and `"Murray"` are arguments of the call.

In the first call to `AddOne`, the value of `start` would be `100`. During the second call, the value would be `200`, and during the third call, it would be `300`.

Now take another look at the header:

```
int AddOne(int start)
```

The word `AddOne` is the name of the function, as you probably figured out already. And that leaves that thing at the beginning, the `int`. That's the *type* of the return value. The final line in the function before the closing brace is

```
return newnumber;
```

The variable `newnumber` inside the function is an integer. And the return type is integer. That's no accident: As we've all heard before, friends don't let friends return something other than the type specified in the function header. The two must match in type. And further, take a look at this line from inside `main`:

```
result = AddOne(testnumber);
```

What type is the `result` variable? It's also an integer. All three match. Again, no accident. You can copy one thing to another (in this case the function's return value to the variable called `result`) only if they match in type. And here, they do. They're both integers.

And notice one more thing about the function header: It has no semicolon after it. This is one of the places you do *not* put a semicolon. If you do, the compiler gets horribly confused. The CodeBlocks compiler shows an error that says, "`error: expected unqualified-id before '{' token.`"

Here's a recap of some of the rules we just mentioned regarding functions:

✦ **Header line:** The header line starts with a value for the return type, the name of the function, and the list of parameters.

✦ **Parameters:** The parameters are written like variable declarations, and indeed, you can use them as variables inside the function.

✦ **Return type:** Whatever you return from the function must match in type with the type you specified in your function header.

✦ **More on format:** The function header does not have a semicolon after it.

✦ **Even more on format:** After the function header, you use an open brace. The function ends with a closing brace. The final brace tells the compiler where the function ends.

Finally, ponder this line of code for a moment:

```
testnumber = AddOne(testnumber);
```

This takes the value stored inside `testnumber`, passes it into `AddOne`, and gets back a new number. It then takes that new number and stores it back into `testnumber`. Thus, `testnumber`'s value changes based on the results of the function `AddOne`.

Multiple parameters or no parameters

You don't need to write your functions with only one parameter each. You can have several parameters, or you can have none at all. It may seem a little strange that you would want a function — a machine — that takes no inputs. But you may run into lots of cases where this may be a good idea. Here are some ideas:

✦ **Day function:** This would be a function that figures out the day and returns it as a string, as in `"Monday"` or `"Tuesday"`.

✦ **Number-of-users function:** This could be a function that figures out the current number of users logged into a Web-server computer.

✦ **Current font function:** This function would be in a text editor program (such as Notepad) and would return a string containing the current font name, such as `"Arial"`.

✦ **Editing time function:** This function would return the amount of time you have been using the word processor program.

✦ **Username function:** If you are logged onto a computer, this function would give back your username as a string, such as `"Elisha"`.

All the functions in this list have something in common: They look something up. Because no parameters are in the code, for the functions to process some information, they have to go out and get it themselves. It's like sending people out into the woods to find food but not giving them any tools: It's totally up to them to do it, and all you can do is sit back and watch and wait for your yummy surprise.

If a function takes no parameters, you write the function header as you would for one that takes parameters, and you include the parentheses; you just don't put anything *in* the parentheses, as Listing 4-6 shows. So if nothing good is going in, there really can be something good coming back out, at least in the case of a function with no parameters.

Listing 4-6:   Taking No Parameters

```
#include <iostream>

using namespace std;

string Username()
{
    return "Elisha";
}

int main()
{
  cout << Username() << endl;
  return 0;
}
```

When you run Listing 4-6, you see the following output:

```
Elisha
```

Your function can also take multiple parameters. Listing 4-7 shows this. Notice that the function, `ConnectNames`, takes the two strings as parameters and combines them, along with a space in the middle. Notice also that the function uses the two strings as variables.

Listing 4-7:   Taking Multiple Parameters

```
#include <iostream>

using namespace std;

string ConnectNames(string first, string last)
{
  return first + " " + last;
}

int main()
{
  cout << ConnectNames("Richard", "Nixon") << endl;
  return 0;
}
```

In the function header in Listing 4-7, we had to put the type name `string` for each parameter. If we only listed it for the first, we would get a compile error. (Okay, we admit it — we did forget it, and that's how we remembered to tell you. But that shows that even experienced programmers came make mistakes. Occasionally.)

Now here are some points about this code:

✦ We didn't create variables for the two names in `main`. Instead, we just typed them as string constants (that is, as actual strings surrounded by quotes).

✦ You can do calculations and figuring right inside the `return` statement. That saves the extra work of creating a variable. In the function, we could have created a return variable of type `string`, set it to `first + " " + last`, and then returned that variable, as in the following code:

```
string result = first + " " + last;
return result;
```

But instead, we chose to do it all on one line, as in this:

```
return first + " " + last;
```

Although you can save yourself the work of creating an extra variable and just put the whole expression in the `return` statement, sometimes this is a bad thing. If the expression is really long like the following

```
return (mynumber * 100 + somethingelse / 200) *
  (yetanother + 400 / mynumber) / (mynumber + evenmore);
```

then it can get just a tad complicated. Breaking it into variables, such as this, is best:

```
double a = mynumber * 100 + somethingelse / 200;
double b = yetanother + 400 / mynumber;
double c = mynumber + evenmore;
return a * b / c;
```

Returning nothing

In the preceding section, "Multiple parameters or no parameters," we presented a list of functions that take no parameters; these functions go and bring back something, whether it's a number, a string, or some other type of food.

One such example gets the username of the computer you're logged into. But what if you are the great computer guru, and *you* are writing the program that actually logs somebody in? In that case, your program doesn't ask the computer what the username is — your program tells the computer what the username is, by golly!

In that case, your program would call a function, like `SetUsername`, and pass the new `username`. And would this function return anything? It could; it could return the name back, or it could return a message saying that the username is not valid or something like that. Or, it may not return anything at all.

Take a look at the case where a function doesn't return anything at all. In C++, the way you state that the function doesn't return anything is by using the word *void* as the return type in the function header. Listing 4-8 shows this.

Listing 4-8: Returning Nothing at All

```
#include <iostream>

using namespace std;

void SetUsername(string newname)
{
  cout << "New user is " << newname << endl;
}

int main()
{
  SetUsername("Harold");
  return 0;
}
```

When you run the program, you see

```
New user is Harold
```

Notice the function header: It starts with the word void, which means that it returns nothing at all. It's like in outer space: There's just a big void with nothing there, and nothing is returned, except for static from the alien airwaves, but we won't go there. Also notice that, because this function does not return anything, there is no return statement.

Now, of course, this function really doesn't do a whole lot other than print the new username to the console, but that's okay; it shows you how you can write a function that does not return anything.

A function of return type void returns nothing at all.

Do not try to return something in a function that has a return type of void. Void means the function returns nothing at all. If you try to put a return statement in your function, you get a compile error.

Keeping your variables local

Everybody likes to have their own stuff, and functions are no exception. When you create a variable inside the code for a function, that variable will be known only to that particular function. When you create such variables, they are called *local variables*, and people say that they are local to that particular function. (Well, *computer* people say that, anyway.)

For example, consider the following code:

```
#include <iostream>

using namespace std;

void PrintName(string first, string last)
{
  string fullname = first + " " + last;
  cout << fullname << endl;
}

int main()
{
  PrintName("Thomas", "Jefferson");
  return 0;
}
```

Notice in the `PrintName` function that we declared a variable called `fullname`. We then use that variable in the second line in that function, the one starting with `cout`. But we cannot use the variable inside `main`. If we try to, as in the following code, we would get a compile error:

```
int main()
{
  PrintName("Thomas", "Jefferson");
  cout << fullname << endl;
  return 0;
}
```

However, we can *declare* a variable called `fullname` inside `main`, as in the following code. But, if we do that, this `fullname` is local only to `main`, while the other variable, also called `fullname`, is local only to the `PrintName` function. In other words, each function has its own variable; they just happen to share the same name. *But they are two separate variables.*

```
int main()
{
  string fullname = "Abraham Lincoln";
  PrintName("Thomas", "Jefferson");
  cout << fullname << endl;
  return 0;
}
```

When two functions declare variables by the same name, they are two separate variables. If you store a value inside one of them, the other function will not know about it. The other function only knows about its own variable by that name. Think of it the way two people could each have a storage bin in the closet labeled "tools." If Sally puts a hammer in her bin labeled "tools" and Hal opens another bin also labeled "tools" at *his* house, he won't see the very same hammer in Sally's bin, will he? We hope not, or something is seriously awry in the universe. With variables it works the same way.

If you use the same variable name in two different functions, forgetting that you're working with two different variables is very easy. Only do this if you're sure that no confusion can occur.

If you use the same variable name in two different functions (such as a counter variable called `index`, which you use in a `for` loop), matching the case is usually a good idea. Don't use `count` in one function, and `Count` in another. Although you can certainly do that, you may find yourself typing the name wrong when you need it. But that won't cause you to access the other one. (You can't because it's in a different function.) Instead, you get a compile error, and you have to go back and fix it. Being consistent is a timesaver.

Forward references and function prototypes

In all the examples in this chapter, we have put the code for any function we write above the code for `main`. The reason is that the compiler scans through the code from start to finish. If it has not encountered a function yet but sees a call to it, it won't know what it's seeing, and it issues a good old compile error.

Such an error can be especially frustrating and could cause you to spend hours yelling at your computer (or, if you're like us, running to the refrigerator and getting something sweet and fattening). Nothing is more frustrating than looking at your program, being told by the compiler it's wrong, yet knowing it's right because you know you wrote the function.

You can, however, put your functions after `main`; or you can even use this method to put your functions in other source-code files (something we talk about in Minibook I, Chapter 5).

What you can do is include a function prototype. A *function prototype* is nothing more than a copy of the function header. But instead of following it with an open brace and then the code for the function, you follow the function header with a semicolon and are finished. A function prototype, for example, looks like this:

```
void PrintName(string first, string last);
```

Then you actually write the full function (header, code, and all) later. The full function can even be later than `main` or later than any place that makes calls to it.

Notice that this looks just like the first line of a function. In fact, we cheated! To write it, we simply copied the first line of the original function we wrote and added a semicolon.

So where would you use this fellow? Take a look at Listing 4-9.

Listing 4-9: Using a Function Prototype

```cpp
#include <iostream>

using namespace std;

void PrintName(string first, string last);

int main()
{
  PrintName("Thomas", "Jefferson");
  return 0;
}

void PrintName(string first, string last)
{
  string fullname = first + " " + last;
  cout << fullname << endl;
}
```

Notice, in this listing, that we have the function header copied above `main` and ending with a semicolon. Then we have `main`. Finally we have the function itself (again, with the header but no semicolon this time). Thus, the function comes after `main`.

"Whoop-de-do," we can hear you saying. The function comes after. But why bother when now we have to type the function header twice?

But rest assured, dear readers, that this step is useful. If you have a source code file with, say, 20 functions, and these functions all make various calls to each other, it could be difficult to carefully order them so that each function calls *only* functions that are above it in the source code file. Instead, most programmers put the functions in some logical order (or maybe not), but they don't worry much about the calling order. Then they have all the function prototypes toward the top of the source code file, as we did earlier in Listing 4-9.

When you type a function prototype, many people say that you are specifying a *forward reference*. This phrase simply means that you are providing a reference to something that happens later. It's not a big deal, and it mainly comes from some of the older programming languages. But some people use the jargon, and we hope that if you hear that phrase, it will trigger happy memories of this book.

Writing two versions of the same function

There may be times when you want to write two versions of the same function, the only difference being that they take different parameter types. For example, you may want a function called `Combine`. One version takes two strings and puts the two strings together, but with a space in the middle. It then prints the resulting string to the console. Another version takes two numbers, adds them, and writes all three numbers — the first two and the sum — to the console.

The first version would look like this:

```
void Combine(string first, string second)
{
  cout << first << " " << second << endl;
}
```

There's nothing magical or particularly special about this function. It's called `Combine`; it takes two strings as parameters; it does not return anything. The code for the function prints the two strings with a space between them.

Now the second version looks like this:

```
void Combine(int first, int second)
{
  int sum = first + second;
  cout << first << " " << second << " " << sum << endl;
}
```

Again, nothing spectacular here. The function name is `Combine`, and it does not return anything. But this version takes two integers, not two strings, as parameters. The code is also different from the previous code in that it first figures the sum of the two and then it prints the different numbers.

Well this is all fine and dandy, but can you have two functions by the same name like this? Yup! Listing 4-10 shows the entire code. Both functions are present in the listing.

Listing 4-10:   Writing Two Versions of a Function

```
#include <iostream>

using namespace std;

void Combine(string first, string second)
{
  cout << first << " " << second << endl;
}

void Combine(int first, int second)
{
  int sum = first + second;
  cout << first << " " << second << " " << sum << endl;
}

int main()
{
  Combine("David","Letterman");
  Combine(15,20);
  return 0;
}
```

Note in `main` that we called each function. How did we specify which one we want? *By simply passing the right types.* Take a close look at the first call:

```
Combine("David","Letterman");
```

This call includes two strings. so the compiler knows to use the first version, which takes two strings. Now look at the second function call:

```
Combine(15,20);
```

This call takes two integers, so the compiler knows to use the second version of the function.

This process of writing two versions of the same function is called *overloading* the function. Normally, overloading is a bad thing, like when we go to a nice restaurant and overload our stomachs. But here it's a good thing and even useful.

When you overload a function, the parameters must differ. For example, the functions can take the same type of information but use a different number of parameters. Of course, the previous example shows that the parameters can also vary by type. You can also have different return types, but they must differ by *more than just the return type*.

Calling All String Functions

To get the most out of strings, you need to make use of some special functions that cater to the strings. However, using these functions is a little different from the other functions used so far in the chapter. Instead of just calling the function, you type first the variable name that holds the string, then a period (or *dot*, as the netheads prefer to call it), and then the function name along with any parameters (*arguments,* if any purists are reading).

The reason you code string functions differently is because you're making use of some *object-oriented programming* features. Minibook I, Chapter 7 describes in detail how these types of functions (called *member* functions) work.

One function that you can use is called `insert`. You can use this function if you want to insert more characters into another string. For example, if you have the string `"Something interesting and bizarre"` and you insert the string `"seriously "` (with a space at the end) into the middle of it starting at index 10, you'll get the string `"Something seriously interesting and bizarre"`.

When you work with strings, the first character is the 0th index, and the second character is the 1st index, and so on.

The following lines of code perform an insert by using the `insert` function:

```
string words = "Something interesting and bizarre";
words.insert(10, "seriously ");
```

The first of these lines simply creates a string called `words` and stuffs it full with the phrase `"Something interesting and bizarre"`. The second line does the insert. Notice the strange way of calling the function: You first specify the variable name, `words`, and then a dot, and then the function name, `insert`. Next, you follow it with the parameters in parentheses, as usual. For this function, the first parameter is the index where you want to insert the string. The second parameter is the actual string you are going to insert.

After these two lines run, the string variable called `words` contains the string "Something seriously interesting and bizarre".

You can also erase parts of a string by using a similar function called, believe it or not, `erase`. Although computer folks like to obfuscate through their parlance (that is, confuse people through choices of words!), they do occasionally break down and pick names that actually make sense.

The following line of code erases from the string called `words` 16 characters starting with the 20th index:

```
words.erase(19,16);
```

Consequently, if the variable called `words` contains the string `"Something seriously interesting and bizarre"`, after this line runs, it will contain `"Something seriously bizarre"`.

Another useful function is `replace`. This function replaces a certain part of the string with another string. To use this, you specify where in the string you want to start the replacement and how many characters you want to replace. Then you specify the string you want to replace the old, worn-out parts with.

So, for example, if your string is `"Something seriously bizarre"` and you want to replace the word `"thing"` with the string `"body"`, you would tell `replace` to start at index 4, and replace 5 characters with the word `"body"`. To do this, you would enter:

```
words.replace(4, 5, "body");
```

Notice the number of characters you replace does not have to be the same as the length of the new string. If the string starts out with `"Something seriously bizarre"`, after this `replace` statement runs, the string will contain `"Somebody seriously bizarre"`. But the string will not actually contain somebody who is seriously bizarre; it contains just the string.

Listing 4-11 shows all these functions working together.

Listing 4-11:   Operating on Strings

```
#include <iostream>

using namespace std;

int main()
{
  string words = "Something interesting and bizarre";
  cout << words << endl;

  words.insert(10, "seriously ");
  cout << words << endl;

  words.erase(19,16);
  cout << words << endl;

  words.replace(4, 5, "body");
  cout << words << endl;

  return 0;
}
```

When you run this program, you see the following output:

```
Something interesting and bizarre
Something seriously interesting and bizarre
Something seriously bizarre
Somebody seriously bizarre
```

The first line is the original string. The second line is the result of the insert function. The third line is the result of the erase function. And the final line is the result of the replace function.

Understanding main

All the programs so far have had a main. This main is actually a function. Notice its header, which is followed by code inside braces:

```
int main()
```

You can see that this is definitely a function header: It starts out with a return type, then the function name, main. This is just one form of the main function — the form that CodeBlocks uses by default. However, you may decide that you want to give users the ability to provide input when they type the name of your program at the console. In this case, you use this alternative form of the main function that includes two parameters.

```
int main(int argc, char *argv[])
```

Who, what, where, and why return?

The main function header starts with the type int. This means the function main returns something. But what? And to whom? And why and when and all those *w* words?

The result of main is sometimes used by the computer to return error messages if the program, for some reason, didn't work or didn't do what it was supposed to do. But here's the inside scoop: *Outputting a return value just doesn't work* — at least, not in the graphical environment that most of you use.

It's true. For many computers, particularly Windows computers, the return value is of very little use to anybody. The return type is specifically designed to work with batch files (files with a BAT extension that originally appeared as part of DOS, or Disk Operating System). Consequently, unless you plan to work with batch files (and many people still do), just return 0.

On some high-powered Unix systems, the return value of main *is* used. Some of these systems running so-called *mission-critical applications* (a fancy word that means the computer programmers feel like what they're doing is important to the safety of the universe) do indeed use the return values from main. These computers may run hundreds of programs. If one of these programs returns something other than 0, another program detects this and notifies somebody (usually by sending the poor sap a page in the middle of the night). When you're still learning C++, you're not likely to need to return things other than 0, but if you're lucky enough to be working for a company that builds applications vital to the well-being of the universe, you may want to find out from your teammates if you do, in fact, need to return something other than 0.

So what about those seriously bizarre looking parameters in main? The first is reasonably straightforward; it's an integer variable with the goofy name argv, which sounds like something Scooby-Doo would say. But what about that second goofiness? To understand the second, you need to know that these two parameters are actually used as *command-line parameters*. When you run a program, especially from the command prompt, you type the name of the program and press Enter. But before pressing Enter, you can follow the program name with other words. Many of the commands you use in Unix and in the Windows command-line tool (also known as DOS) have a program name and then various parameters. For example, on Unix you could type the following command to copy the file called myfile to a new file called yourfile:

```
cp myfile yourfile
```

On Windows, you could type the following command to copy the file called `myfile` to a new file called `yourfile`:

```
copy myfile yourfile
```

When you run such a command, you are actually running a program called `copy`. The program takes two command-line parameters, in this case `"myfile"` and `"yourfile"` and passes these two strings into the `main` function as parameters.

For the `main` function, the first parameter in the header is `argc`, pro-nounced *arg-SEE*, which represents the number of command-line param-eters. In the case of the `copy` or `cp` command (see the two preceding lines of code), you have two (`"myfile"` and `"yourfile"`), so `argc` would be 2.

The second parameter in the `main` function is the cryptic-looking `char *argv[]`. The name of the variable is called `argv`, and it is pronounced *arg-VEE*. Minibook I, Chapter 8, deals with a topic called an array. An *array* is a sequence of variables stored under one name. The `argv` variable is one such animal. To access the individual variables stored under the single umbrella known as `argv`, you do something like this:

```
cout << argv[0] << endl;
cout << argv[1] << endl;
```

(In the preceding example, you're using brackets as you did similarly with accessing the individual characters in a string.)

In the case of the two command-line parameters `myfile` and `yourfile`, these two lines of code would print the lines

```
myfile
yourfile
```

You can access the command-line parameters using a `for` loop. Listing 4-12 shows how.

Listing 4-12:   Accessing the Command-Line Parameters

```cpp
#include <iostream>
#include <stdlib.h>
int main(int argc, char *argv[])
{
  for (int index=0; index < argc; index++)
  {
    cout << argv[index] << endl;
  }
  return 0;
}
```

When we run this program from the prompt using the following command-line parameters

```
CommandLineParameters Command Line Parameters
```

we see the following output:

```
c:\CommandLineParameters Command Line Parameters
CommandLineParameters
Command
Line
Parameters
```

The first item in the `argv` list is always the name of the program.

Chapter 5: Dividing Between Source-Code Files

In This Chapter

✔ Creating multiple source-code files

✔ Creating header files

✔ Sharing variables among source files

✔ Making use of the mysterious header wrappers

*J*ust as you can divide your work into functions, you can also divide your work into multiple source-code files. The main reason to do so is, simply, to help keep your project more manageable. Also, with multiple source-code files, you can have several people working on a single project, each working on a different source-code file at the same time. The goal, of course, is to make sure that your coworkers work on the harder parts that are more grueling and no fun while you get all the credit.

The key to multiple source files is knowing where to break the source code into pieces. Like anything else, if you break the source code in the wrong place, it will, well, break.

In this chapter, we show you how to divide your source code into multiple files (and in all the right places). The examples we give use CodeBlocks; however, we also provide a few Makefile tips if you're using other tools.

Creating Multiple Source Files

In this section, we talk about how to create multiple source-code files, first for CodeBlocks and then for other compilers. This process is far simpler in CodeBlocks, and we highly recommend that approach.

When you create a second source-code file, this code becomes part of your project. And when you compile, the compiler compiles all the source-code files in your project, assuming that you have changed them since the last time you compiled. You can put your functions in separate source-code files, and they can call each other. In this way, they all work together in the single program. In the section "Sharing with Header Files," later in this chapter, we talk about how you can have a function call another function in a different source file.

You cannot break a single function up and put it into two source files. That would be quite painful for the little fellow, and certainly not a good programming practice either because it simply wouldn't compile. The compiler requires that your functions stay in one piece in a single source file.

Multiple source files in CodeBlocks

If you're using CodeBlocks, cutting your program into multiple source-code files is as easy as cutting a cake. The following steps show you how to perform this task:

1. **Choose File⇨New⇨File.**

You see the New from Template dialog box shown in Figure 5-1. Notice that you can choose from a header, source code, or an empty file. Normally, you'll choose either the C/C++ Header or C/C++ Source option. The Empty File option is for non-source files, such as a text file used as a ReadMe.

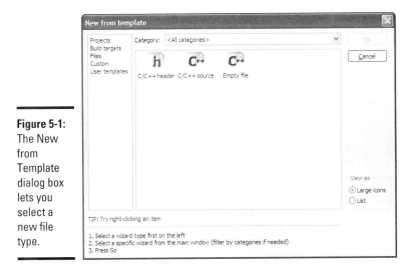

Figure 5-1: The New from Template dialog box lets you select a new file type.

2. **Highlight the template you want to use and click Go.**

You see a wizard associated with the particular file you've chosen.

3. **Click Next to get past the initial Welcome page.**

If you chose the Empty File template, skip to Step 5. When using the C/C++ Header or C/C++ Source templates, you see a language selection page.

4. **Highlight the language you want to use — either C or C++ — and click Next.**

The wizard asks what you want to call the file, where you want to store it, and which builds should use the file, as shown in Figure 5-2.

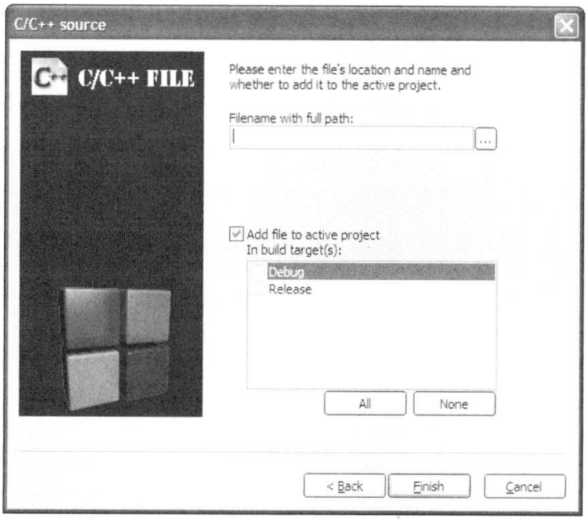

Figure 5-2:
Provide
the file
information
required by
the wizard.

5. **Type a path and filename for the file in the Filename with Full Path field.**

You must provide a full path, even if you want the file in the current folder. Click the ellipses to display a Select Filename dialog box where you can choose the location of the file. The default path shown in the Select Filename dialog box is the current folder.

6. **Check the individual builds that should use the file.**

As an alternative, you can click All to add the file to all builds.

7. **Click Finish.**

The wizard adds the new file to your project. CodeBlocks automatically opens the file so you can begin editing it. You also see the file you added in the Management window, as shown in Figure 5-3. In this case, you see both the source files and a header file. Notice that the source files appear in dark type, while the header file appears in gray type. This shows that the source files are compiled to create the project and the header file isn't. The "Sharing with Header Files" section of the chapter discusses how the compiler works with header files in more detail.

Figure 5-3:
The Management window displays the files used to compile the project.

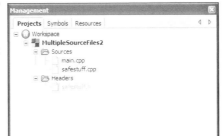

If you add a file to CodeBlocks that you really don't need, right-click the file in the Management window and choose Remove File from Project from the context menu. The file will disappear from the project but still appear in the directory in which you created it. If you later decide that you really do want that file, right-click the project entry in the Management window, choose Add Files from the context menu, and select the file you want to add back into the project using the options in the Add Files to Project dialog box.

If CodeBlocks doesn't automatically open the file you added, you can open it by double-clicking its name in the tree. When you do, an additional tab appears at the top of your source-code files. These tabs represent the different files that are open. You can click a tab to have that file's code appear in the source-code window. When you click another tab, the window shows the source for that file, instead. And, thankfully, it remembers any changes you make if you switch to another tab. So you can bounce all around the screen and switch all you want, and the computer shouldn't get confused.

After you have multiple files in your project, you can put some of your source in one file and some in another. But before you do, you may want to read some of the other sections in this chapter because we explain how to properly divide your source code without it ending up like cake that got smooshed while you were trying to cut it.

Multiple source files in other compilers

If you're using CodeBlocks, you don't really need to read this section because CodeBlocks mucks around with the Makefile for you automatically. Life is good. If you want to see how CodeBlocks performs this task, look at the `.depend` file for your project, such as `MultipleSourceFiles.depend`. The `.depend` file is simple XML, so you can view it with any XML-capable application (including Internet Explorer or Firefox). Otherwise, you'll want to read this section.

To add source-code files to other compilers, you need to modify the Makefile, and you need to understand Makefile rules and the compile rocess. Yuck. (Makefiles are described in Appendix A.) Many ways to modify a Makefile are available. If you use implicit rules, you probably just need to add the name of the file to the list of source files. If you use a separate rule for each file, you need to add another rule for this new file. In that case, you may still have a list of all source-code files or a list of all object files (which are just the source-code filenames with either an .o or .obj extension), in which case you'll have to make another entry.

For example, you may have separate rules for each source file, as in the following:

```
main.o: main.cpp
    $(CC) -c main.cpp -o main.o $(CFLAGS)
```

In this case, you need to add another line similar to this one for your new file. If your new file is orangegoo.cpp, your new rule will look like this:

```
orangegoo.o: orangegoo.cpp
    $(CC) -c orangegoo.cpp -o orangegoo.o $(CFLAGS)
```

Note that you must indent the second line by using a tab. If you use spaces, it may not work properly.

You probably also have a rule listing the object files. Remember that it will likely be the object files and not the source files, because the object files are the temporary things that the compiler generates — or *makes*. Thus, you may have a macro such as this:

```
OBJ = main.o orangegoo.o
```

This macro would be listed in the rule for the final executable file. That way, when you make the executable file, the make utility first sees whether these two .o files are up-to-date. If not, make first makes these two .o files, based on the rules you supplied earlier. Nice and simple; too bad Makefiles are so ugly.

Creating multiple files

Before two source files can work together, they must somehow find out about each other. Just because they're both sitting on the computer doesn't mean that they know about each other. Computers are kind of goofy about that sort of thing. So to get two source files to finally open up and get to know each other, you need to tell each of them about what's in the other file.

When you write a function, normally the function must appear before any calls to it appear within the same source file. That's because of the way the compiler goes through the code: If it encounters a call to a function but has not yet heard of that function, it issues an error. But the way around this is to use a function prototype. A *function prototype* is simply the header line from a function, ending with a semicolon, as in the following:

```
void BigDog(int KibblesCount);
```

Later in the source file is the actual function, with this header line duplicated. But instead of a semicolon, the function would have an open brace, the function code, and a closing brace, as in the following:

```
void BigDog(int KibblesCount)
{
    cout << "I'm a lucky dog" << endl;
    cout << "I have " << KibblesCount << " pieces of food" << endl;
}
```

So after the function prototype, you can call the function whether the function code itself is before or after the call.

For the compiler to understand a function call, all it needs at the point the code makes the call is a function *prototype*. It's up to the linker to determine whether that function really exists.

Because the function call only needs a function prototype, you can put the function *itself* in another source-code file. You could, therefore, have two separate source-code files, as in the following example. The first source-code file, main.cpp, is shown in Listing 5-1. The second source-code file, mystuff.cpp, is shown in Listing 5-2.

Listing 5-1: Calling a Function with Only a Prototype

```
#include <iostream>

using namespace std;

void BigDog(int KibblesCount);

int main()
{
  BigDog(3);
  return 0;
}
```

Listing 5-2: Using a Function from a Separate File

```
#include <iostream>

using namespace std;

void BigDog(int KibblesCount)
{
    cout << "I'm a lucky dog" << endl;
    cout << "I have " << KibblesCount << " pieces of food" << endl;
}
```

A quick overview of namespaces

The `using namespace std;` line in Listing 5-2 tells the compiler to use a specific namespace, `std`. A *namespace* is a grouping of classes and functions. The `std`, or standard, namespace contains a host of useful classes and functions, such as `string`. If you don't include this declaration, you need to preface every use of the classes or functions found in `std` by typing `std::<class or function>`. For example, to use a `string` you need to type `std::string`. Because this is a painful way to write code, you add the `using namespace std;` line.

In Listings 5-1 and 5-2, we broke the function away from the prototype. When you compile these two files together as a single program (either by pressing F9 in CodeBlocks or by using the methods described in the "Multiple source files in other compilers" section, earlier in this chapter), they all fit together nicely. You can then run the program, and you see this somewhat interesting output:

```
I'm a lucky dog
I have 3 pieces of food
```

Notice also that we had to put the same `#include` lines at the start of the `mystuff.cpp` file. That's because `mystuff.cpp` uses `cout`, and to use `cout`, it needs the `#include <iostream>` line.

Sharing with Header Files

Breaking source code apart into multiple files is easy, but soon you may run into a problem. If you have a function, say, `SafeCracker`, and this function is extremely useful and is likely to be called many times from within several other source-code files, you would need a prototype for `SafeCracker` in every file that calls it. The prototype may look like this:

```
string SafeCracker(int SafeID);
```

But instead of putting this line in every file that uses the function, we know of an easier way. (We computer people are always looking for the easier way so we can finally retire.) Simply put this line inside its own file, called a *header file,* and give the filename an `.h` or an `.hpp` extension. (It's your choice which extension you use, because it really doesn't matter; we usually just go with `.h`.) For example, we might save the line `string SafeCracker (int SafeID);` in a file called `safestuff.h`.

Then, instead of typing the header line at the start of each file that needs the function, you type

```
#include "safestuff.h"
```

You would then have three source-code files, which we have shown in Listings 5-3, 5-4, and 5-5. The first is main.cpp, which calls the function. The second is safestuff.h, which contains the function prototype. The third is safestuff.cpp, which contains the actual code for the function whose prototype appears in the header file. Lots of files, but now the code is broken into manageable pieces. Also, make sure that you save all three of these files in the same directory.

Listing 5-3:   Including the Header File in the main File

```
#include <iostream>
#include "safestuff.h"

using namespace std;

int main()
{
  cout << "Surprise, surprise!" << endl;
  cout << "The combination is (once again)" << endl;
  cout << SafeCracker(12) << endl;
  return 0;
}
```

Listing 5-4:   Containing the Function Prototype in the Header File

```
using namespace std;

#ifndef SAFESTUFF_H_INCLUDED
#define SAFESTUFF_H_INCLUDED

string SafeCracker(int SafeID);

#endif // SAFESTUFF_H_INCLUDED
```

Listing 5-5:   Containing the Actual Function Code

```
#include <iostream>

using namespace std;

string SafeCracker(int SafeID)
{
    return "13-26-16";
}
```

Before you compile this program, however, we need to give you a couple pointers. First, the compiler *does not* compile the header file into a separate `.o` or `.obj` file. With the program in Listings 5-3 through 5-5, the compiler compiles only two files: `main.cpp` and `mystuff.cpp`. Instead of compiling the header file, when it reads through the `main.cpp` file and gets to the `#include` line for the header file, it temporarily switches over and reads that file, pretending that it's still reading the same `main.cpp` file. As it continues, it compiles everything as if it's all part of the `main.cpp` file. And if you include this header file in other source-code files, it does the same thing again for those source files.

To get this code to compile, remember the following rules:

+ Makefiles: If you are using a compiler where you have to handle your own Makefiles, do not add a rule for compiling the header files, which usually start with `.hpp` or `.h`. Only compile the source files, which usually start with `.cpp` or `.cc`.

+ Visual C++: Although we've said very little so far about Microsoft Visual C++ (VC++), if you use VC++, do not add header files to your project. Only add source files. VC++ will keep a listing of the header files in a tree called dependencies, but you don't add them yourself.

+ CodeBlocks: What could be easier? You just make the files, and CodeBlocks handles all the file connectivity for you. Nothing to worry about. The header and source files all show in the project list, and CodeBlocks also handles the details of which ones need to be compiled.

After you follow these rules, you can go ahead and compile and run the code in Listings 5-3 through 5-5. When you run the program, you see the following output:

```
Surprise, surprise!
The combination is (once again)
13-26-16
```

If you have a source file containing some functions, creating a header file that contains the associated function prototypes is generally a good practice. Then you can name the header file the same as the source file, except with a different extension. We did this in Listings 5-4 and 5-5: We named the header file `safestuff.h`, and the source file `safestuff.cpp`.

Instead of saying *header file,* some people prefer to say *include file.* We usually say *header file* because, to us, *include* is usually a verb, and it gets kind of awkward to say something like this: "We're pretty sure that we included the include file, but if we didn't include the correct include file, would you please include us in your meeting; and in the discussion, we will be sure to include a few questions about how to include the proper include file. Then you can include an answer to our inclusions about the inclusions of an include file." It's just difficult to say, you know? So we say *header file.*

Adding the header only once

CodeBlocks includes several lines in the header file by default. These lines create a symbol that tells the compiler whether a header file is already included in the source file so that the compiler doesn't add it twice. Adding a header twice is an error because then you'd define the forward reference for a function twice. Here is what you see when you initially create a header file with CodeBlocks:

```
#ifndef SAFESTUFF_H_INCLUDED
#define SAFESTUFF_H_INCLUDED

#endif // SAFESTUFF_H_INCLUDED
```

When you type the header code into CodeBlocks, type it between the `#define SAFESTUFF_H_INCLUDED` and `#endif // SAFESTUFF_H_INCLUDED` lines. The "Using the Mysterious Header Wrappers" section of the chapter describes these automatic entries in detail.

Using brackets or quotes

You may have noticed something about the code in Listing 5-3. When we included the `safestuff.h` file, we did not put it inside brackets as we did in the other `#include` lines. Instead, we put it inside quotes:

```
#include "safestuff.h"
```

That's because programmers for years have been fighting over the rules of *where* exactly on the hard drive to put the header files. Do you put them in the same directory or folder as your project? Or do you put them in a special directory all by themselves? Or do you just put them out in the back yard to dry out?

Regardless of where you put your header files, here is the rule for when to use quotes and when to use brackets: The compiler looks in several directories to find include files. And it can, possibly, look in the same directory as the source file. If you use angled brackets (that is, less-than and greater-than signs), as in `#include <string>`, the compiler does not look in the same directory as the source file. But if you use double quotes, as in `#include "safestuff.h"`, the compiler *first* looks in the same directory as the source file. And if the compiler doesn't find the header file there, it looks in the remaining directories, as it would with angle brackets.

Some people always like to use double quotes. That way, whether the header file is in the same file as the source file or not, the compiler should find it.

Most professional programmers today *always* use angle brackets. This forces programmers to put their header files in a common area. With really big projects, programmers like to have a directory dedicated to source files and another directory dedicated to header files. No header file is ever in the same directory as the source file.

For small projects, some people like to lump all the source and header files into a single directory. These people typically use angle brackets around system header files (such as `#include <string>`) and double quotes around their own header files. In the projects in this book, we generally follow this rule. The header files that we write are in the same directory as the source files, and we use double quotes for `#include` lines of our own files and angle brackets for the `#include` lines of system headers.

If you follow the same approach that we use here, you immediately know whether the `#include` line refers to one of your own header files or another header file. If it refers to your own, it has double quotes.

If you start working on a large C++ project, you will probably find that project managers use the rule of always using angle brackets. For large projects, this is typically the best policy.

If you try to compile and you get a `No such file or directory` error on the `#include` line, it's probably because you put the header file in a source file directory but used angle brackets instead of double quotes. Try switching that line to double quotes.

Sharing Variables Among Source Files

When you declare a variable inside a function, it remains local to the function. But you may want functions to share a single variable: One function may store something, and another may read its contents and write it to the console. To do this, declare the variable outside a function. That works until you try to share a variable between multiple source files. If you're not careful, the source files end up with a separate copy of the variable. Within a single source file, the variable can be shared between functions but not between source files. That could be confusing.

There's a trick to making this work. Declare the variable inside one and only one of the source files. Then, you declare it *again* inside one (and only one) header file, but you precede it with the word *extern*, as in `extern int DoubleCheeseburgers;`.

Listings 5-6, 5-7, and 5-8 demonstrate the use of a single variable that is shared between multiple source files.

Listing 5-6: Making Use of a Global Variable

```
#include <iostream>
#include "sharealike.h"

using namespace std;

int main()
{
  DoubleCheeseburgers = 20;
  EatAtJoes();
  return 0;
}
```

Listing 5-7: Using a Header File to Declare a Global Variable

```
#ifndef SHAREALIKE_H_INCLUDED
#define SHAREALIKE_H_INCLUDED

extern int DoubleCheeseburgers;
void EatAtJoes();

#endif // SHAREALIKE_H_INCLUDED
```

Listing 5-8: Declaring the Actual Storage for the Global Variable

```
#include <iostream>
#include "sharealike.h"

using namespace std;

int DoubleCheeseburgers;

void EatAtJoes() {
  cout << "How many cheeseburgers today?" << endl;
  cout << DoubleCheeseburgers << endl;
}
```

Be careful when you do this; getting it exactly right is very tricky. You declare the variable once inside the header file, but you must remember the word extern. That tells the various files, "This variable is declared elsewhere, but here's its name and type so you can use it." Then you declare the variable in one of the source files, *without* the word extern; this creates the actual storage bin for the variable. Finally, you include the header file in each of your source files that use the global variable.

When you share a variable among multiple source files, it is a *global variable.* A variable used by a single function is called a *local variable.* If you share a variable between functions within a single source file but not between multiple source files, people call this a *global variable* or a *global variable that is local to the source file.*

Use the word `extern` in your header file when using a global variable. If you forget to do that, you give each source file its own variable that happens to have the same name.

Using the Mysterious Header Wrappers

When you include a header file, you usually only want to include it *once* per source file. But that can create a problem: Suppose we have a huge software project, and several header files include another of our header files, called `superheader.h`. If we include all these other header files, how can we be sure to pick up the `superheader.h` file only once?

The answer looks strange but does the trick. We start each header file with these lines:

```
#ifndef SHAREALIKE_H
#define SHAREALIKE_H
#endif
```

Depending on which C++ IDE you use, your editor may add these lines automatically, just as CodeBlocks does. In this case, you type the header file content between the `#define SHAREALIKE_H` and `#endif` lines. However, if your IDE doesn't add the lines automatically, be sure to add them so your code looks like the code in Listing 5-7. Otherwise, the compiler may spout errors that you may not recognize immediately.

These *header wrappers,* as they are often called, ensure that the code in the header gets processed only once per source-code file each time you compile. The wrappers use special lines called *preprocessor directives.* Basically, the *second* line defines something that is sort of like a variable but is used only during compilation; this something is called a *symbol.* The symbol is called `SHAREALIKE_H`, and we picked it by taking the filename, making it all caps, and replacing the dot with an underscore.

The first line checks to see whether this symbol has been defined. If *not,* it proceeds with the lines of code that follow. The next line goes ahead and defines the symbol, so now it's actually defined for later. Then the compiler does all the rest of the lines in the file. Finally, the last line, `#endif`, simply finishes the very first line.

Now consider what could happen if you include this same file twice, as in

```
#include "sharealike.h"
#include "sharealike.h"
```

(That can happen indirectly if you include two different files that each include sharealike.h.) The *second* time the compiler goes through sharealike.h, it sees the first line, which checks to see whether the SHAREALIKE_H symbol is defined. But this time it is! So instead of going through all the lines again, the compiler *skips* to the #endif line at the very end of the file. Thus, your header file gets processed only once per source-code file. Tricky, no? And confusing? Yes, a bit. So remember the following rule.

When you create a header file, be sure to put the header wrappers around it. You can use any symbol name you like, provided it uses only letters, numbers, and underscores and doesn't start with a number, and provided it's not already a variable name in your source or a C++ word. But most people base their choice on some variation of the filename itself, such as MYFILE_H or MYFILE_H_ or even _MYFILE_H_.

Chapter 6: Referring to Your Data through Pointers

In This Chapter

✔ Using two types of memory: the stack and heap

✔ Accessing variable addresses through pointers

✔ Creating variables on the heap by using the new keyword

✔ Taking pointers as parameters and returning pointers

✔ Modifying variables the easy way

*W*here do you live? Don't say it out loud because thousands of people are reading this book, and you don't want them all to know. So just think about your address. Most places have some sort of address so the mail service will know where to deliver your packages and the cable guy can show up sometime between now and 5:00 next Thursday. (So make sure that you're there.)

Other things have addresses too. For example, a big corporation in an office building likely has all its cubes numbered. And offices in buildings usually have numbers; and apartments normally have numbers, too.

Now suppose someone named Sam works in office number 180. Last week, however, Sam got booted out the door for spending too much time surfing the Web. Now Sally gets first dibs on office number 180, even though she's not taking over Sam's position. Sam moved out; Sally moved in. Same office — different person staying there.

The computer's memory works similarly. Every little part of the computer's memory is associated with a number that represents its location, or *address*. In this chapter, we show you that after you determine the address of a variable stored in memory, you can do powerful things with it, which gives you the tools to create powerful programs.

If any single topic in C++ programming is most important, it is the notion of pointers. Therefore, if you want to become a millionaire, read this chapter. Okay, so it may not make you a millionaire, but suggesting it could give you the incentive to master this chapter. Then you can become an ace programmer and make lots of money.

Heaping and Stacking the Variables

C++ programs use two kinds of memory: heap and stack. The *heap* is a common area of memory that your program *allocates* — that is, sets aside — for the different functions in your program to use. Global variables go in this heap.

Whenever your program calls a function, however, the function gets its own little private area of memory storage in an area of memory known as a *stack*. The reason that this is called a stack is because it's treated like a stack of papers: You can put something on the stack, and you can take something off, but you can't put anything in the middle or take anything from the middle. The computer uses this stack to keep track of all your function calls.

For example, suppose you have a function called GoFishing. The function GoFishing calls StopAndBuyBait, which then calls PayForBait, which calls GetOutCreditCard, which calls UseFakeCreditCard. How can the computer keep track of all this mess? It uses the *stack* metaphor. First it saves the original function, GoFishing. Then when that function calls StopAndBuyBait, the computer remembers that function by putting it *on top* of GoFishing — not in the same storage bin, but in one on top of the preceding item so that the preceding item is still there. Then, when that function calls PayForBait, the computer once again remembers that function by putting it on top of StopAndBuyBait, and so on, until it has all the items piled one on top of the other, with UseFakeCreditCard on the top and GoFishing on the bottom. This process *pushes* items onto the top of the stack.

Next, when the computer is finished with UseFakeCreditCard, it *pops* off the top of the stack. What it picks up is the place it left off before calling UseFakeCreditCard, which happens to be GetOutCreditCard. And when that function is finished, once again the computer pops the top off the stack to find PayForBait. And, as before, that's where it left off last. It continues this until it gets all the way back to the beginning, which was GoFishing.

Every position in memory has a number associated with it. When your program starts, the computer sets aside a large chunk of memory and then works closely with the microprocessor itself to assign a bunch of numbers to the memory. Your program's variables and your program's code goes in this memory. And consider this: If your program sits in memory, each function sits in a particular place in memory, a place with a number or address associated with it. In other words, each function has an address.

Each function and each variable in your program has a place where it resides in memory. That place has a number associated with it. Therefore, each function and each variable has an *address*.

Placing a hex on C++

Sooner or later in your computer programming, you will encounter a strange way of notating numbers on the computer. This strange way is called *hexadecimal,* or sometimes just *hex.* In C++, you can recognize a hex number because it starts with the characters 0x. These characters aren't actually part of the number; they just notate it in the same way double quotes denote a string. Whereas our usual decimal numbers consist of the digits 0, 1, 2, 3, 4, 5, 6, 7, 8, and 9, a hex number consists of these digits plus six more: A, B, C, D, E, and F. That makes a total of 16 digits. (Yes, we know, the letters A through F are not digits. But in hex, they are considered digits.) A good way to picture counting with regular decimal numbers is by using the odometer in a car, which (if you're honest) only goes forward, not backward. It starts out with 00000000 (assuming eight digits, which is a lot). The rightmost digit runs from 0 through 9, over and over. When any digit reaches 9 and all digits to the right of that are nine, the

next digit to the left goes up by 1. For example, when you reach 00000999, the next digit to the left goes up by 1 as each 9 goes back to 0, to get 00001000.

With hex numbers, you count this same way, except instead of stopping at 9 to loop back, you then go to A, then B, and then up to F. And then you loop back. So the first 17 hex numbers are, using eight digits, 00000000, 00000001, 00000002, 00000003, 00000004, 00000005, 00000006, 00000007, 00000008, 00000009, 0000000A, 0000000B, 0000000C, 0000000D, 0000000E, 0000000F, 00000010. Notice when we hit F toward the end there, we wrapped around again, adding 1 to the next digit to the left. When working with hex numbers, you may see such numbers as 0xAAAA0000 and 0X0000A3FF. (We included the 0x for C++ notation.) And incidentally, 1 more than each of these is 0xAAAA0001 and 0x0000A400.

The stack where the computer keeps track of the function calls is just a bunch of memory, too. What the computer considers the *top* of the stack is really the next position in memory. And the way the computer puts a function on the stack is by putting on the stack the *address* of where the computer left off in the preceding function.

When the computer calls one of your functions, not only does it save the address of the return location on the stack, it also reserves some space on the stack for your local variables.

This means that your variables can live in two places:

✦ **Heap:** The *heap* is a common area in memory where you can store global variables.

✦ **Stack:** The *stack* is the area where the computer stores both the information about the functions being called and the local variables for those functions.

A stack is an example of all sorts of wonderful things called *data structures.* Computer programmers have a tendency to try to model things from real life on the computer. A stack of papers apparently wasn't good enough for the computer folk; they wanted to be able to do the same type of thing with their data in the computer, and they called this thing a stack. They have come up with many types of data structures, including a similar one called a queue: With a *queue,* you put data in one end and take it out the other. It's like putting sheets of paper on top but taking them only from the bottom. You experience a queue when you wait in line at a store. The people are forming a queue, and some even call a line of people a queue.

Every hex number has a decimal equivalent. When you make a list showing decimal numbers side by side with hex numbers, you see, for example, that 0x0000001F is next to the decimal number 31. Thus, these two numbers represent the same quantity of items, such as apples. Remember that when you want to buy some apples: "I would like to buy one-ef apples."

Looks can be deceiving. The hex number 10 represents the same number of apples as the decimal number 16. That's why it's a good idea to use the 0x notation. Thus instead of hex 10, we would write 0x10, making it clear that we're not talking about a decimal number.

Converting between hexadecimal and decimal

If you want to convert between hex and decimal, you can use the calculator program that comes with Windows. However, you need to make sure it's running in *scientific mode.* To turn on this mode, choose View➪Scientific (if it's not already chosen). When you do, you will see the calculator magically transform into a much bigger, more powerful calculator.

To convert a hex number to decimal, click the Hex option in the upper left. Then type the hex number by using the number keys and the letters A through F, such as FB1263. (You don't need to type the zeros at the beginning, such as 00FB1263 — they won't show up — nor do you type the 0x used in C++.) After you finish

typing it all in, click the Dec option, which is next to the Hex option. The calculator instantly transforms this beautiful hex thing into an equally beautiful thing — a decimal number! In this case, you see 16454243. You can go the other way, too: If you have a decimal number, such as 16454243, you can click the Hex option to convert it to hex. If you convert 16454243 to hex, you get back FB1263, which is what you started with.

You can convert words, too (if you're bored). The hex number and disco group ABBA is 43962 in decimal. And the hex number FADE is 64222. And Jeff's house, which he calls hex number FACADE, is 16435934. Have fun!

You can represent hex numbers by using either uppercase or lowercase letters. However, do not mix cases within a single number. Don't use 0xABab0000. Instead use either 0xabab0000 or 0xABAB0000.

Getting a variable's address

Because every variable lives somewhere in memory, every variable has an address. If you have a function that declares an integer variable called NumberOfPotholes, then when your program calls this function, the computer will allocate space for NumberOfPotholes somewhere in memory.

If you want to take the address of (which is computerspeak for *find the address of*) the variable NumberOfPotholes, you simply throw an ampersand, &, in front of it.

Listing 6-1 shows an example of taking the address of a variable and printing it.

Listing 6-1: Using the & Character to Take the Address of a Variable

```
#include <iostream>

using namespace std;

int main()
{
  int NumberOfPotholes = 532587;
  cout << &NumberOfPotholes << endl;
  return 0;
}
```

When you run this program, a hexadecimal number appears on the console. This may or may not match ours, and it may or may not be the same each time you run the program. The result depends on exactly how the computer allocated your variable for you and the order in which it did things. This could be very different between versions of compilers. When we run Listing 6-1, we see

```
0x22ff74
```

The output you see from this program is the address of the variable called NumberOfPotholes. In other words, that number is the hex version of the place where the NumberOfPotholes variable is stored in memory. The output is not the *contents* of the variable or the contents of the variable converted to hex; rather, it's the address of the variable converted to hex.

A pointer example

Suppose `NumberOfPotholes` contains the number 5000. That means the computer stores the number 5000 somewhere in memory. When you take the address of `NumberOf Potholes`, you are taking the address of the memory where you can find the number 5000.

And so, when you set

```
ptr = &NumberOfPotholes;
```

`ptr` points to a memory location that contains the number 5000.

That output is not very useful, unless you want to sound like a computer techie. You could walk around announcing that the variable lives at 0x22ff74, but that's not going to get you very far in life. (It may get you some interesting looks, though, which may be worth it.) But when you take that address, you can use it for other purposes. For example, you can use it to modify the variable itself by using what are called pointer variables. A *pointer variable* is just like any other variable except that it stores the *address of* another variable.

To declare a pointer variable, you need to specify the type of variable it will point to. Then you precede the variable's name with an asterisk, as in the following:

```
int *ptr;
```

This declares a variable that *points to* an integer. In other words, it can contain *the address* of an integer variable. And how do you grab the address of an integer variable? Easy! By using the & notation! Thus, you can do something like this:

```
ptr = &NumberOfPotholes;
```

This puts the address of the variable `NumberOfPotholes` in the `ptr` variable. Remember that `ptr` doesn't hold the number of potholes; rather, it holds the address of the variable called `NumberofPotholes`.

You specify the type of a pointer by the type of item it points to. If a pointer variable points to an integer, its type is *pointer to integer*. In C++ notation, its type is `int  *` (with a space between them) or `int*` (no space); you are allowed to enter it with or without a space. If a pointer variable points to a string, then its type is *pointer to string*, and notation for this type is `string  *`.

The `ptr` variable holds an address, but what's at that address? That address is the location in memory of the storage bin known as `NumberOfPotholes`. Right at that spot in memory is the data stored in `NumberOfPotholes`.

TIP

Think this pointer concept through carefully. If you have to, read this section over a few times until it's in your head. Then meditate on it. Wake up in the night thinking about it. Call strangers on the telephone and chitchat about it. But the more you understand pointers, the better off your programming career will be — and the more likely you will make a million dollars.

Changing a variable by using a pointer

After you have a pointer variable holding another variable's address, you can use the pointer to access the information in the other variable. That means that we have two ways to get to the information in a variable: We can use the variable name itself (such as NumberOfPotholes) or we can use the pointer variable that points to it.

If we want to store the number 6087 in NumberOfPotholes, we could do this:

```
NumberOfPotholes = 6087;
```

Or we could use the pointer. To use the pointer, we first declare it as follows.

```
ptr = &NumberOfPotholes;
```

Then, to change NumberOfPotholes, we don't just assign a value to it. Instead, we throw an asterisk in front of it, like so:

```
*ptr = 6087;
```

If ptr points to NumberOfPotholes, these two lines of code will have the same effect: Both will change the value to 6087. This process of sticking the asterisk before a pointer variable is called *dereferencing* the pointer. By the time you're finished with this book, you will know gobs of words that nobody else does. (And your newly enriched vocabulary makes talking on the telephone difficult at first.)

Take a look at Listing 6-2, which demonstrates all this.

Listing 6-2:   Modifying the Original Variable with a Pointer Variable

```
#include <iostream>

using namespace std;

int main()
{
  int NumberOfPotholes;
  int *ptr;
  ptr = &NumberOfPotholes;
  *ptr = 6087;
  cout << NumberOfPotholes << endl;
  return 0;
}
```

In Listing 6-2, the first line declares an integer variable, while the second line declares a pointer to an integer. The next line takes the address of the integer variable and stores it in the pointer. Then the fourth line modifies the original integer by dereferencing the pointer. And just to make sure that the process really worked, the next line prints the value of NumberOfPotholes. When you run the program, you will see the following output:

```
6087
```

This is correct; it is the value that the program stored in the original variable by using the pointer variable.

You can also read value of the original variable through the pointer. Take a look at Listing 6-3. This code accesses the value of NumberOfPotholes through the pointer variable, ptr. When the code gets the value, it saves it in another variable called SaveForLater.

Listing 6-3:   Accessing a Value through a Pointer

```
#include <iostream>

using namespace std;

int main()
{
  int NumberOfPotholes;
  int *ptr = &NumberOfPotholes;
  int SaveForLater;
  *ptr = 6087;
  SaveForLater = *ptr;
  cout << SaveForLater << endl;
  *ptr = 7000;
  cout << *ptr << endl;
  cout << SaveForLater << endl;
  return 0;
}
```

When you run this program, you see the following output.

```
6087
7000
6087
```

Notice also in this listing that we changed the value through ptr again, this time to 7000. When we run the program, you can see that the value did indeed change, but the value in SaveForLater remained the same. That's because SaveForLater is a separate variable and is not connected to the other two. The other two, however, are connected to each other.

Pointing at a string

Pointer variables enjoy pointing. Pointer variables can point to any type, including strings. However, after you say that a variable points to a certain type, it can only point to that type. That is, like any variable, you cannot change its type out from underneath it. The compiler won't let you do it.

To create a pointer to a string, you simply make the type of the variable `string *`. You can then set it equal to the address of a string variable. Listing 6-4 demonstrates this.

Listing 6-4:   Pointing to a String with Pointers

```
#include <iostream>

using namespace std;

int main()
{
  string GoodMovie;
  string *ptrToString;
  GoodMovie = "Best in Show";
  ptrToString = &GoodMovie;
  cout << *ptrToString << endl;
  return 0;
}
```

In Listing 6-4, you can see that the pointer variable called `ptrToString` points to the variable called `GoodMovie`. But when you want to use the pointer to access the string itself, you need to dereference the pointer by putting an asterisk, `*`, in front of it.

When you run this code, you see the results of the dereferenced pointer, which is the value of the `GoodMovie` variable:

```
Best in Show
```

You can change the value of the string through the pointer, again by dereferencing it, as in the following code:

```
*ptrToString = "Galaxy Quest";
cout << GoodMovie << endl;
```

Here, we dereferenced the pointer to set it equal to the string `"Galaxy Quest"` (a fine movie, we might add). Then to show that it really changed, we printed the variable itself, `GoodMovie`. The result of this code, when added at the end of Listing 6-4 (but prior to the `return 0`) is

```
Galaxy Quest
```

You can also use the pointer to access the individual parts of the string, as we did in Listing 6-5.

Listing 6-5:   Using Pointers to Point to a String

```cpp
#include <iostream>

using namespace std;

int main()
{
  string HorribleMovie;
  string *ptrToString;

  HorribleMovie = "L.A. Confidential";
  ptrToString = &HorribleMovie;

  for (unsigned i = 0; i < HorribleMovie.length(); i++)
  {
    cout << (*ptrToString)[i] << " ";
  }

  cout << endl;
  return 0;
}
```

When you run this program, you see the letters of the terrible movie appear one with spaces between them, as in the following.

```
L . A .   C o n f i d e n t i a l
```

Okay, so we didn't like *L.A. Confidential*. But it won two Oscars and was nominated for seven more, and it won a boatload of other awards, so we don't feel so bad saying so.

When you access the characters of the string through a pointer, you need to put parentheses around the asterisk and the pointer variable. Otherwise, the compiler gets confused and first tries to do the index in brackets with the variable name and afterwards applies the asterisk. That's backwards, and it won't make sense to the computer, so the compiler gives you an error message. But you can make it all better by using parentheses, as we did in Listing 6-5.

This program loops through the entire string, character by character. We used the `length` function for the string to find out how many characters are in the string. And inside the loop we grabbed the individual characters of the string, printing them with a space after each.

Notice that `i` is of type `unsigned`, rather than `int`. The length function returns an `unsigned` value, rather than an `int` value. If you try to use an `int` for `i`, the compiler will display the following warning:

```
warning: comparison between signed and unsigned integer
```

It's important to use the correct data types for loop variables. Otherwise, when the loop value increases over the amount that the loop variable can support, the application will fail. Trying to find such an error can prove frustrating even for the best developers.

You can also change the individual characters in a string through a pointer. You can do this by using a line like `(*ptrToString)[5] = 'X';`. Notice, as before, that we had to put parentheses around the variable name along with the dereferencing (that is, the asterisk) character.

The length of a string is also available through the pointer. You can call the length function by dereferencing the pointer, again with the carefully placed parentheses, such as in the following:

```
for (unsigned i = 0; i < (*ptrToString).length(); i++)
{
  cout << (*ptrToString)[i] << " ";
}
```

Pointing to something else

When you create a pointer variable, you must specify what type of data it points to. After that, you cannot change the type of data it points to, but you can change *what* it points to. For example, if you have a pointer to an integer, you make it point to the integer variable called `ExpensiveComputer`. Then, later, in the same program, you can make it point to the integer variable called `CheapComputer`. We demonstrate this in Listing 6-6.

Listing 6-6:   Using Pointers to Point to Something Else and Back Again

```
#include <iostream>

using namespace std;

int main()
{
  int ExpensiveComputer;
  int CheapComputer;
  int *ptrToComp;

  ptrToComp = &ExpensiveComputer;
  *ptrToComp = 2000;
  cout << *ptrToComp << endl;

  ptrToComp = &CheapComputer;
  *ptrToComp = 500;
```

This code starts out by initializing all the goodies involved — two integers and a pointer to an integer.

Next, the code points the pointer to `ExpensiveComputer` and uses the pointer to put something inside `ExpensiveComputer`. It then writes the contents of `ExpensiveComputer`, again by using the pointer.

Then the code changes what the pointer points to. To do this, we set the pointer to the address of a different variable, `&CheapComputers`. Pretty simple. And the next line stores 500 in whatever the pointer points to. But that's `CheapComputers`. And again we print it.

Now just to drive the point home in case the computer isn't listening, we then point the pointer back to the original variable, `ExpensiveComputer`. But we don't store anything in it. This time we just print what's already inside this high-powered supermachine. We do this again by dereferencing the pointer. And when we run the program, we see that `ExpensiveComputer` still has 2000 in it, which is what we originally put in it. That means that after we pointed the pointer to something else and did some finagling, the original variable remained unchanged. That's a good thing, considering that nobody was pointing at it and it was just being left alone, totally ignored in a world all by itself, feeling neglected.

Be careful if you use one pointer to bounce around several different variables. It's easy to lose track of which variable the pointer is pointing to.

Tips on pointer variables

Here are some pretty good tips on using pointer variables.

You can declare two pointer variables of the same type by putting them together in a single statement, as you can with regular variables. However, you must precede *each one* with an asterisk, as in the following line.

```
int *ptrOne, *ptrTwo;
```

If you try to declare multiple pointers on a single line but put an asterisk only before the first pointer, only that one will be a pointer. The rest will not be. This can cause serious headaches and muscle spasms later because this line will compile fine. The following line is just such an example:

```
int *ptrOne, Confused;
```

Here, `Confused` is not a pointer to an integer; rather, it's just an integer. So beware!

Some people like to put the asterisk right after the type, as in the following, to emphasize the fact that the type is *pointer to integer*.

```
int* ptrOne;
```

However, we prefer not to do that simply because it makes it easy for a forgetful persons like ourselves to not remember that any variables that follow, separated by a comma, need their own asterisks if they are to be pointers.

When we declare a pointer variable, we usually start its name with the letters `ptr`, which is an abbreviation for *pointer*. That way, we immediately know (when we're looking at our code) that it's a pointer variable. That makes life a little easier sometimes, at least in the sanity areas of life.

Dynamically Allocating with new

The heap is a special place where you can declare storage. However, to use this storage, you take a different approach from just declaring a variable.

When you create a variable, you go through the process of actually typing a variable, giving it a type, a name, and (sooner or later) a value. When you write the code, that's when you decide that you want a variable. However, you can also write code that can cause the computer to allocate space only after it's running. The computer allocates this space on the heap. This process is called *dynamic allocation*.

Using new

To declare a storage bin on the heap, first you need to set up a variable that will help you keep track of the storage bin. This variable must be a pointer variable.

For example, suppose you already have an integer declared out on the heap somewhere. (We show you how to do that in the next paragraph.) We won't give it a name, because such variables don't have names. Just think of it as an integer on the heap. Then, with the integer variable, you could have a *second* variable. This second variable is not on the heap, and it's a pointer holding the address of the integer variable. So if you want to access the integer variable, you do so by dereferencing the pointer variable.

To allocate memory on the heap, you need to do two things: First, declare a pointer variable. Second, call a function called `new`. The `new` function is a little different from other functions in that you don't put parentheses around its parameter. For this reason, it's actually considered to be an *operator*. Other operators are + and – for adding and subtracting integers. These other operators behave similar to functions, but you don't use parentheses.

To use the `new` function, you specify the type of variable you want to create. For example, the following line creates a new integer variable:

```
int *somewhere = new int;
```

After the computer creates the new integer variable on the heap, it stores the address of the integer variable in the somewhere variable. And that makes sense: The somewhere variable is a pointer to an integer. Thus, it holds the address of an integer variable. Listing 6-7 demonstrates this.

Listing 6-7: Allocating Memory by Using new

```
#include <iostream>

using namespace std;

int main()
{
    int *ptr = new int;
    *ptr = 10;
    cout << *ptr << endl;
    return 0;
}
```

When you run this program, you see the sweet and simple output:

```
10
```

In this program, we first allocated a pointer variable, which we called ptr. Then we called new with an int type, which returns a pointer to an integer. We saved that return value in the ptr variable.

Then we started doing our magic on it. Okay, so it's not all that magical, but we saved a 10 *in the thing that ptr points to.* And then we printed the value stored in *the thing that ptr points to.*

But what exactly is *the thing that ptr points to,* and why does it fancy itself so important as to justify italics? It's the memory that was allocated by the new operator. Think of it as a variable out there somewhere. But unlike regular variables, this variable doesn't have a name. And because it doesn't have a name, the only way you can access it is through the pointer. It's kind of like an anonymous author with a publicist. If you want to send fan mail to the author, you have to go through the publicist. Here, the only way to reach this unnamed but famous variable is through the pointer.

But this doesn't mean that the variable has a secret name such as BlueCheese and that, if you dig deep enough, you might discover it; it just means that the variable has no name. Sorry.

When you call new, you get back a pointer. This pointer is of the type that you specify in your call to new. You can then store the pointer only in a pointer variable of the same type.

When you use the `new` operator, the usual terminology is that you are *allocating memory on the heap.*

Now at this point, you may be asking the all-important question: Why? Why would we go through the trouble of creating an integer variable somewhere out on the heap, a variable that has no name, if we just have to create a second variable to point to it? Doesn't that seem counterproductive?

The answer is this: You can take advantage of many features if you allocate your variables on the heap. You can use pointers along with something called an array. An *array* is simply a large storage bin that has multiple slots, each of which holds one item. And if you set up an array that holds pointers, you can store away all these pointers without having to name them individually. And these pointers can point to complex things, called objects. (We cover objects in Minibook I, Chapter 7, and arrays in Minibook I, Chapter 8.) And then if you want to, for example, pass all these variables (which could be quite large, if they're strings) to a function, you need to pass only the array, not the strings themselves. That step saves memory on the stack.

In addition to objects and arrays, you can also have a function create and return a variable. Then, when you get the variable back from the function, you can use it, and when you are finished with the variable, delete it. Finally, you can pass a pointer into a function. When you do so, the function can actually modify the pointer for you. See "Passing Pointer Variables to Functions" and "Returning Pointer Variables from Functions," later in this chapter.

Using an initializer

When you call `new`, you can provide an initial value for the memory you are allocating. For example, if you are allocating a new integer, you can, in one swoop, also store the number 10 in the integer.

Listing 6-8 demonstrates this.

Listing 6-8:   Putting a Value in Parentheses to Initialize Memory That You Allocate

```
#include <iostream>

using namespace std;

int main()
{
  int *ptr = new int(10);
  cout << *ptr << endl;
  return 0;
}
```

In this code, we called `new`, but we also put a number in parentheses. That number will get put in the memory initially. This line of code is equivalent to the following two lines of code:

```
int *ptr = new int;
*ptr = 10;
```

When you initialize a value in the `new` operator, the technical phrase for what you are doing is *invoking a constructor*. The reason is that the compiler adds a bunch of code to your program, code that operates behind the scenes. This code is called the *runtime library*. The library includes a function that initializes an integer variable if you pass an initial value. The function that does this is known as a *constructor*. When you run it, you are *invoking* it. Thus, you are invoking the constructor. For more information on constructors, see Minibook I, Chapter 7.

Making new strings

You can use `new` to allocate almost any type, including strings. You simply type `new` followed by `string`.

You cannot allocate one special type with `new`. If a function has no return, you specify the return type as `void`. You cannot use `new` to allocate a void type. For that matter, you also cannot create a variable of type `void`. The compiler won't let you do it.

Listing 6-9 is an example of calling `new` for a string. As usual, remember the include line for `<string>`.

Listing 6-9:   Using the new Operator with Strings

```
#include <iostream>

using namespace std;

int main()
{
  string *Password = new string;
  *Password = "The egg salad is not fresh.";
  cout << *Password << endl;
  return 0;
}
```

This code allocates a new string by using the `new` keyword and saves the results in the `Password` variable. Next, it stores an interesting commentary in the newly allocated string by dereferencing the pointer. Finally, it prints the commentary, again by dereferencing the pointer. Remember, the `string` variable itself is off in the heap somewhere and has no name. And if it's going to make comments like those heard at a fine restaurant, it's probably best that it remain nameless.

Freeing Pointers **139**

Book I
Chapter 6

Referring to Your
Data through
Pointers

When you store a string of characters in a `string` variable that you allocated by using `new`, you are storing the string in the allocated memory, *not* in the pointer variable. The pointer variable still holds the address of the allocated memory. The pointer is just the publicist for the memory, handling all its deals and transactions for it, whether ethical or not.

When you are working with strings, you can use a shortcut to the somewhat cumbersome method of putting parentheses around the name preceded by an asterisk in order to call the various string functions. (That was even hard to type!) Instead of typing `(*Password).length()`, for example, you can use a shortcut notation that looks like the following line of code. (The characters after `Password` are a minus sign and then a greater than sign, which together resemble an arrow.)

```
cout << Password->length() << endl;
```

You can initialize a string by using parentheses when you call `new` for a string type. To do this, simply put the string in quotes and then in parentheses after the word `string`, as in the following line of code:

```
string *Password = new string("The egg salad is still not fresh.");
```

This line of code is equivalent to the first two lines of code inside `main` in Listing 6-9, shown previously.

Even though the pointer points to a string, the pointer itself still holds a number (in particular, the address of the string it's pointing to). This is a number, but do not confuse it with an integer. However, you can do some basic arithmetic with pointers, as detailed in Minibook I, Chapter 8.

Freeing Pointers

When you allocate memory on the heap by calling the `new` function and you're finished using the memory, you need to let the computer know, whether it's just a little bit of memory or a lot. The computer doesn't look ahead into your code to find out if you're still going to use the memory. So in your code, when you are finished with the memory, you *free* the memory.

The way you free the memory is by calling the `delete` function and passing the name of the pointer:

```
delete MyPointer;
```

This line would appear after you're finished using a pointer that you allocated by using `new`. (Like the `new` operator, `delete` is also an operator and does not require parentheses around the parameter.)

Listing 6-10 shows a complete example that allocates a pointer, uses it, and then frees it.

Listing 6-10: Using delete to Clean Up Your Pointers

```cpp
#include <iostream>

using namespace std;

int main()
{
  string *phrase = new string("All presidents are cool!!!");
  cout << *phrase << endl;

  (*phrase)[20] = 'r';
  phrase->replace(22, 4, "oked");
  cout << *phrase << endl;

  delete phrase;
  return 0;
}
```

When you run this program, you see the following output:

```
All presidents are cool!!!
All presidents are crooked
```

In this code, we first allocated a new string and initialized it, saving its address in the pointer variable called `phrase`. Then we wrote the phrase, manipulated it (providing some editorial content), and then wrote it again. Finally, we freed the memory used by the phrase.

Although people usually say that you're *deleting the pointer* or *freeing the pointer*, really you're freeing the *memory* that the pointer points to. The pointer can still be used for subsequent new operations. Nevertheless, we will abide by tradition and use these phrases.

You can actually get away with not freeing your pointers because the computer frees all the memory used by your program when it ends. That way, your memory is available to all the other cool programs you want to run. However, getting into the habit of freeing your pointers when you are finished using them is a good practice; otherwise, you may use all the memory allotted for the heap while your program is running. And some big software systems at big companies run on and on, shutting down maybe once a week or every two weeks. If one part of the program continues to refuse to free its data, eventually the heap probably fills and the whole program shuts down.

If you free a pointer, the memory it points to is now free. However, immediately after the call to delete, the pointer still points to that particular memory location, even though it's no longer being used. Therefore, do not try to use the pointer after that until you set it to point to something else through a call to new or by setting it to another variable.

Whenever you free a pointer, a good habit is to set the pointer to the value 0. (Some people set it to the value *null*, but that's the same thing, and 0 is guaranteed to work on all compilers.) Then, whenever you use a pointer, first check whether it's equal to 0 and only use it if it's not 0. This always works because the computer will never allocate memory for you at address 0. So the number 0 can be reserved to mean *I point to nothing at all.*

The following code sample shows this. First, this code frees the pointer and then clears it by setting it to 0:

```
delete ptrToSomething;
ptrToSomething = 0;
```

This code checks if the pointer is not 0 before using it:

```
ptrToComp = new int;
*ptrToComp = 10;
if (ptrToComp != 0)
{
  cout << *ptrToComp << endl;
}
```

Only call delete on memory that you allocated by using new. Although the free compiler that ships with this book doesn't seem to complain when you delete a pointer that points to a regular variable, it serves no purpose to do so. You can free only memory on the heap, not local variables on the stack.

Passing Pointer Variables to Functions

One of the most important uses for pointers is this: If they point to a variable, you can pass the pointer to a function, and the function can modify the original variable. This lets you write functions that can actually modify the variables passed to them.

Changing variable values with pointers

Normally, when you call a function and you pass a few variables to the function, the computer just grabs the values out of the variables and passes those values. Take a close look at Listing 6-11.

Listing 6-11: A Function Cannot Change the Original Variables Passed into It

```
#include <iostream>

using namespace std;

void ChangesAreGood(int myparam)
{
    myparam += 10;
    cout << "Inside the function:" << endl;
    cout << myparam << endl;
}

int main()
{
    int mynumber = 30;
    cout << "Before the function:" << endl;
    cout << mynumber << endl;

    ChangesAreGood(mynumber);
    cout << "After the function:" << endl;
    cout << mynumber << endl;

    return 0;
}
```

Listing 6-11 includes a function called ChangesAreGood that modifies the parameter it receives. (It adds 10 to its parameter called myparam.) It then prints the new value of the parameter.

The main function initializes an integer variable, mynumber, to 30 and prints its value. It then calls the ChangesAreGood function, which changes its parameter. After coming back from the ChangesAreGood function, main prints the value again.

When you run this program, you see the following output:

```
Before the function:
30
Inside the function:
40
After the function:
30
```

Before the function call, mynumber is 30. And after the function call, it's still 30. But the function added 10 to its parameter. This means that when the function modified its parameter, *the original variable remained untouched.* The two are separate entities. Only the value 30 went into the function. The actual variable did not. It stayed in main.

That keeps mean and nasty functions from messing things up in the outside world. But what if you write a function that you *want* to modify the original variable?

A pointer contains a number, which represents the address of a variable. If you pass this address into a function and the function stores that address into one of its own variables, its own variable also points to the same variable that the original pointer did. Make sense? The pointer variable in `main` and the pointer variable in the function *both point to the same variable* because *both pointers hold the same address.*

That's how you let a function modify data in a variable: You pass a pointer. But when you call a function, the process is easy, because you don't need to make a pointer variable. Instead, you can just call the function, putting an & in front of the variable. Then, you are not passing the variable or its value — instead, you are passing the address of the variable.

Listing 6-12 is a modified form of Listing 6-11; this time the function actually manages to modify the original variable.

Listing 6-12:   Using Pointers to Modify a Variable Passed into a Function

```
#include <iostream>

using namespace std;

void ChangesAreGood(int *myparam)
{
    (*myparam) += 10;
    cout << "Inside the function:" << endl;
    cout << (*myparam) << endl;
}

int main()
{
  int mynumber = 30;
  cout << "Before the function:" << endl;
  cout << mynumber << endl;

  ChangesAreGood(&mynumber);
  cout << "After the function:" << endl;
  cout << mynumber << endl;

  return 0;
}
```

When you run this program, you see the following output:

```
Before the function:
30
Inside the function:
40
After the function:
40
```

Notice the important difference between this and the output from Listing 6-11: The final line of output is `40`, not `30`. The variable was modified by the function!

To understand how this happened, first look at `main`. The only difference we had to make to `main` was a little one: We threw an ampersand, `&`, in front of the `mynumber` argument in the call to `ChangesAreGood`. That's it: Instead of passing the value stored in `mynumber`, we passed the address of `mynumber`.

Now the function has some major changes. We rewrote the function header so it takes a pointer rather than a number. We did this by adding an asterisk, `*`, so the parameter is a pointer variable. This pointer receives the address being passed into it. Thus, it points to the variable `mynumber`. Therefore, any modifications we make by dereferencing the pointer will attack the original variable. And attack it, it does: It changes it! The following line changes the original variable. Excellent!

```
(*myparam) += 10;
```

When you pass a pointer to a function, you are still passing a number. In Listing 6-11, you are passing to the function the value stored in `mynumber`. In Listing 6-12, you aren't somehow passing the variable itself. Instead, you are passing the *value* of `mynumber`'s address. The value is still a number either way. However, in Listing 6-12, because the number is an address now, we had to modify the function header so it expects an address, not just a number. To do that, we used a pointer variable because it is a storage bin *that holds an address*. Then we had to modify the remainder of the function to make use of the pointer, instead of a number.

The `ChangesAreGood` function in Listing 6-12 no longer modifies its own parameter. The parameter starts holding the address of the original `mynumber` variable, and that never changes. Throughout the function, the pointer variable `myparam` holds the `mynumber` address. And any changes the function performs are on the dereferenced variable, which is `mynumber`. *The pointer variable does not change.*

Modifying string parameters

Modifying a string parameter is just as easy as modifying an integer variable. But with string variables, you have the added benefit that if you're working with pointers, you can use the shortcut `->` notation.

Listing 6-13 is an example of a function that modifies the original `string` variable that is passed into it. The function expects a pointer to a `string`. Inside, the function uses the `->` notation to access the `string` functions. Then the function returns. `main` creates a `string`, initializes it, prints the string's value, calls the function, and prints the value again. As you see when you run the program, the value of the string has changed.

Listing 6-13:   **Using a Function to Modify a String Passed into It by Using Pointers**

```
#include <iostream>

using namespace std;

void Paranoid(string *realmessage)
{
  (*realmessage)[6] = 'i';
  realmessage->replace(9, 1, "");
  realmessage->insert(18, "ad");
  realmessage->replace(15, 2, "in");
  realmessage->replace(23, 7, "!");
  realmessage->replace(4, 3, "ali");
}

int main()
{
  string message = "The friends are having dinner";
  cout << message << endl;

  Paranoid(&message);
  cout << message << endl;

  return 0;
}
```

In Listing 6-13, we chose to not make the message variable a pointer. It's just a string variable. We then put a string into it and called the Paranoid function. But instead of passing the value stored in message, we passed the address of message. The function then receives a pointer as a parameter. Because it's a string pointer, we made extensive use of the shortcut notation, ->. Remember, (*realmessage). equals the pointer.

When you run this program, you see the original value stored in message and then the revised value after the function has its way with it:

```
The friends are having dinner
The aliens are invading!
```

Returning Pointer Variables from Functions

Functions can return values, including pointers. To set up a function to return a pointer, specify the type followed by an asterisk at the beginning of the function header. Listing 6-14 shows this. The function returns a pointer that is the result of a new operation.

Listing 6-14:   Returning a Pointer from a String Involves Using an Asterisk in the Return Type

```
#include <iostream>
#include <sstream>

using namespace std;

string *GetSecretCode()
{
  string *code = new string;
  code->append("CR");

  int randomnumber = rand();
  ostringstream converter;
  converter << randomnumber;

  code->append(converter.str());
  code->append("NQ");

  return code;
}

int main()
{
  string *newcode;
  int index;

  for (index = 0; index < 10; index++)
  {
    newcode = GetSecretCode();
    cout << *newcode << endl;
  }

  return 0;
}
```

In this code, we wedged the asterisk against the function name in the function header. This is a common way of doing it. If you prefer, you can do any of the following lines:

```
string *GetSecretCode() {
string* GetSecretCode() {
string * GetSecretCode() {
```

In the main function, we created a pointer to a string, not just a string. My function is returning a pointer to a string, and we needed the pointer and the string to match. When we used the string, we had to dereference it.

When you run this program, you see something like the following output.

```
CR41NQ
CR18467NQ
CR6334NQ
CR26500NQ
```

Returning Pointer Variables from Functions **147**

Book I
Chapter 6

Referring to Your
Data through
Pointers

```
CR19169NQ
CR15724NQ
CR11478NQ
CR29358NQ
CR26962NQ
CR24464NQ
```

Never return from a function the address of a local variable in the function. The local variables live in the stack space allocated for the function, not in the heap. When the function is finished, the computer frees the stack space used for the function, making room for the *next* function call. If you try this, the variables will be okay for a while, but after enough function calls that follow, the variable's data will get overwritten. Wiped out. Gone to the great variable home in the sky.

Just as the parameters to a function are normally values, a function normally *returns* a value. In the case of returning a pointer, the function is still returning just a value — it is returning the value of the pointer, which is a number representing an address.

Random numbers and strings

Some special code is right smack in the middle of the function in Listing 6-14, and we need to explain that. It's a little trick we used for generating a random number and putting it into the middle of the string. First, we had to add another `include` line. This one is

```
#include <sstream>
```

This line provides some of the special features we're about to talk about, specifically the `ostringstream` type. Now here are the three lines that perform the magic:

```
int randomnumber = rand();
ostringstream converter;
converter << randomnumber;
```

The first of these creates a random number by calling a function called `rand`. You get back from this function an integer, which is random. The next one creates a variable of a type called `ostringstream`, which is a type that's handy for converting numbers to strings. A variable of this type has features similar to that of a console. You can use the `insertion` operator, `<<`, except instead of going to the console, anything you write goes into the string itself. But this isn't just any old string; it's a special string of type `ostringstream` (which comes from the words *output, string,* and *stream;* usually things that allow the insertion operator `<<` or the extraction operator `>>` to perform input and output are called *streams*). After we do this, we can add the resulting string onto our string variable called `code`. To do that, we use the line

```
code->append(converter.str());
```

The part inside parentheses, `converter.str()`, returns an actual `string` version of the `converter` variable. And that we can easily append to our `code` variable by using the `append` function. It's kind of tricky, but it works quite nicely.

Returning a Pointer as a Nonpointer

You may find it annoying to dereference a pointer returned from a function every time you want to use it. Listing 6-14, in the preceding section, is an example of how you need to dereference a pointer each time. But you can avoid this issue by dereferencing the pointer as soon as it comes cranking out of the machine. Listing 6-15 shows this: We preceded the call to the function with an asterisk, which dereferences the result immediately. We then place the result in a local nonpointer variable. After that, we have the value in the variable, and we don't need to dereference the pointer when we want to use the value. Thus, when we call cout, we just use the variable directly without the use of asterisks and other pointer paraphernalia.

Listing 6-15:   Dereferencing Your Return Value Immediately So You Don't Need to Use It as a Pointer

```
#include <iostream>

using namespace std;

string *GetNotSoSecretCode()
{
  string *code = new string("ABCDEF");
  return code;
}

int main()
{
  string newcode;
  int index;

  for (index = 0; index < 10; index++)
  {
    newcode = *GetNotSoSecretCode();
    cout << newcode << endl;
  }

  return 0;
}
```

When you run this program, you see the following secret but highly enticing output:

```
ABCDEF
ABCDEF
ABCDEF
ABCDEF
ABCDEF
ABCDEF
ABCDEF
ABCDEF
ABCDEF
ABCDEF
```

Passing by Reference

C++ is based on the old C language, which was a simple language. C++ has some features to make it cushier. One feature is references. A *reference* is another way of specifying a parameter in a function whereby the function can modify the original variable. Instead of following the parameter type with an asterisk, *, to denote a pointer, you follow it with an ampersand, &. Then, throughout your function, you can use the parameter just as you normally would, not as a pointer. But every change you make to the parameter affects the original variable! A concept ahead of its time. Or behind its time, considering that other languages have had this feature for years.

Take a look at Listing 6-16 and notice how we didn't use any pointers.

Listing 6-16: With References, You Don't Need Pointers!

```
#include <iostream>

using namespace std;

void MessMeUp(int &myparam)
{
    myparam = myparam * 2 + 10;
}

int main()
{
    int mynumber = 30;
    MessMeUp(mynumber);
    cout << mynumber << endl;
    return 0;
}
```

Look at that code! No more pointers! In `main`, we don't need to take the address of anything, and we don't need to use that *dereference* word, which the spelling checker insists is wrong. And the function itself has no pointers either. We just throw the old ampersand thing in front of the parameter name in the function header.

If you have `string` parameters, and you use the & to pass them by reference, skip the shortcut -> notation to call the string functions. And don't dereference anything. There are no pointers. Just type the dot (or period) and the function. No asterisks needed.

If you write a function that uses a reference and somebody else uses your function in code (see Minibook I, Chapter 5, for information on how to do this), you could end up making that other person angry. The other person may not realize that *Hey man, this thing just messed up my variable!* WHAM! Their variable gets changed. How do you avoid this? Warn them. Make it clear to anybody using your function that it uses references and will modify variables, even the unsuspecting little ones.

Remembering the Rules

When you use pointers and references, make your life easier:

+ **Understand pointers and references:** Your C++ programming ventures will be much happier.

+ **Free your pointers:** Whenever you call new, you should (sooner or later) call delete. Don't leave memory in the heap when you're finished with it.

+ **Know your references:** If you write a function that has references, make sure that everybody knows it. And if you *use* a function that somebody else wrote, make sure that you check both the person's references and the function's references.

Chapter 7: Working with Classes

In This Chapter

✔ Understanding objects and classes and the difference between the two

✔ Becoming familiar with member functions and variables in a class

✔ Making parts of a class public, private, and protected

✔ Using constructors and destructors

✔ Building hierarchies of classes

*B*ack in the early 1990s, the big buzzword in the computer world was *object-oriented*. For anything to sell, it had to be *object-oriented*, whatever *that* meant. Programming languages were object-oriented. Software applications were object-oriented. Computers were object-oriented. Refrigerators were object-oriented. What did that all mean? *Nothing*. It was simply a catchphrase that was cool at the time.

Those days are gone, and now we can explore what object-oriented *really* means and how you can use it to organize your C++ programs. In this chapter, we introduce object-oriented programming and show how you can do it in C++. Although people disagree on the strict definition of object-oriented, in this book it means programming with objects and classes.

Understanding Objects and Classes

Consider a pen, a regular, old pen. One of us actually has a pen on our desk. Here's what we can say about it:

+ **Ink Color:** Black

+ **Shell Color:** Light gray

+ **Cap Color:** Black

+ **Style:** Ballpoint

+ **Length:** Six inches

+ **Brand:** Office Depot

+ **Ink Level:** 50 percent full

+ **Capability #1:** Write on paper

+ **Capability #2:** Break in half
+ **Capability #3:** Run out of ink

Now, look around for other things. We see a printer. Let us describe that:

+ **Kind:** Laser
+ **Brand:** Lexmark
+ **Model:** E260
+ **Ink Color:** Black
+ **Case Color:** Cream
+ **Input trays:** Two
+ **Output trays:** Two
+ **Connection:** USB
+ **Capability #1:** Reads print job requests from the computer
+ **Capability #2:** Prints on sheets of paper
+ **Capability #3:** Prints a test page
+ **Capability #4:** Needs the toner cartridge replaced when empty

We're just describing the things we see. We're giving dimensions, color, model, brand. And we're also describing what the things can do. The pen can break in half and run out of ink. The printer can take print jobs, print pages, and have its cartridge replaced.

When we describe what the things can do, we're carefully writing it from the perspective of the thing itself, not from the perspective of the person using the thing. A good way to name the capability is to test it by preceding it with the words "I can" and see if it makes sense. Thus, because "I can *write on paper*" works from the perspective of a pen, we chose *write on paper* for one of the pen's capabilities.

Instead of saying the word *thing*, we will say the word *object*. The two meanings are the same: An object is just a thing. Anything, really. A book. A dirty plate. A stack of writeable CD-ROMs. These are all objects.

But is seeing all the objects in the universe possible, or are some of those objects hidden? Certainly some objects are physical, like atoms or the dark side of the moon, and we can't see them. But other objects are abstract. For example, we have a checking account. What is a checking account, exactly?

Using enumerations

We think that the number 12 is a good representation of the color blue, and the number 86 is a good representation of the color red. Purple? That's 182. Beige? That's getting up there — it's 1047. Yes, this sounds kind of silly. But let's suppose you want to create a variable that holds the color blue. Using the standard types of integers, floating-point numbers, characters, and letters, you don't have a lot of choices. In the old days, people would just pick a number to represent each color and store that number in a variable. Or, you could have saved a string, as in `blue`. But C++ presents a better alternative. It's called an *enumeration*. Remember that for each type, there's a whole list of possible values. An integer, for example, can be a whole number within a particular range. (This range varies between computers, but it's usually pretty big.) Strings can be any characters, all strung together. But what if you want a value called `blue`? Or `red`? Or even `beige`? Then you need enumerations. (Hurray!) This line creates an enumeration type:

```
enum MyColor {blue, red, green, yellow,
         black, beige};
```

You now have a new *type* called `MyColor`, which you can use the same way you can use other types, such as `int` or `double` or `string`. For example, you can create a variable of type `MyColor` and set its value to one of the values in the curly braces:

```
MyColor inkcolor = blue;
MyColor shellcolor = black;
```

The variable `inkcolor` is type `MyColor`, and its value is `blue`. The variable `shell color` is also of type `MyColor`, and its value is `black`.

Can you point to it? Can you drop it, throw it? You can throw your checkbook across the room and, if you're brave, can even try to get into the room where the main computer is holding your checking account. But is the checking account something physical you can touch? No. It's abstract.

Classifying classes and objects

When we pick up a pen, we can ask somebody, "What type of thing is this an instance of?" Most people would probably say, "a pen." In computer programming, instead of using *type of thing*, we say *class*. This thing in my hand belongs to the pen class.

Now if we point to the thing parked out in the driveway, and ask you, "What class does that belong to?," you will answer, "class Car." Of course, you could be more specific. You may say that the thing belongs to class 1999 Ford Taurus.

Class names and class files

In Listings 7-3 and 7-4, nearby in this chapter, we chose filenames that match the name of our class. That's usually the way we like to do it: When we create a class, we put the class definition in a header file of the same name as the class but with an `.h` extension. And we put the class member function code in a source-code file of the same name as the class but this time with a `.cpp` extension. We usually like our filenames capitalized the same as the class name; thus, we called the files `Pen.h` and `Pen.cpp`. Naming the files the same as classes has lots of advantages that can help you in your quest to become a millionaire. First, you automatically know the name of the header file you need to include if you want to use a certain class. Second, it provides a general consistency, which is always good in life, whether dealing with programming or pancake syrup. And finally, if we see a header file, we know what class is probably inside it.

When we show you the pen, we are asking you what class this object belongs to. If we then pick up another pen, we're showing you another example of the same class. One class, several examples. If we stand next to a busy street, we see many examples of the class called car. Or we may see many examples of the class Ford Explorer, a few instances of the class Volkswagen Beetle, and so on. It depends on how you *classify* those things roaring down the road. But regardless, we likely see several examples of any given class.

So when you organize things, you specify a *class,* which is the type of object. And when you're ready, you can start picking out examples (or *instances*) of the class. Each class may have several instances. Some classes have only one instance. That's a *singleton class*. For example, at any given time, the class United States President would have one instance.

Describing member functions and data

If we choose a class, we can describe some characteristics. However, because we're only describing the class characteristics, we don't actually specify them. We may say the pen has an ink color, but we don't actually say *what* color. That's because we don't yet have an example of the class pen. We have only the class itself. When we finally find an example, it may be one color, or it may be another. So, if we're describing a class called pen, we may list the following characteristics:

+ **Ink Color**
+ **Shell Color**
+ **Cap Color**
+ **Style**

✦ **Length**

✦ **Brand**

✦ **Ink Level**

We don't specify ink color, shell color, length, or any of these. We're listing only general characteristics for all instances of the class pen. That is, every pen has these characteristics. But the actual values for these characteristics might vary from instance to instance. One pen may have a different ink color from another, but both might have the same brand. Nevertheless, they are both separate instances of the class pen.

After we actually have an instance of class pen, we can give the specifics for the characteristics. For example, Table 7-1 lists the characteristics of three actual pens.

Table 7-1   Specifying Characteristics of Instances of Class Pen

Characteristic	First Pen	Second Pen	Third Pen
Ink Color	Blue	Red	Black
Shell Color	Grey	Red	Grey
Cap Color	Blue	Black	Black
Style	Ballpoint	Felt-tip	Ballpoint
Length	5.5 inches	5 inches	6 inches
Brand	Office Depot	Superrite	Easy-Ink
Ink Level	30%	60%	90%

In Table 7-1, the first column holds the names of the characteristics. The second column holds values for those characteristics for the first pen. The third column holds the values of characteristics for the second pen, and the final column holds the values for the third pen.

All the pens in the class share characteristics. But the values for these characteristics may differ from pen to pen. When we build a new pen (assuming that we could do such a thing), we would follow the list of characteristics, giving the new pen its own values. We may make the shell purple with yellow speckles, or we may make it transparent. But we would give it a shell that has some color, even if that color is *transparent*.

In Table 7-1, we didn't list capabilities. But all these pens have the same capabilities:

✦ **Capability #1:** Write on paper

✦ **Capability #2:** Break in half

✦ **Capability #3:** Run out of ink

Unlike characteristics, these capabilities don't change from instance to instance. They are the same for each class.

In computer programming, capabilities are *member functions.* That's because you'll be writing functions to perform these, and they are part of a class. The characteristics are *member variables,* because they are variables that are part of the class.

When you describe classes to build a computer program using a class, you are modeling. In the preceding examples, we modeled a class called Pen. In the following section, we implement this model by writing a program that mimics a pen.

If you work with enums (the code form of enumerations), you need to decide what to name your new type. For example, you can choose MyColor or MyColors. Many people, when they write a line such as enum MyColor {blue, red, green, yellow, black, beige};, make the name plural (MyColors) because this is a list of colors. We make it singular, as in MyColor. When you declare a variable, it makes more sense: MyColor inkcolor; would mean that inkcolor is a *color* — not a group of *colors.*

Implementing a class

To implement a class in C++, you use the word class. We know it's profound. And then you add the name of the class, such as Pen. You then add an open brace, list your member variables and member functions, and end with a closing brace.

Most people capitalize the first letter of a class name in C++, and if their class name is a word, they don't capitalize the remaining letters. Although you don't have to follow this rule, many people do. You can choose any name for a C++ class provided it is not a C++ word; it consists only of letters, digits, and underscores; and it does not start with a number.

The code in Listing 7-1 shows a class in C++, which we put inside a header file called Pen.h. (See Minibook I, Chapter 5, for information on how to put code in a header file.) Take a look at the header file, and you can see how we implemented the different characteristics. The characteristics of a header file are just like variables: They have a type and a name. And we implemented the capabilities simply as functions. But all this stuff goes inside curly brackets and is preceded by a class header. The header gives the name of the class. And, oh yes, the word *public* is stuck in there, and it has a colon after it. We explain the word *public* in "Accessing members," later in this chapter. By itself, this code isn't very useful, but we put it to use in Listing 7-2, a program that you can compile and run.

Listing 7-1:   Pen.h Contains the Class Description for Pen

```cpp
#ifndef PEN_H_INCLUDED
#define PEN_H_INCLUDED

using namespace std;

enum Color
{
    blue,
    red,
    black,
    clear
};

enum PenStyle
{
    ballpoint,
    felt_tip,
    fountain_pen
};

class Pen
{
public:
    Color InkColor;
    Color ShellColor;
    Color CapColor;
    PenStyle Style;
    float Length;
    string Brand;
    int InkLevelPercent;

    void write_on_paper(string words)
    {
        if (InkLevelPercent <= 0)
        {
            cout << "Oops! Out of ink!" << endl;
        }
        else
        {
            cout << words << endl;
            InkLevelPercent = InkLevelPercent - words.length();
        }
    }

    void break_in_half()
    {
        InkLevelPercent = InkLevelPercent / 2;
        Length = Length / 2.0;
    }

    void run_out_of_ink()
    {
        InkLevelPercent = 0;
    }
};

#endif // PEN_H_INCLUDED
```

When you write a class, you always end it with a semicolon. Write that down on a sticky note and hang it on the refrigerator. The effort spent in doing this will be well worth avoiding the frustration of wondering why your code won't compile.

In a class definition, you describe the characteristics and capabilities (that is, supply the member variables and member functions, respectively).

Note in Listing 7-1, earlier in this chapter, that the member functions access the member variables. However, we said that these variables don't have values yet, because this is just a class, not an *instance* of a class. How can that be? When you create an instance of this class, you can give values to these member variables. Then you can call the member functions. And here's the really great part: You can make a *second instance* of this class and give it its own values for the member variables. Yes, the two instances will each have their own sets of member variables. And when you run the member functions for the second instance, these functions operate on the member variables for the second instance. Isn't C++ smart?

Now take a look at Listing 7-2. This is a source file that uses the header file in Listing 7-1. In this code, we make use of the Pen class.

Listing 7-2: main.cpp Contains Code That Uses the Class Pen

```cpp
#include <iostream>
#include "Pen.h"

using namespace std;

int main()
{
  Pen FavoritePen;

  FavoritePen.InkColor = blue;
  FavoritePen.ShellColor = clear;
  FavoritePen.CapColor = black;
  FavoritePen.Style = ballpoint;
  FavoritePen.Length = 6.0;
  FavoritePen.Brand = "Pilot";
  FavoritePen.InkLevelPercent = 90;

  Pen WorstPen;

  WorstPen.InkColor = blue;
  WorstPen.ShellColor = red;
  WorstPen.CapColor = black;
  WorstPen.Style = felt_tip;
  WorstPen.Length = 3.5;
  WorstPen.Brand = "Acme Special";
  WorstPen.InkLevelPercent = 100;

  cout << "This is my favorite pen" << endl;
  cout << "Color: " << FavoritePen.InkColor << endl;
  cout << "Brand: " << FavoritePen.Brand << endl;
```

```
        cout << "Ink Level: " << FavoritePen.InkLevelPercent << "%" << endl;

        FavoritePen.write_on_paper("Hello I am a pen");
        cout << "Ink Level: " << FavoritePen.InkLevelPercent << "%" << endl;

        return 0;
}
```

There are two variables of class `Pen`: `FavoritePen` and `WorstPen`. To access the member variables of these objects, we type the name of the variable, a dot (or period), and then the member variable name. For example, to access the `InkLevelPercent` member of `WorstPen`, we type:

```
WorstPen.InkLevelPercent = 100;
```

Remember, `WorstPen` is the variable name, and this variable is an *object*. It is an object or instance of class `Pen`. This object has various member variables, including `InkLevelPercent`.

You can also run some of the member functions that are in these objects. In the code, we called

```
FavoritePen.write_on_paper("Hello I am a pen");
```

This called the function `write_on_paper` for the object `FavoritePen`. Take a look at the code for this function, which is in the header file, Listing 7-1:

```
void write_on_paper(string words)
{
    if (InkLevelPercent <= 0)
    {
        cout << "Oops! Out of ink!" << endl;
    }
    else
    {
        cout << words << endl;
        InkLevelPercent = InkLevelPercent - words.length();
    }
}
```

This function uses the variable called `InkLevelPercent`. But `InkLevelPercent` is not declared in this function. The reason is that `InkLevelPercent` is part of the object and is declared in the class. Suppose you call this method for two different objects, as in the following:

```
FavoritePen.write_on_paper("Hello I am a pen");
WorstPen.write_on_paper("Hello I am another pen");
```

The first of these lines calls `write_on_paper` for the `FavoritePen` object; thus, inside the code for `write_on_paper`, the `InkLevelPercent` refers to `InkLevelPercent` for the `FavoritePen` object. It looks at and possibly decreases the variable for that object only. But `WorstPen` has its *own*

`InkLevelPercent` member variable, separate from that of `FavoritePen`. So in the second of these two lines, `write_on_paper` accesses and possibly decreases the `InkLevelPercent` that lives inside `WorstPen`.

In other words, each object has its own `InkLevelPercent`. When you call `write_on_paper`, the function modifies the member variable based on which object you are calling it with. The first line calls it with `FavoritePen`. The second calls it with `WorstPen`. When you run this program, you see the following output:

```
This is my favorite pen
Color: 0
Brand: Pilot
Ink Level: 90%
Hello I am a pen
Ink Level: 74%
```

Now notice something about the color line. Here's the line of code that writes it:

```
cout << "Color: " << FavoritePen.InkColor << endl;
```

We're writing the `InkColor` member for `FavoritePen`. But what type is `InkColor`? It's the new enumerated type we created called `Color`. But something is wrong. It printed 0. Yet here's the line where we set it:

```
FavoritePen.InkColor = blue;
```

We set it to `blue`, not 0. Unfortunately, that's the breaks with using `enum`. You can use it in your code, but *under the hood,* it just stores numbers. And when we print it, we get a number. Well, that stinks. The compiler chooses the numbers for you, and it starts the first in the `enum` list as 0, the second as 1, then 2, then 3, and so on. Thus, `blue` is stored as 0, `red` as 1, `black` as 2, and `clear` as 3. But, as we always say (because we're forever the optimists), fear not! People have found a way to create a new class that handles the `enum` for you (that is, it *wraps* around the `enum`), and then you can print what you really want: `blue`, `red`, `black`, and `clear`. Take a look at Minibook I, Chapter 8 for tips on how to do this astounding feat.

Remember that you can create several *objects* (also called *instances*) of a single class. Each object gets its own member variables, which you declare in the class. To access the members of an object, you use a period, or dot.

Separating member function code

When you work with functions, you can either make sure that the code to your function is positioned before any calls to the function, or you can use a *forward reference,* also called a *function prototype.* We talk about this handy little feature in Minibook I, Chapter 4.

The string class

If you've been reading the previous chapters of Minibook I and trying the programs, you have seen the string type. Now for the big secret: string is actually a class. When you create a variable of type string, you are creating an object of class string. That's why, to use the string functions, you first type the variable name, a dot, and then the function name: You are really calling a member function for the string object that you created. Similarly, when you work with pointers to strings, instead of a dot you can use the -> notation to access

the member functions. (See "Using classes and pointers," later in this chapter, for more information.) When working with newer versions of C++, the string class is part of the std namespace, which is why you add using namespace std; to the beginning of your code. If you use an older version of C++, the string class appears as part of the string file. In this case, you include <string> to provide the necessary header files to declare the string class.

When you work with classes and member functions, you have a similar option. Most C++ programmers prefer to keep the code for their member functions outside the class definition. The class definition contains only function prototypes, or, at least, mostly function prototypes. If the function is one or two lines of code, people may leave it in the class definition.

When you use a function prototype in a class definition, you write the prototype by ending the function header with a semicolon where you would normally have the open brace and code. If your member function looks like

```
void break_in_half()
{
    InkLevelPercent = InkLevelPercent / 2;
    Length = Length / 2.0;
}
```

a function prototype would look like

```
void break_in_half();
```

Yes, it's true: To type this, we just copied the first line of the function, put the cursor at the end, pressed backspace a couple times, and typed a semicolon. We're telling you that not to brag about our prowess with the keyboard when writing books but rather because that's how we do it when we actually write code. That way, we can be assured that the two lines *match*. Ah, the beauty of computers. Imagine how hard it would be to write a computer program without the help of computers.

Now after you have the function prototype in the class, you write the function again *outside* the class definition. However, you need to doctor it up just a bit. In particular, you need to throw in the name of the class, so that the compiler knows which class this function goes with.

The following is the same function we described earlier but souped-up with the class information:

```
void Pen::break_in_half()
{
    InkLevelPercent = InkLevelPercent / 2;
    Length = Length / 2.0;
}
```

You would put this after your class definition. And you would want to put this inside one of your source-code files if your class definition is in a header file.

You can use the same function name in different classes. Like variables in different functions, function names are totally separate things. Although you don't want to go overboard on duplicating your function names, if you feel a need to, you can certainly do it without a problem.

Listings 7-3 and 7-4 show the modified version of the Pen class, which originally appeared earlier in this chapter in Listing 7-1. You can use these two files together with Listing 7-2, which did not change.

Listing 7-3: Using Member Function Prototypes with the Modified Pen.h file

```
#ifndef PEN_H_INCLUDED
#define PEN_H_INCLUDED

using namespace std;

enum Color
{
    blue,
    red,
    black,
    clear
};

enum PenStyle
{
    ballpoint,
    felt_tip,
    fountain_pen
};

class Pen
{
public:
    Color InkColor;
    Color ShellColor;
    Color CapColor;
    PenStyle Style;
```

```
    float Length;
    string Brand;
    int InkLevelPercent;

    void write_on_paper(string words);
    void break_in_half();
    void run_out_of_ink();
};

#endif // PEN_H_INCLUDED
```

Listing 7-4: Containing the Member Functions for Class Pen in the New Pen.cpp File

```cpp
#include <iostream>
#include "Pen.h"

using namespace std;

void Pen::write_on_paper(string words)
{
    if (InkLevelPercent <= 0)
    {
        cout << "Oops! Out of ink!" << endl;
    }
    else
    {
        cout << words << endl;
        InkLevelPercent = InkLevelPercent - words.length();
    }
}

void Pen::break_in_half()
{
    InkLevelPercent = InkLevelPercent / 2;
    Length = Length / 2.0;
}

void Pen::run_out_of_ink()
{
    InkLevelPercent = 0;
}
```

All the functions from the class are now in a separate source (.cpp) file. The header file now just lists prototypes and is a little easier for us humans to scan through. And for the source file, we included the header file at the top. That's required; otherwise, the compiler won't know that Pen is a class name, and it will get confused (as it so easily can).

The parts of a class

Here is a summary of the parts of a class and the different ways classes can work together.

✦ **Class:** A class is a type. It includes *characteristics* and *capabilities*. Characteristics describe the class, and capabilities describe its behavior.

✦ **Object (or instance):** An object is an example of a class. Or, to put it another way, an object's type is the class. If you like analogies, the object `Fred` is to the `Human` class as `17` is to `int`.

✦ **Class definition:** The class definition describes the class. It starts with the word *class*, then has the name of the class, and then an open brace and closing brace. Inside the braces are the members of the class.

✦ **Member variable:** A member variable is the C++ version of a characteristic in a class. You list the member variables inside the class. Each instance of the class gets its own copy of each member variable.

✦ **Member function:** A member function is the C++ version of a capability of a class. Like member variables, you list the member functions inside the class. When you call a member function for a particular instance, the function accesses the member variables for the instance.

When you divide the class, you put part in the header file and part in the source-code file. The following list describes what goes where:

✦ **Header file:** Put the class definition in the header file. You can include the function code inside the class definition itself if it's a short function. Most people prefer not to put any function code longer than a line or two in the header or don't put any function code in the header. You may want to name the header file the same as the class but with an `.h` or `.hpp` extension. Thus, the class `Pen`, for instance, might be in the file `Pen.h`.

✦ **Source file:** If your class has member functions, and you did not put the code in the class definition, you need to put the code in a source file. When you do, precede the function name with the class name and two colons. (Do not put any spaces between the two colons, but you can put spaces on either side of the pair of colons.) If you named the header file the same as the class, you probably want to name the source file the same as the class as well but with a `.cpp` or `.cc` extension.

Working with a Class

Many handy tricks are available for working with classes. In this section, we explore several clever ways of working with classes, starting with the way you can hide certain parts of your class from other functions that are accessing them.

Accessing members

When you work with an object in real life, there are often parts of the object that you interact with and other parts that you don't. For example, when we use the computer, we type on the keyboard but don't open the box and poke around with a wire attached to a battery. For the most part, the stuff inside is off-limits except when we're upgrading it.

In object terminology, we use the words *public* and *private* to refer to characteristics and capabilities. When you design a class, you might want to make
some member variables and functions freely accessible by users of the class.
You may want to keep other classes tucked away.

First, let us explain what we mean by *users of the class.* When the `main`
function of your program creates an instance of a class and calls one
of its member functions, `main` is a *user* of the class. If you have a function
called `FlippityFlop`, and it creates an instance of your class and does
a few things to the instance, like change some its member variables,
`FlippityFlop` is a *user* of your class. In short, a user is any function that
accesses your class.

If you're designing a class, it's possible that you want only these users
calling certain member functions. Other member functions you may want
to keep hidden away, to be called only by other member functions within
the class. Suppose you're writing a class called `Oven`. This class includes a
method called `Bake`, which takes a number as a parameter representing the
desired oven temperature. Now you may also have a member function called
`TurnOnHeatingElement` and one called `TurnOffHeatingElement`.

Here's how it would work. The `Bake` method starts out calling `TurnOn`
`HeatingElement`. Then it keeps track of the temperature, and when the
temperature is correct, it calls `TurnOffHeatingElement`.

Now would you want somebody walking in the kitchen and calling the `Turn`
`OnHeatingElement` function without touching any of the dials, only to
leave the room as the oven gets hotter and hotter with nobody watching it? No.
You allow the users of the class to call only `Bake`. The other two member
functions, `TurnOnHeatingElement` and `TurnOffHeatingElement`, are
reserved for use only by the `Bake` function.

You bar users from calling functions by making specific functions *private.*
Functions that you want to allow access to you make *public.*

After you have such a class designed, if you write a function (not a member
function) that has an object and you try to call one of an object's private
member functions, you get a compiler error when you try to compile it. The
compiler won't allow you to call it.

Listing 7-5 shows a sample `Oven` class and a `main` that uses it. Take a look
at the class definition. It has two sections: one private and the other public.
After the class definition, we put the code for the functions. The two private
functions don't do much other than print a message. (Although they're also
free to call other private functions in the class.) The public function, `Bake`,
calls each of the private functions, because it's allowed to.

Listing 7-5: Using the Public and Private Words to Hide Parts of Your Class

```
#include <iostream>

using namespace std;

class Oven
{
private:
    void TurnOnHeatingElement();
    void TurnOffHeatingElement();

public:
    void Bake(int Temperature);
};

void Oven::TurnOnHeatingElement()
{
    cout << "Heating element is now ON! Be careful!" << endl;
}

void Oven::TurnOffHeatingElement()
{
    cout << "Heating element is now off. Relax!" << endl;
}

void Oven::Bake(int Temperature)
{
    TurnOnHeatingElement();
    cout << "Baking!" << endl;
    TurnOffHeatingElement();
}

int main()
{
    Oven fred;
    fred.Bake(875);
    return 0;

}
```

When you run this program, you see some messages:

```
Heating element is now ON! Be careful!
Baking!
Heating element is now off. Relax!
```

Nothing too fancy here. Now if you tried to include a line in your `main` such as the one in the following code, where you call a private function

```
fred.TurnOnHeatingElement();
```

you see an error message telling you that you can't do it because the function is private. In CodeBlocks, we see this message:

```
error: `void Oven::TurnOnHeatingElement()' is private
```

When you design your classes, consider making all the functions private by default, and then only make those public that you want users to have access to. Some people, however, prefer to go the other way around: Make them all public, and only make those private that you are sure you don't want users to access. There are good arguments for either way; however, we prefer to make public only what must be public. That way, we minimize the risk of some other program, that's using your class, messing things up by calling things the programmer doesn't really understand.

You don't necessarily need to list the private members first followed by the public members. You can put the public members first if you prefer. Some people put the public members at the top so they see them first. That makes sense. Also, you can have more than one private section and more than one public section. For example, you can have a public section, a private section, and then another public section, as in the following code:

```
class Oven
{
public:
    void Bake(int Temperature);

private:
    void TurnOnHeatingElement();
    void TurnOffHeatingElement();

public:
    void Broil();
};
```

But we recommend having only one public section and only one private section (or no private sections). This minimalism keeps your code neater.

Using classes and pointers

As with any variable, you can have a pointer variable that points to an object. As usual, the pointer variable's type must match the type of the class. This creates a pointer variable that points to a `Pen` instance:

```
Pen *ptrMyPen;
```

The variable `ptrMyPen` is a pointer, and it can point to an object of type `Pen`. The variable's own type is *pointer to* `Pen`, or in C++ notation, `Pen *`.

A line of code like `Pen *ptrMyPen;` creates a variable that serves as a pointer to an object. But this line, by itself, does not actually create an instance. By itself, it points to nothing. To create an instance, you have to call `new`. This is a common mistake among C++ programmers; sometimes people forget to call `new` and wonder why their programs crash.

After you create the variable `ptrMyPen`, you can create an instance of class `Pen`, and point `ptrMyPen` to it using the `new` keyword like so:

```
ptrMyPen = new Pen;
```

Or you can combine both `Pen *ptrMyPen;` and the preceding line:

```
Pen *ptrMyPen = new Pen;
```

Now you have two variables: You have the actual object, which is unnamed and sitting on the heap (see Minibook I, Chapter 6, for more information on pointers and heaps). You also have the pointer variable, which points to the object: two variables working together.

Because the object is out on the heap, the only way to access it is through the pointer. To access the members through the pointer, you use a special notation that is a minus sign followed by a greater-than sign, which looks like an arrow, as in the following line:

```
ptrMyPen->InkColor = red;
```

This goes through the pointer to set the `InkColor` of the object to `red`.

Get used to working with pointers and using the pointer notation for accessing the members of an object. It's not just a programming language; it's a way of life!

Although we like to begin a pointer variable's name with `ptr`, we sometimes forgo that when we're working with objects. Most object work involves objects on the heap, so you are always accessing objects through pointers. In our minds, we connect the two into one, and we feel like the pointer variable is the object, so we don't use the `ptr` prefix.

If we decide not to start our pointer variable names with `ptr`, the previous lines of code would look like this instead:

```
Pen *MyPen = new Pen;
MyPen->InkColor = red;
```

As with other variables you created with `new`, after you are finished using an object, you should call `delete`. To do so, start with the word `delete` and then the name of the object, as in this:

```
delete MyPen;
```

Store a 0 in the pointer after you *delete* it (which really means *delete the object it's pointing to*). When you call `delete` on a pointer to an object, you are deleting the object itself, not the pointer. If you don't store a 0 in the pointer, it still points to where the object *used to be*.

Listing 7-6 shows a process of declaring a pointer, creating an object and pointing to it, accessing the object's members through the pointer, deleting the object, and clearing the pointer back to 0.

Listing 7-6:   Managing an Object's Life

```
#include <iostream>
#include "Pen.h"

using namespace std;

int main()
{
    Pen *MyPen;
    MyPen = new Pen;

    MyPen->InkColor = red;
    cout << MyPen->InkColor << endl;

    delete MyPen;
    MyPen = 0;

    return 0;
}
```

Table 7-2 reiterates the process (steps) shown in Listing 7-6 in a more formal way. We call Table 7-2 "Steps to Using Objects," rather than something more specific such as "Using Objects with Pointers," because the majority of your work with objects will be through pointers. Therefore, this is the most common way of using pointers.

Table 7-2		Steps to Using Objects
Step	*Sample Code*	*Action*
1	`Pen *MyPen;`	Declares the pointer
2	`MyPen = new Pen;`	Calls `new` to create the object
3	`MyPen->InkColor = red;`	Accesses the members of the object through the pointer
4	`delete MyPen;`	Deletes the object
5	`MyPen = 0;`	Clears the pointer

Now that you have an overview of the process through Listing 7-6 and understand the basics through Table 7-2, let's formalize the procedure. The following steps describe precisely how to work with pointers and objects:

1. **Declare the pointer.**

The pointer must match the type of object you are going to work with, except the pointer's type name in C++ is followed by an asterisk, *.

2. **Call new, passing the class name, and store the results of new in the pointer.**

You can combine Steps 1 and 2 into a single step.

3. **Access the object's members through the pointer with the shorthand notation ->.**

You could dereference the pointer and put parentheses around it, but everyone uses the shorthand notation.

4. **When you are finished with the pointer, call delete.**

This step frees the object from the heap. Remember that this does not delete the pointer itself, although programmers usually say that they're *deleting the pointer.*

5. **Clear the pointer by setting it to 0.**

If your delete statement is at the end of the program, you don't need to clear the pointer to 0.

Passing objects to functions

When you write a function, normally you base your decision about using pointers on whether or not you want to change the original variables passed into the function. Suppose you have a function called AddOne, and it takes an integer as a parameter. If you want to modify the original variable, you can use a pointer (or you can use a reference). If you don't want to modify the variable, just pass the variable *by value* as it's called.

The following prototype represents a function that can modify the variable passed into it:

```
void AddOne(int *number);
```

And this prototype represents a function that cannot modify the variable passed into it:

```
void AddOne(int number);
```

With objects, you can do something similar. For example, this function takes a pointer to an object and can, therefore, modify the object:

```
void FixFlatTire(Car *mycar);
```

But what do you suppose this would do:

```
void FixFlatTire(Car mycar);
```

Based on what we said previously, most likely the function gets its own `Car` instance that cannot be modified. That's correct, but consider that for a moment: The function gets its own instance. In other words, every time you call this function, it creates an entirely new instance of class `Car`. This instance would be a duplicate of class `Car` — except that it wouldn't be the same instance. Just a copy of it.

When you work with objects, a *copy* is not always a sure thing. What if the object has member variables that are pointers to other objects? Will the copy get copies of those pointers, which in turn point to those same other objects? Or does this object's members point to its own *other objects*? Are those objects copies or the originals?

Always pass objects as pointers. Don't pass objects directly into functions. Yes, it risks bad code changing the object, but careful C++ programmers want the actual object, not a copy. That outweighs the risk of an accidental change. This chapter explains how to prevent accidental changes by using the `const` parameters.

So just do this:

```
void FixFlatTire(Car *mycar);
```

If you like references, you are welcome to do this:

```
void FixFlatTire(Car &mycar);
```

But don't just pass the object. It's messy and not nice.

Because your function receives its objects as pointers, you continue accessing them by using the `->` notation. For example, the function `FixFlatTire` may do this:

```
void FixFlatTire(Car *mycar)
{
    mycar->RemoveTire();
    mycar->AddNewTire();
}
```

Or, if you prefer references, you would do this:

```
void FixFlatTire2(Car &mycar)
{
    mycar.RemoveTire();
    mycar.AddNewTire();
}
```

In this code, because you're dealing with a reference, you access the object's members using the dot rather than the `->` notation.

Another reason to use only pointers and references as parameters for objects is that a function that takes an object as a parameter usually wants to change the function. Such changes require pointers or references. When you don't want the function to modify the object, use `const`, which is covered in the following section.

Using const parameters in functions

If a function takes an object as a parameter and you're passing it by using a pointer or reference but don't want the function modifying the object, use the word `const` in the function header. If you insert `const` before the type in the parameter list, the compiler does not let the function code modify the object. Such code causes a compiler error.

The `const` word is useful because you generally don't want to pass an object directly. That involves copying the object, which is messy. Instead, you normally pass by using a pointer or reference, which would allow you to change the object. If you put the word `const` before the parameter, the compiler will not allow you to change the parameter. In Listing 7-7, we have inserted `const` before the parameter. The function can look at the object but can't change it.

**Listing 7-7: The Inspect Function Is Not Allowed to
                    Modify Its Parameter**

```
#include <iostream>
#include "Pen.h"

using namespace std;

void Inspect(const Pen *Checkitout)
{
    cout << Checkitout->Brand << endl;
}

int main()
{
    Pen *MyPen = new Pen();
    MyPen->Brand = "Spy Plus Camera";

    Inspect(MyPen);

    return 0;
}
```

Now suppose that you tried to change the object in the `Inspect` function. You may have put a line in that function like this:

```
Checkitout->Length = 10.0;
```

If you try this, the compiler issues an error. In CodeBlocks, we get

```
error: assignment of data-member `Pen::Length' in read-only structure
```

If you have multiple parameters, you can mix `const` and `non-const`. If you go overboard, this can be confusing. The following line shows two parameters that are `const` and another that is not. The function can modify only the members of the object called `one`.

```
void Inspect(const Pen *Checkitout, Spy *one, const Spy *two);
```

Using the this pointer

Consider a function called `OneMoreCheeseGone`. It's not a member function, but it takes an object of instance `Cheese` as a parameter. Its prototype looks like this:

```
void OneMoreCheeseGone(Cheese *Block);
```

This is just a simple function with no return type. It takes an object pointer as a parameter. For example, after you eat a block of cheese, you can call:

```
OneMoreCheeseGone(MyBlock);
```

Now consider this: If you have an object on the heap, it has no name. You access it through a pointer variable that points to it. But what if the code is currently executing inside a member function of an object? How do you refer to the object itself?

C++ has a secret variable that exists inside every member function: `this`. It's a pointer variable. The `this` variable always points to the current object. So if code execution is occurring inside a member function and you want to call `OneMoreCheeseGone`, passing in the current object (or block of cheese), you would pass `this`.

Listing 7-8 demonstrates `this`. The `this` listing has four main parts. First is the definition for the class called `Cheese`. The class contains a couple of member functions.

Next is the function `OneMoreCheeseGone` along with a global variable that it modifies. This function subtracts one from the global variable and stores a string in a member variable, `status`, of the object passed to it.

Next come the actual member functions for class `Cheese`. (We put these functions after the `OneMoreCheeseGone` function because they call it. If we used a function prototype as a forward reference for `OneMoreCheeseGone`, the order wouldn't matter.)

Finally we have `main`, which creates two new instances of `Cheese`. Then it sets the global variable to 2, which keeps track of the number of blocks left. Next, it calls the `eat` function for the `asiago` cheese and `rot` for the `limburger` cheese. And then it prints the results of everything that happened: It displays the `Cheese` count, and it displays the `status` variable of each object.

Listing 7-8: Passing an Object from Inside Its Member Functions by Using the this Variable

```cpp
#include <iostream>

using namespace std;

class Cheese
{
public:
    string status;
    void eat();
    void rot();
};

int CheeseCount;

void OneMoreCheeseGone(Cheese *Block)
{
    CheeseCount--;
    Block->status = "Gone";
};

void Cheese::eat()
{
    cout << "Eaten up! Yummy" << endl;
    OneMoreCheeseGone(this);
}

void Cheese::rot()
{
    cout << "Rotted away! Yuck" << endl;
    OneMoreCheeseGone(this);
}

int main()
{
    Cheese *asiago = new Cheese();
    Cheese *limburger = new Cheese();

    CheeseCount = 2;

    asiago->eat();
    limburger->rot();

    cout << endl;
    cout << "Cheese count: " << CheeseCount << endl;
    cout << "asiago: " << asiago->status << endl;
    cout << "limburger: " << limburger->status << endl;

    return 0;
}
```

When you run the program in Listing 7-8, you see this output:

```
Eaten up! Yummy
Rotted away! Yuck

Cheese count: 0
asiago: Gone
limburger: Gone
```

The first line is the result of calling `asiago->eat()`, which prints one message. The second line is the result of calling `limburger->rot()`, which prints another message.

The third line is simply the value in the variable `CheeseCount`. This variable was *decremented* once each time the computer called the `OneMoreCheeseGone` function. Because the function was called twice, `CheeseCount` went from 2 to 1 to 0.

The final two lines show the contents of the `status` variable in the two objects. (The `OneMoreCheeseGone` function had stored the string `Gone` in these variables.)

Take a careful look at the `OneMoreCheeseGone` function. It operated on the current object that came in as a parameter by setting its status variable to the string `Gone`. Where did the parameter come from? The member function `eat` called it, passing the object itself by using the `this` pointer. The member function `rot` also called it, again passing the object itself via the `this` pointer.

Overloading member functions

You may want a member function in a class to handle different types of parameters. For example, you might have a class called `Door` and a member function called `GoThrough`. You might want the `GoThrough` function to take as parameters an object of class `Dog`, an object of class `Human`, or an object of class `Cat`. Depending on which class is entering, you might want to change the `GoThrough` function's behavior.

A way to handle this is by *overloading* the `GoThrough` function. C++ lets you design a class that has multiple member functions that are all named the same. However, the parameters must differ between these functions. With the `GoThrough` function, one version will take a `Human`, another a `Dog`, and another a `Cat`.

Go through the code in Listing 7-9 and notice the `GoThrough` functions. There are three of them. Now look at `main`. It creates four different objects — a cat, a dog, a human, and a door. It then sends each creature through the door.

Listing 7-9:   Overloading Functions in a Class

```cpp
#include <iostream>

using namespace std;

class Cat
{
public:
    string name;
};

class Dog
{
public:
    string name;
};

class Human
{
public:
    string name;
};

class Door
{
private:
    int HowManyInside;

public:
    void Start();
    void GoThrough(Cat *acat);
    void GoThrough(Dog *adog);
    void GoThrough(Human *ahuman);
};

void Door::Start()
{
    HowManyInside = 0;
}

void Door::GoThrough(Cat *somebody)
{
    cout << "Welcome, " << somebody->name << endl;
    cout << "A cat just entered!" << endl;
    HowManyInside++;
}

void Door::GoThrough(Dog *somebody)
{
    cout << "Welcome, " << somebody->name << endl;
    cout << "A dog just entered!" << endl;
    HowManyInside++;
}

void Door::GoThrough(Human *somebody)
{
    cout << "Welcome, " << somebody->name << endl;
    cout << "A human just entered!" << endl;
    HowManyInside++;
}
```

```
int main()
{
    Door entrance;
    entrance.Start();

    Cat *SneekyGirl = new Cat;
    SneekyGirl->name = "Sneeky Girl";

    Dog *LittleGeorge = new Dog;
    LittleGeorge->name = "Little George";

    Human *me = new Human;
    me->name = "Jeff";

    entrance.GoThrough(SneekyGirl);
    entrance.GoThrough(LittleGeorge);
    entrance.GoThrough(me);

    delete SneekyGirl;
    delete LittleGeorge;
    delete me;

    return 0;
}
```

The program allows them to enter like humans. The beginning of this program declares three classes, Cat, Dog, and Human, each with a name member. Next is the Door class. A private member, HowManyInside, tracks how many beings have entered. Then we have a public function called Start, which activates the door. Finally, the class contains the overloaded functions. They all have the same name and the same return type. You can have different return types, but they must differ by parameters. These do; one takes a Cat pointer; one takes a Dog pointer; and one takes a Human pointer.

Next is the code for the member functions. The first function, Start, is easy to activate. It sets HowManyInside to 0. The next three functions are overloaded. They do similar things, but they write slightly different messages. Each takes a different type.

Then we have main, which creates a Door instance. We didn't make this a pointer (just to show that you can mix pointers with stack variables in a program). After creating the Door instance, we called its Start function. Next, we created three creature instances: one Cat, one Dog, and one Human. We also set the name member variables for each.

Then we call the entrance.GoThrough function. The first time we pass a Cat, then we pass a Dog, and then we pass a Human. (Sounds painful.) Because you can see the Door class, you know that we're calling three different functions that happened to be all named the same. But when we're *using* the class, we consider them all one function that happens to accept either a Cat, a Dog, or a Human. That's the goal of overloading: to create what feels like *versions* of the one function.

Starting and Ending with Constructors and Destructors

You can add two special functions to your class that let you provide special startup and shutdown functionality. These are called a *constructor* and a *destructor.* The following sections provide the secret details about these nifty functions.

Starting with constructors

When you create a new instance of a class, you may want to do some basic setup on the object. Suppose you have a class called `Apartment`, with a private member variable called `NumberOfOccupants` and a member function called `ComeOnIn`. The code for `ComeOnIn` adds 1 to `NumberOfOccupants`.

When you create a new instance of `Apartment`, you probably want to start `NumberOfOccupants` at 0. The best way to do this is by adding a special member function, a *constructor,* to your class. This member function has a line of code such as

```
NumberOfOccupants = 0;
```

Whenever you create a new instance of the class `Apartment`, the computer first calls this constructor for your new object, thereby setting `NumberOfOccupants` to 0.

Think of the constructor as an *initialization function:* The computer calls it when you create a new object.

To write a constructor, you add it as another member function to your class, and you make it public. You name the constructor the same as your class. For the class `Apartment`, we would name our constructor `Apartment`. The constructor has no return type, not even `void`. You can have parameters in a constructor; see "Adding parameters to constructors," later in this chapter.

Listing 7-10, later in this section, shows a sample constructor along with a *destructor,* which we cover in the next section.

Ending with destructors

When you delete an instance of a class, you might want some *cleanup* code to straighten things out before the object goes off to the classroom in the sky. For example, your object may have member variables that are pointers to other objects. You may want to delete those other objects.

You put cleanup code in a special function called a destructor. A *destructor* is a finalization function that the computer calls before it deletes your object.

The destructor function gets the same name as the class, except it has a tilde, ~, at the beginning of it. (The tilde is usually in the upper-left corner of the keyboard.) For a class called Squirrel, the destructor would be ~Squirrel. The destructor does not have a return type, not even void, because you can't return anything from a destructor (the object is gone, after all). You just start with the function name and no parameters.

The next section, "Sampling constructors and destructors," shows an example that uses both constructors and destructors.

Constructors and destructors are a way of life for C++ programmers. Nearly every class has a constructor, and many also have a destructor.

Sampling constructors and destructors

Listing 7-10 uses a constructor and destructor. This program involves two classes, the main one called Squirrel that demonstrates the constructor and destructor, and one called Walnut, which is used by the Squirrel class.

The Squirrel class has a member variable called MyDinner that is a pointer to a Walnut instance. The Squirrel constructor creates an instance of Walnut and stores it in the MyDinner variable. The destructor deletes the instance of Walnut.

In main, we create two instances of Squirrel. Each instance gets its own Walnut to eat. Each Squirrel creates its Walnut when it starts and deletes the Walnut when the Squirrel is deleted.

Listing 7-10:   Initializing and Finalizing with Constructors and Destructors

```
#include <iostream>

using namespace std;

class Walnut
{
public:
    int Size;
};

class Squirrel
{
private:
    Walnut *MyDinner;

public:
    Squirrel();
    ~Squirrel();
```

(continued)

Listing 7-10: *(continued)*

```
};

Squirrel::Squirrel()
{
    cout << "Starting!" << endl;
    MyDinner = new Walnut;
    MyDinner->Size = 30;
}

Squirrel::~Squirrel()
{
    cout << "Cleaning up my mess!" << endl;
    delete MyDinner;
}

int main()
{
    Squirrel *Sam = new Squirrel;
    Squirrel *Sally = new Squirrel;

    delete Sam;
    delete Sally;

    return 0;
}
```

Notice in this code that the constructor has the same name as the class, Squirrel. The destructor also has the same name, but with a tilde, ~, tacked on to the beginning of it. Thus, the constructor is Squirrel and the destructor is ~Squirrel.

When you run this program, you can see the following lines, which were spit up by the Squirrel in its constructor and destructor. (You see two lines of each because we created two squirrels.)

```
Starting!
Starting!
Cleaning up my mess!
Cleaning up my mess!
```

If our Walnut class also had a constructor and destructor, and we made the MyDinner member an actual variable in the Squirrel class rather than a pointer, the computer would create the Walnut instance after it creates the Squirrel instance but before it calls the Squirrel constructor. It then deletes the Walnut instances when it is deleting the Squirrel instance, after it finishes calling the ~Squirrel destructor. It would do this for each instance of Squirrel, so that each Squirrel gets its own Walnut, as before.

Constructors and destructors with stack variables

In Listing 7-10, we created the two `Squirrels` on the heap by using pointers and calling

```
Squirrel *Sam = new Squirrel;
Squirrel *Sally = new Squirrel;
```

But we could have made them on the stack by just declaring them without pointers:

```
Squirrel Sam;
Squirrel Sally;
```

You can do this, and the program will run fine, provided you remove the `delete` lines. You do not delete stack variables. The computer calls the destructor when the `main` function *ends*. That's the general rule with objects on the stack: They are created when you declare them, and they stay until the function ends.

Adding parameters to constructors

Like other functions, constructors allow you to include parameters. When you do, you can use these parameters in constructors in your initialization process. To use them, you list the arguments inside parentheses when you create the object.

Although `int` has a constructor, it is not actually a class. However, the *runtime library* (that big mass of code that gets put in with your program by the linker) includes a constructor and destructor that you can use when calling `new` for an integer.

Suppose that you want the `Squirrel` class to have a member variable called `name`. Although you could create an instance of `Squirrel` and then set its `name` variable, you can specify the `name` directly by using a constructor.

The constructor's prototype would look like this:

```
Squirrel(string StartName);
```

Then, you would create a new instance like so:

```
Squirrel *Sam = new Squirrel("Sam");
```

The constructor is expecting a `string`, so you pass a `string` when you create the object.

Listing 7-11 shows a program that includes all the basic elements of a class with a constructor that accepts parameters.

Listing 7-11: Placing Parameters in Constructors

```cpp
#include <iostream>

using namespace std;

class Squirrel
{
private:
    string Name;

public:
    Squirrel(string StartName);
    void WhatIsMyName();
};

Squirrel::Squirrel(string StartName)
{
    cout << "Starting!" << endl;
    Name = StartName;
}

void Squirrel::WhatIsMyName()
{
    cout << "My name is " << Name << endl;
}

int main()
{
    Squirrel *Sam = new Squirrel("Sam");
    Squirrel *Sally = new Squirrel("Sally");

    Sam->WhatIsMyName();
    Sally->WhatIsMyName();

    delete Sam;
    delete Sally;

    return 0;
}
```

In `main`, we passed a string into the constructors. In the code for the constructor, we're taking the string parameter called `StartName` and copying it to the member variable called `Name`. In the `WhatIsMyName` function, we write it to the console.

You cannot include parameters in a destructor. The C++ language does not allow it.

Building Hierarchies of Classes

When you start going crazy describing classes, you usually discover *hierarchies* of classes. For example, you might say you have a class `Vehicle`. But we might say, we can divide your class `Vehicle` into classes `Car`, `Pickup Truck`, `Tractor Trailer`, and `SUV`.

Then you might say that you can take the `Car` class and divide it into such classes as Station Wagon, `Four-door Sedan`, and `Two-door Hatchback`.

Or we could divide `Vehicle` into car brands, such as `Ford`, `Honda`, and `Toyota`. Then we could divide the class `Toyota` into models, such as `Tercel`, `Celica`, `Camry`, and `Corolla`.

You can create similar groupings of objects for the other class hierarchies; your decision depends on how you categorize things and how the hierarchy is used.

In the hierarchy, class `Vehicle` is at the top. This class has characteristics that you find in every brand or model of vehicles. For example, all vehicles have wheels. How many they have varies, but it doesn't matter at this point because classes don't have specific values for the characteristics.

Each brand has certain characteristics that might be unique to it, but each has all the characteristics of class `Vehicle`. That's called *inheritance.* The class `Toyota`, for example, has all the characteristics found in `Vehicle`. And the class `Celica` has all the characteristics found in `Toyota`, which includes those inherited from `Vehicle`.

Creating a hierarchy in C++

In C++, you can create a hierarchy of classes. When you take one class and create a new one under it, such as creating `Toyota` from `Vehicle`, you are *deriving* a new class.

To derive a class from an existing class, you write the new class as you would any other class, but you extend the header after the class name with a colon, `:`, the word `public`, and then the class you're deriving from, as in the following class header line:

```
class Toyota : public Vehicle {
```

When you do so, the class you create (`Toyota`) *inherits* the member variables and functions from the previous class (`Vehicle`). For example, if `Vehicle` has a public member variable called `NumberOfWheels` and a public member function called `Drive`, the class `Toyota` has these members, although you didn't write the members in `Toyota`.

Listing 7-12 shows a class inheritance. We started with a class called `Vehicle`, and we derived a class called `Toyota`. In `main`, we created an instance of `Toyota`, and we called two member functions for the instance, `MeAndMyToyota` and `Drive`. The definition of the `Toyota` class does not show a `Drive` function. The `Drive` function was inherited from the `Vehicle` class. You can call this function like a member of the `Toyota` class because in many ways it *is*.

Listing 7-12: Deriving One Class from Another

```cpp
#include <iostream>

using namespace std;

class Vehicle
{
public:
    int NumberOfWheels;

    void Drive()
    {
        cout << "Driving, driving, driving..." << endl;
    }
};

class Toyota : public Vehicle
{
public:
    void MeAndMyToyota()
    {
        cout << "Just me and my Toyota!" << endl;
    }
};

int main()
{
    Toyota MyCar;
    MyCar.MeAndMyToyota();
    MyCar.Drive();

    return 0;
}
```

When you run this program, you see the output from two functions:

```
Just me and my Toyota!
Driving, driving, driving...
```

Some people use the term *parent* class for the first class in a hierarchy and *child* for the one that is derived. However, these are not the best terms because some people use them to mean that one class has an instance of another class as a member variable. In that case, the parent class has as a member the child class. A better term is *base* class and *derived* class. You derive a class from the base class. The result is a derived class.

Understanding types of inheritance

When you create a class, member functions can access both public and private member variables and functions. Users of the class can access only the public member variables and functions. But when you derive a new class, the picture changes. The derived class *cannot* access the private members in its own class. Private members are reserved for a class itself and not for any derived class.

When members need to be accessible by derived classes, there's a specification you can use beyond public and private: *protected.*

REMEMBER

Protected members and private members work the same way, but derived classes can access only protected members, not private members. Users can't access either class.

TECHNICAL STUFF

We avoid private members unless we know that we won't derive classes from a member. When we've derived classes from other people's classes with private unprotected members, we couldn't add all the cool features we wanted. My derived class required access to those private members, so we had to mess up the original code to modify the original class. If the original programmer had used *protected* members, our derived class could access the members without changing the original code!

Chapter 8: Using Advanced C++ Features

In This Chapter

✓ Using comments

✓ Working with conversions, consoles, and preprocessor directives

✓ Manipulating constants, enums, and random numbers

✓ Structuring your code with switch statements

✓ Managing arrays of data

C++ has so much to offer that we thought we'd give you a mixture of advanced topics you can explore in C++. So for starters, we're going to talk a bit about some fundamental issues in C++ that become important as you advance your programming career.

Filling Your Code with Comments

We have a task for a friend of ours. We want him to turn our refrigerator around and repair the compressor. We're not going to give him any details about how to do this, and we don't want him to look in a manual. Just grab the tools, go at it, and try to fix the thing. Now doesn't that sound like fun?

Unless he happens to be an expert on refrigeration devices, it's doubtful that he'd get very far, especially without hurting himself.

Now in computer programming, the risk of hurting yourself is pretty low, barring things like monitors falling on you or keyboards jumping up and attacking you. Nevertheless, other people occasionally have to fix your programs, so it's a good idea for you to provide adequate explanations of what your programs do.

How do you explain your programs? You put what are called comments in your code. A *comment* is simply some words in the code that the compiler ignores and you put in for the benefit of the humans reading the code.

For example, you may have some code like this:

```
total = 10;
for (i = 0; i < 10; i++)
{
    total = (total + i) * 3;
}
```

But this code may not be very clear to your coworkers (or to you if you put it away for six months and come back later to look at it). So instead, you can add some comments. You denote a comment in C++ by starting a line with two slashes, as follows:

```
// Initialize total to the number
// of items involved.
total = 10;

// Calculate total for the
// first ten sets.
for (i = 0; i < 10; i++)
{
    total = (total + i) * 3;
}
```

Now the people working on the project can understand what the code does. Note the white space between the groups of code. Using white space helps someone looking at the code see where one thought ends and another begins. You should always include white space in your code so that other developers can read the code more easily.

Of course, you could put comments like this:

```
// My salary is too low
// I want a raise
total = 10;

// Someday they'll recognize
// my superior talents!
for (i = 0; i < 10; i++)
{
    total = (total + i) * 3;
}
```

However, comments like this don't have much use in the code; besides, they may have the reverse effect from what you're hoping for!

A comment is ignored by a compiler (but not always by other humans). You can write whatever you want as comments, and the compiler pretends that it's not even there. (Your boss, however, may notice, so use discretion.)

A comment begins with //, and it can begin anywhere on the line. In fact, contrary to what you might think, you can even put comments at the end of a line containing C++ code, instead of on a separate line. Using comments on a code line lets you focus a comment on just that line, as follows:

```
int subtotal = 10;   // Initialize the subtotal value to 10.
```

This comment gives a little more explanation of what the line does. You normally use line comments like this when you want to tell others what kind of information a variable holds or explain a complex task. Normally, you explain blocks of code as shown earlier in this section.

You can use two kinds of comments in C++. One is the double-slash (as we've already described). When the compiler sees two slashes, it treats the rest of that line as a comment. That is, the comment runs from the two slashes to the end of the line. The other kind of comment begins with a slash-asterisk, /*, and ends with an asterisk-slash, */. The comments go between these *delimiters* and can span several lines, as in the following example:

```
/* This program separates the parts of the
   sandwich into its separate parts. This
   process is often called "separation of
   parts".
   (c) 1964 Sandwich Parts Separators, Inc.
*/
```

This is all one comment, and it spans multiple lines. You normally use this kind of comment to provide an overview of a task or describe the purpose of a function. This kind of comment also works well for the informational headings that some large company applications require. As with other comments, you can put these anywhere in your code, provided you don't break a string or word in two by putting a comment in the middle. Nobody likes to be broken in two, and C++ words are no different.

Much of the code in the remainder of this chapter has comments in it so you can see how we use comments and so you can get a few more ideas about how the code works.

Some beginning programmers get the mistaken idea that comments appear in the program window when the program runs. That is not the case. A comment does not write anything to the console. To write things to the console, use `cout`.

Converting Types

Sometimes you just don't have the type of things you want. You might want to trade in your 1999 Ford Taurus for that brand-new Porsche. But, needless to say, unless you have plenty of money, that might be pretty hard.

But converting between different types in C++, now *that's* a lot easier. For example, suppose you have a string variable called `digits`, and it holds the string `"123"`. Further, you want to somehow get the numbers inside that string into an integer variable called `amount`. Thus, you want `amount` to hold the value `123`; that is, you want to *convert the string to a number.*

In Listing 8-1, later in this chapter, we show you how you can convert between numbers and strings. Minibook I, Chapter 6 shows some sample code for converting a number to a string. Here we employ that same technique along with a similar technique for converting a string back to a number.

Converting strings is an interesting concept in C++ because a really great feature lets you *write to* and *read from* a string just as you would to and from a console. For example, although you can write a number `12` out to a console by using code like this:

```
cout << 12;
```

you can actually do the same thing with strings: You can write a number `12` to a string, as in

```
mystring << 12;
```

After this line runs, the string contains the value `"12"`. However, to do this, you need to use a special form of string called a `stringstream`. In the never-ending world of computer terminology, a *stream* is something that you can write to and read from in a flowing fashion (think about bits flowing through a wire — much as a stream flows along a waterbed). For example, you might write the word `"hello"` to a `stringstream`, then the number `87`, and then the word `"goodbye"`. After those three operations, the string contains the value `"hello87goodbye"`.

And you can similarly read from a stream. In the section "Reading from the Console," later in this chapter, we show you how you can read from a console by using the > notation. When you read from the console, although your program stops and waits for the user to enter something, the real stream technology takes place *after* the user types something: After the console has a series of characters, your program reads in the characters as a stream, one data type after other. You can read a string, then a series of numbers, and another string, and so on.

With `stringstream`, you can do something similar. You would fill the string with something, rather than having the user fill it, as in the case of a console. From there, you can begin to read from the string, placing the values into variables of different types. One of these types is integer. But because the `stringstream` is, at heart, just a string, that's how you convert a string of digits to an integer: You put the digit characters in the string, and read the string as a stream into your integer. Pretty snazzy!

The only catch to using these is that you need to know in advance which kind of streaming you want to do. If you want to write to the `stringstream`, you create an instance of a class called `ostringstream`. (The o is for *output*.) If you want to read from a `stringstream`, you create an instance of a class called `istringstream`. (The i is for *input*.)

Listing 8-1 includes two handy functions that you may want to save for your own programming experience later. One is called `StringToNumber`, and the other is called `NumberToString`.

Listing 8-1: Converting Between Types Is Easy

```cpp
#include <iostream>
#include <sstream>    // for istringstream, ostringstream

using namespace std;

int StringToNumber(string MyString)
{
    istringstream converter(MyString); // Converts from string to number.
    int result;                        // Contains the operation results.

    // Perform the conversion and return the results.
    converter >> result;
    return result;
}

string NumberToString(int Number)
{
    ostringstream converter; // Converts from number to string.

    // Perform the conversion and return the results.
    converter << Number;
    return converter.str();
}

int main()
{
    float NumberOfKids; // Contains the theoretical number of kids.
    int ActualKids;     // Contains an actual number of kids.

    /* You can theoretically have 2.5 kids, but in the real world,
       you can't. Convert the theoretical number of kids to a real
       number by truncating NumberOfKids and display the results. */
    cout << "Float to Integer" << endl;
    cout << "(Truncated)" << endl;
    NumberOfKids = 2.5;
    ActualKids = (int)NumberOfKids;
    cout << NumberOfKids << " " << ActualKids << endl;

    // Perform the same task as before, but use a theoretical 2.1
    // kids this time.
    NumberOfKids = 2.1;
    ActualKids = (int)NumberOfKids;
    cout << NumberOfKids << " " << ActualKids << endl;

    // This time we'll use 2.9 kids.
```

(continued)

Listing 8-1 *(continued)*

```
NumberOfKids = 2.9;
ActualKids = (int)NumberOfKids;
cout << NumberOfKids << " " << ActualKids << endl;
cout << "Float to Integer" << endl;

// This process rounds the number, instead of truncating it.
// We do it using the same three numbers as before.
cout << "(Rounded)" << endl;
NumberOfKids = 2.5;
ActualKids = (int)(NumberOfKids + .5);
cout << NumberOfKids << " " << ActualKids << endl;

// Do it again using 2.1 kids.
NumberOfKids = 2.1;
ActualKids = (int)(NumberOfKids + .5);
cout << NumberOfKids << " " << ActualKids << endl;

// Do it yet again using 2.9 kids.
NumberOfKids = 2.9;
ActualKids = (int)(NumberOfKids + .5);
cout << NumberOfKids << " " << ActualKids << endl;
cout << endl << "Integer to Float" << endl;

// In this case, use the StringToNumber() function to perform the
// conversion.
ActualKids = 3;
NumberOfKids = ActualKids;
cout << NumberOfKids << endl << endl;
cout << "String to number" << endl;
int x = StringToNumber("12345") * 50;
cout << x << endl << endl;

// In this case, use the NumberToString() function to perform the
// conversion.
cout << "Number to string" << endl;
string mystring = NumberToString(80525323);
cout << mystring << endl;

    return 0;
}
```

StringToNumber takes a string, copies it into an istringstream, and then reads it into an integer. NumberToString takes an integer, writes it to an ostringstream, and then copies it to a string.

Feel free to use the StringToNumber and NumberToString functions in your own code. Sooner or later, you are likely to need to convert between integers and strings, and these functions can help you out without having to go search for the answers yourself.

Another kind of conversion that's useful is converting floating-point numbers (that is, numbers with a decimal point) and integers and vice versa. In C++, this conversion is easy: You just copy one to the other, and C++ takes care of the rest. The only catch is that when C++ converts from a float to an integer, it always *truncates*. That is, it doesn't round up: When it converts

`5.99` to an integer, it doesn't go up to `6`; it goes *down* to `5`. But there's an easy trick around that: Add `0.5` to the number before you convert it. If the number in the upper half (that is, from .5 to .9999 and so on), that `0.5` first takes the number above or equal to the upper whole number. Then, when the function rounds the number, the number will round *down* to the *upper* whole number.

So, for example, if you start with `4.6`, just converting it gets you a `4`. But if you add `.5`, you first get `5.1`, and then when you convert that, you get `5`. It works!

Going the other direction is even easier: To convert an integer to a float, you just copy it. If `i` is an integer, and `f` is a float, you just set it as follows to convert it:

```
f = i;
```

Whenever you convert from a `float` to an `int` or from an `int` to `float`, you must tell the compiler that you know what you're doing by adding `(int)` or `(float)` in front of the variable. Adding these keywords is called *coercion* or *type conversion*. The act of coercing one type to another is called *casting*. For example, the following tells the compiler that you know you're converting from a `float` to an `int`:

```
ActualKids = (int)NumberOfKids;
```

If you leave the `(int)` part out, the compiler displays a warning like this one:

```
warning: converting to 'int' from 'float'
```

Using the proper coercion code is important because it also tells other developers that you really do mean to perform the type conversion. Otherwise, other developers will point to that area of your code and deem it the source of an error, when it might not be the true source. Using proper coding techniques saves everyone time.

When you run this program, you see the results of all these conversions. The first big batch inside `main` puts different floating-point values into `NumberOfKids` (starting with the usual `2.5` number of kids, of course) and then converts these two integers. In the first batch, we didn't add `0.5`, so it just rounds it down. You can see in the output for this section that all the numbers were rounded down. The first number in each pair is the original floating-point value, and the second number is the number converted to an integer. Notice that the program always rounded down:

```
Float to Integer
(Truncated)
2.5 2
2.1 2
2.9 2
```

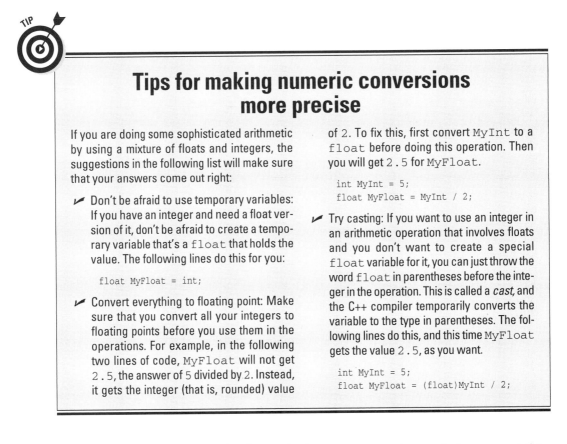

Tips for making numeric conversions more precise

If you are doing some sophisticated arithmetic by using a mixture of floats and integers, the suggestions in the following list will make sure that your answers come out right:

✔ **Don't be afraid to use temporary variables:** If you have an integer and need a float version of it, don't be afraid to create a temporary variable that's a `float` that holds the value. The following lines do this for you:

```
float MyFloat = int;
```

✔ **Convert everything to floating point:** Make sure that you convert all your integers to floating points before you use them in the operations. For example, in the following two lines of code, `MyFloat` will not get `2.5`, the answer of 5 divided by 2. Instead, it gets the integer (that is, rounded) value

of `2`. To fix this, first convert `MyInt` to a `float` before doing this operation. Then you will get `2.5` for `MyFloat`.

```
int MyInt = 5;
float MyFloat = MyInt / 2;
```

✔ **Try casting:** If you want to use an integer in an arithmetic operation that involves floats and you don't want to create a special `float` variable for it, you can just throw the word `float` in parentheses before the integer in the operation. This is called a *cast,* and the C++ compiler temporarily converts the variable to the type in parentheses. The following lines do this, and this time `MyFloat` gets the value `2.5`, as you want.

```
int MyInt = 5;
float MyFloat = (float)MyInt / 2;
```

In the next block of code, we do the same conversions as before, except this time we add `0.5` to each float. The result is an actual round to the nearest whole number. Note that the higher decimal numbers rounded up, while the lower ones rounded down:

```
Float to Integer
(Rounded)
2.5 3
2.1 2
2.9 3
```

Next is a quick one. We just converted the integer to a float. It doesn't print with a decimal point, but it is a float:

```
Integer to Float
3
```

Then we convert between numbers and strings. The first block of these converts a string to a number. Just to prove it really *is* a number, we go ahead and work some mathematical arithmetic on it — something you can't do with a string.

```
String to number
617250
```

And finally, we convert a number to a string:

```
Number to string
80525323
```

The output of these digits, of course, would look the same whether we print them as a string or a number, but you can see in the code that what we printed is indeed a string, not a number.

Reading from the Console

Throughout this book, we have used the console to demonstrate several topics. Many of the programs write some sort of output to the console. You can also use the console to get information from the user, something we briefly mention in Minibook I, Chapter 2.

To do this, instead of using the usual << with cout to write to the console, you use the >> operator along with cin (pronounced *see-in*).

In the old days of the C programming language, reading data from the console and placing its variables was somewhat nightmarish because it required you to use pointers. Now, in C++, that's no longer the case. If you want to read a set of characters into a string called MyName, you just type

```
cin >> MyName;
```

That's it! The program pauses, and the user can type something at the console. When the user presses Enter, the string he or she typed will go into the string called MyName.

Reading from the console has some catches. First, the console uses spaces as delimiters. That means that if you put spaces in what you type, only the letters up to the space are put into the string. Anything after the space, the console saves for the next time your program calls cin. That situation can be confusing. Second, if you want to read into a number, the user can type any characters, not just numbers. The computer then goes through some bizarre process and converts any letters into a meaningless number. Not good.

But fear not. As usual, we have found ways around such problems! Listing 8-2 shows you how to read a string and then a number from the console.

Next, it shows you how you can force the user to type only numbers. And finally, it shows how you can ask for a password with only asterisks appearing when the user types.

To make these last two tasks work correctly, we had to use a library called `conio`. This library gives you more direct access to the console, bypassing `cin`. But that's okay. We also used a special function called `StringToNumber` that is described in "Converting Types," earlier in this chapter.

Listing 8-2: Having the User Type Something

```cpp
#include <iostream>
#include <sstream>
#include <conio.h>

using namespace std;

int StringToNumber(string MyString)
{
    istringstream converter(MyString); // Holds the string.
    int result;                        // Holds the integer result.

    // Perform the conversion.
    converter >> result;
    return result;
}

string EnterOnlyNumbers()
{
    string numAsString = ""; // Holds the numeric string.
    char ch = getch();       // Obtains a single character from the user.

    // Keep requesting characters until the user presses Enter.
    while (ch != '\r')  // \r is the enter key
    {
        // Add characters only if they are numbers.
        if (ch >= '0' && ch <= '9')
        {
            cout << ch;
            numAsString += ch;
        }

        // Get the next character from the user.
        ch = getch();
    }
    return numAsString;
}

string EnterPassword()
{
    string numAsString = ""; // Holds the password string.
    char ch = getch();       // Obtains a single character from the user.

    // Keep requesting characters until the user presses Enter.
    while (ch != '\r')  // \r is the enter key
    {
```

```
        // Display an asterisk instead of the input character.
        cout << '*';

        // Add the character to the password string.
        numAsString += ch;

        // Get the next character from the user.
        ch = getch();
    }

    return numAsString;
}

int main()
{
    // Just a basic name-entering
    string name;
    cout << "What is your name? ";
    cin >> name;
    cout << "Hello " << name << endl;

    // Now you are asked to enter a number,
    // but the computer allows you to enter anything!
    int x;
    cout << endl;
    cout << "Enter a number, any number! ";
    cin >> x;
    cout << "You chose " << x << endl;

    // This time you can only enter a number.
    cout << endl;
    cout << "This time you'll only be able to enter a number!" << endl;
    cout << "Enter a number, any number! ";
    string entered = EnterOnlyNumbers();
    int num = StringToNumber(entered);
    cout << endl << "You entered " << num << endl;

    // Now enter a password!
    cout << endl;
    cout << "Enter your password! ";
    string password = EnterPassword();
    cout << endl << "Shhhh, it's " << password << endl;
    return 0;
}
```

The first parts of main are straightforward. You can see that we called
cin >> name; to read a string from the console; then we printed it. Then
we called cin >> x; to read an integer from the console, and we again
printed it.

Next, we made sure that the user could enter only digits by calling the
EnterOnlyNumbers function. Take a close look at that function. The first
thing it does is declare a string called numAsString. When the user types
things, they come in as characters, so we save them one by one in a string
variable (because a string is really a *character string*). To find out what the
user types, we call the getch function. That function returns a single character. (For example, if the user presses Shift-A to get a capital *A*, the getch
function will return the character A.)

Avoiding getch function problems

Some compilers will complain if you use the getch function. In this case, try the _getch function instead. Both functions perform the same task. Some vendors claim that _getch is International Standards Organization (ISO) compliant, but it isn't. The getch and _getch functions are useful low-level library functions that you can use without hesitation, but they don't appear as part of any standard. The GNU GCC compiler provided with CodeBlocks can use either form of the function.

After retrieving a single character, we start a loop, watching for the `'\r'` character. (Remember that the backslash in a character or string means that the character is special.) The loop continues processing characters until the user presses the Enter key. At that point, the character we get from getch is `\r`, so we exit the loop and return the number as a string.

Inside the loop, we test the *value* of the character, seeing if it's in the range `'0'` through `'9'`. Yes, characters are associated with a sequence, and fortunately, the digits are all grouped together. So we can determine if we have a digit character by checking to see if it's in the range `'0'` through `'9'` as follows:

```
if (ch >= '0' && ch <= '9')
```

If the user presses a number key, we wind up inside this if statement, or at least the computer does. Because the user pressed a number key, we go ahead and write that out to the console and add the digit character to the end of our string. We have to write it to the console because, when you call getch, the computer doesn't automatically print anything. But that's a good thing here, because after we're out of the if statement, we go ahead and call getch again for another round. Thus, if the user pressed something other than the Enter key, the character the user pressed doesn't even appear on the console, and it won't get added to the string either. Nifty, huh?

The EnterPassword routine is similar to the EnterOnlyNumbers routine, except it allows the user to enter any character (including spaces). So no if statement is *filtering out* certain letters. And further, instead of just printing the character that the user types, it just prints an asterisk, *. That gives the feeling of a password entry, which is a good feeling. People want to feel good when they're entering their passwords.

When you run this program, you get output like the following:

```
What is your name? Hank
Hello Hank

Enter a number, any number! abc123
You chose 2293728

This time you'll only be able to enter a number!
Enter a number, any number! 5001
You entered 5001

Enter your password! *****
Shhhh, it's hello
```

The first line went well; we didn't type any spaces, and the name `Hank` made it into our variable. But then, when we were asked to enter a number, we got sneaky and typed something we weren't supposed to, `abc123`. And boy, the computer got confused! But the next section didn't allow us to type anything but numbers because it called our `EnterOnlyNumbers` routine. And finally, we entered a password, and you can see that the computer displayed asterisks when we pressed each key. Then the program kept the secret password and wrote it on the screen anyway.

Understanding Preprocessor Directives

When you compile a program, the first thing the compiler does is run your code through something called a *preprocessor*. The preprocessor simply looks for certain statements in your code that start with a # symbol. You have already seen one such statement in every one of your programs, `#include`. These preprocessor statements are known as *directives* because they tell the preprocessor to do something; they direct it.

Think of the preprocessor as just a machine that transforms your code into a temporary, fixed-up version that's all ready to be compiled. For example, take a look at this preprocessor directive:

```
#include <iostream>
```

If the preprocessor sees this line, it inserts the entire text from the file called `iostream` (yes, that's a filename; it has no extension) into the fixed-up version of the source code.

For example, suppose the file called `iostream` looks like this:

```
int hello = 10;
int goodbye = 20;
```

Just two lines are all that's in it. (Of course, the real `iostream` file is much more sophisticated.) And suppose your own source file, `MyProgram.cpp`, has this in it:

```
#include <string>
int main()
{
    cout << "Hello" << endl;
}
```

Then, after the preprocessor gets through with its preprocessing, it creates a temporary fixed-up file (which has the lines from the string file inserted into the `MyProgram.cpp` file where the `#include` line had been) to look like this:

```
int hello = 10;
int goodbye = 20;
int main()
{
    cout << "Hello" << endl;
}
```

In other words, the preprocessor replaced the `#include` line with the contents of that file. Now, the string file itself could have `#include` lines, and those lines would be replaced by the contents of the files *they* refer to. As you may imagine, what started out as a simple program with just a few lines could actually have hundreds of lines after the preprocessor gets through with it. (In fact, that's a conservative estimate: We ran the default CodeBlocks code through the preprocessor, and it contained *25,613 lines!* Many of those are blank lines for various reasons, but nevertheless, it's a very big file!)

Don't worry: Your original source code file doesn't change when the preprocessor goes at it. The preprocessor builds a temporary file, and *that's* what the compiler compiles. Also, you don't have to run the preprocessor manually; the compiler runs it for you.

Although you don't have to run the preprocessor yourself, you can if you're curious to see what its output looks like. The CodeBlocks compiler actually calls on `gcc.exe` to perform the compilation process. However, `gcc` is really just a small program that launches the compiler. But before it launches the compiler, it runs the preprocessor. The preprocessor command is `cpp` (for *C p*reprocessor). If your paths are set up correctly and you want to try it out, just type **cpp**, the name of your source file, the redirection symbol (**>>**), and the name of an output file at the command line, such as `cpp main.cpp >> main.txt`. In most cases, you can set up the path correctly by typing the following at the command line and pressing Enter:

```
path=C:\Program Files\CodeBlocks\MinGW\bin;%path%
```

And prepare yourself for a *lot* of lines. But seeing the output and how your code looks when it's ready to be pushed through the compiler is interesting!

The preprocessor also provides you with a lot of other directives besides #include. One of the more useful ones is the #define directive. Here's a sample #define line:

```
#define MYSPECIALNUMBER 42
```

After the preprocessor sees this line, every time it encounters the word MYSPECIALNUMBER, it replaces it with the *word* 42 (that is, whatever sequence of letters, numbers, and other characters follow the definition). But #define also lets you create what are called *macros.* Take a look at this line:

```
#define oldmax(x, y) ((x)>(y)?(x):(y))
```

After the preprocessor learns this line, every time it sees the word oldmax followed by two things in parentheses separated by a comma, it replaces it with the form ((x)>(y)?(x):(y)), substituting the thing before the comma for x and the thing after the comma for y. For example, if you then have this line

```
q = oldmax(abc, 123);
```

the preprocessor replaces the line with

```
q = ((abc)>(123)?(abc):(123));
```

and does nothing more with the line.

Minibook I, Chapter 2, refers to these as conditional operators. The variable q is set to the value in abc if the abc value is greater than 123; otherwise, the q gets set to 123.

However, the preprocessor doesn't have an understanding of the conditional operator, and q doesn't get set to anything during preprocessing. All the preprocessor knows is how to replace *text* in your source-code file. The pre-processor replaced the earlier line of code that contained oldmax with the next line containing the conditional operator. That's it. The preprocessor doesn't run any code, it doesn't make the comparison, and it doesn't put anything in q. The preprocessor just changes the code.

Although you can still use #define statements in C++, in general you should simply create a function instead of a macro or use a constant instead of a symbol. Using symbols and macros are older and outdated styles of pro-gramming. However, they do have their place in programming in the form of *conditional compilation,* which we discuss next.

You may have times when you want to compile one version of your program for one situation, and compile another for a different situation. For example, you may want to have a *debug* version of your program that has some extra goodies in it that spit out special information for you that you can use during the development of your program. Then, after your program is ready to ship to the masses so millions of people can use it, you no longer want that extra debug information.

To accomplish this, you can use a conditional compilation. Take a look at these lines:

```
#ifdef DEBUG
    cout << "The value of j is " << j << endl;
#else
    cout << j << endl;
#endif
```

The lines that begin with # are preprocessor directives. The preprocessor has its own version of `if` statements. In your code, you can have a line like the following with nothing after it:

```
#define DEBUG
```

This simply *defines* a symbol. It works just like the symbols we described earlier, except that it's not set to be replaced by anything. It's just a symbol. You can also define such symbols in the command-line options to `gcc` or whichever compiler you use. (In CodeBlocks, you choose Project⌁ Build Options. In the Project Build Options dialog box that opens, click the Compiler Settings tab, followed by the #defines subtab, as shown in Figure 8-1. You type your compiler options as shown in the figure.) To define the DEBUG symbol through a command-line option, you add

```
-D DEBUG
```

to your command, either in the `gcc` command or in the Project Build Options dialog box in CodeBlocks. Then, when you include this compiler option, the DEBUG symbol is defined throughout your program, just as if you had included a `#define DEBUG` line at the very beginning.

Now when the preprocessor starts going through your program and gets to the `#ifdef DEBUG` line, it checks whether the DEBUG symbol is defined. If the symbol is defined, it spits out to its fixed-up file the lines that follow, up until the `#else` line. Then it skips any lines that follow that, up until the `#endif` line.

But if the DEBUG symbol is *not* defined, the preprocessor skips over the lines up until the `#else`, and spits out the lines that follow, up until the `#endif`.

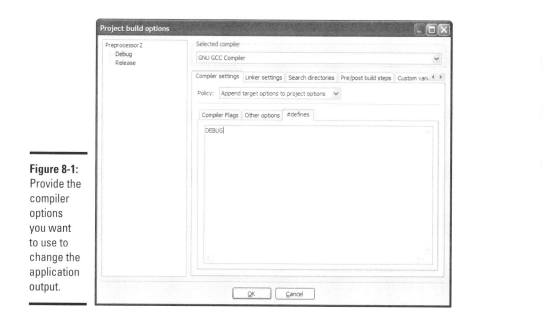

Figure 8-1:
Provide the
compiler
options
you want
to use to
change the
application
output.

Thus, for the example we gave earlier in this section, if DEBUG is defined,
the block of code starting with `#ifdef DEBUG` through the line `#endif` is
replaced by the stuff in the first half of the block:

```
cout << "The value of j is " << j << endl;
```

But if DEBUG is not defined, it is replaced by the stuff following the `#else`
line:

```
cout << j << endl;
```

When the preprocessor goes through your file, it is only creating a new
source-code file to be used by the compiler. That means these `#ifdef` lines
affect your program only when the compiler fires off the preprocessor. When
your program is compiled and you *run* it, these `#ifdef` lines are nowhere to
be found. So please don't forget that these `#ifdef` lines do not affect how
your program runs — only how it compiles.

Using preprocessor directives, you can have two different versions of your
program. In the example we gave, we're gearing up for two versions, a debug
version and a release version. To tell the compiler which version to build,
we then modify the command-line options by either removing or adding the
`-D DEBUG` line.

The `-D` option works either with or without a space after the D. Thus, you
can either use `-DDEBUG` or `-D DEBUG`. They both do the same thing.

Listing 8-3 demonstrates all the things that we covered in this section.

Listing 8-3:   Using Many Different Preprocessor Directives

```
#include <iostream>

using namespace std;

#ifdef UNIVAC
const int total = 200;
const string compname = "UNIVAC";
#elif defined(HAL2000)
const int total = 300;
const string compname = "HAL2000";
#else
const int total = 400;
const string compname = "My Computer";
#endif
// This is outdated, but you might
// see it on occasion. Don't write
// code yourself that does this!
#define oldmax(x, y) ((x)>(y)?(x):(y))
#define MYSPECIALNUMBER 42

int main()
{
    cout << "Welcome to " << compname << endl;
    cout << "Total is:" << endl;
    cout << total << endl << endl;

    // Try out the outdating things.
    cout << "*** max ***" << endl;
    cout << oldmax(5,10) << endl;
    cout << oldmax(20,15) << endl;
    cout << MYSPECIALNUMBER << endl << endl;

    // Here are some standard
    // predefined macros.
    cout << "*** Predefined Macros ***" << endl;
    cout << "This is file " << __FILE__ << endl;
    cout << "This is line " << __LINE__ << endl;
    cout << "Compiled on " << __DATE__ << endl;
    cout << "Compiled at " << __TIME__ << endl << endl;

    // Here's how some people use #define,
    // to specify a "debug" version or
    // "release" version.
    cout << "*** total ***" << endl;
    int i;
    int j = 0;
    for (i = 0; i<total; i++)
    {
        j = j + i;
    }

#ifdef DEBUG
    cout << "The value of j is " << j << endl;
#else
    cout << j << endl;
```

```
#endif

    return 0;
}
```

When we run Listing 8-3 without any symbols (we did not set DEBUG), we see this output:

```
Welcome to My Computer
Total is:
400

*** max ***
10
20
42

*** Predefined Macros ***
This is file C:\0246 - Source Code\BookI\Chapter08\Preprocessor2\main.cpp
This is line 37
Compiled on Apr  7 2009
Compiled at 13:54:09

*** total ***
79800
```

But note, at the beginning, we're testing for the symbol UNIVAC. But that if block is a bit more complex because we also have an #elif (else if) construct. The language of the preprocessor has no elseifdef or anything like it. Instead, you have to write it like so:

```
#elif defined(HAL2000)
```

Now with this block, the preprocessor checks for the symbol UNIVAC; if the preprocessor finds UNIVAC, it spits out the lines

```
const int total = 200;
const string compname = "UNIVAC";
```

Otherwise, the preprocessor looks for HAL2000; if the preprocessor finds it, it adds these lines to the fixed-up code:

```
const int total = 300;
const string compname = "HAL2000";
```

And finally, if neither UNIVAC nor HAL2000 is set, the preprocessor adds these lines:

```
const int total = 400;
const string compname = "My Computer";
```

Now remember that, in each case, these two lines are sent out to the fixed-up version in place of the entire block starting with #ifdef UNIVAC and ending with #endif.

So if we include the command-line option -D UNIVAC, we see different output:

```
Welcome to UNIVAC
Total is:
200

*** max ***
10
20
42

*** Predefined Macros ***
This is file C:\0246 - Source Code\BookI\Chapter08\Preprocessor2\main.cpp
This is line 37
Compiled on Apr  7 2009
Compiled at 14:05:19

*** total ***
19900
```

To see this different output, remember that these #define lines affect only the compilation of your program. Therefore, you need to recompile your program to see the changes. But a catch is involved: If the object file for your source-code file is newer than your source, the compiler won't rebuild the object file, even though you changed the command-line options. You need to type **makeclean** first, if you are using a command-line compiler such as MinGW or Cygwin. In CodeBlocks, you choose Build⇨Clean. Then you can compile your program again and run it to see the new output.

And now, here's a different set of options:

```
-D HAL2000 -D DEBUG
```

When we again clean, compile, and run, we see this output. Notice that the final line is a bit different now that we have DEBUG defined.

```
Welcome to HAL2000
Total is:
300

*** max ***
10
20
42

*** Predefined Macros ***
This is file C:\0246 - Source Code\BookI\Chapter08\Preprocessor2\main.cpp
This is line 37
Compiled on Apr  7 2009
Compiled at 14:07:14

*** total ***
The value of j is 44850
```

Using Constants

When you are programming, you may sometimes want a certain fixed value that you plan to use throughout the program. For example, you might want a string containing the name of your company, such as "Bobs Fixit Anywhere Anyhoo". And you don't want someone else working on your program to pass this string into a function as a reference and modify it by mistake, turning it into the name of your global competitor, "Jims Fixum Anyhoo Anytime". That could be bad. Or, if you're writing a scientific application, you might want a fixed number, such as pi = 3.1415926 or PeachPi=4.1415926.

You can create such *constants* in C++ by using the `const` keyword. When you create a constant, it works just like a variable, except you *cannot change it* later in the program. For example, to declare your company name, you might use

```
const string CompanyName = "Bobs Fixit Anywhere Anyhoo";
```

Of course, you can modify this string in your code, but later in your code, you cannot do something like this:

```
CompanyName = CompanyName + ", Inc.";
```

The compiler issues an error for that line, complaining that it's a constant and you can't change it.

After you declare the constant, then, you can use the string called `CompanyName` to refer to your company throughout your code. Listing 8-4 shows you how to do this. Note the three constants toward the top called `ParkingSpaces`, `StoreName`, and `pi`. In the rest of the program, we use these just like any other variables — except that we don't try to change them.

Listing 8-4:   Using Constants for Permanent Values That Do Not Change

```
#include <iostream>

using namespace std;

const int ParkingSpaces = 80;
const string StoreName = "Joe's Food Haven";
const float pi = 3.1415926;

int main()
{
    cout << "Important Message" << endl;
    cout << "Here at " << StoreName << endl;
    cout << "we believe you should know" << endl;
    cout << "that we have " << ParkingSpaces;
    cout << " full-sized" << endl;
```

(continued)

Listing 8-4 *(continued)*

```
        cout << "parking spaces for your parking" << endl;
        cout << "pleasure." << endl;
        cout << endl;

        cout << "We do realize, however, that parking" << endl;
        cout << "is tight at " << StoreName << endl;
        cout << "and so we are going to double our" << endl;
        cout << "spaces from " << ParkingSpaces << " to ";
        cout << ParkingSpaces * 2;
        cout << ". Thank you again!" << endl << endl;

        float radius = 5;
        float area = radius * pi * pi;

        cout << "And remember, we sell " << radius;
        cout << " inch apple pies" << endl;
        cout << "for a full " << area << " square" << endl;
        cout << "inches of eating pleasure!" << endl;

        return 0;
}
```

When you run this program, you see the following:

```
Important Message
Here at Joe's Food Haven
we believe you should know
that we have 80 full-sized
parking spaces for your parking
pleasure.

We do realize, however, that parking
is tight at Joe's Food Haven
and so we are going to double our
spaces from 80 to 160. Thank you again!

And remember, we sell 5 inch apple pies
for a full 49.348 square
inches of eating pleasure!
```

The biggest advantage to using constants is this: If you need to make a change to a string or number throughout your program, you make the change only once. For example, if you have the string `"Bobs Fixit Anywhere Anyhoo"` pasted a gazillion times throughout your program, and suddenly you incorporate and need to change your program so the string says, `"Bobs Fixit Anywhere Anyhoo, LLC"`, you would need to do some serious search-and-replace work. But if you have a single constant in the header file for use by all your source-code files, you need to change it only *once*. You modify the header file with the new constant definition, recompile your program, and you're ready to go.

There's a common saying in the programming world that goes like this (sing along now): "Don't use any magic numbers." The idea is that if, somewhere in your code, you need to calculate the number of cows that have crossed over the bridge to see if the bridge will hold up and you happen to know the average weight of a cow is 632 pounds, don't just put the number 632 in your code. Somebody else reading it may wonder where that number came from. Instead, make a constant called, perhaps, AverageCowWeight and set that equal to 632. Then, in your code, use AverageCowWeight anytime you need that number. Plus, if cows evolve into a more advanced species and their weight changes, all you need to do is make one change in your code — you change the header file containing the const declaration. Here's a sample line that declares AverageCowWeight:

```
const int AverageCowWeight = 632;
```

Before C++, the original C language did not have constants. The way to use constants was through preprocessor directives. For example, in C++, you could have a constant, such as

```
const int DuckCrossing = 500;
```

But in C, you couldn't do this. Your choice would be to use either a non-constant variable, as in

```
int DuckCrossing = 500;
```

or a preprocessor directive, as in

```
#define DuckCrossing 500
```

Then you can use DuckCrossing as a substitute for 500 in your program. The problem here is that if you try to debug your program (see Minibook III, Chapter 1), the debugger (yes, that's *really* the word) knows nothing of the word DuckCrossing. Therefore, if you see a #define used this way, you know what it means; however, we recommend that you don't write new code that uses this. Use the const keyword instead.

Using Switch Statements

Many times in programming you may want to compare a variable to one thing, and if it doesn't match, compare it to another and another and another. To do this with an if statement, you need to use a whole bunch of else if lines.

That works out pretty well, but you can do it in another way; you can use the switch statement.

The approach we're showing you in this section does not work for all types of variables. In fact, it works only with the various types of integers and characters. It won't even work with character strings. However, when you need to do multiple comparisons for integers and characters, using this approach is very useful.

First, here's a complete `switch` statement that you can refer to as we describe the individual parts in the paragraphs that follow. This compares x to 1, then 2, and finally includes a catchall section called `default` if x is neither 1 nor 2.

```
int x;
cin > x;
switch (x)
{
    case 1:
        cout << "It's 1!" << endl;
        break;
    case 2:
        cout << "It's 2!" << endl;
        break;
    default:
        cout << "It's something else!" << endl;
        break;
}
```

To use the `switch` statement, you type the word `switch` and then the variable or expression you want to test in parentheses. Suppose x is type `int`, and you want to compare it to several different values. You would first type

```
switch (x) {
```

The preceding item in parentheses is *not a comparison*. It's simply a variable. You can also put more complex expressions inside the parentheses, but they must *evaluate* to either an integer or a character. So, for example, if x is an integer, you can test

```
switch (x + 5) {
```

because x + 5 is still an integer.

After the header line for the `switch` statement, you list the items you want to compare the expression to. These have a rather strange format. They start with the word `case`, then have the value to compare the expression against, and then a colon, as in

```
case 1:
```

Next is the code to run in the event the expression matches this case (here, 1).

```
cout << "It's 1" << endl;
```

Finally (here's where it gets really strange) you have the word `break`. Every case in the `switch` statement usually has a `break` line, which means *get out of the switch statement now!* And here's the exceedingly strange part: If you forget the `break` statement, when the computer runs this case, it continues running the code for the *next* case! Yes, C++ can seem stupid at times. And this is one of those rare and less-than-beautiful moments.

Note something peculiar at the end of the `switch` block: The final case is `default`. It applies to the situation when none of the preceding cases apply.

The `default` case isn't required; you can leave it off if you don't need it. However, if you do include it, we recommend putting it at the end of the `switch` block because that's where most people expect to find it.

With the sample code we gave at the beginning of this section, you can enter in a number, which gets put in the x variable. The code then tests the value x against 1; if it matches, it performs the line after the `case 1:` line. But if it doesn't match, it tests it against 2 and performs its lines if it matches. But if none of those match, it does the code after the `default` line.

When the computer encounters the `break` line, it exits the `switch` statement altogether. So you may be wondering: Why did those goofball authors include a `break` line at the very end? Our answer: Tradition. That's all. It's consistent with the other blocks of code. But you certainly don't need it. *However*, if you leave it off, you must remember that if you decide to add any other cases, you will probably want to put it back in. But on the other hand, people typically put the `default` at the end. (You don't have to, but most people expect to see it at the end and not in the middle.)

A `switch` statement only compares a single variable or expression against several different items. If you have more complex comparisons, you can instead use a compound `if` statement.

In many other programming languages, a `switch` statement is called a *case block*. That's because in those languages, the word that starts the whole thing is *case*. Here, however, the whole shebang gets off with a bang on the word `switch`. Thus, in C and C++, we call it a `switch` statement. It's fun to be different. Sometimes.

Listing 8-5 is a complete program that demonstrates a `switch` statement. It also shows you how you can make a simple antiquated-looking *menu* program on the console. You don't need to press Enter after you choose your menu item; you just press the key for your menu selection. That's thanks to the use of `getch` rather than `cin`.

Listing 8-5:   Making Multiple Comparisons in One Big Block

```
#include <iostream>
#include <conio.h>

using namespace std;

int main()
{
    // Display a list of options.
    cout << "Choose your favorite:" << endl;
```

(continued)

Listing 8-5 *(continued)*

```
cout << "1. Apples " << endl;
cout << "2. Bananas " << endl;
cout << "3. Fried worms " << endl;
cout << "4. Poison Apples " << endl;
cout << "5. Lobster " << endl;

// Obtain the user's selection.
char ch = getch();

// Continue getting user selections until the user
// enters a valid number.
while (ch < '1' || ch > '5')
{
    ch = getch();
}

// Use a switch to display the user's selection.
cout << "You chose " << ch << endl;
switch (ch) {
case '1':
    cout << "Apples are good for you!" << endl;
    break;
case '2':
    cout << "Bananas have plenty of potassium!" << endl;
    break;
case '3':
    cout << "That's disgusting!" << endl;
    break;
case '4':
    cout << "All I wanna know is WHY?" << endl;
    break;
case '5':
    cout << "Expensive but good taste you have!" << endl;
    break;
}

return 0;
}
```

Supercharging enums with Classes

When you work with classes, you can use a technique called *wrapping*. In Minibook I, Chapter 7, we discuss the enum keyword and how you can use it to create your own types. However, when you print the enumeration, you don't see the word, such as red or blue; you see a number. Listing 8-6 is a simple class that *wraps* an enum type. You can use this class with enum ColorEnum, as main demonstrates. When you run this program, you see the single word red in the console.

Listing 8-6:   Creating a Class for enums

```cpp
#include <iostream>

using namespace std;

class Colors
{
public:
    enum ColorEnum {blue, red, green, yellow, black};
    Colors(Colors::ColorEnum value);
    string AsString();

protected:
    ColorEnum value;
};

Colors::Colors(Colors::ColorEnum initvalue)
{
    value = initvalue;
}

string Colors::AsString()
{
    switch (value)
    {
    case blue:
        return "blue";
    case red:
        return "red";
    case green:
        return "green";
    case yellow:
        return "yellow";
    case black:
        return "black";
    default:
        return "Not Found";
    }
}

int main()
{
    Colors InkColor = Colors::red;
    cout << InkColor.AsString() << endl;
    return 0;
}
```

In the preceding section, "Using Switch Statements," our `switch` statement did not include any `break` statements. Instead we have a `return` statement. The `return` causes the computer to exit the function entirely, so you have no reason to worry about getting out of the `switch` statement. You may wonder why the `switch` statement includes a `default` clause. After all, it will never get called. In this case, if you don't supply a `default` clause, the compiler displays the following message:

```
warning: control reaches end of non-void function
```

Adding cout capabilities

It would be nice if the `Colors` class allowed you to just call `cout`, as in `cout << Ink Color << endl;` without having to call Ink Color.AsString() to get a string version. C++ has a capability called *operator overloading.* When you type `something cout <<` followed by a variable, you are calling a function: `<<`. Several versions of the `<<` functions (they are overloaded) are available; each has a different type. For example, `int` handles the cases when you write out an integer, as in `int x = 5;`, and then `cout << x;`. Because the `<<` function doesn't use parentheses, it is an *operator*.

To add `cout` capabilities to your class, just write another `<<` function for your class. Here's the code. This is not a class member function; it goes *outside* your class. Add it to Listing 8-6 anywhere after the `class` declaration but before `main`. Here goes:

```
ostream& operator << (ostream& out,
                Colors& inst)
{
  out << inst.AsString();
  return out;
}
```

Because this function is an operator, you have to throw in the word `operator`. The type of `cout` is `ostream`, incidentally; thus, you take an `ostream` as a parameter, and you return the same `ostream`. The other parameter is the type you are printing: in this case, it's a `Colors` instance, and once again, it's passed by reference. After you add this code, you can change the line `cout << InkColor.As String() << endl;` to simply

```
cout << InkColor << endl;
```

Whenever possible, add the code required for your application to compile without warnings. Adding the `default` clause simply ensures that the `AsString` function always returns a value, no matter what happens.

The expression `Colors::red` may be unfamiliar to you. That means we're using the `red` value of the `ColorEnum` type. However, because `ColorEnum` is declared *inside* the class `Color`, we cannot just say `red`. We have to first say the class name, then two colons, and then the value. Thus we type `Colors::red`.

In `main`, we created the `InkColor` instance and set it not to a `Color` object but to an `enum`! We just violated An Important Rule about setting things equal to something of the same type. Why? C++ has a neat little trick: You can create a constructor that takes a certain type. In this case we have a constructor that takes a `ColorEnum`. Then when you create a `stack` variable (not a pointer) you can just set it equal to a value of that type. The computer will *implicitly* call the constructor, passing it that value.

Working with Random Numbers

Sometimes, you need the computer to generate random numbers for you. But computers aren't good at doing things at random. We humans can toss dice or flip a coin, but the computer must do things in a predetermined fashion.

The computer geniuses of the last century have come up with algorithms that generate *pseudorandom numbers*. These are numbers that are *almost* random or *seemingly* random. They're sufficiently random for many purposes.

The only catch with these random number generators is that you need to *seed* them. But a computer scientist beheld a great idea. *The current time* is random. If we run a program and you run a program, most likely we won't start running them at *precisely the same moment in time*. Our scientist realized that would be a good starting point for a random number generator. In Listing 8-7, we obtain the current time to start the random number generator. To do that, we include `time.h`. We create a variable called `now` of a special type called `time_t` (which is just a number), and then we call the `time` function, passing the address of `now`. That gives us the number of seconds since January 1, 1970. Then we call `srand`, passing that time. That process seeds the generator.

Then we print several random numbers by calling `rand`, which returns a random number. But we noticed something strange when we ran this program. Each time, the first call to `rand` got just a little bit bigger, and it seemed to be affected by the current time. With each second that passed, the supposedly random number got just a bit bigger. The rest seemed fine, so we decided to skip the first random number. Thus, right after we seed the random number, we call `rand` and ignore the return value.

Then we go ahead and print five random numbers. But we wanted to limit the numbers in the range from 0 through 99, so we took the *modulus 100* of the number. (That's the remainder when we divide the number by 100.) You can choose a different number than 100 if you need a different range.

Listing 8-7: Seeding the Random Number Generator

```
#include <iostream>

using namespace std;

int main()
{
    // Re-seed the random-number generator
    time_t now;
    time(&now);
```

(continued)

Listing 8-7 (continued)

```
srand(now);
rand();

// Print out a list of random numbers
for (int i=0; i<5; i++)
{
    cout << rand() % 100 << endl;
}

return 0;
}
```

The first time we ran Listing 8-7, we saw the following output:

```
19
69
85
83
47
```

The *second* time, we saw this output. It's very different than before:

```
79
67
38
72
73
```

Storing Data in Arrays

Most programming languages support a data structure called an array. An *array* is a list of variables, all stored side by side in a row. You access them through a single name. Each variable in the array must be of the same type.

When you create an array, you specify how many items the array holds. For example, you can have an array of 100 integers. Or you can have an array of 35 strings or an array of 10 pointers to the class BrokenBottle. If the code you're working with represents a type, you can create an array out of it.

When you create an array, you give it a name. You can access the array's *elements* (items) by using that name followed by an *index* number in brackets. The first element is always 0. Thus, if you have an array of five integers called AppendixAttacks, the first element is AppendixAttacks[0]. The second is AppendixAttacks[1], then AppendixAttacks[2], Appendix Attacks[3], and finally AppendixAttacks[4].

Because an array starts with element number 0, the final element in the array has an index that is 1 less than the size of the array. Thus, an array of 89 elements has indexes ranging from 0 to 88.

Declaring and accessing an array

Here's how you declare an array:

```
int GrilledShrimp[10];
```

This declares an array of 10 integers called `GrilledShrimp`. You first put the type (which is really the type of each element in the array), then the name for the array, and then the number of elements in brackets. And because this declares 10 integers, their indexes range from 0 to 9.

To access the first element of the array, you put the number 0 in brackets after the type name, as in

```
GrilledShrimp[0] = 10;
```

Sometimes people call the act of referring to a single element in the array as *subscripting*. But we avoid that word. Our brains prefer simpler words.

Often people use a loop to fill in an array or access each member. People usually call this *looping through the array*. Listing 8-8 shows an example.

Listing 8-8:   Using a Loop to Loop Through the Array

```
#include <iostream>

using namespace std;

int main()
{
    int GrilledShrimp[5];

    for (int i=0; i<5; i++)
    {
        GrilledShrimp[i] = i * 2;
        cout << GrilledShrimp[i] << endl;
    }

    return 0;
}
```

If you use a `for` loop to go through all the elements in the array, start your loop at 0. You end the loop with 1 less than the size of the array. If you store the array size in the variable `size` and your loop index is `i`, the middle clause in your `for` loop can be either `i < size` or `i <= size - 1`. Do *not* use `i <= size`. That goes 1 more than you want.

When you use arrays, don't go beyond the array bounds. Due to some old rules of the early C language, the compiler does not warn you if you write a loop that goes beyond the upper boundary of an array. You may not get an error when you run your program, either.

Arrays of pointers

Arrays are particularly useful for storing pointers to objects. If you have lots of objects of the same type, you can store them in an array.

Although you can store the actual objects in the array, most people don't. Most people fill the array with pointers to the objects. To declare an array of pointers to objects, remember the asterisk in the type declaration, like this:

```
CrackedMusicCD *missing[10];
```

Listing 8-9 declares an array of pointers. In this example, after declaring the array, we fill the elements of the array with 0's. Remember, each element is a *pointer;* that way, we can immediately know whether the element points to something by just comparing it to 0. If it's 0, it's not being used. If it has something other than 0, it has a pointer in it.

Listing 8-9:   Using an Array to Store a List of Pointers to Your Objects

```
#include <iostream>

using namespace std;

class CrackedMusicCD
{
public:
    string FormerName;
    int FormerLength;
    int FormerProductionYear;
};

int main()
{
    CrackedMusicCD *missing[10];

    for (int i=0; i<10; i++)
    {
        missing[i] = 0;
    }

    return 0;
}
```

If you want to create a whole group of objects and fill the array with pointers to these objects, you can do this kind of thing:

```
for (int i=0; i<10; i++)
{
    missing[i] = new CrackedMusicCD;
}
```

Because each element in the array is a pointer, if you want to access the member variables or member functions of one of the objects pointed to by the array, dereference the pointer by using the shortcut -> notation:

```
missing[0]->FormerName = "Shadow Dancing by Andy Gibb";
```

This example line accesses the FormerName member variable of the object whose address is in the first position of the array.

Though the array contains pointers to objects, because of the mental connection between a pointer and the object it points to, some people just refer to the objects *in the array.*

When you're finished with the objects in the array, you can delete the objects by calling delete for each member of the array, as in this code:

```
for (int i=0; i<10; i++)
{
    delete missing[i];
    missing[i] = 0;
}
```

In the preceding code, we clear each array element to 0. When you are working with arrays of pointers, we recommend that you do the same. That way, the pointer is *reset* to 0 and no longer points to anything after its object is gone.

Passing arrays to functions

Sometimes you need to pass an entire array to a function. While passing entire objects to arrays can be unwieldy, passing an entire array can be dangerous. Arrays can be enormous, with thousands of elements. If each element is a pointer, each element can be several bytes. If you pass a really big array onto the stack, you may overflow your program's stack.

As with passing objects, your best bet is to pass an array's address. You *pass to a function a pointer to the array.* But passing an array's address to a function is confusing to code. Listing 8-10 is a sample that passes an array, without worrying about any pointers and addresses.

Listing 8-10:   Passing an Array to a Function by Declaring the Array in the Function Header

```
#include <iostream>

using namespace std;

const int MyArraySize = 10;

void Crunch(int myarray[], int size)
```

(continued)

Listing 8-10 *(continued)*

```
{
    for (int i=0; i<size; i++)
    {
        cout << myarray[i] << endl;
    }
}

int main()
{
    int BigArray[MyArraySize];

    for (int i=0; i<MyArraySize; i++)
    {
        BigArray[i] = i * 2;
    }

    Crunch(BigArray, MyArraySize);

    return 0;
}
```

When you run this program, it prints the nine members of the array. We declared the parameter in the function header: We declared an array but did not specify a size. This means that you can pass an array of any size to the function. We included a size parameter, so the function knows the size of the array that we're passing in. Therefore, we included the array size when we called this function from main. Also, we used a constant rather than 10 for the array size; then if we decide later to modify the program by changing the size of the array, we need to change only the one constant at the top of the program. Otherwise, we risk missing one of the 10s.

How do you pass a pointer to an array? There's a pointer symbol in the data type for argv. argv is a pointer to a set of character pointers.

That's exactly what we did in Listing 8-10. *We did not actually pass the array itself. We passed the array's address.* When you pass an array this way, the *compiler* writes code to pass a pointer to the array. You don't worry about it.

The name of an array is actually a pointer to the first element in the array.

In the main of Listing 8-10, when we call the function, we pass the array name, BigArray. The compiler treats this name as the first array element address.

Thus, BigArray is the same as &(BigArray[0]). (We put parentheses around the BigArray[0] part so the computer knows that the & refers to the combination of BigArray[0], not just BigArray.) So you could have used this in the call:

```
Crunch(&(BigArray[0]), MyArraySize);
```

But there's no reason to do that. Just pass `BigArray`. It's the same thing!

The name of the array is a pointer to the array.

Adding and subtracting pointers

You can do interesting things when you add numbers to and subtract numbers from a pointer to an array element that is stored in a pointer variable as an address. If you take the address of an element in an array and store it in a variable, such as one called `cur` (for current), as in

```
cur = &(Numbers[5]);
```

where `Numbers` is an array of integers, you can access the element at `Numbers[5]` by dereferencing the pointer, as in the following:

```
cout << *cur << endl;
```

Then you can add and subtract numbers from the pointer, like these lines:

```
cur++;
cout << *cur << endl;
```

The compiler knows how much memory space each array element takes. When you add 1 to `cur`, *it advances to the next element in the array.* And so the `cout` that follows prints the next element, in this case, `Numbers[6]`.

Listing 8-11 shows an example of moving about an array. Note that we declare a variable called `cur`, which is a pointer to an integer. The array holds integers, so this pointer can point to elements in the array.

We start `cur` out pointing to the first element. The array name is the address of the first element, so to accomplish that we just typed

```
cur = Numbers;
```

That puts the address of the first element of the array in the variable `cur`.

Listing 8-11:   Moving by Using Pointer Arithmetic

```
#include <iostream>

using namespace std;

int main()
{
    int Numbers[100];

    for (int i=0; i<100; i++)
    {
```

(continued)

Listing 8-11 *(continued)*

```
        Numbers[i] = i * 10;
    }

    int *cur;
    cur = Numbers;

    cout << *cur << endl;
    cur++;
    cout << *cur << endl;
    cur++;
    cout << *cur << endl;
    cur += 3;
    cout << *cur << endl;
    cur--;
    cout << *cur << endl;

    return 0;
}
```

When you run the program, here is the output you see:

```
0
10
20
50
40
```

In the code, the ++ and – operators add 1 to and subtract 1 from the pointer. We also directly added a 3 to the pointer to advance it three "notches" in the array. You can also subtract from a pointer, as in

```
cur -= 2;
```

You cannot do multiplication and division with pointers.

Book II

Understanding Objects and Classes

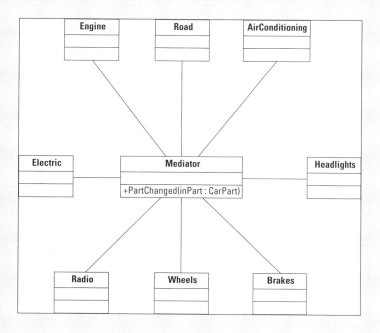

Contents at a Glance

Chapter 1: Planning and Building Objects

In This Chapter

✔ Recognizing objects so you can create classes

✔ Encapsulating classes into self-contained capsules

✔ Building hierarchies of classes through inheritance

✔ Discovering classes

Step outside for a moment and look down. What is the thing you are standing on? (Hint: It's giant, it's made of rock and sand and stone and molten lava, and it's covered with oceans and land.) The answer? A thing! (Even a planet is a thing.) And now go back inside. What's the thing that you opened, the thing with a doorknob? It's a thing, too! It's a slightly *different* kind of thing, but a *thing* nevertheless. And what are you inside? Okay, you get the idea. Everything you can imagine is a *thing*. Or, to use another term, an *object*. Remember that word: object.

Over the years, researchers in the world of computer programming (now, doesn't *that* sound like an exciting job?) have figured out that the best way to program computers is to divide whatever it is you're trying to *model* into a bunch of objects. These objects have capabilities and characteristics. (Eventually they have relationships, but that comes later.)

In this chapter, we show you how to make use of objects to create a software application. In the process, you get to twist some of the nuts and bolts of C++ that relate to objects and get tips on how to get the most out of them.

Recognizing Objects

Let's get to the meat of it: Think of an *object* as any *thing* that a computer can describe. (Object = thing. How's that for an obvious definition?) Just as physical things have characteristics, such as size, weight, or color, objects in a program can have *attributes* — say, a particular number of accounts, an engine, or even other objects that it contains, just as a car contains engines, doors, and other objects.

Further, just as real-world things have uses — for example, serving as containers, vehicles, or tools — an object in a program has *capabilities*. For example, it might be able to withdraw money or send a message or connect to the Internet.

Here's an example of an object: Outside, in front of your house, you might see a mailbox. That mailbox is an object. (See how easy this is?) A mailbox is a useful device. You can receive mail, and depending on the style (kind) of mail, you can send mail. (The style of mail is important — you can send a letter because you know how much postage to attach, but you can't send a package because the amount of postage is unknown.) Those are the mailbox's *capabilities.* And what about its characteristics? Different mailboxes come in different shapes, sizes, and styles. So those are three *characteristics.* Now some mailboxes, such as the kind often found at apartment buildings, are great big metal boxes with several little boxes inside, one for each apartment. The front has doors for each individual box, and the back has a large door for the mail carrier to fill the boxes with all those wonderful ads addressed to your alternate name, *Resident.*

In this case, you could think of the apartment mailbox as one big mailbox with lots of little boxes, or you could think of it as a big *container* for smaller mailboxes. In a sense, the little boxes each have a front door that a resident uses, and the back of each has an entry that the mail carrier uses. The back opens when the big container door opens.

So think about this: The mail carrier interacts with the container, which holds mailboxes. The container has a big door, and when that door opens, it exposes the insides of the small mailboxes inside, which open, too. Meanwhile, when a resident interacts with the system, he or she interacts with only his or her own particular box.

Take a look at Figures 1-1 and 1-2. Figure 1-1 shows the general look of the back of the mailbox container, where the mail carrier can open the container and put mail in all the different boxes. Figure 1-2 shows the front of the container, with one box open so a resident can take the mail out.

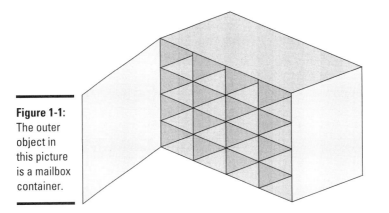

Figure 1-1:
The outer object in this picture is a mailbox container.

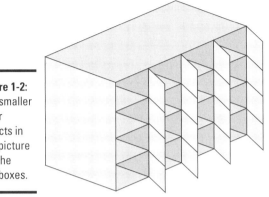

Figure 1-2:
The smaller inner objects in this picture are the mailboxes.

So far, there are two objects here: the container box and the mailboxes. But wait! There are multiple mailboxes. So, really, we have one container box and multiple mailboxes. But each mailbox is pretty much the same, except for a different lock and a different apartment number, right? In Figure 1-2, each box that's open is an example of a single mailbox. The others are also examples of the type of object called *mailbox*. In Figure 1-2, you can see 16 examples of the objects classified as *mailbox*. In other words, Figure 1-2 shows 16 *instances* of the *class* called *mailbox*. And all those mailboxes are inside an instance of the class that we would probably call *mailboxes*.

There is no hard and fast rule about naming your classes. However, Microsoft recommends that developers use a singular name for objects and a plural name for collections. A single `mailbox` object would appear as part of a `mailboxes` collection. Using this naming convention makes it easier for other developers to understand how your code works. Of course, the most important issue is consistency — once you decide on a naming convention, use the same convention all the time.

Observing the mailboxes class

What can you say about the `Mailboxes` collection object?

✦ The `Mailboxes` collection contains 16 mailbox instances.

✦ The `Mailboxes` collection object is 24 inches by 24 inches in front and back, and it is 18 inches deep. (Really, it's on legs, but we're not going to consider those to be part of it.)

✦ When the carrier unlocks the mailboxes and pulls, its *back door opens*.

✦ When the mailboxes' back door opens, it *exposes the insides of each contained mailbox.*

✦ When the mail carrier pushes on the door, the door shuts and relocks. (Okay, really, the mail carrier probably has to lock it, but we're not going to worry about that part. We'd rather keep this example nice and simple.)

By using this list, you can discover some of the characteristics and capabilities of mailboxes. The following list shows its characteristics:

✦ Width: 24 inches

✦ Height: 24 inches

✦ Depth: 18 inches

✦ Mailboxes: 16 mailbox objects are inside it

And here's a list of some of the mailboxes' capabilities:

✦ It can open its door. (Well, some external thing — such as a human — opens the door, but we'll get to that shortly.)

✦ It can give the mail carrier access to the mailboxes.

✦ It can close its door. (And yes, again, some external force such as a push causes the door to close, but again, we'll get to that . . . right now!)

Think about the process of the carrier opening or closing the door. Here we seem to have a bizarre thing: *The mail carrier asks mailboxes to close its door, and the door closes.* That's the way you need to look at modeling objects: Nobody does anything to an object. Rather, someone asks the object to do something, and the object *does* it *itself.*

For example, when you reach up to shove a slice of pizza into your mouth, your brain sends signals to the muscles in your arm. Your brain just sends out the signals, and your arms just move up, and so does the pizza. The point is that you make the command; then the arms carry it out, even though you feel like you're causing your arms to do it.

Objects are the same way: They have their capabilities, and we tell them to do their job. We don't do it for them. At least, that's the way computer scientists view it. We know: It's a stretch sometimes. But the more you think in this manner, the better you understand object-oriented programming.

The mailboxes contain 16 mailboxes. In C++, that means the Mailboxes collection would have as member variables 16 different Mailbox instances. These Mailbox instances could be an array or some other collection, and most likely the array would hold pointers to Mail instances.

Observing the mailbox class

Consider the characteristics and capabilities of the mailboxes. Each mailbox has these characteristics:

+ Width: 6 inches

+ Height: 6 inches

+ Depth: 18 inches

+ Address: A unique integer. But what number exactly? That depends on *which* mailbox you're talking about.

And each mailbox has these capabilities:

+ It can open its door.

+ It can close its door.

Notice we wrote the capabilities from the perspective of the mailbox, not from the person opening the mailbox.

Now think about the question regarding the address printed on the mailbox. What number goes on it? There are 16 different mailboxes, and each one gets a different number. So we can say this: The mailbox *class* includes an address, which is an integer. Each *instance* of the mailbox class gets its own number. The first may get 1, the second may get 2, and so on.

And so you have two concepts here for the mailboxes:

+ **Mailbox class:** This is the general description of a mailbox. It includes no specifics, such as the actual address. It simply states that each mailbox *has* an address.

+ **Mailbox instance:** This is the actual object. The mailbox instance belongs to the class mailbox. There can be several instances of the mailbox class.

Think of the mailbox class as a cookie cutter. Or, in C++ terminology, the *type*. The mailbox instance is an actual example of the *class*. In C++, we can create a variable of class `Mailbox`, and set its `Address` integer to 1. Then we can create another variable of class `Mailbox` and set its `Address` integer to 2. Thus, we've created two distinct mailbox objects, each of class `Mailbox`.

But all these have a width of 6, a height of 6, and a depth of 18. These are the same throughout the mailbox. Thus, we would probably not set those manually; instead, we would probably set them in the constructor for the class `Mailbox`. Nevertheless, the values of width, height, and depth go with each instance, not with the class; and the instances could, conceivably, each have their own width, height, and depth. However, when we design the class, we would probably put some stipulation in the class that these member variables cannot be changed. (We would do that by making them private and including a single function for each of them that retrieves their values.)

Finding other objects

If you are dealing with a `Mailboxes` instance and an instance of `Mailbox`, you can probably come up with some other classes. When we start considering the *parts* involved, we can think of the following objects:

✦ `Lock`: Each `Mailbox` instance would have a `Lock`, and so would the `Mailboxes` instance.

✦ `Key`: Each lock would require a `Key`.

✦ `Mail`: Each `Mailbox` instance can hold several `Mail` instances. The carrier puts these in the `Mailbox` instances, and the residents take them out.

✦ `LetterOpener`: Some residents would use these to open the `Mail`.

So you now have four more types of objects (`Lock`, `Key`, `Mail`, and `LetterOpener`). But are these classes necessary? Their need depends on the application you're building. In this case, we're modeling the mailbox system simply as an exercise. Therefore, we can pretty much choose which classes we need. But if this were an actual program for a post office, for example, you would have to determine whether the classes are necessary for the people using the software. If the application is a training exercise for people learning to be mail carriers, the application may need more detail, such as the `Key` objects. If the application were a video game, it may need all the classes we mentioned and even more.

In deciding if you need certain classes, you can follow some general rules. First, some classes are so trivial or simple that it doesn't make sense to include them. For example, a letter opener serves little purpose beyond opening mail. If you're designing a `Mail` class, you would probably have a capability *Open the envelope.* Because some people would use a letter opener and others wouldn't, you have little reason to pass into that function a `LetterOpener` instance. Therefore, you would probably not include a class as trivial as `LetterOpener`. But then again, if the program teaches residents how to use the mailbox (a strange idea, we know), it might include a section on *How to use your letter opener.* Yes, that's kind of silly, but you get the idea: Whether you include the class depends on the situation.

Encapsulating Objects

People have come up with various definitions for what exactly *object-oriented* means. And the phrase *various definitions* in the last sentence really means that there aren't simple discussions around a table at a coffeehouse about what the term means. Rather, there are outright arguments! Believe it or not, one of the central points of contention is whether C++ is object-oriented. And in such arguments (sorry, *discussions*), one of the words that usually pops up is *encapsulation*. People who defend C++ as being object-oriented point out that it supports encapsulation.

Instead of arguing, let's just all agree that yes, C++ lets you program objects and classes. Now that we've put that argument to rest and can all live peacefully, what exactly does *encapsulation* mean?

First, think about the word itself. A big part of it is *capsule*. A capsule is a small container. In the bigger picture, it's, well, a self-contained container that contains things. On the computer world, *encapsulation* refers to the process of creating a standalone object that can take care of itself and do what it must do, while holding on to information.

For example, to model a cash register, it would likely be a class. We'd *encapsulate* the cash register by putting everything about the register (its capabilities and characteristics) into a single class. In C++, the capabilities would be *member functions* and the characteristics would be *member variables.*

Book II
Chapter 1

Planning and
Building Objects

When we create the class, we would make some of the member variables and member functions *public;* we would make others *private.* (Some members can be *protected,* so derived classes could access them, but they still would not be public.) What exactly would private and protected member variables and member functions be?: the parts that you don't want other functions modifying. For example, the cash register would probably have a value inside it representing the total dollar amount that the register contains. But the functions that use the class would not directly modify that value. Instead, they would call various member functions to perform transactions. One transaction might be `Sale`. Another transaction might be `Refund`; another might be `Void`. These would be the capabilities of the register in the form of public methods, and they would modify the cash value inside the register, making sure that it balances with the sales and returns. If a function could just modify the cash value directly, the balance would get out of whack.

The cash amount, therefore, would be a *private* or *protected member variable.* It would be hidden from the other functions and classes. As for which it would be, private or protected, that depends on whether we expect to derive new classes from the cash register class and whether we want these new classes to have access to the members. In the situation of a cash register, we would probably not want other parts of the program to access the cash register if we're worried about security. But on the other hand, if we think that we'll be creating derived classes that have added features involving the cash (such as automatically sending the money to a bank via an electronic transaction), we would want the members to be protected. (In general, we choose protected, rather than private, as we have been bitten too many times by using classes that have a gazillion private members. In those cases we're unable to derive useful classes because everything is private!)

Encapsulation, then, is this: You combine the methods and member variables into a single entity, hiding some of them and making some accessible. The accessible ones together make up the *interface* of the object. And finally (this is important!), when you create an object, you create one that can perform on its own. In other words, the users of the class tell it what to do (such as perform a sales transaction) by calling its member functions and supplying parameters, and the object does the work. *The calling function doesn't care how the object does its thing, just that it can do it.* For example, a cash register class knows how to perform a sales transaction. As the designer of the class, don't force users to first call `Sale`, and then call separate functions to manually modify the amount of cash in the register and modify the running total. Rather, the `Sale` function does all the hard work, and users of the class don't have to worry about how that work takes place.

And now the really big question: Why do you need to know the word *encapsulation*? Because it's a common term that computer scientists like to throw around. If they use it, however, they are likely to use it as a verb: "Look at me! I am going to encapsulate this information into an object!"

But the process matters more than the word itself. When you design objects and classes, you encapsulate your information into individual objects. If you keep the process in mind, you will be better off. Here are the things you need to do each time you design a class:

+ **Encapsulate the information.** Combine the information into a single entity that becomes the class. This single entity has member variables representing its characteristics and member functions representing its capabilities.

+ **Clearly define the public interface of the class.** Provide a set of functions that are public (and possibly member variables that are public, although it's best to keep them protected or private), and make the rest of the members either protected or private.

+ **Write the class so that it knows how to do its own work.** The class's users should need only to call the functions in the public interface, and these public functions should be simple to use.

+ **Think of your class as a *black box*.** The object has an interface that provides a means so that others can use it. The class includes details of how it does its thing; users only care that it does it. In other words, the users don't see into the class.

Accessing read-only member variables

Suppose that you have a class that contains a member variable, and you want to allow users to retrieve the value of the variable but not change it. For example, in the Dog class, you might set the weight in the constructor, and that's it — after that, users can get the weight but can't change it. The way to do that is to simply not have a method that sets the value. Instead, you have a method that only retrieves the value. Thus, the Dog class would have the GetWeight method, but you would not have the SetWeight method. Then users can only read the value, not set it.

✦ **Never change the class interface after you publish the class.** Many application errors occur when a developer changes how methods, events, or access methods in the class work after publishing the class. If application developers rely on one behavior and the class developer introduces a new behavior, all applications that rely on the original behavior will break. You can always add to a class interface but never subtract from it or modify it. If you find that you must introduce a new behavior to Sale, add the new behavior to a new method, Sale2.

A common saying in object-oriented programming is that you should never make your member variables public. The idea is that if users of the object can easily make changes to the object's member variables, a big mess could result. (For example, making the cash member variable public in a CashRegister class is asking for functions that just modify it directly, screwing up the balance.) By allowing users to only call member functions, you can put *checking code* inside to handle bad situations. For example, if you have a class called Dog that contains a member variable called Weight, you wouldn't want a user of the class to take a Dog object and set the Weight to a negative number. But if you make the Weight member public, that's exactly what any user can do.

So instead, you make the Weight member either private or protected, and then give the class *access methods* (other languages use the term *properties* instead of access methods — see the "Access methods versus properties" sidebar for details). For example, you might have a method called SetWeight. It would take an integer parameter and then check the parameter to make sure that it's greater than 0. If it is, only then would it save the number in the Weight member variable. For example, the class might look like this:

```
class Dog
{
protected:
    int Weight;

public:
    void SetWeight(int NewWeight);
};
```

And the code for the function that sets the weight might look like this:

```
void Dog::SetWeight(int NewWeight)
{
    if (NewWeight > 0)
    {
        Weight = NewWeight;
    }
}
```

Note that the `Weight` member is protected, and the `SetWeight` is public. Thus the users of the class can't modify the `Weight` member directly; they can only call `SetWeight` to set it, which provides built-in checking. Now this works all fine and dandy, except when the users of the class need to find Fido's weight to make sure that he's not rapidly shrinking. The only problem is that `Weight` is protected, so the user can't read it. So you need to add a function that retrieves the value of `Weight`, as in the following:

```
int Dog::GetWeight()
{
    return Weight;
}
```

We must modify the class to accommodate this function:

```
class Dog
{
protected:
    int Weight;

public:
    void SetWeight(int NewWeight);
    int GetWeight();
};
```

Now when you use this class, instead of accessing the `Weight` variable directly, you use the access methods, as in the following sample lines:

```
int main()
{
    Dog fido;
    fido.SetWeight(10);
    cout << fido.GetWeight() << endl;
    fido.SetWeight(-5);
    cout << fido.GetWeight() << endl;
    return 0;
}
```

To set the weight, you call `SetWeight`. Note in the first call to `SetWeight`, we're passing a legitimate value, 10. And when the next line runs, we see the number 10 appear on the console. But in the second call to `SetWeight`, we're passing an invalid weight, –5. The `SetWeight` function rejects this value and doesn't change the weight. So the second time we write the weight by calling `GetWeight`, we still see 10. The number did not change. The –5 value was rejected, and the weight remained the same.

Access methods versus properties

Many modern languages support a third aspect to classes called properties, in addition to the usual member methods and member variables. C++ doesn't support a named entity called properties, but it does support the equivalent methodality. In your programming career you're likely to move between lots of different languages. And so we want to take a moment to introduce you to properties, which are found in languages such as C#, VB.NET, and Object Pascal. Properties are essentially a combination of member variables and methods. Think of a public member variable in C++. Anyone using an object can freely modify a member variable. But sometimes when you're creating a class, you want to place restrictions on what people can do with the member variables. For example, you might want to limit the access to reading the member variable but not changing it. Or you might want to restrict what values the variable can take on, such as limiting the variable to integers between 1 and 100 and not allowing it to contain any other integers.

In C++, the way to impose such limitations is to make the member variable private, and then write two member methods, one for reading the value of the variable and one for setting the value. The method that sets the value would impose the limits; if the caller tries to set the value to 101, for example, the method might automatically knock the value down to 100, if that's the limit you're imposing. And similarly, if you want people to be able to read the value but not change it, you might provide only a method that returns the value, and not a method for modifying the variable.

These two methods — one for setting a member variable, and one for "getting" (that is, reading) a member variable — are called *accessor*

methods. Some languages besides C++ let you combine these member methods into what are called properties. Since C++ doesn't support properties, we can't really show you sample code, but the idea would be like this:

```
mydog.weight = 10
cout << mydog.weight << endl;
```

Although the first line looks like we're just storing a 10 in the weight variable, if this were a property-based language, instead such code would cause your "property setter" method to get called. In that method you'd write code that tests the value and makes sure it's a valid value before storing it. Similarly, the second line, which appears to just read the `weight` variable, would indirectly call the method that retrieves the value of `weight`. So the code would perform just like this code:

```
mydog.SetWeight(10);
cout << mydog.GetWeight() <<
    endl;
```

See how we're calling two methods, one that sets the weight and one that gets the weight? That's the idea behind properties. They let you write code that appears to read and write member variables, but in fact the code calls "getter" and "setter" methods, respectively. (When working with other languages, you can write properties such that they let the user read values, write values, or read and write values, so the background functionality still relies on what amounts to two methods — one for setting the value and one for getting the value.) C++ doesn't have properties, but many modern languages do. Learning about them now while studying objects will help you understand properties should you end up using other languages that support them.

When you use access functions, you can do much more than just guard against invalid values and return the current value. The `Set` function, for example, can process the value and make calculations or modify it. For example, the `Dog` class might have a maximum weight. If the user passes a larger weight to the `SetWeight` function, the function could change it to the maximum weight. For example, the following function limits the weight to an upper level of 100 and a lower level of 1:

```
void Dog::SetWeight(int NewWeight)
{
    if (NewWeight < 0)
    {
        Weight = 0;
    }
    else if (NewWeight > 100)
    {
        Weight = 100;
    }
    else
    {
        Weight = NewWeight;
    }
}
```

You can use a `Get` function to send a modified form of a member variable. For example, if you have a `SalesTransaction` class that contains a `CreditCardNumber` variable, which is a string containing the digits and the spaces, you may not want to reveal only the last four digits instead of the entire number. A `Get` function, then, might retrieve the `CreditCardNumber`, extract only the final four digits, and build a string of the form "XXXX XXXX XXXX 1234." It would then return that string, rather than the actual `CreditCardNumber` value.

Building Hierarchies

One of the great powers in C++ is the capability to take a class and build new classes from it. When you use any of the available C++ libraries, such as the Standard C++ Library, you will probably encounter many classes, sometimes dozens of classes, that are all related to each other. Some classes are derived from other classes, although some classes are standalone. This gives programmers great flexibility. And it's good to be flexible. The blood flows more easily through your system, and you will be more relaxed. And for programming, it's good for a class library to be flexible, too, because when you are using a flexible library, you have many choices in the different classes you want to use.

Establishing a hierarchy

When you design a class, you can derive a new class from that original *base* class. The new class inherits the capabilities and characteristics of the base class. Normally, the members that are public in the base class will remain public in the derived class. The members that are protected in the base class will remain protected in the derived class; thus if you derive even further, those final classes will also inherit the protected members. Private members, however, live only in the base class.

Suppose you have a base class called `FrozenFood`, and from there you derive a class called `FrozenPizza`. From `FrozenPizza`, you then derive a class called `DeepDishPizza`. `FrozenPizza` is at the top of the hierarchy. It includes various members common to all classes.

Now suppose the `FrozenFood` class has the following member variables:

+ `intPrice` (private): This is a private variable that represents the price of the product.

+ `intWeight` (protected): This is a protected variable that represents the weight of the product.

The `FrozenFood` class also has these member functions:

+ constructor: The constructor is public and takes a price and a weight as a parameter. It saves them in the `Price` and `Weight` member variables, respectively.

+ `GetPrice`: This is a public access method that returns the value in the private `Price` member variable.

+ `GetWeight`: This is a public access method that returns the value in the protected `Weight` member variable.

To make this a little more clear to myself, we're going to list these items in a box, putting the name of the class (`FrozenFood`) at the top of the box. Then the box has a horizontal line through it, and under that we list the member variables. Under the member variables, we have another line, and then we list the member functions. We show this in Figure 1-3.

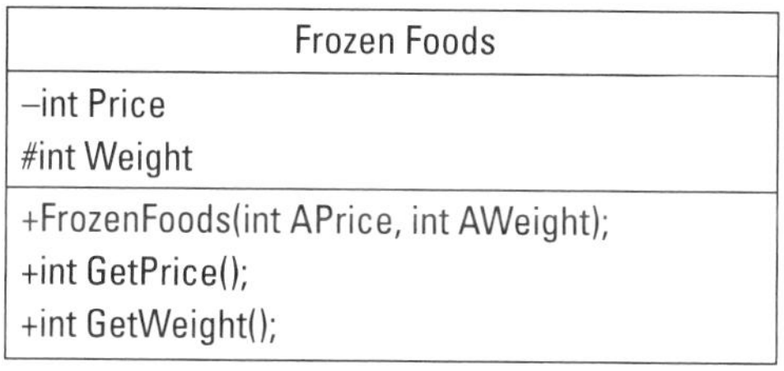

Figure 1-3:
You can draw a class by using a box divided into three horizontal sections.

Frozen Foods
−int Price
#int Weight
+FrozenFoods(int APrice, int AWeight);
+int GetPrice();
+int GetWeight();

Note that, in this figure, we did one other thing: Before each member variable and function, we place either a plus sign (+), a minus sign (–), or a pound sign (#). This is shorthand notation: The + means the item is public, the – means it's private, and the # means it's protected.

In Figure 1-3, note that we wrote the lines for the member variables and functions in C++ form. Normally, you don't do this; you use a special notation called UML in place of the C++, which we introduce a little of later in this chapter and then discuss for the remainder of this minibook.

Protecting members when inheriting

In C++, you have options for how you derive a class. To understand this, you need to remember that when you derive a class, the derived class inherits the members from the base class. With the different ways to derive a class, you can specify whether those inherited members will be public, protected, or private in the derived class. Here are the options:

+ **Public:** When you derive a new class as *public,* all the members that were public in the base class will remain public in this derived class.

+ **Protected:** When you derive a new class as *protected,* all the members that were public in the base class will now be protected in this new class. This means the members that were public in the base class will not be accessible by users of this new class.

+ **Private:** When you derive a new class as *private,* all the members in the base class that this new class can access will be private. This means these members will not be accessible by any classes that you later derive from this new class — they are private, after all.

Think of it as an order: The highest access is public. When a member is public, users can access the member. The middle access is protected. Users cannot access protected members, but derived classes will have access to the protected members. The lowest access is private. Users cannot access private members, and derived classes can't either.

We're talking about inheritance here: Thus, if we have a base class called `FrozenFood` and a derived class called `FrozenPizza`, the derived class is a combination of the members in `FrozenFood` and additional `FrozenPizza` members. However, only the methods in the `FrozenFood` portion of `FrozenPizza` can access the private members of the `FrozenFood` portion. Nevertheless, the methods in the `FrozenFood` portion of `FrozenPizza` and the private members of `FrozenFood` are part of the derived class.

When you derive a class as public, the base class portion of the derived class remains unchanged: Those items that were private remain in the base class portion; therefore, the derived class does not have access to them. Those that were protected are still protected, and those that were public are still public.

But when you derive a class as protected, the base class portion is different from the original base class: Its public members are now protected members of this derived class. (But remember, the actual base class itself did not change! We're talking only about the base class *portion* of the derived class.) Thus, the members that were public in the base class but are now protected in the derived class are not accessible to other functions and classes: They are now protected.

And finally, if you derive a class as private, the base class portion is again different from the original base class: All its members are now private. Because its members are private, any classes you derive from this newly derived class can't access these members: They're private. However, as before, the original base class itself didn't change; we're still talking about the base class portion of the derived class.

REMEMBER

All these derivation approaches can be complicated. Remember that when you derive a class, you are specifying what level the inherited public and protected members will have in the derived class.

In C++, you specify the type of inheritance you want in the header line for the derived class. Take a look at Listing 1-1. Notice the three classes at the top of the listing: FrozenFood, FrozenPizza, and DeepDishPizza. Frozen Food is the base class of FrozenPizza, and FrozenPizza is the base class of DeepDishPizza. Figure 1-4 shows this by using a special notation called UML, where the arrows point toward the *base* class.

Listing 1-1:   Specifying the Access Levels of the Inherited Members

```
#include <iostream>

using namespace std;

class FrozenFood
{
private:
    int Price;

protected:
    int Weight;

public:
    FrozenFood(int APrice, int AWeight);
    int GetPrice();
    int GetWeight();
};

class FrozenPizza : public FrozenFood
{
protected:
    int Diameter;

public:
    FrozenPizza(int APrice, int AWeight, int ADiameter);
```

(continued)

Listing 1-1 *(continued)*

```cpp
    void DumpInfo();
};

class DeepDishPizza : public FrozenPizza
{
private:
    int Height;

public:
    DeepDishPizza(int APrice, int AWeight, int ADiameter, int AHeight);
    void DumpDensity();
};

FrozenFood::FrozenFood(int APrice, int AWeight)
{
    Price = APrice;
    Weight = AWeight;
}

int FrozenFood::GetPrice()
{
    return Price;
}

int FrozenFood::GetWeight()
{
    return Weight;
}

FrozenPizza::FrozenPizza(int APrice, int AWeight, int ADiameter) :
FrozenFood(APrice, AWeight)
{
    Diameter = ADiameter;
}

void FrozenPizza::DumpInfo()
{
    cout << "\tFrozen pizza info:" << endl;
    cout << "\t\tWeight: " << Weight << " ounces" << endl;
    cout << "\t\tDiameter: " << Diameter << " inches" << endl;
}

DeepDishPizza::DeepDishPizza(int APrice, int AWeight,
int ADiameter, int AHeight) :
FrozenPizza(APrice, AWeight, ADiameter)
{
    Height = AHeight;
}

void DeepDishPizza::DumpDensity()
{
    // Calculate pounds per cubic foot of deep-dish pizza
    cout << "\tDensity: ";
    cout << Weight * 12 * 12 * 12 * 14 / (Height * Diameter * 22 * 16);
    cout << " pounds per cubic foot" << endl;
}

int main(int argc, char *argv[])
{
    cout << "Thin crust pepperoni" << endl;
```

```
FrozenPizza pepperoni(450, 12, 14);
pepperoni.DumpInfo();
cout << "\tPrice: " << pepperoni.GetPrice() << " cents" << endl;

cout << "Deep dish extra-cheese" << endl;
DeepDishPizza extracheese(650, 21592, 14, 3);
extracheese.DumpInfo();
extracheese.DumpDensity();
cout << "\tPrice: " << extracheese.GetPrice() << " cents" << endl;
return 0;
}
```

**Book II
Chapter 1**

**Planning and
Building Objects**

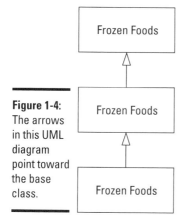

Figure 1-4:
The arrows
in this UML
diagram
point toward
the base
class.

When you run Listing 1-1, you see the following output:

```
Thin crust pepperoni
        Frozen pizza info:
                Weight: 12 ounces
                Diameter: 14 inches
        Price: 450 cents
Deep dish extra-cheese
        Frozen pizza info:
                Weight: 21592 ounces
                Diameter: 14 inches
        Density: 35332 pounds per cubic foot
        Price: 650 cents
```

The first five lines show information about the object of class FrozenPizza. The remaining lines show information about the object of class DeepDishPizza, including the fact that it weighs 21592 ounces (which happens to be 1349.5 pounds) and has a density of 35,332 pounds per cubic foot (35,332 pounds per cubic foot is a bit more than 17 tons per cubic foot, which is still nowhere near that of a neutron star, which measures about three trillion tons per cubic foot. Nevertheless, that's one serious pizza).

The derivations are all public. Thus, the items that were public in Frozen Food are still public in FrozenPizza and DeepDishPizza. Note where the different information in the output comes from. The line Frozen pizza info: and the two lines that follow (`Weight:` and `Diameter:`) come from the public function `DumpInfo`, which is a member of `FrozenPizza`. `DumpInfo` is public in the `FrozenPizza` class. Since `DeepDishPizza` derives from `FrozenPizza` as *public,* `DumpInfo` is also a public member of `DeepDishPizza`.

Now try changing the header for `DeepDishPizza` from

```
class DeepDishPizza : public FrozenPizza
```

to

```
class DeepDishPizza : protected FrozenPizza
```

You're changing the word `public` to `protected`. Make sure that you change the right line, or it will spoil the effect of this nifty thing we're showing you.

Now try compiling the program. You will get an error. We got

```
In function `int main(int, char**)':
error: `void FrozenPizza::DumpInfo()' is inaccessible
error: within this context
error: `FrozenPizza' is not an accessible base of `DeepDishPizza'
error: `int FrozenFood::GetPrice()' is inaccessible
error: within this context
error: `FrozenFood' is not an accessible base of `DeepDishPizza'
```

This refers to the line in `main`:

```
  extracheese.DumpInfo();
```

Why is that an error now? Because `DumpInfo` is now a `protected` member of `DeepDishPizza`, thanks to the word `protected` in the class header. By putting the word `protected` in the class definition, you are saying that inherited members that are public are instead going to be protected. Because the `DumpInfo` member is protected, you can't call it from `main`. However, `DumpInfo` is still public in the `FrozenPizza` class, so this call is fine:

```
pepperoni.DumpInfo();
```

Go ahead and change the line back to a public inheritance as it was in Listing 1-1:

```
class DeepDishPizza : public FrozenPizza
```

And now change the header of `FrozenPizza`, so it looks like this:

```
class FrozenPizza : private FrozenFood
```

Again, make sure you change the right lines. Now try compiling the program. When we do so in CodeBlocks, we get the following error:

```
In function `int main(int, char**)':|
error: `void FrozenPizza::DumpInfo()' is inaccessible|
error: within this context|
error: `FrozenPizza' is not an accessible base of `DeepDishPizza'|
error: `int FrozenFood::GetPrice()' is inaccessible|
error: within this context|
error: `FrozenFood' is not an accessible base of `DeepDishPizza'|
```

This error refers to the line inside `DeepDishPizza::DumpDensity` where the code is trying to access the `Weight` member. Why doesn't the compiler let us access the member now? Because the member, which was public in the original `FrozenFood` class, became private when it became a part of `FrozenPizza`. And because it's private in `FrozenPizza`, the derived class `DeepDishPizza` cannot access it from *within its own member functions*. *Remember:* The rule with private members is that derived classes will not have access to them. And that was the case here.

Overriding member functions

One of the cool things about classes is that you can declare a member function in one class, and then when you derive a new class, you can give that class a different version of the same function. This is called *overriding* the function. For example, if you have a class `FrozenFood` and a derived class `FrozenPizza`, you may want to include a member function in `FrozenFood` called `BakeChemistry`, which modifies the food when it's baked. Because all foods are different, the `BakeChemistry` function would be different for each class derived from `FrozenFood`.

In C++, you can provide a different *version* of the function for the different derived classes by dropping the word `virtual` before the function name in the base class declaration, as in this line of code:

```
virtual void BakeChemistry();
```

This line is the prototype inside the class definition. Later, you would provide the code for this function.

In the class for your derived class, you would then just put the function prototype, without the word `virtual`:

```
void BakeChemistry();
```

And as before, you would include the code for the function later on. For example, you might have something like this. First, here are the classes:

```
class FrozenFood
{
private:
```

```
    int Price;

protected:
    int Weight;

public:
    FrozenFood(int APrice, int AWeight);
    int GetPrice();
    int GetWeight();
    virtual void BakeChemistry();
};

class FrozenPizza : public FrozenFood
{
protected:
    int Diameter;

public:
    FrozenPizza(int APrice, int AWeight, int ADiameter);
    void DumpInfo();
    void BakeChemistry();
};
```

You can see that we put the word `virtual` in the `FrozenFood` class, and then we put the function declaration again in the `FrozenPizza` class. Now here are the `BakeChemistry` functions:

```
void FrozenFood::BakeChemistry()
{
    cout << "Baking, baking, baking!" << endl;
}

void FrozenPizza::BakeChemistry()
{
    cout << "I'm getting crispy!" << endl;
}
```

Note we did not put the word `virtual` in front of the functions; that only goes in the class declaration. Now, when you make an instance of each class and call `BakeChemistry` for each instance, you call the one for the given class. Consider the following two lines of code:

```
FrozenPizza pepperoni(450, 12, 14);
pepperoni.BakeChemistry();
```

Because pepperoni is an instance of `FrozenPizza`, this code calls the `BakeChemistry` for the `FrozenPizza` class, not for the `FrozenFood` class.

You may not want any code in your base class for the `BakeChemistry` function. If so, you can do this:

```
virtual void BakeChemistry() {}
```

Wait! Now why would you want a function that has no code? Well, we're not as goofy as we look. Okay, we are goofy. But regardless, you may not want any code here, but you do want code in the derived classes, and you want them to be different versions of the same code. The idea then is to provide a basic, default set of code that the classes inherit if they don't override the function. And sometimes, that basic, default set of code is simply *nothing*. And so, you would just put an open brace and a closing brace, and you can do that inside the class itself:

```
class FrozenFood
{
private:
    int Price;

protected:
    int Weight;

public:
    FrozenFood(int APrice, int AWeight);
    int GetPrice();
    int GetWeight();
    virtual void BakeChemistry() {}
};
```

Book II
Chapter 1

Planning and
Building Objects

Some people prefer to put the word `virtual` in the overridden function's prototype in the derived class. Technically speaking, this step is not required, although many people who have been programming in C++ for a long time do this. You can if you want, if you think that it looks cool. We do it for one reason besides looking cool: It reminds us that the function *is* `virtual`. Thus, in the `FrozenPizza` class definition, your function prototype would look like this, just as it did in the `FrozenFood` class:

```
virtual void BakeChemistry();
```

Specializing with polymorphism

Suppose you have a function called `Bake`, and you want it to take as a parameter a `FrozenFood` instance. If you derive `FrozenPizza` from `FrozenFood` and then derive `DeepDishPizza` from `FrozenPizza`, then by the "is a" rule, objects of the class `FrozenPizza` and `DeepDishPizza` are both examples of `FrozenFood` objects. This is true in general: If you have a class called `Base` and you derive from that a class called `Derived`, instances of class `Derived` are *also* instances of class `Base`. Think of it like a family name. If your last name is Swaddlebug and you have a child who grows up, marries, and takes the name Higglequack, then although the child bears the name Higglequack, at heart he or she is and always will be a Swaddlebug.

And so it is with frozen foods and C++, too. You can treat an object of any class derived from `FrozenFood` as if it *is* a `FrozenFood` instance. Therefore, if you have a function called `Bake` and you declare it as follows, you are free to pass to this function a `FrozenFood` instance or to pass an instance of any class derived from `FrozenFood`, such as `FrozenPizza` or `DeepDishPizza`:

```
void Bake(FrozenFood *)
{
    cout << "Baking" << endl;
}
```

But here's where the fun begins: Suppose that in this `Bake` function you're going to set the oven temperature to a fixed amount, turn on the oven, and then cook the food. Every food behaves differently in the oven. For example, a deep-dish frozen pizza might rise and become thicker, but a regular frozen pizza will become crispier but not get any thicker.

Now you don't really want to put all the different food types inside the `Bake` function, with a million `if` statements: If it's this type of food, have it rise; `if` it's that type of food, have it brown; and `if` it's another type of food, have it scream and yell. Instead — and this is where things start to get seriously cool — you can put the actual baking chemistry in the class for the food itself! Yes! The `FrozenPizza` would have its own `BakeChemistry` member function, and the `DeepDishPizza` would also have its own `BakeChemistry` function. Then the `Bake` function would simply call `BakeChemistry` for whatever object it receives as a parameter! And how does C++ know how to do this? By virtue of the virtual functions! The `BakeFunction` itself doesn't even know or care what type of `FrozenFood` it receives. It just calls `BakeChemistry` for whatever object it receives. And thanks to the miraculous beauty of C++, it automatically calls the correct `BakeChemistry` function, whether it's the one for `FrozenPizza` or the one for `DeepDishPizza` or even a class that you add later when you modify the program! And when you modify the program, if you write a new class and derive it from `Frozen Food` and give it its own `BakeChemistry` function, then you can pass an instance of this class to `Bake`, without even having to modify `Bake`! In other words, you don't need to tell `Bake` about this class! Isn't that great! Can you tell we're excited?

In short, what this means is that the `Bake` function can take an object of class `FrozenFood` (or any class derived from `FrozenFood`) and call its `BakeChemistry` function. Each class can have its own version of `BakeChemistry`, and the computer will call the appropriate `BakeChemistry` function. This whole process is called *polymorphism*.

Polymorphism is one of the most powerful aspects of object-oriented programming. The idea is that you can expand and enhance your program by simply adding new classes derived from a common base class. Then you have to make very few (if any) modifications to the rest of your program. Because you used virtual functions and polymorphism, the rest of your program automatically understands the new class you created. In essence, you are able to *snap* in the new class, and the program will run just fine.

Getting abstract about things

When you create a base class with a virtual function and then derive other classes, you may want to override the virtual function in all the derived classes. Furthermore, you may want to make sure that nobody — and we mean *nobody* — ever creates an instance of the base class!

Now, why would you do that? Because the base class might contain basic things that are common to all the other classes, but the class itself doesn't make much sense as an instance. For example, we want you to go to the store and pick up a frozen food. We hear they're on sale at the grocery store down the street. We like the purple kind. See, it doesn't make much sense to have an instance of a class called `FrozenFood`. What kind of frozen food? Well, it could be a (you guessed it!) `FrozenPizza`, or even better, a `DeepDishPizza`. But by itself, a `FrozenFood` item isn't realistic.

Philosophers have a word for such things: *abstract*. The class `FrozenFood` is abstract; it doesn't make sense to create an instance of it. In C++, you can make a class abstract, but when you do, the compiler will not allow you to make any instances of the class.

Now this is where things get a little strange: In C++, you don't actually specify that the class itself is abstract. The word *abstract* does not appear in the language. Instead, you have to be, well, more abstract about it. To specify that the class is abstract, you must have at least one virtual function that has no code. But instead of just putting an empty code block, as in `{}`, you follow the function prototype in the class definition with `= 0`, as in:

```
class FrozenFood
{
private:
    int Price;

protected:
    int Weight;

public:
    FrozenFood(int APrice, int AWeight);
    int GetPrice();
    int GetWeight();
    virtual void BakeChemistry() = 0;
};
```

In this class definition, the function `BakeChemistry` has `= 0` after it (but before the semicolon — *don't forget the semicolon*). The `= 0` magically transforms the virtual function into an *abstract virtual function*. And if you have an abstract virtual function inside you, then, face it, you are an abstract class. No ifs, ands, or buts. You're abstract.

This is the rule for creating an abstract class: You must have at least one abstract virtual function in your class. If you don't, the class will not be abstract, and users of the class will be able to create instances of it. But if you do have at least one abstract virtual function, the compiler will issue

Book II
Chapter 1

Planning and
Building Objects

an error message when you and other users try to create an instance of the class.

TIP

In your extensive travels throughout the virtual world of C++, you are likely to encounter a slightly different term for *abstract virtual function.* That term is *pure virtual function.* Although the name sounds all pristine and pure, it means the same thing. You can use either term.

So now that you have your abstract class and can't make an instance of it, are you home free? Nope. Now in your derived classes, you *must* override the abstract virtual function. Otherwise, the derived classes will also be *abstract.* And when your class is abstract, you can't create instances of it.

To override the abstract virtual function, you override as you would with any virtual function. This class includes a function that overrides the BakeChemistry function:

```
class FrozenPizza : public FrozenFood
{
protected:
    int Diameter;

public:
    FrozenPizza(int APrice, int AWeight, int ADiameter);
    void DumpInfo();
    void BakeChemistry();
};
```

Then you provide the code for the BakeChemistry function, as in

```
void FrozenPizza::BakeChemistry()
{
    cout << "I'm getting crispy under this heat!" << endl;
}
```

There's nothing magical about defining the override function, but you are *required* to override it if you want to create an instance of this class.

Discovering Classes

In your studies of object-oriented programming, you could spend weeks and weeks searching for the answer to this question: How do you know what classes to put in your program? Oddly, many of the books on object-oriented programming don't even tackle this question. Too many people, even self-proclaimed experts, simply don't know the answer to this question.

In this section, we show you how to discover the classes you need for your project, and we put the concepts in the context of the bigger picture of software engineering.

Engineering your software

Ready to write your program? Okay, sit down and start coding. And call us in six months. Oh, and in case we forgot to mention, this software that you build has to do exactly what we, your customers, need. And please, please don't let it mess up, okay?

Well now isn't that nice? How are you supposed to know what we need, and much less, how are you supposed to get it perfect the first time? Yet, believe it or not, many young programmers build their software this way. The shoot-from-the-hip approach goes something like this:

1. "Hey! I have a *really* great idea!"
2. Open up the compiler.
3. Write the code.
4. Sell it.

And people wonder why so many programs crash and screw up. Have you ever seen a program mess up? Who hasn't? But fortunately, your software doesn't have to be in this group! You have, in your hands, an instruction guide for building software.

When you have a great idea, the first thing you need to ask yourself is this: Who will be using your software? You? Your friends? Business people? Children? People at home? Teachers? Non-profit agencies? Airline pilots? Doctors in the middle of surgery? Hackers? The dog?

Ask yourself this question and be honest. The truth is this: No software package will be used by *everyone*. Yes, certain programs are used by a *lot* of people. Examples of this are the software that runs the telephone system or the software in your cable TV box. But even then, we could probably find a couple dozen people on some island somewhere who will never use your software. So when you answer this question, be realistic. And be as detailed as possible. For example, one answer might be the following: This software will be used by VPs and CEOs at Fortune 500 companies who need to divide time between surfing the Web and playing solitaire.

Once upon a time, people believed that, to create software, you should create a complete model that duplicates the real world. But people designing software quickly realized a slight, shall we say, *difficulty* in this approach: What if the real-world process you're modeling is, frankly, screwed up and a total joke? Want to find out for sure? Ask the workers who actually *use* the process you're trying to computerize. And this spawned an interesting profession that a lot of computer programmers took up: Business process reengineering. Sounds pretty cool. "What do you do?" "I'm a business process reengineer." "Cool. We bet you have a big house."

Business process reengineering simply means helping a company fix its internal processes so that they actually function correctly. And we're talking about the actual processes, not just the computer software they use. One of the creators of the software modeling language we advocate in this book (UML), a guy named Ivar Jacobson, even wrote one of the early great books on business process reengineering. (And we suppose he probably *does* have a big house, although we've never seen it.)

It boils down to this: When you model a process, you may find inefficiencies in the process. So you probably won't want to model the process exactly. Besides, if the process were exactly the same, why bother? The computer should make the process better. So think of ways that the people who use your software will find that it not only automates what they do but makes their life easier, too. Here are the steps, then, to engineering your software.

The following are the general steps in building good software. Each step is called a *workflow*. As you gain experience, you will get better at actually doing these steps. Like anything else in the real world, building software that *works* and is *good* requires practice and patience.

1. Determine who will be using the software and gather the requirements. In other words, find out what the people who will be using it need the software to do. This is called the *requirements workflow*. In doing so, build a *glossary of terms*. That's important! The glossary contains all the words involved in the process you are modeling. For instance, if you are writing the software that will automate a beach, you will probably encounter terms such as *surfboard, sand castle, high tide, undertow, shark, broken glass, foot, swimsuit, umbrella, volleyball, net*, and *volleyball court*. These are all nouns. But your glossary can also have verbs (possibly with a noun tacked on to the end — that's called a *direct object*, by the way), as in *dive, swim, ward off shark, avoid broken glass, rent umbrella*, and *throw volleyball*.

2. Next, begin the *analysis workflow*. To do this, determine your analysis classes. For more information on this, see "Finding those pesky classes," later in this chapter. Note that while doing this, you may realize some things were missing or not quite right in Step 1. That's okay — you can go back to Step 1 and fix things. Then, after you fix things in Step 1, you can return to Step 2. And remember that in this workflow, you are not worrying about the details of *how* you're going to be writing the code. In fact, you *won't* be writing any code here, nor will you be worrying about things like how you will be storing your files, how you're going to sort a list of numbers, and so on. Save all that for the implementation workflow described in Step 4. Here, you're just designing some classes. After you have your analysis classes, have the people who will be using the software (or at least some of them if there are millions) review your classes and see if these are the general *parts* of the software they imagined.

During this second step, you can do one thing related to programming: Design some screens. Although many of the textbooks on object-oriented analysis and design do not put that step here, doing so has many benefits. First, it allows you to show the potential users of the program what the program might look like when it's finished. And this allows them to begin analyzing whether or not what you're building will be useful. (And if they don't find it useful, don't quit and don't yell at them. They are, after all, using this thing and paying you mondo-big bucks, so do what they want and laugh all the way to the bank.) And second, doing this lets you show them that, yes, you really are building software and not just surfing the Web.

3. Now comes the *design workflow.* This is where you take the analysis classes and begin building the classes you will use in your program. For this stage, you use UML notation and describe the classes in your program, how they all interact, and the steps that various processes in your program take. You can start thinking about the code now, but you still won't actually write any code! And by the way, it's very possible (or even likely) that you'll discover that something you did in Step 2 or 3 is wrong, or at least not *quite* right. If so . . . that's right — go ahead and return to those steps and fix the things. But if you go back to Step 2, please revisit Step 3 before coming back to Step 4. You may end up having to change some things there, too.

4. And finally the *implementation workflow* has arrived! That's just a fancy term for *coding time.* Now that you've made it this far, you will realize that much of your work is already completed. The first several steps took care of much of the hard work, and now you can do the fun part of focusing on the coding part. And once again, you may have to backtrack a few steps if you find some things that aren't quite right.

5. But you're not finished yet. Nope. Can anyone guess what comes next? That's right: the *testing workflow.* During this workflow, you try to use your program in all the possible ways you intended it to be used. And you can also choose a few other people who you trust to use it. We say *trust* because this is a vital stage of your software. You want to make sure that the people who test it really know what they're doing and are going to seriously put the program through the wringer. And further, you want these people to give you honest, objective comments, not things like, "You messed up! You're fired!" Rather, you want them to report actual problems and difficulties they found in the software so that you, the programmer, can fix them. But remember: Having others help you test your program is to your benefit. Just like editing your own papers; you are likely to miss certain things, and having at least one more set of eyes and fingers trying it out is a good thing.

Our experience in the testing world tells us that most of the bugs you and the other testers find result in you going back to Step 4 and working on the coding to fix problems. However, occasionally you find you have

Book II
Chapter 1

Planning and
Building Objects

to backtrack to Step 3, or even once in a while to Step 2. But that's okay: Your goal is to build the software and build it correctly.

Finding those pesky classes

When you set out to determine the classes to use in your program as part of the *analysis workflow,* the first thing you end up with is a set of analysis classes. These are not classes in a final form that you would type into an editor and compile as a C++ program. Rather, they are more of a descriptive style that depict what you are modeling. Then, after you have these classes, you move to the design workflow of your development: That's when you refine the class descriptions you can easily transform into C++ code.

People use three general ways to determine the classes. None of these approaches are perfect; if they were, a computer could program itself automatically. (Assuming that somebody programmed the computer to program, but that's a separate philosophy altogether, something we won't get into here.) Here are the three general ways people discover classes:

+ Look at the glossary you developed during the requirements workflow, searching out the nouns and the verbs.

+ Use CRC cards, which stands for Class, Responsibilities, and Collaborators (as described in "Using CRC cards," later in this chapter).

+ Look for hidden or missing classes.

We recommend doing all three; or do either of the first two along with the final one. The final item on the list is important in case you missed anything.

Searching for nouns and verbs

As much as it sounds like a drag, searching for nouns and verbs is actually a fun process. Not all computer programmers are known for their love for the English language. (There are exceptions, and we tend to write books!), but you don't have to be a grammar whiz to make it through this stage.

First, go through the glossary and any other documents you accumulated during the requirements workflow, and begin making two lists: all the important nouns and all the important verbs.

After you have compiled your list, think about which of the nouns are particularly important; for instance, some nouns may be major aspects of the program. If you're writing a program that models a grocery store, for example, *cash register* is probably a pretty important noun. If you're writing a program to control an intergalactic space ship, everybody knows that the antigravity booster is vital. These, then, are good candidates for classes. You will make most of the remaining nouns characteristics in your classes. (Remember that, ultimately, characteristics and capabilities will be member variables and functions, but you're not thinking about programming at this point.) If, however, you find a characteristic that just doesn't seem to work with any class, you probably want to make it a class as well. Finally, the verbs will become the capabilities of the classes. You should not have any capabilities that are without a class: Either you don't need the capability, or you are probably missing a class. Go ahead and add it.

Using CRC cards

People love CRC (Class, Responsibilities, and Collaborators) cards because they find that creating them is fun. Big corporations like to do this type of thing during team-building exercises to help employees get along. In addition to climbing ropes and such, they design software with CRC cards.

People often use sticky notes for CRC cards, although we usually just draw them on a whiteboard. (But we're not supposed to admit that because our fellow object-oriented people will be angry with us.)

A CRC card consists of three parts. The top part is the name of the class. The left side shows the responsibilities (what we call *capabilities*) of the class. The right side features the collaborations, which means you just list other classes that this class works together with. For example, an antigravity booster class certainly works together with a high-energy proton accelerator class, as everybody knows. You list the names of these classes on the right side of the card because they are collaborations.

Some people prefer to put their CRC cards as sticky notes right on a whiteboard; then instead of writing the names of the related classes on the right side of the card, they just draw a line between the cards. You can either list the classes or draw lines, whichever you like best.

By coming up with collaborations, you will spot missing classes. For example, because you know that the antigravity booster works with a high-energy proton accelerator, when you fill in the collaborators for the antigravity booster class, you will know whether you forgot about the high-energy proton accelerator class.

Look for hidden or missing classes

It's possible that when you do a class analysis, you will have left out some classes. Some of these missing classes may not be obvious, and to find them, you will probably have to get back with the people who helped suggest requirements. This is a good time to have them review the classes. Remember, the classes that you are building right now are not final classes ready for C++. Instead, these are less technical classes that are understandable by people who don't program. Therefore, the people who offered the requirements and the people who will be using the program can probably look over the classes and help you determine if you are missing anything.

After you determine that you have missing classes, go ahead and add them by making another CRC card.

Completing the analysis with the design workflow

After you have your classes, you can move to the *design workflow* and write the classes in UML form. This is a simple form in that you will have a box with the class name at the top followed by the characteristics of the class and finally followed by the capabilities of the class. (Refer to Figure 1-3 for an example of a class in this form.) These are the classes you will use in the coding phase (*implementation workflow*), where you actually transform them into real, breathing C++ classes. The remaining chapters in this minibook show you how to do all this!

Chapter 2: Describing Your Program with UML

In This Chapter

✔ Moving up to UML and modeling with it

✔ Designing with diagrams

✔ Going through iterations

✔ Stepping through phases

✔ Performing workflows

The ancient people knew something that we don't know. Instead of wasting their time writing these big, long sentences and descriptions, they used hieroglyphics, pictures that just got right to the point. One picture = one statement. It wasn't until the twentieth century that people in the computer world started getting back to their ancient roots and realized that maybe there was something to be said for all those drawings and pictures. One day, while working late, a small group of researchers realized that a nifty way to describe software is through drawings. And thus they came up with the Unified Modeling Language, or UML for short (pronounced, well, just *You-Em-Ell*).

In this chapter, we talk about what UML is and how you can use it to model your programs. We give a brief overview of the types of diagrams it includes, and we talk about the difference between a *methodology* and a *modeling language*.

Moving Up to UML

The Unified Modeling Language has an interesting history. When object-oriented programming was just getting off the ground in the late 1980s, several people came up with different ways to draw various diagrams to help people design their classes. This, of course, was nothing new. In addition to ancient people who used drawings in their hieroglyphics, people have always had a tendency to draw diagrams to describe something. For example, people might draw a chart listing the different parts of their programs. Or they might draw a chart that shows the steps that a program goes through, using a form called a flowchart.

A *flowchart* is simply a diagram that shows the step-by-step nature of a process, complete with the decision making that the process might involve. For example, we might have a step-by-step process (or *algorithm*) we use that helps us decide what to do on Mondays. This might look like Figure 2-1.

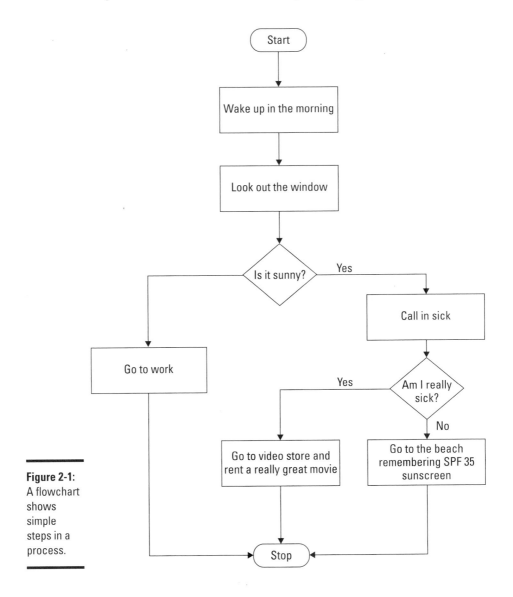

Figure 2-1:
A flowchart
shows
simple
steps in a
process.

In Figure 2-1, we start at the top in the spot called *Start,* and then we follow the arrow down to the first box. The first box is a command or statement — something that we *do.* Then after we do that, we follow the arrow down to the next box. After that we follow the arrow again, but this time we encounter a diamond. A diamond contains a decision. We answer the question, and if our answer is *yes,* we go one way, but if our answer is *no,* we go the other way. In this case, if it's *yes,* we go to the right, and begin the boxes on the right, following the arrows, responding to any decisions we find. If the first decision was *no,* we follow the arrows on the left, again doing what the boxes tell us and answering any questions we see in the diamonds.

Well, this whole flowcharting business works great for small, simple tasks. But over the years, software has become far more complex. For one thing, people now build their programs around objects and classes, which simply don't fit to the flowchart idea. And second, software has become *big.* Just a quick look at some of the software you use on a daily basis, such as the word processors that run under Microsoft Windows, and you can see that these programs were written by lots and lots of people who seemed like they wanted to add every bell and whistle — whether you even use it or not! And the flowcharts are more suited to small portions of a software package, such as a single function or an algorithm.

And so, over the years, people have pretty much ditched the flowcharting and left it in a time capsule somewhere to be found hundreds of years from now. (Although, a portion of UML — called an *activity diagram* — is similar to a flowchart.) And during the years since programmers have started ditching flowcharts, a few well-respected researchers in the field of computer science have come up with new ways to draw pretty pictures that will describe a computer program. Several different attempts have been made, but it seems like programmers have finally come up with one that everyone can live with: UML.

UML takes the concept of flowcharting to a whole new level. Yes, that sounds like it came from a marketing brochure, but it's true. UML is much *more* than just flowcharting. UML uses symbols that show how all the classes and objects fit together in your program, and it shows how they interact and *collaborate.* You then use UML as you design and build your entire software systems. Figure 2-2 is an example of a UML diagram.

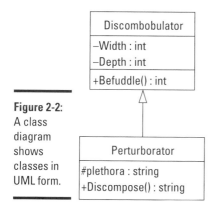

Figure 2-2:
A class
diagram
shows
classes in
UML form.

The three amigos

In your explorations of UML, sooner or later you're going to come across the term *Three Amigos*. Although that was a goofy movie back in the Greatest Decade (why, the 1980s of course), in the context of UML, it refers to the three guys who developed UML. Why are they called that? Because after about seven years or so, they finally became *friends*. It's true.

For several years, there were three guys who wrote books on object-oriented programming, and they each had their own way of doing things. But worse, the *rumor* is that these guys couldn't stand each other. (Who knows if that's even true.) "My way is better, and I don't like you, anyway." Come on guys, can't we all just get along? Well, in fact, they did end up getting along.

One day, it dawned on them: "Hey! You know what? Like Superman, Batman, and Spiderman, we can all just join forces in one great big hall of justice and make it a better world for all!" That and, "Hey, you know what? Our ideas really aren't all *that* different. Let's combine them into a new, better way of doing object-oriented programming." Like any time three greats join and put their heads together, the result was something pretty nifty: UML.

By the way, movieland's *Three Amigos* are Chevy Chase, Steve Martin, and Martin Short. In UML circles, the three amigos are Grady Booch, Ivar Jacobson, and James Rumbaugh.

This shows two classes, one called `Discombobulator` and another called `Perturborator`. Each is inside a box divided into three rows, with the class name at the top, the member variables in the middle, and the member functions at the bottom. The format is slightly different from regular C++ format; the types go at the end, after a colon. (Remember that in C++ you put the types first, as in `int Height;`)

The first class, `Discombobulator`, has two member variables, `Width` and `Depth`. (Everybody knows that an actual discombobulator has no height; thus, we didn't include one in this class.) The two member variables are private; therefore, they start with a minus sign, (–), and each is an integer type. The `Befuddle` member function is public, and therefore starts with a plus sign, +. In the `Perturborator` class, the `plethora` member variable is protected, and therefore it starts with a # sign.

Notice the arrow. The arrow shows inheritance, but it goes in the opposite direction of what a lot of people might expect. *It points toward the base class.* Thus, in this diagram, `Pertuborator` is derived from `Discombobulator`.

The Unified Modeling Language has been accepted by millions of engineers as the standard way for modeling software. The Object Management Group (or OMG, found at `www.omg.org`) has adopted UML as its official modeling language. The OMG is a consortium of hundreds of software companies that have all joined to oversee the big sea of software development standards.

Modeling a methodology

A lot of people will start reading a book on UML and become a bit disoriented at the beginning because they quickly realize that an important question sometimes goes unanswered: How do you use UML to actually design a complete software package from start to finish? How do you use UML to go through the process of determining what classes you need, building those classes, writing your software, testing it, and all that good stuff? Some books on UML seem to avoid this question for a good reason:

UML is *not* a methodology. It's not a set of rules and steps for building software. Rather, UML is simply a set of diagrams that you can use while modeling your software. That's actually a point that many software engineers don't realize. "What methodology do you use?" "We use UML." If that's their answer, it proves they don't really know what UML is. You use UML *with* a methodology, and then you have a powerful set of tools for building software.

Modeling with UML

The idea behind UML is that it can be used for modeling pretty much any type of information — not just object-oriented systems — even information not computer-related. As such, UML has many parts. But the great thing about UML is that you don't need to *learn* all the parts to use it. You need to learn only the parts useful to your projects.

UML covers all the aspects of the usual software development process. Now we have said that UML itself is not a step-by-step process or methodology for building software. However, the designers of UML have provided enough diagram types and symbols that it can be used with all the different steps of software development. Therefore, to learn UML, learning a methodology along with it is a good idea. In fact, the people who designed UML, *The Three Amigos* (see the nearby sidebar by that name), have also designed a methodology. Theirs is called the Unified Process. That's the methodology we use. (And to be quite frank, most methodologies are more-or-less the same.)

Diagramming and designing with UML

The diagrams in UML are simple enough that they can be drawn by hand on a sheet of paper. Of course, this is the age of computers, and using a computer makes sense, so why resort to the old-fashioned method of pencil and paper? But beyond that, there's a slight technicality as to why paper drawings are not suited to a software design.

When you use UML to design a system, you typically use a computer program called a Computer-Aided Software Engineering (CASE) tool. When you use the CASE tool, you specify all your objects; and as you do, you create your diagrams that describe the classes and how they interact. However, the model itself is the collection of classes — *not the diagrams*. You can change the diagrams and create new diagrams, but underneath it all is the collection of classes. The collection of classes itself is known as the *model*. When you draw a diagram, you are simply providing a visual representation of the model. Most of the better CASE tools (such as Rational Rose or Paradigm Plus) include a way to create and modify the model itself. You can usually do so directly or by using the drawing tools included in the CASE program.

When you build a software system by using UML, you work out your classes by using the drawings. In the process, you are creating and modifying the model and the drawings simultaneously. But the model itself is still a separate entity from the diagrams.

A good CASE tool has two ways of looking at your system: The first is through the model itself, which is often depicted as an Explorer-style tree, with the classes and their members listed. The second is through the diagrams. You can use the diagrams to add information to the model; for example, you can use a class diagram to add classes and modify the member variables and functions.

Most CASE tools have a slight catch: If you remove a class from a diagram, you don't actually remove it from the model. The class is still in the model, just in case you still want to continue working on it and add it to more diagrams. If you *really* want to remove a class, you have to go to the model itself and remove the class. Fortunately, this applies only to removing classes. You can modify and add classes from the diagrams.

In UML, you can use nine types of diagrams. As you work on these diagrams, your model will evolve. You can make changes to the diagrams, and thereby make changes to the underlying model.

Tables 2-1 and 2-2 show you the nine models. We grouped them into two kinds: *static* and *dynamic*. The static diagrams represent the parts of the software system you are building. The dynamic diagrams show how the parts work together and how things take place over time.

The words *static* and *dynamic* come up again and again in the computer world. *Static* refers to something fixed and unchanging, while *dynamic* refers to something that changes:

✦ In your program, a class is static because you describe it in your code; and after you have described your class, it does not change while the program is running. A class has a certain set of member variables and member functions that you specify in the code. Although the program is running, the members of a class do not change.

✦ The objects, however, are considered to be dynamic, because they can come to life while the program is running, their member variables can change, and they can be deleted.

Table 2-1	Static Diagrams of UML
Diagram Type	*What It Shows*
Class diagram	The different classes
Component diagram	The different parts of the system; each part contains classes related to each other
Deployment diagram	The different computers and hardware involved

The following list describes the items in Table 2-1 in a bit more detail:

✦ **Class diagram:** The class diagram shows the different classes and their relationships to each other. For example, a class diagram might show that the class called Skiddle is derived from the class Skaddle, and it might show that the class Skaddle contains as a member a list of Ruddle instances. Typically as you work on a class diagram, you will also be adding and modifying the classes from the model itself.

✦ **Component diagram:** The component diagram shows the major parts of your software system. For example, all the parts dealing with Discombobulation, including the Discombobulator class and the Perturburator class as well as other related classes, might all be grouped into a single component called SuperSystem.

✦ **Deployment diagram:** The deployment diagram shows a hardware view of your system. This might include specific computers (such as a Compaq Presario with a gigabyte of RAM), or it might include more abstract hardware components, such as *Internet connection.* Or it might show hardware components even more generic, such as *network node* or *database server.* Nevertheless, these are all hardware components.

In Windows, a single component often lives in the form of a Dynamic Link Library, or DLL for short. Most DLLs that you find on your computer were built as components. When you use multiple DLLs that other people built, you are building with various software components. You can show these components on a component diagram.

Table 2-2	Dynamic Diagrams of UML
Diagram Type	*What It Shows*
Use case diagram	The different functions of the software system
Object diagram	Instances of the classes and their relationships to each other
Collaboration diagram	How instances work together with other instances
Sequence diagram	The time sequence of objects working together with other objects
Statechart diagram	The lifecycle of a single object in terms of states
Activity diagram	A sequence of steps; much like a flowchart

The following list describes the dynamic diagrams in a bit more detail:

✦ **Use case diagram:** The use case diagram shows the different individual functions that the software package can perform. Here we mean *function* in a generic sense, like a process, not like a C++ function consisting of a set of code. A word processor might have a use case called *Set italic.* This use case represents the function of setting the italic style for the highlighted text. A Web browser might have a use case called *Go,* which takes a Web address and pulls down and displays the appropriate Web page.

✦ **Object diagram:** The object diagram describes the instances of the classes. This is in contrast to the class diagram, which shows the classes but not the actual instances. The reason that the object diagram is considered a dynamic diagram rather than a static diagram is because objects themselves are considered dynamic. Objects can change while the program is running. Classes, on the other hand, do not change while the program is running.

✦ **Collaboration diagram:** As your program runs, the code for an object's member function might call a member function in another object. In this sense, the two objects are working together, or *collaborating,* just as two people might collaborate to rob a bank. A collaboration diagram shows how the different objects collaborate.

✦ **Sequence diagram:** A sequence shows the collaborations of the objects over time. So if your program is a model of two bank robbers failing because they get into a severe argument over which door to leave the bank through, and you have two objects that represent the two bank robbers, this diagram would show them calling each other's member functions over time. These functions might be things like `Insult` and `Criticize` and `PolitelyDisagree`.

✦ **Statechart diagram:** A statechart diagram is like a sequence diagram, but it shows only one object. It shows how an object changes over time, from the time it is created until it is deleted.

✦ **Activity diagram:** An activity diagram shows the step-by-step nature of a single member function. It is actually a type of statechart:

- A *statechart diagram* shows how an *object* changes from state to state.

- An *activity diagram* shows how a *member function* moves from one activity to the next. In that sense, each state in the activity diagram is an activity.

In the world of UML, when an object's member function calls a member function of a second object, the process is called *sending a message*. The first object sends a message to the second object. This terminology is not new to UML; the original object-oriented language, Smalltalk, used the same terminology. In Smalltalk, objects sent messages to other objects. You use a collaboration diagram to show how one object *sends a message to* another object. Or you can say that the collaboration diagram shows member functions calling the member functions of other objects. They both mean the same thing.

A popular word among software engineers is *lifecycle*. Really, the word basically means life. A software development process has a lifecycle: You start building the software, go until it's all built, update the software as needed, and then retire the software when you're finished using it; that's the lifecycle of the project. However, in many senses, it does cycle back: You get bug reports from customers, and you fix the bugs, and you eventually release another version of the software. Objects have lifecycles too: When you create an instance, you are beginning the life of the object. Then, during the object's lifecycle, you do things to the object like call its member functions and modify its member variables. Then, when you're finished, you delete the object. That finishes the lifecycle.

Software engineers like to think in terms of states. A *state* is simply the current situation in which something exists, like the state of the nation or the state of affairs. These represent the current situation for the nation or the affairs. Or somebody could be in a state of all-out confusion. That represents the current state the person is in. An object also has a particular state: The `Caboodle` class might have member variables `PenCount` and `NotebookCount`, which represent the number of pens and the number of notebooks inside an instance of the `Caboodle` class. A particular instance of the `Caboodle` class might have the value 7 for `PenCount` and the value 3 for `NotebookCount`. Thus, the current state of this particular instance is `PenCount=7, NotebookCount=3`. The `Caboodle` class might also include a member function called `AddPen`, which takes no parameters and simply adds 1 to `PenCount`. When you call `AddPen`, you are *changing the state of the object*.

When you consider the state of an object, you need to look at only the member variables. The values of the member variables together represent the state. The member functions may modify the state, but because the functions themselves do not change during the life of the program, they do not represent part of the object's state. Also, remember that one object can contain as a member another object. The current state of the outer object would include the state of the object that it contains.

In the world of UML, the concept of a *metadescription* comes up again and again. *Meta* is a prefix to a word, and it usually means *the next level up*. For example, with metadescription, we could first describe a tree by writing information about the tree. Then we could describe the description: "It was a beautiful paragraph with flowing words that brought the tree to life." Now that previous sentence itself is what we are referring to right now in this sentence. Do you see what is happening here? We're describing something, and then we describe the description, and then we describe *that* description. Each time we move up "one level of abstraction." The term *metadescription,* then, means a description of a description.

In UML, you encounter meta terminology all the time. For example, a class represents a type of object. But the word *class* is a kind of classifier. Another kind of classifier is *type*. So consider this somewhat philosophical concept: A class is a kind of classifier, at least from the perspective of the UML diagrams. But a particular class itself has certain attributes about it, such as the class name and the names and types of the members. That information is a *metaclass*. If you're not totally confused and you find this fascinating, we highly recommend reading *Gödel, Escher, Bach: An Eternal Golden Braid*, by Douglass R. Hofstadter (Basic Books, 1999) or, for a slightly easier read, *Metamagical Themas: Questing for the Essence of Mind and Pattern*, also by Hofstadter (Basic Books, 1996).

Building with UML and the Unified Process

UML is not a methodology. That means that UML, by itself, is not a step-by-step process for building software. Rather, you can think of UML as a language you use for describing your software as you are building it. The language, however, is not a verbal talking language with a bunch of engineers in a room yelling and arguing. Yes, that sometimes happens, but fortunately it's neither a part of UML nor required. UML is a visual language. There's that adage about a picture being worth a whole bunch of words, or something like that, and it holds up here, too. You describe your software with diagrams. These diagrams provide a full description of your software.

But you create the diagrams as you move through a process. The process *is* a methodology that you use; the one that we use and describe in this book is the Unified Process. There are five main steps (which tend to be the same for most methodologies). These main steps, which are called *workflows,* are as follows: requirements, analysis, design, implementation, and testing. When you think of the steps you would do to accomplish pretty much anything that's not computer-related, you can probably see that you often use these steps.

For example, suppose that you're going to build a time warp device so you can skip that dentist appointment next week. First, you decide what you need to build; this is called the *requirement collection.* In this case, you need a device that takes you forward into time, probably a specified amount of time. So you'll want a display on the device and a keypad so you can enter the amount of time to move forward. And you'll probably need a button to start the time warp. Those are the requirements for the project.

Then you think about how you're going to do the time warp and what you'll need, and you analyze the project. In this case, you'll need the actual time warping portion consisting of the relativistic universe bender as well as the main interface portion, where you get to control the thing. This step is called the *analysis.*

Next, you begin carefully designing the invention but not actually building it. This is the meat of your work, where you draw diagrams of what you'll be building and how the different parts work out. You draw how your particular version of the relativistic universe bender works and the parts involved in it as well as all the other major components of the system. This is the *design* step.

Then you build, or *implement,* the thing. This is the fun part, where you go into the shop and start hammering and pounding and defying gravity to build the device! And of course, this step is called the *implementation.*

But you're not finished yet; finally, you have to *test* it. For this, you pay off the guy next door to take a ride in your time machine to see whether it works. If not, he can report back to you and let you know what went wrong. (Assuming that he makes it back.)

Now this is all good, but some issues can come up that these basic five steps don't handle. For example, many people who try building a large software system quickly discover the chicken-and-egg syndrome. The problem is this: If we're in the middle of the analysis workflow and we're supposed to be getting our rough classes down, how can we possibly know all the classes we're going to need until we get down into the code and start writing the thing?

For this reason, many people have the attitude *skip engineering and just code the stupid thing!* But just imagine what your time warp device would be like if you tried to build it without planning it. After you get the thing completely built (more or less), do you really *trust* it? Would you take a ride in it, rather than just pay the unsuspecting neighbor? Well the same is true for software. If you just dive in and start grinding out code, racing for the finish line, how can you be sure that you covered everything? Did you miss anything? Most likely. And does what you wrote run perfectly? Doubtful.

Fortunately, there's a way to fit everything together. It uses steps called *iterations*.

Speaking iteratively

Suppose we want to build a new kind of Web browser. This Web browser will be super-smart and will just automatically know what Web site you want to go to by tapping into your brain waves. When you wake up in the morning, you will hear your ears ringing with the message of a faint distant phrase, "Where do you want to go?" You think, "Wouldn't it be fun to see the Smithsonian?" Then you walk to your computer, sit down, and first the browser brings up the site for the Smithsonian, and then it brings up a site that shows flights, hotels, rental car information, and maps to get there. Now wouldn't that be a seriously cool Web browser?

So, being a good engineer, you follow the formal steps of building it. You draw your requirements, and you even interview your friends to see what ideas they have about such an amazing work of software. Then you analyze the different parts and come up with the functionality of the software, and you even draw some sample screens. Next, you move into the design work-flow, fleshing out the basic classes you built in the analysis workflow. And finally, you begin coding. You code for weeks, when suddenly — WHAM! — you discover that something is *seriously* wrong: You completely forgot that you need to write a portion of the software that does the grunt work of connecting to the Internet, then to a specific site, anddownloading the appropriate Web page. In effect, you failed to consider the low-level *communications portion* of your super-cool program. And while ruminating over this problem, you also start to think of some other things you failed to consider earlier: After you receive the Web page, are you going to draw it on the screen, or are you going to buy some C++ library that will display it in a window for you? The latter would make your life easier, but regardless, you had not considered this.

That's when you get frustrated and start considering that position your cousin offered you to be a mime out in front of City Hall downtown, drawing customers in to buy hotdogs from your cousin's hotdog stand in front of the Hall of Justice.

What exactly happened? Here's what happened:

1. You didn't realize until coding time that the display part of the browser, the part that shows the Web page on the screen, would be extremely complicated and might require the purchase of a library that displays the browser pages for you.

2. You didn't even consider that you would need a low-level communications system. Or did you? Maybe Windows already provides it. But either way, you hadn't thought of that during the analysis or design workflow.

As you dwell on these problems, you notice more *bad things*. For starters, if you decide to do the low-level communications system, do you make it its own library that you could potentially use in other programs? Or do you buy a library? Or is one already available on the computer? You've heard that Windows has such things built-in, but you're not sure.

So you know *what* happened, but *why* did it happen? Finally, you put your finger on it: It's another chicken-and-egg syndrome, and it goes like this: How could you have known you needed a low-level communications system until you finally started coding the thing? Yet, you needed that information while you were in the analysis and design workflows, before you started coding it! In effect, which comes first, the chicken (the analysis and design) or the egg (the realization that you need a low-level communications system)?

Although this might sound horribly apocryphal, it happens all the time in the software world. If you want to see tempers flare, visit some software engineers when such an abysmal situation arises.

Well, we think we've made our point, but before you rush off to the psychiatrist for a nice, big supply of antidepressants, fear not: The Unified Process is here to save the day!

The designers of the Unified Process knew well that these problems occur. And thus, they made a set of higher-level processes called *phases,* and put the five workflows inside these higher levels. During each phase, you cycle through several of the five workflows. Then when you're finished, you can cycle through them again, or you can move on to the next phase. And you once again cycle through several of the five workflows.

The idea is that each time you cycle through several of the workflows, you finish an *iteration*.

Phasing in and out

The Unified Process consists of four main phases. In each phase, you focus on various workflows, such as analysis or design, but you are free to move forward to later workflows. The only catch is that, although you can start and stop at any workflow, you must complete all the workflows in between for a single iteration. For example, you can't jump from analysis to test; you must first do analysis, then design, then implementation, and finally test. Here are the phases of the Unified Process:

✦ **Inception:** During this phase, you determine the objectives of your software.

✦ **Elaboration:** In this phase, you analyze and design your software.

✦ **Construction:** This is when you focus primarily on coding the software.

✦ **Transition:** This final phase is when you deliver the software. For retail software, this means sending it to the disc duplicators and packagers; for in-house software, it means shipping it to the groups who will be using it.

And here's the really great part: Each of these four phases can be a whole set of workflows: Requirements, analysis, design, implementation, and testing. *But how can that be, my dear friend*, you ask? It goes like this: In the inception phase, you gather requirements and go through the process of getting some basic analysis and design down. And if need be, you even do some rough prototypes of the software, where you basically play around and try out some things. In effect, you do a basic coding (implementation). And yes, you might even spend a little time testing it. But you're not building a full-scale software system, by any means! You're just doing pieces and parts and parts and pieces. But more so, you're doing a *proof of concept* just to see if you think, as a professional engineer, this idea is going to fly. And undoubtedly, you will run into some issues that the original requirements failed to take into account.

For example, suppose that you're going to build a word processor program that beats Microsoft Word hands down. Now, if you have used Microsoft Word and opened up a really big document (like several hundred pages), you may have noticed something happens on occasion. Sometimes when you make a substantial change that will drastically affect the page count, such as changing the margins, Microsoft Word *repaginates*. And as it repaginates, you might find that some vital paragraphs get split, with maybe one line of text at the end of one page and the rest of the paragraph on the next page. That can create an ugly document, and thus, Microsoft Word includes a feature called *Keep paragraphs together* as an option in a dialog box.

Now if you're building a word processor, it's possible that you won't think of this hair-splitting, paragraph-splitting issue until well into the coding. So what do you do? Most likely, during one of the first two phases, after you have a basic prototype, you might notice that sometimes paragraphs are getting broken up at inconvenient places. The solution? Include an option to keep paragraphs together. And so you go back to the requirements and add a piece to the required functionality: an option for keeping paragraphs together!

Now if you're building a super-cool Web browser that specializes in mind-reading, during the inception phase you might do a basic prototype that has all the major features, even if they don't work well. But during that time, you spot something you left out: the communications system. But now you know that you need it! So you return to the analysis phase, where you can actually add it, perhaps as a component! Cool, no?

Now each time you backtrack through your workflows and change something, you begin a new iteration. Therefore, you can see that the phases are broken up into iterations, each with several of the five workflows. And you may go through several iterations within a single phase.

You don't have to get all the way to the end, to the testing workflow, before you back up. Thus, each iteration might consist of only one or two workflows.

If all this sounds a little strange, look at it this way: If you discover that you don't have something quite right, what do you do? You go back and fix it! But software engineers like to sound a bit more technical than that, so instead they say that they *begin a new iteration*.

The inception phase

The *inception phase* is the first phase, where you start getting things off the ground. During this phase, you may not make it to the point where you're coding a prototype and finding problems. But if you're building a big project, you just may make it to the point of coding a prototype. However, if you are, you will probably be writing small prototypes of only various portions of the project.

And during the inception phase, you try to do the following:

✦ **Determine whether the project is feasible.** The term *feasibility* is a word that comes up again and again, and it's primarily the result of people having great ideas but later determining that, well, frankly, those ideas are not practical or reasonable. But instead, businesses prefer the kinder, gentler term, *feasible*.

✦ **Determine the primary requirements.**

Requirements gathering is a particularly touchy issue because, during that time, people are going to want to include everything. Not only will they want the software to browse the Web, but they will also want it to inject the Web page back into your brain and also give you the ability to download it straight from your brain to your friends' brains and print a copy by just laying your finger on the printer. They want the software to do *everything*.

But thankfully, during this time, you start to map out the project, probably build some prototypes, and determine what it really *should* do. Is it feasible to transfer the pages back into the brain, or is that technology not going to come for another year or two? If not, it probably isn't feasible.

The goal in this phase is to solidify the requirements and do some basic analysis. During this time, you will get people to agree to what it is you're going to build. (These people are called *stakeholders* because they hold a big stake — like their *jobs* — in the success of this software. And when you finish writing it for them and they become millionaires, they will treat themselves to a nice, big steak.) You will also get them to agree on things such as what computers the software will run on and the software's limits. For example, can the browser read multiple people's brains or just one person's brain at a time? (That's a *limit.*) And will it run on Windows, or will it also run on Macintosh, Unix, and Linux?

And, of course, the business folks will want a bit of say in all this, too. So the goals of this phase will also include things such as a schedule and cost for the project: How soon will you have it completed, and how much will it cost the business? Will you need to hire more engineers to work on the project? And will you need to buy more computers and tools, such as compilers?

And finally at the end of this phase, you will want to have a basic architecture of the system, consisting of UML diagrams. Now these diagrams may be rough and basic, but they will provide an overall outline of the system.

The elaboration phase

During the *elaboration phase,* you solidify the functionality of your software. You use tools called *use cases* — descriptions of individual pieces of the software functionality. For example, a word processor would have use cases such as *set italic on, set italic off, print, set left-align,* and *delete a page.* The use cases are all the things you can do with the software.

Also during the elaboration phase, you develop a plan for when you build the thing. This means elaborating on the basic designs you created in the inception phase by going through more analysis and design.

Some of the major goals of the elaboration phase are to finalize the scope of the software and to incorporate any changes to the software (for example, after further inspection, you may have determined that more things were not feasible and that other parts were); to finalize the project plan, including the number of people you need and how long it will take; and to make sure the stakeholders are all happy and hunky-dory with the project.

And during the elaboration phase, you also create a first, rough-draft version of the software. Yes, you may have built some code in the inception phase, but that was just prototyping for determining feasibility. You don't use that rough code from the inception phase in the real coding. Here, however, you make a first run of coding the real program. To get there, you continue with your analysis and design, and get into coding (implementation). Of course, the software is just a rough draft, but it is more than a prototype; unlike the preceding phase, in the elaboration phase you'll be saving much of the code and reusing it for the next phase. Thus, you once again move through iterations, cycling through workflows, such as analysis, design, and implementation.

The construction phase

During the *construction phase,* you continue with the implementation. But by now, all your analysis and design should be pretty much finished. Everybody (including the famous stakeholders) agrees by now on what the software will and won't do, how much it will cost, how long it will take to build it, and how many people will work on it. But further, you have drawn up your groups of classes that you will be designing and have decided how the classes fit together and how they communicate with each other. The analysis and design is ready for prime time, and now you can focus on actually making the system work. Here you look for parts that don't quite fit together, and you fix problems to make them fit together. You make sure that your system has no major holes whereby the entire thing could come to a crashing halt under a strange, unexpected situation. In a word, you make your software *stable.*

If you were involved with computers in the early 1990s, when things were finally settling down and we were starting to see practical, real software, you probably also saw something else: little error messages that popped up called *general protection faults (GPFs)*. GPFs appeared when the program *really screwed up bad,* and the only way to fix the program was to attempt to click the Ignore button to *ignore* the error (an option that, trust us, never worked) or *abort* the program. We remember those days well because they made us start to consider job offers from distant cousins who rented beach umbrellas on the Gulf of Mexico.

Now why did these errors happen? Because the software wasn't *stable.* You managed to put the software into a situation that the programmers didn't expect, and the thing choked, coughing up a general protection fault. And why did the programmers create software that allowed this situation to occur? Because they didn't thoroughly go through the construction phase!

The construction phase includes *implementation* and *testing* workflows. You may have some analysis and design flaws, but they will be little; the main time you'll see these flaws is if you find you forgot something or need to change something in the classes. By now, you will be going through iterations of writing code, testing, testing, testing, and finally more testing. When the testers encounter errors, you go back and fix the code. Then, eventually, the testers determine that they can't find any more bugs! The day is done! You are ready to ship!

Thus, if you follow the construction phase properly, you will limit the number of operating system errors that pop up when your program goes haywire — because if you did everything correctly, it shouldn't go haywire!

If you are heading up a project where you will be using the Unified Process to design a large-scale software system, you will want to give your testers a certain amount of authority. Think of the testers as the quality assurance people. And in fact, some companies call them *Q/A engineers* instead of testers. Your testers shouldn't allow your company to put its name on the software until they say it *works*. This has multiple benefits because it allows the Q/A engineers to feel a certain amount of authority, and it also puts a heavy responsibility on them, which will help ensure that they do a *thorough* job. And that will help ensure that your software is both good and stable. Sounds like a good plan to us!

The transition phase

The *transition phase* is both the happiest time and the scariest. As a software engineer, we know that this can be a frightening time because the final moment of truth has arrived: Did you and the rest of the team build a product that is actually going to work? Or is it going to get out on the customer's computer and crash and burn?

Most likely, because you did everything correctly in the first three phases, the software will run on the customer's computers. However, just because you did it right doesn't mean that you won't be anxious. But relax: If you are shipping a piece of software to one specific customer, you and the other engineers will probably be on hand that day for the big installation. It may not go perfectly at first, but in our experience most of the problems will not involve faulty software. Rather, the customer's computers will not be set up quite right. Fortunately, such problems are pretty easy to track down and fix.

But if you're shipping software that will be sold through the retail chains to potentially millions of people, the transition phase has an important step that many companies don't think of. In this final step, you choose a workday and invite all the employees who want to come in for a giant beat-up-the-software party! Yeah! They all come in, and you pass out CD-ROMs containing your software. These are copies of the CD-ROM you intend to ship, assuming that all goes well today. The employees get free pizza and soft drinks (beer isn't allowed on company property; besides you want them thinking clearly!), and they get to beat the stuffing out of your software. They install it, play with it, manipulate it, use it, fiddle with it, and do everything they can with it; and in the process, give it a pounding it will never forget. And if they encounter a problem, they let you know (politely, of course). But your personal job, on this day, is not to join them in testing the software. Your job is to get to work fixing any problems they find. Generally, they will be minor problems, and you'll be able to crank out the fixes in no time.

If you actually have a big test day like this, try to make it as exciting as possible. Free pizza, free soft drinks, maybe loud, fun music blasting, and maybe a relaxation room where people can go and goof off for a few minutes and forget about the project. Believe us, these folks will enjoy this special day if you make it exciting for them. And the result, of course, is a successful software package!

Moving Forward with UML

Although you spend much of the time on the construction phase, a lot of the brainwork is in the analysis and design phases. That's where UML comes into play. You use UML to map your classes, draw them, work with them, and design them. Therefore, for the rest of Minibook II, you find various discussions about UML and processes that usually take place during analysis and design. However, some take place during the requirements phase.

The next two chapters focus on the nine types of diagrams you use during your requirements gathering, analysis, and design. The first chapter focuses on the static diagrams, and the next chapter focuses on the dynamic diagrams.

**Book II
Chapter 2**

**Describing Your
Program with UML**

Chapter 3: Structuring Your Classes with UML

In This Chapter

✔ Drawing classes in UML

✔ Drawing inheritance and other relationships

✔ Building components with UML

✔ Deploying the software

*W*hen you use the Unified Modeling Language (UML) to design software, your diagrams have two aspects. One is *static*, and the other is *dynamic*. The static diagrams represent the things that do not change while your program is running. For example, a class does not change while the program is running. When you write the code, you write the class name, member variables, and member functions, and you notate what is private, protected, and public. After you compile the program, this information does not change; it remains static. This is in contrast to the information you represent in the dynamic diagrams, where the information can change. Dynamic diagrams include things like object creation and deletion as well as object collaborations (objects working together, or collaborating, conspiring, plotting, and scheming like good little classes).

In this chapter, we discuss the different types of static diagrams. These are

✦ **Class diagram:** A class diagram represents the different classes in your program.

✦ **Component diagram:** A component diagram represents the major parts, or components, of your program.

✦ **Deployment diagram:** A deployment diagram represents the different computers and hardware that your program will ultimately run on.

In this chapter, we talk about the UML diagrams. And although you'll rarely hear us say this, there is one thing we don't talk about much — at least, not in this chapter: We do not cover the methodology. (We cover that in Minibook II, Chapter 2.) UML is a *language* that you use to design software. A *methodology* is the process you use to design software. The process that we recommend is the Unified Process. In this chapter, we discuss the diagrams and we mention the parts of the process where you might use the diagrams. So in this chapter, you get to make lots of pretty pictures.

Drawing Classes

Like so many things around us, objects can have other objects inside of them. For instance, an alligator object could have inside it . . . well, that's probably not the best example. Rather, a printer object would have a toner cartridge inside it. These could be separate objects, each belonging to its own class. One might be the `LaserPrinter` class, and the other might be the `TonerCartridge` class.

In this sense, the two classes are connected. The connection is not by inheritance; nevertheless, they have a *relationship*.

You can take this relationship a step further. We have a container of blank, writeable CD-ROMs (or CD-Rs). The container could be an instance of class `CDROMHolder`. The items inside the container might each be an instance of class `CDR`. In this case, a single instance of `CDROMHolder` might contain several instances of `CDR`. So whereas the `LaserPrinter` instance contained a single `TonerCartridge` instance, the `CDROMHolder` contains several `CDR` instances. Another example is the class `Porsche` parked in our driveways. It contains exactly four instances of `GoodyearTire`. (Yes, we're dreaming.) And so you can see there are several possibilities here:

✦ **Exactly one instance:** An instance of a class might contain exactly one instance of another class.

✦ **Fixed amount of instances, greater than 1:** Each instance of a class might contain an exact number of instances of another class. This number does not change between instances.

✦ **Varying number of instances:** Each instance of a class might have a different number of instances of another class. This amount might vary from instance to instance, and it might even change over time for a single instance.

As for the final item, you can see that when we remove a `CDR` instance from the `CDROMHolder` instance, the number of instances the holder contains decreases by 1. Or if we put a `CDR` instance back, the holder goes up by 1. If we buy more and refill the holder, it goes up by more than 1. But with the `Porsche` that we really believe is parked outside, the number of tires stays the same.

As you analyze the classes to build your program, you might find some disagreement here: When we go in to get new tires, the car will be raised up, and the mechanics will remove the old tires, one by one, until no tires are on the car. Then they will put new ones on, one by one. Thus, the number of tires isn't fixed throughout the life of the instance. But how you build your class depends on the needs of the people using the program. It's possible that you won't need to consider that aspect and can therefore treat the number of tires as fixed. Or you may need to include the tire replacements, in which case you would not treat the number as fixed.

And here's another example: If you're writing a program for a racing game or simulator, you may want to have the ability for wrecks to occur and tires to come off the car. Then you would need to vary the tire count.

How you design your classes depends on the situation. Always assuming the same thing for a similarly named class as it appears in different programs is not practical. Some programs may require a class to be different from a class in another program, even though both classes happen to have a similar name.

Another kind of relationship is inheritance. The `LaserPrinter` class might be derived from the `Printer` class.

Inheritance can also be complex. You may have a class and also have two classes derived from it. One of these two classes might have two classes derived from it, and another might have only one. And from there, you might have no more classes derived. C++ offers great flexibility.

You can look at design issues in another way. A class is a kind of *classifier*. In this regard, you can imagine an inheritance showing different words for *kind*. One would be *class* and one would be *classifier*. Then *class* is derived from *classifier*. Another classifier is *type*, and therefore *type* would be derived from *classifier* as well. (Remember, that integers are types, for example.) So from this perspective of the *metainformation* or *metadata,* you can think of `int` as an instance of the classifier *type*. And you can think of `LaserPrinter` as an instance of the classifier *class*. And the particular printer on our desks, then, is an instance of `LaserPrinter`. This requires an abstract way of looking at things, but if you can keep up with this, you're ready for some serious class designs. That's because you'll understand how classes all fit together in the greater scheme of things.

Mapping classes with UML

You can create a UML diagram that shows several classes and their various relationships. Take a look at Figure 3-1. This figure shows three classes, `Printer`, `LaserPrinter`, and `TonerCartridge`. Pay close attention to the lines connecting these three classes. The lines are different because these classes relate to each other in different ways.

First, the line connecting `Printer` and `LaserPrinter` shows inheritance. The fat, hollow arrow points to the base class. Thus, `LaserPrinter` is derived from `Printer`.

Although you won't hear us use this term much, an opposite to the term *derived from* is *generalizes*. Thus, if `LaserPrinter` is derived from `Printer`, another way to say this is `Printer` generalizes `LaserPrinter`. The idea is that `Printer` is a general form of `LaserPrinter`, while `LaserPrinter` is a specific form of `Printer`. The reason why we prefer not to use the term *generalize* is that when you create a hierarchy of classes, you typically create the base class first. Then you derive a new class. So to us, the term *generalize* is counterintuitive. And our brains don't do well with counterintuitive ideas. (However, we should add, in all fairness, that a common way to come up with classes is by noticing similarities between two classes and then coming up with a single class to serve as a base class. So in this sense, generalization makes sense.)

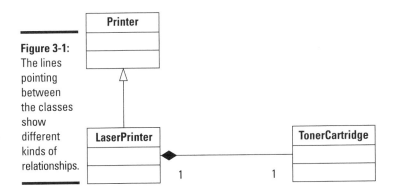

Figure 3-1: The lines pointing between the classes show different kinds of relationships.

Now look at the line connecting `LaserPrinter` to `TonerCartridge`. This is called a *composition,* and this word means that the two classes are *associated.* Therefore, each `LaserPrinter` instance will contain exactly one `TonerCartridge` instance. How you implement this later is your choice, but most likely you will include in the `LaserPrinter` class a pointer to a `TonerCartridge` instance.

In this second line, the end with the filled diamond refers to the *whole* that *contains* the *part.* Thus, `LaserPrinter` is the whole, and it contains the part `TonerCartridge`. Notice also that two numbers are below the composition line. The one on the left means that one `LaserPrinter` instance is in the association, and the one on the right means that one `TonerCartridge` instance is in the association.

Now look at Figure 3-2. Here, you have a diamond and a line, which again mean *composition.* But this time, the `Porsche` class has a 1 by it, and the `GoodyearTire` class has a 4 by it. That combination means that exactly one instance of `Porsche` will have exactly four instances of `GoodyearTire`. In other words, one car has four tires.

Next, look at Figure 3-3. Again, you see an association, but this time it is between the `Pasture` class and the `Cow` class. But in this case, the `Pasture` class has a 1 by it, while the `Cow` class has an asterisk (*) by it. The * means that any number of `Cow` instances can be associated with any single `Pasture` instance. In other words, a single pasture can have multiple cows running around on it. When you put * in the UML diagram, it means that any number of instances can be in the association, including 0. Therefore, a `Pasture` might have no cows in it (they're all in the barn getting milked), or just 1 could be in the pasture, or 100 cows could be out in the pasture, lounging around.

Figure 3-2:
The diamond and the line together mean composition.

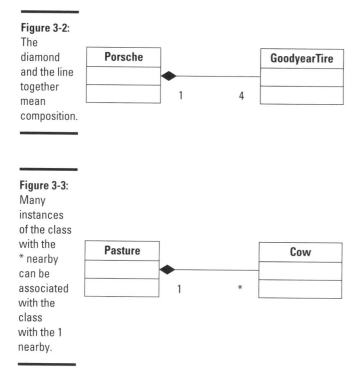

Figure 3-3:
Many instances of the class with the * nearby can be associated with the class with the 1 nearby.

Other possibilities for denoting the number of items in a relationship are also available. These possibilities are called *multiplicities*. Table 3-1 lists them.

Attributes and methods

In the object-oriented world, you're likely to hear two words many times over: attribute and method. An *attribute* is simply a member variable, and a *method* is just another name for *member function*. These two terms are the official UML terms. However, most people in C++ usually don't use them, except perhaps when drawing UML diagrams. Instead, most C++ programmers prefer the terms *member variables* and *member functions*. You can use whichever terms you prefer, and whichever terms you hear other people saying. In this book, we use *attribute* and *method* when talking specifically about UML diagrams and not referring to C++ code.

Table 3-1	Multiplicities
Symbols	*What They Mean*
1	Exactly one instance
n	Exactly *n* instances (where *n* is any number)
m..n	Anywhere from *m* to *n* instances allowed; examples are 0..1 or 1..10
*	Any number of instances, including 0
0..*	Any number of instances, including 0.(same as *)

For example, if you have two classes, one called Vacuum and another called ExtensionTube, and you see a 1 on the side with the Vacuum and a 1..4 on the side of the ExtensionTube, that means for each (1) instance of Vacuum, you can have anywhere from one to four (1..4) instances of ExtensionTube.

But wait. We thought these class diagrams were supposed to be static, not dynamic! And that's true: They are still static diagrams, although the line between static and dynamic is a little blurred. We could go into a big philosophical explanation about why class diagrams are indeed static (for example, you write a class that contains a single array, and that does not change), but instead, let us say this: Just consider a class diagram to be static, and recognize that some blurry distinctions exist. It's not a big deal.

Inheriting in UML

If you want to specify inheritance in UML, you simply draw an arrow from the derived class up to the base class and don't fill in the arrow. But you can show other types of inheritance with UML.

If you want to specify that a base class has abstract virtual functions, you specify those in the class using italics. For example, in Figure 3-4 we have a base class called Person. This is an abstract class because it contains an abstract virtual function, work. The function is *abstract virtual* because it is in italics. (And thus, the class itself is virtual. Remember that a class that has at least one abstract virtual function is therefore itself abstract.)

The two classes derived from Person, BankRobber and MiddleManager (we just thought those made for an interesting combination), each override the work function. Therefore, they are *not* abstract. And thus, you can create instances of BankRobber and MiddleManager.

You may have noticed that, so far, we have not mentioned a way to specify a virtual function in UML. You can specify a member function as abstract, but what about just plain old virtual? You can't. The virtual keyword is unique to C++, and the word simply means that you can override a function. So how do you specify virtual? Many CASE tools include an option in the model that lets you specify a member function as virtual.

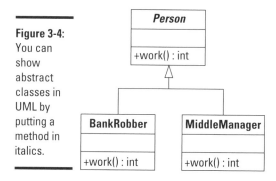

Aggregating and composing classes

When you associate two classes but not by inheritance, you can do it in two common ways: composition and aggregation. Consider the `LaserPrinter` class and its association with the `TonerCartridge` class. A toner cartridge is a fundamental part of a laser printer, but a toner cartridge can't be inside more than one laser printer at a time. This is composition. Think of *composition* as a very strong bond between two objects.

Aggregation, on the other hand, refers to two objects that are more loosely connected. In an office, you may find hundreds of computers and a dozen or so laser printers. The laser printers can function on their own, and they interact with many different computers. Meanwhile, the computers can each interact with many different laser printers. This is a much looser connection; this is aggregation.

But this does *not* imply composition is only for one-to-one relationships, and aggregation is for many-to-many. Instead, composition simply means a much stronger, tighter relationship. A toner cartridge is an intimate *part* of a printer and therefore is in a composition relationship. But a printer is not such a tight, important part of a computer. The computer can live without the printer, and vice versa, which suggests an aggregation.

In UML, you can distinguish the two based on the quality of the diamond. Doesn't that sound nice? However, in this case, we're talking about the diamond shape on the diagram, not an actual diagram. For composition, the diamond is filled in solid black. For aggregation, it's not filled in; it's just an outline. Figures 3-1 through 3-3 show composition. Figure 3-5 shows aggregation.

Notice that Figure 3-5 has the same classes that we put in Figure 3-3. But this time the diamond is not filled in. This means we modified the diagram to make it an aggregation rather than a composition.

Composition and attributes

A close similarity exists between a composition and an attribute. When each LaserPrinter instance has its own TonerCartridge instance, you have a choice: You can either draw a composition line between LaserPrinter and TonerCartridge, with the diamond on the side of TonerCartridge, or you can simply give the LaserPrinter class a member variable (*attribute*) of type TonerCartridge. After all, when you take the composition and write the code for the class, the composition will manifest itself in the form of a member variable. So which do you do? Really, it's up to you (but don't do both at once). But here's one rule. (And as we would like it with most rules and laws, this is not strict.) If you have a common class that you use throughout your program (one that you might think of as a utility class) and it appears as a member variable in many classes, it is probably best to make it an attribute, rather than show it through a composition line, simply because it will keep your diagrams from getting cluttered.

Figure 3-5:
When the diamond is not filled in, you have an aggregation.

When you use UML, you can't have two diagrams showing two conflicting associations; thus, we can't have both Figure 3-3 and Figure 3-5 in a single UML model. Instead, we changed Figure 3-3 to show an aggregation, and we showed aggregation in Figure 3-4.

Another way to look at composition is through ownership. If it makes sense for one object to own another object, this is composition. For example, one LaserPrinter instance would have its own TonerCartridge instance. Another LaserPrinter would have a *different* TonerCartridge instance. That is, the two LaserPrinters cannot share a single TonerCartridge. Thus, you can think of each LaserPrinter instance as owning a TonerCartridge instance. In that case, you can use composition.

Building Components

When you are building software, grouping various classes together into *components* is often convenient. Ultimately, when you are developing by using C++ on Windows, a component often ends up as a Dynamic Link Library, or DLL for short. (Unpronounceable; so we just say Dee-El-El.) A *DLL* is simply a file that contains a bunch of code that other programs can use. The other programs *load* the DLL and then *call* its functions. But nothing particularly magical surrounds the DLL. It's just a bunch of compiled classes and functions stuffed into a single file. (And it's compiled; it's not source code.)

Or a component might end up in the form of something called a *static library.* A static library is much like a DLL in that it contains a bunch of code for your program to use. However, when you build your program, the linker (which is the tool that performs the link process) combines the code in the library right into your final executable file. This means that your executable file will be bigger than it would be if you link it to a DLL; but when you link to a DLL, you need to either ship the DLL with your program or make sure it's already installed in the user's program. With a static library, you don't need to worry about it. (Incidentally, if you're using a Unix system, a static library gets the .a extension, which stands for *archive*, and a dynamic library gets the .so extension, which stands for *shared object.*)

If you're doing some sophisticated programming, you could also group classes into a *component* that you will ultimately put into an ActiveX control or a COM object. (These are special kinds of libraries that run on Windows.)

Therefore, you can think of a *component* as a generic way to group classes together. Figure 3-6 shows a component. It's a box with a couple added little boxes to its left. Inside this component called `MyLibrary`, you can see that we put two classes, one called `Safe` and one called `Lock`.

Figure 3-6:
A
component
is a box with
two smaller
boxes added
to its left.

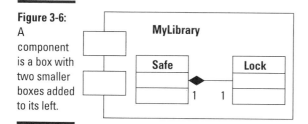

UML provides another way to notate components, which we have shown in Figure 3-7. Notice here that we drew the classes outside the component, and instead pointed dotted arrows at them from the component. We also put the word *reside* in double angle brackets. (These double angle brackets are actually called *guillemots*, and the French use them in place of double-quotes. Write it down in case somebody quizzes you on it.)

Stereotyping

Most people accept that stereotyping is a bad thing, but in UML it's actually a good thing. In UML, you can take an existing symbol, such as the component symbol, and slightly modify it to make your own customized version of the symbol. This modification process is called *stereotyping.* When you do so, you add a word inside the top of the component symbol. You put the word in double angle brackets. << and >>. (Guillemots again! One for everybody!) In fact, in UML, anytime you see a word in guillemots, you're seeing a stereotype. Just think of a *stereotype* as a modified form of the symbol, or your own version of the symbol.

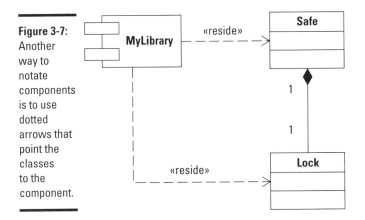

Figure 3-7:
Another way to notate components is to use dotted arrows that point the classes to the component.

When you create a component diagram, you can use stereotypes in your components. Think of it this way: Suppose you have several components that you are going to build into a DLL. Because the component symbol itself doesn't have any place to notate that it's a DLL, you can create your own *DLL component* symbol. You do this by putting a stereotype inside the component symbol. Figure 3-8 shows three components all working together. Two will ultimately be DLLs, and one will be the final executable file that calls into the DLLs. To show these, we stereotyped them all. Notice that because we're creating our own symbol, we can *reuse* the symbol. In this case, we used the DLL component symbol twice. If we have more executables, we can also reuse the executable component symbol.

CASE tools differ on how you add stereotypes. With many tools, you use a menu item; and in a dialog box that opens, you add a name for the stereotype. Then you choose the base class. Now don't confuse that with what you normally think of as a base class. We're talking about metainformation here. Look at it this way: You have a symbol, such as component. Now you're making your own specialized symbol based on component, called, for example, DLL component. This DLL component is, in a sense, derived from the component symbol. Thus, the base class in this hierarchy is the component symbol. And so, when you create a stereotype for a component, the base class is component.

Before you make your own stereotype, first check to see whether it already exists. Many stereotypes are already available in UML. For example, in the CASE tool that we're using, *executable* already exists for the component symbol.

In Figure 3-8, you can see how we used stereotypes to create a special DLL component symbol and a special executable component symbol. Notice also that we drew an arrow from the executable called SpyProgram to the two DLLs, called AccountingLibrary and MathLibrary. These arrows are dashed and have no stereotype with them. The dashed arrows mean that they depend on the two libraries. Meanwhile, the two libraries each have two classes in them. To show that the classes reside in the libraries, we used a dependency arrow (again, a dashed line), but we used stereotypes to show that these are *reside* forms of the dependencies. So again, this is a special version of the symbol, which we denote through stereotypes.

Book II
Chapter 3

Structuring Your
Classes with UML

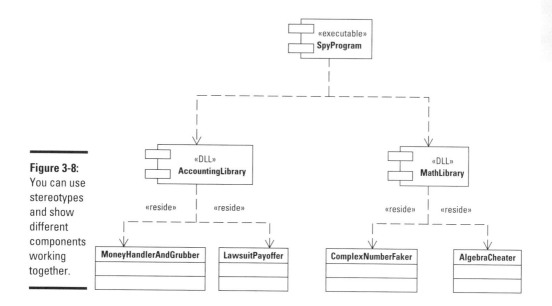

Figure 3-8:
You can use stereotypes and show different components working together.

Deploying the Software

During your designs, you can create a diagram that shows how your software will run and will be configured on the final computer system. In UML, the diagram you use is called a *deployment diagram.* This is a static diagram because the information in it does not change while the program is running.

Figure 3-9 shows an example of a deployment diagram. In this figure, we included two nodes. In a hardware system, a *node* is any computer component.

In this case, one node is a PC, and the other node is some shared drive on the network. You can see in the diagram that the shared drive contains the two DLLs. The executable itself, however, resides on the user's PC. Note also that the components have connections between them because we used the same CASE model that we used in Figure 3-8. When we added the components to the two nodes, the CASE tool automatically drew the lines to connect them.

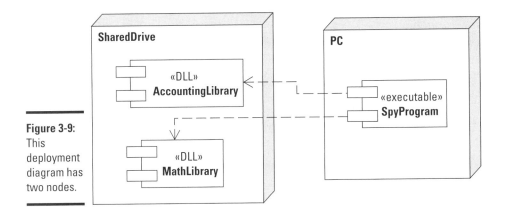

Figure 3-9:
This deployment diagram has two nodes.

One particularly fun thing about deployment diagrams is that the UML standard lets you make your own versions of the symbols. However, this creative capability goes beyond just stereotyping, where you add a word inside those funny angle brackets. Instead, you can actually use clip art! Yes, clip art! Take a peek at Figure 3-10 to see an example.

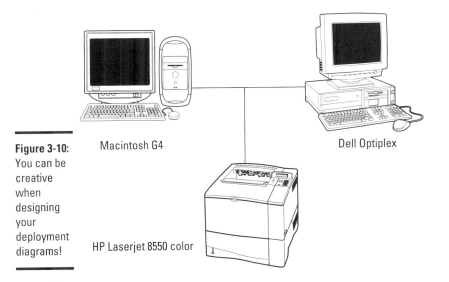

Figure 3-10:
You can be creative when designing your deployment diagrams!

Macintosh G4

Dell Optiplex

HP Laserjet 8550 color

Chapter 4: Demonstrating Behavior with UML

In This Chapter

✔ Drawing out objects in UML

✔ Expanding use cases into use case diagrams

✔ Ordering steps with sequence diagrams

✔ Showing how objects collaborate

✔ Noting the flow of activities

✔ Stating the different states of an object

*I*n this chapter, we take you through the five dynamic diagrams in UML. These are the diagrams that show how objects work together and change over time. Some of them you may find more useful than others, and that's fine — you don't have to use all the diagrams you see in this chapter. You are free to use those that you find the most useful.

Drawing Objects

In UML, you can draw class diagrams that show the classes in your system, or you can get right down to it and draw an *object diagram,* which contains actual instances or objects. Because you are drawing instances, you might have multiple objects of a single class on a single object diagram.

When you draw objects on a UML diagram, they look pretty much the same as class diagrams, but with one important difference: For an object, the name at the top of the rectangle is underlined. With classes, the name is not underlined. Be sure to remember this difference so your diagrams don't confuse other people. Probably the best way to explore an object diagram is to see it compared to a class diagram. Take a peek at Figure 4-1, and you can see a class diagram at the top and an object diagram at the bottom.

Two classes are in the diagram. The names are not underlined and the two classes are related by composition. The composition is *one-to-many* — one Pasture instance to multiple Cow instances. In effect, instances of the Pasture class contain 0 or more instances of Cow. We included some attributes for each class.

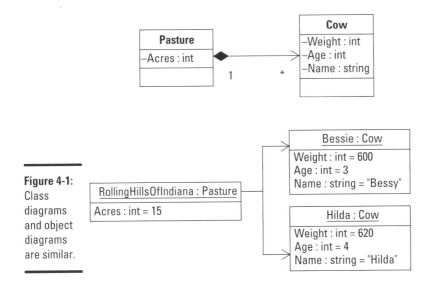

Figure 4-1:
Class
diagrams
and object
diagrams
are similar.

The lower half of the diagram shows instances of the classes. When you program, you sometimes give a name to an instance in the way of a variable name. Or you may be using a language that allows its objects to be named. (C++ does not allow this; you have to use a variable name.) In the object diagram, we named the instances. At the top of each rectangle is an underlined name, a colon, and the class type. Thus, RollingHillsOfIndiana is an instance of type Pasture. Bessie is an instance of type Cow, and Hilda is also an instance of type Cow. Inside the object boxes, we also gave values to the member variables (or attributes). For these, the name goes first, then a colon, then the type, just as in the class symbols. But then you see an equal sign and a value. (Because these are actual instances of the class, they can have values for the member variables.)

Look carefully at the line connecting the RollingHillsOfIndiana object to the Bessie and Hilda objects (as well as the line connecting the two classes). You can see an arrow pointing to each of the Cow instances but not to the Pasture instance. Thus, the Pasture instance contains a pointer to each Cow instance but not vice versa. That means the Cow instances don't know about the Pasture instances. That is, the Cow instance does not contain a member variable that points to the Pasture instance. You can see this is the case also with the class diagram, because an arrow is pointing to the Cow class.

If you want both instances to *know about* each other, you simply remove the arrows and use just lines. This change is called a *bidirectional association*. When you have an arrow, the arrow means that the relationship is unidirectional. In the case of Pasture and Cow, the arrow means that the Pasture instance can call methods in the Cow instance but not vice versa. The Cow instances are not aware of the Pasture instance.

Sometimes, people really like to show that the objects are instances of the class by drawing a dashed arrow from the instance to the class and adding the <<instantiate>> stereotype. When you have lots of instances, this technique can make for a messy diagram, but if you have only one instance per class, you can easily show it in the diagram. We did just that in Figure 4-2. Notice that the word <<instantiate>> is present and the arrow points to the class. To us, this setup seems a little backward, but lots of stuff seems backwards in the world of computers, so we're not surprised.

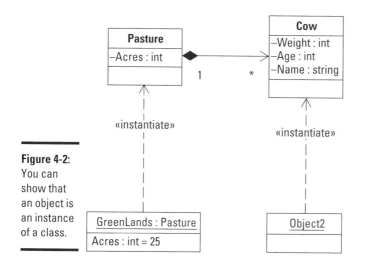

Figure 4-2:
You can
show that
an object is
an instance
of a class.

Casing Out the Use Cases

Talk about disagreement. People have argued and bickered about use cases for years. The term *use case* (pronounced with a soft *s*, as in *use,* because *use* is a noun here) refers to one single case or instance of functionality in your program. Most programs have many, many things you can do with them; for example, a Web browser enables you to click the Go button to go to a Web address that you typed into a box; or it enables you to click a link to go to a page. These two things are each a single use case.

Use cases have become an important aspect in modeling software. So why the contention? Because use cases focus on the functions (that is, verbs!) of a software package, while objects focus on the things, or nouns. So it would make sense by that argument that use cases have no big place in object-oriented analysis and design. However, the flaw in this argument is in saying that object-oriented means you focus only on the nouns. It's true that it's oriented to the objects, but that doesn't mean you ignore or have a disdain for verbs. Personally, we like verbs. Life without verbs boring. Talking difficult with no verbs. Me car grocery store.

And the same is true with object-oriented programming. Although we focus our building around the objects, we still have functions, which are verbs. And we still have functionality. And we can organize and group the functionality, such as through menus or through dialog boxes.

And so, when we design software, one thing we do is go through and list all the use cases we can think of for the software. This often takes place in the analysis phase.

Figure 4-3 shows an example of a use case diagram. The actual use cases are the oval shapes. And you certainly noticed the other goofy symbol: The stick man figure! The stick man figure is called an *actor* because it represents the user interacting with the application similar to the way an actor interacts with the audience. Yes, this is one time when we, the software engineers of the world, get to revert to our childhood roots and draw pretty pictures. In this case, we get to draw stick figures. Now, just to be crystal clear, please realize that this a unisex stick figure. It is neither a man nor a woman, or both a man and a woman. Thus, we don't need to draw a skirt to show a woman as so many other fields do. Here, we believe all people are, at heart, all the same. Thus, we draw our stick figures all the same.

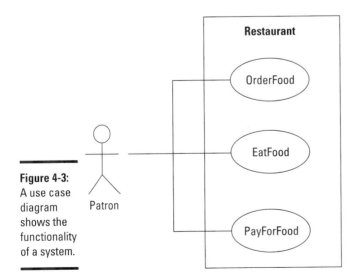

Figure 4-3:
A use case diagram shows the functionality of a system.

Now, if you look at Figure 4-3, you can see that the use cases each have names. These are the things that the user can do with the *system*. (We use the word *system* to mean a collection of software that you're building.) The system in this example is called `Restaurant`.

Use case: Order food

Ordering food is a handy and tasty example of how events flow in a use case:

ID: UC1000

Actors: Patron

Preconditions: Patron must be seated at the table with a napkin covering the shirt. Hands must be clean.

Flow of events:

1. The patron waits for the server to arrive.

2. When the server arrives, the patron orders the food.

3. The server takes the order to the kitchen.

4. The cook prepares the food.

5. The server delivers the food to the table.

6. The patron eats the food.

Postconditions: The patron has a full stomach and is ready to pay for the food.

For some steps, you may have what amounts to an `if-then-else` block in your code. You can notate this in different ways, but here's a handy one: The flow of events goes beyond Step 6, like this:

7. The server asks the patron whether he or she will be having dessert.

8. If the patron wants dessert.

    8.1. The patron looks at the dessert menu.

    8.2. The patron chooses a dessert.

    8.3. The server fetches the dessert.

    8.4 The patron eats the dessert.

9. else

    9.1 The server relaxes for a moment, dreaming about what life could have been like if he or she had only had dessert.

Steps 1 through 9 can easily be a function or an algorithm. You can also use `for` loops and `while` loops by putting the `for` or `while` condition and following it with steps:

    9.2 For each dessert on the menu the patron imagines.

        9.2.1 Eating one single bite.

        9.2.2 Contemplating the flavor.

        9.2.3 Devouring the rest.

The stick figure guy (or gal) represents the *user* of the system. In the case of a word processor, that could be you sitting there using it, or it could be another human. Either way, it represents a user, a human being. The lines point to the different use cases the user has access to.

Expanding use cases

After you draw your use cases on the diagrams, you can define what they do on paper. The way you do this is to write the information in a single-column table, with each row specifying different information about the use case. This information includes:

✦ **Name:** The name of the use case as you described it in the diagram.

✦ **Unique Identifier:** Some people like to include a special code, such as UC (which stands for use case), followed by a number, as in UC1000.

✦ **Actors:** The actors involved with the use case.

✦ **Preconditions:** The situation that must exist before the use case can begin to operate.

✦ **Flow of events:** A step-by-step flow of the events that take place when the use case *runs*.

✦ **Postconditions:** The situation that will exist after the use case runs.

A sample use case makes an exclusive guest appearance in a nearby sidebar.

Matching use cases and requirements

When you are designing software, making sure that every requirement has at least one use case associated with it is a good idea. *Remember:* The requirements describe what the software does.

Table 4-1 shows an example of how to ensure that each requirement has at least one associated use case. Remember that you normally give each use case an identifier (the need for the identifier increases as project complexity increases). You can do the same with the requirements.

Table 4-1	Sample Requirements			
	UC1	*UC2*	*UC3*	*UC4*
REQ1	✓	✓		
REQ2	✓			
REQ3			✓	
REQ4			✓	✓

In this grid, each requirement has at least one use case associated with it. Further, each use case satisfies at least one requirement. If a requirement was missing, you would need to add a use case. If you have a use case that does not satisfy a requirement, you must make a decision: Either you discovered a new use case and, therefore, a new requirement, and you need to add that requirement; or you went overboard and added an unnecessary feature, in which case you can eliminate the use case.

Sequence Diagrams

When you are working with objects, showing a time sequence of how objects interact with each other is helpful. You can do this by using a sequence diagram. A sequence diagram can be a little mind-boggling when you first look at it (at least it was for us), but after you understand the layout, a sequence diagram makes more sense. In a *sequence diagram*

✦ Time moves from top to bottom. In effect, things positioned higher on the diagram happen earlier; things positioned lower happen later.

✦ Objects are drawn side by side, left to right.

✦ When one object *sends a message to* (calls a member function of) another object, you show this as a solid arrow with a filled-in arrowhead. Above the arrow, you put the name of the function (or the name of the message if you prefer that jargon).

Refer to Figure 4-3 for a moment, and you can see how this sequencing business works. We took the use case shown in that figure and built a sequence diagram from it. Note, however, that we did not include the added part about the dessert. We will add that shortly, because the process of adding it is a bit more complex. Also, note that to build this sequence diagram, we first had to come up with some classes. They are as follows:

✦ Server: This is a class whose instances receive an order, send it to a Cook instance for preparation, and then take the order and deliver it to the patron.

✦ Cook: This is a class that can receive an order and prepare it.

✦ Food: This is a class that represents, well, food!

Notice that we did not create a class for the Patron. That's because the Patron is outside the system and not a part of it. The Patron, instead, *uses* the system.

Figure 4-4 is an example of a sequence diagram. Remember, the stuff at the top takes place earlier in time, and as you move your eyes down the diagram, you are advancing forward in time. And you can even move your eyes up on the diagram, although be careful because you don't want to go back in time and relive your past!

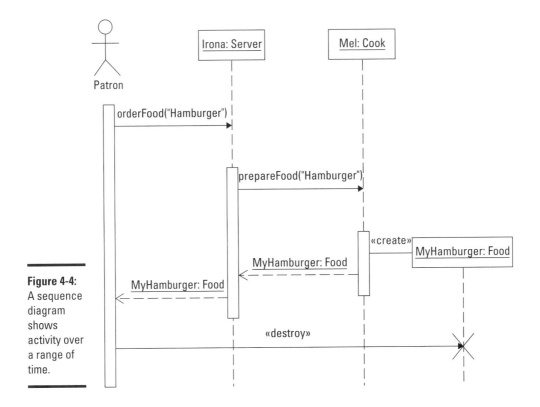

Figure 4-4:
A sequence
diagram
shows
activity over
a range of
time.

Here's how this diagram works. The objects are listed at the top, along with
the user who initiates the use case. Below the objects are dashed lines that
represent the lifeline of the object. The top of the lifeline represents the time
the object is created. For example, if you create an object in the middle of a
use case, you would begin the object at that time position (that is, vertical
position) on the use case. Here, most of our objects existed before the use
case (because they're at the top of the diagram) and their lifeline stretches
to the bottom of the diagram; it does not end. That means the objects are
around for the full duration of the use case. However, one object, the Food
instance, comes to life in the middle of the use case.

Now, notice that a *bar* (a tall, thin rectangle) replaces the lifeline in some
places. This is where the object has *focus* in the use case. Or you can say the
object is *active*. Before and after, the object is sitting there, but this use case
isn't actually using the object. Although the bar is present, the use case is
using the object.

Finally, look at the horizontal arrows. This is where an object to the left calls a member function in an object to the right. The first arrow has a label `orderFood("Hamburger")`. This arrow starts on the bar for the user (called `Patron`) and points to the `Server` object called `Irona`. In effect, the user calls the `orderFood` member function in the `Server` object. Then right under that, the `Server` lifeline becomes a bar, which means it's active. The `Server` then calls `prepareFood("Hamburger")` for the `Cook` object called `Mel`.

When the `Mel` object receives the `prepareFood("Hamburger")` message, it creates a new instance of `Food`. Notice that the arrow to the right of the `Mel` lifeline calls a function in the `Food` object, but this is not a typical function. Instead, it's a stereotype with the word `create` in double angle brackets. This means that the `Mel` object creates a new instance of `Food` and calls it `MyHamburger`. Because the object was just created, its lifeline begins midway down the diagram.

Then the returns follow: The `Cook` object returns an object called `MyHamburger` (which is of class `Food`). The `Server` object receives this and returns it back to the user.

Now think about this: How can the user call a function? A user can do it through a *user interface,* such as a window on the screen with buttons on it or perhaps a menu item. That is, the user interface is the part that you see on the screen! And the name makes sense: It's the interface to the program for the user. Thus, you have a deeply philosophical concept here: Through the screen, keyboard, and mouse, you are interfacing with the computer program, calling member functions. Pretty good!

And finally, notice that the user deletes the object. How can this be? Remember that this use case has a function that the user called. That function then calls destroy. The object's lifeline ends with the deletion, and you see a big X to show that the line ends.

When an object on a sequence diagram calls a member function of an object to the right, a common term for this process is that the first object is *sending a message* to the second object. If you are using a tool to help you draw UML diagrams, the arrows might be called something like *message* arrows.

Notating sequence diagrams

When you create a sequence diagram, you are free to put some notes to the left of the sequence diagram. These notes on the left describe what the thing does. Figure 4-5 shows an example of this.

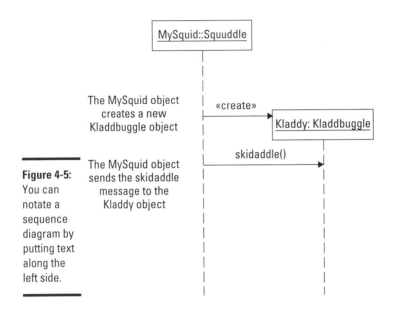

Figure 4-5:
You can notate a sequence diagram by putting text along the left side.

Looping and comparing in sequence diagrams

To show a loop (such as a *for loop* or a *while loop*) in a sequence diagram, you enclose part of your sequence diagram in a rectangle and put the loop condition immediately below the rectangle. You can see this in Figure 4-6, where we put the rectangle around the point when the Server object calls the payBill method on the CashRegister object.

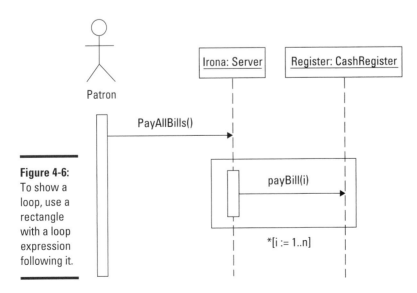

Figure 4-6:
To show a loop, use a rectangle with a loop expression following it.

TIP

Believe it or not, UML does not have a standard syntax for specifying a loop condition beyond the fact that you must start it with an asterisk. However, a common approach is to use notation, such as i := 1..5, which means the loop counter i increases from 1 to 5. Thus, there are five iterations; in the first, i is 1; in the second, i is 2; and so on; and in the final i is 5. So you can see in Figure 4-6 that Patron sends a message to the Server to pay for all the meals in the restaurant. (Apparently this Patron just won the lottery or something.) The Server then goes to the CashRegister object and processes all the orders.

Now suppose in our little restaurant model that the restaurant is out of a particular food, such as french fries. In that case, the Server object might go back and ask the cook if any french fries are still available. If they are, the Server will request that they be included in the order. The Server will then return the order of fries to the Patron; otherwise the Server will send a message back to the Patron (that is, *return* a message, in computerese) that there are no more fries. You can show this as we did in Figure 4-7.

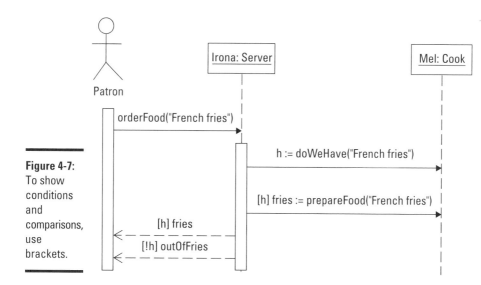

Figure 4-7:
To show
conditions
and
comparisons,
use
brackets.

Look at how this works. First, the Server object sends the message doWeHave("French fries") to the Cook object. (We simplified this part of the diagram by not showing how the Cook object does this.) The result of this comes back as either true or false, which we store in the h symbol. Then, in the next step, the Server calls prepareFood only if h is true. That's what the brackets with the h in them mean.

Colons in assignment statements?

In UML, you often see an assignment state-ment with a colon, rather than just an equals sign. For example, you might see `index :=` `10`. Why the colon? Well, it turns out that this syntax is borrowed from some languages *other than* C and C++. Lucky us. C++ is probably the single most popular language on the planet, and the designers of UML used another language for some of its syntax. In the two languages, Pascal (which is the underlying language for a programming tool called Delphi) and Ada (which is *supposedly* used a lot by the military), the colon always precedes the equals sign in an assignment statement. And to make matters more complicated, these two languages also use a single equals sign for comparison. C++, of course, uses two equals signs for a compar-ison. Maybe someday we'll have a standard computer programming language. Until then, life is messy in the programming world. But we'll survive.

Finally, if h is true, the `Server` object returns the order of fries in the form of a new `Food` object. This is the return line that starts with `[h]`, which means that h is true. (We didn't show the process of the `Cook` creating the `Food` object; you can see that kind of thing in Figure 4-3.) But if h is not true, the `Server` object returns a symbol that represents there are no more french fries. (You will probably make this symbol an `enum` in C++, or perhaps a 0.)

At this point, we're actually getting into some local variable names, such as the value of whether there are french fries. However, most CASE tools aren't sophisticated enough to take a sequence diagram such as this and generate C++ code that works. Most can generate some basic code, and some let you type the code through the CASE tool. You will most likely take this diagram and use it as a guide to write your own code. Designing it through the diagram is a lot easier than with the code. And other people — those who *don't program* — can get a basic idea of the flow of events by looking at the sequence diagram. It's less likely that they would understand code. That way, the people called *stakeholders* (those who run the company and eat lots of steak) can look at the diagram and tell you if you're building what they want you to build.

As you refine your sequence diagrams, you may discover member functions that you didn't include in a class, or you might even discover new classes. As we built the sequence diagrams in this section, we discovered that we didn't have methods for paying the bills. And so we ended up adding a `CashRegister` object and some methods in various objects for paying the bills. We also discovered that we needed some methods for finding out whether a certain food item existed. As you can see, we *refined* the software system as we worked on these diagrams. And that's the goal of UML: To refine it and get it all right! If you're curious, check out Figure 4-8, which is the updated class diagram we created as we were working on these sequence diagrams.

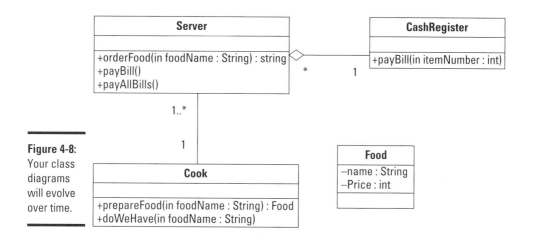

Figure 4-8:
Your class diagrams will evolve over time.

Collaboration Diagrams

Collaboration diagrams are similar to sequence diagrams, but they don't show the time ordering. The idea is that they give an overview of the interactions between the diagrams. Frankly, we always opt for sequence diagrams and tend to skip the collaboration diagram; in many ways, a sequence diagram is a type of collaboration diagram that has the benefit of showing a time sequence. However, if you don't want to show time sequence and instead want to focus on interactions between the objects, you can use a collaboration diagram.

If you look back at Figure 4-7, earlier in this chapter, you can see an example of a sequence diagram. Now in Figure 4-9, we have the same information, but it is in the form of a collaboration diagram.

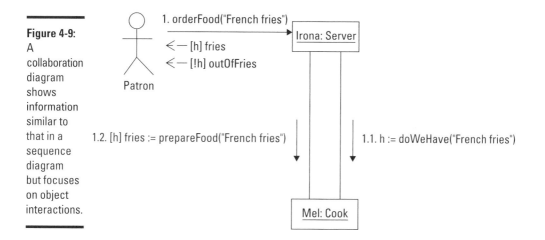

Figure 4-9:
A collaboration diagram shows information similar to that in a sequence diagram but focuses on object interactions.

In Figure 4-9, no time sequence is given. The diagram focuses on the interactions between the objects and between the user and the objects. However, we did give a basic notion of steps by numbering the messages (1, 1.1, and 1.2). First, the user sends a message to the `Server` object; second, the `Server` asks the `Cook` if there are more fries. And third, if there are, the `Server` puts in the order for the fries.

We didn't just number these things 1, 2, 3. We started with 1, then 1.1, and then 1.2. The reason is that we imagine the second and third steps as being *substeps* to Step 1. Ultimately, these will be inside a single function, such as this *pseudocode* (simplified code that illustrates the basic point):

```
orderFood() {
    h = doWeHave("French fries")
    if (h) {
        fries = prepareFood("French fries")
        return fries
    }
    else {
        return outOfFries
    }
}
```

This is almost C++ code, and it would be easy to change it to real C++ code (such as declaring the variables and making this an actual member function with a return type and a parameter list). This is partly how we envision the collaboration diagram looking in C++ code; the calls to `doWeHave` and `prepareFood` are inside the code for `orderFood`. And thus, they get substep numbers 1.1 and 1.2 (like an outline) rather than their own Steps 2 and 3.

Activity Diagrams

An *activity diagram* is essentially a flowchart. It shows a sequence of steps. Yes, so does a sequence diagram and, in some senses, a collaboration diagram. However, there's a slight difference: You normally use a sequence diagram to show the steps in a use case. You can use an activity diagram to show individual parts of a sequence diagram, such as a single member function.

The idea behind an activity diagram is that it shows the *lowest level* of steps possible. In effect, the steps (*activities*) in an activity diagram can't be divided into substeps. The word that computer people like here is that the activities are *atomic* and cannot be divided, as people once believed atoms could not be divided. (But this time the theory will stick.)

Figure 4-10 shows an example of an activity diagram. The diagram shows the starting point with a filled-in circle (in this case, at the top of the diagram). Then an arrow points to the first activity (Eat first bite), which is inside an oval. Next comes a decision. Unlike traditional flowcharting, you do not put any text inside the decision. Instead, you show arrows extending away from the diamond; beside them, you put a Boolean condition inside brackets. Or you can put the word *else* for all other cases. Thus, in this diagram, if the food is yummy, you can move down to the oval on the lower right (`Eat another bite`). Otherwise you move down to the oval on the lower left (`Throw food away`).

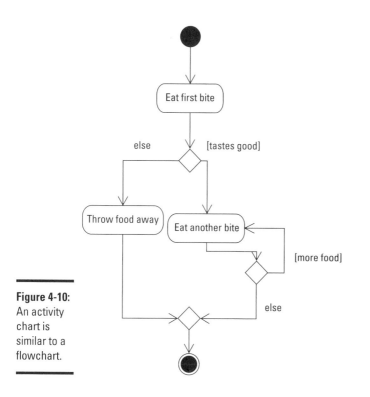

Figure 4-10:
An activity
chart is
similar to a
flowchart.

We followed the `Eat another bite` activity with a decision. If the condition `[more food]` is true, you go back to `Eat another bite`. Otherwise you move to the final diamond.

The final diamond shows all the steps coming together. A diamond represents a return from a decision, where the different paths come back together. We did not put any conditions around it. We show two arrows going in but only one coming out.

And then the final thing is a filled circle with a border around it. That represents the *final state* or, more simply put, the end of the activity diagram.

Sometimes, you might want your activity diagram to include a step that is not atomic; you might want to show that you perform a complex step next, but you just give the name of the step without showing all the steps. Such a step is called a *subactivity.* A subactivity is not atomic, and it can be broken up into further subactivities. In Figure 4-11, we created a subactivity called `Eat Food`. We don't show the detailed steps on eating the food; we just point out that the computer must perform the function called `Eat Food`. To make this clear, we used a slightly different diagram. It's an oval with two ovals inside, with one pointing up to the other.

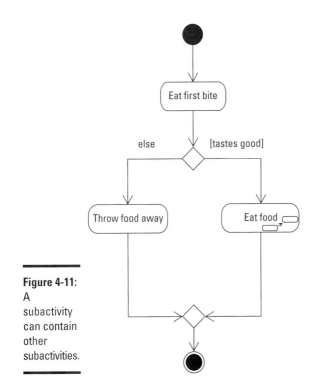

Figure 4-11:
A subactivity can contain other subactivities.

State Diagrams

A *state diagram* shows the different states in which an object can live. We don't mean Nebraska or California, but a state such as this collection:

✦ The food name is `Hamburger`.

✦ The burger's top bun is present (or `true`).

✦ The burger's meat is present (or `true`).

✦ The burger's bottom bun is present (or `true`).

✦ The food is accompanied by ketchup and mustard.

✦ There are ten remaining bites.

These items together all show the current state of an object. An object's *state* is represented by the values in the member variables, what function the object is presently running (if any), and how it is currently associated with other objects. For example, this `Hamburger` object might be in the hands of the `Server` and not the `Patron`. That is one part of the object's current state.

A state diagram is similar to an activity diagram. A state diagram shows flow from state to state. But it also shows how to get from one state to the next.

States on a diagram are rounded rectangles (rectangles with rounded corners).

We show a basic state diagram in Figure 4-12. The burger has two states: `Hamburger present` (meaning it's all there) and `Bottom-only Burger` (meaning the top bun has been eaten away by somebody or something). These two states are shown in rounded rectangles, and their names are present.

Book II
Chapter 4

Demonstrating
Behavior with UML

Figure 4-12:
A state diagram shows the different states an object can be in.

How does the burger transform from one state to the next? In the diagram, you can see an arrow pointing from one state, `Hamburger present`, to the next, `Bottom-only Burger`. That arrow is the only one in the diagram, which means that it's the only possible *state transition*. That is, the burger can be in the `Hamburger present` state, and next it can move to the `Bottom-only Burger` state, but not back. And the burger gets there when the situation written above the arrow takes place. Here's what that means:

1. The first portion of the text is `biteTopBun`. This is a process or activity or step that takes place.

2. The next portion is `[didn't miss]`. That's a condition. If the bite worked (and the assailant didn't miss), you get to go on to the new state.

3. To go on to the new state, you do what follows: `removeTopBun`. Of course, the biting and the removing really are one step. But in computers, we can break it up. The biting is the process of starting to remove the bun, and it's possible that the biting will fail (if you miss the bun, that is). But if the biting doesn't fail, the computer must perform the activity called `removeTopBun`.

Finally, notice how this is all divided. First is the process that takes place. Next is the condition in brackets. Then there's a slash, and finally the activity that puts the object in the next state appears. Thus the state diagram shows an entire transition between two states.

Chapter 5: Modeling Your Programs with UML

In This Chapter

✔ Using some UML extras, such as packages, notes, and tags

✔ Taking advantage of the freedom UML gives you

✔ Creating C++ enumerations in UML

✔ Using static members in UML

✔ Notating templates with UML

*I*n this chapter, we give you some miscellaneous details about using UML. After you understand how to use the diagrams and have a feel for a methodology or process, read this chapter for interesting details about UML. For example, you can use several symbols in any of your diagrams to make them more descriptive; we discuss those here. We also talk about how to show various C++ features in UML.

Using UML Goodies

The UML specification is huge. We're talking *big*. So in this section we give you some additional information you can use when creating UML diagrams.

Packaging your symbols

In computer programming, a common term is *namespace*. When you have functions and classes and variables, you can put them into their own namespace, which is nothing more than just a grouping. When you do so, the names of the functions, classes, and variables must be unique within the namespace. But if you create another namespace, you can reuse any of the names from the other namespace. In technical terms, *identifiers* must be unique *within a namespace*.

To make this clear, let us show you a C++ example. In C++, you can create a namespace by using none other than the `namespace` keyword. Have a gander at Listing 5-1 — and bear in mind that `using namespace std;` line you see in each of these programs, too.

Listing 5-1: Using the Namespace Keyword to Create a Namespace in C++

```cpp
#include <iostream>

using namespace std;

namespace Work
{
    int FavoriteNumber;

    class Info
    {
    public:
        string CompanyName;
        string Position;
    };

    void DoStuff()
    {
        cout << "Doing some work!" << endl;
    }
}

namespace Play
{
    int FavoriteNumber;

    class Info
    {
    public:
        string FullName;
        string Hobby;
    };

    void DoStuff()
    {
        cout << "Having fun!" << endl;
    }
}

int main()
{
    // Work stuff
    Work::FavoriteNumber = 7;
    Work::Info WorkInformation;
    WorkInformation.CompanyName = "Spaceley Sprockets";
    WorkInformation.Position = "Worker";
    Work::DoStuff();

    // Play stuff
    Play::FavoriteNumber = 13;
    Play::Info PlayInformation;
    PlayInformation.FullName = "George Jetson";
    PlayInformation.Hobby = "Playing with the dog";
    Play::DoStuff();

    return 0;
}
```

In Listing 5-1, we created two different namespaces, one called `Work` and one called `Play`. Just to prove the point, we created a global variable, a class name, and a function inside each namespace, and they are each named the same as in the other namespace. To make use of these items, down in `main` we precede them with the namespace name and two colons. So you can see we have two separate global variables:

```
Work::FavoriteNumber = 7;
Play::FavoriteNumber = 13;
```

And we created instances of two separate classes:

```
Work::Info WorkInformation;
Play::Info PlayInformation;
```

These are completely separate classes and variables; they just happen to have the same name. But they're inside their own namespaces, so this is perfectly legal. And you can see that we also called the function in each namespace. Again, we put the namespace name, two colons, and then the function name. As before, these are each separate functions; they just happen to share the same name.

Think of a namespace as a grouping mechanism. You can group related items, and it frees you from having to worry about whether the name you came up with is unique.

To keep everything neat and tidy, the designers of C++ have put all their own features, such as `cout`, in their own namespace. This namespace is called `std`, which is short for *standard*. To make use of `cout` and other standard features, you need to use the `std` namespace. This means you would normally type `std::cout` to access `cout`. However, having a lot of `cout` entries in your code can be cumbersome. To simplify access to the `std` namespace, then, you can just put `using namespace std;` near the start of your code. Then each time the compiler comes across an identifier it doesn't recognize, it follows up by checking the `std` namespace. Thus you can have `cout` without the `std::cout` before it. The compiler at first won't recognize `cout`, but then the compiler will check the `std` namespace, thus locating `cout`.

And now on to UML. In UML, you can show namespaces in your diagrams by using packages. In UML, a *package* is equivalent to a namespace in C++ and other languages. A package looks like a file folder. (Not the kind in your computer, but the kind in those wondrous and archaic things past generations of the late twentieth century called *file cabinets*.)

Figure 5-1 shows an example of a package. You can see that it's a file-folder-looking thing, and the classes are inside it. We put two packages in this diagram, one called `Work` and one called `Play`, to match the classes in Listing 5-1.

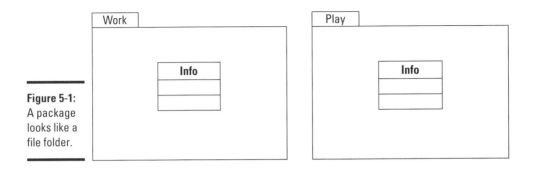

Figure 5-1:
A package
looks like a
file folder.

Different Computer-Aided Software Engineering (CASE) tools and diagramming software do packages differently. If you are using Microsoft Visio to do your diagrams, for example, its built-in UML tool does not let you draw your classes inside the package symbol. Instead, when you create a package symbol, you get a new blank page on which you put your symbols.

In UML, by default, a namespace already exists. It's called `topLevel`. If you don't explicitly put your data inside a namespace, they automatically go in the `topLevel` package.

Notating your diagrams

UML has a handy little symbol called a *note* whose only purpose is to provide comments on a UML diagram. A note is much like a comment in C++ code: It has no bearing on the actual diagrams but is rather there for the benefit of us humans and other creatures with highly evolved brains to read.

Figure 5-2 shows an example of a note. The note symbol is a sheet of paper with a folded corner, like an actual note.

Figure 5-2:
A note
contains a
comment.

When the discombobulator itself becomes discombobulated, the users will want to run the disDiscombobulate member function followed by the recombobulate member function.

Tagging your symbols

Sometimes, you want to add some extra information, such as a class diagram, directly to a symbol. Although you could put a note symbol on the page, another possibility is to put the information right into the symbol itself through a *tag* (or sometimes called a *tagged property*). A tag gets a name and

a value. For example, you might want to put a date on a symbol, such as
Date = January 1, 2010. You can notate this through a tag. Figure 5-3
shows two tags added to a class symbol and a single tag added to a
component symbol.

Figure 5-3:
You can add
tags to your
symbols.

Discombobulator
{Date = January 1, 2010,
Owner = Discombs, Inc.}
+size[1] : int

The tags in Figure 5-3 are of the format name = value, and they are
surrounded by *curly brackets*.

To have tags show up in some CASE tools, you have to make them visible
for the symbol. For example, some CASE tools have an option called
ShowProperties. Using this allows the tags to show up in the symbol.

Free to Be UML

One of the great things about UML is that it gives you a great deal of
freedom. For example, if you find a diagram you don't care to use, you don't
have to use it; you can still move though an entire software development
process or methodology. For example, some people prefer to use sequence
diagrams while staying away from collaboration diagrams. And some people
don't use state diagrams and activity diagrams. Now some purists might
complain about this, but as a software engineer, you need to do what works
best for you and your team.

Further, UML is not intended to be used just for software engineering. The
creators of UML designed it to be a general-purpose language for modeling,
and it can be used for all sorts of projects. For example, in one book, every
chapter started out with a UML activity diagram showing the flow of sections
in the book.

Of course, most people are going to use UML for software engineering,
primarily because many people outside the software field have simply never
heard of UML.

Another area where UML allows freedom is in the methodology you choose. Although this book focuses on the Unified Method, UML contains a rich set of diagrams and symbols that work with nearly any methodology.

Thanks to stereotypes, you can even add symbols to UML; so if you're using a methodology with its own symbols, you are not trapped with those built into UML. A *stereotype* is a way of creating a new symbol. Normally, you take an existing symbol and from it *derive* a new symbol that has similar but more specialized features. You put the name in the funny angle brackets, as in <<MyStereotype>>. However, there's an alternative: Instead of putting the name inside those things (called *guillemots*), you can use your own custom icon. In Figure 5-4, for example, we used a scroll symbol.

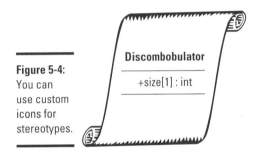

Figure 5-4:
You can use custom icons for stereotypes.

In Figure 5-4, the scroll symbol is a stereotype based on a class diagram. Because a stereotype creates a new type of symbol derived from another symbol, this is still a class, but a class used for certain purposes. In our case, we defined this as a class that's stored as a document. From now on, every time we create a new class, we use this symbol to mean a type of class that can be stored. When we finally implement this class, we will probably derive it from a base class called something like Storable. That means, then, that instead of creating a stereotype, we could recognize how this stereotype will be used when we ultimately code it in C++, and instead just draw our diagram as a base class, Storable, and then derive a new class, Discombobulator, as shown in Figure 5-5. Either is fine.

However, stereotypes go beyond just classes. Remember that stereotypes in UML give you the opportunity to *extend UML*. That is, stereotypes let you add new symbols with their own new meanings. In the case of our scroll symbol, we extended the class symbol and still ultimately have a class. But we can stereotype other symbols, and that gives them a totally different (or slightly related) meaning from the original symbol.

For example, we may have a special association in our program that specifically means that one class (the composite) holds instances of the other class (the parts) in the form of a sorted list. We can do this in one of two ways: We can stereotype it, or we can create a tagged property. Figure 5-6 shows the relationship as a stereotype.

Figure 5-5:
You can get around using stereotyped classes by using abstract classes.

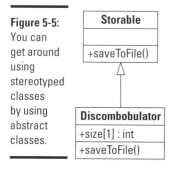

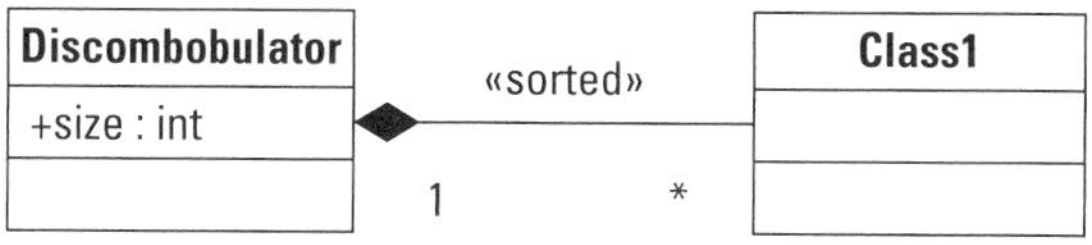

Figure 5-6:
You can use a stereotype to specify a type of association.

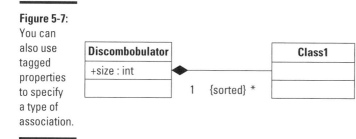

Figure 5-7, in turn, shows the relationship with a tagged property. Notice that, with the tagged property, the tag is in curly brackets.

Figure 5-7:
You can also use tagged properties to specify a type of association.

Not all CASE tools support all the features of UML. If you find a feature is missing, you can typically get around it by using related features. Most UML tools, however, support both stereotypes and tagged properties.

C++ and UML

When you study UML, you may come across various items that you know are present but you can't find in UML. Here we direct you toward some smaller parts of UML that have a direct connection to something in C++. Specifically we talk about enumerated types, static members, and templates.

Drawing enumerations

If you want to show an enumeration in UML, you can use a symbol similar to a class symbol. Remember that in C++, an enumeration is a type. In UML, symbols for types are called *classifiers*. Thus, in UML you use a special classifier to show an enumeration. (However, note that this classifier is really a class diagram that has been stereotyped. This is a good example of how you can use stereotypes!)

Figure 5-8 shows an example of an enumeration in UML. At the top is the stereotype name, <<enumeration>>. Under the name is the type, in this case Color. In the compartment following are the enumerations themselves.

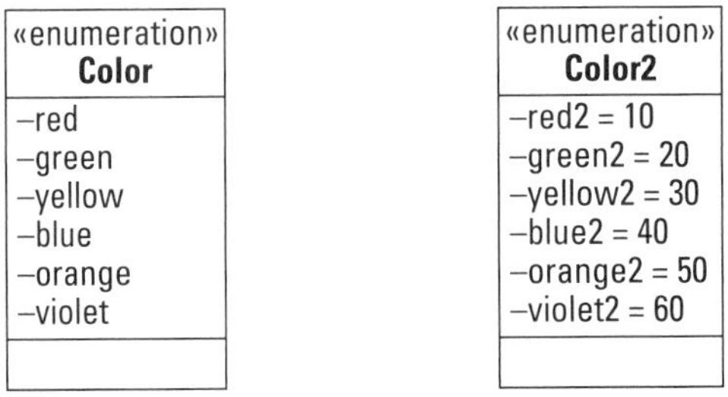

Figure 5-8:
UML includes a special classifier for enumerations.

«enumeration» Color
–red
–green
–yellow
–blue
–orange
–violet

«enumeration» Color2
–red2 = 10
–green2 = 20
–yellow2 = 30
–blue2 = 40
–orange2 = 50
–violet2 = 60

In Figure 5-8, we gave two enumerations. The first one, called Color, simply lists the symbols for the enumeration. The second one, called Color2, includes values for each enumeration. In C++, these two enumerations would look like this:

```
enum Color {red, green, yellow, blue, orange, violet};
enum Color2 {red2 = 10, green2 = 20, yellow2 = 30, blue2 = 40,
    orange2 = 50, violet2 = 60};
```

Including static members

In C++, you can include static members in a class. *Static members* are those members that are part of the class but shared among all instances of the class. Normally, instances of a class all get their own member variables. But if a member variable is static, there is only one copy of the variable for all the instances to share. For this reason, people associate such variables as being part of the class itself, not part of the instances. In UML language, these variables have a *class scope*. Regular member variables have an *instance scope*.

Member functions can also have a class scope. Such functions do not operate on an individual instance (and therefore can't access the member variables that are of the instance scope).

A common use of class-scoped members is to maintain a count of the number of instances. Here, you would have a class-scoped member variable called, for example, `instanceCount`. This would be an integer. In the constructor you would increment `instanceCount`, and in the destructor you would decrement it. Because there's only one copy of the `instance Count` member, each time you create an instance, you would increment this single copy. Thus, you would have a count of the number of instances.

Figure 5-9 shows an example in UML of a class with two class-scoped members. The class-scoped members are underlined. In this case, the class is called `MessedUpWebSite`. We suppose the idea is that every time you visit a crummy Web site, you would create a new instance of this class and save its Web address in the instance. This has two class-scoped members, `siteCount`, which is a private integer, and `getSiteCount`, which is a public function that returns the value of `siteCount`. (We made `siteCount` private so other objects can't change it.) And although we didn't show it, you would increment and decrement `siteCount` in the constructor and destructor, respectively.

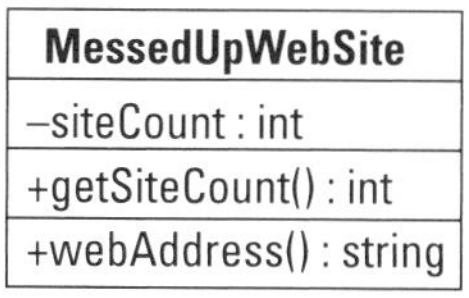

Figure 5-9:
You can show static members in UML by using a class scope.

MessedUpWebSite
–siteCount : int
+getSiteCount() : int
+webAddress() : string

In C++, the class in Figure 5-9 looks like the following lines of code:

```
class MessedUpWebSite
{
private:
    static int siteCount;

public:
    static int getSiteCount();
```

```
    string webAddress();
    MessedUpWebSite() { siteCount++; }
    ~MessedUpWebSite() { siteCount--; }
};

int MessedUpWebSite::getSiteCount()
{
    return siteCount;
}

int MessedUpWebSite::siteCount = 0;
```

Parameterizing classes with templates

UML includes a notation that you can use along with C++ templates. (We discuss templates in Minibook IV, Chapter 5.) In UML terms, a *template* is a *parameterized class.* If you think about how a template works in C++, you can see that this makes sense, because a template takes several parameters that are used by the compiler to build the class.

When you add the template parameters, the UML standard states that if the parameter is of type class, you can leave the parameter type blank. That's what we did in Figure 5-10. Note that the parameter called MyType has no type after it; thus, its type is class.

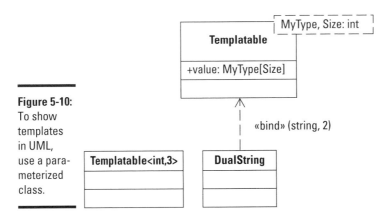

Figure 5-10: To show templates in UML, use a para-meterized class.

Figure 5-10 shows a UML parameterized class. It looks just like a regular old class symbol, except that it has a nifty little dashed rectangle in the upper-right corner. This dashed rectangle contains the template parameters.

Note in Figure 5-10 that we then declared two classes that use the template type. The first one is unnamed and simply specifies the parameters. The second is named and shows an association back to the template class. A stereotype name called <<bind>> appears next to the association arrow. After the stereotype name come the two parameters for the template.

Here is the C++ equivalent of this UML diagram. Notice the `MyType` parameter is of type `class`:

```
template <class MyType, int Size> class Templatable
{
public:
    MyType value[Size];
};
```

And here is some sample code that uses this template. In this code we also use the two classes based on the template. Note that, to get the named template instantiation, we use a `typedef`:

```
Templatable<int,3> inst;
inst.value[0] = 10;
inst.value[1] = 20;
inst.value[2] = 30;
cout << inst.value[2] << endl;
typedef Templatable<string,2> DualString;
DualString inst2;
inst2.value[0] = "abc";
inst2.value[1] = "def";
cout << inst2.value[1] << endl;
```

Chapter 6: Building with Design Patterns

In This Chapter

✓ Understanding what design patterns are and how you can use them

✓ Implementing an Observer pattern

✓ Building a Mediator pattern

*W*hen you work as a software designer, eventually you start to notice that you do certain things over and over. For example, you may get mad and shut off the computer. But that's not directly related to software design.

For an example related to software design, whenever we need to keep track of how many instances of a certain class get created, we always create a static member variable called something like `int InstanceCount`; and in the constructor, we include a line that increments `InstanceCount`; and in the destructor, we put a line that decrements `InstanceCount`. Further, we typically make `InstanceCount` private and include a static method that retrieves the value, such as `int GetInstanceCount()`.

We have used this design so many times we know that it works. The first time we used it, we had to think about it and how we would design and implement it. Now, we barely have to think about it; we just do it, sometimes even when we're driving down the road. Well, maybe not then, but we do use it when we're designing software. Thus it's a *design pattern* that we use.

Way back in 1995, a book came out that became an instant best seller in the computer programming world. It was called *Design Patterns: Elements of Reusable Object-Oriented Software*, by Erich Gamma, Richard Helm, Ralph Johnson, and John Vlissides. The four authors of this groundbreaking book would become known in the field of programming as *The Gang of Four*. They drew on a body of knowledge in the field of architecture — not software architecture, but rather the field of those people who build tall buildings, brick-and-mortar style, for Superman to leap over and see through. That kind of architecture has been around for at least two and a half centuries, so the field is just a wee bit more mature than the field of software engineering. And, in the field of designing buildings, people have come up with common ways to design and build buildings and towns, without having to start over from scratch each time with a new set of designs. Some guy (apparently famous in that field) named Christopher Alexander wrote a book in 1977 that teaches building architecture by using patterns. The Gang of Four drew on this knowledge and applied it to software engineering principles. They then wrote their *Design Patterns* book.

In it, they pointed out something that seems obvious in hindsight (but then again, great discoveries are often deceptively simple): The best software engineers reuse techniques in the sense of patterns. Our description of the class that keeps an instance count is an example of a technique that can be used over and over.

Now, if you heavily explore the field of object-oriented programming (and computer science in general, really), you will keep seeing the term *reusable*. One of the goals of object-oriented programming is to make code reusable by putting it in classes. You then derive your own classes from these classes, thereby reusing the code in the base classes.

That's all fine and dandy, but it doesn't always work. Yes, we could probably put our instance-counting class in a base class and always derive from it. But for some other designs, this doesn't always work. Instead, software engineers simply apply the same design to a new set of classes. Yes, they reused the design by pulling it from the back dusty caverns of their brains (isn't that pleasant), but they didn't actually reuse any code. That's okay! They drew on experience. And that's the idea behind design patterns. You don't just write up your design patterns and stuff them into a bunch of base classes. Instead, you simply know the patterns. Or you keep a list or catalog of them. So in this chapter, we present you with some of the more common design patterns.

Introducing a Simple Pattern: the Singleton

In this section we take you step-by-step through creating a design pattern, so you can see what it is and, more important, how you can use it.

Here's the situation: You are designing this truly great piece of software that is so good that everybody from the North Pole to the South Pole will not only buy a copy but will invest in your company as well. And while designing the software, you discover many situations where you need a class such that *only one instance can exist at any given time.*

You've come across this many times. For example, you may have a class that represents the computer itself. You want only one instance of it. You also may have a class that represents the planet Earth. Again, you need only one instance. And you might want a class that models the great leader of the universe (you). Again, only one instance. If people try to create a second instance of the class in their code, they will receive a compiler error. How do you do this?

You could spend a couple hours coming up with an approach. Or you could look at a pattern that already exists somewhere, such as what we're about to show you.

To understand how to create a pattern, you need to first understand an unusual concept that a lot of C++ programmers don't usually consider: You can make a constructor of a class *private or protected*! Now why would you do that? It turns out that making a constructor private prevents you from directly creating an instance of a class. We can hear you now, *Oh boy! Doesn't that sound like a useful class, if you can't make an instance of it? This guy's a nutjob!* But you *can* make an instance of the class. There's a trick: You include a static member function that creates the instance for you.

Remember: Static member functions do not have an instance associated with them. You call them directly by giving the class name, two colons, and the function name. But as it happens, the static member function is itself a member of the class, so it can call the constructor and create an instance for you.

One of the more popular examples for basic pattern creation is a *singleton* class — a class that lets you instantiate only one object. A singleton class is useful because it ensures that only one object is available across an application. Developers often use a singleton to coordinate the activities of other parts of the application.

Here's how you make a singleton class: First, make the constructor private. Next, add a public static member function that does the following:

1. Checks if a single instance of the class already exists. If so, it returns the instance's pointer.

2. Creates a new instance and returns its pointer if an instance doesn't already exist.

Finally, where do you store this single instance? You store its pointer in a static member of the class. Because it's static, only one member variable is shared throughout the class, rather than a separate variable for each class. Also, make the variable private so that users can't just modify it at will.

And voilà! You have a singleton class! Here's how it works: Whenever you need the single instance of the class, you don't try to create it. (You'll get a *compile* error! Yes, the *compiler itself* won't let you do it.) Instead, you call the static member function.

The following lines of code are an example of such a class:

```
class Planet
{
private:
```

```
    static Planet *inst;
    Planet() {}

public:
    static Planet *GetInstance();
};

Planet *Planet::inst = 0;

Planet *Planet::GetInstance()
{
    if (inst == 0)
    {
        inst = new Planet();
    }
    return inst;
}
```

To use this class, you do not just create an instance directly. Instead, you call the `GetInstance` member function:

```
Planet *MyPlanet = Planet::GetInstance();
```

You call this any time you want to get a copy of the single instance.

Each time you call `GetInstance`, you will always get a pointer to the same instance.

Now, take a look at the constructor: It's private. Therefore, if you attempt something like this somewhere outside the class (such as in `main`)

```
Planet MyPlanet;
```

you get a compiler error. In CodeBlocks, we get this error:

```
error: `Planet::Planet()' is private
error: within this context
```

Or if you try to create a pointer, you get the same error when you call `new`:

```
Planet *MyPlanet = new Planet();
```

When you have a class such as this, you probably also want to ensure that nobody attempts to delete the single instance. Just as you would make the constructor private, you would also make the destructor private, as in the following:

```
class Planet
{
private:
    static Planet *inst;
    Planet() {}
    ~Planet() {}

public:
```

```
    static Planet *GetInstance();
};
```

If you try to delete an instance after you obtain it, as in the following

```
Planet *MyPlanet = Planet::GetInstance();
delete MyPlanet;
```

then once again you receive an error message, this time for the destructor:

```
`Planet::~Planet()' is private
```

You may be tempted to make a constructor that takes a parameter. You could pass parameters into the GetInstance member function, which would in turn pass them to the constructor. This would work the first time, but there's a catch: Remember that after the GetInstance function creates the instance, it never does so again. That means it won't call the constructor again. Therefore, if you have a class that looks like this:

```
class Planet
{
private:
    static Planet *inst;
    Planet(string name)
    {
        cout << "Welcome to " << name << endl;
    }
    ~Planet() {}

public:
    static Planet *GetInstance(string name);
};
```

and your GetInstance method has this code in it:

```
Planet *Planet::GetInstance(string name)
{
    if (inst == 0)
    {
        inst = new Planet(name);
    }
    return inst;
}
```

and you make two calls like this:

```
Planet *MyPlanet = Planet::GetInstance("Earth");
Planet *MyPlanet2 = Planet::GetInstance("Venus");
```

the results may not be as you expect. You end up with only one instance, which will get created with the first line, the one with "Earth" passed in. In your second call to the GetInstance function, GetInstance will see that an instance already exists and will not even use the "Venus" parameter. So be careful if you're using parameters in constructors.

Watching an Instance with an Observer

A common task in computer programming is when one or more instances of a class (or different classes) need to keep an eye on a certain object and perform various actions when that object changes. For example, you may be writing a program that monitors various activities around your house when you're away. Your program could be configurable; you could set it up so the user can choose various actions to take if something goes awry. You might have the following options:

✦ The program saves a note in a file so you can later review it.

✦ The program sends an e-mail to you.

✦ If the computer is linked to a telephone security system, it can notify the police.

✦ The robotic dog can receive a signal to go on high alert.

. . . and so on. Each of these different things can exist in a different class, each with its own code for handling the situation. The one about saving a note to a file is easy; you would open a file, write to it, and close the file. The e-mail one might involve launching Microsoft Outlook, somehow telling it to compose an e-mail, and sending it. To notify the police, your computer would have to be hooked up to an online security system accessible via the phone lines or perhaps via the Internet, and the police would need a similar system at their end. The class for this would send a signal out the lines to the police, much like the way a secret button that notifies the police of a robbery at a gas station works. Finally, you might have a similar contraption hooked up into the brain of your little robotic watchdog, Fido; and when he receives a high-voltage jolt, he can go on high alert and ward off the intruders. Sounds like fun, no? We call all these classes `Observer` classes (and by this we mean that each class will be derived from a base class called `Observer`).

Now, you would also have a class whose object detects the problem in the house. This object might be hooked up to an elaborate security system, and when the change takes place, the computer calls a method inside this object. We call this class the `Subject` class.

So think about what is happening here:

1. When a security issue happens, the computer calls a method inside the single `Subject` instance.

2. The `Observer` classes have objects that watch the `Subject` instance. The method in the `Subject` class then calls methods in each of the `Observer` objects. These methods do the appropriate action, whether it's write to a file, notify the police, zap the robotic dog, or whatever.

Now here's the catch: The people using your computer program can determine which Observer classes they want to respond to the event (possibly through an options dialog box). But just to be difficult and to make sure that we design this with great flexibility, we're going to add the following requirement: Over the next year, you might add new Observer classes as they come up. One might signal a helicopter to fly in and chase a robber as he's making his getaway. But you can't be sure what you'll come up with over the next year. All you know is that you may add Observer subclasses and instances of these subclasses. So the point is this: You want to make the Subject class as flexible as possible.

Here are the issues that come up when designing such a set of classes. First, you could just keep a big list of instances inside the Subject class, and whenever an event takes place, the event handler calls a routine in all the Observer instances. The Observer instances then decide whether or not they want to use the information. The problem with this situation is that you have to call into the Observer classes, even if the individual instances don't want the information. The robotic dog might be sleeping and not want to be bothered by the break-in. Or the police might be on break themselves. (Because this is a serious book, we'll avoid any donut shop jokes.)

But on the other hand, you could have each Observer instance constantly check the Subject instance, looking for an event. (This process is called *polling.*) The problem here is that this process can push the computer to its limits, believe it or not: If every single Observer instance is constantly calling into the Subject class, you're going to have a lot of activity going on for possibly hours on end, keeping the CPU nice and toasty. That's not a good idea either.

The way you can perform polling without overextending the CPU is by using the *Observer pattern.* In this pattern, the Observer class contains a method called Respond. Meanwhile, the Subject class includes a list of Observer instances. Further, the Subject class includes a method called Event, which the computer calls whenever something happens, such as a break-in.

Now here's the twist that makes it work: Your program will add and remove Observer instances to and from the Subject's list of Observer instances, based on the options the people choose when using your program.

As you can imagine, this is a recurring pattern that a lot of programs use. Although zapping a robotic dog might not be common, other programs use this general model. For example, in some C++ editors, we can open the same document in multiple windows, all under one instance of the editor program. When we change the code in one window, we can immediately see the change in the other windows. Each class probably has a window, and these windows are the Observer classes. The Subject represents the underlying document. Or, for another example, you can open multiple browser windows all looking at the same Web page. As the page comes down from the Internet, it gradually appears in all windows. Again, the windows are associated with the Observer classes, and the actual Web document is associated with a Subject class.

So on to the code already! First, the Observer class contains a member function called Respond. In the Observer class itself, this is a pure abstract function; it's up to the derived classes to respond to the event in their own ways.

The following lines are an example of the Observer class:

```
class Observer
{
public:
    virtual void Respond() = 0;
};
```

As you can see, there's not much there. So we're going to add some derived classes. Here are a couple:

```
class Dog : public Observer
{
public:
    void Respond();
};

class Police : public Observer
{
protected:
    string name;

public:
    Police(string myname) { name = myname; }
    void Respond();
};
```

And here are the Respond member functions for these two classes. For now, to keep it simple, we're just writing something to the console:

```
void Dog::Respond()
{
    cout << "Bark bark" << endl;
}

void Police::Respond()
{
    cout << name << ": 'Drop the weapon! Now!'" << endl;
}
```

Again, so far there's nothing particularly interesting about this. These lines of code represent just a couple member functions that do their thing, really. But next, things get exciting. Here we make the Subject class:

```
class Subject
{
```

```
protected:
    int Count;
    Observer *List[100];

public:
    Subject() { Count = 0; }
    void AddObserver(Observer *Item);
    void RemoveObserver(Observer *Item);
    void Event();
};
```

This class has a list of `Observer` instances in its `List` member. The `Count` member is the number of items in the list. Two methods for adding and removing `Observer` instances are available: `AddObserver` and `RemoveObserver`. A constructor initializes the list (by just setting its count to 0, really), and there's the famous `Event` member function.

Here's the code for the `AddObserver` and `RemoveObserver` methods. These functions just manipulate the arrays:

```
void Subject::AddObserver(Observer *Item)
{
    List[Count] = Item;
    Count++;
}

void Subject::RemoveObserver(Observer *Item)
{
    int i;
    bool found = false;
    for (i=0; i < Count; i++)
    {
        if (found)
        {
        }
        else if (List[i] == Item)
        {
            found = true;
            List[i] = List[i+1];
        }
    }
    if (found)
    {
        Count--;
    }
}
```

The `RemoveObserver` function uses some little tricks (again, a pattern!) to remove the item. It searches through the list until it finds the item; after that, it continues through the list, pulling items back one slot in the array. And finally, if it found the item, it decreases `Count` by 1.

And now here's the fun part! The `Event` method looks like this:

```
void Subject::Event()
{
    int i;
```

```
    for (i=0; i < Count; i++)
    {
        List[i]->Respond();
    }
}
```

This code just climbs through the list, calling `Respond` for each item in the list. When you put this all together, you can have a `main` that sets up these items. Here's one possibility:

```
Dog Fido;
Police TJHooker("TJ");
Police JoeFriday("Joe");
Subject Alarm;
Alarm.AddObserver(&Fido);
Alarm.AddObserver(&TJHooker);
Alarm.AddObserver(&JoeFriday);
Alarm.RemoveObserver(&TJHooker);
Alarm.Event();
```

We make three `Observer` instances (one dog and two cops) and a `Subject` instance called `Alarm`. We then add all three instances to the list; but then TJ Hooker backs out, so we remove him from the list.

Then we call `Event`. (If this were an actual system, we wouldn't call `Event` right now; we would call `Event` when an actual break-in event occurs.) And when we run this code, we get the responses of each of the *registered* observers:

```
Bark bark
Joe: 'Drop the weapon! Now!'
```

Notice that `TJHooker` didn't respond because he was no longer interested. And so he didn't receive a notification. He is, however, still an instance.

In this example, the three observers (Fido, TJ Hooker, and Joe Friday) are *watching* the alarm, ready to respond to it. They are observers, ready for action. The alarm is their subject of observation. That's why we use the metaphor of `Observer` and `Subject`.

Observers and the Standard C++ Library

If you're interested in using templates and the Standard C++ Library, you can make the `Subject` class a bit more sophisticated by using a list rather than an array. You can do this by using the standard `list` class. The only catch is that the `list` class doesn't seem to do well with abstract classes. So you need to "de-abstractify" your `Observer` class by setting it up like this:

```
class Observer
{
public:
    virtual void Respond() {}
};
```

Then, you can modify the `Subject` class and its methods like so:

```
class Subject
{
protected:
    list<Observer *> OList;

public:
    void AddObserver(Observer *Item);
    void RemoveObserver(Observer *Item);
    void Event();
};

void Subject::AddObserver(Observer *Item)
{
    OList.push_back(Item);
}

void Subject::RemoveObserver(Observer *Item)
{
    OList.remove(Item);
}

void Subject::Event()
{
    list<Observer *>::iterator iter;
    for (iter = OList.begin(); iter != OList.end(); iter++)
    {
        Observer *item = (*iter);
        item->Respond();
    }
}
```

Note that, in the list, we're saving pointers to `Observer`; we're not saving the `Observer` instances themselves. That's because, by default, the `list` class makes a copy of whatever you put in the array. If you put in an actual instance, the `list` class will make a copy (which creates problems with derived classes because the `list` just copies the object being stored as an `Observer` instance, not a class derived from `Observer`). With pointers, a copy of a pointer still points to the original object, and therefore the items in the list are the originals (at least their addresses are in the list).

Automatically adding an observer

When you have a program that lets the users configure various observers, you may want to create and delete observers based on the configurations. In that case, it's possible to add an `Observer` to a `Subject`'s list automatically when you create the `Observer`, and remove the `Observer` from the list when you delete the `Observer`. To do this, you can call the `AddObserver` method from within the constructor and the `RemoveObserver` method from within the destructor. But to make this work, you need to tell the object who the `Subject` is. That's easy; just pass the name as a parameter to the constructor. The following code does this. Note that we had to move the `Subject` class above the `Observer` class because the `Observer`'s constructor and destructor call into `Subject`. Also, note that we made the

AddObserver and RemoveObserver functions protected. But because we want the Observer class to use these functions, we used a little trick called a *friend*: We put the word friend followed by the word Observer in the Subject class; now the Observer member functions can call the protected and private member functions of Subject. The code for the complete program is in Listing 6-1.

Listing 6-1: Using the Add and Remove Items in the Constructor and Destructor

```
#include <iostream>

using namespace std;

class Observer;

class Subject
{
    friend class Observer;

protected:
    int Count;
    Observer *List[100];
    void AddObserver(Observer *Item);
    void RemoveObserver(Observer *Item);

public:
    Subject() { Count = 0; }
    void Event();
};

class Observer
{
protected:
    Subject *subj;

public:
    virtual void Respond() = 0;

    Observer(Subject *asubj)
    {
        subj = asubj;
        subj->AddObserver(this);
    }

    virtual ~Observer() { subj->RemoveObserver(this); }
};

class Dog : public Observer
{
public:
    void Respond();
    Dog(Subject *asubj) : Observer(asubj) {}
};

class Police : public Observer
{
protected:
```

```
        string name;
public:
        Police(Subject *asubj, string myname) : Observer(asubj) { name = myname; }
        void Respond();
};

void Dog::Respond()
{
        cout << "Bark bark" << endl;
}

void Police::Respond()
{
        cout << name << ": 'Drop the weapon! Now!'" << endl;
}

void Subject::AddObserver(Observer *Item)
{
        List[Count] = Item;
        Count++;
}

void Subject::RemoveObserver(Observer *Item)
{
        int i;
        bool found = false;
        for (i=0; i < Count; i++)
        {
                if (found)
                {
                }
                else if (List[i] == Item)
                {
                        found = true;
                        List[i] = List[i+1];
                }
        }

        if (found)
        {
                Count--;
        }
}

void Subject::Event()
{
        int i;
        for (i=0; i < Count; i++)
        {
                List[i]->Respond();
        }
}

int main()
{
        Subject Alarm;

        Police *TJHooker = new Police(&Alarm, "TJ");

        cout << "TJ on the beat" << endl;
```

(continued)

Listing 6-1 *(continued)*

```
Alarm.Event();
cout << endl;
cout << "TJ off for the day" << endl;
delete TJHooker;
Alarm.Event();

return 0;
}
```

Mediating with a Pattern

Suppose you're going to design a sophisticated, complex model of a car. You're going to include the following parts, each of which will have its own class:

✦ The engine

✦ The electrical supply (for the technical folks, we mean the battery and alternator together)

✦ The radio

✦ The wheels

✦ The brakes

✦ The headlights

✦ The air conditioner

✦ The road

Now see if you can keep up (read this as fast as you possibly can): When the electrical supply goes up, the headlights get brighter. When the engine speeds up, the electrical supply increases. When the electrical supply goes down, the radio volume goes down. When the air conditioner turns on, the electrical supply goes down. When the air conditioner turns off, the electrical supply goes up. When the engine increases, the wheels accelerate. When the electric supply increases, the radio volume increases. When the road ascends due to a hill, the speed of the wheels goes down. When the brakes come on, the speed of the wheels decreases. When the electrical supply goes down, the headlights get dimmer. When the engine slows down, the electrical supply decreases. When the road descends due to a hill, the speed of the wheels goes up.

Now your job is to model all this behavior. Sound like fun? Not particularly. In fact, it's a total mess! How can you model this?

Here's the problem: You have a million objects (well, eight actually) all interacting with each other in different ways. You could try to make all the objects communicate. In the code, making them communicate would mean that most of the classes would have to contain references to objects of the other classes. That technique could get pretty confusing.

If you followed all this, the UML diagram in Figure 6-1 shows the interactions. As you can see, it's kind of messy. It's a *little* cleaner now in UML form than in the long-winded paragraph earlier, but it's still messy, and the code itself is still going to be complicated.

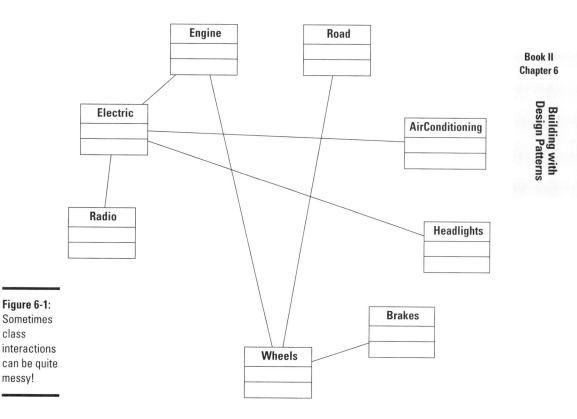

Figure 6-1:
Sometimes
class
interactions
can be quite
messy!

When you have this kind of a mess, first try to rearrange things visually to see if there's some way to simplify it. Figure 6-2 shows our cleaned-up version. Looking at this figure, we still get a little confused, but the figure does help us see the connections a bit more clearly.

So now we introduce the theme of this pattern. The idea is that when you have a set of classes that interact in a complex way, a *mediator* class through which the classes all communicate is often easiest to create. That way, only the mediator class needs to know about all the instances. The instances themselves communicate only with the mediator.

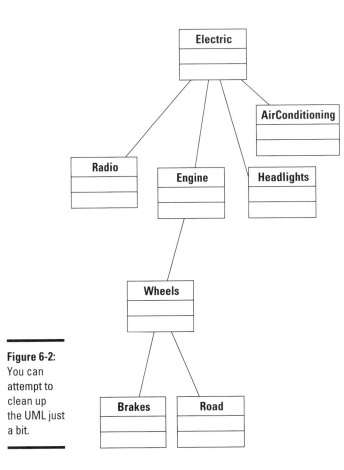

Figure 6-2:
You can attempt to clean up the UML just a bit.

In the example, when there's a hill, the road goes up. The road does not need to know about all the other car parts. Instead, it just informs the mediator of the change. The mediator then informs the necessary car parts.

This may seem like overkill: Why can't the road just talk directly to the car parts? The idea is that if you enhance this program later, you may want to add more car parts. Rather than having to go through and hook up connections to all the necessary car parts, you just make a connection with the mediator object. Suppose you add a new part called automatic transmission. When the car begins to climb a hill, the automatic transmission might detect this and automatically shift to a lower gear, resulting in an increase to the engine speed. To add this class, you only need to define its behavior and how it responds to various events, and then hook it up to the mediator. You will also modify the mediator so it knows something about the automatic transmission's behavior. Thus, you don't need to hook it up to all the other instances.

Figure 6-3 is the revised UML with the addition of a mediator. Now it looks a bit cleaner!

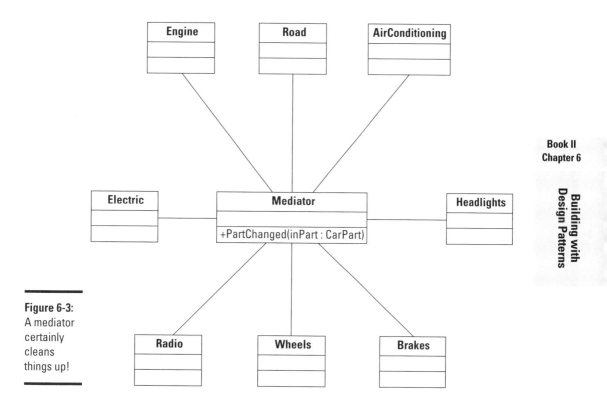

Figure 6-3:
A mediator
certainly
cleans
things up!

One thing we're not showing in Figure 6-3 (for the purpose of keeping things uncluttered) is that we're going to derive all the various car parts (including the road!) from a base class called CarPart. This class will have a single member: a pointer to a Mediator instance. Each of the car parts, then, will inherit a pointer to the Mediator instance.

The Mediator class has a member function called PartChanged. This is the key function: Any time any of the car parts experiences a change, it calls PartChanged. But remember, a car part can experience a change in only two ways: either through an outside force unrelated to the existing classes (such as the driver pushing the gas pedal or turning the steering wheel) or through the Mediator instance. If the change comes from the Mediator instance, it was triggered through one of the other objects.

For example, look at the following steps:

1. The driver pushes the gas pedal by calling a method in the `Engine` instance.

2. The `Engine` instance changes its speed and then tells the `Mediator` of the change.

3. The `Mediator` instance knows which objects to notify of the change. For this change, it notifies the wheels to spin faster.

Here's another possible sequence:

1. The road has a hill. To tell the car about the hill, the main routine calls a member function in the `Road` instance. The hill has a ten-degree incline.

2. The `Road` instance notifies `Mediator` of the change.

3. The `Mediator` instance handles this by figuring out how much to decelerate; it then notifies the wheels to slow down.

So you can see most of the *smarts* are in the `Mediator` class.

You may have noticed what seems like a contradiction in things we have told you and other OOP (Object-Oriented People) have told you. Here we're saying to put the smarts in the `Mediator` class. Elsewhere you are hearing that objects must be able to do their own work. But that's not really a contradiction. In fact, the `Mediator` class is handling all smarts dealing with *collaborations* between objects. After the `Mediator` instance figures out, for example, that the wheels must spin faster, it notifies the wheels and tells them to spin faster. That's when the wheels take over and do their thing. At that point, they know how to spin faster without outside help from other classes and objects. So it's not a contradiction after all.

Putting up a Façade (pattern)

In the car system example, we felt as though it would be cumbersome to have to manipulate the car system by paying separate attention to all the different parts, such as the engine and the wheels, simultaneously. Imagine what life would be like if you had to drive a car while constantly worrying about every little thing. Instead, we created a class called `CarControls` through which you can interact with the system. The `CarControls` class is a pattern itself, called a Façade pattern. A façade is a front of something. (It's a French word.) This pattern is also a front: It's the interface into the system through which you interact. That way, you don't have to keep track of the individual classes. When you add a class through which users can interact with the system, you are using a Façade pattern.

Now take a look at Listing 6-2. This is a header file that contains the class declarations for the car parts.

Listing 6-2:   Using the carparts.h File

```
#ifndef CARPARTS_H_INCLUDED
#define CARPARTS_H_INCLUDED

#include "mediator.h"

class CarControls; // forward reference

class CarPart
{
protected:
    Mediator *mediator;
    CarPart(Mediator *med) : mediator(med) {}
    void Changed();
};

class Engine : public CarPart
{
protected:
    friend class Mediator; friend class CarControls;
    int RPM;
    int Revamount;

public:
    Engine(Mediator *med) : CarPart(med),
        RPM(0), Revamount(0) {}
    void Start();
    void PushGasPedal(int amount);
    void ReleaseGasPedal(int amount);
    void Stop();
};

class Electric : public CarPart
{
protected:
    friend class Mediator; friend class CarControls;
    int Output;
    int ChangedBy;

public:
    Electric(Mediator *med) : CarPart(med),
        Output(0), ChangedBy(0) {}
    void ChangeOutputBy(int amount);
};

class Radio : public CarPart
{
protected:
    friend class Mediator; friend class CarControls;
```

(continued)

Listing 6-2 *(continued)*

```cpp
    int Volume;

public:
    Radio(Mediator *med) : CarPart(med),
        Volume(0) {}
    void AdjustVolume(int amount) { Volume += amount; }
    void SetVolume(int amount) { Volume = amount; }
    int GetVolume() { return Volume; }
};

class Wheels : public CarPart
{
protected:
    friend class Mediator; friend class CarControls;
    int Speed;

public:
    Wheels(Mediator *med) : CarPart(med),
        Speed(0) {}
    int GetSpeed() { return Speed; }
    void Accelerate(int amount);
    void Decelerate(int amount);
};

class Brakes : public CarPart
{
protected:
    friend class Mediator; friend class CarControls;
    int Pressure;

public:
    Brakes(Mediator *med) : CarPart(med),
        Pressure(0) {}
    void Apply(int amount);
};

class Headlights : public CarPart
{
protected:
    friend class Mediator; friend class CarControls;
    int Brightness;

public:
    Headlights(Mediator *med) : CarPart(med),
        Brightness(0) {}
    void TurnOn() { Brightness = 100; }
    void TurnOff() { Brightness = 0; }
    void Adjust(int Amount);
    int GetBrightness() { return Brightness; }
};

class AirConditioner : public CarPart
{
protected:
    friend class Mediator; friend class CarControls;
    int Level;
    int ChangedBy;

public:
    AirConditioner(Mediator *med) : CarPart(med),
```

```
        Level(0), ChangedBy(0) {}
    void TurnOn();
    void TurnOff();
    bool GetLevel() { return Level; }
    void SetLevel(int level);
};

class Road : public CarPart
{
protected:
    friend class Mediator; friend class CarControls;
    int ClimbAngle;
    int BumpHeight;
    int BumpWhichTire;

public:
    Road(Mediator *med) : CarPart(med) {}
    void ClimbDescend(int angle);
    void Bump(int height, int which);
};

#endif
```

**Book II
Chapter 6**

**Building with
Design Patterns**

These classes know little of each other. That's a good thing. However, they do know all about the mediator, which is fine. In this source, we used an important small feature of the latest ANSI version of C++. Notice the constructor line in the Engine class definition:

```
Engine(Mediator *med) : CarPart(med),
    RPM(0), Revamount(0) {}
```

After the constructor definition, you see a colon and the name of the base class, CarPart. This calls the base class constructor. Then there's a comma and the name of a member variable (RPM) and a value in parentheses, which together form an *initializer*. When you create an instance of Engine, the RPM variable will get set to the value 0. Further, the Revamount variable will also get set to the value 0. Using the constructor with an initializer causes the constructor to behave just like this code:

```
Engine(Mediator *med)
{
    RPM = 0;
    Revamount = 0;
}
```

Next, in Listing 6-3, is the header file for the mediator along with a special class called CarControls, which provides a central place through which you can control the car. You may have noticed that we gave the CarControls class friend access to the car parts in the carparts.h file. We also included in this file several forward declarations. Remember: This class knows about the various CarParts classes. This file also includes a class derived from Mediator that provides a general interface to the whole system.

Listing 6-3: Using the mediator.h File

```
#ifndef MEDIATOR_H_INCLUDED
#define MEDIATOR_H_INCLUDED

// Define all of the required forward references.
class CarPart;
class Engine;
class Electric;
class Radio;
class SteeringWheel;
class Wheels;
class Brakes;
class Headlights;
class AirConditioner;
class Road;

class Mediator
{
public:
    Engine *MyEngine;
    Electric *MyElectric;
    Radio *MyRadio;
    SteeringWheel *MySteeringWheel;
    Wheels *MyWheels;
    Brakes *MyBrakes;
    Headlights *MyHeadlights;
    AirConditioner *MyAirConditioner;
    Road *MyRoad;
    Mediator();
    void PartChanged(CarPart *part);
};

class CarControls : public Mediator {
public:
    void StartCar();
    void StopCar();
    void PushGasPedal(int amount);
    void ReleaseGasPedal(int amount);
    void PressBrake(int amount);
    void Turn(int amount);
    void TurnOnRadio();
    void TurnOffRadio();
    void AdjustRadioVolume(int amount);
    void TurnOnHeadlights();
    void TurnOffHeadlights();
    void ClimbHill(int angle);
    void DescendHill(int angle);
    void TurnOnAC();
    void TurnOffAC();
    void AdjustAC(int amount);
    int GetSpeed();
    CarControls() : Mediator() {}
};

#endif
```

Next is the code for the member functions for all the car parts. These are in
Listing 6-4. Note in these functions that we never, ever call the functions in
other car parts. We do, however, call a general `Changed` method that's in the
car parts base class, `CarParts`. This calls into the `Mediator` to let it know
that a change took place.

The magic words: high cohesion, low coupling

In the world of software engineering, two buzzwords are *cohesion* and *coupling*.

Cohesion refers to the process of keeping similarly minded functions grouped together. If you create good classes, this shouldn't be a problem. Functions involving the wheels should go in the `Wheels` class, not, for example, the `Engine` class.

Coupling is a bit more complex. It refers to the process of tying together classes so they can't function independently. In effect, the classes are coupled. In good object-oriented programming, having lots of coupling is not good. You want your classes to be as independent as possible; you want *low coupling*. The `Mediator` pattern helps a great deal toward the low-coupling goal. In the car system example, if we had instead given the `Electric` class pointers to an `Engine` instance and a `Radio` instance, and so on, then we would be forcing these classes to all work dependently. In effect, we would have coupled them. But by using the `Mediator` instance, each class works only with the `Mediator`. We have low coupling. You should, therefore, try to design for *high cohesion and low coupling*. It's a good thing!

Listing 6-4:   Presenting the carparts.cpp File

```cpp
#include <iostream>
#include "carparts.h"

using namespace std;

void CarPart::Changed()
{
    mediator->PartChanged(this);
}

void Engine::Start()
{
    RPM = 1000;
    Changed();
}

void Engine::PushGasPedal(int amount)
{
    Revamount = amount;
    RPM += Revamount;
    Changed();
}

void Engine::ReleaseGasPedal(int amount)
{
    Revamount = amount;
    RPM -= Revamount;
    Changed();
}

void Engine::Stop()
{
```

(continued)

Listing 6-4 *(continued)*

```cpp
    RPM = 0;
    Revamount = 0;
    Changed();
}

void Electric::ChangeOutputBy(int amount)
{
    Output += amount;
    ChangedBy = amount;
    Changed();
}

void Wheels::Accelerate(int amount)
{
    Speed += amount;
    Changed();
}

void Wheels::Decelerate(int amount)
{
    Speed -= amount;
    Changed();
}

void Brakes::Apply(int amount)
{
    Pressure = amount;
    Changed();
}

void Headlights::Adjust(int Amount)
{
    Brightness += Amount;
}

void AirConditioner::TurnOn()
{
    ChangedBy = 100 - Level;
    Level = 100;
    Changed();
}

void AirConditioner::TurnOff()
{
    ChangedBy = 0 - Level;
    Level = 0;
    Changed();
}

void AirConditioner::SetLevel(int newlevel)
{
    Level = newlevel;
    ChangedBy = newlevel - Level;
    Changed();
}

void Road::ClimbDescend(int angle)
{
    ClimbAngle = angle;
    Changed();
```

```
}

void Road::Bump(int height, int which)
{
    BumpHeight = height;
    BumpWhichTire = which;
    Changed();
}
```

And now, in Listing 6-5, is the mediator source code and the source code for the `CarControls` class.

Listing 6-5: Using the carparts.cpp File

```
#include <iostream>
#include "mediator.h"
#include "carparts.h"

using namespace std;

Mediator::Mediator()
{
    MyEngine = new Engine(this);
    MyElectric = new Electric(this);
    MyRadio = new Radio(this);
    MyWheels = new Wheels(this);
    MyBrakes = new Brakes(this);
    MyHeadlights = new Headlights(this);
    MyAirConditioner = new AirConditioner(this);
    MyRoad = new Road(this);
}

void Mediator::PartChanged(CarPart *part)
{
    if (part == MyEngine)
    {
        if (MyEngine->RPM == 0)
        {
            MyWheels->Speed = 0;
            return;
        }

        if (MyEngine->Revamount == 0)
        {
            return;
        }

        // If engine increases, increase the electric output
        MyElectric->ChangeOutputBy
            (MyEngine->Revamount / 10);

        if (MyEngine->Revamount > 0)
        {
            MyWheels->Accelerate(
                MyEngine->Revamount / 50);
        }
    }
```

(continued)

Listing 6-5 *(continued)*

```
    else if (part == MyElectric)
    {
        // Dim or brighten the headlights
        if (MyHeadlights->Brightness > 0)
          MyHeadlights->Adjust(MyElectric->ChangedBy / 20);

        if (MyRadio->Volume > 0)
          MyRadio->AdjustVolume(MyElectric->ChangedBy / 30);
    }

    else if (part == MyBrakes)
    {
        MyWheels->Decelerate(MyBrakes->Pressure / 5);
    }

    else if (part == MyAirConditioner)
    {
        MyElectric->ChangeOutputBy(
            0 - MyAirConditioner->ChangedBy * 2);
    }

    else if (part == MyRoad)
    {
        if (MyRoad->ClimbAngle > 0)
        {
            MyWheels->Decelerate(MyRoad->ClimbAngle * 2);
            MyRoad->ClimbAngle = 0;
        }

        else if (MyRoad->ClimbAngle < 0)
        {
            MyWheels->Accelerate(MyRoad->ClimbAngle * -4);
            MyRoad->ClimbAngle = 0;
        }
    }
}

void CarControls::StartCar()
{
    MyEngine->Start();
}

void CarControls::StopCar()
{
    MyEngine->Stop();
}

void CarControls::PushGasPedal(int amount)
{
    MyEngine->PushGasPedal(amount);
}

void CarControls::ReleaseGasPedal(int amount)
{
    MyEngine->ReleaseGasPedal(amount);
}

void CarControls::PressBrake(int amount)
{
    MyBrakes->Apply(amount);
```

```
    }

    void CarControls::TurnOnRadio()
    {
        MyRadio->SetVolume(100);
    }

    void CarControls::TurnOffRadio()
    {
        MyRadio->SetVolume(0);
    }

    void CarControls::AdjustRadioVolume(int amount)
    {
        MyRadio->AdjustVolume(amount);
    }

    void CarControls::TurnOnHeadlights()
    {
        MyHeadlights->TurnOn();
    }

    void CarControls::TurnOffHeadlights()
    {
        MyHeadlights->TurnOff();
    }

    void CarControls::ClimbHill(int angle)
    {
        MyRoad->ClimbDescend(angle);
    }

    void CarControls::DescendHill(int angle)
    {
        MyRoad->ClimbDescend( 0 - angle );
    }

    int CarControls::GetSpeed()
    {
        return MyWheels->Speed;
    }

    void CarControls::TurnOnAC()
    {
        MyAirConditioner->TurnOn();
    }

    void CarControls::TurnOffAC()
    {
        MyAirConditioner->TurnOff();
    }

    void CarControls::AdjustAC(int amount)
    {
        MyAirConditioner->SetLevel(amount);
    }

    int main()
    {
        // Create a new car.
        Mediator *MyCar = new Mediator();
```

(continued)

Listing 6-5 *(continued)*

```
    // Start the engine.
    MyCar->MyEngine->Start();
    cout << "Engine Started!" << endl;

    // Accelerate.
    MyCar->MyWheels->Accelerate(20);
    cout << "The car is going: " << MyCar->MyWheels->GetSpeed() << endl;

    // Apply the brakes.
    MyCar->MyBrakes->Apply(20);
    cout << "Applying the brakes." << endl;
    cout << "The car is going: " << MyCar->MyWheels->GetSpeed() << endl;

    // Stop the car.
    MyCar->MyBrakes->Apply(80);
    cout << "Applying the brakes." << endl;
    cout << "The car is going: " << MyCar->MyWheels->GetSpeed() << endl;

    // Shut off the engine.
    MyCar->MyEngine->Stop();
    cout << "Engine Stopped" << endl;

    return 0;
}
```

The CarControls part runs a bit long, but it's handy because it provides a central interface through which you'll be able to operate the car. The work-horse of the pattern, however, is in the Mediator class. This is a bunch of if statements that look at the change that took place and then call into other classes to modify the objects of the other classes. That's the whole goal with the Mediator pattern: *It has a Mediator class containing a general function that looks for changes and then changes other classes.*

If you look back at Listing 6-4, you can see that, after each change, we call the Changed function. This function is in the base class, and it calls into the Mediator's PartChanged function, which does all the hard work. Also note that in some of the car parts classes, the Mediator doesn't respond to their changes (such as the Wheel class); however, we still call Change in the member functions for the class. The reason is that we may add features whereby the Mediator would respond to these changes. Then we wouldn't have to check to see whether or not we included a Change method; it's already there. This helps avoid the bug of wondering why the Mediator isn't doing what it's supposed to do if we forgot the call to Change.

At some point, you'll want to test the new class. The main function in this example does precisely that. The code doesn't provide a complete test, but it does demonstrate some of what you can do. In this case, the code turns the engine once, accelerates the car, applies the brake a little, applies the brake more to come to a stop, and then stops the engine.

Documenting your work

Imagine that somebody else will use your set of car classes. You have saved your header files and your source files, along with a static library containing the compiled code, on a network drive. Your coworker begins looking at your header files. What does he or she see? A big collection of classes. How does the coworker know how to use the classes? Does the coworker know to use the main Façade class called CarControls? Or will he or she have to just dig through the code to figure out which classes to use and which ones not to?

The answer is no. Instead, clearly document your classes. Somewhere, put together a simple document (no more than a page or two) that explains how to use your class library. Write this document for other programmers to use (but make it readable, please!), and explicitly state that programmers are to interact with the system through the CarControls class. You should then describe the public member functions (the *interface*) to the CarControls class and provide concrete examples. You might also include a reference section for advanced programmers who want to understand how the whole thing works. But whatever you do, don't just hand over the classes and expect other people to understand them without sufficient documentation!

Book III

Fixing Problems

EXPERIMENTING WITH THE WIRELESS LASER BEAM NETWORK

"Okay – did you get that?"

Contents at a Glance

Chapter 1: Dealing with Bugs

In This Chapter

↙ **Distinguishing bugs from features**

↙ **Anticipating every move the user makes**

↙ **Avoiding mistakes the easy way**

↙ **Dealing with errors**

*W*ho knows whether it's true, but as the story goes, back when the first computer was built over a half century ago, it filled an entire room with circuitry (yet was about as powerful as one of today's digital wristwatches). One day, the thing was misbehaving, and some brave engineers climbed deep into the thing. (The version we're thinking of has them wearing white radiation suits, of course.) Deep in *The Bowels of the Machine* (sounds like a movie title), they found none other than . . . an insect! A bug! It was a great *big* bug that had gotten messed up in the circuitry, causing the computer to malfunction. So the story goes, anyway. Today, we use the term *bug* to mean something that is wrong with a program. In this minibook, we show you how to track down bugs and fix them in your software. In this chapter, we talk about what exactly a bug is (and is not!), how bugs occur, and how you can try to avoid them.

It's Not a Bug. It's a Feature!

So we're using Microsoft Word, and all of a sudden, the program freaks out and saves our file automatically. We didn't tell it to do that; we didn't ask for it. Then we're using the same copy of Word, and we try to do a copy-and-paste procedure (that's called a *use case,* by the way), and suddenly the Font dialog box pops up. And then later, we're sitting with our laptops at Starbucks, and it automatically begins the shutdown procedure. We didn't tell it to do that.

Bugs! Bugs! They're all bugs! Or are they? Seems that these pesky little incidents might be considered *features* by some programmers.

Turns out that Microsoft Word has an optional *autosave* feature that causes it to automatically save *recovery* information in case our computer goes dead. And that Font dialog box that popped up was a mistake of ours: we meant to press Ctrl+V, but our fingers slipped and caught the *D* key instead. As it happens, by default Ctrl+D opens the Font dialog box in Microsoft

Word. (Why *D*? We have no idea.) And newer versions of Windows understand laptop computers: When the battery is just about to be completely drained, Windows saves the entire state of your machine to a giant file on the hard drive and shuts down. This is called *hibernation.* So these aren't bugs after all. We guess we can close up that bug report we just sent to Microsoft.

Now consider this: Suppose you're using some program that we won't name here, and in the middle of it, you get a message box that says something like `Exception Error`, and the program just closes. All your work was lost. So you call tech support, and the helpful friend on the other end says, "You must have typed something it didn't like. This program has a built-in protection scheme whereby if you type something you're not supposed to, it shuts down."

Oh, yeah. We get it. That's when the guy says, "It's a *feature*, not a bug!" Tell me another one. But sometimes situations walk the fine line between bug and feature. We don't think that a program crashing could be considered a feature, but consider this instead: When Microsoft Internet Explorer 6.0 messes up, a message asks if you want it to send Microsoft a trouble report. *That's* a feature that handles bugs.

But the unnamed program that shut down definitely has a bug. And other programs have bugs. For example (we can pick on Internet Explorer, right?), we have been quickly switching between Internet Explorer windows, typing, resizing, doing things quickly as we go back and forth between the windows (too much caffeine perhaps), when suddenly the thing crashes, and we get the trouble-report message. That really was a bug: The program choked when we, the user, *did something that the programmers did not anticipate.*

Now why did the program choke? Well, in addition to what we did that the programmers hadn't expected, it's possible that the programmers simply messed up. Either they didn't include code to handle a rough situation (rapidly switching, resizing, that sort of thing), or perhaps they wrote code that did something wrong, such as freed a pointer but then continued to use the memory address.

Here's an example of programmers not expecting something. Suppose we're writing a program that reads a number from the console. You should type a single character for your first choice and then another character for your second choice. The code might look like this:

```
char x, y;
cout << "Enter your first choice" << endl;
cin >> x;
cout << "Enter your second choice" << endl;
cout << x << endl;
cin >> y;
cout << y << endl;
```

A simple little code, but suppose that you respond to the first request by typing an entire word for what you want, such as *Read* rather than a single letter such as *R.* Our program would then take the letters *e, a,* and *d* and use those for the subsequent cin calls, something we might not have antici-pated. The *e* would go into the cin > y line and get put in y. That's the bug of not anticipating something: You, the programmer, must make sure that your program can handle all situations. All of them. Every single one. But fortunately, there are ways around such problems, and we share these with you in this chapter.

You can group these situations into the following categories:

✦ Real features, not bugs at all

✦ A situation that the programmers didn't anticipate

✦ A mistake, plain and simple

Make Your Programming Features Look Like Features

The last thing you want is to get calls from users complaining about *a bug* in your program that was, in fact, *a feature.* This can happen, and it does. But the technical support people are embarrassed when they have to explain, "No, sir/ma'am. That really is the way it's supposed to work." And it's also not fun for the technical support people to get called mean names after this, especially when they didn't write the software — *you did.*

Book III
Chapter 1

Dealing with Bugs

But as programmers, we want to make everybody's lives easier (starting with our own, of course!), so building our software so that it's easy to use and *makes sense* is best. The key, then, in creating software where the fea-tures actually look like features is to make it all sensible. Don't have your software start the Zapper automatically unless the user explicitly asks that the Zapper come on:

Smiling technical support representative: "It's a feature! The Zapper comes on after the computer has been sitting idle for ten minutes."

Angry customer: "Yes, but I would kind of like to be at least ten feet away from the thing when the Zapper starts up!"

Smiling technical support representative: "But why would you be sitting there for ten minutes not using the computer if you're not away from it?"

Angry customer: "I was reading the manual on how to configure the Zapper!"

You know the rest: Lawsuits follow and people get fired. Not a pretty sight, and that says nothing for the poor customer who was in the vicinity of the computer when the Zapper kicked in at full force.

With features, the rules are simple: Let the user choose which features they want to happen when. If they don't want autosave, then let them turn it off. Let them configure the software, and don't let it do anything surprising.

Anticipating (Almost) Everything

When you write a program, try to anticipate the different things that users can do to your program — much of which may not exactly be associated with the proper use of your program. Most of this kind of protection — that is, ensuring that your program doesn't choke when the users do something you don't anticipate — you build into your software centers around the *user interface,* the area where the users interact with your program.

If your program is a console-based application or if users can enter things into text boxes in a windowing program, you must guard against invalid input. Take a look at this output from a hypothetical program:

```
What would you like to do?
    A. Add random information to the system
    B. Boil information
    C. Compress information
    D. Delete the information
    Your choice:
```

Now suppose that the user chose *D* for Delete, and the following menu appeared:

```
What would you like to delete?
    A. None of the data — forget it!
    B. Some of the data.
    C. Most of the data.
    D. All the data! Get rid of it all!
```

Now imagine that a user just starts this program and sees the first menu. The user doesn't know whether to type **A** for the first choice or **Add** for the first choice. The user types **Add** and presses Enter. Oops. The *A* went to the first choice, and the system added the random information and printed the same first menu again. The *d* (the second character the user typed) then went to choice `Delete the information`. That caused the second menu, the Delete menu to appear. The third character the user typed, *d,* caused the second menu's *D* selection to take place, `All the data! Get rid of it all!`, all in one shot, without the user realizing what happened.

Oops! What was supposed to be `Add` turned into `Add`, `Delete`, `Delete all the data`. Not good! How can you avoid this kind of thing?

+ Restrict the user's choices.

+ Clearly state what the user should do.

+ Support multiple options.

+ Anticipate what could go wrong.

For example, you might tell the user to type only a single character, with a message such as this:

```
Please enter a single character for your choice:
```

But now, does the user have to press Enter afterwards? This message suggests so. But maybe not. So you must be more specific. Maybe one of these would be better:

```
Type a single character and do not press Enter:
```

```
Type a single character and then press Enter:
```

But even these aren't good enough. First, you should generally allow the user to press Enter. Doing something automatically with a single keystroke may surprise the user. Further, you may want to support multiple options. If the user wants to choose option A in the menu, then you might support any of the following for input:

+ A

+ a

+ Add

+ ADD

+ add

This can all be wrapped up into some short code that looks like this:

```
string choice;
cin >> choice;
char ch = choice[0];
ch = toupper(ch);
switch (ch)
{
    case 'A':
        cout << "Adding random data..." << endl;
        break;
    case 'B':
        cout << "Boiling it down!" << endl;
        break;
    case 'C':
        cout << "Compressing!" << endl;
        break;
    case 'D':
        cout << "Deleting..." << endl;
        break;
}
```

**Book III
Chapter 1**

Dealing with Bugs

Now the user can type any word, and the only thing that the program checks is the first letter. But if you don't like the idea that *aompress* can be taken as *add* and not *compress* (who knows what they meant to type?), you can do something like this:

```
string choice;
cin >> choice;
choice = MyUppercase(choice);
if (choice == "A" || choice == "ADD")
{
    cout << "Adding random data..." << endl;
}
else if (choice == "B" || choice == "BOIL")
{
    cout << "Boiling it down!" << endl;
}
else if (choice == "C" || choice == "COMPRESS")
{
    cout << "Compressing!" << endl;
}
else if (choice == "D" || choice == "DELETE")
{
    cout << "Deleting..." << endl;
}
else
{
    cout << "I don't know that word" << endl;
}
```

Now this code looks for only the first letter, or the exact word, and the letter or word can be in either uppercase or lowercase. This choice is probably the best one. However, you may notice that we used a function called MyUppercase. That's our own function because support in C++ for converting an entire string to uppercase leaves a bit to be desired. So we wrote our own function. Here it is:

```
string MyUppercase(string str)
{
    char *buf = new char[str.length() + 1];
    strcpy(buf, str.c_str());
    strupr(buf);
    return string(buf);
}
```

But be careful if you're dealing with a sophisticated program. Suppose you are writing a program that looks up information in a database for a particular customer name. You could run into the following situations:

+ The names in the database are all in uppercase (for example, *GEORGE WASHINGTON*), and the user can enter names in mixed case (for example, *George Washington*).

+ The first and last names are stored separately, so your program must look in the database for the situation where the last name is *Washington* and the first name is *George*. The user doesn't know to enter just the last name, and may enter both names into a single text box. Or you might allow the user to enter both names at once, but the user didn't know he or she was supposed to put last name first, or perhaps last name, then a comma, then the first name.

✦ The user can type some spaces at the beginning or end of the name. The program will then look for *George Washington* and not find it because it's stored as George Washington (with no spaces before or aft).

✦ The user might include middle initials when the name is not stored in the database with middle initials.

All these problems are easy to avoid. Here are some tips:

✦ You must know how the names are stored in the database before you go looking for them. If they are stored in all caps, you shouldn't require the user to enter them in all caps. Instead, accept words in any case and *convert them* to all uppercase.

✦ You must know if the names are stored with first name separate from last. Then allow any format. If the user types **George Washington** (no comma), you can split the string at the space and pull out the first and last name. But if the user types the name with a comma between the first and last name, you can split it at the comma and extract the last name and then the first.

✦ Spaces should not be a problem. You can strip the spaces off a string after a user types it in.

✦ Are middle initials required? Document things well. Your program should clearly tell the user whether to enter a middle name, a middle initial, or neither. If you are using text controls, don't even include a middle name field if you don't want a middle name. Or if you do, specify right on the window whether the user should type a middle initial or an entire middle name. If the entry is just an initial, you can remove a trailing period, or add it, depending on what's stored in the database.

All these steps will help make your program bulletproof. The idea is to encourage the users to do things the way they prefer, but to prevent them from doing things in ways that your program doesn't like. If your program doesn't want middle initials, don't give the users the opportunity to enter them.

Listing 1-1 shows you how you can strip spaces, strip a possible period off the end of a middle initial, and split a string based on either spaces or commas. In this listing, we used a special class called `vector`. The `vector` class is much like an array, except that the `vector` class is a bit more powerful: `vector` is a class, and you can add things to it and remove things from it easily by using member functions. `vector` is also a *template,* so when you declare it, you must state what type of variables you want it to hold. You put the type of variables in angled brackets. We're putting strings in it, so we declared it as `vector<string>`. But to make our lives simpler, we used a `typedef` to make an easier name for this type: `StringList`.

The myth of the bulletproof application

Anyone who has spent time reviewing the trade press knows that Internet Explorer and many other applications seem to have a recurring problem with bugs. Just as soon as the vendor fixes one bug, another bug turns up. Some developers may think that the developers at these companies are morons and are giving us all a black eye. However, these developers, more often than not, are just like us. Because they're human and humans make mistakes — both at the developer and user end of the application @md applications will never become bug free. Sure, you may be able to create a nearly bulletproof simple application, but as application complexity increases, so do the number of interactions and the number of potential bugs. At some point, the number of interactions between application parts increases to the point that a bug-free application becomes impossible.

Over the years we have read any number of articles and books that purport to give you the magic required to create an application that not only lacks bugs but also prevents unanticipated user actions. The bulletproof application is a myth. If you buy into this myth, you may be tempted to stop looking for bugs the moment the development staff can't find anymore. Unfortunately, this attitude leads to headlines proclaiming your application as the next significant Windows security hole. Don't buy into the bulletproof application myth — always be alert for potential errors.

Listing 1-1:   Processing Strings to Reduce Bugs

```
#include <iostream>
#include <vector>

using namespace std;

typedef vector<string> StringList;

StringList Split(string orig, string delims)
{
    StringList list;
    int pos;

    while((pos = orig.find_first_of(delims)) != -1)
    {
        list.push_back(orig.substr(0, pos));
        orig = orig.substr(pos + 1);
    }

    list.push_back(orig);

    return list;
}

string MyUppercase(string str)
{
    char *buf = new char[str.length() + 1];

    strcpy(buf, str.c_str());
    strupr(buf);
```

```
        return string(buf);
}

string stripspaces(string orig)
{
    int left;
    int right;

    // If string is empty, just return it.
    if (orig.length() == 0)
        return orig;

    // Strip right
    right = orig.find_last_not_of(" \t");
    if (right > -1)
        orig.resize(right + 1);

    // Strip left
    left = orig.find_first_not_of(" \t");
    if (left > -1)
        orig.erase(0, left);

    // If left still has a space, it
    // means the whole string is whitespace.
    // So just remove it all.
    if (orig[0] == ' ' || orig[0] == '\t')
    {
        orig = "";
    }

    return orig;
}
void ProcessName(string name)
{
    StringList list;
    string first, middle, last;
    int size, commapos;
    name = stripspaces(name);
    commapos = name.find(",");

    if (commapos > 0)
    {
        // Name has a comma, so start with last name.
        name.erase(commapos, 1);
        list = Split(name, " ");
        size = list.size();

        if (size > 0)
            last = list[0];
        if (size > 1)
            first = list[1];
        if (size > 2)
            middle = list[2];
    }
    else
    {
        // Name has no comma, so start with first name.
        list = Split(name, " ");
        size = list.size();
```

(continued)

Listing 1-1 *(continued)*

```
        if (size > 0)
            first = list[0];
        if (size > 2)
        {
            middle = list[1];
            last = list[2];
        }
        if (size == 2)
        {
            last = list[1];
        }
    }

    // If middle name is just initial and period,
    // then remove the initial.
    if (middle.length() == 2)
    {
        if (middle[1] == '.')
        {
            middle.erase(1,1);
        }
    }

    // Convert all to uppercase
    first = MyUppercase(first);
    middle = MyUppercase(middle);
    last = MyUppercase(last);

    cout << "first: " << first << endl;
    cout << "middle: " << middle << endl;
    cout << "last: " << last << endl;
    cout << endl;
}

int main()
{
    string name;

    name = "   Washington, George Zeus    ";
    ProcessName(name);

    name = "Washington, George Z.";
    ProcessName(name);

    name = "George Z. Washington";
    ProcessName(name);

    name = "George Zeus Washington";
    ProcessName(name);

    name = "George Washington";
    ProcessName(name);

    return 0;
}
```

Listing 1-1 is rather bugproof, but it still won't handle some situations properly. For example, if somebody tries to process a string with a middle name such as *Zeus.* (notice a period is present after the name), the program won't remove the period. But is that correct or not? Who knows, but people don't normally format names like that. And so here are some improvements you might make to this program:

✦ **Eliminate improper characters:** You could make sure that no improper characters appear in the names. We would probably do this after we found the first, middle, and last names; that way, we wouldn't kill the attempt to find the data based on the presence of a single comma that might be needed to specify the name order. You can use various `if` statements to do this kind of thing.

✦ **Handle more names than three:** We would probably have a special precaution for the case of more than three names. Some people have lots of names — like 10 or 11 — especially if they're British royalty. But if this program is to be used, for example, in an oil change operation, we don't think you'll see Charles Philip Arthur George, Prince of Wales coming through (although it's possible). And so, as usual, how you handle the names depends on your particular situation.

✦ **Perform initial processing:** We would also do some initial processing. Right after the user enters the names, we would make sure that the names are not empty strings, that is, `" "` (one pair of quotation marks with no space between them).

Avoiding Mistakes, Plain and Simple

Even though many programmers take measures to prevent bugs, programmers still sometimes let problems slip through. However, if you're careful, you can avoid a lot of these problems. When you create software, you should be in the right frame of mind to watch for potential problems *as you're writing the code*. (Getting into the right frame of mind includes ensuring you have enough sleep, avoiding distractions, and doing other things that help you concentrate on your work, but this section also describes some specifics you should consider.)

The list of potential problems that we're giving you here could probably go on and on for thousands of pages. However, the point is not to have a big checklist but rather for you to go through this list and start to recognize the things you need to do to write good code. Writing code is conscious and deliberate. It's like when you are going down a sidewalk and are vaguely aware of such things as whether cars are coming or whether you need to step over any holes. These hazards are always in the back of your mind as you carefully walk along. Writing code is the same way: Certain *gotchas* should stay in the back of your mind, too:

✦ **Indexes:** Strings and arrays run from index 0 to 1 less than the length. Using a loop, such as `for (i=0; i<=size; i++)`, is a common mistake. The less-than-or-equal-to symbol is incorrect, yet people make this mistake a lot. The scary thing is that sometimes the code will still function, and you'll just end up overwriting something else. And worse, you might not immediately catch this coding error, so it will manifest itself as a bug in the program later.

✦ **For every new, there's a `delete`:** Whenever you allocate an object using `new`, remember to free it. But forgetting the `delete` doesn't usually create noticeable bugs in your program; read the next item to see what's more likely to cause a noticeable bug.

✦ **Remember what you deleted:** Worse than forgetting to delete an object is forgetting *that* you deleted it and continuing to use it. When you delete a pointer, make sure that you didn't pass it to some other object that stored it away and plans to use it again.

✦ **Don't forget to create an object:** You may have seen this one: An error message pops up that says:

```
The instruction at 0x00402119 referenced memory at 0x00000000. The memory
    could not
be written.
```

This means someone had a pointer variable and forgot to call `new`. We generated this message easily on purpose with the following code:

```
int *x = 0;

*x = 10;
```

We created a pointer variable and initialized it to 0, meaning it's not being used. But before calling `new` or setting the variable equal to some object's address, we tried to stuff something into the memory it points to (which is address 0, something the operating system doesn't like). And the operating system responded with the error message. This is a bug we see far more than we would expect in commercial software.

These are just a few items to think about, but you can see that they mostly deal with memory issues, such as allocating memory and using it incorrectly. Most important, you can avoid them if you're conscientious with your programming. As you code, bear in mind the repercussions of what you're doing. And as crazy as this sounds, remember what you might be forgetting! Ask yourself, am I forgetting to delete some pointers or that someone else has a copy of this pointer I'm about to delete? If you keep these things in mind, you should avoid some of the most common bugs.

Chapter 2: Debugging a Program

In This Chapter

✔ Working with debuggers

✔ Using the CodeBlocks debugger

✔ Tracing through a program and in and out of functions

✔ Using other debuggers

✔ Getting seriously advanced debuggers

*I*n this chapter, we talk about how you can use a debugger to track down problems and bugs in your program. Sooner or later, things don't work the way you planned them. In this case, you have several plans of attack. One plan involves a hammer and the computer, but we don't recommend that one. Instead, we suggest using a debugger to try to *fix* the program.

Programming with Debuggers

A *debugger* is a special tool that you use for tracing line by line through your program. Take a look at Listing 2-1. This is just a basic program with a main and a couple of functions that we use to demonstrate the debugger.

Listing 2-1:   Tracing a Simple Program

```cpp
#include <iostream>

using namespace std;

int CountRabbits(int original)
{
    int result = original * 2;
    result = result + 10;
    result = result * 4;
    cout << "Calculating " << result << endl;
    return result * 10;
}

int CountAntelopes(int original)
{
    int result = original + 10;
    result = result - 2;
    cout << "Calculating " << result << endl;
```

(continued)

Listing 2-1 *(continued)*

```
        return result;
}

int main()
{
        int rabbits = 5;
        int antelopes = 5;
        rabbits = CountRabbits(rabbits);
        cout << "Rabbits now at " << rabbits << endl;
        antelopes = CountAntelopes(antelopes);
        cout << "Antelopes now at " << antelopes << endl;
        // system("PAUSE"); // add this for Windows
        return 0;
}
```

When you type and run this program, you see the following output:

```
Calculating 80
Rabbits now at 800
Calculating 13
Antelopes now at 13
```

Now look closely at `main` and follow it through, line by line. The first thing `main` does is declare a couple of integers. Then `main` calls into the `CountRabbits` functions. The `CountRabbits` function declares an integer and does a few lines of calculations. Then the `CountRabbits` function prints a message. Finally it returns. Once back in `main`, the program prints another message and then calls into the `CountAntelopes` function. This function also declares an integer, does some calculations, prints a message, and then returns. Back in `main`, the program prints another message, and the program finally finishes.

What we just gave you is a linear description of the entire process of this program. You can see these same steps by using a debugger. With a debugger, you see the computer going line by line through your code. A debugger performs the first line of your program and then waits for you to tell it to perform the next line — then the next, and the next, and so on, until the end of the program.

In this example, we use the debugger that comes with the CodeBlocks application. If you prefer to use some other debuggers, we recommend that, for most of this chapter, you at least try the CodeBlocks debugger. It is a nice tool, and we think that you'll be happy with it. But besides that, it allows you to follow through the examples we give. Then you can return to whatever other tool you're using.

You must know one important aspect before using a debugger. For the debugger to understand your code, you must compile it with debugging information. The compiler adds extra information into the final executable so that the debugger can locate your source code and variable information. Here's how you turn on debug information:

Adding debug and symbol information

When you compile with debug information, you are adding debug and symbol information to the final executable file. This information includes data about the source-code files, including the line numbers and the variable names. This is the primary difference between a *debug* version and a *release* version of your product: People typically don't include debug and symbol information in a version of the product that they release to the general public. One reason is that including it makes it too easy for competitors and hackers to reverse-engineer the product. (Another reason is that including

the debug and symbol information makes the application run slower and consume more system resources.) However, the actual source code is not in the debug and symbol information; that stays in the source-code file. The debug information, instead, just contains line numbers, which serve as references (pointers, if you will!) into the source-code file. So hackers and competitors won't have the complete source to your program, but they will have variable names and other information that could make their job easier (and yours harder).

+ **CodeBlocks:** Choose Debug in the Build Target drop-down list box.

+ **Dev-C++ 5.0:** Open the project and choose Tools⇨Compiler Options. In the Linker tab, make sure that Generate Debugging Information is turned on.

+ **gcc under MinGW and Cygwin:** Add the -g option to the compiler. You will probably do this inside a `Makefile`.

After you change the compiler options to generate debug information, you must rebuild your project. The reason is that the compiler and linker must regenerate object files and executable files with the debug information.

Running the debugger

After you have rebuilt your project, you can run the debugger. To start the debugger, click Debug/Continue, choose Debug⇨Start, or press F8. (If you click Run, the application runs as normal without entering debug mode.) When you start the debugger, you should see a screen like that shown in Figure 2-1. (You also get a console window behind that screen. This console window contains the output for the program you are debugging.)

Figure 2-1 shows two special features you need to know to debug programs. The first is the red circle and the second is the yellow triangle. The red circle is a *breakpoint* — a place where you want the debugger to stop. You add breakpoints to the Editing window by clicking the left side next to the instruction where you want to stop. When you click that spot again, the red circle goes away, showing that you have cleared the breakpoint. You can place as many breakpoints as you want in the application, but you can place breakpoints only on instructions.

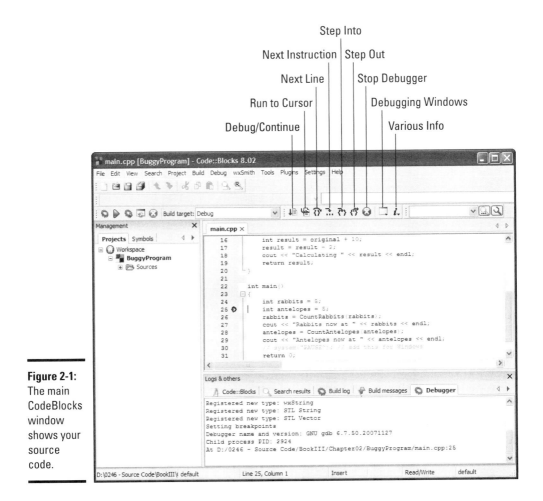

Figure 2-1:
The main
CodeBlocks
window
shows your
source
code.

The yellow triangle is the *instruction pointer,* which shows the instruction that the debugger will execute next. As you tell the debugger to execute instructions, the yellow triangle moves. Whenever you start the application in debug mode, the yellow pointer automatically stops at each breakpoint. Figure 2-1 shows how the debugger looks when the yellow triangle stops at a breakpoint.

When you start the debugger again by clicking Debug/Continue, execution begins as if the application is in normal run mode until the debugger encounters another breakpoint. If the debugger doesn't encounter a breakpoint, the dialog box closes, and the program returns to the source screen.

If you don't set any breakpoints and try to debug your program, it will run without letting you trace through the code. That is, the program will run as if you're not running it in the debugger.

Look at the Debugger tab of the Logs and Others window shown in Figure 2-1. This tab contains debugging messages from your application. Whenever you see the At message, you know that the debugger has stopped at a particular location. The remainder of the message tells you where the debugger has stopped. In Figure 2-1, the debugger has stopped at line 25 of the `D:/0246 - Source Code/BookIII/Chapter02/BuggyProgram/ main.cpp` file.

So go ahead and run the program. Begin by setting a breakpoint at line 22, the `int main()` entry. Click Debug/Continue, choose Debug⇨Start, or press F8 to start the debugger. You'll see a number of messages appear in the Debugger tab and then you'll see the At message when the debugger stops at line 23. (If you spaced your program slightly different from the way we did in Listing 2-1, you may see a slightly different line number.) The yellow triangle should appear on line 23, which contains a curly bracket, meaning that the program is stopped at that line. The instruction pointer stopped at the curly bracket because it is the first instruction after the `main()` entry.

Click Next Line, which is the third button on the Debugger toolbar. The button you want is the one with an icon with two braces, {}, and an arrow pointing over it from the left side to the right side. (You can also press F7.) The yellow triangle (instruction pointer) moves to the first assignment statement on line 24, which is

```
int rabbits = 5;
```

Click Next Line. When you click the button, the instruction pointer advances to the next line. The computer just performed the first line in `main()`, and next the computer will perform the second line in `main()`, which is this:

```
int antelopes = 5;
```

Click Next Line again. Now the instruction pointer is on the third line of `main()`, which looks like this:

```
rabbits = CountRabbits(rabbits);
```

This third line of `main()` is a function call, and now you have a choice. (*Don't* click Next Line!) You can either tell the computer to just perform what's inside this function without stopping on each line for you to see, or you can "step into it" and see the individual lines.

Click the fifth button from the left, the one called Step Into, which shows two braces, {}, and an arrow going from the left into them. (Or press Shift+F7.) When you do, the instruction pointer moves into the `CountRabbits()` function. The highlight will be on the first line in that function:

```
int result = original * 2;
```

When the highlight moved into the function, the computer *stepped into* the function. Now think about the symbol for the icon that caused this to happen: The icon has two braces, {}, and an arrow pointing into them. The two braces represent a function. (They're supposed to be the open and closing brace for the function.) And the arrow points into the middle of the braces, which means that you're going to *step into* the function. That's the idea behind the odd symbols. The one you've been clicking before, the Next Line icon that has an arrow going over, means *stepping over* the function.

Now, before stepping into this function, because you were clicking lines that were not functions but just individual lines, you used the Next Line (that is, the step over) button. But you could have used either the Next Line button or the Step Into button, because *stepping into a function* doesn't bear much meaning on statements that are not functions.

Normally, we use the Next Line button by default and choose the Step Into button only when we specifically want to go into a function. The reason is that some lines of code that may not appear to be functions really are. For example, cout << "a"; is, in fact, a function, and you might not want to step into that code, because either the source code for it might not be present or you simply might not be interested in the details of the function.

It's time to see how these debugging features work. The following procedure takes you through the debugging process so that you can see the CodeBlocks debugger in action:

1. **Click Next Line three times until the instruction pointer appears on the cout line:**

    ```
    cout << "Calculating " << result << endl;
    ```

    This line writes output to the console. Remember, in addition to the main CodeBlocks window, you also have a console window. That's where the output from this line goes.

2. **Click Next Line.**

3. **Click the console window.**

    You see the results of the cout statement:

    ```
    Calculating 80.
    ```

    Then the instruction pointer lands on the return statement.

4. **Click Next Line again.**

    The instruction pointer is on the closing brace of the function. Note that CodeBlocks highlights both the opening brace and the closing brace in blue. This feature helps you see where a function begins and ends in the Integrated Development Environment (IDE).

5. Click Next Line yet again.

The instruction pointer returns to `main()`, on the line following the call to the `CountRabbits()` function:

```
cout << "Rabbits now at " << rabbits << endl;
```

6. Click Next Line again.

The instruction pointer is on the second function call:

```
antelopes = CountAntelopes(antelopes);
```

7. But this time, instead of stepping into the function, just press Next Line to step over it.

The instruction pointer advances to the next line, which is this:

```
cout << "Antelopes now at " << antelopes << endl;
```

Take a look at the console. The `CountAntelopes()` function itself contained a call to `cout`. You can see on the console that this `cout` line did its stuff:

```
Calculating 13
```

You saw the output from the `CountAntelopes()` function because, although you stepped over the function, you didn't actually skip it: The function ran in its entirety during that one click of the Next button. The debugger just didn't go through it line by line, that's all.

8. Click Next Line to do the final `cout` line.

Your entire output now looks like this:

```
Calculating 80
Rabbits now at 800
Calculating 13
Antelopes now at 13
```

and the instruction pointer ends on the final `return` statement:

```
return 0;
```

9. Click Next Line one more time and the highlight is on the closing brace of `main()`.

Now things get just a little strange. Unbeknownst to us, there's really more code than we see. When you compile and link your program, the linker includes some special startup code that calls your `main()` function.

10. Click Next Line one more time, and you are timewarped out of your source file and into some assembly language code. The Debugger window shows the following message:

```
In __mingw_CRTStartup () ()
```

11. To see the assembly language code, you must click a new button, Next Instruction (four buttons from the left on the Debugger toolbar).

CodeBlocks automatically displays a new window called Disassembly, as shown in Figure 2-2. The numbers in your figure may differ from ours, but the code is the same.

Figure 2-2:
The Disassembly window displays the assembly language version of your code.

```
Disassembly                                                    ☒
Function:    __mingw_CRTStartup
Frame start: 0022FFB8
    00401150    push    %ebp
    00401161    mov     %esp,%ebp
    00401163    push    %ebx
    00401164    sub     $0x24,%esp
    00401167    movl    $0x401000,(%esp)
    0040116E    call    0x41533c <SetUnhandledExceptionFilter@4>
    00401163    sub     $0x4,%esp
    00401166    call    0x40ce0c <__cpu_features_init>
    0040116B    call    0x40cf0c <fpreset>
    00401170    movl    $0x0,-0x8(%ebp)
    00401177    lea     -0x8(%ebp),%eax
    0040117A    mov     %eax,0x10(%esp)
    0040117E    mov     0x4410a0,%eax
    00401183    movl    $0x446004,(%esp)
    0040118A    mov     %eax,0xc(%esp)
    0040118E    lea     -0xc(%ebp),%eax
    00401191    mov     %eax,0x8(%esp)
    00401195    mov     $0x446000,%eax
    0040119A    mov     %eax,0x4(%esp)
    0040119E    call    0x416234 <__getmainargs>
    004011A3    mov     0x449b10,%eax
    004011A8    test    %eax,%eax
    004011AA    je      0x401210 <__mingw_CRTStartup+192>
    004011AC    mov     %eax,0x4410b0
                                              Save to text file
```

Yuck. This is assembly, a human-readable form of the language that the computer understands. You don't have to know what all this means, but you can probably figure out that the line

```
(hexadecimal number) call    (another hexadecimal number) <__main>
```

is where this code stuff calls into your `main`.

12. To get out of this, just click the first button (called Debug/Continue) or the sixth button (called Step Out), the one with an arrow pointing to the left of the two braces, {}. (Or just press Ctrl+F7 or Ctrl+Shift+F7, respectively.)

Clicking Debug/Continue causes the program to run to the real end of your program (or the next breakpoint) and then finish. Clicking Step Out tells the debugger to step out of the current function, which in this case is the same as running to the end of the program.

13. If you want to avoid going into the crazy assembly-code stuff, you can avoid it by clicking Debug/Continue when you get to the final `return` line of your program.

And that's how you trace through your program line by line. But you can do a lot more with the program when you're tracing through it. You can look at the values in your variables, you can change the values of the variables, and you can get a list of all the function calls that led up to the current position in your program. You can do plenty, and we explain all this in the remainder of this minibook.

Recognizing the parts of the CodeBlocks debugger

The CodeBlocks debugger displays the Debugger toolbar whenever you debug an application. The previous sections of this chapter have discussed many of the buttons on the Debugger toolbar: Debug/Continue, Next Line, Next Instruction, Step Into, and Step Out. However, the toolbar contains a number of other interesting buttons you should know about.

Sometimes you examine a piece of code in the editor and want to see what the variables look like when you get to that point. To see what happens, place your text cursor at the place you want to stop (using only the mouse cursor isn't enough) and click Run to Cursor (the second button on the Debugger toolbar). The debugger stops at the line where your cursor is resting. In this case, the text cursor acts as a kind of breakpoint for the debugger.

After you debug your application for a while and locate problems you want to fix, you may not want to run the rest of the application. When this situation occurs, simply click Stop Debugger (the button that looks like a stop sign). The debugger stops immediately. You can make any required changes and restart the debugger as normal.

CodeBlocks provides access to a number of debugging windows. In fact, you saw one of these windows previously in the chapter — the Disassembly window. You access these windows by clicking the Debugging Windows button (the one that looks like a window, to the right of the stop sign buttons). Later chapters in this minibook describe these windows in detail. Here is a quick summary of the windows for now:

Book III
Chapter 2

Debugging a Program

+ **Breakpoints:** Presents all the breakpoints you've set in your application. Double-clicking a breakpoint entry takes you to that breakpoint in the editor. You can use this window also to remove one or more breakpoints.

+ **Call Stack:** Displays the function calls used to get to the current point in the code.

+ **CPU Registers:** Shows the contents of the hardware registers in the processor. You won't normally need to view these registers unless you're performing low-level programming tasks.

+ **Disassembly:** Let's you see the underlying machine code used to make your code work. You won't normally need to view this information unless you're performing low-level programming tasks.

+ **Memory Dump:** Displays the precise way that the application stores data in memory, which may not look very much like the C++ view. This is a useful window because it helps you better understand how memory works and how your application uses memory. In some cases, knowing how a variable stores memory can help you locate problems with your code.

✦ **Running Threads:** Shows a list of threads, other than the main thread, associated with the current application. You use this window for debugging multithreaded applications.

✦ **Watches:** Displays a list of local variables and function arguments. You can also add other variables to monitor as a watch. The Watches window is probably the most useful debugger window because it illustrates the C++ view of your data and shows how the application code manipulates that data.

The debugger also provides access to a number of information windows. You access these windows by clicking the Various Info button (the one with an *i* in italics far down on the left). Here is a quick summary of the information windows:

✦ **Current Stack Frame:** Shows the current stack frame information. C++ creates something called a *stack frame* when certain events occur, such as calling a function. This stack frame contains the data and data references for the current function. You won't normally need to view this information unless you're performing low-level programming tasks.

✦ **Loaded Libraries:** Contains a list of all of the libraries loaded to run your application. It's important to know which libraries your application uses when you deploy (load) it on other machines. In many cases, you may not even know that C++ requires certain libraries to run your application, so this is an exceptionally useful window.

✦ **Targets and Files:** Provides a detailed view of how the loaded libraries are used in your application. You won't normally need to view this information unless you're performing low-level programming tasks.

✦ **FPU Status:** Displays the register information for the Floating-Point Unit (FPU) in your processor. At one time, the FPU was a separate chip, but now it appears as part of your main processor. The FPU is exceptionally adept at performing real number (versus integer) math. You won't normally need to view this information unless you're performing low-level programming tasks.

✦ **Signal Handling:** Shows how CodeBlocks handles signals between the hardware and your application, such as an arithmetic exception or a segmentation fault. You won't normally need to view this information unless you're performing low-level programming tasks.

Debugging with Different Tools

You can use several tools for debugging your code. However, which compiler you usually use dictates which debugging tools you can use. For example, Microsoft Visual C++ has a really good debugger. But getting it to debug a program compiled with Dev-C++, for example, is difficult because different compilers use different forms of debugging and symbol information. The type used by the various breeds of gcc compilers is different from the type used by Microsoft Visual C++.

Standard debuggers

Here's a quick rundown of some of the debuggers that are available:

✦ **Visual C++:** This debugger works similarly to the CodeBlocks debugger. It's primarily for debugging programs that were built by using Visual C++. However, if you are brave and need to debug something for which you have no code or symbol information, its support for assembly-code debugging is good.

✦ **gdb:** This is the standard debugger that ships with MinGW and Cygwin. It's a command-line tool, but we don't recommend using it as such. Instead, we suggest using the Insight debugger with it so you can use a graphical *front end.* This makes life a lot easier. But if you insist on using the command-line version, you can learn about it by typing gdb at the command prompt and then typing help.

✦ **Dev-C++ 5.0:** Starting with Version 5.0, Dev-C++ has an integrated debugger that works similarly to the Insight debugger. You may want to give this a try. (If you're using a version of Dev-C++ prior to 5.0, you have to use the Insight debugger.)

Chapter 3: Stopping and Inspecting Your Code

In This Chapter

✔ Setting, enabling, and disabling breakpoints

✔ Temporarily setting or disabling a breakpoint

✔ Inspecting a variable

✔ Watching all the local variables

✔ Watching any variable

Sometimes, things break. But what we're talking about here is the code. Now this is one of those instances when a word or phrase has lots of different meanings. Programmers talk about *breaking the code.* This phrase usually means one of two things: It may mean that the programmer made a mistake and the code no longer *works*. But in this chapter, we're using a different definition for the term. When you're debugging a program, you can have the program run until it gets to a certain line in the code. The debugger then stops at that line, and you can look at the values of variables, inspect things about the code, or even change the variables. When the program stops, that's called *breaking.* The reason it stops on that particular line is because you put a *breakpoint* on that line.

In this chapter, we talk about setting and manipulating breakpoints in your code (if nothing else in your code is broken) and inspecting and modifying various aspects of your code, such as variables, after your code stops at a breakpoint.

In the examples in this chapter, we use the debugger supplied with the CodeBlocks IDE. If you use a different product, the debugger will probably work about the same but not precisely the same. For example, everything we show you how to do here you can do in Microsoft Visual C++. The keystrokes and mouse clicks may be different, but the features are present. Make sure you check the vendor documentation for precise details on using your debugger.

To work through the examples in this chapter, make sure that you compile with debug information turned on. (In CodeBlocks, you can compile with debug information by choosing Debug in the Build Target field of the Compiler toolbar. If you can't see the Compiler toolbar, choose View➪ Toolbars➪Compiler to place a checkmark next to the Compiler entry.)

When you are developing software, you should always have debug information on. That way, you're always ready to debug your code and fix things. Only when you're ready to release the product formally should you recompile it without debug information. (Although we do recommend doing a full test of the software again without debug information, just to make sure that it still functions correctly.)

Setting and Disabling Breakpoints

A *breakpoint* is a place in your code where you tell the debugger to stop.

In the sections that follow, we talk about breakpoints. Please use the code in Listing 3-1 for these sections. Remember what you're supposed to do? Make sure that you compile it with debug information on!

Listing 3-1: Using a Program for Breakpoints and Inspections

```
#include <iostream>

using namespace std;

class BrokenMirror
{
private:
    int NumberOfPieces;

public:
    int GetNumberOfPieces();
    void SetNumberOfPieces(int newamount);
    BrokenMirror() : NumberOfPieces(100) {}
};

int BrokenMirror::GetNumberOfPieces()
{
    return NumberOfPieces;
}

void BrokenMirror::SetNumberOfPieces(int newamount)
{
    newamount = newamount * 20;
    NumberOfPieces = newamount;
}

int main()
{
    BrokenMirror mirror;
    mirror.SetNumberOfPieces(10);
    cout << mirror.GetNumberOfPieces() << endl;

    return 0;
}
```

Setting a breakpoint in CodeBlocks

Go ahead and compile the program in Listing 3-1 (with debug information turned on). Look at the left margin of the window, to the right of the line numbers. Figure 3-1 shows a small circle on line 16. When you view the IDE, this circle is red. The red circle is a breakpoint that we set. To set this breakpoint in your code, click in the area between the left margin and the code, as shown in the figure on line 16. (It's line 16 on our screens, but if you formatted your code differently, you may see it on a different line number.) If you haven't done so, go ahead and click the mouse in the left margin of the `int BrokenMirror::GetNumberOfPieces()` line. You see a red circle appear in the left margin. You just placed a breakpoint on that line! Hurray!

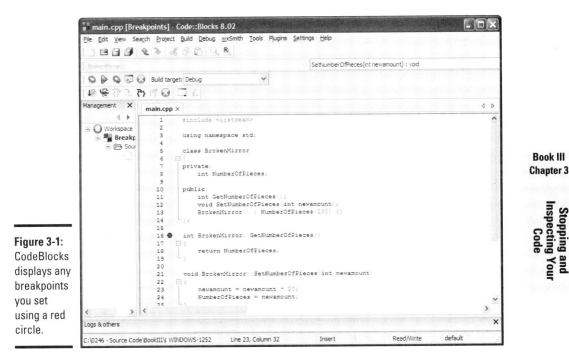

Figure 3-1:
CodeBlocks displays any breakpoints you set using a red circle.

Click again in the left margin of the same line. The red circle disappears. When the circle disappears, the breakpoint is gone.

Finally, click a third time, because for now you do want a breakpoint there.

Now, run the program by clicking the Debug/Continue button (it looks like a sheet of paper with a down-pointing arrow next to it) on the Debugger toolbar. If you don't see the Debugger toolbar, choose

View➪Toolbars➪Debugger to place a checkmark next to the Debugger entry. (Don't click the Run button, the blue right-pointing triangle, on the Compiler toolbar because choosing this option simply runs the program without debugging it.) When you click Debug/Continue, the console window may pop in front, so just click the CodeBlocks window to bring it back to the front.

The program runs until it gets to the breakpoint you chose for the int BrokenMirror::GetNumberOfPieces line, as shown in Figure 3-2. Note that execution actually ends with the opening curly brace because this is the beginning of execution for this function. The yellow right-pointing triangle tells you the current instruction that the CodeBlocks debugger will execute. You can now click the Next Line button (it's the button with two braces, {}, and an arrow pointing over it from the left to the right) to move to the next line, or you can click Debug/Continue to run the rest of the program.

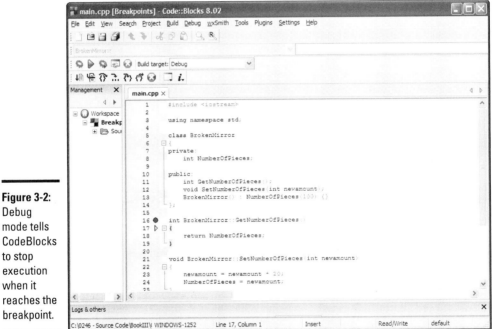

Figure 3-2:
Debug mode tells CodeBlocks to stop execution when it reaches the breakpoint.

Enabling and disabling breakpoints

You may have times when you have several breakpoints set, and you want to turn them off momentarily, but you don't want to lose them because you may want to turn them back on later. You can do this by *disabling* the breakpoints. Disabling the breakpoint is faster than removing the breakpoints and then going back and finding them again to turn them back on. Use the following steps to disable a breakpoint:

1. **Right-click the red circle and choose Edit Breakpoint from the context menu.**

You see the Edit Breakpoint dialog box, as shown in Figure 3-3.

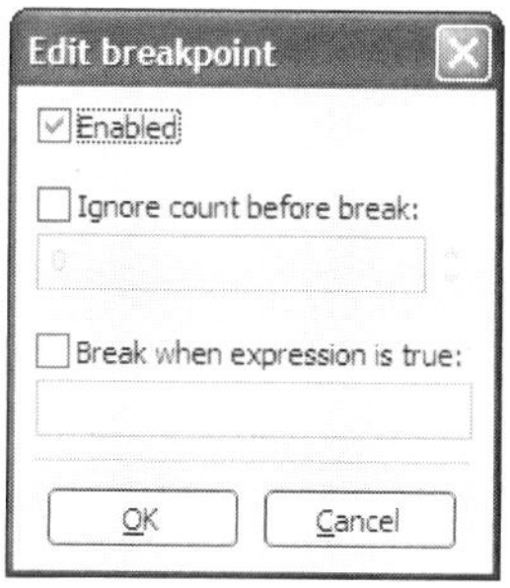

Figure 3-3:
Use the Edit
Breakpoint
dialog box
to enable
and disable
breakpoints.

2. **Clear the Enabled option and click OK.**

CodeBlocks disables the breakpoint so that it no longer stops application execution.

Many debuggers show a disabled breakpoint using a hollow red circle. Unfortunately, CodeBlocks doesn't provide this visual cue. To see that disabling the breakpoint actually does work, set a new breakpoint at the line that reads `return NumberOfPieces;`. Click Debug/Continue and you'll see that the debugger bypasses the first breakpoint and stops at the second, as shown in Figure 3-4.

In some cases, you want to enable or disable a number of breakpoints. Use the following steps to perform this task:

1. **Choose Debug⇨Debugging Windows⇨Breakpoints.**

You see the Breakpoints window shown in Figure 3-5. The window shows the kind of breakpoint, the breakpoint location, and the line in the code file where the breakpoint appears.

2. **Right-click the breakpoint entry and choose Breakpoint Properties from the context menu.**

You see the Edit Breakpoint dialog box (refer to Figure 3-3), where you can change the breakpoint status.

Book III
Chapter 3

**Stopping and
Inspecting Your
Code**

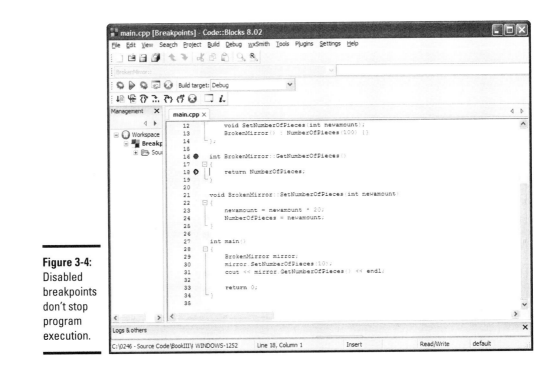

Figure 3-4:
Disabled
breakpoints
don't stop
program
execution.

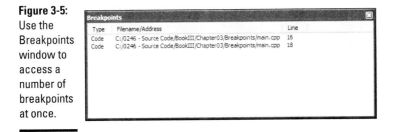

Figure 3-5:
Use the
Breakpoints
window to
access a
number of
breakpoints
at once.

Watching, Inspecting, and Changing Variables

When you stop at a breakpoint in a program, you can do more than just look at the code. You can have fun with it! You can look at the current values of the variables, and you can change them.

Listing 3-2 is a sample program that you can use to try out these examples of inspecting, changing, and watching variables. Please note that this program is similar to Listing 3-1, earlier in this chapter, but you should see some differences. Specifically, we added a line to the `SetNumberOfPieces` member function

```
newamount = newamount * 20;
```

We added a new function called SpecialMath, and we added an i variable to main that is initialized to 10; then we doubled it, and we passed it into the SetNumberOfPieces function.

Listing 3-2: Using a Program for Breakpoints and Inspections

```cpp
#include <iostream>

using namespace std;

class BrokenMirror
{
private:
    int NumberOfPieces;

public:
    int GetNumberOfPieces();
    void SetNumberOfPieces(int newamount);
    BrokenMirror() : NumberOfPieces(100) {}
};

int BrokenMirror::GetNumberOfPieces()
{
    return NumberOfPieces;
}

void BrokenMirror::SetNumberOfPieces(int newamount)
{
    newamount = newamount * 20;
    NumberOfPieces = newamount;
}

int SpecialMath(int x)
{
    return x * 10 - 5;
}

int main()
{
    int i = 10;
    BrokenMirror mirror;

    i = i + SpecialMath(i);

    mirror.SetNumberOfPieces(i);
    cout << mirror.GetNumberOfPieces() << endl;

    // Clear this comment if you want the application to stop to
    // display the results.
    // system("PAUSE");

    return 0;
}
```

Watching the local variables

To watch the local variables in your program, follow these steps:

1. **Compile this program with debug information on.**

2. **Set a breakpoint at the int i = 10; line in main.**

3. **Click Debug/Continue.**

4. **When the debugger stops at the breakpoint, click the Next Line button on the Debugger toolbar so that you are one line beyond the following line:**

    ```
    int i = 10;
    ```

5. **Choose Debug⇨Debugging Windows⇨Watches.**

    You see the Watches window, as shown in Figure 3-6.

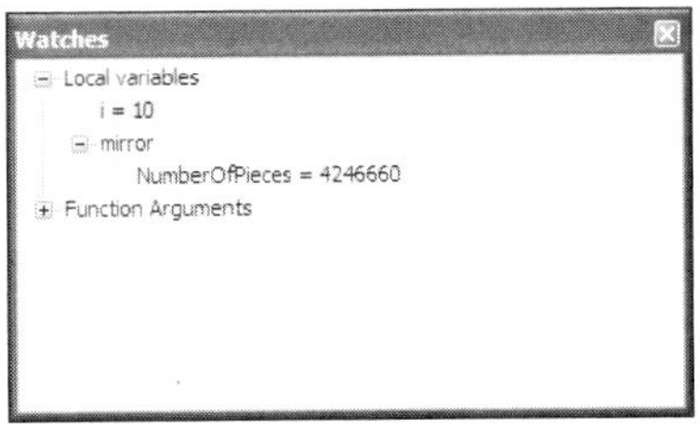

Figure 3-6:
The
Watches
window
shows the
value of
variables
and objects.

6. **Open the Local Variables folder.**

    You see the current value of i, which is 10.

Figure 3-6 also shows the mirror variable because it's a local variable. When we click the plus symbol next to the mirror variable, we see what's inside the object. In this case, you see something like:

```
NumberOfPieces   4246660
```

(Your number may not precisely match the one shown in Figure 3-6.) Oops! That's a strange value. Well, the reason is this: We haven't run the following line yet:

```
BrokenMirror mirror;
```

The debugger is sitting on this line, waiting to perform it. It turns out that C++ allocates the space for all the local variables at the beginning of the function. And so the space for mirror is there, but the space is not set up yet. Meanwhile, there's just garbage in the space. (Yes, that is really the term programmers use for whatever may be in something before it's initialized: *garbage*. We're not making this up!)

To run the next line and see the results, follow these steps:

1. **Position your windows so that you can see both the Watches window (at least the line showing NumberOfPieces) and the source-code window.**

    At this point, you have several options:

    *   You can click Next Line and the debugger proceeds directly to the next line of main, skipping through all the code required to initialize NumberOfPieces.

    *   As an alternative, you can click Step Into on the Debugger toolbar to see how the application initializes NumberOfPieces.

2. **In the source-code window, click Next Line so the BrokenMirror mirror; line runs.**

    The value in the NumberOfPieces member variable has changed. In the Watches window, the value for NumberOfPieces now says:

    ```
    NumberOfPieces = 100
    ```

    The line showing the value is now red. That color change gives you a visual indication that the value has changed.

    When you look at an object in the Watches window, you are looking at a particular instance, not the class. Therefore, all the member variables have values stored in them. (But if the member variables are uninitialized, those values will be garbage.)

3. **Click the Next Line button again to run this line:**

    ```
    i = i + SpecialMath(i);
    ```

    The NumberOfPieces line in the Local Variables window changes back to black. The reason is that with the running of this single line of code, the NumberOfPieces value did not change. Only the values that changed under the most recent running of the code get red. The others get black. The yellow triangle will now point to this line:

    ```
    mirror.SetNumberOfPieces(i);
    ```

4. **Click the Step Into button to go into the function.**

    The Watches window changes drastically. The Local Variables folder shows that there aren't any local variables. Open the Function Arguments folder, however, and you see the variables for the current function, including the this pointer, which is the pointer to the current object. Figure 3-7 shows the new information (the precise numbers you see may vary from those shown in the figure).

Book III
Chapter 3

**Stopping and
Inspecting Your
Code**

Figure 3-7:
Function
arguments
appear in
a special
folder.

5. **Click the Next Line button so that the instruction pointer is on the line that reads**

   ```
   NumberOfPieces = newamount;
   ```

6. **Take a look at the `newamount` value in the Watches window.**

   It now says 2100.

7. **Right-click the `newamount` line in the Watches window and choose Change Value from the context menu.**

   Voilà! A Change Variable's Value dialog box appears, and you can actually type a new value for `newamount`! Excellent!

8. **Type 1000 and press Enter.**

   You just changed the value of `newamount`.

9. **Go back to the main CodeBlocks window and click Next Line a few more times until you're one line past the `cout` line.**

10. **Take a look at the console window, and you will see the output from this line:**

    ```
    cout << mirror.GetNumberOfPieces() << endl;
    ```

    The output looks like this:

    ```
    1000
    ```

    Yes, that is the value you stuffed inside the `newamount` variable, not the value that it used to have, which was 2100.

Watching other variables

You can watch any variables you want by using the Watches window. To watch any variables, not necessarily the locals, follow these steps:

1. **Go ahead and run the program in Listing 3-2 inside CodeBlocks from the beginning, stopping at the `int i = 10;` line.**

2. **Right-click `i` and choose Watch 'i' from the context menu.**

   CodeBlocks adds a watch for `i` to the Watches window.

3. **Click the Next Line button.**

The value of i in the Watches window shows 10. Now, as you step through the program, you can watch the value of i at any time. Further, you can change the value of i by double-clicking its line in the Watch Expressions window.

Adding a watch is useful for global variables that do not show up in the Local Variables folder of the Watches window. This feature is handy when you are stepping through the code, going from function to function, and you have a global variable that you want to monitor.

Now for something really great. Here's how you can perform complex expressions inside the Watch Expression window: Right-click the Watches window and choose Add Watch from the context menu. In the Keyword field of the Edit Watch dialog box type: **i * 50 + 3 / 2**. Click OK. The result of this expression shows up in the Watches window, as shown in Figure 3-8. Very nice indeed!

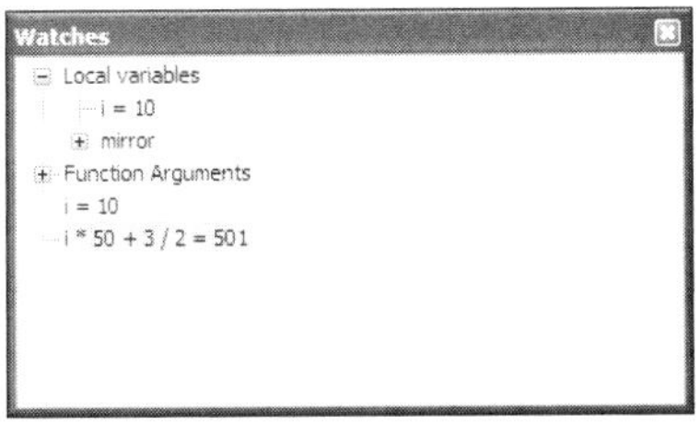

Figure 3-8:
The Watches window can contain complex expressions.

```
Watches                                   ☒
⊟ Local variables
    ├─ i = 10
    ⊞ mirror
⊞ Function Arguments
    i = 10
    └─ i * 50 + 3 / 2 = 501
```

Chapter 4: Traveling About the Stack

In This Chapter

✔ **Moving about the stack**

✔ **How local variables are stored**

✔ **Viewing threads**

✔ **Tracing through assembly code**

✔ **Viewing memory**

Debuggers can be powerful things. They can leap tall computer programs in a single bound and see through them to find all their flaws. The more you know about these little debuggers, the more you can put them to use. In this chapter, we show you how to move about the stack and to make use of advanced debugger features.

Stacking Your Data

A stack is a common thing in the computer world. We have stacks of bills, and stacks of paychecks, and stacks of data. The stacks of data are interesting because, unlike the bills and paychecks, they live inside the computer's memory. But the stack metaphor is appropriate. When the operating system runs a program, it gives that program a *stack,* which is simply a big chunk of memory. But the data is stored just like a stack of cards: With a stack of real cards, you can put a card on the top, then another, and do that six times over; then you can take a card off and take another card off. You can put cards on the top and take them off the top. And if you follow these rules, you can't insert them into the middle or bottom of the stack. You can only look at what's on the top. A stack *data structure* works the same way: You can store data in it by *pushing* the data *onto* the stack, and you can take data off by *popping* it *off* the stack. And yes, because the stack is really just a bunch of computer memory, sneaking around and accessing memory in the middle of the stack is possible. But under normal circumstances, you don't do that: You put data on and take data off.

But what's interesting about the stack is that it works closely with the main CPU, such as the Intel Pentium, AMD Athlon 64, or whatever is inside your computer. The CPU has its own little storage bin right on the chip itself.

(This isn't in the system memory or RAM; it's inside the CPU itself.) This storage bin holds what are called *registers*. One such register is the *stack pointer*, called the ESP. (That stands for Extended Stack Pointer, because the earlier Intel processors just had a Stack Pointer, or SP. Then, when the folks at Intel replaced that chip, they made the registers bigger and just stuck on the letter *E* for *extended* to denote the bigger registers.)

The stack is useful in many situations and is used extensively behind the scenes in the programs you write. The compiler generates code that uses the stack to store local variables, to function parameters, and the order that functions are called. It's all stacked onto the stack and stuck in place, ready to be unstacked.

Moving about the stack

The CodeBlocks debugger, like most debuggers, lets you look at the stack. But really, you're not looking directly at the stack. When a debugger shows you the *stack,* it is showing you the list of function calls that led up to the application's current position in the program code. However, that information is stored in the stack, and the debugger uses the stack to get that information. So that's why programmers always call the list of function calls the *stack,* even though you're not actually looking at the stack.

Figure 4-1 shows an example of the Call Stack window in CodeBlocks. To see the Call Stack window, simply choose Debug⇨Debugging Windows⇨Call Stack. You can see the Call Stack window in front of the main CodeBlocks window. No information appears in the Call Stack window until you start running a program.

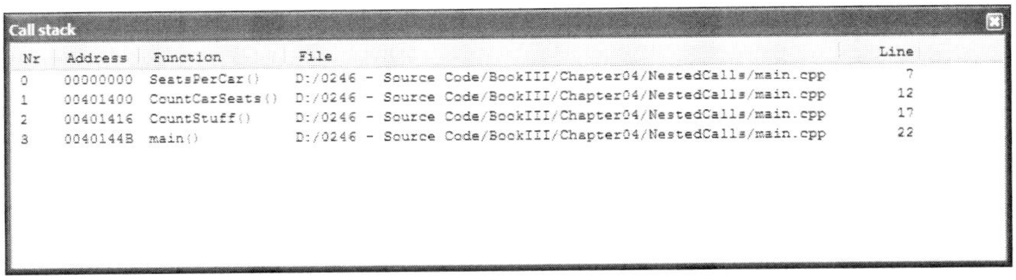

Figure 4-1:
The Call Stack window shows the function calls that led up to the current position.

```
Call stack
 Nr   Address    Function        File                                                              Line
 0    00000000   SeatsPerCar()   D:/0246 - Source Code/BookIII/Chapter04/NestedCalls/main.cpp         7
 1    00401400   CountCarSeats() D:/0246 - Source Code/BookIII/Chapter04/NestedCalls/main.cpp        12
 2    00401416   CountStuff()    D:/0246 - Source Code/BookIII/Chapter04/NestedCalls/main.cpp        17
 3    0040144B   main()          D:/0246 - Source Code/BookIII/Chapter04/NestedCalls/main.cpp        22
```

You can try viewing the stack yourself. Take a look at Listing 4-1. This listing shows a simple program that makes several nested function calls.

Listing 4-1:   Making Nested Function Calls

```
#include <iostream>

using namespace std;

int SeatsPerCar()
{
    return 4;
}

int CountCarSeats()
{
    return 10 * SeatsPerCar();
}

int CountStuff()
{
    return CountCarSeats() + 25;
}

int main()
{
    cout << CountStuff() << endl;
    system("PAUSE");
    return 0;
}
```

To try out the Call Stack window, follow these steps:

1. **Compile this program (set the Build Target field to Debug).**

2. **Set a breakpoint at the `int main()` line.**

3. **Run the application in the CodeBlocks debugger by pressing F8.**

4. **Step into the `CountStuff` function, then into the `CountCarSeats` function, and then into the `SeatsPerCar` function.**

(Or just put a breakpoint in the `SeatsPerCar` function and run the program until it stops at the breakpoint.)

5. **Choose Debug➪Debugging Windows➪Call Stack.**

A window like the one in Figure 4-1 appears. Note the order of function calls in the Call Stack window:

```
SeatsPerCall()
CountCarSeats()
CountStuff()
main()
```

This information in the Call Stack window means that your program started out with `main()`, which called `CountStuff()`. That function then called `CountCarSeats()`, which in turn called `SeatsPerCall()`. And that's where you currently are.

This window is handy if you want to know what path the program took to get to a particular routine. For example, you might see a routine that is called from many places in your program and you're not sure which part is calling the routine when you perform a certain task. To find out which part calls the routine, set a breakpoint in the function. When you run the program and the debugger stops at that line, the Call Stack window shows you the path the computer took to get there, including the name of the function that called the function in question.

In the Call Stack window, you can double-click any function name, and the Debugger moves the cursor to the function's body in the source code. This feature makes it easy for you to locate any function within the call stack and see why the code followed the path it did.

Stack features are common to almost all debuggers. We won't say *all* because we're sure some really bad debuggers that don't have stack features are out there. But the good debuggers, including those built into CodeBlocks and Microsoft Visual C++, include features for moving about the stack.

Debuggers use different terminology for the window that shows stack information. Borland C++ Builder and Borland Delphi (a Pascal tool) both use the term Call Stack, just like CodeBlocks. To get the Call Stack window in C++ Builder, choose View➪Debug Windows➪Call Stack. The Insight debugger uses the term Stack window; you access it by choosing View➪Stack. No matter what a particular product calls the window that contains stack information, the essential functionality is the same — to show how you arrived at a particular point in the code.

Storing local variables

As you get heavily into debugging, it always helps to fully understand what goes on under the hood of your program. Now at this point, we're going to be speaking on two levels — one level is your C++ code, and the other level is the resulting assembly code that the compiler generates based on your C++ code. (*Assembly* is the human-readable form of machine code that the processor on your machine understands.) So throughout this chapter, we make sure that we clearly state which level we're referring to.

Suppose you write a function in C++, and you call the function in another part of your program. When the compiler generates the assembly code for the function, it inserts some special code at the beginning and at the end of the function. At the start of the function, this special code allocates space for the local variables. At the end of the function, the special code deallocates the space. This space for the variables is called the *stack frame* for the function.

Now this space for the local variables lives on the stack. The storage process works as follows: When you call your function, the computer pushes the return address onto the stack. After the computer is running inside the function, the special code the compiler inserted saves some more of the stack space — just enough for the variables. This extra space becomes the local storage for the variables; and just before the function returns, the special code removes this local space. Thus, the top of the stack is now the return address. The return then functions correctly.

This process with the stack frame takes place with the help of the internal registers in the CPU. Before a function call, the assembly code pushes the arguments to the function onto the stack. Then it calls the function by using the CPU's built-in `call` statement. (That's an assembly-code statement.) This `call` statement pushes the return address onto the stack and then moves the instruction pointer to the function address. After the execution is inside the function, the stack contains the function arguments and then the return address. The special function startup code (called a *prolog*) saves the value in one of the CPU registers, called the Extended Base Pointer, or *EBP register*.

Where does the prolog save the value? On the stack! The prolog code first pushes the EBP value onto the stack. Then the prolog code takes the current stack pointer (which points to the top of the stack in memory) and saves that back in the EBP register for later use. Then the prolog code adjusts the stack pointer to make room for the local variable storage. The code inside the function then accesses the local variables as offsets above the position of EBP on the stack and the arguments as offsets below the position of EBP on the stack.

Finally at the end of the function, the special code (now called an *epilog*) undoes the work: The epilog copies the value in EBP back into the stack pointer; this deallocates the local variable storage. Then it *pops* the top of the stack off (as opposed to *blow* the top of the stack off) and restores this value back into EBP. (That was, after all, the original value in EBP when the function started.) Now the top of the stack contains the function return address, which is back to the way it was when the function began. The next assembly statement is a `return`, which *pulls* the top of the stack off and goes back to the address that the epilog code pulled off the stack. Now just think: Every single time a function call takes place in your computer, this process takes place. Kinda gives you new respect for this big pile of bits and bytes, doesn't it!

Inside the computer, the stack actually runs upside down. When you push something on the stack, the stack pointer goes *down* in memory — it gets *decremented*. When you pop something off the stack, the stack pointer gets *incremented*. Therefore, in the stack frame, the local variables are actually *below* EBP in memory, and you access their addresses by subtracting from the value stored in the EBP register. The function arguments, in turn, are *above* the EBP in memory, and you get their addresses by adding to the value stored in EBP.

The one thing we didn't discuss in the previous technical discussion is the return value of a function. In C++, the standard way to return a value from a function is for the function's assembly code to move the value into the Extended Accumulator, or EAX, register. Then the calling code can simply inspect the EAX register after the function is finished. However, if you are returning something complex, such as a class instance, things get a more complex. Suppose you have a function that returns an object, but not as a pointer, as in the function header `MyClass MyFunction();`. Different compilers handle this differently, but when the gcc compiler that's part of CodeBlocks, Dev-C++, MinGW, and Cygwin encounters something such as `MyClass inst = MyFunction();`, it takes the address of `inst` and puts that in EAX. Then, in the function, it allocates space for a local variable, and in the `return` line it copies the object in the local variable into the object whose address is in EAX. So when you return a nonpointer object, you are, in a sense, passing your object into the function as a pointer!

Debugging with Advanced Features

Most debuggers, including CodeBlocks, have some advanced features that are handy when going through your program. These features include the capability to look at threads and assembly code.

Viewing threads

If you are writing a program that uses multiple threads and you stop at a breakpoint, you can get a list of all the current threads by using the Running Threads window. To open the Running Threads window, in the main CodeBlocks window choose Debug⇔Debugging Windows⇔Running Threads. A window showing the currently running threads opens. Each line looks something like this:

```
2 thread 2340.0x6cc  test() at main.cpp:7
```

The first number indicates which thread this is in the program; for example, this is the second thread. The two numbers after the word `thread` are the process ID and the thread ID, separated by a dot. Then you see the name of the function where the thread is currently stopped along with the line number where the thread is currently stopped.

Interestingly enough, CodeBlocks shows only running threads, so if your application has just one thread (as the example in Listing 4-1), the Running Threads window is blank when you pause the application for debugging. Consequently, you can't see the main (and only) thread of the application because the thread isn't running.

Tracing through assembly code

If you really feel the urge, you can view the actual assembly code. The only time we ever do this is when we absolutely must get down to the hard-core nitty-gritty. CodeBlocks lets you do this. Choose Debug⇨Debugging Windows⇨Disassembly to see the Disassembly window shown in Figure 4-2.

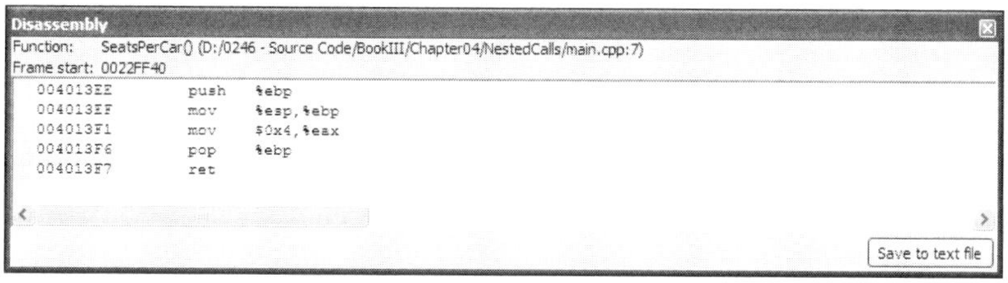

Figure 4-2:
The Disassembly window shows the assembly code that results from the C++ code you write.

```
Disassembly
Function:    SeatsPerCar() (D:/0246 - Source Code/BookIII/Chapter04/NestedCalls/main.cpp:7)
Frame start: 0022FF40
    004013EE        push    %ebp
    004013EF        mov     %esp,%ebp
    004013F1        mov     $0x4,%eax
    004013F6        pop     %ebp
    004013F7        ret
                                                    Save to text file
```

The window shown in Figure 4-2 is the disassembly of the `SeatsPerCar()` function shown in Listing 4-1. Here's the function again so you can compare it to Figure 4-2.

```cpp
int SeatsPerCar()
{
    return 4;
}
```

The following lines create the stack frame:

```
004013EE    push    %ebp
004013EF    mov     %esp,%ebp
```

After the code creates a stack frame, it moves a value of 4 (the `return 4;` part of the code) into EAX as shown here:

```
004013F1    mov     $0x4,%eax
```

The code then pops EBP and returns to the caller (the `CountCarSeats()` function) using this code:

```
004013F6    pop     %ebp
004013F7    ret
```

Now, if you move into the `CountCarSeats()` function, you see assembly like that shown in Figure 4-3.

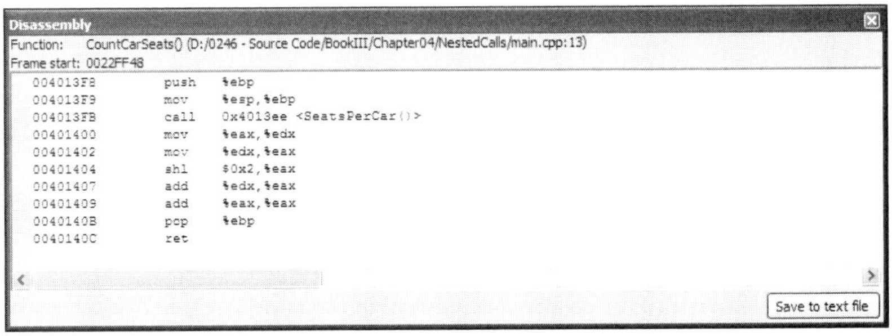

Figure 4-3:
This Disassembly window shows the CountCar Seats() function code.

```
Disassembly                                                                    [X]
Function:    CountCarSeats() (D:/0246 - Source Code/BookIII/Chapter04/NestedCalls/main.cpp:13)
Frame start: 0022FF48
    004013F8        push    %ebp
    004013F9        mov     %esp,%ebp
    004013FB        call    0x4013ee <SeatsPerCar()>
    00401400        mov     %eax,%edx
    00401402        mov     %edx,%eax
    00401404        shl     $0x2,%eax
    00401407        add     %edx,%eax
    00401409        add     %eax,%eax
    0040140B        pop     %ebp
    0040140C        ret
                                                                   [Save to text file]
```

As before, the assembly begins by creating a stack frame. It then issues a call to the SeatsPerCar() function. When the function returns, the assembly performs the multiplication part of the task. Finally, the code performs the usual task of placing the return value in EAX, popping EBP, and returning to the caller. Notice that what appears to be simple multiplication to you may not be so simple in assembler. Let's say you changed the code to read

```
int CountCarSeats()
{
    return 4 * SeatsPerCar();
}
```

The math is simpler now because you're using 4, which is easily converted into a binary value. Figure 4-4 shows the assembly that results from this simple change.

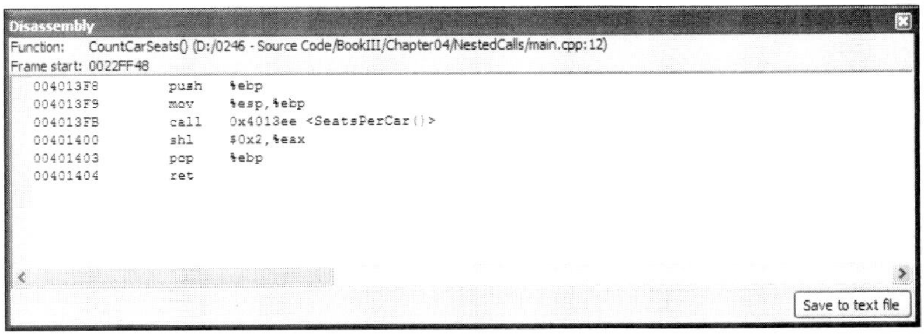

Figure 4-4:
Small C++ code changes can result in large assembly-code changes.

```
Disassembly                                                                    [X]
Function:    CountCarSeats() (D:/0246 - Source Code/BookIII/Chapter04/NestedCalls/main.cpp:12)
Frame start: 0022FF48
    004013F8        push    %ebp
    004013F9        mov     %esp,%ebp
    004013FB        call    0x4013ee <SeatsPerCar()>
    00401400        shl     $0x2,%eax
    00401403        pop     %ebp
    00401404        ret
                                                                   [Save to text file]
```

Now all the code does is perform a shift left (SHL) instruction. Shifting the value in EAX left by 2 is the same as multiplying it by 4. The reason the assembler uses the SHL instruction is that shifting takes far fewer clock cycles than multiplication, which makes the code run faster. The result is the same, even if the assembler code doesn't quite match your C++ code.

If you want to see the values in the registers so you can more easily follow the assembler code, choose Debug⇨Debugging Windows⇨CPU Registers. You see the CPU Registers window shown in Figure 4-5. This window reflects the state of the registers at the current stopping point in the code. Consequently, you can't see each step of the assembler shown in the Disassembly window reflected in these registers.

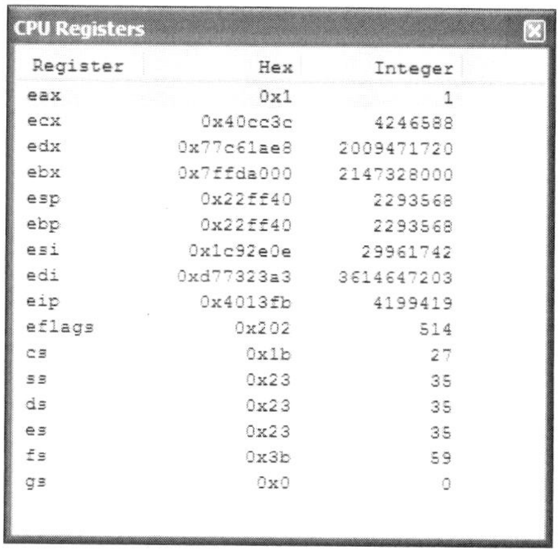

Figure 4-5:
Viewing the CPU registers can give you insights into how code interacts with the processor.

CPU Registers		
Register	Hex	Integer
eax	0x1	1
ecx	0x40cc3c	4246588
edx	0x77c61ae8	2009471720
ebx	0x7ffda000	2147328000
esp	0x22ff40	2293568
ebp	0x22ff40	2293568
esi	0x1c92e0e	29961742
edi	0xd77323a3	3614647203
eip	0x4013fb	4199419
eflags	0x202	514
cs	0x1b	27
ss	0x23	35
ds	0x23	35
es	0x23	35
fs	0x3b	59
gs	0x0	0

**Book III
Chapter 4**

**Traveling About
the Stack**

Book IV

Advanced Programming

The 5th Wave   By Rich Tennant

"Shoot, that's nothing. Watch me spin him!"

Contents at a Glance

Chapter 1: Working with Arrays, Pointers, and References

In This Chapter

✔ Working with arrays and multidimensional arrays

✔ Understanding the connection between arrays and pointers

✔ Dealing with pointers in all their forms

✔ Using reference variables

*W*hen the C programming language, predecessor to C++, came out in the early 1970s, it was a breakthrough because it was *small*. C had only a few keywords. Tasks like printing to the console were handled not by built-in keywords but by functions.

Technically, C++ is still small. So what makes C++ big?

✦ The language itself is small, but its libraries are huge.

✦ The language is small, but it's extremely sophisticated, resulting in millions of things you can do with the language.

In this chapter, we give you the full rundown of topics that lay the foundation for C++: arrays, pointers, and references. In C++, these items come up again and again.

We assume that you have a basic understanding of C++ — that is, that you understand the material in Minibook I and Minibook II, Chapter 1. You know the basics of pointers and arrays (and maybe just a teeny bit about references) and you're ready to grasp them thoroughly.

Building Up Arrays

As you work with arrays, it seems like you can do a million things with them. This section provides the complete details on arrays. The more you know about arrays, the less likely you are to use them incorrectly, resulting in a bug.

Know how to get the most out of arrays when necessary — not just because they're there. Avoid using arrays in the most complex way imaginable.

Declaring arrays

The usual way of declaring an array is to simply put the type name, followed by a variable name, followed by a size in brackets, as in this line of code:

```
int Numbers[10];
```

This declares an array of 10 integers. The first element gets index 0, and the final element gets index 9. Always remember that in C++ arrays start at 0, and the highest index is one less than the size. (Remember, *index* refers to the position within the array, and *size* refers to the number of elements in the array.)

A common question that the usual programming student asks is, Can I just declare an array without specifying a size, like this:

```
int Numbers[]
```

In certain situations, you can declare an array without putting a number in the brackets. For example, you can initialize an array without specifying the number of elements:

```
int MyNumbers[] = {1,2,3,4,5,6,7,8,9,10};
```

The compiler is smart enough to count how many elements you put inside the braces, and then the compiler makes that count the array size.

Another time you can skip the number in brackets is when you use the `extern` word. (Remember, the `extern` statement refers to variables in other source files. See Minibook I, Chapter 5 for more information.) Suppose you have one source file, perhaps `numbers.cpp`, that contains this line:

```
int MyNumbers[] = {1,2,3,4,5,6,7,8,9,10};
```

Then, in another source file, say `main.cpp`, you can declare an external reference to the array in `numbers.cpp`:

```
#include <iostream>

using namespace std;

extern int MyNumbers[];
int main(int argc, char *argv[])
{
    cout << MyNumbers[5] << endl;
    return 0;
}
```

When you compile these two source files (`numbers.cpp` and `main.cpp`), you get the correct result for `MyNumbers[5]`:

```
6
```

(Remember that `MyNumbers[5]` refers to the sixth element because the first element has index 0. The sixth element has a 6 in it.)

Although you can get away with leaving out the size in an external array declaration, we do not recommend doing so because you would be asking for errors. Instead, include it. In fact, we would rewrite `numbers.cpp` to have an explicit array size as well, as in

```
int MyNumbers[10] = {1,2,3,4,5,6,7,8,9,10};
```

Then `main.cpp` would look like this:

```
extern int MyNumbers[10];
```

Specifying the array size helps decrease your chances of having bugs, bugs, everywhere bugs. Plus, it has the added benefit that, in the actual declaration, if the number in brackets does not match the number of elements inside braces, the compiler issues an error, at least if the number is smaller anyway. The following

```
int MyNumbers[5] = {1,2,3,4,5,6,7,8,9,10};
```

yields this compiler error

```
excess elements in aggregate initializer
```

But if the number in brackets is greater than the number of elements, as in the following code, you will not get an error. So be careful!

```
int MyNumbers[15] = {1,2,3,4,5,6,7,8,9,10};
```

You also can skip specifying the array size when you pass an array into a function, like this:

```
int AddUp(int Numbers[], int Count) {
    int loop;
    int sum = 0;
    for (loop = 0; loop < Count; loop++) {
        sum += Numbers[loop];
    }
    return sum;
}
```

This technique is particularly powerful because the `AddUp` function can work for any size array. You can call the function like this:

```
cout << AddUp(MyNumbers, 10) << endl;
```

But this is kind of annoying because you have to specify the size each time you call into the function. However, you can get around this. Look at this line of code:

```
cout << AddUp(MyNumbers, sizeof(MyNumbers) / 4) << endl;
```

With the array, the `sizeof` operator tells you how many bytes it uses. But the size of the array is usually the number of elements, not the number of bytes. So you divide the result of `sizeof` by 4 (the size of each element).

But now you have that magic number, 4, sitting there. (By *magic number,* we mean a seemingly arbitrary number that is stuffed somewhere into your code.) So a slightly better approach would be to enter this:

```
cout << AddUp(MyNumbers, sizeof(MyNumbers) / sizeof(int)) << endl;
```

Now this line of code works, and here's why: The `sizeof` the array divided by the `sizeof` each element in the array gives the number of elements in the array.

Arrays and pointers

The name of the array is a pointer to the array itself. The *array* is a sequence of variables stored in memory. The *array name* points to the first item.

This is an interesting question about pointers: Can we have a function header, such as the following line, and just use `sizeof` to determine how many elements are in the array? If so, this function wouldn't need to have the caller specify the size of the array.

```
int AddUp(int Numbers[]) {
```

Consider this function and a `main` that calls it:

```
void ProcessArray(int Numbers[]) {
    cout << "Inside function: Size in bytes is "
      << sizeof(Numbers) << endl;
}
int main(int argc, char *argv[])
{
    int MyNumbers[] = {1,2,3,4,5,6,7,8,9,10};
    cout << "Outside function: Size in bytes is ";
    cout << sizeof(MyNumbers) << endl;
    ProcessArray(MyNumbers);
    return 0;
}
```

When you run this program, here's what you see:

```
Outside function: Size in bytes is 40
Inside function: Size in bytes is 4
```

Outside the function, the code knows that the size of the array is 40 bytes. But why does the code think that the size is 4 after it is inside the array? The reason is that even though it appears that you're passing an array, you're really passing a *pointer* to an array. The size of the pointer is just 4, and so that's what the final `cout` line prints.

Declaring arrays has a slight idiosyncrasy. When you declare an array by giving a definite number of elements, such as this:

```
int MyNumbers[5];
```

the compiler knows that you have an array, and the `sizeof` operator gives you the size of the entire array. The array name, then, is *both* a pointer and an array! But if you declare a function header without an array size like this

```
void ProcessArray(int Numbers[]) {
```

the compiler treats this as simply a *pointer* and nothing more. This last line is, in fact, equivalent to this:

```
void ProcessArray(int *Numbers) {
```

Thus, inside the functions that either line declares, the following two lines of code are *equivalent*:

```
Numbers[3] = 10;
*(Numbers + 3) = 10;
```

This equivalence means that if you use an `extern` declaration on an array, such as this:

```
extern int MyNumbers[];
```

and then take the size of this array, the compiler will get confused. Here's an example: If you have two files, `numbers.cpp` and `main.cpp`, where `numbers.cpp` declares an array and `main.cpp` externally declares it, you will get a compiler error if you call `sizeof`:

```
#include <iostream>

using namespace std;

extern int MyNumbers[];
int main(int argc, char *argv[])
{
    cout << sizeof(MyNumbers) << endl;
    return 0;
}
```

In CodeBlocks (which is the compiler we're using for most of this book; see Appendix B for more information), the gcc compiler gives us this error:

```
error: invalid application of `sizeof' to incomplete type `int[]'
```

The solution is to put the size of the array inside brackets. Just make sure that the size is the same as in the other source-code file! You can fake out the compiler by changing the number, and you *won't get an error*. But that's bad programming style and just asking for errors.

Although an *array* is simply a sequence of variables all adjacent to each other in memory, the *name* of an array is really just a pointer to the first element in the array. You can use the name as a pointer. However, do that only when you really need to work with a pointer. After all, you really have no reason to write code that is cryptic, such as * (Numbers + 3) = 10;.

The converse is also true. Look at this function:

```
void ProcessArray(int *Numbers) {
    cout << Numbers[1] << endl;
}
```

This function takes a pointer as a parameter, yet we access it as an array. Again, we do not recommend writing code like this; instead, we recommend that you understand *why code like this works*. That way, you gain a deeper knowledge of arrays and how they live inside the computer, and this knowledge, in turn, can help you write code that works properly.

Even though, throughout this chapter, we're telling you that the array name is just a pointer, the name of an array of integers isn't the exact same thing as a pointer to an integer. Check out these lines of code:

```
int LotsONumbers[50];
int x;
LotsONumbers = &x;
```

We're trying to point the LotsONumbers *pointer* to something different: something declared as an integer. The compiler doesn't let you do this; you get an error. That wouldn't be the case if LotsONumbers were declared as int *LotsONumbers; then this code would work. But as written, you get a compiler error. And believe it or not, here's the compiler error we get in CodeBlocks:

```
error: incompatible types in assignment of `int*' to `int[50]'
```

This error implies the compiler does see a definite distinction between the two types, int * and int[]. Nevertheless, the array name is indeed a pointer, and you can use it as one; you just can't do everything with it that you can with a normal pointer, such as reassign it. (If we were philosophers, we might argue that an array name's type is not equivalent to its equivalent. But we're not philosophers, so when we suggest something like that, we're only being equivalent to philosophers.)

When using arrays, then, we suggest the following tips. These will help you keep your arrays bug-free:

✦ Keep your code consistent. If you declare, for example, a pointer to an integer, do not treat it as an array.

✦ Keep your code clear and understandable. If you pass pointers, it's okay to take the address of the first element, as in `&(MyNumbers[0])` if this makes the code clearer — though it's equivalent to just `MyNumbers`.

✦ When you declare an array, always try to put a number inside the brackets, unless you are writing a function that takes an array.

✦ When you use the `extern` keyword to declare an array, go ahead and also put the array size inside brackets. But be consistent! Don't use one number one time and a different number another time. The easiest way to be consistent is to use a constant, such as `const int ArraySize = 10;` in a common header file and then use that in your array declaration: `int MyArray[ArraySize];`.

Using multidimensional arrays

Arrays do not have to be just one-dimensional. You can declare a multidimensional array, as shown in Listing 1-1.

Listing 1-1:   Using a Multidimensional Array

```
#include <iostream>

using namespace std;

int MemorizeThis[10][20];

int main(int argc, char *argv[])
{
    int x,y;
    for (x = 0; x < 10; x++) {
        for (y = 0; y < 20; y++ ) {
            MemorizeThis[x][y] = x * y;
        }
    }
    cout << MemorizeThis[9][13] << endl;
    cout << sizeof(MemorizeThis) / sizeof(int) << endl;
    system("PAUSE");
    return 0;
}
```

When you run this, `MemorizeThis` gets filled with the multiplication tables (thus the clever name!). Here's the output for the program, which is the contents of `MemorizeThis[9][13]`, and then the size of the entire two-dimensional array:

**Book IV
Chapter 1**

Working with
Arrays, Pointers,
and References

And indeed, 9 times 13 is 117. The size of the array is 200 elements. Because each element, being an integer, is 4 bytes, that means that the size in bytes is 800.

You can have many, many dimensions, but be *careful*. Every time you add a dimension, the size multiplies by the size of that dimension. Thus an array declared like the following line has 48,600 elements, for a total of 194,400 bytes:

```
int BigStuff[4][3][5][3][5][6][9];
```

And the following array has 4,838,400 elements, for a total of 19,353,600 bytes. That's about 19 megabytes!

```
int ReallyBigStuff[8][6][10][6][5][7][12][4];
```

If you really have this kind of a data structure, consider redesigning it. Any data stored like this would be downright confusing. And fortunately, the compiler will stop you from going totally overboard. Just for fun we tried this giant monster:

```
int GiantMonster[18][16][10][16][15][17][12][14];
```

This is the error we got:

```
error: size of array `GiantMonster' is too large
```

(That would be 1,974,067,200 bytes: more than a gigabyte!)

Initializing multidimensional arrays

Just as you can initialize a single-dimensional array by using braces and separating the elements by commas, you can initialize a multidimensional array with braces and commas and all that jazz, too. But to do this, you combine arrays inside arrays, as in this code:

```
int Numbers[5][6] = {
    {1,2,3,4,5,6},
    {7,8,9,10,12},
    {13,14,15,16,17,18},
    {19,20,21,22,23,24},
    {25,26,27,28,29,30}
};
```

The hard part is remembering whether you put five batches of six or six batches of five. Think of it like this: Each time you add another dimension, it goes *inside* the previous. That is, you can write a single-dimensional array like this:

```
int MoreNumbers[5] = {
    100,
    200,
    300,
    400,
    500,
};
```

Then, if you add a dimension to this, each number in the initialization is replaced by an array initializer of the form {1,2,3,4,5,6}. Then you end up with a properly formatted multidimensional array.

Passing multidimensional arrays

If you have to pass a multidimensional array to a function, things can get just a bit hairy. That's because you don't have as much freedom in leaving off the array sizes as you do with single-dimensional arrays. Suppose you have this function:

```
int AddAll(int MyGrid[5][6]) {
    int x,y;
    int sum = 0;
    for (x = 0; x < 5; x++) {
        for (y = 0; y < 6; y++) {
            sum += MyGrid[x][y];
        }
    }
    return sum;
}
```

So far, the function header is fine because we're explicitly stating the size of each dimension. But you may want to do this:

```
int AddAll(int MyGrid[][]) {
```

or maybe pass the sizes as well:

```
int AddAll(int MyGrid[][], int rows, int columns) {
```

But unfortunately, when we compile either of these two lines, we get this error:

```
declaration of `MyGrid' as multidimensional array
must have bounds for all dimensions except the first
```

That's strange: The compiler is telling us that we must explicitly list all the dimensions, but it's okay if we leave the first one blank as with one-dimensional arrays.

So that means this crazy thing will compile:

```
int AddAll(int MyGrid[][6]) {
```

How about that? The reason is that the compiler treats multidimensional arrays in a special way. A multidimensional array is not really a two-dimensional array, for example; rather, it's an array of an array. Thus, deep down inside C++, the compiler treats the statement MyGrid[5][6] as if it were MyGrid[5] *where each item in the array is itself an array of size 6*. And you're free to not specify the size of a one-dimensional array. Well, the first brackets represent the one-dimensional portion of the array. So you can leave that space blank, as you can with other one-dimensional arrays. But then, after that, you have to give the array *bounds*. Sounds strange, we know. And perhaps just a bit contrived. But it's C++, and it's the rule: You can leave the first dimension blank in a function header, but you must specify the remaining dimension sizes.

When using multidimensional arrays, it's often easier on our brains if we think of them as an *array of arrays*. Then we use a `typedef` so that, instead of it being an array of arrays, it's an array of some user-defined type, such as `GridRow`. Either of the following function headers are confusing:

```
int AddAll(int MyGrid[][6]) {
```

```
int AddAll(int MyGrid[][6], int count) {
```

Here's our recommendation: Use a `typedef`! So here's a cleaner way:

```
typedef int GridRow[6];
int AddAll(GridRow MyGrid[], int Size) {
    int x,y;
    int sum = 0;
    for (x = 0; x < Size; x++) {
        for (y = 0; y < 6; y++) {
            sum += MyGrid[x][y];
        }
    }
    return sum;
}
```

The `typedef` line defines a new type called `GridRow`. This type is an array of six integers. Then, in the function, you are passing an array of `GridRow`s.

Using this `typedef` is the same as simply using two brackets, except it emphasizes that you are passing an *array of an array* — that is, an array in which each member is itself an array of type `GridRow`.

Arrays and command-line parameters

In a typical C++ program, the `main` function receives an array and a count as parameters. However, to beginning programmers, the parameters can look intimidating. But they're not: Think of the parameters as an array of strings and a size of the array. However, each string in this *array of strings* is actually a character array. In the old days of C, and earlier breeds of C++, no `string` class was available. Thus, strings were always character arrays, usually denoted as `char *MyString`. (Remember, an array and a pointer can be used interchangeably for the most part). Thus, you could take this thing and turn it into an array either by throwing brackets at the end `char *MyString[ ]` or by making use of the fact that an array is a pointer and adding a second pointer symbol, as in `char **MyString`. The following code shows how you can get the command-line parameters:

```
#include <iostream>

using namespace std;

int main(int argc, char *argv[])
{
    int loop;
    for (loop = 0; loop < argc; loop++) {
        cout << argv[loop] << endl;
    }
    return 0;
}
```

When you compile this program, name the executable
CommandLineParams, and then run it from the command prompt using the
following command

```
CommandLineParams abc def "abc 123"
```

You see the following output. (Note that the program name comes in as the
first parameter and the quoted items come in as a single parameter.)

```
CommandLineParams
abc
def
abc 123
```

You can also specify command-line arguments using the IDE for debugging
purposes when working with the CodeBlocks compiler. Choose Project⇨
Set Program's Arguments. CodeBlocks displays the Select Target dialog box,
where you choose a target in the first field and type the arguments in the
Program Arguments field. Click OK and then click Run. CommandLineParams
displays the command-line arguments in the command window as it did
when you typed the command at the command prompt.

Allocating an array on the heap

Arrays are useful, but it would be a bummer if the only way you could use
them were as stack variables. If you could allocate an array on the heap by
using the new keyword, that would be nice. Well, good news! You can! But
you need to know about a couple little tricks to make it work.

First, you can easily declare an array on the heap by using new int[50],
for example. But think about what this is doing: It declares 50 integers on the
heap, and the new word returns a pointer to the allocated array. But, unfortunately, the makers of C++ didn't see it that way. For some reason, they
made the array pointer type based on the first element of the array (which
is, of course, the same as all the elements in the array).

Thus, the call

```
new int[50]
```

returns a pointer of type int *, not something that explicitly points to an array, just like this call does:

```
new int;
```

Nice, huh? But that's okay. We can deal with it. So if you want to save the results of new int [50] in a variable, you have to have a variable of type int *, as in the following:

```
int *MyArray = new int[50];
```

But here's the bizarre part: An array name is a pointer and vice versa. So now that you have a pointer to an integer, you can treat it like an array:

```
MyArray[0] = 25;
```

And now for the *really* bizarre part. When you're all finished with the array, you can call delete. But you can't just call delete MyArray;. The reason is that the compiler knows only that MyArray is a pointer to an integer; it doesn't know that it's an array! Thus, delete MyArray will only delete the first item in the array, leaving the rest of the elements sitting around on the heap, wondering when their time will come. So the makers of C++ gave us a special form of delete to handle this situation. It looks like this:

```
delete[] MyArray;
```

Whenever you allocate an array by using the new keyword, remember to delete the array by using delete[] rather than just plain old delete.

If you're really curious about the need for delete[] and delete, recognize the distinction between allocating an array and allocating a single element on the stack. Look closely at these two lines:

```
int *MyArray = new int[50];
int *somenumber = new int;
```

The first allocates an array of 50 integers, while the second allocates a single array. But look at the types of the pointer variables: They are both the same! How about that? They are both a pointer to an integer. And so the statement

```
delete something;
```

is ambiguous if something is a pointer to an integer: Is it an array, or is it a single number? The designers of C++ knew this was a problem, so they *unambiguated* it. They declared and proclaimed that delete shall only delete a single member. Then they invented a little extra that must have given the compiler writers a headache; they said that if you want to delete an array instead, just throw on an opening and closing bracket after the word `delete`. And all will be good.

All this stuff about pointers and arrays raises an interesting question: How do you specify a pointer to an array? Well, remember that if you have a line like this

```
int LotsONumbers[50];
```

`LotsONumbers` is really a pointer to an integer — it points to the first position in the array. So, by that regard, you already have a pointer to an array. In fact, if you were to write a function declared with a header like this

```
int AddUp(int Numbers[], int Count) {
```

and look at the generated assembly code, you would see that the `Numbers` array really does get passed in as a pointer. To view the disassembly in CodeBlocks, create a breakpoint, start the debugger by pressing F8, and choose Debug⊏➢Debugging Windows⊏➢Disassembly. CodeBlocks displays the Disassembly window, which contains an assembler view of the code.

So the real question is this: When you have an array, how do you *not* use a pointer with it? The answer? You don't! C++ simply does not have a fundamental array type. Other languages do (Pascal, for example), but C and C++ don't. Yet, even though that's the case, the compiler does have a basic feel for the brackets and does seem to understand arrays. Strange, but true.

Storing arrays of pointers and arrays of arrays

Because of the similarities between arrays and pointers, you are likely to encounter some strange notation. For example, in `main` itself, we have seen both of these at different times:

```
char **argc
char *argc[]
```

If you work with arrays of arrays and arrays of pointers, the best bet is to make sure that you completely understand what these kinds of statements mean. Remember that, although you can treat an array name as a pointer, you're in for some technical differences. The following lines of code show these differences. First, think about what happens if you initialize a two-dimensional array of characters like this:

```
char NameArray[][6] = {
    {'T', 'o', 'm', '\0', '\0', '\0'},
    {'S', 'u', 'z', 'y', '\0', '\0'},
    {'H', 'a', 'r', 'r', 'y', '\0'}
};
```

This is an array of an array. Each *inner* array is an array of 6 characters. The *outer* array stores the 3 inner arrays. (The individual content of an array is sometimes called a *member* — the inner array has 6 members and the outer array has 3 members.) Inside memory, the 18 characters are stored in one consecutive row, starting with T, then o, and ending with y and finally \0, which is the null character.

But now take a look at this:

```
char* NamePointers[] = {
    "Tom",
    "Suzy",
    "Harry"
};
```

This is an array of character arrays as well, except that it's not the same as the code that came just before it. This is actually an array holding three pointers: The first points to a character string in memory containing Tom (which is followed by a null-terminator, \0); the second points to a string in memory containing Suzy ending with a null-terminator; and so on. Thus, if you look at the memory in the array, you won't see a bunch of characters; instead, you see three numbers, each being a pointer.

It's often helpful to see the content of memory as you work with arrays. To see memory in CodeBlocks, choose Debug⇨Debugging Windows⇨ Examine Memory. You see the Memory window. Type the name of the variable you want to view in the Address field and click Go.

So where on earth (or in the memory, anyway) are the three strings, Tom, Suzy, and Harry when you have an array of three pointers to these strings? When the compiler sees string constants such as these, it puts them in a special area where it stores all the constants. These then get added to the executable file at link time, along with the compiled code for the source module. (For information on linking, see Appendix A.) And that's where they reside in memory. The array, therefore, contains pointers to these three constant strings in memory.

Now if you try to do the following (notice the type of PointerToPointer)

```
char **PointerToPointer = {
    "Tom",
    "Suzy",
    "Harry"
};
```

you will get an error:

```
error: initializer for scalar variable requires one element
```

A *scalar* is just another name for a regular variable that is not an array. In other words, the PointerToPointer variable is a regular variable (that is, a scalar), *not* an array!

Yet, inside the function header for `main`, you can use `char **`, and you can access this as an array. What's going on? As usual, there's a slight but definite difference between an array and a pointer. You cannot always just treat a pointer as an array; for example, you can't initialize a pointer as an array. But you can go the other way: You can take an array and treat it as a pointer *most of the time*. Thus, you can do this:

```
char* NamePointers[] = {
    "Tom",
    "Harry",
    "Suzy"
};
char **AnotherArray = NamePointers;
```

This compiles, and you can access the strings through `AnotherArray[0]`, for example. Yet, you're not allowed to skip a step and just start out initializing the `AnotherArray` variable like so because this is the same as the code just before this example, and it yields a compiler error!

```
char** AnotherArray = {
    "Tom",
    "Harry",
    "Suzy"
};
```

Thus, this is an example of where slight differences between arrays and pointers occur. But it does explain why you can see something like this

```
int main(int argc, char **argv)
```

and you are free to use the `argv` variable to access an array of pointers — specifically, in this case, an array of character pointers, also called *strings*.

Building constant arrays

If you have an array and you don't want its contents to change, you can make it a constant array. The following lines of code demonstrate this:

```
const int Permanent[5] = { 1, 2, 3, 4, 5 };
cout << Permanent[1] << endl;
```

This array works like any other array, except you cannot change the numbers inside it. If you add a line like the following line, you get a compiler error, because the compiler is aware of constants:

```
Permanent[2] = 5;
```

Here's the error we got when we tried this in CodeBlocks:

```
error: assignment of read-only location
```

Being the inquisitive sorts, we asked ourselves this question: What about a constant array of nonconstants? Can we do that? Well, sometimes, depending on the compiler. As horrible as the following looks (and it's not ANSI-standard!), you are allowed to do this with the gcc compilers. (Microsoft Visual C++ and Borland C++ Builder don't allow it, and the CodeBlocks compiler presents you with an `error: ISO C++ forbids assignment of arrays` error message.)

```
int NonConstant[5] = { 1, 2, 3, 4, 5 };
int OtherList[5] = { 10, 11, 12, 13, 14 };
OtherList = NonConstant;
```

In other words, that third line is saying, "Forget what `OtherList` points to; instead, make it point to the first array, {1,2,3,4,5}!" Now, we *really* don't recommend writing code like this (remember, keep things simple and understandable!), so if you want to prevent this kind of thing, you can make the array constant:

```
const int NonConstant[5] = { 1, 2, 3, 4, 5 };
const int OtherList[5] = { 10, 11, 12, 13, 14 };
OtherList = NonConstant;
```

Now when the compiler gets to the third line, it gives us an error:

```
error: assignment of read-only variable `OtherList'
```

But you may notice that the way we made the array constant was the same way that we made its elements constant in the code that came just before this example! Oops! What's that all about? Turns out there are some rules.

The following list describes the rules, in detail, for making arrays constant:

+ If you want to make an array constant, you can precede its type with the word `const`. When you do so, the array name is constant, and the elements inside the array are *also* constant. Thus, you cannot have a constant array with nonconstant elements, nor can you have a nonconstant array with constant elements.

+ The notion of a *nonconstant array* exists only in gcc and is not ANSI-standard.

If you really want to get technical, the C++ ANSI standard says that when you put the word `const` in front of an array declaration, you're not making the array constant; you're saying that the array holds only constants. Yet, when you do this, most compilers also make the array itself constant. But that's fine; people shouldn't be taking an array name and copying it to something else. It's not good programming style, and it's just asking for bugs — or, at the very least, confusion — later.

Pointing with Pointers

To fully understand C++ and all its strangeness and wonders, you need to become an expert in pointers. One of the biggest sources of bugs is when programmers who have a so-so understanding of C++ work with pointers and mess them up. But what's bad in such cases is that the program may run properly for a while, and then suddenly not work. Those bugs are the hardest bugs to catch, because the user may see the problem occur and then report it; but when the programmer tries to reproduce the problem, he or she can't make the bug happen! (It's just like when you take your car in to be fixed and suddenly it doesn't misbehave.) Both the car repair person and the programmer together say, "Worked fine when I tried it!" How frustrating is that?

In this section, we show you how you can get the most out of pointers and use them correctly in your programs, so you won't have these strange problems.

Becoming horribly complex

We're not making this up, we have seen a function header like this:

```
void MyFunction(char ***a) {
```

Yikes! What are all those asterisks for? Looks like a pointer to a pointer to a pointer to . . . something! How confusing. Now we suppose that some humans have brains that are more like computers, and they can look at that code and understand it just fine. Not us. So don't worry if you don't either.

So to understand the code, think about this: Suppose that you have a pointer variable, and you want a function to change *what the pointer variable points to*. Now be careful: We're not saying that the function wants to change the contents of the thing it points to. Rather, we're saying the function wants to make the pointer *point to something else*. There's a difference. So how do you do that? Well, any time you want a function to change a variable, you have to either pass it by reference or pass its address. And this can get confusing with a pointer. So what we like to do is take a detour. First, we're going to define a new type using our friend, the `typedef` word. It goes like this:

```
typedef char *PChar;
```

This is a new type called `PChar` that is equivalent to `char *`. That is, `PChar` is a pointer to a character.

Now look at this function:

```
void MyFunction(PChar &x)
{
    x = new char('B');
}
```

Book IV
Chapter 1

Working with
Arrays, Pointers,
and References

This function takes a pointer variable and points it to the result of `new char('B')`. That is, it points it to a newly allocated character variable containing the letter B. Now think this through carefully: A `PChar` simply contains a memory address, really. We pass it by reference into the function, and the function modifies the `PChar` so that the `PChar` contains a different address. That is, the `PChar` now points to something different from what it previously did.

To try out this function, here's some code you can put in `main` that tests `MyFunction`:

```
char *ptr = new char('A');
char *copy = ptr;
MyFunction(ptr);
cout << "ptr points to " << *ptr << endl;
cout << "copy points to " << *copy << endl;
```

Think it through carefully: The first line declares a variable called `ptr` that is a pointer to a character. (Notice that we're just using `char *` this time, but that's okay — `char *` is the same as `PChar` because of our `typedef`.) The first line also allocates a new character A on the heap and stores its address in the `ptr` variable.

The second line allocates a second variable that's also a pointer to a character. The variable is called `copy`, and it gets the same value stored in `ptr`; thus it also points to that character A that's floating around out in the heap.

Next we call `MyFunction`. That function is supposed to change what the pointer points to. Then we come back from the function and print the character that `ptr` points to and the character that `copy` points to. Here's what we get when we run it:

```
ptr points to B
copy points to A
```

This means that it worked! The `ptr` variable now points to the character allocated in `MyFunction` (a B), while the `copy` variable still points to the original A. In other words, they no longer point to the same thing: `MyFunction` managed to change what the variable points to.

Now consider the same function, but instead of using references, try it with pointers. Here's a modified form:

```
void AnotherFunction(PChar *x)
{
    *x = new char('C');
}
```

Now because the parameter is a pointer, we have to dereference it to modify its value. Thus, we have an asterisk, `*`, at the beginning of the middle line.

And here's a modified `main` that calls this function:

```
char *ptr = new char('A');
char *copy = ptr;
AnotherFunction(&ptr);
cout << "ptr points to " << *ptr << endl;
cout << "copy points to " << *copy << endl;
```

Because our function uses a pointer rather than a reference, we have to pass the address of the `ptr` variable, not the `ptr` variable directly. So notice the call to `AnotherFunction` has an ampersand, `&`, in front of the `ptr`. And this code works as expected. When we run it, we see this output:

```
ptr points to C
copy points to A
```

This version of the function, called `AnotherFunction`, made a new character called C. And indeed it's working correctly: `ptr` now points to a C character, while `copy` hasn't changed. Again, the function pointed `ptr` to something else.

Now we can unravel things. We created a `typedef`, and honestly, we would prefer to keep it in our code because we think that using `typedefs` makes it much easier to understand what the functions are doing. However, not everybody does it that way; therefore, we have to understand what other people are doing when we have to go in and fix their code. You may have to, too. So here are the same two functions, `MyFunction` and `AnotherFunction`, but without `typedef`. Instead of using the new `PChar` type, they directly use the equivalent `char *` type:

```
void MyFunction(char *&x)
{
    x = new char('B');
}

void AnotherFunction(char **x)
{
    *x = new char('C');
}
```

To remove the use of the `typedefs`, all we did was replace the `PChar` in the two function headers with its equivalent `char *`. You can see that the headers now look goofier. But they mean exactly the same as before: The first is a reference to a pointer, and the second is a pointer to a pointer.

But think about `char ** x` for a moment. Because `char *` is also the same as a character array in many regards, `char **x` is a pointer to a character array. In fact, sometimes you may see the header for `main` written like this

```
int main(int argc, char **argv)
```

instead of

```
int main(int argc, char *argv[])
```

Notice the `argv` parameter in the first of these two is the same type as we've been talking about: a pointer to a pointer (or, in a more easily understood manner, the address of a `Pchar`). But you know that the argument for `main` is an array of strings.

So now follow this somewhat convoluted thought. Go slowly if you have to: What if you have a pointer that points to an array of strings, and you have a function that is going to make it point to a different array of strings?

Better `typedef` this one; it's going to get ugly. And just as a reminder, we're still using the previous `typedef`, PChar, too:

```
typedef char **StringArray;
typedef char *PChar;
```

Make sure that you believe us when we tell you that `StringArray` is a type equivalent to an array of strings. In fact, if you put these two lines of code before your `main`, you can actually change your `main` header into the following and it will compile!

```
int main(int argc, StringArray argv)
```

Now here's a function that will take as a parameter an array of strings, create a new array of strings, and set the original array of strings to point to this new array of strings. (Whew!)

```
void ChangeAsReference(StringArray &array)
{
    StringArray NameArray = new PChar[3];
    NameArray[0] = "Tom";
    NameArray[1] = "Suzy";
    NameArray[2] = "Harry";
    array = NameArray;
}
```

Just to make sure that it works, here's something you can put in `main`:

```
StringArray OrigList = new PChar[3];
OrigList[0] = "John";
OrigList[1] = "Paul";
OrigList[2] = "George";
StringArray CopyList = OrigList;
ChangeAsReference(OrigList);
cout << OrigList[0] << endl;
cout << OrigList[1] << endl;
cout << OrigList[2] << endl << endl;
cout << CopyList[0] << endl;
cout << CopyList[1] << endl;
cout << CopyList[2] << endl;
```

This time in main, we're using the typedef types, because, frankly, the code is getting a bit confusing, and that helps keep what we're doing clear. Note that we first create a pointer to an array of three strings. Then we store three strings in the array. Next, we save a copy of the pointer in the variable called CopyList, and we print all the values.

Now when you run this main, you see the following:

```
Tom
Suzy
Harry

John
Paul
George
```

The first three are the elements in OrigList, which we passed into the function: But they no longer have the values John, Paul, and George. The three original Beatles names have been replaced by three new names: Tom, Harry, and Suzy. However, the Copy variable still points to the original string list. Thus, once again, it worked.

Now we did this change by reference. Next, we do it with pointers. Here's the modified version of the function, this time using pointers:

```
void ChangeAsPointer(StringArray *array)
{
    StringArray NameArray = new PChar[3];
    NameArray[0] = "Tom";
    NameArray[1] = "Harry";
    NameArray[2] = "Suzy";
    *array = NameArray;
}
```

As before, here's the slightly modified sample code that tests the function:

```
StringArray OrigList = new PChar[3];
OrigList[0] = "John";
OrigList[1] = "Paul";
OrigList[2] = "George";
StringArray CopyList = OrigList;
ChangeAsPointer(&OrigList);
cout << OrigList[0] << endl;
cout << OrigList[1] << endl;
cout << OrigList[2] << endl << endl;
cout << CopyList[0] << endl;
cout << CopyList[1] << endl;
cout << CopyList[2] << endl;
```

You can see that when we call ChangeAsPointer, we're passing the address of OrigList. The *output of this version is the same as the previous version.*

And now, as before, we unravel all this. Here are the two function headers without using the `typedef`s:

```
int ChangeAsReference(char **&array) {
```

and

```
int ChangeAsPointer(char ***array) {
```

We have seen code like these two lines from time to time. They're not the easiest to understand, but after you know what they mean, you can interpret them.

Our preference is to go ahead and use a `typedef`, even if it's just before the function in question. That way, it's much more clear to other people what the function does. You are welcome to follow suit. But if you do, make sure that you're familiar with the non-`typedef` version so you understand that version when somebody else writes it without using `typedef`. (Or if the person says to you, "This function takes a pointer to a pointer to a pointer." Yes, we've heard people say that!)

Pointers to functions

When a program is running, the functions in the program exist in the memory; so just like anything else in memory, they have an address. And having an address is good, because that way, people can find you.

You can take the address of a function by taking the name of it and putting the `address-of` operator (`&`) in front of the function name, like this:

```
address = &MyFunction;
```

But to make this work, you need to know what type to declare `address`. The `address` variable is a pointer to a function, and the cleanest way to assign a type is to use a `typedef`. (Fortunately, this is one time when most people are willing to use a `typedef`.)

Here's the `typedef`, believe it or not:

```
typedef int(*FunctionPtr)(int);
```

It's hard to follow, but the name of the new type is `FunctionPtr`. This defines a type called `FunctionPtr` that returns an integer (the leftmost `int`) and takes an integer as a parameter (the rightmost `int`, which must be in parentheses). The middle part of this statement is the name of the new type, and you must precede it by an asterisk, which means that it's a pointer to all the rest of the expression. Also, you must put the type name and its preceding asterisk inside parentheses.

And then you're ready to declare some variables! Here goes:

```
FunctionPtr address = &MyFunction;
```

This line declares `address` as a pointer to a function and initializes it to `MyFunction`. Now for this to work, the code for `MyFunction` must have the same prototype declared in the `typedef`: In this case, it must take an integer as a parameter and return an integer.

So, for example, you may have a function like this:

```
int TheSecretNumber(int x) {
    return x + 1;
}
```

Then, you could have a `main` that stores the address of this function in a variable and then calls the function by using the variable:

```
int main(int argc, char *argv[])
{
    typedef int (*FunctionPtr)(int);
    int MyPasscode = 20;
    FunctionPtr address = &TheSecretNumber;
    cout << address(MyPasscode) << endl;
}
```

Now just so you can say that you've seen it, here's what the `address` declaration would look like *without* using a `typedef`:

```
int (*address)(int) = &TheSecretNumber;
```

The giveaway should be that you have two things in parentheses side by side, and the set on the right has only types inside it. The one on the left has a variable name. So this is not declaring a type; rather, it's declaring a variable.

Pointing a variable to a member function

It's surprising to find out that most C++ programmers have no idea that `this` exists. So this is a big secret! Revel in it! What is the secret? The secret is that you can take the address of an object's member function. Ooh-wee!

Now remember that each instance of a class gets its own copy of the member variables, unless the variables are static. But functions are shared throughout the class. Yes, you can distinguish static functions from non-static functions. But that just refers to what types of variables they access: Static functions can access only static member variables, and you don't need to refer to them with an instance. Nonstatic (that is, *normal, regular*) member functions work with a particular instance. However, inside the memory, really only one copy of the function exists.

So how does the member function know which instance to work with? A secret parameter gets passed into the member function: the this pointer. Suppose you have a class called Gobstopper that has a member function called Chew. Next, you have an instance called MyGum, and you call the Chew function like so:

```
MyGum.Chew();
```

When the compiler generates assembly code for this, it actually passes a parameter into the function — the address of the MyGum instance, also known as the *this pointer*. Therefore, only one Chew function is in the code, but to call it you must use a particular instance of the class.

Because only one copy of the Chew function is in memory, you can take its address. But to do it requires some sort of cryptic-looking code. Here it is, quick and to the point. Suppose your class looks like this:

```
class Gobstopper {
public:
    int WhichGobstopper;
    int Chew(string name) {
        cout << WhichGobstopper << endl;
        cout << name << endl;
        return WhichGobstopper;
    }
};
```

The Chew function takes a string and returns an integer. Here's a typedef for a pointer to the Chew function:

```
typedef int (Gobstopper::*GobMember)(string);
```

And here's a variable of the type GobMember:

```
GobMember func = &Gobstopper::Chew;
```

If you look closely at the typedef, it looks similar to a regular function pointer. The only difference is that the classname and two colons precede the asterisk. Other than that, it's a regular old function pointer.

But whereas a regular function pointer is limited to pointing to functions of a particular set of parameter types and a return type, this function pointer shares those restrictions but is further limited in that it can point to only member functions within the class Gobstopper.

To call the function stored in the pointer, you need to have a particular instance. Notice that in the assignment of func in the earlier code there was no instance, just the classname and function, &Gobstopper::Chew. So to call the function, grab an instance, add func, and go! Listing 1-2 shows a complete example with the class, the member function address, and two separate instances.

Listing 1-2:   Taking the Address of a Member Function

```
#include <iostream>
#include <string>

using namespace std;

class Gobstopper
{
public:
    int WhichGobstopper;
    int Chew(string name) {
        cout << WhichGobstopper << endl;
        cout << name << endl;
        return WhichGobstopper;
    }
};

int main()
{
    typedef int (Gobstopper::*GobMember)(string);
    GobMember func = &Gobstopper::Chew;
    Gobstopper inst;
    inst.WhichGobstopper = 10;
    Gobstopper another;
    another.WhichGobstopper = 20;
    (inst.*func)("Greg W.");
    (another.*func)("Jennifer W.");
    return 0;
}
```

You can see in `main` that first we create the type for the function, which we call GobMember, and then we create a variable, func, of that type. Then we create two instances of the Gobstopper class, and we give them each a different WhichGobstopper value.

Finally, we call the member function, first for the first instance and then for the second instance. Just to show that you can take the addresses of functions with parameters, we pass in a string with some names.

When you run the code, you can see from the output that it is indeed calling the correct member function for each instance:

```
10
Greg W.
20
Jennifer W.
```

Now when we say "the correct member function for each instance," *really* what that means is the code is calling the same member function each time but using a different instance. However, when thinking in object-oriented terms, consider each instance as having its own copy of the member function. Therefore, it's okay to say "the correct member function for each instance."

Pointing to static member functions

A static member function is, in many senses, just a plain old function. The difference is that you have to use a class name to call a static function. But remember that a static member function does not go with any particular instance of a class; therefore, you don't need to specify an instance when you call the static function.

Here's an example class with a static function:

```
public:
    static string MyClassName() {
        return "Gobstopper!";
    }
    int WhichGobstopper;
    int Chew(string name) {
        cout << WhichGobstopper << endl;
        cout << name << endl;
        return WhichGobstopper;
    }
};
```

And here's some code that takes the address of the static function and calls it by using the address:

```
typedef string (*StaticMember)();
StaticMember staticfunc = &Gobstopper::MyClassName;
cout << staticfunc() << endl;
```

Note in the final line that, to call `staticfunc`, we didn't have to refer to a specific instance, and we didn't need to refer to the class, either. We just call it. Because the truth is that deep down inside, the static function is just a plain old function.

Referring to References

In this section, we reveal all the ins, outs, upsides, and downsides of using references. And we tell you a few things about them, too.

We're assuming in this section that you already know how to pass a parameter by reference when you're writing a function. (For more information about passing parameters by reference, see Minibook I, Chapter 6.) But you can use references for more than just parameter lists. You can declare a variable as a reference type. And just like job references, they can be both good and devastating. So be careful when you use them.

Reference variables

Declaring a variable that is a reference is easy. Whereas the pointer uses an asterisk, *, the reference uses an ampersand, &. But there's a twist to it. You cannot just declare it like this:

```
int &BestReference; // Nope! This won't work!
```

If you try this, you see an error that says BestReference declared as reference but not initialized. That sounds like a hint: Looks like you need to initialize it.

Yes, references need to be initialized. As the name implies, *reference* refers to another variable. Therefore, you need to initialize the reference so it refers to some other variable, like so:

```
int ImSomebody;
int &BestReference = ImSomebody;
```

Now from this point on, forever until the end of eternity (or at least as long as the function containing these two lines runs), the variable BestReference will refer to — that is, be an *alias* for — ImSomebody.

And so if you do this:

```
BestReference = 10;
```

Then you will *really* be setting ImSomebody to 10. So take a look at this code that could go inside a main:

```
int ImSomebody;
int &BestReference = ImSomebody;
BestReference = 10;
cout << ImSomebody << endl;
```

When you run this, you see the output

```
10
```

That is, setting BestReference to 10 caused ImSomebody to change to 10, which you can see when you print out the value of ImSomebody.

That's what a reference is: A reference refers to another variable.

Because a reference refers to another variable, that implies that you cannot have a reference to just a number, as in int &x = 10. And, in fact, the offending line has been implicated: You are not allowed to do that. You can only have a reference that refers to another variable.

Returning a reference from a function

It's possible to return a reference from a function. But be careful if you try to do this: You do not want to return a reference to a local variable within a function, because when the function ends, the storage space for the local variables goes away. Not good!

But you can return a reference to a global variable. Or, if the function is a member function, you can return a reference to a member variable.

For example, here's a class that has a function that returns a reference to one of its variables:

```
class DigInto
{
private:
    int secret;
public:
    DigInto() { secret = 150; }
    int &GetSecretVariable() { return secret; }
    void Write() { cout << secret << endl; }
};
```

Notice the constructor stores 150 in the `secret` variable, which is private. The `GetSecretVariable` function returns a reference to the private variable called `secret`. And the `Write` function writes out the value of the `secret` variable. Lots of secrets here! And some surprises too, which we tell you about shortly. You can use this class like so:

```
int main(int argc, char *argv[])
{
    DigInto inst;
    inst.Write();
    int &pry = inst.GetSecretVariable();
    pry = 30;
    inst.Write();
    return 0;
}
```

When you run this, you see the following output:

```
150
30
```

The first line is the value in the secret variable right after the program creates the instance. But look at the code carefully: The variable called `pry` is a reference to an integer, and it gets the results of `GetSecretVariable`. And what is that result? It's a reference to the private variable called `secret`. That means that `pry` itself is now a reference to that variable. Yes, a variable outside the class now refers directly to a private member of the instance! After that, we set `pry` to 30. When we call `Write` again, the private variable will indeed change.

Referring to someone else

And now for the $1,000,000 question: After you have a reference referring to a variable, how can you change that reference so it refers to something else? Brace yourself for a wild answer! Here goes: *You can't.* Yes, it's true, and yes, you may know some people who, nevertheless, have managed to do it. Here's the whole story.

Back when C++ first came out, companies that made compilers gave their compilers some sophisticated capabilities in terms of references. Many of them let you *unseat* a reference — that is, make the reference refer to something else. But, lo and behold, when the ANSI standard came out in the late 1990s, the standard outlawed this practice! So now the rule is that you cannot unseat a reference. Further, you cannot have a pointer to a reference, nor can you have

a reference that refers to another reference. This somewhat restrictive rule actually resolves some ambiguity: Suppose you wrote a line of code asking for the address of a reference with the hope of storing it in a `pointer to reference` variable: Because a reference refers to another variable, does that mean you want the address of the other variable, or do you somehow want the address of the reference itself?

The standard clears this up: You don't have a pointer to a reference. But interestingly, the gcc does let you write code that seems to take the address of a reference; however, in fact, you are taking the address of the variable the reference refers to. So, again, no pointers to references, and that means that you can't even take the address of a reference!

Is it just us, or does that seem like a bad idea? We made the variable private. And now the `GetSecretVariable` function pretty much wiped out any sense of the variable actually remaining private. The `main` function was able to grab a reference to it and poke around and change it however it wanted, as if it were not private! Trouble in C++ land!

That's a problem with references: They can potentially leave your code wide open. Therefore, think twice before returning a reference to a variable. One of the biggest risks is this: Somebody else might be using this code and may not understand references, and may not realize that the variable called `pry` has a direct link to the private `secret` variable. Such an inexperienced programmer might then write code that uses and changes `pry` without realizing that the member variable is changing along with it. Later on, then, a *bug* results — a pretty nasty one at that!

Because functions returning references can leave unsuspecting and less-experienced C++ programmers with just a wee bit too much power on their hands, we recommend using caution with references. No, we suggest just plain being careful. Use them only if you really feel that you must. But remember also that a better approach in classes is to have member access functions that can guard the private variables.

However, having issued the usual warnings, references can be a very powerful thing, provided you understand what they do. When you have a reference, you can easily modify another variable without having to go through pointers. Using references makes life much easier sometimes. So please: use your newfound powers carefully.

Chapter 2: Creating Data Structures

In This Chapter

✔ Discovering all the different data types

✔ Casting and converting

✔ Using structures with your data

✔ Comparing and manipulating structures

C++, being a computer language and all, provides you with a lot of ways to manipulate *data* — numbers, letters, strings, arrays — anything you can store inside the computer memory. To get the most out of C++, you should know as much as you can about the fundamental data types. This chapter covers them and how to use them.

In this chapter, we refer to the *ANSI standard* of C++. ANSI is the American National Standards Institute. The information we provide in this chapter deals with *the* ANSI standard (singular) of C++. Fortunately, the GNU gcc compiler that comes with CodeBlocks is ANSI-standard compliant. (Little nuances show up, but not often.)

Working with Data

In the sections that follow, we tell you how you can manipulate your data, including the types of data available to you and how you can change them.

The great variable roundup

The ANSI C++ standard dictates these fundamental C++ types:

♦ `char`: This is a single character. On most computers, it takes 1 byte.

♦ `int`: This is an integer. On most of the computers in the late 1990s and early 2000s, a single integer takes 4 bytes. With 4 bytes, this gives you a range from –2147483648 to 2147483647.

♦ `short int`: This is a half-sized integer. Just a little 2-byte fellow, which leaves just enough room for –32768 to 32767.

✦ `long int`: You would expect a `long int` to be longer than, well, an `int`. But it's not with the gcc compiler. The compiler recognizes two types: `short int` (2 bytes) and `long int` (4 bytes). If you leave off the first word, the compiler considers it a long `int`. So a long int is an `int`.

✦ `bool`: This can take on a value of either `true` or `false`. Inside the computer, it's a single byte, stored as a number. Normally `true` is stored as 1, and `false` is stored as 0. However, you shouldn't have to convert `bool` to a number; you should only compare it to the values `true` or `false`.

✦ `float`: This is a number with a decimal point (a *floating-point* number). The ANSI standard doesn't define this, but gcc uses 4 bytes.

✦ `double`: This is another floating-point type, and it means *double-precision floating-point*. Again, the ANSI standard doesn't say how long it should be. The gcc compiler uses 8 bytes for a double.

✦ `long double`: This is a humongous size, a real space hog. In gcc (at the time of this writing), it takes up a whole 12 bytes of space.

✦ `void`: The ANSI standard considers this an *incomplete type*. You're not allowed to declare a variable of type `void`. However, you can declare a type *pointer to* void.

✦ `wchar_t`: Many computers today support a *wide character* set, primarily for international and non-English characters. The characters in these sets usually are 2 bytes. `wchar_t` represents these characters. Some operating systems (such as Windows CE) require you to use `wchar_t`.

You can use some variations of these. You can have arrays of any of these. And you can also modify some of these just a bit:

✦ `signed`: You can tack the word `signed` to the beginning of `char`, `short int`, `int`, and `long int` to get `signed char`, `signed short int`, `signed int`, and `signed long int`. If you put `signed` in front, the numbers (and underlying numbers for the `char` type) can include negatives or positives.

✦ `unsigned`: You can put the word `unsigned` at the beginning of these types to get `unsigned char`, `unsigned short int`, `unsigned int`, and `unsigned long int`. Unsigned means that the numbers (and underlying numbers for the `char` type) cannot be negative.

Now when you use `signed` and `unsigned`, the size of the variable doesn't change: It takes the same number of bytes. Instead, the range *shifts*. For example, a signed short int ranges from –32768 to 32767, so there are 65536 possibilities. An `unsigned short int` ranges from 0 to 65535; again, there are 65536 possibilities.

The easiest way to see how the signed integers are stored is to use hexadecimal (hex). The hex numbers line themselves up nicely with the bytes. An *unsigned* short int can hold any hex values from 0x0000 through 0xffff.

These two numbers correspond to the decimal numbers 0 through 65535. Now if you put these same numbers into a *signed* short int, you can see how they're stored. Here's how:

```
short int hoopla;
hoopla = 0x0000;
cout << "0x0000: " << hoopla << endl;
hoopla = 0x0001;
cout << "0x0001: " << hoopla << endl;
hoopla = 0x7fff;
cout << "0x7fff: " << hoopla << endl;
hoopla = 0x8000;
cout << "0x8000: " << hoopla << endl;
hoopla = 0xffff;
cout << "0xffff: " << hoopla << endl;
```

When you run this code, here's what you see:

```
0x0000: 0
0x0001: 1
0x7fff: 32767
0x8000: -32768
0xffff: -1
```

These numbers in the output are out of order. Here they are in the correct order:

✦ Negative numbers from −32768 to −1 are stored from 0x8000 to 0xffff.

✦ The number 0 is stored as 0x0000, as you would expect.

✦ Positive numbers from 1 to 32767 are stored from 0x0001 to 0x7fff.

The larger integers behave similarly. For signed long int, the negatives are stored from 0x800000000 to 0xffffffff. The number 0 is 0x00000000. Positives go from 0x00000001 to 0x7fffffff.

When you are working with the different floating-point types, remember this rule: It's not about *range*, it's about *precision*. The double doesn't just hold a bigger range of numbers than the float type; it holds more decimal places.

void * is just a generic type pointer. If you want a pointer and don't want to specify what type it points to, you can make it a void *. If you're writing a C++ program that uses structures from an older C program, you may see void * crop up. When you use a void * pointer, normally you must cast it to another pointer type (such as MyStruct *).

Expressing variables from either side

Occasionally when you look at error messages (or if you read the ANSI standard!) you see the terms lvalue and rvalue. The l and r refer to *left* and *right,* respectively. In an assignment statement, an `lvalue` is any expression that can be on the left side of the equals sign, and an `rvalue` is an expression that can be on the right side of an equals sign.

The terms `lvalue` and `rvalue` do *not* refer to what happens to be on the left side and right side of an assignment statement. They refer to what is *allowed* or *not allowed* on the left side of an assignment statement. You can only have `lvalues` on the left side of an assignment statement and `rvalues` on the right side of an assignment statement.

Here are some examples, where `ploggle` is an `int` type. This is allowed, because `ploggle` is an `lvalue`:

```
ploggle = 3;
```

On the left side, you cannot have items that are strictly an `rvalue`. The following is not allowed, because 2 is strictly an `rvalue`:

```
2 = ploggle;
```

Now how do we know `ploggle` is an `lvalue`? Because it's allowed to appear on the left side of an assignment statement. The number 2 can't appear on the left (setting it equal to something else makes no sense!), therefore it isn't an `rvalue`. In fact, *anything you can set equal to something else is an `lvalue`.*

The main reason you need to know these terms is their tendency to show up in error messages. If you try to compile the line `2 = ploggle`, here are some error messages that appear (one for each of three compilers):

✦ Borland C++ Builder: `Lvalue required`

✦ gcc (whether CodeBlocks, MinGW, or Cygwin): `non-lvalue in assignment`

✦ Visual C++: `left operand must be l-value`

If you don't know what the term `lvalue` means, these messages can be confusing. And while seeing the problem with `2 = ploggle` is pretty easy, sometimes the problem is not that obvious. Look at this:

```
ChangeMe() = 10;
DontKnow() = 20;
```

Do these even make sense? Putting a function call on the left side? In other words: Are the expressions `ChangeMe()` and `DontKnow()` lvalues?

It depends. Take a look at this code:

```
int uggle;

int &ChangeMe()
{
    return uggle;
}

int DontKnow()
{
    return uggle;
}
```

The *function* `ChangeMe` returns a reference to an integer; this line is valid:

```
ChangeMe() = 10;
```

The *expression* `ChangeMe()` refers to the variable `uggle`, and thus this line of code stores 10 in `uggle`. But the second function, `DontKnow`, returns just an integer *value* (a number, not a variable). Therefore, this line is not valid:

```
DontKnow() = 20;
```

The left side, `DontKnow()` is not an `lvalue` — it's an `rvalue` — therefore it cannot appear on the left side of an equation, and that line is an error.

Indeed, when we try to compile these lines, the compiler is happy with the `ChangeMe() = 10;` line. But for the `DontKnow() = 20;` line, it gives us the following error message.

```
error: non-lvalue in assignment
```

The words `lvalue` and `rvalue` are *not* C++ words. You do not type these into a program. (Well, yeah, we suppose you *could* use them as variable names, but we'd really rather not — and we suggest you don't, either.)

Casting a spell on your data

Although C++ has all these great data types, such as `integer` and `char`, the fact is this: Underneath they are just stored as numbers. And sometimes you may have a character and need to use its underlying number. To do this, you can *cast* the data.

The way you cast is to take a variable of one type and type the variable's name preceded with the other type you would like it to be. You put the other type in parentheses.

```
char buddy = 'A';
int underneath = (int)buddy;
cout << underneath << endl;
```

Comparing casting and converting

The idea behind casting is to take some data and, without changing it (and with nothing up our sleeves), use it in another way. For example, we could have an array containing the characters `Applecrisp`. But inside the memory, each letter is stored as a number. For example, the `A` is stored as `65`, `p` is stored as `112`, and `l` as `108`. Therefore, if we wanted to, we could cast each character to an integer, using such code as

```
cout << (int)(str[loop]) << endl;
```

where `str` is the string (`Applecrisp`) and `loop` is a loop counter that cycles through the string. This would print out the numerical equivalents of each letter. In other words, we cast the characters to integers — but we did not actually change any data. Now we can copy the data like this:

```
int num = str[0];
```

This code would copy the data, but again, it wouldn't change it. We'd just have two copies of the same data. That's what casting is all about: using data as a different data type from what it was originally.

Converting, however, is different. If we want to take the number 123, casting it to a string will not create a string `123`. The string `123` is made up of three underlying byte-sized snacks of numbers. The numbers for the string `123` are 49, 50, and 51, respectively. Casting the number 123 just won't give us that. Instead, you would need to convert the number to a string.

But, like most rules, this one has an exception, and that exception comes into play when converting between floats and integers. Instead of using a conversion function, the C++ compiler automatically converts from float to integer and vice versa if you try to cast one to the other. Ugh. That goes against the rest of the rules, so be careful. Here's an example of converting a float to an integer:

```
float f = 6.3;
int i = (int)f;
```

But the crazy part is that you can also do the same thing without even using the cast, although you will get a compiler warning:

```
float f = 6.3;
int i = f;
```

When you run this code, you obtain an output value of 65. If you substituted a lowercase `a`, the output would be 97 because uppercase and lowercase letters have different numeric values.

Back in the old days of the C programming language, casting was a common way of converting data — *but it's actually somewhat dangerous.* In C, you could take any data type and directly cast it to any other data type. The idea was that if you wanted to burrow into the system and manipulate something (just about anything), you could. But over the years, people started to figure out that maybe, just *maybe*, this wasn't such a good idea. (As in, "Hey, bugs, welcome to my computer!") So although we're showing you how to cast, you should *try to avoid casting.* Instead, focus on converting (which sometimes uses castlike syntax) or using safe casts. See Chapter 8 in Minibook 1 as well as the next section ("Casting safely with C++") in this chapter.

Casting safely with C++

With the ANSI standard of C++ came all kinds of new goodies that make life easier than it used to be. Casting is one example. Originally, you could just cast all you wanted and change from one data type to another, possibly causing a mess, especially if you take existing code and compile it under a different operating system or perhaps even under a different compiler on the same operating system. One type may have a different underlying representation, and then, when you convert it on one system, you get one thing; take it to a different system and you get something else. That's bad. It creates bugs!

So the ANSI standard for C++ gives some newer and better ways of casting between data. These include `dynamic_cast` and `static_cast`.

Dynamically casting with dynamic_cast

When the makers of C++ came up with these new ways of casting, their motivation was this: Think in terms of *conversions*. A cast simply takes one data type and tells the compiler to treat it as another data type. So first ask yourself if one of the conversions will work for you. If not, you can consider one of the new ways of casting.

But remember, a *cast* tells the compiler to treat some data as another type of data. But the new ways of casting prevent you from doing a cast that doesn't make sense. For example, you may have a class hierarchy, and you have a pointer to a base class. But because an instance of a derived class can be treated as an instance of a base class, it's possible that this instance that you're looking at could actually be an instance of a derived class.

In the old style of C and C++ programming, you could just cast the instance and have at it:

```
DoSomethingCool( (derivedclass *) someptr);
```

In this case, we're assuming that `someptr` is of type pointer-to-base-class, but we're *hoping* that, in fact, it points to a `derivedclass` instance. Does it? It may, depending on how we wrote the rest of the program. But maybe not. And when the word *hope* meets the word *program*, the word *disaster* tends to show up. Tempers fly and people lose their jobs. It's not a pretty sight.

But have no fear: ANSI is here! With the new ways of casting, you can be sure. Listing 2-1 is a complete program that demonstrates a proper *downcast,* where we take a pointer to a base class and cast it down to a pointer of a derived class.

Listing 2-1:   Casting Instances Dynamically for Safety

```cpp
#include <iostream>
#include <string>

using namespace std;

class King
{
protected:
    string CrownName;
public:
    virtual string &MyName() { return CrownName; }
    virtual ~King(){}
};

class Prince : public King
{
public:
    string School;
};

void KingInfo(King *inst)
{
    cout << "=========" << endl;
    cout << inst->MyName() << endl;
    Prince *asPrince = dynamic_cast<Prince *>(inst);
    if (asPrince != 0)
    {
        cout << asPrince->School << endl;
    }
}

int main()
{
    Prince George;
    George.MyName() = "George I";
    George.School = "School of the Kings";
    KingInfo(&George);
    King Henry;
    Henry.MyName() = "Henry II";
    KingInfo(&Henry);
    return 0;
}
```

Go ahead and run this code. You'll see output that looks something like this:

```
=========
George I
School of the Kings
=========
Henry II

Process returned 0 (0x0)    execution time : 0.062 s
Press any key to continue.
```

Some strange things are going on in this code. But first, we want to point out the main thing that this code demonstrates: In the main `main`, we call the `KingInfo` function, first passing it the address of `George` (a `Prince` instance, derived from `King`) and then the address of `Henry` (a `King` instance).

The `KingInfo` function first prints the information that is common to both due to inheritance; it calls the `MyName` function and prints the resulting name. Then comes the important part, the dynamic cast. To do this, we call `dynamic_cast` and save it in a pointer variable called `asPrince`. Notice the syntax of `dynamic_cast`. It looks like a template in that you include a type in angled brackets. Then you put the thing you want to cast in parentheses (in this case, the instance that was passed into the function).

If the dynamic cast worked, it returns a pointer that you can save as the type inside angled brackets. Otherwise, the dynamic cast will return 0. You can see that after we called `dynamic_cast`, we tested it against 0. If the result is not 0, the dynamic cast worked, which means that we successfully cast the data to the desired type. And then, in the `if` block, we retrieve the `School` member, which is part of `Prince`, not `King`.

You may notice the unique design of the `King` class. Take a look at just the `King` class:

```
class King
{
protected:
    string CrownName;
public:
    virtual string &MyName() { return CrownName; }
    virtual ~King(){}
};
```

For `dynamic_cast` to work, the base class involved must have *at least one virtual function*. Thus the base class — and each of its derived classes — has a virtual table (also needed for `dynamic_cast` to work). In addition, the CodeBlocks compiler raises a warning message when you don't provide a virtual destructor:

```
warning: `class King' has virtual functions but non-virtual destructor
```

Consequently, the example includes a virtual destructor as well.

Originally, we wanted `CrownName` to be public. But because we needed to add a virtual function to class `King`, we decided to make the function useful, rather than just add a function that does nothing at all. So we made it access the `CrownName` member. And for that, we wanted to give the function a reason for its existence, so we made the `CrownName` protected. Then we had the `MyName` function return a reference to it. The end result is that it's like `CrownName` is public, which is the way we wanted the class in the beginning.

You don't need to use references in a class as we did here just to make `dynamic_cast` work. But you do need at least one virtual function.

Some compilers (including Microsoft Visual C++) do not, by default, handle `dynamic_cast`. To use a dynamic cast in Visual C++, you have to go into the project settings and select Enable Run-time Type Information (RTTI) found in C++ Language Settings. Then you need to recompile your program for the change to take effect. Note that if you don't select this setting, you get a warning (not an error) that says, `dynamic_cast used on polymorphic type 'class King' with /GR-; unpredictable behavior may result`. The program will still compile and link, but when you run it, a run-time error message pops up.

Remember, here's the fundamental difference between an old-style direct cast and the new `dynamic_cast`: The compiler generates code that automatically does an old-style cast, regardless of whether the cast is valid. That is, the cast is *hardcoded*. But `dynamic_cast`, on the other hand, tests the types at *runtime*. The dynamic cast may or may not work depending on the type of the object.

When you use a dynamic cast, you can cast either a pointer or a reference. The `KingInfo` function back in Listing 2-1 uses a pointer. Here's a modified form that uses a reference:

```
void KingInfoAsReference(King &inst)
{
    cout << "=========" << endl;
    cout << inst.MyName() << endl;
    try
    {
        Prince &asPrince = dynamic_cast<Prince &>(inst);
        cout << asPrince.School << endl;
    }
    catch (...)
    {
    }
}
```

To make this work, we had to use an *exception handler* (which is a way to deal with unusual situations; see Chapter 3 in this Minibook for more information on exception handlers). The reason for using an exception handler is that with a pointer, you can simply test the result against 0. But with references, you have no such thing as a *null reference* or *0 reference*. The reference *must* work, or you get a runtime error. And in C++, the way you can catch a situation that didn't work is by typing the word `try`, followed by your code that attempts to do the job, in braces. Follow that with the word `catch` and a set of parentheses containing three periods. Following that, you put braces — and possibly any code you want to run — just in case the earlier code didn't work.

In this code, you can see that we didn't do anything inside the `catch` block. We want to do something only if the code works. We would just leave off the `catch` block because we didn't have it do anything, but, alas, C++ doesn't allow that: If you have a `try` block, you must have a `catch` block. Them's the rules.

Statically casting with static_cast

The ANSI C++ standard includes a special type of cast that does no type checking. If you have to cast directly without the help of `dynamic_cast`, you should opt for `static_cast` instead of the old C-style cast.

When you want to do a static cast, call `static_cast` and follow it with angled brackets containing the type you want to cast to. Then put the item being cast inside parentheses, as in the following:

```
FinalType *f = static_cast<FinalType *>(orig);
```

The advantage of using `static_cast` is that it does some type checking at compile time, whereas old C-style casts do not. The compiler allows you to do `static_cast` only between related objects. For example, you can do a `static_cast` from an instance of one class to an instance of a derived or base class. But if two classes are not related, you will get a compiler error.

For example, suppose that you have these two lines of code:

```
class FinalType {};
class AnotherType {};
```

They are unrelated classes. Then if you have these lines of code

```
AnotherType *orig = new AnotherType;
FinalType *f = static_cast<FinalType *>(orig);
```

and you try to compile it, you get an error:

```
static_cast from `AnotherType *' to `FinalType *'
```

But if you instead make the classes related

```
class FinalType {};
class AnotherType : public FinalType {};
```

then these two lines will compile (if you're using the CodeBlocks compiler, you will receive a message, `warning: unused variable 'f'`):

```
AnotherType *orig = new AnotherType;
FinalType *f = static_cast<FinalType *>(orig);
```

A lot of people think that `static_cast` is useless and is essentially identical to old-style C casts. This is not true. Tell them they're wrong! (But be nice, now. Friends come before software, after all.) The mistaken notion is that `static_cast` does no type checking, when in fact it *does*. The difference between `static_cast` and `dynamic_cast` is that `static_cast` does its type checking at compile time; the compiler makes sure the cast is okay. `dynamic_cast`, however, also does the same type checking at compile time, but when it runs, it does more checking to make sure that the instance is precisely what you're converting to. Old C-style casts do none of this type checking.

If you're just doing a conversion between floating-point numbers and integers, you can do an old-style cast. (That's because an old-style cast is really a conversion, not a cast.) Alternatively, of course, you're welcome to use static_cast to get the same job done:

```
float f = static_cast<float>(x);
```

Structuring Your Data

Before C++ came to life, C had something that was similar to classes, called *structures*. The difference was that structures had only member variables — no member functions. Here's an example of a structure:

```
struct Dimensions
{
    int height;
    int width;
    int depth;
    int weight;
    int price;
};
```

This block of code is similar to a class; as you can see, it has some member variables but no member functions. Nor does it have any access control (such as public, private, or protected).

But not only did the designers of C++ add classes to C++, they also enhanced the structures in C++. So now in C++, you can use structures more powerfully than you could in C. The main change to structures in C++ is that they can have member functions and access control. Thus, we can add to the Dimensions structure like so:

```
struct Dimensions
{
private:
    int price;
public:
    int height;
    int width;
    int depth;
    int weight;
    int GetPrice() { return price; }
};
```

Then we can create an instance of Dimensions in our code like this:

```
Dimensions FirstIem;
Dimensions *SecondItem = new Dimensions;
```

Well now, isn't that interesting? This `struct` business is looking *suspiciously* like a class, wouldn't you say? Hmmm. As it happens, the `struct` code *is* a `class`. It's the *same* thing.

When the great founder of the C++ language (Bjarne Stroustrup) created C++, he enhanced structures to the point that classes and structures are *identical*, with one exception. Members of a structure are public by default. Members of a class, however, are private by default.

That's nice. But why would you use a structure? Really, it doesn't matter. Most C++ programmers today never even touch a structure.

However, some C++ programmers use a special convention concerning structures. If a class has only public member variables and no member functions, then make it a structure.

In other words, programmers use structure for simple data types that are themselves a collection of smaller data types. (That is, they use structures in the same way C originally had it.) That's actually a pretty good idea. In the sections that follow, we tell you about some of these data structure issues. (And for what it's worth, keeping structures around in C++ was a good idea because a lot of people originally took C programs and recompiled them with a C++ compiler. It was good that the C++ compiler handled the structures.)

If you're familiar with C and just learning C++, you may be interested to know that when you declare a variable that is a structure type, in C++ you need to give only the name of the structure. You no longer need the word `struct` in the declaration. Thus, the following line will still compile in C++

```
struct Dimensions another;
```

but all you really need is

```
Dimensions another;
```

Structures as component data types

A common use of structures is as an advanced data type made up of underlying data types. For example, a lot of operating systems that deal with graphics include some libraries that require a `Point` structure. Typically, a `Point` structure is simply a grouping of an X-coordinate and a Y-coordinate, all in one package.

You might declare such a structure like this:

```
struct Point
{
    int x;
    int y;
};
```

Then, when you need to call a function that requires such a structure, such as one we made up for this example called DrawDot, you would simply declare a Point and call the function, as in the following.

```
Point onedot;
onedot.x = 10;
onedot.y = 15;
DrawDot(onedot);
```

The DrawDot function would have a prototype that looks like this:

```
void DrawDot(Point pt);
```

Note that the function doesn't take a pointer to a Point, nor does it take a reference to a Point. It just gets right to the Point directly.

If you want, you can initialize the members of a structure the same way you would an array:

```
Point seconddot = { 30, 50 };
DrawDot(seconddot);
```

Equating structures

Setting simple structures that are equal to another structure is easy. The C++ compiler automatically handles this by copying the members one by one. Listing 2-2 is an example of this process in action.

Listing 2-2:   Copying Structures Easily

```
#include <iostream>

using namespace std;

struct Point3D
{
    double x;
    double y;
    double z;
};

int main()
{
    Point3D FirstPoint = { 10.5, 22.25, 30.8 };
    Point3D SecondPoint = FirstPoint;
    cout << SecondPoint.x << endl;
    cout << SecondPoint.y << endl;
    cout << SecondPoint.z << endl;
    return 0;
}
```

Because structures are almost identical to classes, you can take Listing 2-2 and change the structure definition to the following class definition, and the program will continue to function the same:

```
class Point3D
{
public:
    double x;
    double y;
    double z;
};
```

No matter which form of the application you use, the output is simple. When you run this application, you see output similar to this:

```
10.5
22.25
30.8

Process returned 0 (0x0)   execution time : 0.015 s
Press any key to continue.
```

Returning compound data types

Because simple structures are just a grouping of smaller data items, you can treat them as one chunk of data. For that reason, you can easily return them from functions without having to use pointers.

The following function is an example of this:

```
Point3D StartingPoint(float x)
{
    Point3D start;
    start.x = x;
    start.y = x * 2;
    start.z = x * 3;
    return start;
}
```

This function relies on the `Point3D struct` defined in the "Equating structures" section of the chapter. You can easily call this guy, then, by using code like this:

```
Point3D MyPoint = StartingPoint(5.2);
Point3D OtherPoint = StartingPoint(6.5);
cout << MyPoint.x << endl;
cout << MyPoint.y << endl;
cout << MyPoint.z << endl;
cout << endl;
cout << OtherPoint.x << endl;
cout << OtherPoint.y << endl;
cout << OtherPoint.z << endl;
```

These `cout` statements produce the following output:

```
5.2
10.4
15.6

6.5
13
19.5

Process returned 0 (0x0)    execution time : 0.125 s
Press any key to continue.
```

Note that in the function, we simply created a local variable of type `Point3D`. This variable is not a pointer, nor is it a reference. And at the end of the function, we just returned it. When we called it, we copied the value of the returned structure into our own variables, first `MyPoint` and then `OtherPoint`.

You may start to see some trouble in paradise when returning structures (or class instances, because they're the same thing). Does returning a structure work? Why yes, it does, but what happens is sophisticated. When you create an instance of the structure in the function, you're just creating a local variable. That's definitely *not* something you want to return; it would sit on the stack as a local variable. But consider this call:

```
Point3D MyPoint = StartingPoint(5.2);
```

At the assembly level, the `StartingPoint` function receives the address of `MyPoint`. Then at the end of the function, again at the assembly level, the compiled code copies the contents of the local variable (called `start` in this case) into the `MyPoint` structure by using the pointer to `MyPoint`. So nothing is actually *returned*, per se; instead, the data is copied. That means, then, that if your structure includes a pointer variable, for example, you will get a copy of the pointer variable as well — that is, your pointer variable will point to the same thing as the one in the function. That may be what you want, or it may not be, depending on your situation. So be careful and make sure you fully understand what you're doing when you return a structure from a function!

Naming Your Space

It's often nice to be able to use a common name for a variable or other item without fear of the name clashing with a preexisting identifier. For example, somewhere in a header file you may have a global variable called `Count`, and somebody else may want to make a variable called `Count` in one of his or her functions that uses your global header file. Or you may want to name a function `GetData` — but how can you be sure the people who use your function won't include a header file somebody else wrote that already has a `GetData` function? Is it the great Battle of the `GetDatas`, where only one will survive? Not good! What can you do to avoid the clash?

You can use namespaces. A *namespace* is simply a way to group identifiers, such as all your classes. If you called this group `Menagerie`, for example, `Menagerie` would be your namespace. You would then put your classes inside it, like this:

```
namespace Menagerie
{
    class Oxen {
    public:
        int Weight;
        int NumberOfTeeth;
    };
    class Cattle {
    public:
        int Weight;
        int NumberOfChildren;
    };
}
```

The names `Oxen` and `Cattle` are unique within the `Menagerie` namespace. You are free to reuse these names in other namespaces without worrying about a clash. Then, if you want to use either of the two classes inside the `Menagerie` namespace, you would *fully qualify* the names of the classes, like so:

```
Menagerie::Cattle bessie;
bessie.Weight = 643;
```

Unlike class and structure declarations, a namespace declaration *doesn't* have to end with a semicolon.

If you plan to use the names in the `Menagerie` namespace without reusing them, just put a line after the namespace declaration (but somewhere preceding the use of the names `Cattle` and `Oxen` in your code), like this:

```
using namespace Menagerie;
```

Then you can access the names as if they're not in a namespace:

```
Cattle bessie;
bessie.Weight = 643;
```

When you include a line that has `using namespace`, the compiler knows the namespace is only for lines that follow the `using namespace` declaration. Consider the following code:

```
void cattleranch()
{
    Cattle x;
}

using namespace Menagerie;

void dairy()
{
    Cattle x;
}
```

Here the first function won't compile because the compiler won't know the name `Cattle`. To get it to work, you have to replace `Cattle` with `Menagerie::Cattle`. But the second function *will* compile, thanks to some help from our buddy `using namespace`.

The `using namespace` line is good only for lines that follow it. If you put `using namespace` inside a code block — inside curly braces { and }, as you would inside a function — the line applies only to lines that follow it *within the same code block*. Thus, in this case

```
void cattleranch()
{
    using namespace Menagerie;
    Cattle x;
}

void dairy() {
    Cattle x;
}
```

the compiler will be happy with the first function, `cattleranch` but not with the second function, `dairy`. The `using namespace` line is good only for the length of the `cattleranch` function; it's inside that function's code block.

When you have a `using namespace` line, any variables or identifiers you create after that line don't become *part* of the namespace you're using. The `using namespace` line simply tells the compiler that if it finds an identifier it doesn't recognize, it should check next inside the namespaces you're using.

When you have a `using namespace` line, you can follow it with more `using namespace` lines for other namespaces — and doing so won't cause the compiler to forget the previous `using namespace` line. Thus, if you have

```
using namespace Menagerie;
using namespace Ocean;
```

you can successfully refer to identifiers in both the `Menagerie` and the `Ocean` namespaces.

Creating one namespace in many places

After you create a namespace, you can add to it later in your code if necessary. All you have to do is start the first block of code with (for example) `namespace Menagerie {` and then finish it with a closing brace. Then later in your code, do the same line again — starting the block again with `namespace Menagerie {` and ending it with a closing brace. The identifiers in both blocks become part of the `namespace Menagerie`.

Using variables and part of a namespace

You can put variables in a namespace and then later refer to them through the namespace, as in the following:

```
namespace Menagerie
{
    int CattleCount;
}
```

And then again later (for example, in your `main`) like this:

```
Menagerie::CattleCount = 10;
```

But remember: *A namespace is not a class!* Only one instance of the `CattleCount` variable exists; it just happens to have a full name of `Menagerie::CattleCount`. This doesn't mean you can get away with creating multiple instances of `Menagerie`: You can't. It's a namespace. (Think of it like a surname: There could be multiple people named John, and to distinguish between them in a meeting at work, you might tack on their last names: John Squibbledash and John Poltzerbuckin.) Although the namespace name comes first in `Menagerie::CattleCount`, it's analogous to the last name. Two variables can be called `CattleCount`: one in the `Menagerie` namespace and one in the `Farm` namespace. Thus their full names would be `Menagerie::CattleCount` and `Farm::CattleCount`.

If you want to use only a portion of a namespace, you are free to do that, too. With the `Menagerie` namespace that we declared earlier in this section, you could do something like this outside the namespace:

```
using Menagerie::Oxen;
Oxen ollie;
```

(Notice that no `namespace` word appears after `using`.) The first line tells the compiler about the name `Oxen`, and the second line creates an instance of `Oxen`. Of course, if you have `using namespace Menagerie`, the `using Menagerie::Oxen` isn't very useful because the `Oxen` name is already available from the `using namespace Menagerie` line.

Think of a `using` declaration as pulling a name into the current namespace. Therefore a declaration such as `using Menagerie::Oxen` pulls the name `Oxen` into the current namespace. The single name then lives in both namespaces.

To understand how one name becomes a part of two namespaces, take a look at Listing 2-3.

The standard namespace

Sooner or later, you're going to encounter something like this:

```
std::cout << "Hi" << std::endl;
```

You see this because normally cout, cin, endl, and everything else that comes from #include<iostream> is in a namespace called std (which is short for *standard*). But we find that line of code ugly. We don't want to write a namespace name and two colons every time we want to write a cout or endl (or anything else from iostream, for that matter). So what do you do to avoid it? You simply put

```
using namespace std;
```

at the beginning of your program, after the include lines. Fortunately, the gcc compiler automatically recognizes the std namespace, and you don't need the using namespace std; line. But if you're using other compilers (notably Borland C++Builder or Microsoft Visual C++), you need to add std:: before each cout and cin and endl words or take the easier way out and use the using namespace std; line. We prefer the using namespace std; line. So if you look at the code on the accompanying CD-ROM, you see that line at the beginning of every program.

Listing 2-3: Pulling Names into Other Namespaces with the using Declaration

```cpp
#include <iostream>

using namespace std;

namespace A
{
    int X;
}

namespace B
{
    using A::X;
}

int main()
{
    A::X = 2;
    cout << B::X << endl;
    return 0;
}
```

This code has two namespaces, A and B. The first namespace, A, has a variable called X. The second namespace, B, has a using statement that pulls the name X into that namespace. The single variable that lives inside A is now part of both namespaces, A and B. main verifies this: It saves a value in the X variable of A and prints the value in the X variable of B. And lo and behold, the result on the screen is this:

```
2
```

Yes indeed, A::X and B::X *refer to the same variable*, thanks to the using declaration!

Chapter 3: Constructors, Destructors, and Exceptions

In This Chapter

✓ Writing constructors

✓ Using different kinds of constructors

✓ Writing destructors

✓ Understanding the order that takes place in construction and destruction

✓ Throwing and catching exceptions

*N*ow's the time to seriously master C++. In this chapter, we talk about three vital topics: constructors, destructors, and exceptions. Fully understanding what goes on with constructors and destructors is very important. The better you understand how constructors and destructors work, the less likely you are to write code that doesn't function the way that you expected and the more likely you are to avoid bugs.

Exceptions are important also in that they let you handle error situations — that is, you can handle problems when they do come up.

Many developers feel that constructors, destructors, and exceptions are extremely simple. In fact, many developers would doubt that these three topics could fill an entire chapter, but they can. After you read this chapter, you should have a good mastery of constructors, destructors, and exceptions.

So without further ado, you can begin to construct your reading as you destruct any old ways of programming, without exception.

Constructing and Destructing Objects

Classes are goofy little things. They like to have some say in how their instances get started. But that's okay. We're programmers, and we like to do what the computer wants us to do (as opposed to the other way around). And so the great founders of the C++ language gave us constructors. *Constructors* are member functions that the program calls when it creates an instance. *Destructors,* on the other hand, are member functions that the program calls when it deletes an instance.

A single class can have multiple constructors. In fact, several kinds of constructors are available. There aren't as many kinds of destructors. (In fact, there's really only one.) In the sections that follow, we give you all the necessary information so that, when your classes want constructors, you will be able to happily add them.

If you see some older C++ code, you are more than likely to see the word virtual before a constructor in a class definition. The idea was that you can override a constructor when you derive a new class, so you should make it virtual. However, in ANSI C++, this construction is not right. You cannot make a constructor virtual. If you put the word virtual before a constructor, you get a compiler error. If you see an older class that has a virtual constructor, create constructors as you normally would in the derived classes, and all will be fine. (Unfortunately, all is not fine for those million or so C++ programmers who spent years writing code that had the word virtual before a constructor. They get to practice using that Backspace key.)

Overloading constructors

You are allowed to put multiple constructors in your class. The way the user of your class chooses a constructor is by setting up the parameters in the variable declaration. Suppose you have a class called Clutter, and suppose you see the following two lines of code:

```
Clutter inst1("Jim");
Clutter inst2(123, "Sally");
```

These two lines have different types of parameters in the list. Each one is making use of a different constructor for the single class.

You can put multiple constructors in your class. The process of putting multiple constructors is called *overloading* the constructors. Here's an example of a Clutter class that has two constructors:

```
class Clutter
{
protected:
    string ChildName;
    int Toys;

public:
    Clutter(int count, string name)
    {
        ChildName = name;
        Toys = count;
    }

    Clutter(string name)
    {
        ChildName = name;
        Toys = 0;
    }
};
```

The compiler will figure out which overloaded constructor to use based on the parameters. Therefore, the overloaded constructors must differ in their parameter lists — specifically, this means the *types* of parameters; just changing the names doesn't count! If the parameter lists don't differ, the compiler won't be able to distinguish them, and you will get an error when it tries to compile the class definition.

If your constructor doesn't have a parameter provided by other constructors, you should initialize the associated variable within the constructor code. For example, the second constructor doesn't include a parameter for `Toys`, so the constructor code initializes this variable to 0. As an alternative, you can use an initializer as described in the "Initializing members" section of the chapter.

Having multiple constructors makes your class much more flexible and easy to use. Multiple constructors give the users of your class more ways to use the class, allowing them to configure the instances differently, depending on their situations. Further, the constructors force the user to configure the instances only in the ways your constructors allow.

Initializing members

When C++ originally came out, any time you wanted to initialize a member variable, you had to put it inside a constructor. This created some interesting problems. The main problem had to do with references. You can put reference variables in a class, but normally reference variables must be initialized. You can't just have a reference variable floating around that doesn't refer to anything. But if you put a reference variable inside a class and create an instance of the class, the program will first create the instance and then call the constructor. Even if you initialize the reference in the first line of the constructor, there's still a moment when you have an uninitialized reference! Oh, what to do, what to do?

The ANSI standard uses a single approach for setting up member variables: initializers. An *initializer* goes on the same line as the constructor in the class definition; or, if the constructor isn't inline, the initializer goes with the constructor in the code outside the class definition.

Book IV Chapter 3

Here's an example where we have the initializers right inside the class definition:

```
class MySharona
{
protected:
    int OneHitWonders;
    int NumberRecordings;
public:
    MySharona() : OneHitWonders(1), NumberRecordings(10) {}
};
```

Constructors, Destructors, and Exceptions

When you create an instance of this class, the `OneHitWonders` member gets the value 1 and the `NumberRecordings` member gets the value 10. Note the syntax: The constructor name and parameter list (which is empty in this case) is followed by a single colon. The member variables appear after that, each followed by an initial value in parentheses. Commas separate the member variables.

After the member variables is the open brace for any code you would want in the constructor. In this case, we had no code, so we immediately put a closing brace.

You can put any of the class member variables in the initializer list, but you don't have to include them all. If you don't care to initialize some, you don't have to. Note also that you cannot put inherited members in the initializer list; you can include only members that are in the class itself.

You can also pass these initial values in through the constructor. Here's a slightly modified version of this same class. This time the constructor has a parameter that we save in the `NumberRecordings` member:

```
class MySharona
{
protected:
    int OneHitWonders;
    int NumberRecordings;
public:
    MySharona(int Records) : OneHitWonders(1),
        NumberRecordings(Records) {}
};
```

By associating an initializer list with a constructor, you can have different initializers with different constructors. You are not limited to initializing the data the same way for all your constructors.

You may have noticed that the member initialization follows a format similar to the way you initialize an inherited constructor. Take a look at how we're calling the base class constructor in this code:

```
class MusicInfo
{
public:
    int PhoneNumber;
    MusicInfo(int Phone) : PhoneNumber(Phone) {}
};

class MySharona : public MusicInfo
{
protected:
    int OneHitWonders;
    int NumberRecordings;
public:
    MySharona(int Records) : OneHitWonders(1),
        NumberRecordings(Records),
        MusicInfo(8675309) {}
};
```

In the `MySharona` class, the member variables get initialized, and the base class constructor gets called, all in the initialization. The call to the base class constructor is this portion:

```
MusicInfo(8675309)
```

But note that we're passing a number into the constructor. The `MusicInfo` constructor takes a single number for a parameter, and it uses the number it receives to initialize the `Phone` member:

```
MusicInfo(int Phone) : PhoneNumber(Phone) {}
```

Therefore, every time someone creates an instance of the class `MySharona`, the inherited `PhoneNumber` member is automatically initialized to `8675309`.

Thus, you can create an instance of `MySharona` like this:

```
MySharona CD(20);
```

This instance starts out having the member values `OneHitWonders` = 1, `NumberRecordings` = 20, and `Phone` = 8675309. The only thing that the user can specify here for a default value is the `NumberRecordings` member. The other two members are set automatically by the class.

However, you don't have to do it this way. Perhaps you want the users of this class to be able to specify the `PhoneNumber` when they create an instance. Here's a modified form that does it for you:

```
class MusicInfo
{
public:
    int PhoneNumber;
    MusicInfo(int Phone) : PhoneNumber(Phone) {}
};

class MySharona : public MusicInfo
{
protected:
    int OneHitWonders;
    int NumberRecordings;
public:
    MySharona(int Records, int Phone) : OneHitWonders(1),
        NumberRecordings(Records), MusicInfo(Phone) {}
};
```

Look carefully at the difference: The `MySharona` class now has two parameters. The second is an integer, and we pass that one into the base class through the portion:

```
MusicInfo(Phone)
```

So to use this class, you might do something like this:

```
MySharona CD(20, 5551212);
```

This code snippet creates an instance of MySharona, with the members initialized to OneHitWonders = 1, NumberRecordings = 20, and PhoneNumber = 5551212.

If you have overloaded constructors, you can have different sets of initializations. For example, take a look at yet one more modification to the class:

```
class MusicInfo
{
public:
    int PhoneNumber;
    MusicInfo(int Phone) : PhoneNumber(Phone) {}
};

class MySharona : public MusicInfo
{
protected:
    int OneHitWonders;
    int NumberRecordings;
public:
    MySharona(int Records, int Phone) : MusicInfo(Phone),
        OneHitWonders(1), NumberRecordings(Records) {}

    MySharona(int Records) : MusicInfo(8675309),
        OneHitWonders(1), NumberRecordings(Records)  {}
};
```

Now this class has two constructors. We combined the previous two versions, so now you can use either constructor. You can, then, have the following two variables, for example, each using a different constructor:

```
MySharona CD(20, 5551212);
MySharona OldCD(30);
cout << CD.PhoneNumber << endl;
cout << OldCD.PhoneNumber << endl;
```

When you run the cout lines, they have different values for the PhoneNumber member. The first passes a specific value; the second accepts a default value:

```
5551212
8675309
```

You should initialize the base class values first. Otherwise, the compiler is likely to display warning messages when you compile the application.

If the only real difference in the different constructors is whether or not the user supplies a value (as was the case in the previous example), you can use a slightly better approach. Constructors (and any function in C++, really) can have default values. The following example shortens the previous ones by using default values. The result is the same:

```
class MusicInfo
{
public:
    int PhoneNumber;
    MusicInfo(int Phone) : PhoneNumber(Phone) {}
};

class MySharona : public MusicInfo
{
protected:
    int OneHitWonders;
    int NumberRecordings;
public:
    MySharona(int Records, int Phone=8675309) :
        MusicInfo(Phone), OneHitWonders(1),
        NumberRecordings(Records) {}
};
```

In the preceding code, the second parameter to the constructor has an equals sign and a number after it. That means the user of the class doesn't have to specify this parameter. If the parameter is not present, it automatically gets the value 8675309.

You can have as many default parameters as you want in a constructor or any other function, but the rule is that the default parameters must come at the end. After you have a default parameter, all the parameters that follow must have a default value. Therefore, the following type of code is not allowed:

```
MySharona(int Records = 6, int Phone) :
    MusicInfo(Phone), OneHitWonders(1),
    NumberRecordings(Records) {}
```

There's a practical reason for this: When the user calls the constructor (by creating a variable of type `MySharona`, there is no way to leave out just a first parameter and have only a second one. It's not possible, unless C++ were to allow an empty parameter followed by a comma, as in `MySharona(,8675309)`. But that's not allowed.

Adding a default constructor

A *default constructor* is a constructor that takes no parameters. You can have a default constructor in a class in either of two ways: by coding it or by letting the compiler *implicitly* build one for you. By *implicitly build one for you,* we mean that you don't actually have a constructor in your code, but the compiler gives you one when it compiles the code for you.

You've probably seen a default constructor before. This class has no constructor, so the compiler generates an implicit one for you. It works like this:

```
class Simple
{
public:
    int x,y;
    void Write()
    {
        cout << x << " " << y << endl;
    }
};
```

Of course, the preceding class doesn't do much. It's the same as this:

```
class Simple
{
public:
    int x,y;
    void Write()
    {
        cout << x << " " << y << endl;
    }
    Simple() {}
};
```

However, recognizing that the default constructor is there is important. And you need to realize when the compiler *doesn't* create one automatically because you may run into some problems. Take a look at this modified version of the class:

```
class Simple
{
public:
    int x,y;
    void Write()
    {
        cout << x << " " << y << endl;
    }
    Simple(int startx) { x = startx; }
};
```

We included in this code our own constructor that takes a parameter. After we do this, the class no longer gets an implicit default constructor. If we have a line later like this:

```
Simple inst;
```

the compiler will give us an error message like this:

```
In function `int main()'
error: no matching function for call to `Simple::Simple()'
note: candidates are: Simple::Simple(const Simple&)
note:                 Simple::Simple(int)
```

Yet, if we take out the constructor we added (so it goes back to an earlier example), this error goes away! Therefore, if you provide no constructors, the compiler gives you an implicit default constructor.

TIP

If you're using the CodeBlocks compiler, you obtain some helpful additional information. In this case, you see two note lines that tell you about the available constructor candidates. You can use this information as part of your troubleshooting efforts.

Now here's where you could run into trouble: Suppose you build a class and provide no constructors for it. You give the class to other people to use. They're using it in their code, all happy, making use of the default constructor. Then one day somebody else (not you — you don't make mistakes) decides that he wants to enhance the class by adding a special constructor with several parameters. The rogue programmer adds the constructor and then makes use of it. Mr. Rogue thinks all is fine, because he's using only his new constructor. But little does he know: All the other people who were using the implicit default constructor suddenly start getting compiler errors!

Believe it or not, we have seen this happen. One day, all of a sudden, your code won't compile. Any time you try to create an instance of a class, you start getting errors stating that the compiler can't find `Simple::Simple()`. Oops. Somebody changed it.

But you can avoid this problem by making sure that you explicitly include a default constructor, even if it does nothing:

```
class Simple
{
public:
    int x,y;
    void Write()
    {
        cout << x << " " << y << endl;
    }
    Simple() {}
};
```

Then when Mr. Rogue adds his own constructor, the default constructor will still be there (assuming, of course, that *he* doesn't *remove* it. But if he does, move him to that nice secluded inner office that has no windows and no doors). When he adds his extra constructor, he will be overloading it:

```
class Simple
{
public:
    int x,y;
    void Write()
    {
        cout << x << " " << y << endl;
    }
    Simple() {}
    Simple(int startx) { x = startx; }
};
```

Note that now this class has two constructors! And all will be happy, because everybody's code will still compile.

Functional constructors

Every once in a while, you may come across something that looks like this:

```
Simple inst = Simple(5);
```

What *is* that? It looks like a function call. Or it looks like the way you would declare a pointer variable, except there's no asterisk and no new word. So what is it? It's a functional syntax for calling a default constructor. The right side creates a new instance of Simple, passing 5 into the constructor. Then this new instance gets copied into the variable called inst.

This approach can be handy if you're creating an array of objects, where the array contains actual objects, not pointers to objects:

```
Simple MyList[] = { Simple(1), Simple(50), Simple(80),
  Simple(100), Simple(150) };
```

The approach seems a little strange because the variable MyList is not a pointer, yet you're setting it equal to something on the right. But this approach is handy because every once in a while you need a temporary variable. Listing 3-1 shows how you can use the functional syntax to create a temporary instance of the class string.

Listing 3-1:   Creating Temporary Instances with Functional Constructors

```
#include <iostream>
#include <string>

using namespace std;

void WriteMe(string str)
{
    cout << "Here I am: " << str << endl;
}

int main()
{
    WriteMe(string("Sam"));
    return 0;
}
```

When you compile and run this, you see this output:

```
Here I am: Sam
```

In main, we created a temporary instance of the string class. (Remember, string is a class!) But as it turns out, an even shorter version of this is available. If we had called WriteMe, we could have just done this:

```
WriteMe("Sam");
```

This code works out well because you don't even feel like you're working with a class called `string`. The parameter just seems like a basic type, and you're passing a character array, `Sam`. However, the parameter is an instance of a class. Here's how the code works. Suppose you have a class like this, and a function to go with it:

```
class MyNumber
{
public:
    int First;
    MyNumber(int TheFirst) : First(TheFirst) {}
};

void WriteNumber(MyNumber num)
{
    cout << num.First << endl;
}
```

(`WriteNumber` is *not* a member of `MyNumber`.) You can do any of the following calls to `WriteNumber`.

```
MyNumber prime = 17;
WriteNumber(prime);
WriteNumber(MyNumber(23));
WriteNumber(29);
```

The first call uses a previously declared variable of type `MyNumber`. The second call creates a temporary instance, passing the value 23 into the constructor. The third one also creates a temporary instance, but it does so implicitly! The output from this example is

```
17
23
29
```

You may wonder when your temporary variables get destroyed. For instance, if you call `WriteNumber(MyNumber(23));`, how long does the temporary `MyNumber` instance live on? The ANSI standard proudly proclaims that the instance will get deleted at the end of the *full expression.* In other words, after the line is *done,* the temporary instance will be *done for.*

Be careful when using implicit temporary objects. Consider the following class and function:

```
class MyName
{
public:
    string First;
    MyName(string TheFirst) : First(TheFirst) {}
};

void WriteName(MyName name)
{
    cout << "Hi I am " << name.First << endl;
}
```

Seems straightforward. The `MyName` constructor takes a string, so it seems like we should be able to do this when we call the `WriteName` function:

```
WriteName("George");
```

Except we can't. The compiler gives us an error message:

```
In function `int main()'
error: conversion from `const char*' to non-scalar type `MyName' requested
```

Here's the problem: The compiler got shortsighted. The compiler considers the type of the string constant a `const char *` (that is, a pointer to a `const` character, or really a constant character array). Although we don't have any constructors that take a `const char *` parameter, we do have one that takes a `string`, and it has a constructor that takes a `const char * parameter. Unfortunately, the compiler doesn't fall for that, and it complains. So we have to adjust our function call just a tad, like so:

```
WriteName(string("George"));
```

And this time it works. Now we *explicitly* create a temporary string instance. And by using that, we *implicitly* create a temporary instance of our own class, `MyName`. It would be nice if the compiler could wade through this and implicitly create the `string` instance for us, but it doesn't seem to want to. Oh well. Calling `WriteName(string("George"));` works well enough for us.

Calling one constructor from another

If you have some initialization code and you want several constructors to call it, you might try putting the code in one constructor and then having the other constructors call the constructor that has the initialization code.

Unfortunately, that won't work. Some things in life we just can't have, and this is one of them. If you have a constructor and write code to call another constructor, such as this

```
CallOne::CallOne(int ax)
{
    y = 20;
    CallOne();
}
```

where `CallOne` is your class, then this will compile but won't behave the way you may expect. The line `CallOne();` is not calling a constructor for the same instance! The compiler treats this line as a *functional* constructor. Thus the line creates a *separate, temporary instance*. And then at the end of the line `CallOne()`, the program deletes the instance.

You can see this behavior with the following class:

```
class CallOne
{
public:
    int x,y;
    CallOne();
    CallOne(int ax);
};

CallOne::CallOne()
{
    x = 10;
    y = 10;
}

CallOne::CallOne(int ax)
{
    y = 20;
    CallOne();
}
```

When you create an instance by using the second constructor like this, the value of the y member of the instance will be 20, not 10:

```
CallOne Mine(10);
```

To people who don't know any different, it may look like the y would first get set to 20 in the second constructor, and then the call to the default constructor would cause it to get changed to 10. But that's not the case: The second constructor is not calling the default constructor for the same object; it's creating a separate, temporary instance.

If you have common initialization code that you want in multiple constructors, put the code in its own private or protected function (called, for example, Init), and have each constructor call the Init function. If you have one constructor call another constructor, it won't work. The second constructor will be operating on a separate instance.

Copying instances with copy constructors

One nice thing about C++ is that it lets you copy instances of classes. For example, if you have a class called Copyable, you can write code like this:

```
Copyable first;
Copyable second = first;
```

This will create two instances, and second will be a duplicate of first. The program will accomplish this by simply copying all the member variables from first to second.

That works pretty well, except sometimes you want to customize the behavior just a bit. For example, you may have a member variable that contains a unique ID for each instance. In your constructor, you may have code that generates a unique ID. The problem is that the previous sample will not call your constructor: It will just make a duplicate of the object. Thus, your two objects will have the same number for their supposedly "unique" IDs. So much for diversity.

So if you want to have control over the copying, you can create a copy constructor. A *copy constructor* is just a constructor that takes as a parameter a reference to another instance of the same class, as in this example:

```
Copyable(const Copyable& source);
```

When you copy an instance, your program will call this constructor. The parameter to this constructor will be the instance you are copying. Thus, in the case of `Copyable second = first;`, the source parameter will be `first`. And because it's a reference (which is required for copy constructors), you can access its members by using the dot notation (`.`) rather than the pointer notation (`->`).

Listing 3-2 is a complete program that demonstrates copy constructors.

Listing 3-2:   Customizing the Copying of Instances

```cpp
#include <iostream>

using namespace std;

class Copyable
{
protected:
    static int NextAvailableID;
    int UniqueID;
public:
    int SomeNumber;
    int GetID() { return UniqueID; }
    Copyable();
    Copyable(int x);
    Copyable(const Copyable& source);
};

Copyable::Copyable()
{
    UniqueID = NextAvailableID;
    NextAvailableID++;
}

Copyable::Copyable(int x)
{
    UniqueID = NextAvailableID;
    NextAvailableID++;
    SomeNumber = x;
}
```

```
Copyable::Copyable(const Copyable& source)
{
    UniqueID = NextAvailableID;
    NextAvailableID++;
    SomeNumber = source.SomeNumber;
}

int Copyable::NextAvailableID;

int main()
{
    Copyable take1 = 100;
    Copyable take2;
    take2.SomeNumber = 200;
    Copyable take3 = take1;

    cout << take1.GetID() << " "
        << take1.SomeNumber << endl;
    cout << take2.GetID() << " "
        << take2.SomeNumber << endl;
    cout << take3.GetID() << " "
        << take3.SomeNumber << endl;
    return 0;
}
```

Go ahead and run this application to see how it works. The output from this example is

```
0 100
1 200
2 100
```

We need to tell you two things about the copy constructor in this code. First, *we included* `const` *in the parameter of the copy constructor*. That's because of a small rule in C++ where, if you have a constant instance, you won't be able to copy it otherwise. If we left off `const`, this line would not compile properly. And as it happens, that's the case in the following line:

```
Copyable take1 = 100;
```

The second thing we need to tell you is that, in the code for the copy constructor, we had to manually copy the member variables from one instance to the other. That's because now that we're supplying our own copy constructor, the computer will not copy the members as it would when we supply no copy constructor at all.

Listing 3-2 uses a *static* member to keep track of what the next available `UniqueID` is. Remember that a class shares a single static member among all instances of the class. Therefore, you have only one instance of `NextAvailableID`, and it's shared by all the instances of class `Copyable`.

For a long, happy life

◆ Put a `const` in your copy constructor.

◆ Copy the items manually.

When constructors go bad: failable constructors?

Suppose that you're writing a class that will connect to the Internet and automatically download the latest weather report for the country of Upper Zamboni. The question is this: Do you put the code to connect to the Internet in the constructor or not?

People are often faced with this common design issue. Putting the initialization code in the constructor provides many advantages. For one, you can just create the instance without having to first create it and then call a separate member function that does the initialization. And in general, that works fine.

But what if that initialization code can result in an error? For example, suppose that the constructor is unable to connect to the Internet. Then what? Remember: A constructor doesn't return a value. So you can't have it return, for example, a `bool` that would state whether it successfully did its work.

You have many choices for this, and different people seem to have rather strong opinions about which choice is best. (Programmers with strong opinions? Now there's an unlikely concept.) Here are the ones we've seen:

✦ Just don't do it: Write your constructors so they create the object but don't do any work. Instead, put the work code in a separate member function, which can return a `bool` representing whether it was successful.

✦ Let the constructor do the work: If the work fails (such as it can't connect to the Internet), have the constructor save an error code in a member variable. When you create an instance, you can check the member variable to see whether it works.

✦ Let the constructor do the work: If the work fails, throw an exception. In your code, then, you would wrap the creation of the instance with a `try` block and include an exception handler. (See "Programming the Exceptions to the Rule," later in this chapter, for more information on `try` blocks and exception handlers.)

We don't like this choice. If other people are using the class that we wrote, we don't want them to have to go through the motions of wrapping it in a `try` block and exception handler. But other than being a nice guy, there's a practical reason for avoiding this choice: If we have team-mates who are beginners at programming, they may just skip that part. "Oh shoot. It'll never fail," might be their attitude. And when it does fail on a customer's computer (if it can, then it will, Mr. Murphy!) the customer will be very unhappy that his or her program couldn't connect to the Internet and crashed.

Destroying your instances

Although constructors are versatile and it seems like people could write entire books on them (good for family story time reading), destructors are simple, and there's not a whole lot to say about them. But you do need to know some information to make them work properly.

First, destructors don't get parameters, and (like constructors) they do not have return types. So not much more to say about that.

Suppose you have a class that contains, as members, instances of other classes. When you delete an instance of the main class, will the contained instances be deleted automatically? That depends. If your class contains actual instances (as opposed to pointers), they will get deleted. Look at this code:

```
class LittleInst
{
public:
    int MyNumber;
    ~LittleInst() { cout << MyNumber << endl; }
};

class Container
{
public:
    LittleInst first;
    LittleInst *second;
    Container();
};

Container::Container()
{
    first.MyNumber = 1;
    second = new LittleInst;
    second->MyNumber = 2;
}
```

We have two classes, `LittleInst` and `Container`. The `Container` class holds an instance of `LittleInst` (the member variable called `first`) and a pointer to `LittleInst`. In the constructor we set up the two `LittleInst` instances. For `first`, it already exists, and all we have to do is set up its `MyNumber` member. But `second` is just a pointer, so we have to create the instance before we can set up its `MyNumber` member. Thus, we have two instances, one a pointer and one a regular instance.

Now suppose you use these classes like so:

```
Container *inst = new Container;
delete inst;
```

We gave `Container` no destructor. So will its members, `first` and `second`, get destroyed? Here's what we see after these two lines run:

```
1
```

That's the output from the `LittleInst` destructor. The number 1 goes with the `first` member. So you can see that `first` was deleted, but `second` wasn't.

Here's the rule: When you delete an instance of a class, the members that are direct (that is, not pointers) are deleted as well. Any pointers, however, you must manually delete in your destructor (or elsewhere).

Sometimes, you may want an object to hold an instance of another class but want to keep the instance around after you delete the containing object. In that case, you wouldn't delete the other instance in the destructor.

Here's a modification to the `Container` class that deletes the `second` instance:

```
class Container
{
public:
    LittleInst first;
    LittleInst *second;
    Container();
    ~Container() { delete second; }
};
```

Then when you run these two lines again

```
Container *inst = new Container;
delete inst;
```

you see this output, which deletes both instances:

```
2
1
```

In the preceding output, you can see that it deleted the second instance first. The reason is that the program calls the destructor before it destroys the direct members. In this case, when we deleted our `Container` instance, the program first called our destructor before deleting our `first` member. That's actually a good idea, because in the code for our destructor, we may want to do some work on our member variables before they get wiped out.

Virtually inheriting destructors

Unlike constructors, you can (and should) make destructors virtual. The reason is that you can pass an instance of a derived class into a function that takes a base class, like this:

```
void ProcessAndDelete(DeleteMe *inst)
{
    cout << inst->Number << endl;
    delete inst;
}
```

This function takes an instance of class DeleteMe, does some work on it, and deletes it. Now suppose you have a class derived from DeleteMe, say class Derived. Because of the rules of inheritance, you're allowed to pass the instance of Derived into this function. But by the rules of *polymorphism,* if you want the ProcessAndDelete function to call an overloaded member function of Derived, you need to make the member function virtual. And that's the case with all destructors as well. Listing 3-3 shows this.

Listing 3-3:   Making the Destructors Virtual

```
#include <iostream>

using namespace std;

class DeleteMe
{
public:
    int Number;
    virtual ~DeleteMe();
};

class Derived : public DeleteMe
{
public:
    virtual ~Derived();
};

DeleteMe::~DeleteMe()
{
    cout << "DeleteMe::~DeleteMe()" << endl;
}

Derived::~Derived()
{
    cout << "Derived::~Derived()" << endl;
}

void ProcessAndDelete(DeleteMe *inst)
{
    cout << inst->Number << endl;
    delete inst;
}

int main()
{
    DeleteMe *MyObject = new(Derived);
    MyObject->Number = 10;
    ProcessAndDelete(MyObject);
    return 0;
}
```

Ordering your constructors and destructors

When you have constructors and destructors in a base and derived class and you create an instance of the derived class, remember the ordering: The computer first creates the members for the base class, and then the computer calls the constructor for the base class. Next, the computer creates the members of the derived class, and then the computer calls the constructor for the derived class.

The order for destruction is opposite. When you destroy an instance of a base class, first the computer calls the destructor for the derived class and then deletes the members of the derived class. Next the computer calls the destructor for the base class and then deletes the members of the base class.

When you run this program, thanks to the cout calls in the destructors, delete is calling the destructor for Derived (which in turn calls the base class destructor). Here's the output:

```
10
Derived::~Derived()
DeleteMe::~DeleteMe()
```

The first line is the output from the ProcessAndDelete function. The middle line is the output from the Derived destructor, and the third line is the output from the DeleteMe destructor. We passed in a Derived instance, and the program called the Derived destructor.

Now try this: Remove virtual from the DeleteMe destructor:

```
class DeleteMe
{
public:
    int Number;
    ~DeleteMe();
};
```

Then when you compile and run the program, the program calls the base class destructor. Because the ProcessAndDelete function takes a DeleteMe instance, you see this output:

```
10
DeleteMe::~DeleteMe()
```

In the preceding example, the destructor isn't virtual; it's not able to find the proper destructor when you pass in a Derived instance. So it just calls the destructor for whatever type is listed in the parameter.

Getting into the habit of always making your destructors virtual is a good
idea. That way, if somebody else writes a function, such as
`ProcessAndDelete`, you can be assured that his or her function will automatically call the correct destructor.

Programming the Exceptions to the Rule

An *exception* is a bad situation that occurs in your software, causing your
program to have to handle the bad situation. For example, if you try to write
to a file but somehow that file got corrupted and you can't, the operating
system might *throw* an exception. Or you might have a function that processes some data, and if the function encounters corrupted data, it might
throw an exception.

Exceptions were new to C++; they did not exist in C. People were a little sus-
picious of them when they first came out, and some people even consider
them to be Bad (that's with a capital *B*). The reason is this: People who
oppose exceptions feel that writing code that relies too heavily on exceptions is too easy. But you should use them because they help you handle
situations that you might not otherwise anticipate.

Listing 3-4 is an example of a function that we wrote that throws an exception and an entire program that uses the function.

Listing 3-4:   Throwing and Catching Exceptions

```
#include <iostream>
#include <string>

using namespace std;

void ProcessData()
{
    throw new string("Oops, I found some bad data!");
}

int main()
{
    try
    {
        ProcessData();
        cout << "No problems!" << endl;
    }
    catch (string *excep)
    {
        cout << "Found an error. Here's the message.";
        cout << endl;
        cout << *excep;
        cout << endl;
    }
```

Book IV
Chapter 3

Constructors,
Destructors, and
Exceptions

(continued)

Listing 3-4: *(continued)*

```
    cout << "All finished." << endl;

    return 0;
}
```

Go ahead and run this application. You see the following text as output:

```
Found an error. Here's the message.
Oops, I found some bad data!
All finished.
```

Look closely at what this program does. In `main`, there's a call to `ProcessData`, which we put inside a `try` block. Because the call is inside a `try` block, the computer calls the function; and if the function throws an exception, the program automatically comes back out of the function and goes into the `catch` block. The `catch` block receives the item that was thrown as a parameter, much like a parameter to a function.

But if the `ProcessData` function didn't encounter any problems and therefore didn't throw an exception, the function will complete its work and the program will continue with the code after the function call. In this case, one more line is inside the `try` block. If there was no exception, upon completion of the `ProcessData` function, the computer will do the `cout` line after the `ProcessData` call.

Think of an exception handler as a way to catch errors: If an exception gets thrown, your program can catch the error by including a `catch` block.

After the `try`/`catch` block is complete, the program will run any lines that follow, regardless of whether or not an exception was present. Thus, in all cases, Listing 3-4 will execute the line

```
cout << "All finished." << endl;
```

Now in the listing, note that our `ProcessData` function calls `throw`, meaning that it generates an exception. Normally, you probably wouldn't just have a function throw an exception for no reason, as this function does (unless you're trying to have fun with your users), but we do that just to demonstrate how the exceptions work. And besides, this is fun!

This particular `throw` looks like this:

```
throw new string("Oops, I found some bad data!");
```

We create a new `string` instance, and *that's* what we throw. You can create an instance of any class you want, and it can be either a pointer or a direct instance, depending on whether you prefer to work with pointers or references (it's your choice).

Now look at the `catch` block in Listing 3-4. Notice that it starts with this:

```
catch (string *excep)
```

Because in the function we threw a pointer to a `string` instance, here we catch a pointer to a `string` instance. Everything must match.

You can have more than one `catch` block. Suppose different types of exceptions could get thrown. For example, you might have another function like this:

```
void ProcessMore()
{
    throw new int(10);
}
```

Whereas the other function threw a pointer to a string, this throws a pointer to an integer. Watch out! Lots of things getting thrown around!

Then, when you call the two functions, your `try`/`catch` block can look like this:

```
try
{
    ProcessData();
    ProcessMore();
    cout << "No problems!" << endl;
}
catch (string *excep)
{
    cout << "Found an error. Here's the message.";
    cout << endl;
    cout << *excep;
    cout << endl;
}
catch (int *num)
{
    cout << "Found a numerical error. Here it is.";
    cout << endl;
    cout << *num;
    cout << endl;
}
cout << "All finished." << endl;
```

If you add this code and the `ProcessMore` function to Listing 3-4, you probably want to comment out the `throw` line from the `ProcessData` function if you want to see this program handle the integer exception. That's because the execution of the lines in the `try` block cease as soon as a `throw` statement occurs, and *control will be transferred* to the appropriate `catch` block. Which `catch` block depends on the type of the object thrown.

Throwing direct instances

You can throw a direct instance that is not a pointer. In your `throw` line, you would do this

```
void ProcessData()
{
    throw string("Oops, I found some bad data!");
}
```

or this

```
void ProcessMore()
{
    throw 10;
}
```

Instead of throwing pointers, we're throwing the object or value itself. In the `catch` block, then, you can catch the type itself without a pointer:

```
try
{
    ProcessData();
    ProcessMore();
}
catch (string excep)
{
    cout << excep;
}
catch (int num)
{
    cout << num;
}
```

Or if you prefer, you can use references in the `catch` block. (The `throw` line does not change.)

```
try
{
    ProcessData();
    ProcessMore();
}
catch (string &excep)
{
    cout << excep;
}
catch (int &num)
{
    cout << num;
}
```

You may notice something just a little strange. For the integer version, the `throw` statement looks like this:

```
throw 10;
```

That is, the line of code is throwing a value, not an object. But the `catch` line looks like this:

```
catch (int &num) {
```

The `catch` statement is catching a reference. Normally you can have references to only variables, not values! But it works here because inside the computer, the program makes a temporary variable, and that's what you're referring to in the `catch` block. So all is fine.

Catching any exception

If you want to write a general `catch` handler that will catch any exception and you don't care to actually catch the object that was thrown, you can write your handler like this:

```
try
{
    ProcessData();
    ProcessMore();
    cout << "No problems!" << endl;
}
catch (...)
{
    cout << "An unknown exception occurred." << endl;
}
```

That is, instead of putting what is effectively a `function` parameter in the `catch` header, you just put three dots, called an ellipsis.

Some word processors (Microsoft Word being one) can transform three typed periods into a single ellipses character. Don't paste that character into the code editor because the compiler won't know what to do with it. Instead, type three periods.

You can use the ellipses also as a general exception catcher in addition to your other handlers. Here's an example:

```
try
{
    ProcessData();
    ProcessMore();
    cout << "No problems!" << endl;
}
catch (string excep)
{
    cout << "Found an error. Here's the message.";
    cout << endl;
    cout << excep;
    cout << endl;
}
catch (int num)
```

```
{
    cout << "Found a numerical error. Here it is.";
    cout << endl;
    cout << num;
    cout << endl;
}
catch (...)
{
    cout << "An unknown exception occurred." << endl;
}
```

If your function calls throw an exception and you don't have any exception handler for it (because your `catch` blocks don't handle the type of exception being thrown or you don't have any `try`/`catch` blocks), your program will *stop*. The gcc compiler that comes with CodeBlocks, Dev-C++, MinGW, and Cygwin prints the following message on the console and then immediately terminates the program:

```
abnormal program termination
```

That's not good at all! Imagine the looks on your users' faces if they saw this. We know that we wouldn't want to be standing there with them, knowing that we're the ones who wrote the program.

Visual C++ also prints this same message but shows it in a message box. Borland C++ Builder shows the same message, too, and writes it to the console.

Two programming rules keep your users happily ignorant of exceptions:

✦ Know when you are calling a function that could throw an exception.

✦ When you are calling a function that could throw an exception, include an exception handler.

It doesn't matter how *deep* the exception is thrown; somewhere, *somebody* needs to catch it. A function could call a function that calls a function that calls a function that calls a function that throws an exception. If no intermediate function has an exception handler, put one in your outer function.

Rethrowing an exception

When inside a `catch` block, a `throw` statement without anything after it will simply rethrow the same exception. Although this may seem a bit convoluted (and indeed it can be), you may have a function that contains a `try`/`catch` block. But this function might also be called by another function that has a `try`/`catch` block. In other words, you might have something like this:

```
#include <iostream>

using namespace std;

void Inner()
{
    throw string("Error!");
}

void Outer()
{
    try
    {
        Inner();
    }
    catch (string excep)
    {
        cout << "Outer caught an exception: ";
        cout << excep << endl;
        throw;
    }
}

int main()
{
    try
    {
        Outer();
    }
    catch (string excep)
    {
        cout << "main caught an exception: ";
        cout << excep << endl;
    }

    return 0;
}
```

In the preceding code, main calls Outer. Outer, in turn, calls Inner. Inner throws an exception, and Outer catches it. But main also wants to catch the exception. So we had inner *rethrow* the exception. You do that by calling throw without anything after it, like this:

```
throw;
```

When you run this program, you see the following output.

```
Outer caught an exception: Error!
main caught an exception: Error!
```

Chapter 4: Advanced Class Usage

In This Chapter

✔ Using polymorphism effectively

✔ Adjusting member access between private, protected, and public when deriving new classes

✔ Multiple-inheriting new classes

✔ Making virtual inheritance work correctly

✔ Keeping your friends straight, especially in class

✔ Putting one class or type inside another

Classes are amazingly powerful. You can do so much with them. In this chapter, we talk about many of the extra features you can use in your classes. But these aren't just little extras that you may want to use on occasion. If you follow the instructions in this chapter, you should find that your understanding of classes in C++ will greatly improve, and you will want to use many of these topics throughout your programming.

We also talk about many issues that come up when you are deriving new classes and inheriting members. This discussion includes virtual inheritance and multiple inheritance, topics that people mess up a lot. We describe the ways you can put classes and types inside other classes, too.

Inherently Inheriting Correctly

Without inheritance, doing object-oriented programming would be nearly impossible. Yes, you could divide your work into objects, but the real power comes from inheritance. However, you have to be careful when using inheritance, or you can really mess things up. In the sections that follow, we talk about different ways to use inheritance and how to keep it all straight.

Morphing your inheritance

Polymorphism refers to using one object as an instance of a base class. For example, if you have the class Creature and from that you derive the class Platypus, you can treat the instances of class Platypus as if they're instances of class Creature. This concept is useful if you have a function that takes as a parameter a pointer to Creature. You can pass a pointer to Platypus.

However, you can't go further than that. You can't take a pointer to a pointer to Creature. (**Remember:** When you say a "pointer to a pointer," the first pointer really means "the address of the second pointer variable." We need to phrase things like that, or our brains might explode under certain situations.)

So if you have a function such as this:

```
void Feed(Creature *c)
{
    cout << "Feed me!" << endl;
}
```

you are free to pass the address of a Platypus object, as in the following:

```
Platypus *plato = new Platypus;
Feed(plato);
```

With a function that takes the address of a pointer variable, like this:

```
void Eat(Creature **c)
{
    cout << "Feed me!" << endl;
}
```

(note the two asterisks in the parameter), you *cannot* pass the address of a pointer to a Platypus instance, as in this example:

```
Platypus *plato = new Platypus;
Eat(&plato);
```

If you try to compile this code, you get a compiler error.

You don't always use polymorphism when you declare a variable. If you do, you would be declaring variables like this:

```
Creature *plato = new Platypus;
```

The type plato is a pointer to Creature. But the object is a Platypus. You can do this because a pointer to a base class can point to an object of a derived class. But now the compiler thinks that plato is a pointer to a Creature instance, so you can't use plato to call a member function of Platypus — you can use plato to call only members of Creature! For example, if your two classes look like this:

```
class Creature
{
public:
    void EatFood()
    {
        cout << "I'm eating!" << endl;
    }
};
```

```
class Platypus : public Creature
{
public:
    void SingLikeABird()
    {
        cout << "I'm siiiiinging in the rain!" << endl;
    }
};
```

the following would not work:

```
Creature *plato = new Platypus;
plato->SingLikeABird();
```

Although the first line would compile, the second wouldn't. When the compiler gets to the second line, it thinks that plato is only an object of class type Creature. And Creature does not have a member called SingLikeABird, so the compiler gets upset. You can fix the situation by casting like this:

```
Creature *plato = new Platypus;
static_cast <Platypus *>(plato)->SingLikeABird();
```

If you save work and start by declaring plato as what it is:

```
Platypus *plato = new Platypus;
plato->SingLikeABird();
```

You may need to do it at times. For example, you may have a variable that can hold an instance of an object or its derived object. Then you would have to use polymorphism, as in the following code:

```
Creature *plato;
if (HasABeak == true)
{
    plato = new Platypus;
}
else
{
    plato = new Creature;
}
```

In this code, we have a pointer to Creature. In that pointer, we store the address of either a Platypus instance or a Creature instance, depending on what's in the HasABeak variable.

But if you use an if statement like that, you shouldn't follow it with a call to SingLikeABird, even if you cast it:

```
static_cast <Platypus *>(plato)->SingLikeABird();
```

The reason is that if the `else` clause took place and `plato` holds an instance of `Creature`, not `Platypus`, then the `Creature` instance won't have a `SingLikeABird` member function. Either you get some type of error message when you run the program or you don't, but the program will mess up later. And those messing-up-later errors are the worst kind to try to fix.

Adjusting access

You may have a class that has protected members; and in a derived class, you may want to make the member public. You do this by adjusting the access. You have two ways to do this: One is the older way, and the other is the newer ANSI way. If your compiler supports the newer way, the creators of the ANSI standard ask that you use the ANSI way.

In the following classes, `Secret` has a member, `X`, that is protected. The derived class, `Revealed`, makes the member `X` public. Here's the older way:

```
class Secret
{
protected:
    int X;
};

class Revealed : public Secret
{
public:
    Secret::X;
};
```

We declared the member `X`: We used the base classname, two colons, and then the member name. We didn't include any type information; that was implied. So in the class `Secret`, the member `X` is protected. But in `Revealed`, it is public.

Here's the ANSI way. We've thrown in the word `using`. Otherwise, it's the same:

```
class Secret
{
public:
    int X;
};

class Revealed : public Secret
{
public:
    using Secret::X;
};
```

And now, when you use the `Revealed` class, the inherited member `X` is public (but `X` is still protected in the base class, `Secret`).

If you want to make a protected member public in a derived class, don't just redeclare the member. If you do, you end up with *two member variables of the same name* within the class; and needless to say, that can be confusing! Take a look at the following two classes:

```
class Secret
{
protected:
    int X;

public:
    void SetX()
    {
        X = 10;
    }

    void GetX()
    {
        cout << "Secret X is " << X << endl;
    }
};

class Revealed : public Secret
{
public:
    int X;
};
```

The Revealed class has two int X members! Suppose you try this code with it:

```
Revealed me;
me.SetX();
me.X = 30;
me.GetX();
```

The first line declares the variable. The second line calls SetX, which stores 10 in . . . which variable? The inherited X, because SetX is part of the base class! The third line stores 10 in . . . which one? The new X declared in the derived class! So then GetX is again part of the base class, but will it print 10 or 30? It will print 10!

Personally, having two member variables of the same name is downright confusing. (Fortunately, our brains didn't quite explode because we're still here, writing away.) We think that it would be best if the compiler didn't allow you to have two variables of the same name. But even though the compiler allows it, that doesn't mean you should do it; having two variables of the same name is a perfect way to increase the chances of bugs creeping into your program.

Now think about this: Suppose you have a class that has several public members, and when you derive a new class, you want all the public members to become *protected*, except for one. You can do this task in a couple of ways.

You could adjust the access of all the members except for the one you want left public. Or if you have lots of members, you can take the opposite approach. Look at this code:

```
class Secret
{
public:
    int Code, Number, SkeletonKey, System, Magic;
};

class AddedSecurity : protected Secret
{
public:
    using Secret::Magic;
};
```

Notice what we did: We derived the class as protected, as you can see in the header line for the `AddedSecurity` class. That means all the inherited public members of `Secret` will be protected in the derived class. But then we promoted `Magic` back to public by adjusting its member access. Thus, after all is said and done, `Magic` is the only public member of `AddedSecurity`. All the rest are protected.

If you have a member that is private and you try to adjust its access to protected or public in a derived class, you quickly discover that the compiler won't let you do it. The reason is that the derived class *doesn't even know about the member* because the member is public. And because the derived class doesn't know about the member, you can't adjust its access.

Returning something different, virtually speaking

Two words that sound similar and have similar meanings but are, nevertheless, different are *overload* and *override*. Although both words appear in movies ("Danger, danger! The system is overloaded, so we need to override the built-in security!"), they're less glamorous in computer programming. But the real danger that results in an overloading of your brain is in confusing the two words where one meaning overrides the other. Whew!

So first, let us clarify: To *override* means to take an existing function in a base class and give the function new code in a derived class. The function in the derived class has the same prototype as the base class: It takes the same parameters and returns the same type.

To *overload* means to take a function and write another function of the same name that takes a different set of parameters. An overloaded function can optionally return a different type, but the parameters must be different, whether in number or type or both. The overloaded function can live in the same class or in a derived class. The idea here is to create what appears to be a single function that can take several types of parameters. For example, you may have a function called `Append` that works on strings. By using `Append`, you would be able to append a string to the end of the string represented by the instance, or you could append a single character to the end of the string represented by the instance. Now, although it feels like one function called `Append`, really you would implement it as two separate functions, one that takes a string parameter and one that takes a character parameter.

In this section, we talk about one particular issue dealing with *overriding* functions (that is, replacing a function in a derived class). We said something a few paragraphs back that many others have said: We mentioned that the function must have the same parameter types and must return the same type.

A situation exists under which you can violate this rule, although only slightly. You can violate the rule of an overridden function returning the same type as the original function if *all three* of the following are true:

✦ The overridden function returns an instance of a class derived from the type returned by the original function.

✦ You return either a pointer or a reference, not an object.

✦ If you return a pointer, the pointer doesn't refer to yet another pointer.

Typically, you want to use this approach when you have a *container* class that holds multiple instances of another class. For example, you may have a class called `Peripheral`. You may also have a container class called `PeripheralList`, which holds instances of `Peripheral`. You may later derive a new class from `Peripheral`, called `Printer`, and a new class from `PeripheralList`, called `PrinterList`. If `PeripheralList` has a function that returns an instance of `Peripheral`, you would override that function in `PrinterList`. But instead of having it return an instance of `Peripheral`, you would have it return an instance of `Printer`.

We did exactly this in Listing 4-1.

Listing 4-1: Overriding and Returning a Derived Class

```
#include <iostream>
#include <string>
#include <map>

using namespace std;

class Peripheral
{
public:
    string Name;
    int Price;
    int SerialNumber;
    Peripheral(string aname, int aprice, int aserial) :
        Name(aname), Price(aprice),
        SerialNumber(aserial) {}
```

(continued)

Listing 4-1 *(continued)*

```cpp
};

class Printer : public Peripheral
{
public:
    enum PrinterType {laser, inkjet};
    PrinterType Type;
    Printer(string aname, PrinterType atype, int aprice,
        int aserial) : Type(atype),
        Peripheral(aname, aprice, aserial) {}
};

typedef map<string, Peripheral *> PeripheralMap;

class PeripheralList
{
public:
    PeripheralMap list;
    virtual Peripheral *GetPeripheralByName(string name);
    void AddPeripheral(string name, Peripheral *per);
};

class PrinterList : public PeripheralList
{
public:
    Printer *GetPeripheralByName(string name);
};

Peripheral *PeripheralList::GetPeripheralByName
  (string name)
{
    return list[name];
}

void PeripheralList::AddPeripheral(string name, Peripheral *per)
{
    list[name] = per;
}

Printer *PrinterList::GetPeripheralByName(string name)
{
    return static_cast<Printer *>(
        PeripheralList::GetPeripheralByName(name));
}

int main(int argc, char *argv[])
{
    PrinterList list;
    list.AddPeripheral(string("Koala"),
        new Printer("Koala", Printer::laser,
        150, 105483932)
    );

    list.AddPeripheral(string("Bear"),
        new Printer("Bear", Printer::inkjet,
        80, 5427892)
    );
```

```
Printer *myprinter = list.GetPeripheralByName("Bear");

if (myprinter != 0)
{
    cout << myprinter->Price << endl;
}

return 0;
}
```

We used a special type called `map`, which is simply a container or list that holds items in pairs. The first item in the pair is called a *key,* and the second item is called a *value.* You can then retrieve items from the `map` based on the key. In this example, we're storing peripherals (the value) based on a name, which is a string (the key). To create the `map`, we use a `typedef` and specify the two types involved: first the key and then the value. The key is a string, and the value is a pointer to `Peripheral`. The `typedef`, then, looks like this:

```
typedef map<string, Peripheral *> PeripheralMap;
```

This creates a type of a `map` that enables us to store a set of `Peripheral` instances, and we can look them up based on a name. To put an item in the map, we use a notation similar to that of an array, where `list` is the `map`, `name` is a `string`, and `per` is a pointer to `Peripheral`. The key goes inside square brackets, like this:

```
list[name] = per;
```

To retrieve the item, we simply refer to the `map` using brackets again, as in this line from the listing:

```
return list[name];
```

In Listing 4-1, we have a `Peripheral` class, and from that we derive a `Printer` class. We then have a `container` class that we created called `PeripheralList`, and from that we derived a class called `PrinterList`. The idea is that the `PrinterList` holds only instances of the class called `Printer`. So in the code, we overrode the `GetPeripheralByName` function. The version inside `PrinterList` casts the item to a `Printer`. We did this because the items in the list are instances of `PeripheralList`. But if we were to leave this function as is, then every time we want to retrieve a `Printer`, we would get back a pointer to a `Peripheral` instance, and we would have to cast it to a `(Printer *)` type. But that's annoying. We don't want to have to do that every time because we're lazy. Instead, we overrode the `GetPeripheralByName` function and did the cast right in there.

Even though we overrode it, we're allowed to return from the function a slightly different (but related) type. And it works!

The code in Listing 4-1 has a small bug: Nothing is stopping you from putting an instance of `Peripheral` in the `PrinterList` container. Or, for that matter, you could put an instance of any other class derived from `Peripheral` if there were more. But when we retrieve the instance in the `GetPeripheralByName`, we automatically cast it to a `Printer`. That would be a problem if somebody had stuffed something else in there other than a `Printer` instance. To prevent that, create a special `AddPeripheral` function for the `PrinterList` class that takes, specifically, a `Printer`. To do that, you would make the `AddPeripheral` function in `PrinterList` virtual and then override it, modifying the parameter to take a `Printer` rather than a `Peripheral`. When you do so, you will *hide* the function in the base class. But that's okay: You don't want people calling that one because that can take any `Peripheral`, not just a `Printer` instance. When you run this application, you should get an output value of 80.

Multiple inheritance

In C++, having a single base class from which your class inherits is generally best. However, it is possible to inherit from multiple base classes, a process called *multiple inheritance*.

One class may have some features that you want in a derived class, and another class may have other features you want in the same derived class. If that's the case, you can inherit from both through multiple inheritance.

Multiple inheritance is messy and difficult to pull off properly. But when used with care, you can make it work.

Listing 4-2 is a complete example of multiple inheritance.

Listing 4-2:   Deriving from Two Different Classes

```
#include <iostream>
using namespace std;

class Mom
{
public:
    void Brains()
    {
        cout << "I'm smart!" << endl;
    }
};

class Dad
{
public:
    void Beauty()
    {
        cout << "I'm beautiful!" << endl;
    }
};
```

```
class Derived : public Mom, public Dad
{
};

int main(int argc, char *argv[])
{
    Derived child;
    child.Brains();
    child.Beauty();
    return 0;
}
```

When you run this code, you see this output:

```
I'm smart!
I'm beautiful!
```

In the preceding code, the class `Derived` inherited the functions of both classes `Mom` and `Dad`. Because it did, the compiler allowed us to call both functions for the instance `child`. Also notice how we caused that to happen:

```
class Derived : public Mom, public Dad
```

We put the base classes to the right of the single colon as with a single inheritance, and we separated the classes with a comma. We also preceded each class with the type of inheritance, in this case public.

As with single inheritance, you can use inheritance other than public. But you don't have to use the same access for all the classes. For example, the following, although a bit confusing, is acceptable:

```
class Derived : public Mom, protected Dad
```

What this means is that the public members that are derived from `Dad` are now protected in the class called `Derived`. This means users cannot call the `member` functions inherited from `Dad`, nor can they access any `member` variables inherited from `Dad`. If you used this type of inheritance in Listing 4-2, this line would no longer be allowed:

```
child.Beauty();
```

If you try to compile it, you will see the following error, because the `Beauty` member is protected now:

```
`void Dad::Beauty()' is inaccessible
```

When you are working with multiple inheritance, be careful that you understand what your code is doing. Although it may compile correctly, it still may not function correctly. That leads to the famous creepy crawling thing called a *bug*.

Strange, bizarre, freaky things can happen with multiple inheritance. What if both base classes have a member variable called `Bagel`. What happens if you multiply derive a class from both of these classes? The answer is this: The compiler gets confused. Suppose you enhance the two base classes with a `Bagel` effect:

```
class Mom
{
public:
    int Bagel;
    void Brains()
    {
        cout << "I'm smart!" << endl;
    }
};

class Dad
{
public:
    int Bagel;
    void Beauty()
    {
        cout << "I'm beautiful!" << endl;
    }
};

class Derived : public Mom, public Dad
{
};
```

In the preceding code, each of the two base classes, `Mom` and `Dad`, has a `Bagel` member. The compiler will let you do this. But if you try to access the member as in the following code, you get an error:

```
Derived child;
child.Bagel = 42;
```

Here's the error message we see in CodeBlocks:

```
Error: request for member `Bagel' is ambiguous
```

Aha! We're being *ambiguous!* It means the compiler isn't sure which `Bagel` we're referring to: The one inherited from `Mom` or the one inherited from `Dad`! If you write code like this, make sure you know which inherited member you're referring to. Now this is going to look bizarre, but we promise that it's correct. Suppose we're referring to the `Bagel` inherited from `Mom`. Then we can put the name `Mom` before the word `Bagel`, separated by two colons:

```
child.Mom::Bagel = 42;
```

Yes, that really is correct, even though it seems a little strange. And if we want to refer to the one by `Dad`, we do this:

```
child.Dad::Bagel = 17;
```

Both lines compile properly because we're removing any ambiguities.

When you use multiple inheritance, remove any ambiguities by specifying the name of the base class. But don't worry if you forget: The compiler will give you an error message because it won't know which item you're referring to.

Virtual inheritance

At times, you may see the word *virtual* thrown in when deriving a new class, as in the following:

```
class Diamond : virtual public Rock
```

This inclusion of `virtual` is to fix a strange problem that can arise. When you use multiple inheritance, you can run into a crazy situation where you have a diamond-shaped inheritance, as in Figure 4-1.

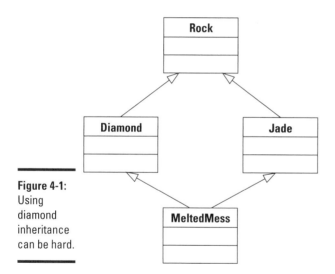

Figure 4-1:
Using
diamond
inheritance
can be hard.

In Figure 4-1, you can see the base class is `Rock`. From that we derived two classes, `Diamond` and `Jade`. So far, so good. But then something strange happened: We used multiple inheritance to derive a class `MeltedMess` from `Diamond` and `Jade`. Yes, you can do this. But you have to be *careful*.

Think about this: Suppose `Rock` has a public member called `Weight`. Then both `Diamond` and `Jade` inherit that member. Now when you derive `MeltedMess` and try to access its `Weight` member, you get an ambiguously melted mess: The compiler claims that it doesn't know which `Weight` you are referring to: the one inherited from `Diamond` or the one inherited from

Jade. Now you know and we know that there should only be one instance of `Weight`, because it came from a single base class, `Rock`. But the compiler sees the situation differently and has trouble with it.

To understand how to fix the problem, recognize what happens when you create an instance of a class derived from another class: Deep down inside the computer, the instance has a portion that is itself an instance of the base class. Now when you derive a class from multiple base classes, instances of the derived class have one portion for each base class. Thus, an instance of `MeltedMess` has a portion that is a `Diamond` and a portion that is a `Jade`, as well as a portion for anything `MeltedMess` added that wasn't inherited.

But remember, `Diamond` is derived from `Rock`. Therefore, `Diamond` has a portion inside it that is a `Rock`. Similarly, `Jade` is derived from `Rock`. That means `Jade` has a portion inside it that is a `Rock`.

And melting all these thoughts together, if an instance of `MeltedMess` has both a `Diamond` in it and a `Jade` in it, and each of *those* in turn has a `Rock` in it, then by the powers of logic vested in us, we declare that `MeltedMess` must have *two* `Rock`s in it! And with each `Rock` comes a separate `Weight` instance. Listing 4-3 shows the problem. In this listing, we declare the classes `Rock`, `Diamond`, `Jade`, and `MeltedMess`.

Listing 4-3:   Cracking up Diamonds

```
#include <iostream>
using namespace std;

class Rock
{
public:
    int Weight;
};

class Diamond : public Rock
{
public:
    void SetDiamondWeight(int newweight)
    {
        Weight = newweight;
    }

    int GetDiamondWeight()
    {
        return Weight;
    }
};

class Jade : public Rock
{
public:
    void SetJadeWeight(int newweight)
```

```
    {
        Weight = newweight;
    }

    int GetJadeWeight()
    {
        return Weight;
    }
};

class MeltedMess : public Diamond, public Jade
{
};

int main(int argc, char *argv[])
{
    MeltedMess mymess;
    mymess.SetDiamondWeight(10);
    mymess.SetJadeWeight(20);
    cout << mymess.GetDiamondWeight() << endl;
    cout << mymess.GetJadeWeight() << endl;
    return 0;
}
```

There is one member called `Weight`, and it's part of `Rock`. In the `Diamond` class, we included two accessor methods, one to set the value of `Weight` and one to get it. We did the same thing in the `Jade` class.

We derived the class `MeltedMess` from both `Diamond` and `Jade`. We created an instance of it and called the four member functions that access the `Weight` member. First, we called the one for `Diamond`, setting `Weight` to 10. Then we called the one for `Jade`, setting the `Weight` to 20.

In a perfect world where each object only has one `Weight`, this would have first set the `Weight` to 10 and then to 20. When we print it, we should see 20 both times. But we don't. Here's the output:

```
10
20
```

When we asked the `Diamond` portion to cough up its `Weight`, we saw 10. But when we asked the `Jade` portion to do the same, we saw 20. They're different! Therefore, we have two different `Weight` members. That's not a good thing.

To fix it, add the word `virtual` when you inherit it. According to the ANSI standard, you put `virtual` in the two middle classes. In our case, that means `Diamond` and `Jade`. Thus, you need to modify the class headers back in Listing 4-3 for `Diamond` and `Jade` to look like this:

```
class Diamond : virtual public Rock {

class Jade : virtual public Rock {
```

Polymorphism with multiple inheritances

If you have multiple inheritance, you can safely treat your object as any of the base classes. In the case of the diamond example, you can treat an instance of `MeltedMess` as a `Diamond` instance or as a `Jade` instance. For example, if you have a function that takes as a parameter a pointer to a `Diamond` instance, you can safely pass a pointer to a `MeltedMess` instance. Casting also works: You can cast a `MeltedMess` instance to a `Diamond` instance or to a `Jade` instance. However, if you do, we suggest using the `static_cast` keyword, rather than the old C-style casts where you simply put the type name in parentheses before the variable you are casting.

When you do that and then run the program, you find that you have only one instance of `Weight` in the final class `MeltedMess`! It's not such a mess after all! Here's the output after we made the change:

```
20
20
```

Now this makes sense: Only one instance of `Weight` is in the `MeltedClass` object, so the following line changes the `Weight` to 10:

```
mymess.SetDiamondWeight(10);
```

Then the following line changes the *same* `Weight` to 20:

```
mymess.SetJadeWeight(20);
```

Then the following line prints the value of the one `Weight` instance, 20:

```
cout << mymess.GetDiamondWeight() << endl;
```

The following line again prints the value of the one `Weight` instance!

```
cout << mymess.GetJadeWeight() << endl;
```

With a diamond inheritance, use *virtual inheritance* in the middle classes to clean them. Although you *can* also add the word `virtual` to the final class (in the example's case, that's `MeltedClass`), you don't need to.

Friend classes and functions

You may encounter a situation where you want one class to access the private and protected members of another class.

Friends of a same class

Can an instance of a class access the private and protected members of other instances of the *same class*? Yes, the compiler allows you to do it. Should you? That depends on your situation. Now think about how you would do that: Inside a member function for a class you would have a pointer to another instance of the same class, perhaps passed in as a parameter. The member function is free to modify any of its members or the object passed in. For your situation, you may need to use `friend` classes, but always be careful.

Normally, this isn't allowed. But it is if you make the two classes best friends. Okay, that sounds corny, but C++ gives us that word: `friend`. Only use `friend` when you really need to. If you have a class, say `Square`, that needs access to the private and protected members of a class called `DrawingBoard`, you can add a line inside the class `DrawingBoard` that looks like this:

```
friend class Square;
```

This will allow the member functions in `Square` to access the private and protected members of any instance of type `DrawingBoard`. (Remember that ultimately we're talking about instances here.)

The `friend` word is powerful because it allows object two to grind up object three, possibly against the will of object one (the object that created object three). And that can create bugs! As Grandma always warned us, "Please use discretion when picking your friends, especially when writing object-oriented programming code in C++."

Some compilers will let you declare a friend without the word `class`, like so:

```
friend Square;
```

However, the gnu compiler under CodeBlocks doesn't allow this. Instead, you must use the `class` keyword:

```
friend class Square;
```

Using Classes and Types within Classes

Sometimes a program needs a fairly complex internal structure to get its work done. Three ways to accomplish this goal with relatively few headaches are nesting classes, embedding classes, and declaring types within classes. The following sections discuss the two most common goals: nesting classes and declaring types within classes. The "Nesting a class" section also discusses protection for embedded classes.

Nesting a class

You may have times when you create a set of classes, and in the set you have a primary class that people will be using, while the other classes are supporting classes. For example, you may be a member of a team of programmers, and your job is to write a set of classes that log on a competitor's computer at night and lower all the prices on the products. Other members of your team will use your classes in their programs. You're just writing a set of classes; the teammates are writing the rest of a program.

In the classes you are creating, you want to make the task easy on your coworkers. In doing so, you may make a primary class, such as EthicalCompetition, that they will instantiate to use your set of classes. This primary class will include the methods for using the system. In other words, it serves as an *interface* to the set of classes.

In addition to the main EthicalCompetition class, you might create additional auxiliary classes that the EthicalCompetition class will use, but your coworkers will not directly create instances of. One might be a class called Connection that handles the tasks of connecting to the competitor's computer.

Here's the first problem: The class Connection may be something you write, but *another* class somewhere may be called Connection, and your coworkers might need to use that class. And here's the second problem: If you have that Connection class, you may not want your coworkers using it. You just want them using the main interface, the EthicalCompetition class.

To solve the unique name problem, you have several choices. For one, you can just rename the class something a bit more unique, such as EthicalCompetitionConnection. But that's a bit long. And why go through all that trouble if it's not even going to be used except internally in the code for EthicalCompetition? However, you could shorten the classname and call it something that's likely to be unique, such as ECConnection.

Yet at the same time, if the users of your classes look at the header file and see a whole set of classes, which classes they should be using may not be clear. (Of course, you would write some documentation to clear this up, but you do want the code to be at least somewhat self-explanatory.)

One solution is to use *nested* classes. With a nested class, you write the declaration for the main class, `EthicalCompetition`, and then, inside the class, you write the supporting classes, as in the following:

```
class EthicalCompetition
{
private:
    class Connection
    {
    public:
        void Connect();
    };

public:
    void HardWork();
};
```

Note that we wrote a class inside a class. We did not provide the code for the functions themselves, so here they are:

```
void EthicalCompetition::HardWork()
{
    Connection c;
    c.Connect();
    cout << "Connected" << endl;
}

void EthicalCompetition::Connection::Connect()
{
    cout << "Connecting..." << endl;
}
```

The header for the `Connect` function in the `ConnectionClass` requires first the outer classname, then two colons, then the inner classname, then two colons again, and finally the function name. This follows the pattern you normally use where you put the classname first, then two colons, and then the function name. But in this case, you have two classnames separated with a colon.

If you want to declare an instance of the `Connection` class, you do it differently, depending on where you are when you declare it. By that we don't mean whether you're in an office cube or sitting on the beach with a laptop; rather, we mean where in the code you are trying to declare an instance.

If you are inside a member function of the outer class, `EthicalCompetition`, you simply refer to the class by its name, `Connection`. You can see we did that in the member function `HardWork`, with this line:

```
Connection c;
```

If you're outside the member functions, you can declare an instance of the inner class, `Connection`, without an instance of the outer class, `EthicalCompetition`. To do this, you *fully qualify* the classname, like this:

```
EthicalCompetition::Connection myconnect;
```

This line would go, for instance, in the `main` of your program if you want to create an instance of the inner class, `Connection`.

However, you may recall that one of the reasons for putting the class inside the other was to shield it from the outside world, to keep your nosey coworkers from creating an instance of it. But so far, what you've done doesn't really stop them from using the class. They can just use it by referring to its fully qualified name, `EthicalCompetition::Connection`.

In a sense, so far, you've created a handy grouping of the class, and you also set your grouping up so you can use a simpler name that won't conflict with other classes. If you just want to group your classes, you can use a nested class.

You can add higher security to a class that will prevent others from using your inner class. For that, you use a few tricks.

Don't put the inner class definition inside a private or protected section of the outer class definition. It doesn't work.

Here's how you create the inner class definition. For the first trick, we need to show you how you can declare the class with a forward definition but put the class definition outside the outer class. The following code does this:

```
class EthicalCompetition
{
private:
    class Connection;

public:
    void HardWork();
};

class EthicalCompetition::Connection
{
public:
    void Connect();
};
```

Inside the outer class, we wrote a header for the inner class and a semicolon instead of writing the whole inner class; that's a *forward declaration*. Then we wrote the rest of the inner class after the outer class. To make this work, we had to again fully qualify the name of the class, like this:

```
class EthicalCompetition::Connection
```

If we skipped the word `EthicalCompetition` and two colons, the compiler compiles this class like a different class. Later, the compiler would complain that it can't find the rest of the declaration for the `ConnectionClass`. The error is `aggregate 'class EthicalCompetition::Connection c'` `has incomplete type and cannot be initialized`. Remember that message, so you know how to correct it when you forget the outer class-name.

By declaring the inner class after the outer class, you can now employ another trick. The idea is to write it so that only the outer class can access the members. To accomplish this, you can make all the members of the inner class either private or protected and then make the outer class, `EthicalCompetition`, a friend of the inner class, `Connection`.

Here's the modified version of the `Connection` class:

```
class EthicalCompetition::Connection
{
protected:
    friend class EthicalCompetition;
    void Connect();
};
```

Only the outer class can access most of its members. But we say *most* because we left something out. Although the members are protected, nothing stops users outside `EthicalConnection` from creating an instance of the class. To add this security, you need a constructor for the class that is either *private or protected*. And when you do that with a constructor, following suit with a destructor is a good idea. Make the destructor private or protected too. Even if the constructor and destructor don't do anything, by making them private or protected you prevent others from creating an instance of the class — others, that is, except any friends to the class.

So here's yet one more version of the class:

```
class EthicalCompetition::Connection
{
protected:
    friend class EthicalCompetition;
    void Connect();
    Connection() {}
    ~Connection() {}
};
```

This does the trick. When we try to make an instance of the class outside `EthicalCompetition` (such as in main), as in this:

```
EthicalCompetition::Connection myconnect;
```

we see the message

```
EthicalCompetition::Connection::~Connection()' is protected
```

Yet, we can still make an instance from within the member functions of `EthicalCompetition`. It worked! Listing 4-4 shows the final program.

Listing 4-4: Protecting Embedded Classes

```cpp
#include <iostream>
using namespace std;

class EthicalCompetition
{
private:
    class Connection;

public:
    void HardWork();
};

class EthicalCompetition::Connection
{
protected:
    friend class EthicalCompetition;
    void Connect();
    Connection() {}
    ~Connection() {}
};

void EthicalCompetition::HardWork()
{
    Connection c;
    c.Connect();
    cout << "Connected" << endl;
}

void EthicalCompetition::Connection::Connect()
{
    cout << "Connecting..." << endl;
}

int main(int argc, char *argv[])
{
    // EthicalCompetition::Connection myconnect;
    EthicalCompetition comp;
    comp.HardWork();
    return 0;
}
```

We purposely left in a commented-out line where we attempted to make an instance of the inner class, `Connection`. Previously, we had the line there, but not commented out, so we could see what error message it would print and then tell you about it. If you want to see the error message, you can remove the two slashes so the compiler will try to compile the line.

Types within classes

When you declare a type, such as an enum, associating it with a class can be convenient. For example, you may have a class called Cheesecake. In this class, you may have the member variable SelectedFlavor. The SelectedFlavor member can be your own enumerated type, such as Flavor, like this:

```
enum Flavor
{
    ChocolateSuicide,
    SquishyStrawberry,
    BrokenBanana,
    PrettyPlainVanilla,
    CoolLuah,
    BizarrePurple
};
```

To associate these with a class, you can put them in a class, like this:

```
class Cheesecake
{
public:
    enum Flavor
    {
        ChocolateSuicide, SquishyStrawberry, BrokenBanana,
        PrettyPlainVanilla, CoolLuah, BizarrePurple
    };

    Flavor SelectedFlavor;
    int AmountLeft;

    void Eat()
    {
        AmountLeft = 0;
    }
};
```

The type Flavor now can be used anywhere in your program, but to use it outside the member functions of the Cheesecake class, you must fully qualify its name by putting the classname, two colons, then the type name like this:

```
Cheesecake::Flavor myflavor = Cheesecake::CoolLuah;
```

As you can see, for an enum, we also had to fully qualify the enumeration itself. If we had just put CoolLuah on the right side of the equals sign, the compiler would complain and say that CoolLuah is undeclared.

Listing 4-5 shows an example of where we use the Cheesecake class.

Listing 4-5:   Using Types within a Class

```
#include <iostream>

using namespace std;

class Cheesecake
{
public:
    enum Flavor
    {
        ChocolateSuicide, SquishyStrawberry, BrokenBanana,
        PrettyPlainVanilla, CoolLuah, BizarrePurple
    };

    Flavor SelectedFlavor;
    int AmountLeft;

    void Eat()
    {
        AmountLeft = 0;
    }
};


int main()
{
    Cheesecake yum;
    yum.SelectedFlavor = Cheesecake::SquishyStrawberry;
    yum.AmountLeft = 100;
    yum.Eat();
    cout << yum.AmountLeft << endl;
    return 0;
}
```

Notice in Listing 4-5 that I had to fully qualify the name
SquishyStrawberry.

When you declare a type (using a typedef or an enum) inside a class, you
do not need an instance of the class present to use the type. But you must
fully qualify the name. Thus, you can set up a variable of type
Cheesecake::Flavor and use it in your program without creating an
instance of Cheesecake.

Do you have types that you want used only within the class? Make them protected or private. That way, you cannot use them outside the class.

Unlike nested classes, you can make a type within a class private or protected. If you do, you can use the type only within the member functions
of the class. If you try to use the type outside the class (including setting a
member variable, as in yum.SelectedFlavor = Cheesecake::Squishy
Strawberry;), you get a compiler error.

You can also put a `typedef` inside your class in the same way you would put an `enum`, as in the following example:

```
class Spongecake
{
public:
    typedef int SpongeNumber;
    SpongeNumber weight;
    SpongeNumber diameter;
};

int main(int argc, char *argv[])
{
    Spongecake::SpongeNumber myweight = 30;
    Spongecake fluff;
    fluff.weight = myweight;
    return 0;
}
```

Chapter 5: Creating Classes with Templates

In This Chapter

✔ Creating class templates

✔ Using parameters in templates

✔ Deriving with templates

✔ Creating function templates

*I*f C++ programming has any *big secret*, it would have to be templates. Templates seem to be the topic that beginning programmers strive to understand because they've heard about them and seem to think that templates are the big wall over which they must climb to ultimately become The C++ Guru.

We can't say whether understanding templates will make you a C++ guru (we like to think that it will!), but we can say that it will open your abilities to a whole world out there, primarily because the entire Standard C++ Library is built around templates. Further, understanding templates can help you understand all that cryptic code that you see other people posting on the Internet. (And it will help you realize that it didn't have to be so cryptic! Simplify, simplify, we always say!)

So, in this chapter, we show you how to program templates in C++.

 Templates have an interesting history. Back when people started building C++ compilers, no standard for how to do templates existed. As a result, different compilers supported different ways of doing templates. The whole template thing was a mess and very confusing. So if you're using a compiler that's older than around 1999 or 2000 and you're interested in using templates, you should seriously consider upgrading to a newer compiler (such as the GNU gcc compiler included with CodeBlocks on the CD that comes with this book).

Templatizing a Class

Templates are complicated and difficult to understand. That was a lie. We don't know why people make creating and using templates so hard, but they're really not. In this section, we show you just how simple templates are to understand.

First, think of a class. Pick one, any class. We'll pick OldGasStation. That's a class, and it has some members. Remember, a class is a *type*. You can declare variables of the type. Thus, we can declare a variable of type OldGasStation called, for example HanksGetGas. We can also create another variable of type OldGasStation; maybe this one would be called FillerUp. And, of course, we could create a third one; this one might be called GotGasWeCanFillIt.

Each of these variables, HanksGetGas, FillerUp, and GotGasWeCanFillIt, are each instances of the type (or class) OldGasStation.

In the same way, we can take an existing type, say int, and make some instances of it. We can name one CheckingAccountBalance, and we can name another BuriedTreasuresFound. Each of these is an instance of the type called int. Although int isn't a class, it is a type.

Now, think about this so far: You have the two different types available to you that we mentioned; one is called OldGasStation, and the other is called int. One of these is a type you make; the other is built into C++.

We want to focus on the one you create, OldGasStation. This is a type that you create by declaring it in your program when you write the code. The compiler takes your declaration and builds some data inside the resulting program that represents this type. After the program runs, the type is created, and it does not change throughout the course of the program.

The variables in your program may change at runtime; you can create new instances of a type and delete them and change their contents. But the *type* itself *is created at compile time* and *does not change at runtime*. Remember this as one property of types in general. You will need to keep this in mind when dealing with templates.

Suppose that you have a class called MyHolder. This class is going to hold some integers. Nothing special, but it looks like this:

```
class MyHolder
{
public:
    int first;
    int second;
    int third;
    int sum()
    {
        return first + second + third;
    }
};
```

This class is easy to use; you just create an instance of it and set the values of its members. But remember: After the program is running, the class is a done deal. But at runtime, you're free to create new instances of this class.

For example, the following creates ten instances of the class, calls `sum`, and prints the return value of `sum`:

```
MyHolder *hold;
int loop;
for (loop = 0; loop < 10; loop++)
{
    hold = new MyHolder;
    hold->first = loop * 100;
    hold->second = loop * 110;
    hold->third = loop * 120;
    cout << hold->sum() << endl;
    delete hold;
}
```

This creates an instance at runtime, does some work with it, and then deletes the instance. It then repeats this over and over for a total of ten times. Instances (or variables) are created, changed, and deleted — all at runtime. But the class, which we'll say one more time, is created at compile time.

Suppose you're coding away, and you discover that this class `MyHolder` is pretty handy, except it would be nice if you had a version of it that holds `float`s instead of `int`s. You could create a second class just like the first that uses the word `float` instead of `int`, like this:

```
class AnotherHolder
{
public:
    float first;
    float second;
    float third;
    float sum()
    {
        return first + second + third;
    }
};
```

This works the same way as the previous class, but it stores three `float` types instead of `int` types. But you can see, if you have a really big class, this method would essentially require a lot of copying and pasting followed by some search-and-replacing — in other words, busywork. But you can minimize this busywork by using templates. Instead of typing two different versions of the class, type one version of the class that you can, effectively, modify when you need different versions of the class.

Take a look at this code:

```
template <typename T>
class CoolHolder
{
public:
    T first;
    T second;
    T third;
```

```
    T sum()
    {
        return first + second + third;
    }
};
```

Think of this as a rule for a class that does exactly what the previous two classes did. In this rule is a placeholder called T that is a placeholder for a type. Imagine, in your mind, this set of code; then remove the first line and replace all the remaining Ts with the word int. If you did that, you would end up with this:

```
class CoolHolder
{
public:
    int first;
    int second;
    int third;
    int sum()
    {
        return first + second + third;
    }
};
```

This is, of course, the same as the earlier class called MyHolder, just with a different name. Now imagine doing the same thing but replacing each T with the word float. You can probably see where we're going with this. Here it is:

```
class CoolHolder
{
public:
    float first;
    float second;
    float third;
    float sum()
    {
        return first + second + third;
    }
};
```

And once again, this is, of course, the same as the earlier class called AnotherHolder, but with a different name.

That's what a template does: It specifies a placeholder for a class. But it doesn't actually *create* a class . . . yet. You have to do one more thing to tell the compiler to take this template and create a class. The way you do this is by writing code to create a variable or by using the class somehow. Look at this code:

```
CoolHolder<int> IntHolder;
IntHolder.first = 10;
IntHolder.second = 20;
IntHolder.third = 30;
```

Do you see what's happening? This code is telling the compiler to take the CoolHolder template and make a version of it where T is replaced by the word int. In other words, the compiler creates a class. What is the class called? It's called CoolHolder<int>. And then these four lines of code first create an instance of CoolHolder<int> called IntHolder; then they set the members of IntHolder.

And when does the computer create this class? (That is, not the instance, but the class itself?) At *compile time*. Remember, types are created at compile time, and this is no exception to this rule.

Here's an easy way to look at a template. When you see a line like CoolHolder<int> IntHolder; you can think of it like CoolHolderint IntHolder. Although that's not really what the template is called, you are telling the compiler to create a new class. In your mind, you may think of the class as being called CoolHolderint, that is, a name without the angle brackets. (But remember that the name really isn't CoolHolderint. It's CoolHolder<int>.)

Listing 5-1 shows a complete program that uses the CoolHolder template.

Listing 5-1:   Using Templates to Create Several Versions of a Class

```
#include <iostream>

using namespace std;

template <typename T>
class CoolHolder
{
public:
    T first;
    T second;
    T third;
    T sum()
    {
        return first + second + third;
    }
};

int main()
{
    CoolHolder<int> IntHolder;
    IntHolder.first = 10;
    IntHolder.second = 20;
    IntHolder.third = 30;

    CoolHolder<int> AnotherIntHolder;
    AnotherIntHolder.first = 100;
    AnotherIntHolder.second = 200;
    AnotherIntHolder.third = 300;

    CoolHolder<float> FloatHolder;
    FloatHolder.first = 3.1415;
```

(continued)

Listing 5-1 *(continued)*

```
FloatHolder.second = 4.1415;
FloatHolder.third = 5.1415;

cout << IntHolder.first << endl;
cout << AnotherIntHolder.first << endl;
cout << FloatHolder.first << endl;

CoolHolder<int> *hold;
for (int loop = 0; loop < 10; loop++)
{
    hold = new CoolHolder<int>;
    hold->first = loop * 100;
    hold->second = loop * 110;
    hold->third = loop * 120;
    cout << hold->sum() << endl;
    delete hold;
}

return 0;
}
```

When you run this program, you see a bunch of results from calls to sum():

```
10
100
3.1415
0
330
660
990
1320
1650
1980
2310
2640
2970
```

Look closely at the code. Near the beginning is the same template that we showed you earlier. Remember that the compiler doesn't create a type for this template. Instead, the compiler uses it as a rule to follow to create additional types. That is, the code indeed serves as a template for other types, thus its name.

Here's the first line of the template:

```
template <typename T>
```

All this means is that a template class is going to follow, and that it has a type with a placeholder called T. That means that inside the class anywhere a T appears, it will be replaced by the typename. (The T is standalone; if you have it as part of a word, it won't be replaced.) The standard practice is for people to use T for the placeholder, but you can use any identifier (starting with a letter or underscore, followed by any combination of letters, numbers, or underscores).

Down inside the `main` for this class, we then declare several variables of types based on this template. Here's one such line:

```
CoolHolder<int> IntHolder;
```

This line declares a variable called `IntHolder`. For this variable, the compiler creates a type called `CoolHolder<int>`, which is a type based on the `CoolHolder` template, where `T` is replaced by `int`.

Here's another line where we declare a variable:

```
CoolHolder<int> AnotherIntHolder;
```

This time, the compiler doesn't have to create another type because it just created the `CoolHolder<int>` type earlier. But again, this line uses the same type based on the template, where `T` is replaced by `int`.

Here we create another class based on the template, and we declare a variable of this new type:

```
CoolHolder<float> FloatHolder;
```

When the compiler sees this line, it creates another type by using the template, and it replaces `T` with the word `float`. So in this case, the three members of the instance `FloatHolder`, called `first`, `second`, and `third`, each hold a floating-point number. And the member function called `sum` returns a floating-point number.

The following line uses the type created earlier called `CoolHolder<int>`, and it declares a pointer to `CoolHolder<int>`. Yes, you can do that; pointers are allowed:

```
CoolHolder<int> *hold;
```

Then the code that follows cycles through a loop where we call `new` to create instances of type `CoolHolder<int>` by using the line

```
hold = new CoolHolder<int>;
```

We access the members using the pointer notation, `->`, like so:

```
hold->first = loop * 100;
```

And that's the basics of templates. They're really not as bad as people make them out to be. Just remember that when you see an identifier followed by angle brackets containing a type or class, it's a template. So see what you think of this line of code:

```
vector<string> MyList;
```

Any idea what this code does? It uses some template called `vector` and tells `vector` to use the string type inside it. In fact, `vector` is part of the Standard C++ Library, and it works similar to an array. Its *template parameter* (the thing in angle brackets) represents the type of the items the `vector` holds. So this declares a variable called `MyList`, which is a `vector` that holds `string` instances.

Separating a template from the function code

In the earlier days of templates and C++, the rule was that you had to put member function code for a class template inside the template itself; you couldn't put a forward declaration and then put the function code outside the template as you could do with classes. However, the ANSI standard changed this and made putting the code outside the template legal. If you are using an ANSI-compliant compiler, you can put the function code outside the template. The GNU gcc compiler is, for the most part, ANSI-compliant; with it, you can put the code outside the template. However, you have to place the code carefully to get it to compile correctly. The code in Listing 5-2 shows you how to do this.

Listing 5-2:   Separating a Template from Function Code

```
#include <iostream>

using namespace std;

template <typename T>
class ImFree
{
protected:
    T x;

public:
    T& getx();
    void setx(T);
};

template <typename T>
T &ImFree<T>::getx()
{
    return x;
}

template <typename T>
void ImFree<T>::setx(T newx)
{
    x = newx;
}

int main()
{
    ImFree<int> separate;
    separate.setx(10);
    cout << separate.getx() << endl;
    return 0;
}
```

As you can see, the format is ugly. To be honest, whenever we do this, we have to look up the format; it's hard to memorize. (Maybe you can memorize it, but our brains are too prone to explosions.)

Look closely at one of the member functions:

```
template <typename T>
T &ImFree<T>::getx()
{
    return x;
}
```

The first line is the same as the first line of the template definition. It's just the word `template` followed by the parameter in angle brackets.

The next line looks almost like you might expect it to. With classes you put the function prototype, adding the classname and two colons before the function name itself, but after the return type. Here you do that too; the sticky part is how you write the template name. You don't just give the name; instead, you follow the name by two angle brackets, with the parameter inside, like this: `T &ImFree<T>::getx()`. Note the `<T>` part.

Earlier compilers didn't allow you to separate the function code the way we did in Listing 5-2. Instead, you would have to put the function code inside the template itself, as in the following:

```
template <typename T>
class ImFree
{
protected:
    T x;
public:
    T& getx()
    {
        return x;
    }
    void setx(T newx)
    {
        x = newx;
    }
};
```

Note one little thing that we did in both Listing 5-2 and in the old type of code: For the `getx` member function, instead of just returning a variable of type `T`, we returned a reference. That is, instead of this:

```
T getx()
```

we declared the function as

```
T& getx()
```

(We added the ampersand.) Although that has the potential of upsetting some people, there's a good reason for doing it. In the `main` of Listing 5-2, we created the class based on the template with an integer parameter:

```
ImFree<int> separate;
```

However, we could instead create the class with some other class:

```
ImFree<SomeOtherClass> separate;
```

If we do that, we don't really want to return just an instance from the function, as in

```
T& getx()
{
    return x;
}
```

Returning just an instance copies the instance rather than just returning the instance itself. The solution might be to use a pointer, as in

```
T* getx()
{
    return &x;
}
```

And, in fact, we tried that when we first wrote the code. But then the code gets annoying because we would have to dereference the result when we use the function, even if the result is just an integer. Our `cout` statement ended up looking like this when we used a pointer:

```
cout << *(separate.getx()) << endl;
```

And frankly, we found that code, shall we say, yucky. So, as in a presidential election, we picked the lesser of the evils by making it a reference. We figured a reference was less evil because the user of the class wouldn't have to do any bizarre coding. Instead, the `cout` is rather straightforward:

```
cout << separate.getx() << endl;
```

Including static members in a template

You can include static members in a template, but you need to be careful when you do so. Remember that all instances of a class share a single static member of the class. You can think of the static member as being a member of the class itself, whereas the nonstatic members are members of the instances.

Now, from a single template, you can potentially create multiple classes. This means that to maintain the notion of static members, you need to either get creative with your rules or make life easy by just assuming that each class based on the template gets its own static members. And the easy way is exactly how this process works.

When you include a static member in a template, each class that you create based on the template gets its own static member. Further, you need to tell the compiler how to store the static member just as you do with static members of classes that aren't created from templates.

Listing 5-3 shows an example of static members in a template.

Listing 5-3:   Using Static Members in a Template

```
#include <iostream>

using namespace std;

template <typename T>
class Electricity
{
public:
    static T charge;
};

template <typename T>
T Electricity<T>::charge;

int main()
{
    Electricity<int>::charge = 10;
    Electricity<float>::charge = 98.6;
    Electricity<int> inst;
    inst.charge = 22;

    cout << Electricity<int>::charge << endl;
    cout << Electricity<float>::charge << endl;
    cout << inst.charge << endl;

    return 0;
}
```

First, see how we declared the storage for the static member; it's the two lines in between the template and `main`. The syntax is somewhat difficult to remember: First, you supply the same template header you would for the class. (That is, notice that the line `template <typename T>` appears both before the class template and the storage line.) Then, you specify the type of the static member (in this case T, which is the template parameter). Next, you refer to the static member by using the usual `class name::member name` syntax. But remember that the class name gets the template parameter in angle brackets after it. Done deal.

In this code, you can also see that we created two classes based on the templates `Electricity <int>` and `Electricity <float>`. Each of these classes has its own instance of the static member; for the `<int>` version, we put a `10` in it, and for the `<float>` version, we put a `98.6` in it. Then, just to show that there's only a single static member per class, we created an instance of `Electricity<int>` and set its static member to `22`. Then we wrote them to the console with the `cout` statement. And, indeed, the two lines for `Electricity<int>` are the same, and the one for `Electricity<float>` is different from the two for `Electricity<int>`. Done deal!

Parameterizing a Template

A template consists of a template name followed by one or more *parameters* inside angled brackets. Then comes the class definition. When you politely ask the compiler to create a new class based on this template, the compiler happily obliges by making a substitution for whatever you supply as the parameter. At least we think that the compiler is happy. It doesn't complain much beyond the occasional error message.

Focus your eyes on this template:

```
template <typename T>
class SomethingForEveryone
{
public:
    T member;
};
```

Not much to it: It's just a simple template with one member called, conveniently enough, `member`. Life is simple sometimes.

But what we want you to notice in particular is what's inside the angled brackets. This is the parameter: `typename T`. Like parameters in a function, first is the type of the parameter (`typename`), and second is the name of the parameter (`T`).

But is `typename` a, um, typename? Not really; it's a special C++ word reserved for use in templates. *typename* means that what follows (in this case, `T`) is a *type*. So when you politely tell the compiler to create a new class based on this template, you specify a *type* for `T`. For example, this line tells the compiler to create the new class and make a variable named `JustForMe` that is of the new class:

```
SomethingForEveryone<int> JustForMe;
```

Now the compiler looks at what you supplied inside angle brackets and uses that as a parameter for the template. Here, `int` goes with the `T` in the template. The compiler will take each instance of `T` that isn't inside a word, and replace it with the parameter, which is `int`.

Putting different types in the parameter

It turns out there's more to this parameter thing than meets the computer screen. You can put many more things inside the parameter beyond just the boring word `typename`. For example, suppose you have a class that does some comparisons to make sure that a product isn't too expensive for a person's budget. Each person would have several instances of this class, one for each product. This class would have a constant in it that represents the maximum price the person is willing to spend.

But there's a twist: Although you would have multiple instances of this class, one for each product the person wants to buy, the maximum price would be different for each person.

You can create such a situation with or without templates. Here's a way you can do it with a template:

```
template <int MaxPrice>
class PriceController
{
public:
    int Price;
    void TestPrice()
    {
        if (Price > MaxPrice)
        {
            cout << "Too expensive" << endl;
        }
    }
};
```

Before we show you an example that uses this template, we'll quickly explain what's going on with it. This time, the template parameter isn't a type at all — it's an integer value, an actual number. Then, inside the class, we use that number as a constant. As you can see in the `TestPrice` function, we compare the `Price` member to the constant, which is called `MaxPrice`. So this time, instead of using `T` for the name of the template parameter, we used something a little more sensible, `MaxPrice`. And `MaxPrice` is a value, not a type.

Listing 5-4 shows a complete example that uses this template.

Listing 5-4:   Using Different Types for a Template Parameter

```
#include <iostream>

using namespace std;

template <typename T>
class SomethingForEveryone
{
public:
    T member;
};

template <int MaxPrice>
class PriceController
{
```

(continued)

Listing 5-4 *(continued)*

```
public:
    int Price;
    void TestPrice()
    {
        if (Price > MaxPrice)
        {
            cout << "Too expensive" << endl;
        }
    }
};

int main()
{
    SomethingForEveryone<int> JustForMe;
    JustForMe.member = 2;
    cout << JustForMe.member << endl;

    const int FredMaxPrice = 30;
    PriceController<FredMaxPrice> FredsToaster;
    FredsToaster.Price = 15;
    FredsToaster.TestPrice();

    PriceController<FredMaxPrice> FredsDrawingSet;
    FredsDrawingSet.Price = 45;
    FredsDrawingSet.TestPrice();

    const int JulieMaxPrice = 60;
    PriceController<JulieMaxPrice> JuliesCar;
    JuliesCar.Price = 80;
    JuliesCar.TestPrice();

    return 0;
}
```

Each person gets a different class. You can see that Fred gets a class called
`PriceController <FredMaxPrice>`. Julie, however, gets a class called
`PriceController <JulieMaxPrice>`. And remember, these really *are*
different classes. The compiler created two different classes, one for each
item passed in as a template parameter. And notice that the parameters are
constant integer values. `FredMaxPrice` is a constant integer holding `30`.
`JulieMaxPrice` is a constant integer holding `60`.

For the first one, `PriceController <FredMaxPrice>`, we created
two instances of that class. And for the second one, `PriceController`
`<JulieMaxPrice>`, we created one instance.

The compiler really does create two separate classes, one called
`PriceController <FredMaxPrice>` and one called `PriceController`
`<JulieMaxPrice>`. These are as separate as they would be if you typed in
two separate classes, one called `PriceControllerFredMaxPrice` and one
called `PriceControllerJulieMaxPrice`. They aren't separate instances
of a class — they are separate classes.

So far in this section, we've shown you that you can use a type as a template parameter or a value of a certain type. You can also use a class as a template parameter. The following list describes each type of parameter:

✦ **Value parameters:** (The ANSI standard calls these *non-type* parameters, but we like *value* better.) You can give the type and name for a value in the parameter, as in template <int MaxPrice>. But for some reason, the ANSI standard forbids you from using a floating-point value here, as in template <float MaxPrice>, or a class, as in template <MyClass inst>, or a void type, as in template <void nothing>. But you're free to use *pointers*, so template <float MaxPrice> is allowed, and so are template <MyClass *inst> and template <void *MaxPrice>. (Although, in general, you should avoid void * because it's not very useful; try to be more specific with your pointers, as in int *MaxPrice.)

✦ **typename parameters:** You can use a type as a parameter to a class, as in template <typename T>. You then use a type when you ask the compiler to create the class based on the template. And when you use typename, you have to make sure that you actually use it as a type inside the class; don't just pass a variable for the parameter.

✦ **Class parameters:** Remember that a class is in itself a type, so you can pass a classname when your template requires a type. But remember that we're not talking about passing an instance of a class to the template; We're talking about passing a class itself by specifying its name in the template parameter.

Parameterizing with a class

When your template is expecting a class for its parameter (remember, a class, not an instance of a class), you can use the word type-name in the template parameter as we did in the examples in this chapter. You would then instruct the compiler to create a class based on the template by passing a classname into the template, as in MyContainer<MyClass> inst;. Typically, you would use a class, called a *container*, as a template parameter if you have a template that you intend to hold instances of a class. However, instead of using the word typename, you can instead use the word class, like so:

```
template <class T>
class MyContainer
{
public:
    T member;
};
```

But whichever you use, typename or class, really doesn't matter: According to the C++ ANSI standard, the word typename and the word class are interchangeable when used in a template parameter.

The GNU gcc compiler that's used for CodeBlocks corrects a strange error message that other compilers sometimes provide when you use something you're not supposed to inside a template. The problem is, these older compilers don't give an error message for the line that has the word *template* in it, such as `template <float MaxPrice>;` instead, they give two error messages for the line that tries to create the class based on the template, such as `PriceController<FredMaxPrice> FredsToaster;`. Here are the two messages we saw:

```
non-constant `FredMaxPrice' cannot be used as template argument
ANSI C++ forbids declaration `FredsToaster' with no type
```

When working with CodeBlocks, you still see the message associated with the class creation. However, you also see the following message, which tells you precisely where the problem lies:

```
error: `float' is not a valid type for a template constant parameter
```

Including multiple parameters

You're not limited to only one parameter when you create a template. For example, the Standard C++ Library has a template called map. The map template works like an array, but instead of storing things based on an index as you would in an array, you store them based on an object called a *key*. In other words, you store things in an array in pairs; the first item in the pair is called a key and the second item is called a value. To retrieve an item from map, you specify the key, and you get back the value. When you create a class based on the map template, you specify the two types map will hold, one for the key and one for the value. Note that we said the *types* that map will hold, not the *objects or instances* it will hold. After you specify the types, the compiler creates a class, and inside that class you can put the instances.

To show how this works, instead of using the actual map template, we're going to make our own template that works similarly to a map. Instances of classes based on this template will hold only as many items as you specify when you create the class, whereas a real map doesn't have any limitations beyond the size of the computer's memory. These days that means map can hold just about as much as you want! So load up on map items! Listing 5-5 shows our map template.

Listing 5-5: Using Multiple Parameters with Templates

```
#include <iostream>

using namespace std;

template<typename K, typename V, int S>
class MyMap
{
```

```
protected:
    K key[S];
    V value[S];
    bool used[S];
    int Count;

    int Find(K akey)
    {
        int i;
        for (i=0; i<S; i++)
        {
            if (used[i] == false)
                continue;
            if (key[i] == akey)
            {
                return i;
            }
        }
        return -1;
    }

    int FindNextAvailable()
    {
        int i;
        for (i=0; i<S; i++)
        {
            if (used[i] == false)
                return i;
        }
        return -1;
    }

public:
    MyMap()
    {
        int i;
        for (i=0; i<S; i++)
        {
            used[i] = false;
        }
    }

    void Set(K akey, V avalue)
    {
        int i = Find(akey);
        if (i > -1)
        {
            value[i] = avalue;
        }
        else
        {
            i = FindNextAvailable();
            if (i > -1)
            {
                key[i] = akey;
                value[i] = avalue;
                used[i] = true;
            }
            else
                cout << "Sorry, full!" << endl;
        }
    }
```

(continued)

Listing 5-5 *(continued)*

```
    V Get(K akey)
    {
        int i = Find(akey);
        if (i == -1)
        {
            return 0;
        }
        else
        {
            return value[i];
        }
    }
};

int main()
{
    MyMap<char,int,10> mymap;

    mymap.Set('X',5);
    mymap.Set('Q',6);
    mymap.Set('X',10);

    cout << mymap.Get('X') << endl;
    cout << mymap.Get('Q') << endl;

    return 0;
}
```

When you run this program, you will see this output:

```
10
6
```

This listing is a good exercise — not just for your fingers as you type it in, but in understanding templates. Notice the first line of the template definition:

```
template<typename K, typename V, int S>
```

This template takes not one, not two, but (count them!) three parameters. The first is a type, and we use it as the key for map, so we call it K. The second is a type, and we use it as the value for map, so we call it V. The final is S, and it's not a type. Instead, S is an integer value; it represents the maximum number of pairs that map can hold.

The member functions that follow allow the user of any class based on this map to add items to map and retrieve items from map. We didn't include any functions for removing items; you might think about ways you could add such an item. You might even take a look at the header files for the map template in the Standard C++ Library to see how the designers of the library implemented a removal system.

Typedefing a Template

If there's a template that you use with particular parameters over and over, often just using `typedef` for the thing is the easiest way to go. For example, if you have a template like this

```
template <typename T>
class Cluck
{
public:
    T Chicken;
};
```

and you find yourself using `Cluck <int>` over and over, you can `typedef` this, as in the following:

```
typedef Cluck<int> CluckNum;
```

Then, anytime you need to use `Cluck<int>`, you can use `CluckNum` instead. This `main` demonstrates the use of `ClickNum`:

```
int main()
{
    CluckNum foghorn;
    foghorn.Chicken = 1;
    return 0;
}
```

We like to `typedef` our templates, because then the classname looks like a regular old classname, rather than a template name. In the preceding example, we get to use the classname `CluckNum` instead of the somewhat cryptic `Cluck<int>`. And interestingly, if you're working as part of a team of programmers and the other programmers aren't as knowledgeable about templates as you are, they tend to be less intimidated if you `typedef` the template. That way, you get to use a regular name, and they won't have a brain overload when they see your code. But don't tell them we said that.

When the compiler creates a class based on a template, people say that the compiler is *instantiating* the template. we know, we know, most people use the word *instantiate* to mean that you create an object based on a class. But if you stretch your imagination, you can see how the template itself is a type from which you can create other types. And thus, a class based on a template is actually an *instance of a template!* And the process of creating a class based on a template is called *template instantiation*.

When you use a `typedef` to give a simpler name to a specific class based on a template, the compiler instantiates the class based on the template. Or, to put it another way, the compiler *instantiates the template class.*

Deriving Templates

If you think about it, you can involve a class template in a derivation in at least three ways. You can

- ✦ Derive a class from a class template
- ✦ Derive a class template from a class
- ✦ Derive a class template from a class template

Or you could do none of these three items. But if you want to find out about them, read the following sections, where we show you how they work.

Deriving classes from a class template

You can derive a class from a template, and in doing so, specify the parameters for the template. In other words, think of it like this, if it's not too round-about: From a template, you create a class, and from that created class, you derive your final class.

Suppose you have a template called `MediaHolder`, and the first two lines of its declaration look like this:

```
template <typename T>
class MediaHolder
```

Then, you could derive a class from a particular case of this template, as in this header for a class:

```
class BookHolder : public MediaHolder<Book>
```

Here we created a new class (based on `MediaHolder`) called `MediaHolder<Book>`. And from that class, we derived our final class, `BookHolder`. Listing 5-6 is an example of the class `MediaHolder`, and the listing includes some good books and magazines to add to your reading list as well.

Listing 5-6   Deriving a Class from a Class Template

```
#include <iostream>

using namespace std;

class Book
{
public:
    string Name;
    string Author;
    string Publisher;
```

```
    Book(string aname, string anauthor, string apublisher) :
        Name(aname), Author(anauthor), Publisher(apublisher)
        {}
};

class Magazine
{
public:
    string Name;
    string Issue;
    string Publisher;
    Magazine(string aname, string anissue,
        string apublisher) :
        Name(aname), Issue(anissue), Publisher(apublisher)
        {}
};

template <typename T>
class MediaHolder
{
public:
    T *array[100];
    int Count;

    void Add(T *item)
    {
        array[Count] = item;
        Count++;
    }

    MediaHolder() : Count(0) {}
};

class BookHolder : public MediaHolder<Book> {
public:
    enum GenreEnum
        {childrens, scifi, romance,
         horror, mainstream, hownotto};

    GenreEnum GenreOfAllBooks;
};

class MagazineHolder : public MediaHolder<Magazine>
{
public:
    bool CompleteSet;
};

int main()
{
    MagazineHolder dl;
    dl.Add(new Magazine(
        "Dummies Life", "Vol 1 No 1", "Wile E."));
    dl.Add(new Magazine(
        "Dummies Life", "Vol 1 No 2", "Wile E."));
    dl.Add(new Magazine(
        "Dummies Life", "Vol 1 No 3", "Wile E."));
    dl.CompleteSet = false;
    cout << dl.Count << endl;
```

(continued)

Listing 5-6 *(continued)*

```
BookHolder bh;
bh.Add(new Book(
    "CEOing for Dumdums", "Gookie Dan", "Wile E."));
bh.Add(new Book(
    "Carsmashing for Dumdums", "Woodie and Buzz",
    "Wile E."));
bh.Add(new Book(
    "Turning off the Computer for Dumdums",
    "Wrath of Andy",
    "Wile E."));
bh.GenreOfAllBooks = BookHolder::hownotto;
cout << bh.Count << endl;

return 0;
}
```

Deriving a class template from a class

A template doesn't have to be at the absolute top of your hierarchy, the total king of the hill. No, a template can be derived from another class that's not a template. The brain acrobatics work like this: When you have a template and the compiler creates a class based on this template, the resulting class will be derived from another class.

For example, suppose you have a class called `SuperMath` that is *not a template*. You could derive a class template from `SuperMath`. Listing 5-7 shows how you can do this.

Listing 5-7: Deriving a Class Template from a Class Template

```
#include <iostream>

using namespace std;

class SuperMath
{
public:
    int IQ;
};

template <typename T>
class SuperNumber : public SuperMath
{
public:
    T value;

    T &AddTo(T another)
    {
        value += another;
        return value;
    }

    T &SubtractFrom(T another)
    {
        value -= another;
        return value;
    }
};
```

```
void IncreaseIQ(SuperMath &inst)
{
    inst.IQ++;
}

int main()
{
    SuperNumber<int> First;
    First.value = 10;
    First.IQ = 206;
    cout << First.AddTo(20) << endl;

    SuperNumber<float> Second;
    Second.value = 20.5;
    Second.IQ = 201;
    cout << Second.SubtractFrom(1.3) << endl;

    IncreaseIQ(First);
    IncreaseIQ(Second);
    cout << First.IQ << endl;
    cout << Second.IQ << endl;

    return 0;
}
```

Note something really great that we did here! The base class is called
SuperMath, and it has a member called IQ. From SuperMath, we derived
a class template called SuperNumber that does some arithmetic. Later, we
put an Incredible IQ-Inflating Polymorphism to use in this function:

```
void IncreaseIQ(SuperMath &inst)
{
    inst.IQ++;
}
```

Note what this function takes: A reference to SuperMath. Because the
SuperNumber class template is derived from SuperMath, that means any
class we create based on the template is, in turn, derived from SuperMath.
And that means that if we have an instance of a class based on the template,
we can pass the instance into the IncreaseIQ function. (Remember, when
a function takes a pointer or reference to a class, you can instead pass an
instance of a derived class.)

Deriving a class template from a class template

If you have a class template and you want to derive another class template
from it, first you need to think about *exactly* what you're doing. Not like what
you're doing spending all your days programming when you could be out
enjoying the sunshine; rather, what we mean is, "What process takes place
when you attempt to derive a class template from another class template?"

Remember that a class template isn't a class: A class template is a cookie
cutter that the compiler uses to build a class. If, in a derivation, the base
class and the derived classes are both templates, really what you have is the
following:

1. The first class is a template from which the compiler builds classes.

2. The second class is a template from which the compiler will build classes that are derived from classes built from the first template.

Now think about this: You create a class based on the base class template. Then you create a second class based on the second template. Does this automatically mean that the second class is derived from the first class? Nope! Here's why: From the first template, you can create many classes. Now if you create a class from the second template, which of those many classes will it be derived from?

To understand what is happening, take a look at Listing 5-8. To keep the code simple, we put the jokes aside and just gave the identifiers basic names. (And notice that we commented one of the lines out. If you're typing this, go ahead and type that line in, too, with the comment slashes, because we want you to try something in a moment.)

Listing 5-8:   Deriving a Class Template from a Class Template

```
#include <iostream>

using namespace std;

template <typename T>
class Base
{
public:
    T a;
};

template <typename T>
class Derived : public Base<T>
{
public:
    T b;
};

void TestInt(Base<int> *inst)
{
    cout << inst->a << endl;
}

void TestDouble(Base<double> *inst)
{
    cout << inst->a << endl;
}

int main()
{
    Base<int> base_int;
    Base<double> base_double;

    Derived<int> derived_int;
    Derived<double> derived_double;
```

```
TestInt(&base_int);
TestInt(&derived_int);

TestDouble(&base_double);
TestDouble(&derived_double);
//TestDouble(&derived_int);

return 0;
}
```

Now compile the program. The preceding example has two functions, each taking a different class and each class based on the first template called `Base`. The first takes `Base<int>` * as a parameter, and the second takes `Base<double>` * as a parameter.

If a function takes a pointer to a class, we can legally pass a pointer to an instance of a derived class. Now note that we created this variable:

```
Derived<int> derived_int;
```

And we pass this variable to the function that takes a `Base<int>`. *And it compiles.* That means `Derived<int>` is derived from `Base<int>`. In the same way, `Derived<double>` is derived from `Base<double>`.

Now just to make sure that this is correct, if you look at the commented out line, you should see that if you uncomment the line, it should not compile. Go ahead and try uncommenting the line `TestDouble(&derived_int)`. When you do this, and you try to compile the listing, you see this message:

```
error: cannot convert `Derived<int>*' to `Base<double>*' for argument `1' to
`void TestDouble(Base<double>*)'
```

Thus, you can't pass a pointer to `Derived<int>` to a function that takes a pointer to `Base<double>`. That's because `Derived<int>` isn't derived from `Base<double>`. Yet, it would appear from the code that the template is derived from the template for `Base<double>`. But that's not true. Here's why.

Templates are not derived from other templates. You can't derive templates because templates are not classes. Rather, templates are cookie cutters for classes, and the class resulting from a template can be derived from a class resulting from another template.

Now that we have that cleared up, look closely at how we declared the second template class. Its header looks like this:

```
template <typename T>
class Derived : public Base<T>
```

The clue here is that the `Derived` template takes a template parameter called `T`. Then the class based on the template is derived from a class called `Base<T>`. But in this case, `T` is the parameter for the `Derived` template.

So if we create a class based on Derived, such as this one:

```
Derived<int> x;
```

We just created a class called Derived<int>; then, in this case, the parameter is int. And thus, the compiler replaces the Ts so that Base<T> in this case becomes Base<int>. And so Derived<int> is derived from Base<int>.

And *that's* how this template derivation stuff works!

When you derive a template class from another template class, you actually make use of the template parameter, and that gets passed into the base class template as a parameter.

Templatizing a Function

A *function template* is a function that allows the user to essentially modify the types used by a function as needed. For example, take a look at these two functions:

```
int AbsoluteValueInt(int x)
{
    if (x >= 0)
        return x;
    else
        return -x;
}

float AbsoluteValueFloat(float x)
{
    if (x >= 0)
        return x;
    else
        return -x;
}
```

If the user of the functions needs to take the absolute value of an integer, he or she would use the AbsoluteValueInt function. But to take the absolute value of a float, he or she would instead use the AbsoluteValueFloat function. What about a double? Or some other numerical type?

But instead of having a separate function for double and a separate function for every other type, we would suggest using a template, as in this:

```
template <typename T> T AbsoluteValue(T x)
{
    if (x >= 0)
        return x;
    else
        return -x;
}
```

Now you need only one version of the function, which handles any numeric type, including `double`. The users of the function can, effectively, create their own versions of the function as they need them. For example, to use an integer version of this function, we just put the typename, `int`, inside angle brackets after the function name when calling the function:

```
int n = -3;
cout << AbsoluteValue<int>(n) << endl;
```

And if we want to use the function for a float, we just do this:

```
float x = -4.5;
cout << AbsoluteValue<float>(x) << endl;
```

Note how we declared the function template itself. The real difference between the function template and a regular run-of-the-mill function is in the header:

```
template <typename T> T AbsoluteValue(T x)
```

First we put the word `template`. Then we follow it with any number of optional spaces, and then an open angle bracket (that is, a less-than sign). Following the angle bracket, we put the word `typename`, a close angle bracket (that is, a greater-than sign), and then an identifier name. Most people like to use the name `T` (since it's the first letter in *type*), so that's what we did, being ones to follow the crowd. Then we put the rest of the function header, which, taken by itself, looks like this:

```
T AbsoluteValue(T x)
```

Remember, `T` represents a type. Therefore, this portion of the function header shows a function called `AbsoluteValue` that takes `T` as a parameter and returns `T`. So if we create a function based on this template by using an integer, the function will take an integer as a parameter and return an integer. Remember, `T` is basically a placeholder for a typename. So when the compiler encounters a line like this:

```
cout << AbsoluteValue<float>(x) << endl;
```

it creates a function based on the template, substituting `float` anywhere it sees `T`.

However, if you have two lines that use the same type, as in this

```
cout << AbsoluteValue<float>(x) << endl;
cout << AbsoluteValue<float>(10.0) << endl;
```

the compiler only creates a single function for both lines. (And these two lines don't need to be one after the other.)

Overloading and function templates

If you really want to go out on a limb and create flexibility in your program, you can use overloading with a function template. Remember, *overloading a function* means that you create two different versions of a single function. Really, what you're doing is creating two separate functions that have different parameters (that is, either a different number of parameters or different types of parameters), but they share the same name.

Look at these two functions:

```
int AbsoluteValue(int x)
{
    if (x >= 0)
        return x;
    else
        return -x;
}

float AbsoluteValue(float x)
{
    if (x >= 0)
        return x;
    else
        return -x;
}
```

These functions are an example of overloading. They take different types as parameters. (One takes an `int`, and the other takes a `float`.) Of course, you could combine these functions into a template:

```
template <typename T> T AbsoluteValue(T x)
{
    if (x >= 0)
        return x;
    else
        return -x;
}
```

But is this really any different? After all, you can use the following two lines of code either after the overloaded functions or after the function template:

```
cout << AbsoluteValue<int>(n) << endl;
cout << AbsoluteValue<float>(x) << endl;
```

(We're assuming that n is an integer and x is a float.) However, the template is a better choice. First, if you use the overloaded form and then try this, you'll get a problem:

```
cout << AbsoluteValue(10.5) << endl;
```

We all know that `10.5` is a `float`; therefore, the compiler should just call the `float` version of the overloaded function. However, the GNU gcc compiler that ships with CodeBlocks gives us this error message:

```
error: call of overloaded `AbsoluteValue(double)' is ambiguous
```

Ambiguous? But look! The message is saying `AbsoluteValue(double)`! Hmmm . . . Apparently, the GNU gcc compiler thinks that our `10.5` is a double, not a float. And you can actually pass a double into either a function that takes an `int` or a function that takes a `float`. The compiler will just convert it to an `int` or a `float`, whichever it needs. And because the compiler thinks that `10.5` is a `double`, it figures it can pass it to either version of the overloaded function. So that leaves you a choice: You can either cast it to a `float` or create a third overloaded version of the function, one that takes a `double`.

Yuck. At least CodeBlocks gives you some clue as to the problem because the extended error information is

```
note: candidates are: int AbsoluteValue(int)
note:                  float AbsoluteValue(float)
```

Creating a template is easier. And that brings us to the second reason the template version is better: If you want a new type of the function, you don't need to write another version of the function.

But what if you want to *overload a function template*? That sounds kind of scary, but you can do it. Listing 5-9 shows an overloaded function template.

Listing 5-9: Overloading a Function Template Provides Even Greater Flexibility

```
#include <iostream>

using namespace std;

template <typename T> T AbsoluteValue(T x)
{
    cout << "(using first)" << endl;
    if (x >= 0)
        return x;
    else
        return -x;
}

template <typename T> T AbsoluteValue(T *x)
{
```

(continued)

Listing 5-9 *(continued)*

```
    cout << "(using second)" << endl;
    if (*x >= 0)
        return *x;
    else
        return -(*x);
}

int main()
{
    int n = -3;
    cout << AbsoluteValue<int>(n) << endl;

    float *xptr = new float(-4.5);
    cout << AbsoluteValue<float>(xptr) << endl;
    cout << AbsoluteValue<float>(10.5) << endl;

    return 0;
}
```

When we pass a pointer (as in the second call to AbsoluteValue in main), the compiler figures out that it needs to use the second version of the template. And just to be sure which version gets used and at what time during application execution, we threw in a cout line at the beginning of each function template. When you run this code, here's what you see:

```
(using first)
3
(using second)
4.5
(using first)
10.5
```

From the middle two lines you can see that the computer did indeed call the second version of the template.

You can make life a little easier by using a little trick. Most compilers let you leave out the type in angle brackets in the function template call itself. The compiler is smart enough to figure out what type of function to build from the template, based on the types that you pass into the function call! Pretty wild. Here's an example main that you can substitute for the main in Listing 5-9:

```
int main()
{
    int n = -3;
    cout << AbsoluteValue(n) << endl;

    float *xptr = new float(-4.5);
    cout << AbsoluteValue(xptr) << endl;
    cout << AbsoluteValue(10.5) << endl;

    return 0;
}
```

In this code, we replaced AbsoluteValue<int>(n) with just AbsoluteValue(n). When you run the modified Listing 5-9, you see the same output as when you run Listing 5-9.

Templatizing a member function

When you write a template for a class, you can put function templates inside the class template. To people who were familiar with some of the early versions of C++ where template support was minimal, this seems a little shocking. But when the electrical current wears off, we all see that putting a template function inside a template class is possible. You simply declare a function template inside a class, as in the following:

```
class MyMath
{
public:
    string name;
    MyMath(string aname) : name(aname) {}

    template <typename T> void WriteAbsoluteValue(T x)
    {
        cout << "Hello " << name << endl;
        if (x >= 0)
            cout << x << endl;
        else
            cout << -x << endl;
    }
};
```

The `WriteAbsoluteValue` member function is a template. It's preceded by the word `template` and a `template` parameter in angle brackets. Then it has a return type, `void`, the function name, and the function parameter.

When you create an instance of the class, you can call the member function, providing a type as need be, as in the following:

```
int main()
{
    MyMath inst = (string("George"));
    inst.WriteAbsoluteValue(-50.5);
    inst.WriteAbsoluteValue(-35);
    return 0;
}
```

In the first call, the function takes a `double` (because, by default, the C++ compiler considers `-50.5` a `double`). In the second call, the function takes an integer. The compiler then generates two different forms of the function, and *they both become members of the class.*

Although you can use function templates as class members, you cannot make them virtual. The compiler will not allow it, and the ANSI standard forbids ("Forbids, we say!") you from doing it. In fact, we tried it with CodeBlocks just to see what friendly message we would get. Here it is:

```
`virtual' can only be specified for functions
```

We guess by *functions* it means actual functions — not function templates.

Chapter 6: Programming with the Standard Library

In This Chapter

✔ **Architecting the Standard C++ Library**

✔ **Storing data in `vector` or `map`**

✔ **Containing data with a list or set**

✔ **Stacking and queuing**

✔ **Copying containers**

*W*hen you get around in the world of C++ programming (a fun world indeed!), you're going to encounter two different *libraries* that people use to make their lives easier. That is, after all, the ultimate point of computers — to make our lives easier, right? These two libraries are

✦ Standard C++ Library

✦ Standard Template Library (STL)

Some people say, "We use STL." Others say, "We use the Standard C++ Library." In this case, *library* means a set of classes that you can use in your programs. These libraries include handy classes, such as `string` and `vector` (which is like an array in that it's a list in which you can store objects).

The difference between the Standard C++ Library and STL is that STL came first. STL was used by so many developers that the American National Standards Institute (ANSI) decided to standardize it. The result is the similar Standard C++ Library that is part of the official ANSI standard and now part of most modern C++ compilers (including CodeBlocks, Microsoft Visual C++, Borland C++ Builder, MinGW, Cygwin, and Dev-C++). We use the Standard C++ Library in this chapter. Because we know that this is C++, we just call it the *Standard Library*.

The concepts that we present here apply to STL, so if you're using STL, you can use this chapter.

Architecting the Standard Library

When people start using the Standard C++ Library, they often ask: Where's the source code? We see the header files, but where are the .cpp files? This question has an easy answer: There are no .cpp files! ANSI architected the Standard C++ Library for ease of use and reliability.

The classes contain their functions inside the class definitions; there are no forward declarations. You don't add source files to your project or linking in compiled libraries. Just add an include line for the libraries you want.

Containing Your Classes

Computers need a place to store things, so the Standard Library includes containers in which you can put things. The classes for containing things are called *container classes.* These classes are templates. When you create an instance of a container class, you specify what class it holds.

When you specify the class in a container, you are saying that the container will contain instances of your specified class or of classes derived from your specified class. You must decide whether the container will hold instances of the class, pointers to the instances, or references to the instances.

Storing in a vector

Listing 6-1 is an example of a container class. This particular container is a datatype called a vector, and it works much like an array.

Listing 6-1:   Using Vectors as Examples of Container Classes

```
#include <iostream>
#include <vector>

using namespace std;

int main()
{
    vector<string> names;

    names.push_back("Tom");
    names.push_back("Dick");
    names.push_back("Harry");
    names.push_back("April");
    names.push_back("May");
    names.push_back("June");

    cout << names[0] << endl;
    cout << names[5] << endl;

    return 0;
}
```

Now, note how we used `vector`. First, it's a template! That means it's going to have a template parameter! And what is the template parameter? Why, you guessed it. (Or you looked at the code.) The template parameter is the type that the template will hold. Thus, the following declares a `vector` that holds strings:

```
vector<string> names;
```

Note also the header files that we included. Among them, we included `<vector>` (with no `.h` after the filename). In general, you include the header file that matches the name of the container you are using. Thus, if there were such a thing as a container called `rimbucklebock`, you would type `#include <rimbucklebock>`. Or, if there were such thing as a container called `set` (which there is), you would type `#include <set>`.

At this point, you may be wondering, what's the advantage to using a `vector` instead of a regular, plain old, no-frills array? The advantage is that, when you declare the `vector` instance, you don't need to know up front how many items will be going in it. With an array, you need to know the size when you declare it.

A `vector` is the closest thing the Standard Library has to an array. In fact, a `vector` is very much like an array, except (being a class template) you get all the goodies that go with a class, such as member functions that operate on `vector`.

Here are some things you can do with `vector`:

✦ Add items to the end of it

✦ Access its members by using bracket notation

✦ Iterate through it, either from beginning to end or from end back to beginning

Listing 6-2 is another example of a `vector`. In this one, we set up several `vector`s, and you can see that each one holds a different type, which we specified in the template parameter.

**Book IV
Chapter 6**

Programming with the Standard Library

Listing 6-2:   Containing the Type You Specify in Classes

```
#include <iostream>
#include <vector>

using namespace std;

class Employee
{
public:
    string Name;
    string FireDate;
    int GoofoffDays;
```

(continued)

Listing 6-2 *(continued)*

```
        Employee(string aname, string afiredate,
            int agoofdays) : Name(aname), FireDate(afiredate),
            GoofoffDays(agoofdays) {}
};

int main()
{
    // A vector that holds strings
    vector<string> MyAliases;
    MyAliases.push_back(string("Bud The Sailor"));
    MyAliases.push_back(string("Rick Fixit"));
    MyAliases.push_back(string("Bobalou Billow"));
    cout << MyAliases[0] << endl;
    cout << MyAliases[1] << endl;
    cout << MyAliases[2] << endl;

    // A vector that holds integers
    vector<int> LuckyNumbers;
    LuckyNumbers.push_back(13);
    LuckyNumbers.push_back(26);
    LuckyNumbers.push_back(52);
    cout << LuckyNumbers[0] << endl;
    cout << LuckyNumbers[1] << endl;
    cout << LuckyNumbers[2] << endl;

    // A vector that holds Employee instances
    vector<Employee> GreatWorkers;
    GreatWorkers.push_back(Employee("George Washington","123100", 50));
    GreatWorkers.push_back(Employee("Thomas Jefferson","052002", 40));
    cout << GreatWorkers[0].Name << endl;
    cout << GreatWorkers[1].Name << endl;

    return 0;
}
```

After you compile and run this program, you see the following output from the cout statements:

```
Bud The Sailor
Rick Fixit
Bobalou Billow
13
26
52
George Washington
Thomas Jefferson
```

Mapping your data

Listing 6-3 is an example of a type of container called map. map works much like vector, except for one main difference: Whereas you look up items in vector by putting a number inside brackets as in this

```
cout << names[0] << endl;
```

with map, you can use any class or type you want for the index, not just numbers. This feature lets you associate objects. Take a gander at Listing 6-3 to see where we're coming from.

Listing 6-3: Associating Objects with map

```
#include <iostream>
#include <map>

using namespace std;

int main()
{
    map<string, string> marriages;

    marriages["Tom"] = "Suzy";
    marriages["Harry"] = "Harriet";

    cout << marriages["Tom"] << endl;
    cout << marriages["Harry"] << endl;

    return 0;
}
```

First, you can see that to use map, we declare a variable of class map, supplying to the template the types of first the keys and then the values:

```
map<string, string> marriages;
```

Then we store something in map by putting a key inside brackets and setting it equal to a value:

```
marriages["Tom"] = "Suzy";
```

And to retrieve that particular item, we grab it based on the key:

```
cout << marriages["Tom"] << endl;
```

And voilà! We get back the item stored in map for that particular key. Think of map like an array, except the indices, which are called *keys,* can be any object, not just a string.

Even though the keys can be any type or class, you must specify the type or class you're using when you set up map. And after you do that, you can use only that type for the particular map. Thus, if you say the keys will be strings, you cannot then use an integer for a key, as in marriages[3] = "Suzy";.

Containing instances, pointers, or references

One of the most common discussions you encounter when people start talking about how to use the container templates is whether to put instances in the containers, pointers, or references. For example, which of these should you type:

```
vector<MyClass>
vector<MyClass *>
vector<MyClass &>
```

In other words, do you want your container to store the actual instance (whatever that might mean), a reference to the actual instance, or a pointer to the instance?

To explore this idea, have a look at Listing 6-4. Here, we're trying out the different ways of storing things in map: instances, pointers, and references.

Listing 6-4:   Making Decisions: Oh, What to Store?

```
#include <iostream>
#include <map>

using namespace std;

class StoreMe
{
public:
    int Item;
};

bool operator < (const StoreMe & first,
const StoreMe & second)
{
    return first.Item < second.Item;
}

int main()
{
    // First try storing the instances
    map<StoreMe, StoreMe> instances;

    StoreMe key1 = {10}; // braces notation!
    StoreMe value1 = {20};
    StoreMe key2 = {30};
    StoreMe value2 = {40};

    instances[key1] = value1;
    instances[key2] = value2;
    value1.Item = 12345;
    cout << instances[key1].Item << endl;

    instances[key1].Item = 34567;
    cout << instances[key1].Item << endl;

    // Next try storing pointers to the instances
    map<StoreMe*, StoreMe*> pointers;

    StoreMe key10 = {10};
    StoreMe value10 = {20};
    StoreMe key11 = {30};
    StoreMe value11 = {40};

    pointers[&key10] = &value10;
    pointers[&key11] = &value11;
    value10.Item = 12345;
    cout << (*pointers[&key10]).Item << endl;
```

```
    // Finally try storing references to the instances.
    // (I commented it out because it will
    // get an error. See the text!)
    // map<StoreMe&, StoreMe&> pointers;
    return 0;
}
```

First, note that to create the instances of `StoreMe`, we used the braces notation. You can do that when you have no constructors. So the line

```
StoreMe key1 = {10};
```

creates an instance of `StoreMe` and puts `10` in the `Item` member variable.

Also note that we commented out the single line

```
// map<StoreMe&, StoreMe&> pointers;
```

This is where we attempt to declare a `map` that holds references. But the line gets a compiler error. When you type this listing, you can try uncommenting the commented line and see the error message. We get several error messages as a result of this line, the main one was

```
error: conflicting declaration 'std::map<StoreMe&, StoreMe&,
std::less<StoreMe&>, std::allocator<std::pair<StoreMe&, StoreMe&> > > pointers'
```

Apparently references are out of the question. But why is that?

Here's why: It turns out `map` is making a copy of everything you put in it. How do we know this? By the output. Here's what you see when you type this program (and recomment out the line that you uncommented out so that it's a recommented-decommented line).

```
20
34567
12345
```

Aha! Tricky. Tricky indeed! But now we need to determine what this output means. For the first line, we stored a pair in `map` for `key1` and `value1`:

```
instances[key1] = value1;
```

And then we changed the `Item` member variable in `value1`:

```
value1.Item = 12345;
```

Next we retrieved the value from the pair in `map` and printed the `Item` member:

```
cout << instances[key1].Item << endl;
```

When we did, we saw 20, *not* 12345. That means the value stored in map is a copy, not the original. We changed the Item member of the original to 12345, but the copy still had the previous value of 20.

But then, we did this:

```
instances[key1].Item = 34567;
```

The hope here was that this action would change the Item member of the value stored in map. And so we printed the value again:

```
cout << instances[key1].Item << endl;
```

And this time it *did* indeed change. We saw 34567. Excellent! Where there's a will, there's a way, and where there's a value, there's a change. (Or something like that.)

And now that we've figured out that map is storing copies of what we put in it, the idea of storing a pointer should be pretty clear: If we have a pointer variable and then we make a copy of it, although we have a separate pointer variable now, the original and the copy both point to the same thing. And that's the idea behind the second part of Listing 6-4. We created map like this:

```
map<StoreMe*, StoreMe*> pointers;
```

Now this map stores pointer variables. Remember that a pointer variable just holds a number that represents an address. If two separate pointer variables hold the same number, it means they point to the same thing. Furthermore, because this map is holding pointers, *really* it's holding numbers, not instances — something to think about.

And so we next set up some instances and then made one association:

```
pointers[&key10] = &value10;
```

Note the ampersand (&) — we're storing the addresses in map. Then we changed the Item member of one the value objects:

```
value10.Item = 12345;
```

And this time, when we printed it by using this carefully parenthesized line

```
cout << (*pointers[&key10]).Item << endl;
```

We see this

```
12345
```

And once again . . . aha! This time the change stuck. Why is that? Because even though map holds a copy, it's holding a copy of a pointer. And that pointer happens to point to the original value10 object. So when we changed the Item member of value10, map picked up the change. map itself didn't change, but map is pointing to that value.

From all this discussion about the containers holding copies, you can come to the following conclusion. Because map holds copies, you can remember these two rules about deleting your original objects:

✦ **The container holds instances:** If you're putting instances in map, you can delete the original instances after they're in map. This is okay because map has its own copies of the instances.

✦ **The container holds pointers:** If you're putting pointers in map, you don't want to delete the original instances because the pointers in map still point to these instances.

So which method is best? It's up to you. But here are a couple of things to consider:

✦ **Keeping instances around:** If you don't want to keep instances lying around, you can put the instances in the container, and it will make copies.

✦ **Copyability:** Are your classes copyable? Some classes, such as classes filled with pointers to other classes or classes that are enormous, don't copy well. In that case, you may want to put pointers in the container.

Comparing instances

When you work with classes that contain other classes (such as vector), you need to provide the class with a way to compare two things. For us humans, having the superbrains that we do, comparing is easy. But it's not that easy for a computer. For example, suppose you have two pointers to string objects. The first points to a string containing abc. The second points to another string containing abc. Are these two pointers the same?

Well, that depends on how you look at it. If you mean do they point to the same sequence of characters, then, yes, they are the same. But if you mean do they point to the same object, then maybe or maybe not. Look at this code:

```
string *pointer1 = new string("abc");
string *pointer2 = new string("abc");
```

Are pointer1 and pointer2 *equal?* Again, it depends on how you look at it. If you mean do they point to strings that are equivalent, then, yes, they are equal in that sense. If you mean do they point to the same object, then, no, they are *not* equal in that sense. Now look at this code:

Book IV
Chapter 6

Programming with the Standard Library

```
string *pointer3 = new string("abc");
string *pointer4 = pointer3;
```

These two pointers point to the same object. So in that sense, they are equal. And because they point to the same object, they also point to the same string of characters. So, again, in that sense, they are equal.

As you can see, you have two kinds of comparisons when dealing with objects:

 ✦ You are comparing two objects and determining whether they are identical, even though they're separate objects. If the two objects are separate but identical, you would say that they are equal.

 ✦ You are comparing two objects and determining if they are the same object. This can happen if you have two pointers and they both point to the same object. In that case, you say that they are equal.

So why do you need to know this besides to drive people batty? ("You say your car and our cars are the same, but in fact, they are different: One is yours, and the others are ours!") You need to know this distinction because when you create a container class that holds instances of your object, often the class needs to know how to compare objects. This is particularly true in the case of map, which holds pairs of items, and you locate the items based on the first of the pair (called the *key*). When you tell map to find an item based on a key, map must search through its list of pairs until it finds one such that the key in the pair is equal to the one you passed in to the search.

Well, that's all fine and dandy; but now, how can the computer know whether two objects are identical? That is, suppose that you are doing your comparison based on whether two separate objects are identical. How does the computer compare the two objects to determine if they are, in fact, identical?

And because we like to get people thinking, how about this: What if you have a list of objects, and you want to keep them in a sorted order? How does the computer determine a sort order?

Here's an example. We create a class called Employee. That's a standard example that you see in lots of books, but in this case it makes for a good example, for once. Now our Employee class contains these member variables: FirstName, LastName, and SocialSecurityNumber.

Next, we have a Salary class that contains payroll information for an employee. This class has member variables MonthlySalary and Deductions. (Yes, in real life, you would probably have more member variables, but this is good enough for now.)

Next, we have a map instance, where each *key,value* pair contains an Employee instance for the key and a Salary instance for the value. So the big question is this: If we want to look up an employee, we would make an instance of Employee and fill in the FirstName, LastName, and SocialSecurityNumber member variables. We would then retrieve the value based on this key. But we can think of two issues here:

✦ We would create an instance and allow map to find the key that matches the instance. Is map looking for the exact same instance or one identical to it?

✦ If map is looking for an instance identical to the object we filled in, what happens if the employee changed his or her name (such as during a marriage). Can you cause map to still find the right key if map has one name and the search object has another? Most likely. In such cases, you would want the value to match only based on the SocialSecurityNumber, without worrying about the others. So in that case, can you tell map to treat the two objects as *identical*?

Here's how to resolve these two issues: If you're dealing with your own classes, in addition to setting up a container class, you also provide a function that compares two instances of your own class. Your comparison function can determine whether two classes are equal, if the first is *less than* the second, or if the first is *greater than* the second.

At first, how *less than* and *greater than* can apply to things like an Employee class may not seem apparent. But the idea behind *less than* and *greater than* is to give the container class a way to determine a sort order. If you have a list class holding Employee instances, for example, and you tell the list to keep them in a sorted order, how does the list know how to sort them? By using the notion of *less than* and *greater than*. The list can determine if one is greater than another and can group them in a sorted order. But if you're dealing with an Employee class, *you* would choose how to sort them: Should an Employee instance with a social security number of 111-11-1111 be less than 999-99-9999? Or should they be sorted based on name, so that the person with social security number 111-11-1111 but the name Zoë Zusseldörf come after the person with social security number 999-99-9999 but the name Aaron Aackman? Well, the answer is this: It's your decision. And after you decide how you want them sorted, you would create a function that determines if one is less than, equal to, or greater than the other. If you want the list to sort by name, you would make your function look strictly at the names. (And will it look at last name, first name, or both? That's your decision.) But if you want your list to sort by social security number, you would write your function to compare the social security numbers.

Listing 6-5 shows an example of a map class, along with a comparison function that determines whether two keys are equal.

Book IV
Chapter 6

Programming with
the Standard Library

Listing 6-5:   Containing Instances and Needing Functions That Compare Them

```
#include <iostream>
#include <map>

using namespace std;

class Employee
{
public:
    string Nickname;
    string SocialSecurityNumber;

    Employee(string anickname, string asocial) :
        Nickname(anickname),
        SocialSecurityNumber(asocial) {}

    Employee() : Nickname(""), SocialSecurityNumber("") {}
};

class Salary
{
public:
    int AnnualRipoff;
    int IRSDeductionsCheat;

    Salary(int aannual, int adeductions) :
        AnnualRipoff(aannual),
        IRSDeductionsCheat(adeductions) {}

    Salary() : AnnualRipoff(0), IRSDeductionsCheat(0) {}
};

bool operator < (const Employee& first, const Employee& second)
{
    return first.Nickname < second.Nickname;
}

int main()
{
    map<Employee, Salary> employees;

    Employee emp1("sparky", "123-22-8572");
    Salary sal1(135000, 18);
    employees[emp1] = sal1;

    Employee emp2("buzz", "234-33-5784");
    Salary sal2(150000, 23);
    employees[emp2] = sal2;

    // Now test it out!
    Employee emptest("sparky", "");
    cout << employees[emptest].AnnualRipoff << endl;

    return 0;
}
```

When you run this program, you will see the AnnualRipoff member of the Salary value, where the key is an Employee with the name sparky:

```
135000
```

Now notice a couple things about this code. First, to locate the salary for Sparky, we didn't need the `Employee` instance for Sparky. Instead, we created an instance of `Employee` and set up the `Nickname` member without worrying about the `SocialSecurityNumber` member. Then we retrieved the value by using the bracket notation for `map`:

```
cout << employees[emptest].AnnualRipoff << endl;
```

Now why did this work? Because the `map` code uses our less-than function that we provided. And in that function, we compared only the `Nickname` members, not the `SocialSecurityNumber` member. We could, however, change things around a bit. Instead of comparing the `Nickname` members, we could compare the `SocialSecurityNumber` members. We could change the less-than function like so:

```
bool operator < (const Employee& first,
const Employee& second)
{
    return first.SocialSecurityNumber <
        second.SocialSecurityNumber;
}
```

And then we can locate Sparky's salary based on his social security number:

```
Employee emptest("", "123-22-8572");
cout << employees[emptest].AnnualRipoff << endl;
```

Wait! This can't be right! How can the computer locate the item with the matching key if all you're giving it is a less-than comparison? Good question. Here's how: Suppose you want to find out if two numbers, say 5 and 5, are equal. (We know, they are equal, but bear with us.) But suppose the only comparison you have available is *less-than*. How can you determine if they are equal? You first see if the first is less than the second: Is 5 less than 5? Nope. Then you see if the second is less than the first: Is the second 5 less than the first 5? Nope. And because neither is less than the other, they must be equal! Aha! And that's how the code for the various containers matches objects: It calls your less-than function twice, the second time flip-flopping the order of the parameters; and if your function returns false both times, the computer determines that they are equal. That approach makes life easier because you need to provide only a single comparison function! Yay!

Iterating through a container

When your house is full of things, sometimes being able to climb over it all so you can look down on it and see what all is there is nice. Containers in the Standard Library are the same way: If you have a container filled with things, being able to climb through it would be nice.

To climb through a container, you use an iterator. And *iterator* works with a container to let you step one-by-one through the container, seeing what all is in it.

Each container class contains an embedded type called `iterator`. To create an iterator instance, then, you need to use the fully qualified name. For example, if you have a `map` that holds integers and strings as in `map<int, string>`, you would create an `iterator` instance like this:

```
map<string, int>::iterator loopy
```

Although `loopy` is an instance of `iterator`, some serious `typedef`ing is going on, and, in fact, `loopy` is a pointer to an item stored inside the container.

Less<MyClass> is more

When we create a class that we will be using in a container, we prefer to write our own overloaded less-than function. The containers in the Standard Library work as follows: When you create a class based on a container template, you provide the types that the container holds, and you also provide a class (or `struct`) that includes a *less-than* member function. However, this class doesn't have a function called <. Instead, it's called `()`, and it takes two parameters, one for each of the two items you're comparing. The container class then calls this function to compare instances.

Well that's all great, but why haven't we seen this in action? The reason is the containers have *default template parameters*. If you don't supply this magical less-than class, the container supplies one *for you*. What does it supply? It supplies a class based on a template called `less`. This template is simple; it includes a single member function that returns the Boolean value

```
x < y
```

For most basic types, that's fine. The compiler can easily use that if, for example, you're working with integers. But what if you're working with one of your own classes? The compiler doesn't understand the < operator unless you provide your own < operator function, as we did everywhere else in this chapter. However, because the container takes a class in its parameter that defaults to the class `less`, you can put together your own class and use that instead of writing your own < operator function. Here's a sample:

```
class MyLess
{
public:
    bool operator()(const MyClass &x,
    const MyClass &y) const
    {
        return x.Name < y.Name;
    }
};
```

Then when you create, for example, a `map`, you would pass this class as a third parameter, rather than relying on the default:

```
map<MyClass, MyClass, MyLess> mymap;
```

And, of course, then you don't need your own *less-than* function.

Now, you want to initialize `loopy` to point to the first item in the container. And you can do this by calling the container's `begin` member function and storing the results in `loopy`. Then `loopy` will point to the first item in the container. You can access the item by dereferencing `loopy`; then when you're finished, you can move to the next item by incrementing `loopy` like this:

```
loopy++;
```

That's pretty easy. And you can tell whether you're finished by checking to see whether `loopy` points to the end of the items. To do this, you call the container's `end` member function and compare `loopy` to the results of `end`. If it's equal, you're done.

The following few lines of code do these steps:

```
vector<string>::iterator vectorloop = Words.begin();

while (vectorloop != Words.end())
{
    cout << *vectorloop << endl;
    vectorloop++;
}
```

You can see the type we used for the iterator, in this case called `vector-loop`. And you can see that we initialized it by calling `begin`. We dereferenced it to get to the data itself, and then incremented `vectorloop` to get to the next item. And in the `while` loop we tested `vectorloop` against the results of `end` to see if we're all done.

Many people seem to forget how to use iterators. We suggest keeping the code in Listing 6-6 handy somewhere. (Print it and hang it on the wall, or save a copy in a directory on your hard drive where you can find it quickly, or maybe print it on really big paper and paste it to the front windshield of your car.) Then if you forget how to put together a simple iterator, you can easily find the answer.

Listing 6-6:   Iterating

```
#include <iostream>
#include <map>
#include <vector>

using namespace std;

int main()
{
    // Iterating through a map
    map<string, int> NumberWords;

    NumberWords["ten"] = 10;
    NumberWords["twenty"] = 20;
    NumberWords["thirty"] = 30;

    map<string, int>::iterator loopy = NumberWords.begin();
```

(continued)

Listing 6-6 *(continued)*

```
while (loopy != NumberWords.end())
{
    cout << loopy->first << " ";
    cout << loopy->second << endl;
    loopy++;
}

// Iterating through a vector
vector<string> Words;

Words.push_back("hello");
Words.push_back("there");
Words.push_back("ladies");
Words.push_back("and");
Words.push_back("aliens");

vector<string>::iterator vectorloop = Words.begin();

while (vectorloop != Words.end())
{
    cout << *vectorloop << endl;
    vectorloop++;
}

return 0;
}
```

When you create a `vector`, it allocates some space for the data you put in it. But after all that space gets filled up and `vector` is stuffed to the brim, `vector` will resize itself, adding more space. But in doing so, it uses the old memory-shuffle trick where it first allocates a bigger chunk of memory; then it copies the existing data into the beginning of that bigger chunk of memory, and finally it frees the original chunk of memory. Now if you use the various iterator functions to home in on a certain item in `vector` (giving you a pointer to the item) and you save that pointer, then after `vector` reallocates itself, that pointer will no longer be valid! It will point to somewhere in the original memory block that's no longer being used. So be careful.

For example, suppose you have the following code to set up a `vector`

```
vector<int> test;
test.push_back(1);
test.push_back(2);
test.push_back(3);
```

and then you use an iterator to get to the beginning; from there you go to the second item in `vector`; then you print the address of the second item:

```
vector<int>::iterator i1 = test.begin();
i1++;
cout << i1 << endl;
```

Then you decide to add a whole bunch of items:

```
for (int loop = 0; loop < 5000; loop++)
{
    test.push_back(loop);
}
```

And now, if you once again use an iterator to get to the second item and then print the address like so

```
vector<int>::iterator i2 = test.begin();
i2++;
cout << i2 << endl;
```

you will likely see a different number than you previously did. If so, it means `vector` reallocated itself, and that means the original pointer is no longer valid.

A map of pairs in your hand

When you iterate through `map`, you get back not just the value of each item nor the key of each item. Instead, you get back a pair of things — the key and the value together. These live inside an instance of a class called `Pair`. (Although, really, it's a template.) This pair instance has two member variables, `first` and `second`. The first member refers to the key in the pair, and the second member refers to the value in the pair. When you iterate through `map`, the iterator points to an instance of `Pair`, so you can grab the key by looking at `first` and the value by looking at `second`. But be careful, because `Pair` is the internal storage bin inside `map`. You're not looking at copies; you're looking at the actual data in `map`. If you change the data as in this

```
while (loopy != NumberWords.end())
{
    loopy->second = loopy->second * 2;
    loopy++;
}
```

you will be changing the value stored in `map` — not a copy of it. So use caution!

The Great Container Showdown

In the sections that follow, we give a rundown of the containers available in the Standard Library. Different containers have different places in life. Some are tall, some are short — wait a minute, that's not right. They each have a different purpose, and in the following sections we show you where you can use each of them.

Associating and storing with a set

First things first. `set` is not a *set*. If you have any background in mathematics, you've likely come across the notion of a set. And in math, a set doesn't have an order to it. It's a group of items stored in, well, a set.

In the Standard Library, `set` has an order to it. However, like a math set, `set` doesn't allow duplicates. If you try to put an item in `set` that's already there, `set` will ignore your attempt to do so.

Listing 6-7 shows you how to use `set`.

Listing 6-7:   Using set to Look up Items

```
#include <iostream>
#include <set>

using namespace std;

class Employee
{
public:
    string Nickname;
    string SocialSecurityNumber;

    Employee(string anickname, string asocial) :
        Nickname(anickname),
        SocialSecurityNumber(asocial) {}

    Employee() : Nickname(""), SocialSecurityNumber("") {}
};

bool operator < (const Employee& first,
const Employee& second)
{
    return first.SocialSecurityNumber <
        second.SocialSecurityNumber;
}

ostream& operator << (ostream &out, const Employee &emp)
{
    cout << "(" << emp.Nickname;
    cout << "," << emp.SocialSecurityNumber;
    cout << ")";
    return out;
}

int main()
{
    set<Employee> employees;

    Employee emp1("sparky", "123-22-8572");
    employees.insert(emp1);

    Employee emp2("buzz", "234-33-5784");
    employees.insert(emp2);
```

```
Employee emp3("coollie", "123-22-8572");
employees.insert(emp3);

Employee emp4("sputz", "199-19-0000");
employees.insert(emp4);

// List the items
set<Employee>::iterator iter = employees.begin();
while (iter != employees.end())
{
    cout << *iter << endl;
    iter++;
}

// Find an item
cout << "Finding..." << endl;
Employee findemp("", "123-22-8572");

iter = employees.find(findemp);
cout << *iter << endl;

return 0;
}
```

In Listing 6-7, we included an `Employee` class, along with a less-than function. The less-than function compares the `SocialSecurityNumber` member of two `Employee` instances. This results in two things:

+ Ordering: The items in `set` will be ordered according to social security number. This is not true with all containers, but it is the way a `set` works.

+ Duplicates: If we try to add two employees with matching `SocialSecurityNumber` members (but the other members can be different), the second addition won't take. The `set` will ignore it.

You can see in this listing that we tried to add two employees with the same `SocialSecurityNumber` members:

```
Employee emp1("sparky", "123-22-8572");
employees.insert(emp1);
```

and

```
Employee emp3("coollie", "123-22-8572");
employees.insert(emp3);
```

Later, when we print all the items in `set`, we see only the one for `"sparky"`, not the one for `"coollie"`. `set` ignored the second employee.

Finding an item in `set` is interesting. Look at how we did it: We created an instance of `Employee`, and we filled in only the `SocialSecurityNumber` member, because that's the only member that the less-than function looks at. Then we called `find`. But what did we get back? If you look at the function header, you will see that the `find` function returns an iterator. But that seems silly. Why an iterator? We're not iterating, by cracky!

The reason we get back an iterator is because the `iterator` type is really a `typedef` for a pointer to an item inside `set`. Oh, okay; that makes sense then: When we call `find`, we get back a pointer to an item in `set`, even if its typename is `iterator`. And so to access the item, we dereference the pointer.

In Listing 6-7, we did something handy: We created a function that lets us use our `Employee` instance with `cout`. We did this by overloading the insertion function. This function's header looks like this:

```
ostream& operator << (ostream &out, const Employee &emp) {
```

The first parameter represents `cout`, and the second is the item we're `cout`ing. And so, inside this function, we write to `cout` the individual members of the `Employee`. Not a problem.

Unionizing and intersecting sets

Everybody has an opinion on unionizing, but fortunately, we're not talking about workers' unions in this section. Instead, we're talking about sets and how you can combine two sets to get the union, or you can find the common elements to get the intersection.

When you `#include <set>`, you automatically get a couple of handy functions for finding the union and intersection of some sets.

Showdown: maps versus sets

And for the first showdown, we'd like to offer you a philosophical (yet practical!) discussion on the difference between `map` and `set`. `map` lets you store information based on a key, through which you can retrieve a value. Elsewhere in this chapter, we use an example where the key is an `Employee` instance and the value is a `Salary` instance. But with `set`, you can achieve something similar: In Listing 6-7, we could have had a single class containing both `Employee` and `Salary` information. And you can see in Listing 6-7 that we were able to look up the `Employee` instance based on nothing but a social security number. So in this sense, we created a `map` where the key is a social security number and the value is the rest of the employee information. Tricky, no? The fact is, you can often accomplish associations with `set`, as you can with `map`. But the advantage to `set` is that you need to store only one instance for each item, whereas with `map`, you must have two instances, both a key and a value. But the advantage to `map` is that you can use the nice bracket notation. The choice is yours.

set does not allow duplicates. A union of two sets is a set that consists of all the elements of the two sets combined, but without any duplicates. The intersection is also itself a set, and therefore it has no duplicates.

Listing 6-8 shows how you can find the intersection and union of two sets.

Listing 6-8:   Finding an Intersection and a Union Is Easy!

```
#include <iostream>
#include <set>

using namespace std;

void DumpClass(set<string> *myset)
{
    set<string>::iterator iter = myset->begin();

    while (iter != myset->end())
    {
        cout << *iter << endl;
        iter++;
    }
}

int main()
{
    set<string> EnglishClass;
    set<string> HistoryClass;

    EnglishClass.insert("Zeus");
    EnglishClass.insert("Magellan");
    EnglishClass.insert("Vulcan");
    EnglishClass.insert("Ulysses");
    EnglishClass.insert("Columbus");

    HistoryClass.insert("Vulcan");
    HistoryClass.insert("Ulysses");
    HistoryClass.insert("Ra");
    HistoryClass.insert("Odin");

    set<string> Union;
    set<string> Intersection;

    insert_iterator<set<string> >
        IntersectIterate(Intersection, Intersection.begin());

    insert_iterator<set<string> >
        UnionIterate(Union, Union.begin());

    set_intersection(EnglishClass.begin(),
        EnglishClass.end(),
        HistoryClass.begin(), HistoryClass.end(),
        IntersectIterate);
    cout << "===Intersection===" << endl;
    DumpClass(&Intersection);

    set_union(EnglishClass.begin(),
        EnglishClass.end(),
        HistoryClass.begin(), HistoryClass.end(),
```

Listing 6-8 *(continued)*

```
        UnionIterate);
    cout << endl << "===Union===" << endl;
    DumpClass(&Union);

    return 0;
}
```

When you run the code in Listing 6-8, you see this output:

```
===Intersection===
Ulysses
Vulcan

===Union===
Columbus
Magellan
Odin
Ra
Ulysses
Vulcan
Zeus
```

But as you can see, something a little bizarre is in the code. Specifically, this part isn't exactly simple:

```
insert_iterator<set<string> >
    IntersectIterate(Intersection, Intersection.begin());
```

This is used in the call to set_intersection. First, recognize that this crazy code is a variable declaration. The first line is the type of the variable, a template called insert_iterator. The template parameter is the type of set, in this case set<string>.

The next line is the instance name, IntersectIterate, and the constructor requires two things: the set that will hold the intersection (called Intersection) and an iterator pointing to the beginning of the Intersection set (even though set is empty).

The variable that these two lines create is an iterator, and it is basically a helper object through which some function that needs to insert multiple items into a list can use. In this case, the function is set_intersection. Now the set_intersection function doesn't take as parameters the sets directly; instead, it takes the beginning and ending iterators of the two sets, along with the IntsersectIterate thingamabob declared earlier. And you can see in Listing 6-8 that those are the five items we passed to the set_intersection function.

Then after calling the set_intersection function, the Intersection object will contain the intersection of the two sets.

The set_union function works precisely the same way, except it figures out the union of the two sets, not the intersection.

To use the `set_intersection` and `set_union` functions, you need to `#include <algorithm>`. This is one of the header files in the Standard C++ Library.

If you find the code in Listing 6-8 particularly ugly, a slightly easier way to call `set_intersection` where you don't need to directly create an instance of `insert_iterator` is available. It turns out there's a function that will do it for you. To use this function, you can remove the declaration for `IntersectIterate` and `UnionIterate`, and then instead call `set_intersection` like this:

```
set_intersection(EnglishClass.begin(),
    EnglishClass.end(),
    HistoryClass.begin(), HistoryClass.end(),
    inserter(Intersection, Intersection.begin()));
```

The fourth line simply calls a function called `inserter`, which creates an instance of `insert_iterator` for you. Then you can do the same for `set_union`:

```
set_union(EnglishClass.begin(),
    EnglishClass.end(),
    HistoryClass.begin(), HistoryClass.end(),
    inserter(Union, Union.begin()));
```

Listing with list

A `list` is a simple container similar to an array, except you can't access the members of `list` by using a bracket notation as you can in `vector` or an array. You don't use `list` when you don't need access to only one item in the list; you use it when you plan to *traverse* through the list, item-by-item.

To add items to a list, use the list's `push_front` member function or its `push_back` member function. The `push_front` function inserts the item in the beginning of the list, in front of all the others that are presently in the list. If you use `push_front` several times in a row, the items will be in the reverse order from which you put them in. The `push_back` function adds the item to the end of the list. So if you put items in a list by using `push_back`, their order will be the same as the order in which you added them.

You can also insert an item before an existing item if you have a pointer to the item inside the list.

For operations where you need a pointer to an item in the list, you need to use an iterator. An *iterator* is simply a `typedef` for a pointer to an item in the list; however, it points to the item *in* the list, not the original item you added to the list. Remember, the containers hold copies. Thus, if you do an `insert` into a list and point to an original item, that item won't be a member of the list, and the `insert` won't work.

Although the `list` template includes an `insert` function, this function has only very special uses. To use `insert`, you must have a pointer to an item in the list — that is, you need to have an iterator. But how do you get this pointer? By traversing the list. It has no `find` function, and so really the only time you would use the `insert` function is if you're already working your way through the list. But if you do need to do an insert and you're willing to use iterators to move through the list to find the location where you want to put the new item, `insert` will do the job.

In Listing 6-9, we demonstrate lists by using a duck metaphor. (They're all in a row.) In this example, we create a list, add our ducks to it, and then reverse it. Next, we create a second list and *splice* its members into the first list.

Listing 6-9: Handling Items in a List Template

```
#include <iostream>
#include <list>

using namespace std;

class Duck
{
public:
    string name;
    int weight;
    int length;
};

ostream& operator << (ostream &out, const Duck &duck)
{
    cout << "(" << duck.name;
    cout << "," << duck.weight;
    cout << "," << duck.length;
    cout << ")";
    return out;
}

void DumpDucks(list<Duck> *mylist)
{
    list<Duck>::iterator iter = mylist->begin();

    while (iter != mylist->end())
    {
        cout << *iter << endl;
        iter++;
    }
}

list<Duck>::iterator MoveToPosition(list<Duck> *mylist, int pos)
{
    list<Duck>::iterator res = mylist->begin();

    for (int loop = 1; loop <= pos; loop++)
    {
        res++;
    }
```

```
    return res;
}

int main()
{
    list<Duck> Inarow;

    // Push some at the beginning
    Duck d1 = {"Jim", 20, 15}; // Braces notation!
    Inarow.push_front(d1);

    Duck d2 = {"Sally", 15, 12};
    Inarow.push_front(d2);

    // Push some at the end
    Duck d3 = {"Squakie", 18, 25};
    Inarow.push_front(d3);

    Duck d4 = {"Trumpeter", 19, 26};
    Inarow.push_front(d4);

    Duck d5 = {"Sneeky", 12, 13};
    Inarow.push_front(d5);

    // Display the ducks
    cout << "===========" << endl;
    DumpDucks(&Inarow);

    // Reverse
    Inarow.reverse();
    cout << "===========" << endl;
    DumpDucks(&Inarow);

    // Splice
    // Need another list for this
    list<Duck> extras;

    Duck d6 = {"Grumpy", 8, 8};
    extras.push_back(d6);

    Duck d7 = {"Sleepy", 8, 8};
    extras.push_back(d7);

    Duck d8 = {"Ornery", 8, 8};
    extras.push_back(d8);

    Duck d9 = {"Goofy", 8, 8};
    extras.push_back(d9);

    cout << "===========" << endl;
    cout << "extras:" << endl;
    DumpDucks(&extras);

    list<Duck>::iterator first =
        MoveToPosition(&extras, 1);

    list<Duck>::iterator last =
        MoveToPosition(&extras, 3);

    list<Duck>::iterator into =
        MoveToPosition(&Inarow, 2);

    Inarow.splice(into, extras, first, last);
```

**Book IV
Chapter 6**

Programming with
the Standard Library

(continued)

Listing 6-9 *(continued)*

```
        cout << "===========" << endl;
        cout << "extras after splice:" << endl;
        DumpDucks(&extras);

        cout << "===========" << endl;
        cout << "Inarow after splice:" << endl;
        DumpDucks(&Inarow);

        return 0;
}
```

We made a function, `MoveToPosition`, that moves to a position in the list. This may seem counterproductive because the `list` template doesn't allow random access. But we needed three iterators to perform the splice: The start and end position of the second list (the one we're splicing members from) and the position in the first list where we want to put the spliced members. For that, we needed an iterator, which `MoveToPosition` finds for us.

The function we created, `MoveToPosition`, is a template function. But when we called the function, we didn't provide the typename in angle brackets. The compiler can figure out which class version we need; the compiler knows that it can look at what we pass into the function as a parameter and use its type to decide the template parameter. (Without the template type in the function parameter, the compiler can't figure it out.) Here's the program output:

```
===========
(Sneeky,12,13)
(Trumpeter,19,26)
(Squakie,18,25)
(Sally,15,12)
(Jim,20,15)
===========
(Jim,20,15)
(Sally,15,12)
(Squakie,18,25)
(Trumpeter,19,26)
(Sneeky,12,13)
===========
extras:
(Grumpy,8,8)
(Sleepy,8,8)
(Ornery,8,8)
(Goofy,8,8)
===========
extras after splice:
(Grumpy,8,8)
(Goofy,8,8)
===========
Inarow after splice:
(Jim,20,15)
(Sally,15,12)
(Sleepy,8,8)
(Ornery,8,8)
(Squakie,18,25)
(Trumpeter,19,26)
(Sneeky,12,13)
```

Showdown: lists versus vectors

With a list, you do not have *random access* to the list, which is a fancy-schmancy way of saying that you can't drop into the middle of the list and look at whatever item is stored there as you can with a vector. If you want to look at the items in the list, you must either start at the beginning or the end and work your way through it one by one. But with a vector, you can refer to any element by using brackets, as in `MyVector[3}`. This may seem like a disadvantage for the list, but the ANSI document claims that "many algorithms only need sequential access anyway." We suppose that there are times when you don't need to drop into the middle of an array, and then a list might do. But lists have definite advantages. The list template allows you to splice together multiple lists, and it has good support for sorting the list, for splicing members out of one list and into another, and for merging multiple lists.

You can see the elements that were inside the two lists before and after the splice; the ducks moved from one list to another.

When you specify the positions for the splice operation, the splice includes the start position *up to but not including* the ending position. Listing 6-9 shows this: We spliced from position 1 to 3 in the second list (`extras`). But we got the ducks from positions 1 and 2 because the code spliced position 1 up to but not including 3 — which is 2.

Stacking the deque

A `deque` (pronounced "deck") container is a sequential list of items like `vector` and `list`. Like `vectors` and unlike `lists`, `deques` allow bracket notation for *random access*. Unlike `vector`, `deque` lets you insert items at the beginning and pop items off the beginning. To create a `deque` that holds integers, do something like this:

```
deque<int> mydek;
mydek.push_front(10);
mydek.push_front(20);
mydek.push_front(30);
mydek.push_back(40);
mydek.push_back(50);
mydek.push_back(60);
```

Then you can loop through the `deque`, accessing its members with a bracket, as if it's an array:

```
int loop;
for (loop = 0; loop < mydek.size(); loop++)
{
    cout << mydek[loop] << endl;
}
```

You can also grab items off the front or back of the deque. Here's an example from the front:

```
while (mydek.size() > 0)
{
    cout << mydek.front() << endl;
    mydek.pop_front();
}
```

Two functions show up here, front and pop_front. The front function returns a reference to the item at the front of the deque. The pop_front function removes the item that's at the front of the deque.

Waiting in line with stacks and queues

Two common programming data structures are in the Standard Library:

✦ **Stack:** With a stack, you put items one-by-one on top of it, and you only take items one-by-one off the top of it. You can add several items, one after the other, before taking an item off the top. This process is sometimes called a First In Last Out (FILO) algorithm.

✦ **Queue:** A queue is like waiting in line at the post office (and some people call such a line a queue). The line gets longer and longer as people arrive, and the new people each go to the back of the line. But people leave only by the front of the line. The queue data structure is like that: You add data at the back of the queue, and take data off one-by-one at the front of the queue. Like the stack, the queue also has an alternate name: it's a First In First Out (FIFO) algorithm.

To use the Standard Library to make a stack, you can use a deque, a list, or a vector as the underlying storage bin. Then you declare the stack, as in the following example:

```
stack<int, vector<int> > MyStack;
```

Or you can optionally use the default, which is queue:

```
stack<int> MyStack;
```

For a queue, you can't use vector because vectors don't include operations for dealing with a front. So, for that situation, you can use either deque or list. For example, here's a line of code that uses list:

```
queue<int, list<int> > MyQueue;
```

Or here's a line of code that uses deque by default:

```
queue<int> MyQueue;
```

Showdown: deques versus vectors

If you go online to any discussion board and use a search phrase like *C++ deque vector*, you will see a lot of discussion, arguments, and confusion between when to use deque and when to use vector. To know which to use when, you need to understand the differences between the two. Under the hood, vector usually stores all its data in a regular old array, making it easy to directly access the members. But that also means that, to insert items, vector must slide everything over to make room for the inserted items. deque, however, does not use the *contiguous* approach that vector does. Inserting is then easier for it because it doesn't need to shuffle things around. Also, deque doesn't have to *regrow* itself if it runs out of space, whereas vector does. And finally, deque includes a push_front member function that allows you to easily add an item at the beginning. The vector template does not include this member.

You normally perform three operations with a stack and a queue:

+ **push:** When you add an item to a stack or queue, you *push* the item. This puts the item on top of the stack or at the back of the queue.

+ **peek:** When you look at the top item of the stack or the front of the queue, you *peek*. The peek operation doesn't remove the item, however.

+ **pop:** When you remove an item from a stack or from the front of the queue, you pop it off. For some libraries, this gives you the item. For the Standard Library, it removes the item. To use an item off the top or front of the stack or queue, first you peek at it and then you pop it off.

In the Standard Library, for peeking at the front of a queue, you call the front member function. For a stack, you call the top member function.

For pushing and popping, the Standard Library uses these terms. The queue and stack each include a push function and a pop function. Listing 6-10 demonstrates both a stack and a queue.

Book IV
Chapter 6

Programming with
the Standard Library

Listing 6-10:   Creating a Stack and a Queue

```
#include <iostream>
#include <stack>
#include <queue>

using namespace std;

void StackDemo()
{
    cout << "===Stack Demo===" << endl;
    stack<int, vector<int> > MyStack;
```

(continued)

Listing 6-10 *(continued)*

```
    // Remember the space between the > >
    MyStack.push(5);
    MyStack.push(10);
    MyStack.push(15);
    MyStack.push(20);
    cout << MyStack.top() << endl;

    MyStack.pop();
    cout << MyStack.top() << endl;

    MyStack.pop();
    MyStack.push(40);
    cout << MyStack.top() << endl;

    MyStack.pop();
}

void QueueDemo()
{
    cout << "===Queue Demo===" << endl;
    queue<int> MyQueue;

    // No container specified in the queue, so it
    // uses deque by default. The same goes for stack.
    MyQueue.push(5);
    MyQueue.push(10);
    MyQueue.push(15);
    cout << MyQueue.front() << endl;

    MyQueue.pop();
    cout << MyQueue.front() << endl;

    MyQueue.pop();
    MyQueue.push(40);
    cout << MyQueue.front() << endl;

    MyQueue.pop();
}

int main()
{
    StackDemo();
    QueueDemo();
    return 0;
}
```

When you specify a container to use inside the stack or queue, remember to put a space between the closing angle brackets. Otherwise, the compiler reads it as a single insertion operator, >>, and gets confused.

Copying Containers

Structures are easy to copy when class libraries are well designed. The Standard C++ Library is that well designed. Each container class contains both a *copy constructor* and an *equal operator.* To copy a container, you either set one equal to the other or pass the first container into the constructor of the second (which copies the first into the second). Listing 6-11 shows this.

Listing 6-11:   Copying Containers Couldn't Be Easier

```cpp
#include <iostream>
#include <map>

using namespace std;

class Scrumptious
{
public:
    string Dessert;
};

bool operator < (const Scrumptious & first,
const Scrumptious & second)
{
    return first.Dessert < second.Dessert;
}

class Nutrition
{
public:
    int VitaminC;
    int Potassium;
};

int main()
{
    map<Scrumptious, Nutrition> ItsGoodForMe;

    Scrumptious ap = {"Apple Pie"}; // Braces notation!
    Nutrition apn = {7249, 9722};

    Scrumptious ic = {"Ice Cream"};
    Nutrition icn = {2459, 19754};

    Scrumptious cc = {"Chocolate Cake"};
    Nutrition ccn = {9653, 24905};

    Scrumptious ms = {"Milk Shake"};
    Nutrition msn = {46022, 5425};

    ItsGoodForMe[ap] = apn;
    ItsGoodForMe[ic] = icn;
```

(continued)

Listing 6-11 *(continued)*

```
ItsGoodForMe[cc] = ccn;
ItsGoodForMe[ms] = msn;

map<Scrumptious,Nutrition> Duplicate = ItsGoodForMe;
map<Scrumptious,Nutrition> AnotherDuplicate(ItsGoodForMe);

ItsGoodForMe[ap].Potassium = 20;
cout << ItsGoodForMe[ap].Potassium << endl;
cout << Duplicate[ap].Potassium << endl;
cout << AnotherDuplicate[ap].Potassium << endl;

return 0;
}
```

You can see in this listing that we created two classes, Scrumptious and Nutrition. We then created a map called ItsGoodForMe that associates Scrumptious instances with Nutrition instances.

We copied map twice, using both an equals sign and a copy constructor:

```
map<Scrumptious,Nutrition> Duplicate = ItsGoodForMe;
map<Scrumptious,Nutrition> AnotherDuplicate(ItsGoodForMe);
```

And that was it! We then changed one of the elements in the original map, to see what would happen. Then we printed that element, as well as the corresponding element in the two copies. Here's the output:

```
20
9722
9722
```

Yep, they're different: This implies that the maps each have their own copies of the instances — that there's no sharing of instances between the maps.

Containers hold copies, not originals. That's true when you copy containers, too. If you put a structure in a container and copy the container, the latter container has its own copy of the structure. To change the structure, you must change all copies of it. The way around this is to put pointers inside the containers. Then the containers each have their own copies of the pointers, but these pointers point to the same one-and-only object.

Book V

Reading and Writing Files

The 5th Wave   By Rich Tennant

"Why, of course. I'd be very interested in seeing this new milestone in the project."

Contents at a Glance

Chapter 1: Filing Information with the Streams Library

In This Chapter

✔ Seeing the need for a streams library

✔ Using the right header files

✔ Opening a file

✔ Dealing with errors

✔ Working with flags to customize your file opening

*F*irst things first. We've all heard of rivers and lakes and streams, and it's interesting just how many common words are used in computer programming. That's handy, because it lets us use words we already know with similar meaning, but it's also a bummer in that it's harder to impress strangers. While we don't have gluggerbumbles and plickershops in computer programming — words most people have never even heard of, mainly because we made them up — we do have *streams!*

Most programmers think of a stream as the same thing as a file. You know — a file that's stored on your hard drive or maybe on a floppy disk or Zip drive. But streams go beyond just files. A *stream* is any type of data structure that you *stream* your data into and out of in a sequence of bytes.

For example, if we open an Internet connection to a top-secret computer that stores all our top-secret data (ooooh), and we start putting our data on the remote computer, we might use a stream-based data structure. By that we mean we write the data in sequence one byte after another as the data goes over the Internet like a stream of water, reaching the remote computer. The data we wrote first gets there first and so on. It's kind of like a stream of water.

You can use the same approach for storing data into a file. Rather than just filling a huge 5MB data structure and then dropping it onto the hard drive, you write your data piece after piece; the information goes into the file.

In this chapter, we talk about different kinds of streams available to you, the C++ programmer.

Seeing a Need for Streams

When you write a program that deals with files, you must use a specific order:

1. **Open the file.**

Before you can use a file, you must open it. In doing so, you specify a filename.

2. **Access the file.**

After you open a file, you either store data into it (this is called *writing* data to the file) or get data out of it (this is called *reading* data from the file).

3. **Close the file.**

After you have finished reading from and writing to a file, you must close the file.

For example, a program that tracks your stocks and writes your portfolio to a file at the end of the day might do these steps:

1. **Ask the user for a name of a file.**

2. **Open the file.**

3. **For each stock object, write the stock data to the file.**

4. **Close the file.**

The next morning, when the program starts, it might want to read the information back in. Here's what it might do:

1. **Ask the user for the name of the file.**

2. **Open the file.**

3. **While there's more data in the file, create a new Stock object, read the data from the file, and put the data into the Stock object.**

4. **Close the file.**

Here are a couple of reasons to close a file after you have finished using it:

✦ **Other programs might be waiting to use the file.** Some operating systems, such as Windows 2000, allow a program to *lock* a file, meaning that no other programs can open the file while the program that locked the file is using it. Thus, in these situations, after you close a file, another program can use it.

✦ **When you write to a file, the operating system decides whether to immediately write the information onto the hard drive or floppy disk or to hold on to it and gather more information, finally writing it all as a single batch.** When you close a file, the operating system puts all your remaining data into the file. This is called *flushing* the file.

You have two ways to write to a file:

✦ **Sequential access:** In sequential access, you write to a file or read from a file from beginning to end. With this approach, when you open the file, you normally specify whether you plan to read from or write to the file, but not both at the same time. After you open the file, if you are writing to the file, the data you write continually gets added to the end of the file. Or if you are reading from the file, you read the data at the beginning, then you read the data that follows, then you read the data that follows that data, and so on, up to the end.

✦ **Random access:** With random access, you can read and write to any byte in a file, regardless of which byte you previously read or wrote. In other words, you can skip around. You can read some bytes, then move to another portion of the file and write some bytes, and then move elsewhere and write some more.

Back in the days of the C programming language, several library functions let you work with files. However, they stunk. They were cumbersome and made life difficult. And so, when C++ came along, people quickly created a set of classes that made life with files much easier. These people used the stream metaphor we've been raving about.

In the sections that follow, we show you how to open files, write to them, read from them, and close them.

Programming with the Streams Library

Before we begin talking about the streams library (the actual libraries include `fstream`, `iostream`, and `sstream`, but don't worry about that now — we'll get into the specifics later), we need to tell you about some compatibility issues. The ANSI C++ standard document gives a complete library of classes that handle streams and general input/output. (There is a joint ANSI/ISO standard today, but we'll focus on the ANSI standard in this book since that is the standard that appears in the GNU gcc documentation.) However, not all compiler systems (commonly called *implementations*) have the header files for these new classes. At the time of this writing, many implementations of the gcc for Windows do have them as an update or as part of the current release. However, some older compilers, perhaps the one on your hard drive, might not be compatible. That's because gcc 2.95 did not yet have full support for the Standard Library, particularly in the stream classes. Newer versions of the gcc compiler are available from 3.1 on up. And a version of MinGW includes gcc3.1.

Fortunately, most of the classes in the Standard Library are available with almost all the compilers currently available. Therefore, in most of this book, we limit ourselves to the classes you can find in most compilers. That way, everyone can be happy (even us!). However, because you may have compilers that use the newer classes, we sometimes discuss them in sidebars.

Getting the right header file

The streams library includes several classes that make your life much easier. It also has several classes that can make your life more complicated, mainly because these are auxiliary classes that you'll probably rarely use. Here are two of the more common classes that you will use. (And remember: These classes are available in pretty much all C++ implementations, whether the complete Standard Library is present or not.)

✦ `ifstream`: This is a stream you instantiate if you want to read from a file.

✦ `ofstream`: This is a stream you instantiate if you want to write to a file.

Before you can use the `ifstream` and `ofstream` classes, you include the proper header file. This is where things get ugly. In the early days of C++, people used the header file `<fstream.h>`. But somewhere in the mid-1990s, people started using the Standard Template Library (and in the late 1990s, the Standard C++ Library), both of which required you to include `<fstream>` (without the `.h` extension).

Because we want to stay up to date, in this book we use the ones without the `.h`. However, the Standard Template Library and the Standard Library put all their classes and objects inside the `std` namespace. (The Standard Template Library and Standard Library are both C++ libraries but implement some functionality differently — the article at `http://en.wikipedia.org/wiki/Standard_Template_Library` describes these differences, but you won't need to worry about them when working through the examples in this book.) Thus, when you want to use an item from the streams library, you must either

✦ Prepend its name with `std`, as in this example:

```
std::ofstream outfile("MyFile.dat");
```

✦ Include a using directive before the lines where you use the stream classes, as in this example:

```
using namespace std;
ofstream outfile("MyFile.dat");
```

By default, the gcc compiler automatically recognizes the std namespace (it's as if you had a line using namespace std; even when you don't). We focus on the gcc compiler, we don't use either of the two preceding methods — putting std:: before our stream class names or including a using namespace std; line.

In the spirit of the rest of this book, if you are using a compiler other than gcc, we recommend that you follow your #include lines with the line using namespace std;. Then you can type all the sample code as-is throughout this book, including the stream examples, without needing to put std:: before every class or object from the Standard Library.

Opening a file

Let's see, what did we call the name of this file? We think it was MyGreatChapter.doc. So we go to the word processor, choose File⇨Open, and type **MyGreatChapter.doc**.

Oops. We get an error message. That file doesn't exist.

Oh, that's right; we haven't written it yet. Instead, we create a new document inside the word processor, type 800 cool pages over the course of a relaxing evening, and then (when we're all finished) we save the file. We give it the name MyGreatChapter.doc. Then we shut down the word processor, hang out by the pool, brag to our friends about the new novels we're writing, and go to bed.

The next morning, we open the document. This time it exists, so the word processor opens it and reads in the information.

As you can see, two issues present themselves in opening a file:

✦ Create a new file

✦ Open an existing file

Here's where life gets a little strange: Some operating systems treat these two items as a single entity. The reason is that when you create a new file, normally you want to immediately start using it, which means you want to create a new file and then open it. And so the process of creating a file is often embedded right into the process of opening a file.

And when you open an existing file that you want to write to, you have two choices:

✦ Erase the current contents; then write to the file.

✦ Keep the existing contents and write your information to the end of the file. This is called *appending* to a file.

Separating a path name

Everybody wants to be different and unique. The people who wrote Microsoft's MS-DOS operating system, instead of following in the tradition of using Unix's / for a path name separator, decided to use \, thus adding the word *backslash* to the vocabularies of millions of people. So today, on Windows, you see such path names as `C:\MyDataFolder\ MyMessyPath\DifficultToType\ LetterToEditor.doc`. But on Unix, you see forward slashes, as in `/usr/something/LetterToEditor.doc`. And if this difference isn't bad enough, think about what the backslash means in a string in C++. It means that a letter follows, and the compiler interprets the two characters together as something else. For example, `\t` means a tab, and `\n` means a newline character. And how do you put a backslash into a string? You put two backslashes. Ugh! That means the earlier MS-DOS-style string (the one with Windows in it, Mr. Bill Gates!) must look like this if you use it in a C++ program:

```
"C:\\MyDataFolder\\MyMessyPath\\
        DifficultToType\\
        LetterToEditor.doc"
```

Yes, you must type every backslash twice if you want the compiler to get the correct string. But instead of doing this, we'd like to propose a much better solution! Don't use backslashes at all, even if you're programming for Windows (or, we suppose, MS-DOS). Yes, it's true! Stop the press! Call the talk radio show! Announce it to the world! When you write a C++ program on Windows, the libraries are smart enough to know that a forward slash works instead of a backslash! Therefore, you can use this string:

```
"C:/MyDataFolder/MyMessyPath/
        DifficultToType/LetterToEditor.
        doc"
```

In this book, you see us using forward paths. That way, our samples work on both Unix and Windows.

The code in Listing 1-1 shows you how to open a brand-new file, write some information to it, and then close it. (But wait, there's more: This version works whether you have the newer ANSI-compliant compilers or the older!)

Listing 1-1: Using Code That Opens a File and Writes to It

```cpp
#include <iostream>
#include <fstream>

using namespace std;

int main()
{
    ofstream outfile("MyFile.dat");
    outfile << "Hi" << endl;
    outfile.close();

    return 0;
}}
```

The short program in Listing 1-1 opens a file called `MyFile.dat`. It does this by creating a new instance of `ofstream`, which is a class for writing to a file. The next line of code writes the string `"Hi"` to the file. It uses the insertion operator, `>>`, just as `cout` does. In fact, `ofstream` is derived from the very class that `cout` is an instance of, and so that means all the things you can do with `cout` you can also do with your file! Wow! We know we're excited!

When we're finished writing to the file, we close it by calling the `close` member function. This is important!

If you want to open an existing file and append to it, you can modify Listing 1-1 slightly. All you do is change the arguments passed to the constructor as follows. This one is for those of you with a slightly older (such as gcc2.95) compiler:

```
ofstream outfile("MyFile.dat", ios::app);
```

And this is for those of you with a newer compiler, such as gcc3.1 or later:

```
ofstream outfile("MyFile.dat", ios_base::app);
```

The `ios::app` item is an enumeration inside a class called `ios`, and the `ios_base::app` item is an enumeration in the class called `ios_base`.

The `ios` class is the base class from which the `ofstream` class is derived. The `ios` class also serves as a base class for `ifstream`, which is for reading files.

For newer compilers, the `ios_base` class is a base for `ofstream` and `ifstream`. (A couple of classes are in between. `ofstream` is a template class derived from a template class called `basic_ofstream`, which is derived from a template class called `basic_ios`, which is derived from the class `ios_base`. You can view a simplified diagram of these classes at `http://www.cplusplus.com/reference/iostream/`.)

You can also read from an existing file. This works just like the `cin` object. Listing 1-2 opens the file created by Listing 1-1 and reads the string back in. The easiest way to read the file for now is to copy it from the Listing 1-1 folder to the Listing 1-2 folder you create. The book's source code includes the file in the proper folder for you.

If you try to run Listing 1-2, it's possible that your program will not find the file created by Listing 1-1. If so, you may want to add a path name to both Listing 1-1 and Listing 1-2, such as:

```
ofstream outfile("/MyFile.dat");
ifstream infile("/MyFile.dat");
```

Finding your files

Whenever you open a new file, you must know where the file is, not just what the file is called. In other words, you need to supply both a *path* and a *filename*, not just a filename. You can obtain a path for your file in different ways, depending on your program. For example, you may be saving all your files in a particular directory; you would then precede your filenames with that directory (that is, *path*) name. The string class makes this easy, as in this code:

```
const string MyPath = "c:\\
    GreatSoftwareInc";
string Filename = MyPath + "\\" +
    "MyFile.dat";
ofstream outfile(Filename.c_str());
```

The reason we had to call c_str on the string is that the ofstream class doesn't have a constructor for a string instance, only a C-style string. The c_str function returns a pointer to a C-style string equivalent of the string. Also, remember to #include <string> when you use the string class!

Also, when you are using a constant path as we did in this example, you may, instead, store the path name in some initialization file that lives somewhere on your user's computer, rather than *hard code* it in your program as we did in this example. You may also include an Options window where your users can change the value of this path.

Listing 1-2:   Using Code to Open a File and Read from It

```cpp
#include <iostream>
#include <fstream>
#include <string>

using namespace std;

int main()
{
    string word;
    ifstream infile("MyFile.dat");
    infile >> word;
    cout << word << endl;
    infile.close();

    return 0;
}}
```

When you run this program, the string you wrote to the file from Listing 1-1, "Hi," appears on the screen. It worked! It read the string in from the file!

Handling Errors When Opening a File

When you open a file, all kinds of things can go wrong. A file lives on a physical device — a fixed disk, for example, or perhaps on a floppy disk — and you can run into problems when working with physical devices. For example,

part of the disk might be damaged, causing an existing file to become corrupted. Or, less disastrous, you might run out of disk space. Or, even less
disastrous, you might try to open a file in a directory that doesn't exist.

If you try to open a file for writing by specifying a full path and filename but
the directory does not exist, the computer responds differently, depending
on the operating system you are using. If you are unsure how your particular operating system will respond, try writing a simple test program that
tries to create and open something like /abc/def/ghi/jkl/abc.txt. (Of course,
you'll want to be sure to use a directory that doesn't exist; we're assuming
/abc/def/ghi/jkl doesn't exist on your hard drive.) Then one of two things
will happen: Either the directory and the file will get created or nothing will
happen.

On our Windows 2000 system, if we attempt to create a file in a directory
that doesn't exist, the system does not create the directory. That's because
deep down inside, the program ultimately calls an operating system function
that does the dirty work of creating the file. And this particular operating
system function (it's called `CreateFile`, if you even care) has a rule that it
will not create a directory for you.

If you want to determine whether the `ostream` class was unable to create
a file, you can call its `fail` member function. This function returns `true` if
the object couldn't create the file. And that's what happens when a directory
doesn't exist. Listing 1-3 shows an example of this.

Listing 1-3:   Returning True When ostream Cannot Create a File

```
#include <iostream>
#include <fstream>

using namespace std;

int main()
{
    ofstream outfile("/abc/def/ghi/MyFile.dat");
    if (outfile.fail()) {
        cout << "Couldn't open the file!" << endl;
        return 0;
    }
    outfile << "Hi" << endl;
    outfile.close();

    return 0;
}}
```

When you run this code, assuming that you don't have a directory called
/abc/def/ghi on your system, you should see the message Couldn't
open the file! We're assuming also that your particular operating
system doesn't create a directory in this case; if it does, your computer will
open the file, write Hi to it, and move on with its happy life after closing
things out.

As an alternative to calling the `fail` member function, you can use an operator available in various stream classes. This is the bang operator, `!`, and you would use it in place of calling `fail`, as in this code:

```
if (!outfile)
{
    cout << "Couldn't open the file!" << endl;
    return 0;
}
```

Most people prefer to use `!outfile` instead of `outfile.fail()`, although our opinion is that `!outfile` stinks. In addition to its aromatic properties, we think it makes confusing code. The reason is that `outfile` is an object, and in our brains, the notion of `!outfile`, which we would pronounce "not outfile," simply doesn't make sense. In fact, `!outfile` trips up many beginning programmers. They know that `outfile` is not a pointer in this sample code, and they wonder how you could test it against 0 as you normally can only do with a pointer. (Remember, by saying `!x`, where `x` is some pointer, you're testing `x` against `0`.) And that simply doesn't make sense! And so to avoid confusion, we prefer to just call `fail`. It makes more sense.

Here are some reasons your file creation may choke:

✦ The directory doesn't exist.

✦ You're out of disk space and out of luck.

✦ Your program doesn't have the right permissions to create a file.

✦ The filename was invalid — that is, it contained characters the operating system doesn't allow in a filename, such as * or ?.

Like any good program, your program should do two things:

1. Check whether a file creation succeeded.

2. If the file creation failed, handle it appropriately. Don't just print a horrible message like `Oops! Aborting!`, leaving your poor users with no choice but to toss the monitor onto the floor. Instead, do something friendlier, like present a message telling them there's a problem and suggest that they might free more disk space.

Flagging the ios Flags

When you open a file by constructing either an `ofstream` or `ifstream` instance, you can modify the way the file will open by supplying what are called flags. In computer terms, a *flag* is simply a small item whose presence or lack of presence tells a function how to do something. With the `ofstream` and `ifstream` classes, the function in question is the constructor.

A flag looks like `ios::app` if you're using a compiler that is not fully ANSI-compliant, or like `ios_base::app` if you're using one that is fully ANSI-compliant. This particular flag means that you want to write to a file, but you want to append to any existing data that may already be in a file. You supply this flag as an argument of the constructor for `ofstream`, as in either of the following examples:

```
ofstream outfile("AppendableFile.txt", ios::app);

ofstream outfile("AppendableFile.txt", ios_base::app);
```

You can see that we added the flag as a second parameter to the constructor. Other flags exist besides `app`, and you can combine them by using the or operator, `|`. For example, one flag is `ios::nocreate` (which isn't included in newer compilers, but we show you how to overcome this limitation later in this section). This one means "only open the file if it already exists." That is, don't create the file if it doesn't exist. (Remember, `ofstream` creates a file if it doesn't already exist.) If the file doesn't exist, the open will fail, and when you call `fail`, you will get back a `true`.

The `ios::nocreate` flag is handy with `ios::app`. Together, these mean *open an existing file and append to it.* That is, the two together will work only if the file already exists, and the call will open the file for an append operation. If the file doesn't already exist, the file won't be created. Here's a sample call:

```
ofstream outfile("/MyFile.dat", ios::app | ios::nocreate);
if (outfile.fail()) {
    cout << "Couldn't open the file!" << endl;
    return 0;
}
outfile << "Hi" << endl;
outfile.close();
```

If `MyFile.dat` doesn't exist when you run this code, you get the message `Couldn't open the file!` But if `MyFile.dat` does exist, the program opens it, appends the string `Hi` to it, and finally closes it.

It turns out that the `nocreate` flag is not available in the new Standard Library. Bummer. Therefore, the code we just gave you works only if you're using an earlier version of the library. When using the CodeBlocks compiler, you see the following error message:

```
error: `nocreate' is not a member of `std::ios'
```

However, you will want to test whether or not your particular compiler includes a library that supports `ios::nocreate`. Your compiler may support it anyway, even if it includes the new Standard Library. As an alternative to `ios::nocreate`, you can use the following code:

```
ifstream infile("/MyFile.dat");
if (infile.fail())
{
    cout << "Couldn't open the file!" << endl;
    return 0;
}
infile.close();

ofstream outfile("/MyFile.dat", ios::app);
outfile << "Hi" << endl;
outfile.close();
```

In this case, you begin by attempting to open the file for reading. If the file doesn't exist, you can't read from it and the code exits with a failure message. If the code can read from the file, it reopens the file for writing. This is a cumbersome workaround, but it works.

Following is a list of the available flags. First, here are the ones for ios, in case you're using a compiler that is not completely ANSI compliant:

+ ios::app: This flag means that you want to open a file and append to it.

+ ios::in: Include this flag if you want to read from a file.

+ ios::out: Include this flag if you want to write to a file.

+ ios::trunc: Include this flag if you want to wipe out the contents of the file before writing to it. It's the opposite of append, and it's also the default if you don't specifically include ios::app.

+ ios::nocreate: Use this flag if you want to ensure that the file will not be created if it doesn't exist, resulting in the file not being opened.

+ ios::noreplace: This flag is the opposite of nocreate. Use this flag if you only want to create a new file. If you use this flag and the file already exists, the file will not open, and fail will return true.

ANSI-compliant compilers don't support the ios::noreplace flag either. In this case, you can use the opposite of the fix for the ios:nocreate flag, as shown here:

```
ifstream infile("/MyFile.dat");
if (!infile.fail())
{
    cout << "The file already exists!" << endl;
    return 0;
}
infile.close();

ofstream outfile("/MyFile.dat");
outfile << "Hi" << endl;
outfile.close();
```

In this case, the code attempts to open the file for reading. If the file exists, the code shows an error message and exits. Otherwise, the code creates a new file and writes to it.

The following flags are available in a complier that's absolutely ANSI-compliant!

✦ `ios::ate`: Use this flag to go to the end of the file after you open it. Normally, you use this flag when you want to append data to the file.

✦ `ios_base::binary`: Use this flag to specify that the file you're opening will hold binary data — that is, data that does not represent character strings.

✦ `ios_base::in`: Specify this flag when you want to read from a file.

✦ `ios_base::out`: Include this flag when you want to write to a file.

✦ `ios_base::trunc`: Include this flag if you want to wipe out the contents of a file before writing to it.

✦ `ios_base::app`: Include this flag if you want to append to the file. It's the opposite of `trunc` — that is, the information that's already in the file when you open it will stay there.

Why do you need an `in` flag and an `out` flag? It seems that the computer should know whether you're writing to a file or reading from it based on whether you use `ofstream` or `ifstream`. The answer to why you have an `in` flag and an `out` flag is that other classes are available besides `ofstream` and `ifstream`. The compilers that don't yet fully support the ANSI standard have a generic class in their libraries called `fstream`. The ANSI-compliant compilers have in their libraries a template class called `basic_filebuf` and a class called `filebuf`. If you use these classes, you can use the `in` and `out` flags.

Chapter 2: Writing with Output Streams

In This Chapter

✔ Using the insertion operator

✔ Working with manipulators

✔ Formatting your output

✔ Using flags to format your output

✔ Specifying a precision for writing numbers

✔ Setting field widths

*Y*ears ago, one of us had an old computer that had 3000 bytes of memory. (Yes, that's *three thousand bytes*, not 3MB.) As an option, this computer came with a floppy disk drive that sat outside it. It did not have a hard drive. Therefore, if you didn't have a disk drive but you wanted to use a program, you had to *type it!* Ah, those were the days.

Nowadays, the notion of a computer without a hard drive seems almost unthinkable. Not only do your programs sit on the hard drive in the form of files, but your programs also create files to store on the hard drive.

When you use a word processor, you save your documents to a file. Imagine if every time you needed the same document, you had to retype it. In this chapter, we show you the different ways you can write to a file.

Inserting with the << Operator

Writing to a file is easy in C++. You're probably already familiar with how you can write to the console by using the cout object, like this:

```
cout << "Hey, I'm on TV!" << endl;
```

Operating the insertion operator

The insertion operator, <<, is an overloaded operator function. For the 100 percent ANSI-compliant libraries, inside the `basic_ostream` class (or, for the non-100 percent ANSI libraries, inside the `ostream` class), you can find several overloaded forms of the << operator function. Each one provides input for a basic type as well as for some of the standard C++ classes, such as `string` or one of its base classes. (We say *or* because most libraries that ship with compilers are written by compiler vendors — who may implement their code slightly differently but get the same results.)

Well, guess what! The `cout` object is a file stream! Amazing! And so to write to a file, you can do it the same way you would with `cout`: You just use the double-less-than symbol, called the *insertion operator,* like this: <<.

If you open a file for writing by using the `ofstream` class, you can write to it by using the insertion operator, as in Listing 2-1.

Listing 2-1:   Using Code to Open a File and Write to It

```
#include <iostream>
#include <fstream>

using namespace std;

int main()
{
    ofstream outfile("outfile.txt");
    outfile << "Lookit me! I'm in a file!" << endl;
    int x = 200;
    outfile << x << endl;
    outfile.close();
    return 0;
}}
```

The first line inside the `main` creates an instance of `ofstream`, passing to it the name of a file called `outfile.txt`.

We then write to the file, first giving it the string, `Lookit me! I'm in a file!`, then a newline, then the integer `200`, and finally a newline. And after that, we show the world what good programmers we are by closing our file.

Placing data in specific folders

Sometimes you want to place data in a specific common folder, such as the current working directory — the directory used by the application. C++ provides a method to obtain this information: `getcwd()`. This method appears in the `<direct.h>` header. Using the `getcwd()` method is relatively straightforward. You create a place to put the information, called a buffer, and then ask C++ to provide the information as shown here:

```
#include <iostream>
#include <direct.h>

using namespace std;

int main()
```

```
{
    char CurrentPath[_MAX_PATH];
    getcwd(CurrentPath, _MAX_PATH);
    cout << CurrentPath << endl;
    return 0;
}
```

The `_MAX_PATH` constant is the maximum size that you can make a path. So, what this code is saying is to create a char array that is the size of `_MAX_PATH`. Use the resulting buffer to hold the current working directory (which is where the name of the method `getcwd()` comes from). You can then display this directory on screen or use it as part of the path for your output stream — amazing!

Formatting Your Output

If you're like us and are saving lists of numbers to a file, you may find that the process works better if the numbers are *formatted* in various ways. For example, you may want them all aligned on the right; or you might want your floating-point numbers to have a certain number of digits to the right of the decimal point.

There are three aspects to setting these formats. They are

+ **Format flags:** A *format flag* is a general style that you want your output to appear in. For example, you may want floating-point numbers to appear in scientific mode, or you may want to be able to print the words *true* and *false* for Boolean values, rather than their underlying numbers. To do these tasks, you specify format flags.

+ **Precision:** This refers to how many digits are on the right of the decimal point when you print floating-point numbers.

+ **Field width:** This refers to how much space the numbers take (both floating point and integer). This feature allows you to align all your numbers.

The next three sections discuss each of these in all their glory and grandeur.

You can use the format flags (detailed in the upcoming section), as well as precision and width specifiers, when writing to your files — and also when writing to `cout`. Because `cout` is a stream object in the `iostream` hierarchy, it accepts the same specifiers as output files. So have at it!

Formatting with flags

The folks who made the ISO C++ standard gave us a slew of *format flags.*

If you're using a compiler that includes a library that's not fully ANSI-compliant, you will be able to use *most* of these format flags but not all of them. Therefore, in this section, we're giving you lists for

+ `ios_base` (for ANSI-compliant libraries)

+ `ios` (for non-compliant libraries)

To use the following format flags, you call the `setf` member function for the file object. (This can be either your own file object or the `cout` object.) For example, to turn on scientific notation, you would do this:

```
cout.setf(ios_base::scientific);
cout << 987654.321 << endl;
```

or, if you're using a non-ANSI-compliant library:

```
cout.setf(ios::scientific);
cout << 987654.321 << endl;
```

To turn off scientific mode, you call the `unsetf` member function:

```
cout.unsetf(ios_base::scientific);
cout << 987654.321 << endl;
```

or, if you're using a non-ANSI library:

```
cout.unsetf(ios::scientific);
cout << 987654.321 << endl;
```

And if you're using your own file, you would do something like this:

```
ofstream myfile("numbers.txt");
myfile.setf(ios_base::scientific);
myfile << 154272.524 << endl;
myfile.close();
```

or, for the non-ANSI folks:

```
ofstream myfile("numbers.txt");
myfile.setf(ios::scientific);
myfile << 154272.524 << endl;
myfile.close();
```

When you run this code for writing to a file, the `numbers.txt` file will contain one of the following examples, depending on your particular compiler and library:

```
1.542725e+005
```

```
1.542725e+05
```

Each of the `ios_base` flags exists both as a format specifier and as a manipulator. (Don't worry about the precise differences for right now; Book V, Chapter 5 explains manipulators in detail.) Therefore, you can, for example, use either of the following lines to set `boolalpha`:

```
cout.setf(ios_base::boolalpha);
```

```
cout << boolalpha;
```

We're talking only about the `ios_base` flags here. The `ios` flags do not coexist as manipulators. You can use these flags as manipulators only with an ANSI-compliant library.

If you use the manipulator form of a format specifier, don't put an `endl` at the end of the line unless you want an endline to print, as in this:

```
cout << boolalpha << endl;
```

Following is a rundown of the format flags available in both the ANSI-compliant and non-ANSI compliant libraries. To set these, you call `setf`. To turn off the flag, you either call `unsetf`, or for some flags, you set a different flag. For example, both of these turn off scientific mode:

```
cout.unsetf(ios_base::scientific);
```

```
cout.setf(ios_base::fixed);
```

In the following list, we point out when you can set another flag to turn off a particular flag. One of these, `boolalpha`, is available only to you ANSI-style folks. Remember, "ANSI-people" must use `ios_base::` before each of these, while "non-ANSI-people" must use `ios::` before each of these.

✦ `boolalpha`: (ANSI only) Setting this flag causes Boolean variables to write with the words *true* or *false* (or the equivalent words for your particular locale). Clearing this flag causes Boolean variables to write 0 for false or 1 for true. (The default is for this flag to be cleared.)

✦ `fixed`: This flag specifies that, when possible, the output of floating-point numbers will not appear in scientific notation. (We say *when possible* because large numbers always appear as scientific notation, whether you specified `scientific` or `fixed`.)

✦ `scientific`: When you specify this flag, your floating-point numbers always appear in scientific notation.

✦ `dec`: When you set this flag, your integers will appear as decimal numbers. To turn this off, you turn on a different *base*, either `hex` (for hexadecimal) or `oct` (for octal).

✦ `hex`: With this flag, all your integers appear in hexadecimal format. To turn this on, choose a different base — `dec` or `oct`. Computer people like hexadecimal because it looks cool to see *letters* in your numbers.

✦ `oct`: When you turn on this flag, your integers will appear in *octal* format. Oh fun, fun.

✦ `left`: When you turn on this flag, all numbers will be left-aligned with a width field. (See "Setting the width and creating fields," later in this chapter, for information on how to set the width.)

✦ `right`: With this flag, all your numbers will be right-aligned with a width field.

✦ `showbase`: When you turn on this flag and print an integer, the integer will be preceded with a super-special character that represents none other than the base — decimal, hexadecimal, or octal. That can be good because the number 153 can represent 153 in decimal or 153 in hexadecimal (which is equivalent to 339 in decimal) or 153 in octal (which is equivalent to 107 in decimal). Yikes.

✦ `showpoint`: With this flag, your floating-point numbers have a decimal point, even if they happen to be whole numbers. (That is, a floating-point variable that contains 10.0 will print as *10.* with a decimal point after it. Without this flag, it will just print as *10* with no decimal point.)

✦ `showpos`: Normally, negative numbers get a minus sign before them, and positive numbers get no sign before them. But when you turn on this flag, your positive numbers *will* get a plus sign before them. Cool!

✦ `unitbuf`: This is for the advanced people. When you turn this on, your output will flush after each output operation. In other words, the library will not accumulate a certain amount of output before writing it in batches. Instead, the library will write the output all out each time you use the insertion operator, <<.

+ `uppercase`: When you write hexadecimal or scientific numbers, the various letters in the number will appear as uppercase. Thus, the letters *A, B, C, D, E,* and *F* will appear in capitals in a hexadecimal number, and the *E* representing the exponent in scientific notation will print as a capital *E.* When this is not set, you will get *a, b, c, d, e,* and *f* for hexadecimal numbers and *e* for the exponent in scientific notation.

Table 2-1 shows the manipulator forms of some flags. We're providing three columns in this table: First is the flag; then the manipulator to turn on the flag. Then comes the manipulator to turn *off* the flag. Yes, you need a way to turn it off. (We coined a new word: *demanipulator.* Yeah, that sounds good.) Remember, if you're pre-ANSI, you don't have access to these manipulators. Instead, you have to call `setf`.

Table 2-1	Using ANSI-Standard Manipulators and Demanipulators	
Flag	*Manipulator*	*Demanipulator*
boolalpha	boolalpha	noboolalpha
showbase	showbase	noshowbase
showpoint	showpoint	noshowpoint
showpos	showpos	noshowpos
skipws	skipws	noskipws
uppercase	uppercase	nouppercase
fixed	fixed	scientific
scientific	scientific	fixed

The `scientific` flag and `fixed` flag are opposites: `fixed` turns off `scientific`, and `scientific` turns off `fixed`. The default if you don't specify either is `fixed`.

Six manipulators aren't in Table 2-1 because they don't have a demanipulator. Instead, they are *three-way*:

+ **Bases:** `dec`, `hex`, and `oct`. Only one base can be active at a time. Activating a base automatically switches off the other bases.

+ **Alignments:** `internal`, `left`, and `right`. Only one alignment can be active at a time. Activating an alignment automatically switches off the other alignments.

Specifying a precision

When you are writing floating-point numbers to a file or to cout (that is, numbers stored in float or double variables), having all the numbers print with the same number of digits to the right of the decimal point is often handy. This feature is called the *precision*.

Do not confuse this form of the word *precision* with the idea that double variables have a greater precision than float variables. Here, we're just talking about the number of digits printed to either the file or cout. The value inside the variable does not change, nor does the precision of the variable's type.

To set or read the precision, call the stream's precision function. If you call precision with no parameters, you can find out the current precision. Or to set the precision, pass a number specifying how many digits you want to appear to the right of the decimal point.

For example, the following line sets the precision of an output:

```
cout.precision(4);
```

The output would take this form:

```
0.3333
```

If you don't set the precision, the stream will have a default precision, probably six, depending on your particular compiler.

Precision has an interesting effect if you use it with the showpoint format flag. In the scientific community, these three numbers have the same precision:

```
3.5672
8432.2259
0.55292
```

Even though the first two of the preceding numbers have the same number of digits to the right of the decimal point, scientists consider precision to mean the same number of total digits not counting leftmost 0s to the left of the decimal (as in the final of the three). Therefore, a scientist would consider the three following numbers to have the same precision because they all have four digits. (Again, for the final one, you don't count the 0 because it's to the left of the decimal point.) Scientific folks call these *significant digits*. You can accomplish significant digits with an output stream by combining precision with the showpoint flag. Listing 2-2 shows an example of showpoint and precision working together in perfect harmony.

```
3.567
8432.
0.1853
```

Listing 2-2: Using the Precision Function to Work with the showpoint Format Flag

```
#include <iostream>

using namespace std;

int main()
{
    int i;
    cout.setf(ios_base::showpoint);
    cout.precision(4);
    for (i=1; i<=10; i++) {
        cout << 1.0 / i << endl;
    }
    cout << 2.0 << endl;
    cout << 12.0 << endl;
    cout << 12.5 << endl;
    cout << 123.5 << endl;
    cout << 1234.9 << endl;
    cout << 12348.8 << endl;
    cout << 123411.5 << endl;
    cout << 1234111.5 << endl;
    return 0;
}}
```

If you're using a non-ANSI-compliant compiler, you need to change `ios_base` to `ios` in the third line in `main`. Also, because Listing 2-2 is for a fully-ANSI-compliant compiler, we included the `using namespace std;` line. (You can always have this line, whether your compiler requires it or not.)

When you run this program, here's the output you see:

```
1.000
0.5000
0.3333
0.2500
0.2000
0.1667
0.1429
0.1250
0.1111
0.1000
2.000
12.00
12.50
123.5
1235.
1.235e+004
1.234e+005
1.234e+006
```

The preceding output has a couple of interesting cases:

+ The last three lines of the preceding output are scientific notation to maintain four significant digits.

+ The fourth line from the end, `1235.`, is rounded up from 1234.9 because of this line:

```
cout << 1234.9 << endl;
```

The `precision` function has an associated manipulator. Instead of calling `precision` as a function, you can use it as a manipulator. But the manipulator's name is slightly different: It's `setprecision`. To use it, you include this header:

```
#include <iomanip>
```

These two lines cause the same thing to happen:

```
cout.precision(4);
```

```
cout << setprecision(4);
```

And these two lines are available for all the recent more-or-less-ANSI-compliant compilers, even those that aren't fully compliant! Yay! Just make sure you remember to `#include <iomanip>`, or you will get a compiler error.

Setting the width and creating fields

This is where you can start making the numbers and data all nice and neat by aligning them in columns. To align your data, use the `width` member function for the stream or `cout`, passing the width of the field, like this:

```
cout.width(10);
```

Then, when you print a number, think of the number as sitting inside a field 10 spaces wide, with the number wedged against the right side of these 10 spaces. For example, look at this:

```
cout.width(10);
cout << 20 << endl;
```

This code produces this output:

```
        20
```

Although seeing this in the printed text is hard, this 20 is pushed to the right of a field of spaces 10 characters wide. That is, because the 20 takes 2 character spaces, there are 8 spaces to the left of it.

If you prefer, you can have the numbers pushed to the left of the field. To do this, set the `left` format flag by using `setf`. (Or, for absolutely perfectly ANSI-compliant libraries, you can use the `left` manipulator.)

For the width function, you can alternatively `#include <iomanip>` and then use a manipulator:

```
cout << setw(10);
```

This works for both the newer 100 percent ANSI-compliant compilers and the slightly older, slightly less compliant compilers.

Due to some oddities in the libraries, when you set the width, it stays that way only for the next output operation. Call it forgetful if you will. Therefore, suppose you have code that looks like this:

```
cout.width(10);
cout << 20 << 30 << endl;
```

Only the first output, 20, will have a field width of 20. The 30 will just take as much space as it needs. Therefore, these lines of code produce this output, which is probably not what most people would intend:

```
        2030
```

This is why we prefer to use the manipulator form: You precede each output item with a width specification. Try this instead:

```
cout << setw(10) << 20 << setw(10) << 30 << endl;
```

which writes this to `cout`:

```
        20        30
```

That looks a little nicer!

Listing 2-3 shows the great things you can do when you set the width. This listing is for the absolute money-back-guarantee ANSI compilers. If yours is slightly less than ANSI compliant, you have to change these two lines:

```
sals << fixed;
sals << left;
```

to this:

```
sals.setf(ios::fixed);
sals.setf(ios::left);
```

Listing 2-3: Setting the Width of a Field Using the setw Manipulator or Width Function

```cpp
#include <iostream>
#include <iomanip>
#include <fstream>

using namespace std;

int main()
{
    ofstream sals("salaries.txt");
    sals << setprecision(2);
    sals << fixed;
    sals << left;

    sals << setw(20) << "Name" << setw(10) << "Salary";
    sals << endl;

    sals << "------------------- "; // 19 hyphens, one space
    sals << "----------" << endl;    // 10 hyphens
    sals << setw(20) << "Hank Williams";
    sals << setw(10) << 28422.82 << endl;

    sals << setw(20) << "Buddy Holly";
    sals << setw(10) << 39292.22 << endl;

    sals << setw(20) << "Otis Redding";
    sals << setw(10) << 43838.55 << endl;
    sals.close();
    return 0;
}}
```

When you run Listing 2-3, you get a file called `salaries.txt`, like this:

```
Name                Salary
------------------- ----------
Hank Williams       28422.82
Buddy Holly         39292.22
Otis Redding        43838.55
```

See how it's neatly lined up? That's pretty! Notice one thing we did, however: The first field, `Name`, is 20 characters wide. For the hyphens, we put only 19 to give the appearance of a space between the two fields. In fact, the two fields are wedged against each other with no space between them.

If you ran Listing 2-3 and each salary printed in a scientific format as in `2.8e+04`, you need to use `sals.setf(ios::fixed);` and `sals.setf(ios::left);`.

We used the `left` format flag so that the data in each field is aligned to the left end of the field. By default, each field is aligned to the right.

Although you can specify the field width, really you're specifying a *minimum.* If the characters in the output are less than the field width, the runtime library will pad them with spaces to make them that minimum size. If they are bigger than that width, the library will not chop them off to make them fit. If you add letters to the Hank Williams line in Listing 2-3 (like this: `sals << setw(20) << "Hank WilliamsABCDEFGHIJ";`), the output looks like the following example instead. The Hank Williams line runs beyond the 20 characters into the next field.

```
Name                Salary
------------------- ----------
Hank WilliamsABCDEFGHIJ28422.82
Buddy Holly         39292.22
Otis Redding        43838.55
```

Chapter 3: Reading with Input Streams

In This Chapter

✔ Reading with the extraction operators

✔ Dealing with the end of the file

✔ Reading various data types

✔ Reading data that is formatted with text

*W*ell, isn't this nice. You have a file that you wrote to, but you need to read from it! After all, what good is a file if it's just sitting on your hard drive collecting dust?

In this chapter, we show you how you can read from a file. Reading a file is tricky because you can run into some formatting issues. For example, you may have a line of text in a file with a sequence of 50 digits. Do those 50 digits correspond to 50 one-digit numbers, or maybe 25 two-digit numbers, or some other combination? If you created the file, you probably know; but the fun part is getting your C++ program to properly read from them. The file might contain 25 two-digit numbers, in which case you make sure that the C++ code doesn't just try to read one enormous 50-digit number. In this chapter, we give you all the dirt on getting the dust off your hard drive and the file into memory. Have at it!

Extracting with Operators

When you read from a file, you can use the *extraction* operator, >>. This operator is very easy to use, provided you recognize that the phrase, "Look mom, no caveats!" just doesn't apply to the extraction operator.

Suppose you have a file called `Numbers.txt` with the following text on one line:

```
100 50 30 25
```

You can easily read in these numbers with the following code. First, make sure you #include <fstream> (but *not* fstream.h, as you'll pick up an old, outdated, yucky file). And you probably will need the line using namespace std; if you're using a newer compiler and library. Then this code will do the work:

```
ifstream MyFile("Numbers.txt");
MyFile >> weight;
MyFile >> height;
MyFile >> width;
MyFile >> depth;
```

In the preceding code, the input file, Numbers.txt, had its numbers separated with spaces. You can also separate them with newlines, like this:

```
100
50
30
25
```

The program doesn't care. It looks for *white space,* which is any number of *spaces, tabs,* and *newlines.* You could have the data like the following example, and the program will still read them in correctly.

```
100        50
                  30
    25
```

When you are dealing with the standard input object, cin, the same rules about white space apply: If you read in four numbers, like the following example, the cin object, like the ifstream object, will separate the numbers based on the white space.

```
cin >> weight;
cin >> height;
cin >> width;
cin >> depth;
```

If the user *accidentally* inserts a space, the computer will apply the separated values in two places — both incorrectly. Be careful!

When you are reading information from a file, make sure that you have clearly defined the order of the information. In other words, make sure that you have agreed upon a protocol for the information. Otherwise, you will likely end up with errors and mistakes, and your coworkers will want to blame somebody. That's the way computer people are, after all.

What's a protocol?

Okay, we're going to give you a list of numbers: 1600 20500 1849 20240. Go ahead and use them the way we intend you to use them, and then send us back the answer, at which point we'll send you our response. What's that? You're not sure what we want you to do with them? Aha! You need a protocol. As defined in this chapter, a *protocol* is simply a rule for how data is ordered. A protocol in general defines rules for exchanging information of any sort between computers (think of it as a diplomatic role).The two systems negotiate the exchange of data based on standardized rules.

As it happens, the first number in the set of numbers we provided is the street address of the White House in Washington, DC, and the second number is the zip code for the White House. The third number is the street address of the main office for the National Park Service headquarters, and the fourth is the National Park Service zip code. Of course, you probably didn't realize that (unless you happen to work for the Park Service and recognized parts of your address!).

But now suppose you tell us, "Send me the White House street address, then its zip code, then the National Park Service street address, and then its zip code." Then we would go ahead and send the four numbers to you. At that point, we wouldn't have any need to send a bunch of extra information, such as English words describing what each number is. If we give them to you in the exact order you requested them, that will be all you need. In fact, if you're writing a computer program that receives this information and we pad it with other information, such as descriptions, your program may not be equipped to handle all that info, and you have a problem. In other words, our program and your program must agree on a protocol. A protocol dictates the order of the information and how it's formatted. Further, a protocol dictates how you'll respond: You may send back a single number 1, which means that you received the data properly, and we may send a single 0, which means that you'll be getting no further information. That's a protocol, and protocols are useful when reading data, whether it's from a file or over the Internet.

Encountering the End of File

When we get to the end of a really good novel, we often feel disappointed that it's done, and we wish that we could just keep reading. But alas, we have encountered the EON (end of novel) condition.

Files have an ending as well, called the *EOF,* which stands for End of File. When you are reading from a file, you need to know when you reach the end. If you know how big the file is going to be, you can write your program so it knows exactly when to stop. So here are the cases we cover in this section: First, how you can read to the end of the file simply because you know how big the file is and, therefore, when to stop reading; and second, how you can keep reading until you reach the EOF without having to know the file size in advance.

You, the programmer, know the format of the file you are reading. (Perhaps your program even wrote the file and now you're writing the part of the program that reads it.) And it's possible your format starts with a *size*. For example, you may be reading in a file, and you start by reading a number from the file, where the number represents how many pieces of information you are to read from the file. This requires that whoever created the file started by writing the size before the rest of the data, and that you agree to this format.

Here's an example. First, Listing 3-1 writes two files that you can later read in.

Listing 3-1:   Using Code to Open a File and Write to It

```
#include <iostream>
#include <fstream>
#include <string>

using namespace std;

void WriteFile(string filename, int count, int start)
{
    ofstream outfile(filename.c_str());
    outfile << count << endl;
    int i;
    for (i=0; i<count; i++)
    {
        outfile << start + i  << endl;
    }
    outfile.close();
}

int main()
{
    WriteFile("/MyData/nums1.txt", 5, 100);
    WriteFile("/MyData/nums2.txt", 6, 200);
    return 0;
}
```

You can see that this program writes two files. Create the \MyData folder before you run the application the first time. We gave a path in the files (/MyData/nums1.txt) to prevent problems with newer operating systems that don't allow root directory access, such as Linux and Windows Vista. The reason we're giving a path is that the next listing reads from the files, and we want to make sure that the program can find the files.

Note that the WriteFile function takes a filename, a count, and a start. It uses this information to write a series of numbers to the file. But before it writes those numbers, it writes the count, like this:

```
outfile << count << endl;
```

Then it uses a loop to write count numbers to the file.

And, of course, when the `WriteFile` function is all done, it closes the file. *Good program, good.*

Listing 3-2 is an example of how to read this data back in.

Listing 3-2:   Using Code to Open a File and Read It Back In

```
#include <iostream>
#include <fstream>
#include <string>

using namespace std;

void ReadFile(string filename)
{
    ifstream infile(filename.c_str());
    int count;
    int i;
    int num;

    cout << "File: " << filename << endl;
    infile >> count;
    cout << "This file has " << count << " items." << endl;
    for (i=0; i<count; i++)
    {
        infile >> num;
        cout << num << endl;
    }
    infile.close();
}

int main()
{
    ReadFile("/MyData/nums1.txt");
    ReadFile("/MyData/nums2.txt");
    return 0;
}
```

You can see in Listing 3-2, like Listing 3-1, `filename` includes the path names for the files the program is reading in.

Now look at the `ReadFile` function. This function opens the file and then immediately reads in a number. This number represents the number of items to read in. It's the first number that was written by the `WriteFile` function in the previous listing, Listing 3-1.

As the writer of both the program that writes the file and the program that reads the file, we agreed (both sides of us agreed, that is, or so we think) on the format of the file both for reading it and for writing it. And by sticking to this format, we can assure ourselves that we can read in the file that we previously wrote. When you run this program, you'll see the following output.

```
File: /MyData/nums1.txt
This file has 5 items.
100
```

```
101
102
103
104
File: /MyData/nums2.txt
This file has 6 items.
200
201
202
203
204
205

Process returned 0 (0x0)   execution time : 0.000 s
Press any key to continue.
```

Now another possibility for reading and writing a file is that you continue reading data from the file until you reach the end of the file. How do you do this? You test the `istream` or `ifstream` object for the EOF.

Listings 3-3 and 3-4 show you how you can do this. As with the earlier listings, the first writes a couple of files, and the second reads them in.

First, here's Listing 3-3.

Listing 3-3:   Using Code to Write to a File but Not Record a Count

```cpp
#include <iostream>
#include <fstream>
#include <string>

using namespace std;

void WriteFile(string filename, int count, int start)
{
    ofstream outfile(filename.c_str());
    int i;
    for (i=0; i<count; i++)
    {
        outfile << start + i  << endl;
    }
    outfile.close();
}

int main()
{
    WriteFile("/MyData/nums1.txt", 5, 100);
    WriteFile("/MyData/nums2.txt", 6, 200);
    return 0;
}
```

As you can probably see, Listing 3-3 is like Listing 3-1, except Listing 3-3 does not start out by writing out a count.

Listing 3-4 reads the numbers back in.

Listing 3-4: Reading from a File and Looking for the EOF Condition

```
#include <iostream>
#include <fstream>
#include <string>

using namespace std;

void ReadFile(string filename)
{
    ifstream infile(filename.c_str());
    int num;

    cout << "File: " << filename << endl;
    bool done = false;
    while (!done)
    {
        infile >> num;
        if (infile.eof() == true)
        {
            done = true;
        }
        else
        {
            cout << num << endl;
        }
    }
    infile.close();
}

int main()
{
    ReadFile("/MyData/nums1.txt");
    ReadFile("/MyData/nums2.txt");
    return 0;
}
```

This listing is like Listing 3-2. However, instead of first reading a count, it just dives in and starts reading.

Note carefully how Listing 3-4 does its thing: The listing first *tries* to read in a number, and *then* it checks if it encountered an EOF. If you're familiar with other styles of reading in files, this approach may seem a little backwards to you. But that's the way the streams do it: First read, and if the read doesn't work, then abort.

Therefore, you have to have some strange logic in your code. Here's the general algorithm:

```
set done to false
while not done
    read a number
    if encounter an end of file
        set done to true
    else
        process the number read in
    end-if
end-while
```

Something bothers us about this approach: We need a big `if` statement, and the `process the number` part goes in an `else` block. We like having a Boolean variable called `done`, because then we can use a `while` loop that reads like this:

```
while (!done) // pronounced "while not done"
```

If lots of processing is needed, the processing will all be piled inside the `else` portion of the `if` block. And that can get ugly with a million indentations. In this case, check for EOF and then break out of the loop, like this:

```
if (infile.eof() == true)
    break;
```

But if you do that, you have no reason for the `done` variable. So what do you put in the `while` loop? A lot of people do this:

```
while (1)
{
    infile >> num;
    if (infile.eof() == true)
        break;
    cout << num << endl;
}
```

Yes, they put `while (1)`. In other words, the `while` loop spins forever until a `break` statement comes along. We're not particularly fond of the `while (1)` construct because it's a bit counterintuitive for our little tiny brains, but a lot of people do it; and we have to admit that we like the short `if` statement, just breaking if the EOF is true. You choose which method you want to use. And heck, you may even be able to dream up a couple more ways to do this.

Reading Various Types

Reading a file is fun, but it can get complicated when you want to read spaces. Suppose we have these two strings that we want to write to a file:

```
"That's the steak by the poodle that I'll have for dinner."
```

```
"I will have the Smiths for dinner, too."
```

Now suppose you wrote these to a file as one big long line to get, "That's the steak by the poodle that I'll have for dinner. I will have the Smiths for dinner, too."

Now later, you want to read back in these two strings. How can you do that? You can't just do this:

```
string first, second;
infile >> first;
infile >> second;
```

If you do this, the variable `first` will hold *That's*, and the variable `second` will hold *the*. Why? Because, when you read in strings, the `ifstream` and `istream` classes use spaces to break (or *delimit*) the strings. Bummer.

But even if you could somehow get the `ifstream` class to go past the spaces, how does the `ifstream` class know when it has reached the end of the first string? Now in this case, you may write your program to follow this protocol: A string ends with a period.

And that protocol is fine, because ending with a period is the case with these two strings that we wrote to the file. But what if they were just sequences of words, like this:

```
"poodle steak eat puddle"

"dinner Smiths yummy"
```

And then, when you write these two strings to a file, you may end up with this inside the file:

```
poodle steak eat puddle dinner Smiths yummy
```

Or worse, you may get this, which contains no space between the two strings:

```
poodle steak eat puddledinner Smiths yummy
```

Here's what we suggest that you do: First, you must agree on a protocol. This, of course, may just mean agreeing with yourself. (Always a good idea. No, it's not! Yes, it is!) Here are some choices for your protocols:

✦ You can write each string on a separate line, and when you read the file, you will know that each line is a separate string.

✦ You can delimit each string with a particular character. Then you would split your strings based on those delimiters.

Writing a string to a separate line is very easy; you simply do this:

```
cout << mystring << endl;
```

Nothing earth shattering there. Reading it in is pretty easy, too; you just use the `getline` function in the `ifstream` or `istream` class. The catch is that the `getline` function wants a character array, not a `string` object. So go ahead and read it into a character array, and then convert it to a `string` object like so:

```
char buf[1024];
infile.getline(&(buf[0]), 1024);
string str(buf);
```

You don't have to convert the array to a `string` object; if you want, you can just work with the character array. But we prefer to work with `string` objects because they're instances of classes and you get all kinds of nice member functions that can manipulate the strings. We're all about making our lives easier.

Listing 3-5 shows how to write the strings with a delimiter. You can see that this has nothing particularly magical about it (other than the quantum physics involved in running the microprocessor, but we don't care about that).

Listing 3-5: Writing Strings with a Delimiter Is Easy

```
#include <iostream>
#include <string>
#include <fstream>

using namespace std;

void WriteString(ofstream &file, string words)
{
    file << words;
    file << ";";
}

int main()
{
    ofstream delimfile("/MyData/delims.txt");

    WriteString(delimfile, "This is a dog");
    WriteString(delimfile, "Some dogs bite");
    WriteString(delimfile, "Some dogs don't bite");
    WriteString(delimfile, "Humans that is");
    WriteString(delimfile, "All dogs bite");
    WriteString(delimfile, "Food that is");
    WriteString(delimfile, "I say, food food food.");

    delimfile.close();
    return 0;
}
```

Listing 3-6 shows you how to read in the file strings. We used a trick for this. The `ifstream` class inherits from the `istream` class the `getline` function. Most people use this to read a line of text. However, a little-known fact is that you can specify the delimiter you prefer to use instead of the end-of-line character. You pass the delimiter as the third parameter. And so we passed a semicolon character for the third character, and lo and behold, the thing worked!

Listing 3-6: Specifying a Delimiter with the getline Function

```
#include <iostream>
#include <string>
#include <fstream>
```

```
using namespace std;

string ReadString(ifstream &file)
{
    char buf[1024]; // Make sure this is big enough!
    file.getline(&(buf[0]), 1024, ';');
    return string(buf);
}

int main()
{
    ifstream delimfile("/MyData/delims.txt");


    while (1)
    {
        string words = ReadString(delimfile);
        if (delimfile.eof() == true)
            break;
        cout << words << endl;
    }
    delimfile.close();
    return 0;
}
```

When you run Listing 3-6, you see this output:

```
This is a dog
Some dogs bite
Some dogs don't bite
Humans that is
All dogs bite
Food that is
I say, food food food.
```

Yay! That's the correct list of strings!

Reading Formatted Input

Sooner or later, you may be reading a file that has this kind of information
in it:

```
Hello there my favorite number is 13. When I go to the
store I buy 52 items each week, except on dates that
start with 2, in which case I buy 53 items.

Hello there my favorite number is 18. When I go to the
store I buy 72 items each week, except on dates that
start with 1, in which case I buy 73 items.

Hello there my favorite number is 10. When I go to the
store I buy 40 items each week, except on dates that
start with 2, in which case I buy 41 items.
```

This file has a general *format* (or protocol!). How can you read in the numbers? One way is to read strings for each of the words and skip them. Here's a sample piece of code that reads up to the first number, the favorite number:

```
ifstream infile("words.txt");
string skip;
for (int i=0; i<6; i++)
    infile >> skip;
int favorite;
infile >> favorite;
```

This code reads in six strings and just ignores them. You can see how we do this through a loop that counts from 0 up to but not including 6. (Ah, you gotta love computers. Most people would just count 1 to 6. We suppose we *could* have, but we're computer guys, no more, no less.)

Then, after we read the six strings that we just ignored, we finally read the favorite number. You can then repeat the same process to get the remaining numbers.

Chapter 4: Building Directories and Contents

In This Chapter

✓ Creating and deleting directories

✓ Getting the contents of a directory

✓ Copying and moving, and why they are related

✓ Moving and renaming files and why they are similar

We're about to say something you might not believe: *C++ provides no functions for creating directories and getting the contents of a directory.*

Really! We know it's hard to believe, but we can say two points about this:

✦ There really is a (more-or-less) good reason for this lack: C++ is a general-purpose language; issues that deal with directories are specific to individual operating systems. Thus, it doesn't make sense to include such features in C++. (Supposedly. So they say. We guess. Whatever.)

✦ Some brave rebels have added some functions — and these functions exist in most C++ implementations. Whew! That's a good thing — otherwise you'd have to call into the operating system to create or modify a directory.

C++ has a holdover from the C programming language in the header file `stdio.h` that includes functions for renaming and removing files and directories. (Interesting.) Oh yes, and there's another one in there for creating a temporary file. (Even more interesting.)

In this chapter we present you with ways to manipulate directories and files. (We have tested these routines only for the GNU gcc compiler that comes with the CodeBlocks product. If you're working with a different compiler or operating system, try them out. They probably will work.)

For the examples in this chapter, you need to add both `#include <stdio.h>` and `#include <io.h>` to the beginning of the source-code file. (Please do not confuse this file with `ios.h`. That's *another* header file but not the right one to mess with just now.) Now again, if you're working with a compiler other than CodeBlocks, we cannot guarantee that you'll find `io.h` in your `include` directory. However, there's a good chance you will. Look for it!

Manipulating Directories

There are a couple functions you can use for creating and deleting directories. These functions are in the io.h header file.

Creating a directory

If you want to create a directory, you can call the mkdir function. If the function can create the directory for you, it returns a 0. Otherwise it returns a nonzero value. (When we ran it we got a −1, but your best bet — always — is to test it against 0.)

Here's some sample code that uses this function:

```
#include <iostream>
#include <stdio.h>
#include <io.h>

using namespace std;

int main()
{
    if (mkdir("c:/abc") != 0)
    {
        cout << "I'm so sorry. I was not" << endl;
        cout << "able to create your directory" << endl;
        cout << "as you asked of me. I do hope" << endl;
        cout << "you are still able to achieve" << endl;
        cout << "your goals in life. Now go away." << endl;
    }
    return 0;
}
```

 Notice (as usual) that we used a forward slash (/) in the call to mkdir. In Windows, you can use either a forward slash or a backslash. But if you use a backslash, you have to use two of them (as you normally would to get a backslash into a C++ string). For the sake of portability, we recommend always using a forward slash.

Clearing up a directory of confusion

We want to make sure we're all clear about a few terms. Back in 1994 when Microsoft created Windows 94 — oops, we mean Windows 95 (it shipped late and had to be renamed) — the kind folks at Microsoft started telling us that we had to use the term *folder* instead of *directory*. Blah, blah, blah. We say they're called *directories*, and in our little private universe that includes only us and revolves around us, we use that term. In fact, that's what most programmers call them, so in this chapter we're calling them directories.

It would be nice to create an entire directory-tree structure in one fell swoop — doing a call such as `mkdir("/abc/def/ghi/jkl")` without having any of the `abc`, `def`, or `ghi` directories already existing. But, alas, you can't. The function won't create a `jkl` directory unless the `/abc/def/ghi` directory exists. That means you have to break this call into multiple calls: First create `/abc`. Then create `/abc/def`, and so on.

If you do want to make all the directories at once, you can use the `system` function, as we describe in "Using the quick-and-dirty method" sidebar, later in this chapter. If you execute `system("mkdir \\abc\\def\\ghi\\ jkl");`, you will be able to make the directory in one fell swoop.

Deleting a directory

It's fun to go on a cleaning spree and just toss everything out. And so it makes sense that deleting a directory is easy. To do it, you just call the `rmdir` function, passing the name of the directory. If you want to find out whether it worked, test its results against 0. Here's some sample code:

```
#include <iostream>
#include <stdio.h>
#include <io.h>

using namespace std;

int main()
{
    if (rmdir("c:/abc") != 0)
    {
        cout << "Life is difficult sometimes, and" << endl;
        cout << "sometimes you just don't get what" << endl;
        cout << "you asked for. And this is one" << endl;
        cout << "such case. I just couldn't remove" << endl;
        cout << "the directory for you. Better" << endl;
        cout << "luck next time, my dear friend." << endl;
    }
    return 0;
}
```

This approach works only if the directory is *not empty*. If the directory has at least one file in it, the function can't remove the directory — and returns a nonzero result. Then you get to see the nice, friendly message that we're particularly proud of.

Getting the Contents of a Directory

If you want to read the contents of a directory, you're really going against what's available in the standard C++ language. However, the Kind Souls of the Great Libraries of C++ (that is, the people who wrote most of the available C++ libraries) usually built in some handy functions for getting the contents of a directory.

A directory usually contains multiple files as well as other directories. Getting a list of contents is involved. You don't just call a function and get something back — we're not sure what that something would be, other than a pretty basic list.

Of course, if the Standard C++ Library included a function for getting information, it would likely be a template class that contains the directory contents. Alas, the library doesn't support it. (Delphi, supports it, but don't get us going.) Instead, you have to climb through some functions. Here's how it works.

1. Call _findfirst, passing it a pathname and a pattern for the files whose names you want to find.

   For example, pass *.* to get all files in the directory, or *.txt to get all files ending in .txt. Also pass it a pointer to a _finddata_t structure.

2. Check the results of _findfirst.

   If _findfirst returned -1, it didn't find any files (which means you're finished). Otherwise it fills the _finddata_t structure with the first file it found, and it will return a number that you use in subsequent calls to the various find functions.

3. Look at the _finddata_t structure to determine the name of the file, and other information such as create date, last access date, and size.

4. Call _findnext and pass it the following values: the number returned from _findfirst and the address of a _finddata_t structure

   If _findnext returns -1, it found no more files; you can go to Step 5. Otherwise look at the _finddata_t structure to get the information for the next file found. Then repeat Step 4.

5. Call _findclose and pass it the number returned from _findfirst.

   You're all finished.

Youch! That's kind of bizarre, but it's the way things used to be done in the old days of programming, before the mainstream languages developed such civilized features as classes and objects. We just had structures; we had to pass a bunch of information around by hand (and walk to school, uphill both ways, in the snow).

Listing 4-1 shows how we implemented this elegant, old-fashioned process.

Listing 4-1:   Using Code to Read the Contents of a Directory

```cpp
#include <iostream>
#include <io.h>
#include <time.h>
#include <string>

using namespace std;

string Chop(string &str)
{
    string res = str;
    int len = str.length();
    if (str[len - 1] == '\r')
    {
        res.replace(len - 1, 1, "");
    }
    len = str.length();
    if (str[len - 1] == '\n')
    {
        res.replace(len - 1, 1, "");
    }
    return res;
}

void DumpEntry(_finddata_t &data)
{
    string createtime(ctime(&data.time_create));
    cout << Chop(createtime) << "\t";
    cout << data.size << "\t";
    if (data.attrib & _A_SUBDIR == _A_SUBDIR)
    {
        cout << "[" << data.name << "]" << endl;
    }
    else
    {
        cout << data.name << endl;
    }
}

int main()
{
    _finddata_t data;

    // Change this entry to match your Windows directory.
    int ff = _findfirst ("C:/Windows/*.*", &data);

    if (ff != -1)
    {
        int res = 0;
        while (res != -1)
        {
            DumpEntry(data);
            res = _findnext(ff, &data);
        }
        _findclose(ff);
    }
    return 0;
}
```

You can see how in `main` we followed the steps we just outlined. And for each of the data structures, we used our own function called `DumpEntry`. The `DumpEntry` function prints out the information about the file. Here are some sample lines from when we ran the program:

```
Wed Jul 26 10:00:00 2000      16730    FeatherTexture.bmp
Thu Sep 28 12:01:54 2000      21692    FOLDER.HTT
Fri Dec 08 06:05:10 2000      0        [Fonts]
```

Note how, in the `DumpEntry` function, we're testing whether the item is a directory. This is another old (but reliable) way to program: We check for the presence of one particular tiny little bit in the middle of the `attrib` member of the structure, like this:

```
if (data.attrib & _A_SUBDIR == _A_SUBDIR)
{
    cout << "[" << data.name << "]" << endl;
}
```

And finally, you'll notice a strange function we included called `Chop`. That's because when we wrote the program, we discovered that the `ctime` function — otherwise handy for formatting the time — adds a carriage return (or *newline*) to the end of the string it creates. So we chop that off. Otherwise the information after the date has to start on the next line of text, which wasn't what we wanted.

You might not have a `C:/Windows` directory on your computer, so you may want to change this code to include some directory you do have, such as `C:/WinNT`. (And as usual, you can see how we get to use those forward slashes!)

Copying Files

Ah, copying a file — something so simple, it happens all the time. Copy this file there; copy that file here. But what exactly takes place when you copy a file? You actually create a *new* file, and fill it with the same contents as the original file. And how do you do that? Well, from what we just said it sounds like you have to read each and every byte from the first file, and write it to the second. Big-time yuck.

But to make matters worse, copying a file means you have to make sure that you copy it exactly the same, that you don't accidentally tack an extra 0 or two at the end of the file, or an extra carriage return or linefeed at the end of the file (which could happen when you copy a text file). When all is done, the two files should be identical — not only contain the *same information*, but also be the *same size*. (We can hear the nonconformists now: "*Super big-time yuck!*")

And on top of all that, most good copy routines do even more! They give the new file a date that matches the date of the original file, and they will set all the attributes — including, say, read-only if the original is a read-only file. (We're pointedly ignoring that if the file is read-only, then maybe we shouldn't be able to copy it in the first place. . . .)

Suddenly copying a file doesn't sound so easy after all!

Now this is going to go against the norm for every computer book you've ever seen, but we're *not* going to give you code and tell you to use it for your file-copying operations. The reason for this heresy? Well, as simple as it may sound, we've seen too many people write code that's *supposed* to copy files but runs too slowly, or screws up the process, or both!

So we tucked a couple of sidebars into this section to give you the *best* way to copy a file. Enjoy!

Copying with windows: You're in luck

If you're programming in Windows, you're in luck! As long as you're not using the ancient Windows 3.1, you get a `CopyFile` function! To get ready to use it, you include the line `#include <windows.h>` in your program. Then here's all you have to do:

```
CopyFile("c:/dog.txt", "c:/dog2.txt", TRUE);
```

This copies from `c:/dog.txt` to `c:/dog2.txt`. But notice the final parameter: It's the word TRUE in all capitals. What's that? That's a preprocessor macro defined somewhere in the bowels of the header windows header files.

You have to use either TRUE or FALSE when calling the Windows functions. That's because in the old days of C, when the early versions of Windows were invented, no `bool` type existed. Those resourceful people of the late twentieth century had to define their own TRUE and FALSE as integers (usually either 1 and 0, respectively, or 0 and 1, respectively). And by the way, that final parameter in `CopyFile` tells the function what to do if the file you're copying to already exists: TRUE means don't overwrite the existing file; just abort. FALSE means overwrite it.

Using the quick-and-dirty method

Okay, time for a secret: There's another way you can copy a file, and you can use this to also move, delete, and rename files. However, this method we're about to show you is absolutely not portable: in effect, if you do this on Windows, for example, you won't be able to run the same program on Unix, and vice versa. That is, you have to make a version for the operating system you're using. Now, if you're familiar with DOS (remember that?) or the Unix shell, you can execute any DOS or Unix-shell commands by using the `system` function. If you use Dev-C++, you've already seen the `system` function many times:

```
system("PAUSE");
```

This runs the DOS `pause` command, which prints the message

```
Press any key to continue . . .
```

and waits for you to press the Any key (or any other key for that matter). Because the `system` function can run any DOS or shell command, you can use it to call the DOS copy command, like this:

```
system("copy c:\\abc.txt c:\\def.txt");
```

Note that we had to use the backslash, not a forward slash; DOS really doesn't like forward slashes. To make the command DOS-friendly, we had to use two backslashes inside the string.

When you use this approach, you can run into some strange situations. For example, if you write a program that calls `system` and you're planning to run it under the `Cygwin` environment in Windows, you can use the Unix-style `cp` command instead of the DOS `copy` command. The resulting weird command looks like this:

```
system("cp c:\\abc.txt c:\\def.txt");
```

But you can only use this command under the `Cygwin` environment. Otherwise it gives you a huffy error message:

```
'cp' is not recognized as an internal
      or external command, operable
      program or batch file.
```

Moral: You have to make sure that whatever command you call in the `system` function really exists in the environment from which you issue the call.

Moving and Renaming Files and Directories

Think about this: We have a file called

```
c:\dog.txt
```

and we're going to rename it to

```
c:\temp\dog.txt
```

Is that a valid way to rename a file? If you notice, the file started out being called `dog.txt`, and afterwards it was called `dog.txt`. Did we rename it or did we just *move* it? Indeed, we moved it from the `root` directory on the `C:` drive to the `temp` directory on the `C:` drive. Why did we call this operation a rename? Because that's *also* what we did! We're thinking of the file's real name as *the entire pathname and filename together*. Thus, the file's name at first is c:\dog.txt, not just dog.txt. When we moved the file, it got a new name, c:\temp\dog.txt.

For that reason, you can move *and* rename by using the same function. If you want to move a file, rename it with a different path. Of course, the path must exist (details, details). If we try to rename c:\dog.txt to c:\temp\dog.txt and there's no c:\temp directory, the rename fails and we get an error message.

The following example renames a file:

```
#include <iostream>
#include <stdio.h>

using namespace std;

int main()
{
    if (rename("/mydata/dog.txt","/mydata/dog.dat") != 0)
    {
        cout << "I quit." << endl;
    }

    if (rename("/mydata/dog.dat","/mydata/temp/dog.dat") != 0)
    {
        cout << "Same old story. No respect at all." << endl;
    }
    return 0;
}
```

We used the rename function, passing first the old filename and then the new filename. The first call renames the file from /mydata/dog.txt to /mydata/dog.dat. The second call renames it from /mydata/dog.dat to /mydata/temp/dog.dat, which (in effect) moves the file.

You can also give the file a new filename when you move it, as in this code:

```
rename("/mydata/dog.dat","/mydata/temp/cat.txt")
```

There are conditions under which the rename operation won't work:

✦ You're renaming the file to move it to a new directory, but that directory does not exist. In this case, create the directory before you move the file.

✦ You're renaming a file but some other file already exists under that name. In this case, either delete the other file or (better yet) make your program ask its users what they want it to do: Delete the old file (that is, "overwrite it")? Abort the operation? Abort! Abort! Abort! (No, wait, that's only for the self-destruct. Never mind.)

✦ You're renaming a file to move it to a new directory, but there's already a file by that name in that directory. In this case, as in the previous example, get your program to ask the users what to do — overwrite or abort?

Now for some really exciting news! Renaming also works with directories! You can move directory names around just as if they were files! But there's a catch: If any program has a file open within that directory, the `rename` function won't work. The operating system lets you move or rename a directory only if you're not accessing any files inside the directory. That's still true if you're using a DOS window and staying inside the `C:` directory like this:

```
C:\>cd dog
C:\dog>
```

If you have a DOS window open with this sort of operation in it, you can't move the `dog` directory unless you either move out of the `dog` directory first or close the DOS window before you move the `dog` directory. (Or you can just make a new directory and move everything out of the old directory.)

Chapter 5: Streaming Your Own Classes

In This Chapter

✔ **Streaming a class to a text file**

✔ **Getting the most out of manipulators**

✔ **Writing your own manipulators**

*T*he C++ stream classes can read and write all sorts of goodies, such as integers, characters, strings, floating-point numbers, and Boolean variables. But sooner or later, being able to stream one of your own classes (like the following) would be nice:

```
MyClass x;
cout << x << endl;
```

Now C++ has a good reason not to have done this already: The compiler and library can't know how to stream your class. What should `cout` write? The name of the class followed by the values of the public member variables? Or maybe just the private member variables? None of the above?

Therefore, you should make the class streamable. In this chapter, we show you how to do it. But recognizing that you have two separate reasons why you may want to make a class streamable is important:

✦ To provide a format for writing the object to a text stream.

✦ To save the information in an object so you can read it back in at a later date, thereby reconstructing the object. A class with this feature is called a *persistent* class.

We cover both topics in this chapter. We also show how you can create your own manipulators. Remember, a *manipulator* is this kind of code:

```
cout << endl;
```

That is, the `endl` is the manipulator. You can make your own manipulators that manipulate the stream in various ways, as we show you later in this chapter.

Streaming a Class for Text Formatting

When dealing with instances of one of your classes, the ability to use the insertion and extraction operators << and >> is nice.

To use these operators, you overload them to take parameters of your class. Sounds easy, doesn't it? When people first find out about overloading the insertion and extraction operators, the process often seems so much harder than it really is.

Here's the scoop: If you have a class, say `MicrowaveOven`, and you have an instance of this class, say `myoven`, all you do to accomplish the overloading of an operator is code a function that takes as a parameter a stream and an object and writes the members of the object *to* the stream. Then you will be able to code one of the following lines:

```
cout << myoven;

outfile << myoven;
```

Now what if you want to code an operator that reads from a stream? Then all you do is write a function that reads the members *from* a stream if you want to code one of the following lines:

```
cin >> myoven;

infile >> myoven;
```

Again, no biggie. The key is *what to call the function*.

Remember that `cout << myoven` actually calls a function called <<. Here's the function header:

```
ostream &operator <<(ostream &out, MicrowaveOven &oven)
```

This technique isn't as hard to remember as you may think. First, always remember that every type in this is a reference. (That makes sense when you look at `cout << myoven`. The second parameter, `myoven`, is not a pointer. And you normally don't want to pass objects around directly, so that leaves only one possibility: passing it by reference.)

Second, remember that the function must return the stream that it's working with. Returning the stream allows you to chain together operators like this:

```
cout << "hi" << myoven << 123 << endl;
```

Finally, remember that the operator function takes two parameters. You can see their order when you look at the order of cout << myoven. The first is the stream, and the second is your class. And thus, when you put this all together, you get the function header we just described, that is

```
ostream &operator <<(ostream &out, MicrowaveOven &oven)
```

Now what do you do with this function that you wrote? You just write to the stream passed into it! What do you write? Whatever you want! It's true: Because you designed the class that the function takes as a parameter, you decide how the output *looks* when you write the object to a stream. So pretend that this is your MicrowaveOven class:

```
class MicrowaveOven
{
public:
    int HighVoltageRadiation;
    int RadioactiveFoodCount;
    int LeakLevel;
    string OvenName;
};
```

Then your insertion function may look like this:

```
ostream &operator <<(ostream &out, MicrowaveOven &oven)
{
    out << "High Voltage Radiation: ";
    out << oven.HighVoltageRadiation << endl;
    out << "Radioactive Food Count: ";
    out << oven.RadioactiveFoodCount << endl;
    out << "Leak Level: ";
    out << oven.LeakLevel << endl;
    out << "Oven Name: ";
    out << oven.OvenName << endl;
    return out;
}
```

Now for some points about the preceding code:

✦ We took complete liberty on how we wanted the object to look on the stream. For each member variable, we wrote a description, a colon, a space, and then a value. We then put an endl. Would you like the output to look different? Then go for it! It's your choice how you want the output to look.

✦ We returned the same output stream that came in as the first parameter. This is important!

✦ When we wrote to the stream, we wrote to out, not to cout. If we messed up and wrote to cout, this function would not work properly when used with a file. If we tried myfile << myoven, the information would just go to cout, not into the file. Oops!

In this function, we accessed only the public member variables of the `oven` instance. As it stands, we can't access the private members because this function is not a member of `MicrowaveOven`. (Now of course, `MicrowaveOven` doesn't actually have any private members, but most of your classes probably do.) To access the private members, make this function a friend of `MicrowaveOven` by adding this inside the `MicrowaveOven` class:

```
friend ostream &operator <<(ostream &out,
    MicrowaveOven &oven);
```

Here's a similar function for reading from a stream:

```
istream &operator >(istream &in, MicrowaveOven &oven)
{
    in >> oven.HighVoltageRadiation;
    in >> oven.RadioactiveFoodCount;
    in >> oven.LeakLevel;
    in >> oven.OvenName;
    return in;
}
```

You can see that the format of this function is like that of the insertion operator: The function returns a reference to the stream, and for parameters, the function takes a reference to a stream and a reference to a `MicrowaveOven` object.

And as before, we had complete freedom on how we wanted to read this in. We chose to just read in each member separately. That means that if we call this function by using `cin` like this

```
cin > myoven;
```

then when we run this line, we could type the member values on one line with spaces, or on separate lines, or any combination:

```
1234 5555
1054 "Buzz"
```

And that's it! Using the insertion and extraction operators isn't really magical at all.

To use the insertion and extraction operators, remember that you simply write two functions, one for each operator. These functions write to a stream or read from it. And always remember the two most important aspects of these functions:

✦ Remember to return the stream at the end!

✦ Remember to use references!

Manipulating a Stream

A lot of people see this kind of thing:

```
cout << "Hello" << endl;
```

and wonder what on Earth endl is. Is it a variable? Is it a keyword? What is it? And how can you add your own things like it? In this section, we answer this and every other question you ever had about these strange little creatures called *manipulators*.

What's a manipulator?

What exactly is endl? Here's the answer, and it might surprise you: endl is a *function*. However, you may notice that it has no parentheses. And so, you're not actually calling the function.

So what are you doing? (Seems as though we've made the story even more complicated.) In this section, we show you that a manipulator is actually the address of a function. How's that for a strange thought? Read on.

To clarify exactly what endl is, think about this:

```
cout << endl;
```

And think about the operator function, <<. By writing cout << endl, you are calling an overloaded insertion operator function and passing in two parameters, cout and endl. The first parameter, cout, is an instance of ostream. The second parameter, endl, is the *address of a function*. Yes, when you type a function name but don't include parentheses, you are giving the address of the function rather than calling the function.

And so, somewhere out there (in the standard header files, actually) is an overloaded insertion function that takes both an ostream and the address of a function. Now the thing about function addresses is that the type of a function pointer is based on the function's return type and parameter types. Thus, pointers to these two functions have the same type:

```
void WriteMe(int x, char c);

void AlwaysAndForever(int y, char x);
```

Even though the names of the parameters are different, the types of the parameters are the same. That's why pointers to the two functions have the same type. But pointers to the following two functions do *not* have the same type:

```
void SomethingForNothing(int x);

int LeaveMeAlone(int y, int z);
```

The functions do not have the same type because their prototypes are different. The first takes a single integer as a parameter and returns a void. The second takes two integers as parameters and returns an integer.

Now here's the prototype for the `endl` function:

```
ostream& endl(ostream& outs);
```

This function takes a reference to `ostream` and returns a reference to `ostream`. And here's a sufficient `typedef` for a pointer to this function:

```
typedef ostream& (*omanip)(ostream&);
```

This defines a new type called `omanip`, which is a pointer to a function that takes as a parameter a reference to `ostream` and returns a reference to `ostream`. Perfect! Therefore, if we have a variable of type `omanip`, we can set it to the address of the `endl` function.

So now back to this:

```
cout << endl;
```

For this manipulator to work, you need an overloaded insertion operator function that takes two parameters: first a reference to `ostream` (for the `cout`) and then `omanip`. Yes, the second parameter must be a reference to `omanip` because the second item in `cout << endl` is `omanip`.

If you're not clear on why `endl` is `omanip`, think about this: There's a function called `endl`, and to call that function, you would type its name, an opening parenthesis, some parameters, and then a closing parenthesis. But if you leave off the parentheses, you're just taking the address of the function. And the type `omanip`, which we defined earlier, is exactly that: an address to a function. But on top of being an address, the `endl` function's prototype matches that for the `omanip` type. Therefore, we can say that `endl` is of the type `omanip`. Whew.

Here's a possibility for the header of the overloaded insertion operator:

```
ostream& operator<<(ostream& out, omanip func);
```

You can see the parameters that this function takes: First, it takes a reference to `ostream` and then `omanip`.

But remember what we're doing. We're trying to explain how this manipulator works:

```
cout << endl;
```

Two functions are involved. Here are their headers:

```
ostream& endl(ostream& outs);

ostream& operator<<(ostream& out, omanip func);
```

When you type `cout << endl`, you are *not* calling the `endl` function. Instead, you are calling this `operator<<` function because `endl` by itself — without parentheses — is nothing more than the *address of the* `endl` *function*. And the address is of type `omanip`.

Thus, when you type **cout << endl**, you are calling this `operator<<` function, passing in `cout` and `endl`.

Here's the `operator<<` function in its entirety:

```
ostream& operator<<(ostream &out, omanip func)
{
    return (*func)(out);
}
```

The second parameter is called `func`. When you call `cout << endl`, you are passing `endl` in as the `func` parameter. And what does this `operator<<` function do? It calls the function passed into it. Thus, it calls `endl`. Huh?

Why did we go through all this rigmarole, if, ultimately, we're just calling this mysterious `endl` function? Here's why. Believe it or not, the use of `endl` is all about aesthetics. The following line is short and clear:

```
cout << "hello" << endl;
```

And to make this line work, you need an overloaded insertion operator. Fortunately, the `operator<<` function we've been talking about does the trick.

Finally, the computer eventually calls the `endl` function itself, and that function does the actual work of adding a newline character to the stream. Wow, all that just for a newline! And you thought you had it rough! Imagine being the compiler!

Now this isn't the only way to accomplish coding a manipulator, as we explain in the following section, "Writing your own manipulator." In that section, we use a slightly different approach that works equally well. But the technique we've been describing works, too.

Time for some honesty: We did doctor the overloaded insertion operator function a bit, because, really, this function is a member of `ostream`. But the overloaded insertion operator function works equally well as a standalone function, as we've described in this section.

Writing your own manipulator

You can write your own manipulators in several ways. The goal is to allow for this type of code

```
cout << mymanipulator;
```

which causes a function, such as this, to get called:

```
ostream &operator << (ostream &out, somespecialtype a);
```

Now think about the overloading that goes on here: Several `operator <<` functions are available; ultimately, they all differ in the type of the second parameter, where we wrote `somespecialtype`. And whatever `mymanipulator` is, it must be the `somespecialtype` type as well. But on top of it, this type must be unique: There cannot already be an overloaded function that has that type! Unique, unique, unique!

Although in the "What's a manipulator?" section, earlier in this chapter, we give all the gory details on how the `endl` manipulator works, we think that amount of detail is a bit too complicated. We'd rather use a slightly different approach for our own manipulators. Here's what we're going to do in the following example: We want to make sure that we have a unique type and that the manipulator is an object of that type. As with other manipulators, function pointers work well. But for the function pointer to be unique, its return type and parameter types must be unique. That's not too hard; to guarantee that no other function has that prototype, we're going to make our own special type — a structure — and use that as the parameter for the function, like this:

```
struct FullOvenManip {};
void FullOvenInfo(FullOvenManip x) {}
```

Check this sample carefully. We created a structure called `FullOvenManip`. This structure has nothing in it; its sole purpose in life is to provide for a unique parameter experience. Yee-hah! And the function `FullOvenInfo` takes this structure as a parameter. Considering that we just invented this structure, we can be quite certain that no other function in the C++ header files matches this prototype. More than certain, in fact. We'd be willing to bet our Hollywood Hills mansion (which we don't have, so we have nothing to lose!).

Now we can provide an overloaded `operator >>` function. That function takes a pointer to the `FullOvenInfo` function. But to do that, we had better `typedef`:

```
typedef void(*FullPtr)(FullOvenManip);
```

This line of code creates a type called `FullPtr`, which is a pointer to a function that takes a `FullOvenManip` parameter and returns a `void`. We can think of only one function that does that! It's the `FullOvenInfo` function. Woo-Hoo!

When writing your own manipulators, don't shy away from using `typedef`. The manipulator concept is confusing and can be a serious struggle for many of us to keep straight. By using a `typedef`, you can simplify your life a bit.

Here's the overloaded `operator >>` function header:

```
ostream &operator << (ostream &out, FullPtr);
```

You can see the second parameter: It's a `FullPtr`. And look at this code:

```
cout << FullOvenInfo;
```

The `FullOvenInfo` item is also a `FullPtr` because it's a pointer to a function that takes a `FullOvenManip`. Voilà. That does the trick.

Listing 5-1 is a really great example of all this!

Listing 5-1:   Using Manipulators

```
#include <iostream>
#include <string>
#include <fstream>
#include <map>

using namespace std;

class MicrowaveOven
{
    friend ostream &operator <<(ostream &out,
        MicrowaveOven &oven);
public:
    typedef map<ostream *, bool> FlagMap;
    int HighVoltageRadiation;
    int RadioactiveFoodCount;
    int LeakLevel;
    string OvenName;
    static FlagMap Flags;
};

MicrowaveOven::FlagMap MicrowaveOven::Flags;
ostream &operator <<(ostream &out, MicrowaveOven &oven)
{
    bool full = true;
    MicrowaveOven::FlagMap::iterator iter =
        MicrowaveOven::Flags.find(&out);
    if (iter != MicrowaveOven::Flags.end())
    {
        full = iter->second;
    }

    if (full)
    {
        out << "High Voltage Radiation: ";
        out << oven.HighVoltageRadiation << endl;
        out << "Radioactive Food Count: ";
        out << oven.RadioactiveFoodCount << endl;
```

(continued)

Listing 5-1 *(continued)*

```
        out << "Leak Level: ";
        out << oven.LeakLevel << endl;
        out << "Oven Name: ";
        out << oven.OvenName;
    }
    else
    {
        out << oven.HighVoltageRadiation << ",";
        out << oven.RadioactiveFoodCount << ",";
        out << oven.LeakLevel << ",";
        out << oven.OvenName;
    }

    return out;
}

istream &operator >(istream &in, MicrowaveOven &oven)
{
    in >> oven.HighVoltageRadiation;
    in >> oven.RadioactiveFoodCount;
    in >> oven.LeakLevel;
    in >> oven.OvenName;
    return in;
}

struct FullOvenManip {};

void FullOvenInfo(FullOvenManip x) {}
typedef void(*FullPtr)(FullOvenManip);

ostream &operator << (ostream &out, FullPtr)
{
    MicrowaveOven::Flags[&out] = true;
    return out;
}

struct MinOvenManip {};

void MinOvenInfo(MinOvenManip x) {}
typedef void(*MinPtr)(MinOvenManip);

ostream &operator << (ostream &out, MinPtr)
{
    MicrowaveOven::Flags[&out] = false;
    return out;
}

int main()
{
    MicrowaveOven myoven;
    myoven.HighVoltageRadiation = 9832;
    myoven.RadioactiveFoodCount = 7624;
    myoven.LeakLevel = 3793;
    myoven.OvenName = "Burnmaster";

    cout << myoven << endl;
    cout << "============" << endl;
    cout << FullOvenInfo << myoven << endl;
```

```
    cout << "============" << endl;
    cout << MinOvenInfo << myoven << endl;

    return 0;
}
```

The code in Listing 5-1 creates two manipulators, one called `FullOvenInfo` and one called `MinOvenInfo`. When you use one of these manipulators, as in the following line, you call our overloaded `operator >>` function:

```
cout << FullOvenInfo << myoven << endl;
```

That function works with a map to keep track of which stream you are manipulating. The map lives as a static member in the `MicrowaveOven` class. So when you use the `FullOvenInfo` manipulator on `cout`, the map's item for `cout` gets a `true`. And when you use the `MinOvenInfo` manipulator on `cout`, the map's item for `cout` gets a `false`.

So why did we bother with the map? The idea is that you may be working with multiple streams, such as one for an `ofstream` file and one for `cout`, and you may want some to show the full information via the `FullOvenInfo` manipulator and some to show the minimal information via the `MinOvenInfo`. And so we keep a map based on the stream. And the really great thing is that the code actually works. In the overloaded `operator >>` function that prints a `MicrowaveOven` object, you can see how we check the map for a `true` or `false` for the current stream.

When you run this program, you see this output:

```
High Voltage Radiation: 9832
Radioactive Food Count: 7624
Leak Level: 3793
Oven Name: Burnmaster
============
High Voltage Radiation: 9832
Radioactive Food Count: 7624
Leak Level: 3793
Oven Name: Burnmaster
============
9832,7624,3793,Burnmaster
```

We printed the same object three times. The first one demonstrates the default: If you provide no manipulators, you get a full listing. We handled that in the overloaded `operator >>` for printing a `MicrowaveOven` object:

```
bool full = true;
MicrowaveOven::FlagMap::iterator iter =
    MicrowaveOven::Flags.find(&out);
if (iter != MicrowaveOven::Flags.end())
{
    full = iter->second;
}
```

Remember that `iterator` is really a pointer to the `map` entry. And so we call `find` to determine if the item is inside the `map` entry. If it's not, `find` returns `Flags.end()`. (That's just the way the `find` function works. If we'd written the `map` class, we would have done things differently. Can you say simplify, simplify, simplify rather than obfuscate, obfuscate, obfuscate?)

And if we don't get back `Flags.end()`, that means we found the item in the map. So in that case, we use `iter->second` to obtain the value.

But notice what happens if we do get back `Flags.end()`, meaning the stream wasn't found in the map. Then we just stick with the default value for `full`, which was `true`:

```
bool full = true;
```

And so you can see that these output lines will function properly:

```
cout << myoven << endl;
cout << "============" << endl;
cout << FullOvenInfo << myoven << endl;
cout << "============" << endl;
cout << MinOvenInfo << myoven << endl;
```

The first line with `myoven` line uses the default, which is a full listing. The second line with `myoven` says to definitely give us a full listing, using the `FullOvenInfo` manipulator. And the third line with `myoven` gives a minimal listing, which we chose with the `MinOvenInfo` manipulator.

Life is good.

Book VI

Advanced C++

The 5th Wave   By Rich Tennant

Well, heck — that's just darn impressive! And you say it's programmed to sew up and dress the incision afterward as well?

Contents at a Glance

Chapter 1: Exploring the Standard Library Further

In This Chapter

✔ Categorizing the Standard Library functions

✔ Working with container functions such as hash

✔ Performing random access with iterator functions

✔ Working with algorithms such as find

✔ Creating random numbers with functors

✔ Working with utilities such as min and max

✔ Creating temporary buffers with allocators

*T*he Standard Library is one of the most important parts of the C++ developer's toolkit because it contains a host of interesting functions that let you write great applications. The Standard Library originally started as the Standard Template Library (STL), and a number of companies, including Silicon Graphics, Inc. (SGI) and IBM, distributed it for everyone to use. The International Standards Organization (ISO) eventually took over STL, made a few minor changes to it, and renamed it the Standard Library. Consequently, when you see the STL online, don't get confused; it's merely an older version of the Standard Library.

For the purposes of this book, the differences between the Standard Library and the STL are so small that you can probably use them interchangeably. Just remember that the Standard Library is newer and does contain some changes to make the various versions of the STL work together.

This chapter provides an overview of the Standard Library and shows you some examples of how to use it. However, if you don't see what you want here, don't worry, we discuss more examples in later chapters and you can always refer to the Standard Library documentation for additional examples. Before the chapter moves on to any examples, however, it's important to know what the Standard Library contains, so the first section of this chapter provides you with a list of Standard Library function categories.

Getting a copy of the Standard Library documentation

The Standard Library is incredibly large, so this book doesn't document it completely. The CodeBlocks product doesn't come with a Standard Library reference either. However, to really use the Standard Library, you really do need a copy of the documentation.

You can join ISO for a bazillion bucks and get a copy of their document free or purchase a copy of it from `http://www.iso.org/iso/iso_catalogue/catalogue_ics/catalogue_detail_ics.htm?csnumber=38110`. As an alternative, you can buy a copy of the Standard Library documentation from an ISO member such as the American National Standards Institute (ANSI) for a more reasonable sum. Check it out at `http://webstore.ansi.org/RecordDetail.aspx?sku=INCITS%2FISO%2FIEC+14882-2003`.

Because the STL and the Standard Library are relatively close, you have a third alternative: use an STL resource. One of the best written and easiest to use resources is from SGI at `http://www.sgi.com/tech/stl/`. You may also want to review the Tiny STL Primer at `http://www.davethehat.com/articles/tiny_stl.htm` for some additional resources (found at the bottom of the Web page).

In addition to the resources mentioned so far, you'll want to check out Bjarne Stroustrup's Web site at `http://www.research.att.com/~bs/C++.html#standard`. Just in case you don't know, he's the guy who designed and originally implemented C++. Finally, you can download most of the C++ 1989 standard at `ftp://ftp.research.att.com/pub/c++std/WP/CD2/`.

Considering the Standard Library Categories

The Standard Library documentation uses a formal approach that you're going to find difficult to read and even harder to understand; it must have been put together by lawyers more interested in the precise meaning of words rather than the usability of the document. This 748-page tome (in the current version) requires quite a bit of time to review. Fortunately, you don't have to wade through all that legal jargon mixed indiscriminately with computer jargon and the occasional bit of English. This chapter provides the overview you need to get going quickly.

The best way to begin is to break the Standard Library into smaller pieces. You can categorize the Standard Library functions in a number of ways. One of the most common approaches is to use the following categories:

+ Containers

+ Iterators

+ Algorithms

+ Functors

+ Utilities

+ Adaptors

+ Allocators

The following sections provide a brief description of each of these categories and tell what you can expect to find in them. Knowing the category can help you locate the function you need quickly on Web sites that use these relatively standard category names.

Containers

Containers work just like the containers in your home — they hold something. You've already seen containers at work in other areas of this book. For example, both queues and deques are kinds of containers. The Containers category doesn't contain any functions, but it does contain a number of types including those in the following table:

basic_string	bit_vector	bitset
char_producer	deque	hash
list	map	multimap
multiset	priority_queue	queue
rope	set	slist
stack	vector	

Iterators

Iterators enumerate something. When you create a list of items, and then go through that list checking items off, you're enumerating the list. Using iterators helps you create lists of items and manipulate them in specific ways. The kind of iterator you create is important because some iterators let you go forward only, some can go in either direction, and some can choose items at random. Each kind of iterator has its specific purpose.

SGI color-coding

The SGI Web site at `http://www.sgi.com/tech/stl/stl_index_cat.html` uses color-coding to tell you about the content. Here are the categories you'll see and their associated color:

- Concept is red

- Type is yellow

- Function is green

- Overview is purple

The Iterators category includes a number of types. These types determine the kind of iterator you create in your code and the capabilities of that iterator. The following is a list of the iterator types:

back_insert_iterator	bidirectional_iterator	bidirectional_iterator_tag
forward_iterator	forward_iterator_tag	front_insert_iterator
input_iterator	input_iterator_tag	insert_iterator
istream_iterator	iterator_traits	ostream_iterator
output_iterator	output_iterator_tag	random_access_iterator
random_access_iterator_tag	raw_storage_iterator	reverse_bidirectional_iterator
reverse_iterator	sequence_buffer	

The Standard Library also includes a number of iterator-specific functions. These functions help you perform tasks such as advance (increment) the iterator by a certain number of positions. You can also measure the distance between the beginning and end of the iterator. The following is a list of iterator functions:

advance	distrance	distance_type
iterator_category	value_type	

Algorithms

Algorithms perform data manipulations such as replacing, locating, or sorting information. You've already seen some algorithms used in the book because it's hard to create a substantial application without using one. There aren't any types in the Algorithms category. The following is a list of algorithm functions:

accumulate	adjacent_difference	adjacent_find
advance	binary_search	copy
copy_backward	copy_n	count
count_if	distance	equal
equal_range	fill	fill_n
find	find_end	find_first_of
find_if	for_each	generate
generate_n	includes	inner_product
inplace_merge	iota	is_heap
is_sorted	iter_swap	lexicographical_compare

lexicographical_compare_3way	lower_bound	make_heap
max	max_element	merge
min	min_element	mismatch
next_permutation	nth_element	partial_sort
partial_sort_copy	partial_sum	partition
pop_heap	power	prev_permutation
push_heap	random_sample	random_sample_n
random_shuffle	remove	remove_copy
remove_copy_if	remove_if	replace
replace_copy	replace_copy_if	replace_if
reverse	reverse_copy	rotate
rotate_copy	search	search_n
set_difference	set_intersection	set_symmetric_difference
set_union	sort	sort_heap
stable_partition	stable_sort	swap
swap_ranges	transform	uninitialized_copy
uninitialized_copy_n	uninitialized_fill	uninitialized_fill_n
unique	unique_copy	upper_bound

Functors

Functors are a special class of object that acts as if it's a function. You call a functor using the same syntax that you use for a function in most cases, but functors possess all the good elements of objects as well. Functors come in a number of forms. For example, a binary function functor accepts two arguments as input and provides a result as output. Functors include a number of types that determine the kind of function the code creates, as shown in the following table:

binary_compose	binary_function	binary_negate
binder1st	binder2nd	divides
equal_to	greater	greater_equal
hash	identity	less
less_equal	logical_and	logical_not
logical_or	mem_fun1_ref_t	mem_fun1_t
mem_fun_ref_t	mem_fun_t	minus
modulus	multiplies	negate

(continued)

not_equal_to	plus	pointer_to_binary_function
pointer_to_unary_function	project1st	project2nd
select1st	select2nd	subtractive_rng
unary_compose	unary_function	unary_negate

The Functors category contains only one function, ptr_fun. This function accepts a function pointer as input and outputs a function pointer adapter, which is a kind of function object. You use ptr_fun when you need to pass a function as input to another function such as transform. Here is an example of such code:

```
#include <iostream>
#include <math.h>
#include <ext/functional>

using namespace std;
using namespace __gnu_cxx;

int main()
{
    const int N = 10;
    double A[N];
    fill(A, A+N, 100);

    cout << A[0] << endl;

    transform(A, A+N, A, compose1(negate<double>(), ptr_fun(fabs)));

    cout << A[0] << endl;

    return 0;
}
```

This example begins by creating a constant that determines the number of elements in the array A. The code then fills every element in A with the value 100 and displays just one of those elements on screen.

The tricky part comes next. The transform algorithm accepts the beginning of an input iterator, the end of an input iterator, and output iterator, and the transformation you want to perform. The transform algorithm takes each of the values in the input iterator, performs the transformation you requested, and places the result in the output iterator.

In this case, the code uses the nonstandard SGI functor compose1, which takes two adaptable unary functions as input. Because fabs is a standard function, you must use ptr_fun to change it into a function pointer adapter before you can use it with compose1. The result is that A contains the negation of the absolute value of the original value in A or -100 when the transformation is complete.

The GNU gcc compiler supports a number of STL features that don't appear as part of the Standard Library. In this case, `compose1` appears in the `ext/functional` header, so you must provide the `#include <ext/functional>` line of code. In addition, because `compose1` is nonstandard, it appears as part of a different namespace. Consequently, you must also provide the using `namespace __gnu_cxx;` line of code to access the functor without having to precede it with the namespace information.

Many C++ examples rely on the nonstandard parts of STL to perform tasks. If you want maximum compatibility and transportability for your code, you should avoid these nonstandard features.

Utilities

Utilities are functions and types that perform small service tasks within the Standard Library. The functions are `min`, `max`, and the relational operators. The types are `chart_traits` (the traits of characters used in other Standard Library features, such as `basic_string`) and `pair` (a pairing of two heterogeneous values).

Adaptors

Adapters perform conversions of a sort. They make it possible to adapt one kind of data to another. In some cases, adaptors perform data conversion, such as negating numbers. The Adaptors category includes one function, `ptr_fun`, which is explained in the "Functors" section of the chapter. In addition, the Adaptors category includes the types shown in the following table:

back_insert_iterator	binary_compose	binary_negate
binder1st	binder2nd	front_insert_iterator
insert_iterator	mem_fun1_ref_t	mem_fun1_t
mem_fun_ref_t	mem_fun_t	pointer_to_binary_function
pointer_to_unary_function	priority_queue	queue
raw_storage_iterator	reverse_bidirectional_iterator	reverse_iterator
sequence_buffer	stack	unary_compose
unary_negate		

Allocators

Allocators manage resources, normally memory. In most cases, you won't ever need to use the members of the Allocators category. For example, you normally create new objects using the `new` operator. The `new` operator allocates memory for the object and then creates it by calling the object's constructor. In rare cases, such as when you want to implement a form of object pooling, you may want to separate the memory allocation process from the construction process. In this case, you call `construct` to perform the actual task of construction the object based on its class definition. The Allocators category has the following functions.

construct	destroy	get_temporary_buffer
return_temporary_buffer	uninitialized_copy	uninitialized_copy_n
uninitialized_fill	uninitialized_fill_n	

The Allocators category also includes a couple of types. These types help you manage memory, and you may find more use for them than you will the functions in this category. The types are

raw_storage_iterator	temporary_buffer

Parsing Strings Using a Hash

Hashes are an important security requirement for applications today. A *hash* creates a unique numeric equivalent of any string you feed it. Theoretically, you can't duplicate the number the hash creates by using another string. A hash isn't reversible — it isn't the same as encryption and decryption.

A common use for hashes is to send passwords from a client to a server. The client converts the user's password into a numeric hash and sends that number to the server. The server verifies the number, not the password. Even if people are listening in, they have no way to ascertain the password from the number and therefore can't steal the password for use with the target application.

Unfortunately, hashes are part of the STL but not part of the Standard Library. However, hashes are so important that you really do need to know how to use them. As with the `ptr_fun` example shown in the "Functors" section of the chapter, you need to do a little extra work to make hashes work with CodeBlocks, as shown in the following example:

```
#include <iostream>
#include <ext/hash_set>

using namespace std;
using namespace  __gnu_cxx;

int main()
```

```
{
    hash<const char*> MyHash;

    cout << "The hash of \"Hello World\" is:" << endl;
    cout << MyHash("Hello World") << endl;
    cout << "while the hash of \"Goodbye Cruel World\" is:" << endl;
    cout << MyHash("Goodbye Cruel World") << endl;

    return 0;
}
```

The example begins by creating a hash function object, MyHash. You use
this function object to convert input text to a hash value. The function
object works just like any other function, so you might provide the input text
as MyHash("Hello World"). Hashes always output precisely the same
value given a particular input. Consequently, you should see the following
output from this example.

Book VI
Chapter 1

Exploring the
Standard Library
Further

```
The hash of "Hello World" is:
952921740
while the hash of "Goodbye Cruel World" is:
1126809588
```

Hashes have uses other than security requirements. For example, you can
create a container that relies on a hash to make locating a particular value
easier. In this case, you use a key/value pair in a *hash map*. The following
code shows how to create a hash map:

```
#include <iostream>
#include <ext/hash_map>

using namespace std;
using namespace __gnu_cxx;

struct eqstr
{
    bool operator()(const char* s1, const char* s2) const
    {
        return strcmp(s1, s2) == 0;
    }
};

int main()
{
    hash_map<const char*, int, hash<const char*>, eqstr> Colors;

    Colors["Blue"] = 1;
    Colors["Green"] = 2;
    Colors["Teal"] = 3;
    Colors["Brick"] = 4;
    Colors["Purple"] = 5;
    Colors["Brown"] = 6;
    Colors["LightGray"] = 7;

    cout << "Brown = " << Colors["Brown"] << endl;
    cout << "Brick = " << Colors["Brick"] << endl;

    // This key isn't in the hash map, so it returns a
    // value of 0.
```

```
cout << "Red = " << Colors["Red"] << endl;

return 0;
}
```

A hash map requires four inputs:

+ Key type

+ Data type

+ Hashing function

+ Equality key

The first three inputs are straightforward. In this case, the code uses a string as a key type, an integer value as a data type, and hash<const char*> as the hashing function. You already know how the hashing function works from the previous example in this section.

The equality key class is a little more complex. You must provide the hash map with a means of determining equality. In this case, the code compares the input string with the string stored as the key. The eqstr structure performs the task of comparing the input string to the key. The structure must return a Boolean value, so the code compares the strcmp function to 0. When the two are equal, meaning the strings are equal, eqstr returns true.

The example goes on to check for three colors, only two of which appear in the hash map Colors. In the first two cases, you see the expected value. In the third case, you see 0, which indicates that Colors doesn't contain the desired key. Always reserve 0 as an error indicator when using a hash map because the hash map will always return a value, even if it doesn't contain the desired key.

Standard Library versus STL headers

You'll find a wealth of STL examples on the Internet because STL was around for a long time before the Standard Library appeared. In fact, some developers continue to prefer the STL simply because they're familiar with it. Here's a little secret: The STL headers use a .h extension and the Standard Library headers don't have an extension. For example, the now familiar iostream header used in every previous example in the book is actually the Standard Library form — the STL form is iostream.h.

Here's another secret. The Standard Library headers often call on the STL headers, so you've also been using STL throughout the book. It's amazing to see how these things work out.

Obtaining Information Using a Random Access Iterator

Most containers let you perform random access of data they contain. For example, the following code shows that you can create an `iterator` and then add to or subtract from the current offset to obtain values within the container that `iterator` supports:

```
#include <iostream>
#include <vector>

using namespace std;

int main()
{
    vector<string> Words;

    Words.push_back("Blue");
    Words.push_back("Green");
    Words.push_back("Teal");
    Words.push_back("Brick");
    Words.push_back("Purple");
    Words.push_back("Brown");
    Words.push_back("LightGray");

    // Define a random iterator.
    vector<string>::iterator Iter = Words.begin();

    // Access random points.
    Iter += 5;
    cout << *Iter << endl;

    Iter -= 2;
    cout << *Iter << endl;

    return 0;
}
```

In this case, the `vector`, `Words`, contains a list of seven items. The code creates an `iterator` for `Words` named `Iter`. It then adds to or subtracts from the `iterator` offset and displays the output on screen. Here is what you see when you run this example:

```
Brown
Brick
```

Sometimes you need to perform a special task using a random access `iterator`. For example, you might want to create a special function to summate the members of `vector` or just a range of members within `vector`. In this case, you must create a specialized function to perform the task as follows because the Standard Library doesn't include any functions to do it for you:

```
#include <iostream>
#include <vector>

using namespace std;

template <class RandomAccessIterator>
float AddIt(RandomAccessIterator begin, RandomAccessIterator end)
{
    float Sum = 0;

    RandomAccessIterator Index;

    // Make sure that the values are in the correct order.
    if (begin > end)
    {
        RandomAccessIterator temp;
        temp = begin;
        begin = end;
        end = temp;
    }

    for (Index = begin; Index != end; Index++)
        Sum += *Index;

    return Sum;
}

int main()
{
    vector<float> Numbers;

    Numbers.push_back(1.0);
    Numbers.push_back(2.5);
    Numbers.push_back(3.75);
    Numbers.push_back(1.26);
    Numbers.push_back(9.101);
    Numbers.push_back(11.3);
    Numbers.push_back(1.52);

    // Sum the individual members.
    float Sum;
    Sum = AddIt(Numbers.begin(), Numbers.end());
    cout << Sum << endl;

    Sum = AddIt(Numbers.end(), Numbers.begin());
    cout << Sum << endl;

    // Sum a range.
    vector<float>::iterator Iter = Numbers.begin();
    Iter += 5;
    Sum = AddIt(Iter, Numbers.end());
    cout << Sum << endl;

    return 0;
}
```

This example builds on the previous example. You still create vector, Numbers, and fill it with data. However, in this case, you create an output variable, Sum, that contains the summation of the elements contained in Numbers.

AddIt is a special function that accepts two RandomAccessIterator values as input. These two inputs represent a range within the vector that you want to manipulate in some way. The example simply adds them, but you can perform any task you want. The output is a float that contains the summation.

AddIt works as you expect. You call it as you would any other function and provide a beginning point and an end point within vector. The first two calls to AddIt sum the entire vector, while the third creates an iterator, changes its offset, and then sums a range within vector. Here is the output from this example:

```
30.431
30.431
12.82
```

A random access iterator can go in either direction. In addition, you can work with individual members within the container supplied to iterator. As a result, the functions you create for iterator must be able to work with the inputs in any order. How you handle this requirement depends on the kind of function you create.

Locating Values Using the Find Algorithm

The Standard Library contains a number of functions to find something you need within a container. Locating what you need as efficiently as possible is always a good idea. Unlike your closet, you want your applications well organized and easy to manage! The four common find algorithms are

+ find
+ find_end
+ find_first_of
+ find_if

The algorithm you use depends on what you want to find and where you expect to find it. You'll likely use the plain find algorithm most often. The following example shows how to locate a particular string within vector — you can use the same approach to locate something in any container type:

```
#include <iostream>
#include <vector>
#include <algorithm>

using namespace std;

int main()
{
```

```
vector<string> Words;

Words.push_back("Blue");
Words.push_back("Green");
Words.push_back("Teal");
Words.push_back("Brick");
Words.push_back("Purple");
Words.push_back("Brown");
Words.push_back("LightGray");

vector<string>::iterator Result =
    find(Words.begin(), Words.end(), "LightGray");

if (Result != Words.end())
    cout << *Result << endl;
else
    cout << "Value not found!" << endl;

Result = find(Words.begin(), Words.end(), "Black");

if (Result != Words.end())
    cout << *Result << endl;
else
    cout << "Value not found!" << endl;
}
```

The example starts with `vector` containing color strings. In both cases, the code attempts to location a particular color within `vector`. The first time the code is successful because `LightGray` is one of the colors listed in `vector`. However, the second attempt is thwarted because `Black` isn't one of the colors in `vector`. Here's the output from this example:

```
LightGray
Value not found!
```

Never assume that the code will find a particular value. Always assume that someone is going to provide a value that doesn't exist and then provide a means of handling the nonexistent value. In this example, you simply see a message stating the value wasn't found. However, in real-world code, you often must react to situations where the value isn't found by

✦ Indicating an error condition

✦ Adding the value to the container

✦ Substituting a standard value

✦ Defining an alternative action based on invalid input

The `find` algorithm is a personal favorite because it's so flexible. You can use it for external and internal requirements. Even though the example shows how you can locate information in an internal `vector`, you can also use `find` for external containers, such as disk drives. Have some fun with this one — experiment with all the containers you come across.

Using the Random Number Generator

Random number generators fulfill a number of purposes. Everything from games to simulations require a random number generator to work properly. Randomness finds its way into business what-if scenarios as well. In short, you need to add random output to your application in many situations.

Creating a random number isn't hard. All you need to do is call a random number function as shown in the following code:

```
#include <iostream>

using namespace std;

int main()
{
    // Always set a seed value.
    srand((unsigned int)time(NULL));

    int RandomValue = rand() % 12;
    cout << "The random month number is: " << RandomValue + 1 << endl;

    return 0;
}
```

Actually, none of the random number generators in the Standard Library works properly — imagine that! Every random number generator is a pseudorandom number generator. The numbers are distributed such that it appears that you see a random sequence, but given enough time and patience, the sequence repeats. In fact, if you don't set a seed value for your random number generator, you can obtain predictable sequences of numbers every time. How boring.

The first line of code in main sets the seed by using the system time. Using the system time ensures a certain level of randomness in the starting value and, therefore, a level of randomness for your application as a whole. If you comment out this line of code, you see the same output every time you run the application. In our case, our system output 6 every time.

The example application uses rand to create the random value. When you take the modulus of the random number, you obtain an output that is within a specific range, 12 in this case. The example ends by adding 1 to the random number because there isn't any month 0 in the calendar, and then outputs the month number for you.

The Standard Library provides access to two types of pseudorandom number generators. The first type requires that you set a seed value. The second type requires that you provide an input value with each call and doesn't require a seed value. Each outputs a different data type, so you can choose the kind of random number you obtain. Table 1-1 lists the random number generators and tells you what data type they output.

Table 1-1	Pseudorandom Number Generator Functions	
Function	*Output Type*	*Seed Required?*
rand	integer	yes
drand48	double	yes
erand48	double	no
lrand48	long	yes
nrand48	long	no
mrand48	signed long	yes
jrand48	signed long	no

Now that you know about the pseudorandom number generators, look at the seed functions used to prime them. Table 1-2 lists the seed functions and their associated pseudorandom number generator functions.

Table 1-2	Seed Functions
Function	*Associated Pseudorandom Number Generator Function*
srand	rand
srand48	drand48
seed48	mrand48
lcong48	lrand48

Performing Comparisons Using min and max

Computer programs perform many comparisons. In most cases, you don't know what the values are in advance or you wouldn't be interested in performing the comparison in the first place. The min and max functions make it possible to look at two values and determine the minimum or maximum value. Here's how you use these two functions:

```
#include <iostream>

using namespace std;

int main()
{
    int Number1, Number2;

    cout << "Type the first number: ";
    cin >> Number1;

    cout << "Type the second number: ";
```

```
    cin >> Number2;

    cout << "The minimum number is: " << min(Number1, Number2) << endl;
    cout << "The maximum number is: " << max(Number1, Number2) << endl;

    return 0;
}
```

In this case, the code accepts two numbers as input and then compares them using min and max. The output you see depends on what you provide as input, but the first output line tells you which number is smaller and the second tells you which is larger.

Working with Temporary Buffers

Temporary buffers are useful for all kinds of tasks. Normally, you use them when you want to preserve the original data, yet you need to manipulate the data in some way. For example, creating a sorted version of your data is a perfect use of a temporary buffer. The following example shows how to use a temporary buffer to sort some strings.

```
#include <iostream>
#include <vector>
#include <memory>

using namespace std;

int main()
{
    vector<string> Words;

    Words.push_back("Blue");
    Words.push_back("Green");
    Words.push_back("Teal");
    Words.push_back("Brick");
    Words.push_back("Purple");
    Words.push_back("Brown");
    Words.push_back("LightGray");

    int Count = Words.size();
    cout << "Words contains: " << Count << " elements." << endl;

    // Create the buffer and copy the data to it.
    pair<string*, ptrdiff_t> Mem = get_temporary_buffer<string>(Count);

    uninitialized_copy(Words.begin(), Words.end(), Mem.first);

    // Perform a sort and display the results.
    sort(Mem.first, Mem.first+Mem.second);

    for (int i = 0; i < Mem.second; i++)
        cout << Mem.first[i] << endl;

    return 0;
}
```

The example starts with the now familiar list of color names. It then counts the number of entries in `vector` and displays the count on screen.

At this point, the code creates the temporary buffer using `get_temporary_buffer`. The output is `pair`, with the first value containing a pointer to the string values and the second value containing the count of data elements. `Mem` doesn't contain anything — you have simply allocated memory for it.

The next task is to copy the data from `vector` (`Words`) to `pair` (`Mem`) using `uninitialized_copy`. Now that `Mem` contains a copy of your data, you can organize it using the `sort` function. The final step is to display the `Mem` content on screen. Here is what you'll see:

```
Words contains: 7 elements.
Blue
Brick
Brown
Green
LightGray
Purple
Teal
```

Chapter 2: Building Original Templates

In This Chapter

- ✔ Determining when to create a template
- ✔ Understanding the elements of good template design
- ✔ Developing a basic math template
- ✔ Creating a structure template
- ✔ Defining a class template
- ✔ Using template specialization to your advantage
- ✔ Building a library of templates
- ✔ Using your custom built template libraries

C++ has been around for many years. Because of its longevity, C++ templates abound. In fact, it may seem that there is a template for every practical purpose. However, the templates that are available to the developer community through standardized and third-party resources usually reflect generalized needs. The individual company you work for or you as a developer may have specialized needs that a generalized template can't address.

Every programming tool in existence offers a certain amount of flexibility. The reason why you see so many generalized tools is that someone developed them and the community as a whole decided to adopt them. Never think that you can't create your own tools. After all, someone created the generalized tools you work with daily — creating a custom tool requires nothing special, just time and thought on your part.

The trick to creating a customized tool is to think the process through, just as you would for any application you create. The fact that you'll use this customized tool to create multiple applications means that you must apply a higher standard than used for one-time applications to its design and the code it contains. A mistake in a customized tool can spell errors in every application you create using it, so this code must work well.

This chapter addresses the thought process behind templates first, and then shows some typical template examples. The examples will help demonstrate ways in which you can use templates to create better applications that require less code because the templates you create meet your needs more completely than any generalized template can. After you see the template examples, you discover the techniques used to place a number of templates in a library. Finally, you discover how to use the template library to create applications.

Deciding When to Create a Template

The first step in creating a template is deciding whether your idea will generate a useful template. Most developers have thousands of creative thoughts that translate into ideas during their careers; however, only a few of these ideas are exceptionally useful. By determining whether the template you want to create is a good idea at the outset, you waste less time on bad ideas and have more time to create that truly useful idea that will help you ascend to the pinnacle of development notoriety (and the astronomical amount of cash that such as position tends to generate).

Before you begin creating the next template to awe and inspire developers everywhere, consider the following questions:

+ **Is there a generic template that is close enough to meet your needs?** A good template idea is unique — it does something more than perform a useful task; it performs a new kind of useful task. Template ideas that fail the uniqueness test usually consume many resources for a small payoff.

+ **Will you use the template more than once?** Some template ideas are so tuned to a particular project that the developer ends up using them precisely once, which means that the template never provides a payback on the investment to create it.

+ **Will the template save more time than you use to create it?** Templates can become complex. In fact, some templates are complex enough that you'd save time by not writing them at all. The reason to use templates is to save time and effort, so a complex template tends to require a larger payback period than a simple one.

+ **Is there a third-party template you can buy or, better yet, obtain free that nearly meets you need?** Someone else may have already had your good idea. Before you invest time in creating a template, you should spend time researching online. Someone else may have created a template that nearly matches your idea. Obtaining a third-party template that's close to what you want is always more time efficient than creating a custom template on your own.

+ **How generic is the template you want to create?** Many good template ideas are simply too specific, which limits their adaptability to other situations. You want to create a unique template, but a unique template that can meet a range of organizational needs.

+ **Is your template concept complete?** Developers often envision only a piece of a template. For example, if you create a math template, you should actually create a library that contains all the equations you plan to use with your applications. Designing a template that contains a single equation is never worthwhile because other developers will have to finish the work you started.

✦ **Do you have the skills to create the template?** Not everyone is a good template designer. A template designer must define a template that goes beyond the original expectations because someone will almost certainly use the template in unexpected ways. The best templates adapt to new situations that the originator never considered. Consequently, creating a template requires a different sort of mindset than creating an application.

A little research at the outset can save significant time, effort, and replicated development. C++ has been around for a long time (at least in computer terms) so you can choose from a wealth of existing code. Always determine in advance whether the template you want to create is worth the effort and will make life easier for other developers.

**Book VI
Chapter 2**

**Building Original
Templates**

Defining the Elements of a Good Template

Minibook IV, Chapter 5 provides you with some insights into basic template creation techniques. However, this introductory chapter doesn't address what makes for a good template. After all, you don't want to appear like the guy who builds in his garage. The template you create has to look professional and work as expected.

The first decision you have to make is what kind of template to create. You can choose between these three types:

✦ **Function:** A function represents the simplest way to create a template and eases debugging requirements. You can group functions in libraries to make them easier to access. However, functions often lack depth and you can't coordinate activities between them as easily as you can between the elements of an object.

✦ **Structure:** A structure provides the best speed in many cases and can reduce the amount of system resources required, depending on how you define the structure. Remember that C++ allocates memory for the entire structure, but structures also present opportunities for optimization that you don't get with a class.

✦ **Class:** A class provides the greatest flexibility because you can express the template using all the elements that a class can provide — methods, properties, and events. You can inherit classes to create new classes. In short, if you have a complex idea to implement, classes are the way to do it.

The second decision you have to make is how to weight design factors when creating the template. C++ offers myriad ways to accomplish any given task. For example, you have multiple ways to create a function. However, one method is normally superior to the others simply because it offers some particular benefit. Consider these requirements when choosing the kind of template to create:

✦ **Security:** Simplicity often translates into easier to secure. In general, functions are easier to secure than structures, which are easier to secure than classes. However, you can easily write an insecure class if you use the wrong approach. Secure templates often require additional checks that can affect reliability (the template tends not to allow specific actions when these actions affect security) and speed (additional code always slows template execution).

✦ **Reliability:** The options you choose will affect the reliability of the template you create. A reliable template produces consistent results for any data type supplied to it. In some cases, ensuring reliability means adding checks to the template, which increases complexity. The additional code affects both the security and the speed of the template.

✦ **Speed:** Templates save the developer time. However, if the resulting template produces slow code, you can be sure that users will complain and the developer will end up rewriting some code to improve application speed. A fast template is usually small and performs the task precisely. The additional checks required to ensure secure and reliable operation always affect speed negatively, so you must work to achieve a balance.

✦ **Usage:** Some templates are so difficult to use that we doubt very much even the originator uses them. If a developer can't determine how to use your template, no one will ever use it and your effort is wasted. Consequently, you must design the template such that it meets security, reliability, and speed goals without becoming overly difficult to use.

✦ **Maintenance:** Someone will have to maintain the code used to create the template. A good template is one in which the code is relatively straightforward. Of course, you need to add comments to the code that explain how the code works and fully document the template design. Most templates see some level of redesign during their lifecycle — they evolve as developers use the template and discover new ways to incorporate it into applications.

The best template is the one that seems obvious. We were recently reading an article about the invention of the safety pin. The safety pin seems obvious, but someone still had to invent it because no one else had thought about it. When you create a template and someone tells you that it seems like an obvious idea, don't get mad. Be glad. You've joined the ranks of people who thought of something that fulfills an obvious need, but no one thought about it before you did.

The third decision you must make is how inclusive to make the template. In some cases, you want to create a template that can handle a range of situations. However, a template can quickly become unwieldy and difficult to manage. A good template is balanced — it includes the elements you need, but nothing beyond.

Creating a Basic Math Template

With a math template, you usually need access to a wealth of calculations but may only use one or two of those calculations at a time. For example, if someone is calculating your mortgage, he or she doesn't need to know the amortization calculation. However, the person might need the amortization calculation when working with the next customer. In short, the calculations all have a purpose and you need them all, but you don't need them all at the same time. Because of the way you use math templates, they work best as a series of function templates. Listing 2-1 shows how to create the series of functions.

Listing 2-1:   Defining a Series of Function Templates

```
#include <iostream>
#include <cmath>

using namespace std;

template<typename T>
T Area(T height, T length)
{
    return height * length;
}

const double PI = 4.0*atan(1.0);

template<typename T>
T CircleArea(T radius)
{
    double result;

    result = PI * radius * radius;

    return (T)result;
}

template<typename T>
T TriangleArea(T base, T height)
{
    double result;

    result = base * height * 0.5;

    return (T)result;
}

int main()
{
    cout << "4 X 4 Areas:" << endl;
    cout << "Square: " << Area<int>(4, 4) << endl;
    cout << "Circle: " << CircleArea<int>(2) << endl;
    cout << "Triangle: " << TriangleArea<int>(4, 4) << endl;
    cout << "Using a value of pi of: " << PI << endl;
    return 0;
}
```

The calculations could consist of any math calculation — the point of the example is that using functions makes each of the calculations discrete, easy to use, and easy to manage. When you run this example, you see the following output:

```
4 X 4 Areas:
Square: 16
Circle: 12
Triangle: 8
Using a value of pi of: 3.14159
```

Note that `CircleArea<int>(2)` uses half the value of the other calculations as input. That's because you calculate the area of a circle using the equation $\pi \times r^2$. If you want to see other area and volume equations, check out the Web site at `http://www.aquatext.com/calcs/calculat.htm`.

For consistency, you could change the circle equation to read like this:

```
radius = radius / 2;
result = PI * radius * radius;
```

Dividing the input by 2, essentially changing the diameter to a radius, means that you could call the equation using the same number as all the other area calculations: `CircleArea<int>(4)`. Whichever approach you choose, you need to document how the template works so that other developers know how to use it.

You should also note that the circle and triangle calculations perform a bit of type coercion to ensure that the user gets the expected results back by modifying the `return` statement to read `return (T)result;`. The type conversions are needed to keep your templates from generating warning messages. It's important to note that the approach used in the example truncates the result when the template returns an `int`.

Building a Structure Template

Structure templates have many interesting uses, such as creating a data repository that doesn't depend on a particular type. The example in Listing 2-2 shows one such use.

Listing 2-2:   Creating a Template from a Structure

```
#include <iostream>

using namespace std;

template<typename T>
```

```
struct Volume
{
    T height;
    T width;
    T length;

    Volume()
    {
        height = 0;
        width = 0;
        length = 0;
    }

    T getvolume()
    {
        return height * width * length;
    }

    T getvolume(T H, T W, T L)
    {
        height = H;
        width = W;
        length = L;

        return height * width * length;
    }

};

int main()
{
    Volume<int> first;

    cout << "First volume: " << first.getvolume() << endl;

    first.height = 2;
    first.width = 3;
    first.length = 4;

    cout << "First volume: " << first.getvolume() << endl;

    Volume<double> second;

    cout << "Second volume: " << second.getvolume(2.1, 3.2, 4.3) << endl;
    cout << "Height: " << second.height << endl;
    cout << "Width: " << second.width << endl;
    cout << "Length: " << second.length << endl;

    return 0;
}
```

In this case, the structure contains height, width, and length data values that the code can use to determine volume. The structure includes a constructor to initialize the values, so even if someone calls getvolume without initializing the structure, nothing bad will happen.

The structure allows independent access of each of the data values. You can set or get them as needed.

The `getvolume` function is overloaded. You can call it with or without input values. The code in `main` tests the structure thoroughly. Here's what you see as output from this example:

```
First volume: 0
First volume: 24
Second volume: 28.896
Height: 2.1
Width: 3.2
Length: 4.3
```

You can use structures for another interesting purpose. The C++ standard says you can't create a `typedef` template. For example, the following code produces an error when you try to compile it:

```
template<typename T>
typedef map<string, T> MyDef;
```

When you try to compile this code, you see the following error in CodeBlocks:

```
error: template declaration of `typedef'
```

However, you can define a `typedef` within a structure template. The code in Listing 2-3 shows a variation of the example found in Listing 6-3 of Minibook IV, Chapter 6.

Listing 2-3: Using a Structure to Define a typedef

```
#include <iostream>
#include <map>

using namespace std;

template<typename T>
struct MyDef
{
    typedef map<string, T> Type;
};

int main()
{
    MyDef<string>::Type marriages;

    marriages["Tom"] = "Suzy";
    marriages["Harry"] = "Harriet";

    cout << marriages["Tom"] << endl;
    cout << marriages["Harry"] << endl;

    return 0;
}
```

This example overcomes the C++ limitations by placing the `typedef` within the `struct`, `MyDef`. The same structure can hold any number of `typedef` entries.

Using a `typedef` in this manner makes it easier to work with `map`. All you need to worry about is the value type — the key type is already defined as `string`.

Except for the `marriages` declaration, this example works precisely the same as the example in Minibook IV, Chapter 6. It still outputs the following results:

```
Suzy
Harriet
```

Developing a Class Template

Class templates perform the heavy lifting of the template types. You use a class template to define objects of nearly any size. Classes are larger and more complex than the other techniques demonstrated in the chapter so far. In most cases, you use classes to represent complex objects or to perform tasks ill suited for function or structure templates.

You normally code classes in a separate file using the name of the class as the filename. The class definition appears in a header file, while the code appears in a code file. To make things a bit easier to understand, this chapter eschews the normal setup and shows the entire example using a single file.

The example shows a specialized queue implementation. It includes many of the features of a standard queue and then adds a few features to meet special development needs. Queues and other containers tend to contain complex code, but you also need to use them with a variety of data types, making a class template the perfect implementation. Listing 2-4 shows the code for this example.

Listing 2-4:   Creating a Specialized Queue

```
#include <iostream>
#include <vector>

using namespace std;

template<typename T>
class MyQueue
{
protected:
    vector<T> data;

public:
    void Add(T const &input);
```

(continued)

Listing 2-4 *(continued)*

```cpp
    void Remove();
    void PrintString();
    void PrintInt();
    bool IsEmpty();
};

template<typename T>
void MyQueue<T>::Add(T const &input)
{
    data.push_back(input);
}

template<typename T>
void MyQueue<T>::Remove()
{
    data.erase(data.begin());
}

template<typename T>
void MyQueue<T>::PrintString()
{
    vector<string>::iterator PrintIt = data.begin();

    while (PrintIt != data.end())
    {
        cout << *PrintIt << endl;
        PrintIt++;
    }
}

template<typename T>
void MyQueue<T>::PrintInt()
{
    vector<int>::iterator PrintIt = data.begin();

    while (PrintIt != data.end())
    {
        cout << *PrintIt << endl;
        PrintIt++;
    }
}

template<typename T>
bool MyQueue<T>::IsEmpty()
{
    return data.begin() == data.end();
}

int main()
{
    MyQueue<string> StringQueue;

    cout << StringQueue.IsEmpty() << endl;

    StringQueue.Add("Hello");
    StringQueue.Add("Goodbye");

    cout << "Printing strings: " << endl;
```

```
StringQueue.PrintString();
cout << StringQueue.IsEmpty() << endl;

StringQueue.Remove();
cout << "Printing strings: " << endl;
StringQueue.PrintString();
StringQueue.Remove();
cout << StringQueue.IsEmpty() << endl;

MyQueue<int> IntQueue;

IntQueue.Add(1);
IntQueue.Add(2);

cout << "Printing ints: " << endl;
IntQueue.PrintInt();

return 0;
}
```

The example starts with the class MyQueue. Note that data is a vector, not a queue as you might expect. A queue is an adapter — as such, it doesn't provide support for many of the features found in containers, such as vector — one of which is the use of iterators.

This example uses an iterator for printing, so it relies on a vector, rather than a queue as a starting point. Whenever you create your own specialized version of a common construct, make sure you begin with the right object. Otherwise, you might find the experience of creating the new class frustrating as a minimum, impossible in the worst case.

MyQueue includes the ability to add, remove, and print elements. In addition, you can check whether a queue is empty or full. You have already seen the code for these tasks in other parts of the book.

You might wonder about the code used for printing. The example includes separate methods for printing strings and integers, which might seem counterintuitive. After all, why not simply declare the iterator as follows so that it accepts any data type:

```
vector<T>::iterator PrintIt = data.begin();
```

The problem is that the iterator requires a specific data type. Consequently, you must declare it as shown in Listing 2-4. Otherwise, you get this unhelpful error message:

```
error: expected `;' before "PrintIt"
```

At some point, you want to test this new class using steps similar to those found in main. The test checks whether the queue actually does detect the empty and filled states, how adding and removing elements works, and whether the print routines work. Here is the output from this example:

```
1
Printing strings:
Hello
Goodbye
0
Printing strings:
Goodbye
1
Printing ints:
1
2
```

Considering Template Specialization

Some templates don't go together quite as easily as you might expect because they express a concept that doesn't translate the same way for every data type. For example, when you `stringify` a data type (turn the data type into its string representation), the technique differs based on data type. For example, when you want to `stringify` an `int`, you might use the following template:

```
#include <iostream>
#include <sstream>

using namespace std;

template<typename T> inline string stringify(const T& input)
{
    ostringstream output;
    output << input;
    return output.str();
}

int main()
{
    // This call works as expected.
    cout << stringify<int>(42) << endl;

    // This call truncates.
    cout << stringify<double>(45.6789012345) << endl;

    return 0;
}
```

The `stringify` function accepts any data type and simply uses an `ostringstream` to convert `input` to a `string`. This approach works fine for the first call in `main`, which is an `int`. However, when the code uses it for a `double`, the result is truncated as shown here:

```
42
45.6789
```

You can fix this problem by adding special handing for a `double`. Here is the modified form of the example that accommodates a `double`.

```cpp
#include <iostream>
#include <sstream>
#include <iomanip>

using namespace std;

template<typename T> inline string stringify(const T& input)
{
    ostringstream output;
    output << input;
    return output.str();
}

template <> inline string stringify<double> (const double& input)
{
    ostringstream output;
    const int sigdigits = numeric_limits<double>::digits10;
    output << setprecision(sigdigits) << input;
    return output.str();
}

int main()
{
    cout << stringify<int>(42) << endl;
    cout << stringify<double>(45.6789012345) << endl;
    return 0;
}
```

When you run this example, you see the expected result because the `double` form of the template uses `setprecision` to modify the `ostringstream` value. As a result, you see the following output:

```
42
45.6789012345
```

As things sit with C++ today, you must create a special template for each data type that requires it. Theoretically, if C++ ever gets a `typeof` function, you could detect the data type and add a `switch` to perform specialized processing within a single template.

You may have also noticed the `inline` keyword used for the template in this example. The `inline` keyword tells the compiler to place the code created by the template in line with the code in which it appears, rather than out of line as a separate function call. In some cases, such as this `stringify` function, the result is code that executes faster. The compiler is under no obligation to comply with the `inline` keyword. In addition, you want template code placed out of line when it must perform some level of instantiation or it doesn't represent critical path code that the application can call often.

Creating a Template Library

You won't normally create a template and stick it in your application project file. The previous examples in this chapter put everything together for ease of explanation, but in the real world, templates usually reside in a library. CodeBlocks provides several kinds of library projects. This chapter looks at the *static library* — a library that is added into the application.

CodeBlocks also supports dynamic link libraries (DLLs) and shared libraries that more than one application can use at a time. Working with DLLs and shared libraries is more complex than working with static libraries, and you won't normally need the ability to share the library when creating a console application. See the "Defining your first project" section of Minibook I, Chapter 1 for details about the various project types that CodeBlocks supports.

Defining the library project

Creating a library project is only a little different than creating a console application. The following steps describe how to create a library project:

1. Choose File⟹New⟹Project.

You see the New From Template dialog box shown in Figure 2-1.

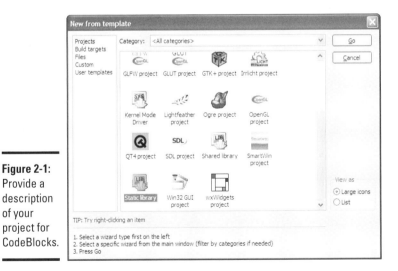

Figure 2-1: Provide a description of your project for CodeBlocks.

2. Highlight the Static Library icon on the Projects tab. Click Go.

You see the Welcome page of the Static Library wizard.

3. Click Next.

You see a list of project-related questions, as shown in Figure 2-2. These questions define project basics, such as the project name.

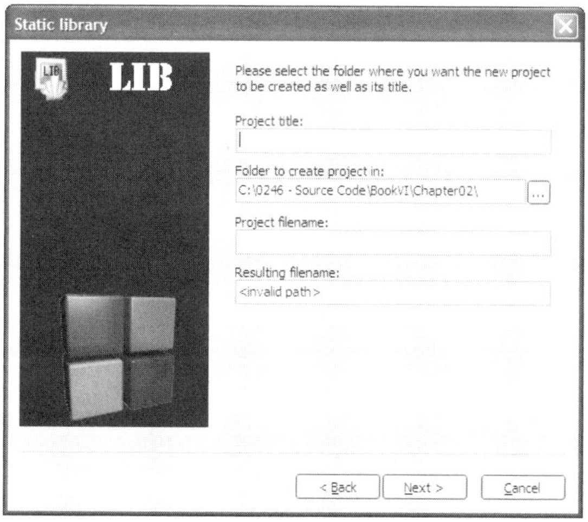

Figure 2-2:
Provide a
description
of your
static
library for
CodeBlocks.

4. Type a name for your project in the Project Title field.

The example uses MathLibrary as the project title. Notice that the wizard automatically starts creating an entry for you in the Project Filename field.

5. Type a location for your project in the Folder to Create Project In field.

6. (Optional) Type a project filename in the Project Filename field.

7. Click Next.

You see the compiler settings shown in Figure 2-3. This example uses the default compiler settings. However, it's important to remember that you can choose a different compiler, modify the locations of the debug and release versions of the project, and make other changes as needed. CodeBlocks provides the same level of customization for libraries as it does for applications.

8. Change any required compiler settings and click Finish.

The wizard creates the application for you. It then displays the CodeBlocks IDE with the project loaded. Note that the Static Library project includes some sample code to get you started. You could compile this library and test it now.

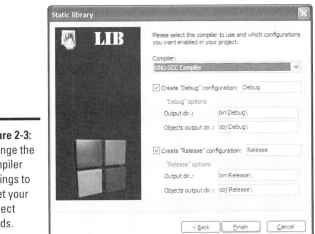

Figure 2-3: Change the compiler settings to meet your project needs.

Configuring the library project

The static library starts with a standard C file. To make this library work well with templates, you need to delete the C file, add a C++ file, and add a header file. The following steps describe how to perform this process:

1. **Right-click main.c and choose Remove File From Project from the context menu.**

   CodeBlocks removes the file from the project tree.

2. **Choose File➪New➪File.**

   You see the New from Template dialog box shown in Figure 2-4.

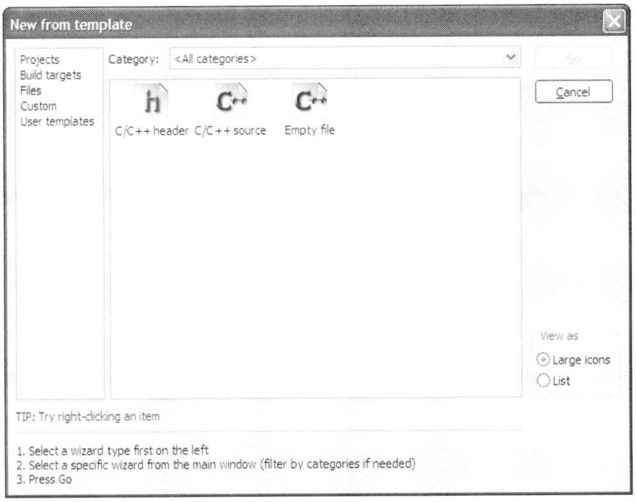

Figure 2-4: Add new files using the New from Template dialog box.

3. **Highlight the C/C++ Header icon and click Go.**

You see the Welcome page of the C/C++ Header wizard.

4. **Click Next.**

The wizard asks you to provide the header configuration information shown in Figure 2-5.

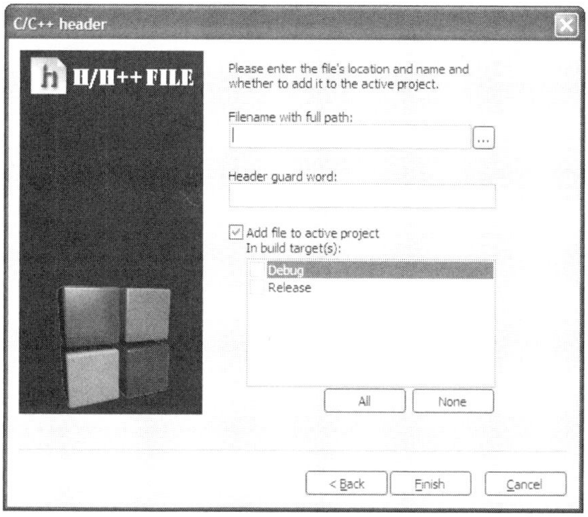

Figure 2-5:
Define the header require- ments.

5. **Type** MathLibrary.h, **click the ellipses button, and click Save.**

CodeBlocks adds the complete project path to the filename you chose. Notice that CodeBlocks also supplies an entry for the Header Guard Word field. This word ensures that the header isn't added more than once to a project.

6. **Click All, and then click Finish.**

The C/C++ Source wizard adds the file to your project. You're ready to begin creating a template library.

Coding the library

At this point, you have what amounts to a blank header file in a static library project. Your static library could conflict with other libraries, so it's impor- tant to add a namespace to your code. The example uses MyNamespace, but normally you'd use something related to you as a person or your company. After all, you should take pride in the library you've created! Listing 2-5 shows what you need to create the library used for this example.

Listing 2-5:   Creating a Static Library

```
#ifndef MATHLIBRARY_H_INCLUDED
#define MATHLIBRARY_H_INCLUDED

#include <iostream>
#include <cmath>

using namespace std;

namespace MyNamespace
{

template<typename T>
T Area(T height, T length)
{
    return height * length;
}

const double PI = 4.0*atan(1.0);

template<typename T>
T CircleArea(T radius)
{
    double result;

    result = PI * radius * radius;

    // This version truncates the value.
    return (T)result;
}

template<typename T>
T TriangleArea(T base, T height)
{
    double result;

    result = base * height * 0.5;

    return (T)result;
}

}

#endif // MATHLIBRARY_H_INCLUDED
```

As you can see, this is a portable form of the math library discussed in the "Creating a Basic Math Template" section of the chapter. Of course, the library form has changes. You have the usual define statements and the use of a namespace to encapsulate all the code. Notice that the namespace comes after all the declarations.

Using Your Template Library

You have a shiny new template library. It's time to test it. The MathLibraryTest console application uses MathLibrary to display some area information. The output is the same as in the "Creating a Basic Math Template" section of the chapter. Listing 2-6 shows the test code used for this example.

Listing 2-6: Testing the Static Library

```
#include <iostream>
#include "..\MathLibrary\MathLibrary.h"

using namespace std;
using namespace MyNamespace;

int main()
{
    cout << "4 X 4 Areas:" << endl;
    cout << "Square: " << Area<int>(4, 4) << endl;
    cout << "Circle: " << CircleArea<int>(2) << endl;
    cout << "Triangle: " << TriangleArea<int>(4, 4) << endl;
    cout << "Using a value of pi of: " << PI << endl;
    return 0;
}
```

When you use your own libraries, you need to tell the compiler where to find them. Because it's likely that you created the example library in the same folder as the test application, you can use the simple path shown in Listing 2-6.

Because the library relies on a namespace, you must also include `using namespace MyNamespace;` in the example code. Otherwise, you'll spend hours trying to figure out why the compiler can't locate the templates in your library. Otherwise, you access and use the template library much as you did before.

Chapter 3: Investigating Boost

In This Chapter

✓ Considering what Boost can do for you

✓ Getting Boost and installing it

✓ Working with the Boost Jam tool

✓ Integrating the Boost Build add-on

✓ Integrating the Boost Regression add-on

✓ Working with the Boost Inspect tool

✓ Using the BoostBook document format

✓ Integrating the Boost QuickBook add-on

✓ Working with the Boost bcp tool

✓ Working with the Boost Wave tool

✓ Creating your first application using Boost

*A*s your skill with C++ improves, you find that you need additional functionality that doesn't come with the Standard Library or with the Standard Template Library (STL). For example, the simple act of checking a string for specific character sequences (such as a telephone number pattern) can prove difficult. You can do it, but most developers will think that someone else has certainly crossed this bridge before. The answer to the question of where to find the additional code you need is third-party libraries. One of the most popular C++ libraries is Boost, which is the topic of this chapter and the next.

Two book chapters can't serve as a complete reference to an entire library — especially not a set of libraries the size of Boost. This chapter introduces you to Boost. It helps you understand why Boost may be helpful to your development efforts, shows you how to obtain and install Boost, demonstrates some Boost tools, and finally helps you create your first application using Boost. Chapter 4 picks up where this chapter leaves off and helps you use Boost to build some interesting applications. In short, these two chapters combined provide you with an overview of a library that you should consider spending more time discovering.

Libraries are simply repositories of code. Consequently, any library can help you produce applications faster and with fewer errors. However, not all libraries are created with the same quality of code. Many developers use the Boost libraries because it provides high-quality code — so high quality that some of Boost is being standardized for inclusion in the Standard Library. The bottom line is that you must choose the libraries you want with care and look at both quality and price (when price is an issue).

Understanding Boost

One of the best things about Boost is that the library itself is free. The Boost Web site, `http://www.boost.org/`, makes a point of letting developers know that they won't pay anything for using Boost, even in a commercial setting. In addition, Boost doesn't have any expenses, so you probably won't ever need to pay for it. A number of people and organizations contribute to Boost, including (but not limited to)

✦ Open Systems Lab at Indiana University

✦ SourceForge

✦ Boost Consulting

✦ MetaCommunications

✦ Individuals, companies, and other organizations that run the regression tests

However, don't get the idea that Boost is completely free. If you want commercial-level support, you'll pay for it, just as you would with any other product. Only the library itself is free. The following sections describe some of the details of Boost.

Boost features

You might think that Boost isn't really all that complete because you can get it free. Actually, Boost includes a significant number of features — far more features than the average developer will use in writing typical applications. It's interesting to note that you probably have an application on your system that relies on Boost, Adobe Acrobat 7.0. That's right, major applications do rely on Boost because it's a feature-rich application development library.

The current version of Boost contains 81 libraries in categories that meet an incredible number of needs. In some cases, you'll need only Boost to meet all your development needs. Because these libraries meet specific conformity requirements, you never find yourself calling a function one way with one library and another way when using a different library. Some of the libraries are so useful that they'll eventually find their way into the Standard Library, so you might have already used Boost without knowing it.

In addition to libraries, Boost also provides a number of tools to make your development experience more enjoyable. Most of this chapter discusses these specialized tools. Because you get the source for all the tools, you can build a version of the tool for every platform in your organization, which means that every developer can use the same toolset. Using a common toolset reduces training time and tends to improve the consistency of development output.

Licensing

The Boost license is friendly to individual users, consultants, and organizations. Even if you work in an enterprise environment, you can use Boost for free. The developers behind Boost are concerned enough about legal matters that they continue working on the license so that usage requirements are easy to understand. You can find a copy of the current license at http://www.boost.org/users/license.html.

The Boost license and the GNU General Public License (GPL) differ in some important ways. The most important consideration for organizations is that the Boost license lets you make changes to the libraries without having to share these changes with anyone. You get to keep your source code secret, which is a big plus for organizations that create commercial applications.

Paid support

When working with Boost, you gain access to the source code and community support. For some organizations, the lack of a formal support mechanism is a problem. Fortunately, you can also get paid support from BoostPro Computing (http://www.boostpro.com/). Most importantly, BoostPro Computing offers formal training in using Boost, which means your organization can get up to speed quickly. You can find additional companies that provide Boost support at http://www.boost.org/support/index.html.

Obtaining and Installing Boost for CodeBlocks

Before you can use Boost, you need to download it. The examples in this chapter rely on version 1.39 of the library, which you can obtain at http://sourceforge.net/project/showfiles.php?group_id=7586. Just the Boost library requires a 58MB download (all file sizes are for the ZIP file). The Web site also contains links for downloading other Boost features, including the following (there may be more when you read this):

+ Boost Build (2MB)

+ Boost Docs (20MB)

+ Boost Jam (1.2MB)

+ Other Boost components, Boost-subparts (5.3MB)

Boost for the Visual Studio Developer

Boost works with a wide variety of programming products, so you shouldn't get the idea that just because we use CodeBlocks in this chapter that you can't use Boost with other products such as Visual Studio. In fact, there is special support for other development products.

Visual Studio developers often find that their development environment is complex enough that getting a good Boost install is difficult.

BoostPro Computing remedies this problem by providing the BoostPro Installer (`http://www.boostpro.com/download`). Download this product and follow the installation instructions on the Web site to get a better Visual Studio installation for Boost. It's important to note that BoostPro Computing currently lacks an installer for the 1.39 version of Boost, but you can use the 1.38 version.

Unpacking Boost

The first step in gaining access to Boost is to unpack the Boost 1.39 library file (`boost_1_39_0.zip`) that you downloaded earlier. When working with CodeBlocks, you'll want to unpack this library into the `\Program Files\CodeBlocks\boost_1_39_0\` folder for ease of access. The documentation often refers to the `boost_1_39_0\` folder as the Boost root directory or `$BOOST_ROOT`. When you unpack the ZIP file, you see the following folders:

+ **boost\:** Contains all the Boost header files.

+ **doc\:** Provides a subset of the Boost documentation. If you want complete documentation, you must either download the separate Boost Docs file or use the Web site directly.

+ **lib\:** Contains all the Boost precompiled libraries after you build them. This folder won't exist when you unpack the Boost library.

+ **libs\:** Provides a root folder for all the Boost library headers.

  • **libs\accumulators\:** Contains a library of incremental statistical computation functions. In addition, you use this library for general incremental calculations.

  • **libs\algorithm\:** Contains algorithms that build on the string functionality found in the Standard Library. These algorithms provide functionality such as trimming, case conversion, predicates, and find/replace functions. You'll also find a min/max library that lets you determine the minimum and maximum of an expression in a single call (among other things).

  • **libs\any\:** Contains a library that helps you interact with variables in a manner reminiscent of scripting languages. You don't need this capability all the time, but it's handy when you want to do things such as convert between an `int` and `string` using a simple `lexical_cast`.

- **libs\array\:** Provides an extension to basic `array` functionality so that you get some of the advantages of using a `vector` without the performance hit that using a `vector` can introduce.

- **libs\more libraries:** Boost contains 81 libraries. You'll want to check them all out.

✦ **more\:** Holds policy and other important documents. The most important document at the outset is `getting_started.html`, which provides essential information for getting started using Boost. The `index.htm` file provides access to basic information about Boost, such as the licensing policy.

✦ **people\:** Tells you about all the people who worked on Boost, which might not seem like a big deal initially, but most of the entries include e-mail addresses. If you want to contact the makers of Boost, this is the place to look.

✦ **status\:** Provides access to a Boost-wide test suite. Generally, you won't need the contents of this folder unless you plan to augment the Boost libraries in some way.

✦ **tools\:** Contains a wealth of tools you use when working with Boost. Much of this chapter tells you about these tools. You must build the tools before you can use them. Each folder contains complete instructions, but you'll also find an example of building the tools later in this section.

✦ **wiki\:** Provides a shortcut to the Boost wiki. Opening `index.html` takes you directly to the wiki site.

**Book VI
Chapter 3**

**Investigating
Boost**

Building the libraries

The Boost library relies on code in headers. Using this approach means that if you include the header in your code, you already have everything you need to use the Boost library. However, these few Boost libraries require separate compilation:

✦ Boost.Filesystem

✦ Boost.IOStreams

✦ Boost.ProgramOptions

✦ Boost.Python

✦ Boost.Regex

✦ Boost.Serialization

✦ Boost.Signals

✦ Boost.System

✦ Boost.Thread

✦ Boost.Wave

You *build* these libraries using a *make* (`.mak`) file at the *command prompt*. All the examples in this book require a build — a combination of compiling and linking to create an executable file that you can run, so building is nothing new or scary. The only difference in this chapter is that you perform the build using a make file instead of relying on CodeBlocks to perform the process. The make file contains instructions that tell the make utility how to create the executable file. Actually, the libraries are object files that you must add to your application to use them. The command prompt is a special window you use to type commands that tell Windows to perform certain tasks or let applications perform the tasks for you. You see how all this works later in the chapter, so don't worry too much about the process for building libraries now.

In addition to required builds for some libraries, a few libraries require that you build external components before you can use them, but only if you use specific features. For example, when working with Boost.DateTime, you must compile an external component when using the `to_string` or `from_string` functions. The documentation tells you when you need to perform a separate compile. Here are the libraries that have external dependencies:

✦ Boost.DateTime

✦ Boost.Graph

✦ Boost.Test

The make files that come with the Boost library are meant for use with Unix and Linux. These files contain a `MkDir` (make directory) command that is incompatible with Windows. Consequently, if you don't create the required directory structure manually, you'll see the following error message:

```
The syntax of the command is incorrect.
```

Make sure you check the individual build instructions for each library before you build it. However, you must modify the instructions as described in this section or the library won't compile. The following procedure shows how to build an example library. In this case, you'll build the RegEx library used in Chapter 4:

1. **Choose Start⇨Programs⇨Accessories⇨Command Prompt.**

Windows opens a command prompt. The command prompt is where you type commands to tell the Minimalist GNU for Windows (MinGW) installation that comes with CodeBlocks to build the library you want to use.

2. **Type** `CD \Program Files\CodeBlocks\boost_1_39_0\libs\regex\build` **and press Enter.**

This command tells Windows to Change Directories (CD) to the directory (folder) that contains the build instructions for the RegEx library. You must be in the correct directory to execute the build commands. Otherwise, the build process will fail because the make program won't be able to find the resources it needs. You may have to modify the directory we've specified if you placed Boost in a different location from our installation or you're using a different version of Boost.

3. **Type** `Path=C:\Program Files\CodeBlocks\MinGW\bin;%Path%` **and press Enter.**

The Path command tells Windows where to find executable programs you want to use. In this case, you tell Windows where to locate the MinGW executables used to build the library. The `%Path%` part of the instruction tells Path to add all the old path elements onto the path you have described. If you don't do this, you may find that you can't access other Windows executables.

4. **Type** `MD gcc` **and press Enter.**

The Make Directory (MD) command creates a new directory. In this case, you create a GNU Compiler Collection (GCC) folder to hold the library when the make program builds it.

5. **Type** `CD gcc` **and press Enter.**

To create subdirectories, you must go to the gcc directory you just created.

6. **Type** `MD boost_regex-gcc-1_38` **and press Enter.**

This new directory holds the gcc version of the Boost RegEx library, and it's version 1.38 of that library. This directory contains the release version of the library.

7. **Type** `MD boost_regex-gcc-d-1_38` **and press Enter.**

This new directory holds the debug version of the RegEx library. You use the debug version of the library when you first create your application and then change to the release version after you get rid of the bugs.

8. **Type** `CD..` **and press Enter.**

Now that you're finished creating the directory structure for the library, you can go back to the build directory. It's time to build the library.

9. **Type** `mingw32-make -fgcc.mak` **and press Enter.**

The Minimalist GNU for Windows 32-bit Make (mingw32-make) utility reads the instructions found in `gcc.mak` and creates the RegEx library using them. Figure 3-1 shows what you should see as the mingw32-make utility does its work.

The -f command-line switch specifies which make file to use for the build process. The mingw32-make utility includes other command-line switches; you can discover them by typing **mingw32-make -?** and pressing Enter.

All the libraries follow a similar process. You build the library after creating a directory structure for it. It's possible to obtain the directory structure by searching for all the `MkDir` commands in the `gcc.mak` file.

```
C:\WINDOWS\system32\cmd.exe                                          _ □ ×

C:\Program Files\CodeBlocks\boost_1_39_0\libs\regex\build>mingw32-make -fgcc.mak

gcc.mak:37: "Building Boost.Regex without ICU / Unicode support:"
gcc.mak:38: "Hint: set ICU_PATH on the nmake command line to point "
gcc.mak:39: "to your ICU installation if you have one."
g++   -o gcc/boost_regex-gcc-1_38/c_regex_traits.o -c -O2 -I../../..   ../src/c_r
egex_traits.cpp
g++   -o gcc/boost_regex-gcc-1_38/cpp_regex_traits.o -c -O2 -I../../..   ../src/c
pp_regex_traits.cpp
g++   -o gcc/boost_regex-gcc-1_38/cregex.o -c -O2 -I../../..   ../src/cregex.cpp
g++   -o gcc/boost_regex-gcc-1_38/fileiter.o -c -O2 -I../../..   ../src/fileiter.
cpp
g++   -o gcc/boost_regex-gcc-1_38/icu.o -c -O2 -I../../..   ../src/icu.cpp
g++   -o gcc/boost_regex-gcc-1_38/instances.o -c -O2 -I../../..   ../src/instance
s.cpp
g++   -o gcc/boost_regex-gcc-1_38/posix_api.o -c -O2 -I../../..   ../src/posix_ap
i.cpp
g++   -o gcc/boost_regex-gcc-1_38/regex.o -c -O2 -I../../..   ../src/regex.cpp
g++   -o gcc/boost_regex-gcc-1_38/regex_debug.o -c -O2 -I../../..   ../src/regex_
debug.cpp
g++   -o gcc/boost_regex-gcc-1_38/regex_raw_buffer.o -c -O2 -I../../..   ../src/r
egex_raw_buffer.cpp
g++   -o gcc/boost_regex-gcc-1_38/regex_traits_defaults.o -c -O2 -I../../..   ../
src/regex_traits_defaults.cpp
```

Figure 3-1:
The make file automates the build process for you.

TIP

To make the libraries easier to access, you can copy them to the boost_1_39_0\lib directory by typing **Copy <LibraryName> "\Program Files\CodeBlocks\boost_1_39_0\lib"** at the command prompt and pressing Enter. (Be sure to include the double quotes or the command won't work properly.) Make sure you create the lib directory before you attempt to use it by typing **MD "\Program Files\CodeBlocks\boost_1_39_0\lib"** and pressing Enter.

Building the Boost tools

Building the Boost tools is considerably different from building the libraries. Boost relies on a tool called Boost Jam to build the Boost tools (see the "Using Boost Jam" section of the chapter for information about this tool). However, before you can use Boost Jam, you have to build it. Use the following procedure to build bjam.exe.

1. **Choose Start⇨Programs⇨Accessories⇨Command Prompt.**

Windows opens a command prompt.

2. **Type** CD \Program Files\CodeBlocks\boost_1_39_0\tools\ jam\src **and press Enter.**

Windows changes the directory to the Boost Jam source code directory.

3. **Type** Path=C:\Program Files\CodeBlocks\MinGW\bin;%Path% **and press Enter.**

Windows adds the MinGW executables to the path.

4. **Type** Build GCC **and press Enter.**

Windows executes the build.bat file. This file contains instructions for building Boost Jam as shown in Figure 3-2. After a few minutes, the build process is complete. You can copy the executable to the root of the tools directory to make it easier to build the rest of the tools.

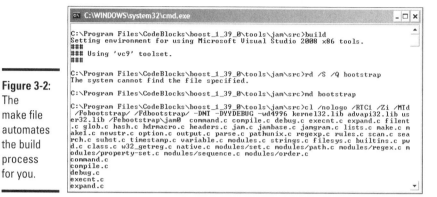

Figure 3-2:
The make file automates the build process for you.

It's essential that you provide the GCC command-line switch with the Build command. Otherwise, the build process will attempt to rely on Visual C++ as the toolset and the build process could fail.

5. Type CD bin.ntx86 **and press Enter.**

You change directories to the executable output directory.

6. Type Copy bjam.exe \Program Files\CodeBlocks\ boost_1_39_0\tools **and press Enter.**

The Boost Jam utility is now at the root of the tools directory where you need it.

Boost Jam is a build tool that you can use for extremely complex build processes. Because the tools require a specific build, you use Boost Jam to ensure that you obtain a good result. The following steps build most of the Boost tools for you and place them in the \Program Files\CodeBlocks\ boost_1_39_0\bin.v2 directory:

1. Using the same command prompt you used to build bjam, type CD \ Program Files\CodeBlocks\boost_1_39_0\tools **and press Enter.**

Windows changes directories to the tool directory.

2. Type bjam toolset=gcc > ToolBuild.log **and press Enter.**

This command line starts the bjam build utility. The bjam utility automatically searches for a Jamfile file and follows the instructions it contains. The tools folder contains such as file.

It sets the toolset to gcc, which is the compiler you use with CodeBlocks. If you choose a different compiler, you need to use the toolset for that compiler. The tool building process is extremely long, so be patient — get a cup of coffee.

The output from this process goes to the ToolBuild.log file. This is a text file that you can examine later for potential errors in the build process.

3. **Copy the tools you want to use to a common `\Program Files\ CodeBlocks\boost_1_39_0\bin` directory.**

   The build process places the executables where you're least likely to find them. For example, the bcp utility appears in the `\Program Files\CodeBlocks\boost_1_39_0\bin.v2\tools\bcp\gcc-mingw-3.4.5\release\link-static` directory on our machines.

The procedure in this section doesn't build all the tools. For example, if you want to work with Boost Build, you need to build it separately. In this case, you change directories to the `\Program Files\CodeBlocks\ boost_1_39_0\tools\build\v2` directory and use Boost Jam to build Boost Build for you.

Using Boost Jam

Boost Jam is a build tool that you can use to build applications at the command line. Normally, you rely on CodeBlocks to perform this task. However, the "Building the Boost tools" section of the chapter has already shown you that building applications at the command prompt need not be difficult — it's more difficult than using CodeBlocks, but it's still quite doable.

The main reason to use a command-line build tool is portability. Not everyone will have a copy of CodeBlocks available to build your application should you decide to release it to the public. In addition, not everyone will use the same platform that you do — the person working with your application might use Windows or Linux or the Macintosh. Standardized C++ code and a command-line make file combine to produce a project that you can move just about anywhere.

Boost Jam relies on the `bjam.exe` file to perform building. You can call `bjam.exe` alone and it automatically locates the `Jamfile` file that contains the building instructions. A `Jamfile` can include a version number, such as `Jamfile.v2` for version 2 of the `Jamfile` format.

You may want to modify the behavior of Boost Jam. For example, in the "Building the Boost tools" section of the chapter, you used the toolset command-line switch to tell Boost Jam to use gcc, rather than Microsoft Visual C++. Here is a list of the command-line switches that Boost Jam understands:

✦ **-a:** Rebuilds the entire application, even if the existing files are up-to-date.

✦ **-d *n*:** Specifies the debugging level you want to use while building the project. You specify a value for *n* from 1 through 13 (the default level is 1). The following list describes each debugging level:

   • **1:** Shows the standard actions that Boost Jam performs to build the project, but doesn't include any detailed information.

- **2:** Shows both the standard and quiet actions that Boost Jam performs to build the project. *Quiet* actions are events that Boost Jam normally doesn't tell you about.

- **3:** In addition to the actions, shows the dependency analysis that Boost Jam performs, along with the target and source timestamps and paths.

- **4:** Adds the build arguments and timing of shell invocations to the output.

- **5:** Includes rule invocations and variable expansions as part of the output.

- **6:** Displays input file information: directory, header file, archive scans, and attempts to bind to the targets.

- **7:** Displays all the variable settings as the build progresses.

- **8:** Increases variable output information by adding variable fetches, variable expansions, and the evaluation results of `if` expressions within the `Jamfile`.

- **9:** Provides maximum variable information by adding variable manipulation, scanner tokens, and memory usage.

- **10:** Displays profile information for build rules. This output includes both timing and memory.

- **11:** Informs you about the parsing progress of the `Jamfiles`.

- **12:** Outputs a text graph of the target dependencies.

- **13:** Displays all available information, including the change target status.

✦ **-d +*n*:** Enables a specific debugging level. See the -d *n* entry for a list of debugging levels.

✦ **-d 0:** Disables all debugging. Boost Jam displays only actual errors experienced during the build process.

✦ **-f *Jambase*:** Specifies an alternative `Jambase` file to read. You use this command line switch when your `Jamfile` uses an alternative name. Boost Jam allows just one -f command-line switch. If you specify a `Jamfile` name of – (hyphen), Boost Jam accepts input from the console until you close the input by pressing Ctrl+Z. When you close the input, Boost Jam treats the input you provided as a `Jamfile`.

✦ **-j *n*:** Performs up to *n* shell commands concurrently. Normally, Boost Jam performs one command at a time. Using multiple commands on a machine that supports it can improve build speed.

✦ **-l *n*:** Stops an action after *n* seconds. This feature prevents your build from becoming stopped by actions that can't complete. You can use this command-line switch only on Windows.

✦ **-n:** Executes everything but updating actions. Using this command-line switch changes the default debug level to 2. See the -d *n* entry for a list of debugging levels.

✦ **-o *file*:** Defines the name of the output file — the file that Boost Jam updates as a result of the build process. The output file should have an executable file extension.

✦ **-q:** Forces Boost Jam to quit immediately after any target failure. Using this feature ensures that you don't wait extended periods while Boost Jam tries to complete a build that can't succeed.

✦ **-s *var=value*:** Sets a Boost Jam variable to a specific value. You can override both internal variables and variables that Boost Jam normally imports from environment variables. An example of an internal variable is JAMVERSION, which tells you the version of the product in use. An example of an environment variable is Path, which should contain the location of the compiler you want to use to build the project. The Web site at `http://www.boost.org/doc/tools/jam/jam/language.html#jam.language.variables` provides additional information about variables and their use.

✦ **-t *target*:** Rebuilds both the target and all the dependencies for the target. Therefore, if you create an application that relies on the RegEx library, Boost Jam rebuilds the RegEx library in addition to your application when you use this command-line switch.

✦ **-- *value*:** Boost Jam ignores this command-line switch and its associated value. However, you can access the value using the $(ARGV) variable, which means you can use this feature to pass values to your build script without affecting normal Boost Jam operation.

✦ **-v:** Prints version information for Boost Jam and then exits.

In addition to the command-line switches, Boost Jam supports a complex scripting language. You use the scripting language to create a Jamfile. A discussion of the scripting language is outside the scope of this book. However, you can discover more about the scripting language at `http://www.boost.org/doc/tools/jam/jam/language.html`.

Using Boost Build

Boost Build (`http://www.boost.org/doc/tools/build/index.html`) isn't a separate executable. It's an add-on product for Boost Jam. Boost Build adds to the capabilities already provided in Boost Jam, making the task of creating and using build files considerably easier.

The instructions at `http://www.boost.org/doc/tools/build/doc/html/bbv2/installation.html` tell you how to install the current version of Boost Build. However, if you installed and built Boost using the instructions found in the "Obtaining and Installing Boost for CodeBlocks" section of the chapter, you already have Boost Build available to you. Use these steps to verify that you have Boost Build:

1. **Choose Start⇨Programs⇨Accessories⇨Command Prompt.**

   Windows opens a command prompt.

2. **Type** `Path=C:\Program Files\CodeBlocks\boost_1_39_0\bin;C:\Program Files\CodeBlocks\MinGW\bin;%Path%` **and press Enter.**

   Windows adds the MinGW executables and the Boost Jam utility to the path. The `C:\Program Files\CodeBlocks\boost_1_39_0\bin` directory is described in the "Building the Boost tools" section of the book — you create this directory to hold the executable tools provided with the Boost library.

   **Book VI
Chapter 3**

Investigating Boost

   When setting the path for the MinGW executables and the Boost library tools make sure you use the correct drive letter. For most people, the correct drive letter is C. However, you might have the MinGW executables installed on drive D and the Boost library tools on drive E, in which case, you'd change the path statement to read `Path=D:\Program Files\CodeBlocks\boost_1_39_0\bin;E:\Program Files\CodeBlocks\MinGW\bin;%Path%`.

3. **Type** `CD \Program Files\CodeBlocks\boost_1_39_0\tools\build\v2\example\hello` **and press Enter.**

   Windows changes the directory to one of the Boost Build examples that installed on your machine. These examples show how to work with Boost Build, and the Hello example is the easiest of the examples.

4. **Type** `bjam --version` **and press Enter.**

   You see the Boost Build and Boost Jam version information for your setup. This information comes from Boost Build. Look through the command-line switches in the "Using Boost Jam" section of the chapter and you notice there is no --version command-line switch for Boost Jam. Here is typical information for the current version of Boost Build.

   ```
   Boost.Build V2 (Milestone 12)
   Boost.Jam 03.1.17
   ```

   Now that you know that Boost Jam is accessible, you must perform a configuration task.

5. **Open the `user-config.jam` file located in the `\Program Files\CodeBlocks\boost_1_39_0\tools\build\v2` folder of your machine using Notepad.**

   You see a number of configuration options. Don't worry about most of these configuration options because you don't need them.

6. **Locate the following lines of configuration information:**

   ```
   # -----------------
   # GCC configuration.
   # -----------------

   # Configure gcc (default version).
   using gcc ;
   ```

7. **Remove the # symbol from in front of using gcc ; and save the file.**

   Boost Build is now configured for CodeBlocks.

8. **At the command prompt, type** bjam **and press Enter.**

   Boost Build builds the Hello example for you using gcc as shown in Figure 3-3.

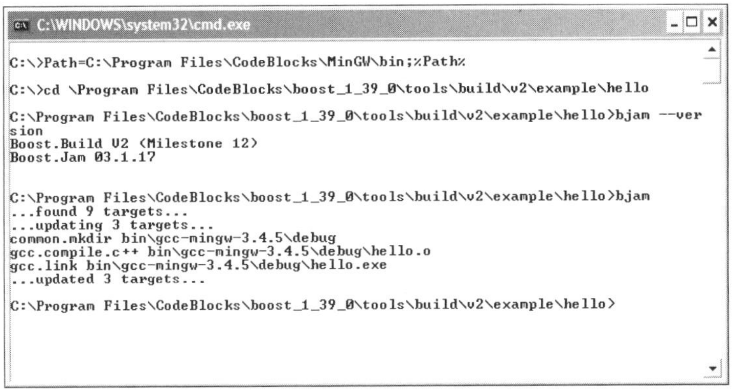

Figure 3-3:
Use the
--version
command-
line switch
to ensure
you have
Boost Build.

At this point, if you go into the \Program Files\CodeBlocks\boost_1_ 39_0\tools\build\v2\example\hello\bin\gcc-mingw-3.4.5 direc-tory, you see debug and release subdirectories, which contain the debug and release versions of the Hello.exe application, respectively. Before you can use Boost Build to build your own applications, you must make it accessible from more than the Boost Build folder. For example, if you try to execute bjam --version in the root directory of your computer right now, you receive the following error message:

```
Unable to load Boost.Build: could not find "boost-build.jam"
------------------------------------------------------------
Attempted search from C:\ up to the root

Please consult the documentation at 'http://www.boost.org'.
```

To make Boost Build generally available, you need to perform an additional configuration task. Type **SET BOOST_BUILD_PATH=C:\Program Files\ CodeBlocks\boost_1_39_0\tools\build\v2** at the command prompt and press Enter. Now when you execute bjam --version in the root directory, you see the proper version information. Boost Build provides an array of configuration options that you can read about at `http://www.boost.org/doc/tools/build/doc/html/bbv2/advanced/configuration.html`.

The example in this section shows just one of many reasons you want to use Boost Build — ease of building your applications. Unlike Boost Jam, Boost Build relies on `.jam` files to hold both build and configuration information. The `.jam` files provide significant additional flexibility over using Boost Jam alone. The overview at `http://www.boost.org/doc/tools/build/index.html` provides you with a list of the added functionality that Boost Build provides.

Using Regression

Regression is an add-on for Boost Build that lets you perform regression testing as part of the build process. *Regression testing* ensures that your application meets specific requirements and that changes you make to your application don't add potential bugs. Larger organization usually employ regression testing as part of major application projects because the testing environment becomes so complex. You never need a product of this sort for smaller applications or for discovering new C++ features.

As with Boost Build, you get Regression when you install Boost according to the instructions found in the "Obtaining and Installing Boost for CodeBlocks" section of the chapter. Regression is an advanced tool that requires that you know a little something about Python as well as C++. Because Regression is such a complex tool, incomplete, and currently in beta, it's well outside the scope of this book to describe. However, you can find the requirements and step-by-step instructions for using Regression at `http://beta.boost.org/development/running_regression_tests.html`.

The Regression add-on provides a number of specific capabilities that you may want to know about. The main Regression Web site at `http://www.boost.org/doc/libs/1_39_0/tools/regression/doc/index.html` provides access to this information. If you do decide to try Regression, make sure you obtain the correct version of Python and perform all required setup testing.

Using Inspect

Many organizations want to make changes to the Boost library to ensure that the library meets their needs or to augment the Boost library to meet a new requirement. Whenever you change something, there is a chance that the change will cause compatibility issues because it doesn't meet the Boost library guidelines. In addition, it's possible for a developer to introduce errors into the Boost library that others will find difficult to fix. The Inspect utility makes it possible for you to scan for potential Boost library errors after you make a change to it.

Normally, the tools build process described in the "Building the Boost tools" section of the chapter builds Inspect for you. However, you can build Inspect manually as well. You find a `.jar` file for building it in the `\Program Files\CodeBlocks\boost_1_39_0\tools\inspect\build` directory.

Start Inspect from the directory that you want to check. Inspect looks for errors in the current directory and all subdirectories. Normally, Inspect performs a complete check of the libraries. However, you can modify Inspect behavior using the following command-line switches to perform specific tests:

+ -license

+ -copyright

+ -crlf

+ -link

+ -path_name

+ -tab

+ -ascii

+ -minmax

+ -unnamed

You can use any number of these command-line switches. If you forget the Inspect command-line switches, type **Inspect -help** and press Enter. Inspect shows you a list of the command-line switches you can use for testing.

Inspect also provides a number of command-line switches that affect how it performs tests. The following list describes these command line switches:

+ **-cvs:** Performs a check of only the `cvs` directory and ignores all other files.

+ **-text:** Outputs the results in pure text format. This option is especially useful when you to save the results to a text file for later analysis. Otherwise, Inspect formats the output as HTML. Figure 3-4 shows a typical report. Click on the links to see details about a particular test, such as the licensed status of each file within a particular directory.

+ **-brief:** Reduces the amount of output text to the minimum required to indicate success or failure of the various tests.

Inspect is sensitive about the ordering of command-line switches. You must place the `-cvs`, `-text`, or `-brief` command-line switch first, and then the test switches; otherwise Inspect displays an error message. The Web site at `http://www.boost.org/doc/libs/1_39_0/tools/inspect/index.html` tells you more about working with Inspect.

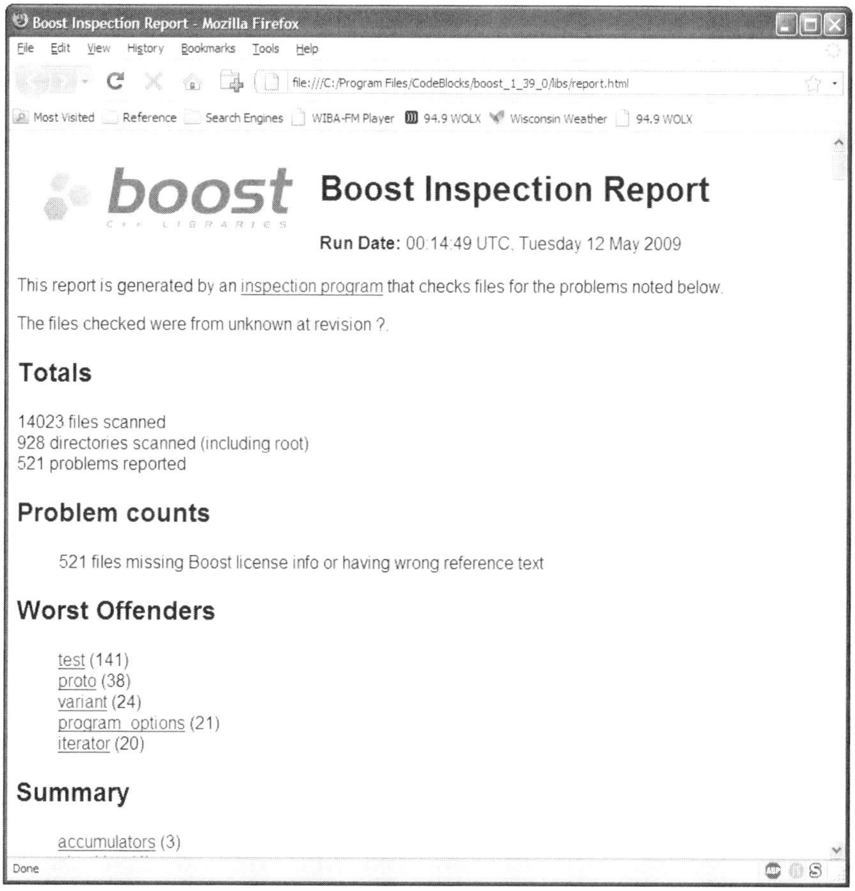

Figure 3-4:
Inspect
normally
outputs its
reports as
HTML.

Understanding BoostBook

The world abounds with documentation formats — everything from `.doc` files produced by Word to the seemingly ubiquitous `.pdf` file. Of all the documentation formats, the most universal and compatible is the lowly `.txt` file. However, `.txt` files lack formatting, which means they limit you solely to words, which may not be enough to describe your documentation. Because you can choose from so many different file formats and formatting code can prove especially difficult, the Boost library relies on a special document format called BoostBook.

Documentation seems to be the bane of developers everywhere. No one seems to want to write the documentation, and the attempts at documentation often leave readers with more questions than answers. BoostBook won't make you a good writer. While it does help you produce highly formatted documentation with a standardized format, it can't overcome deficiencies in writing skill. When creating documentation for your project, the best writer in your group is still the unsurpassed choice for documentation tasks.

If you have installed the Boost library using the instructions in the "Obtaining and Installing Boost for CodeBlocks" section of this chapter, you already have access to BoostBook. However, as with some other Boost utilities, you need to know a bit about Python to use this feature. In addition, you need an Apache server setup and must also download a number of other utilities. In short, even though BoostBook is accessible from a Boost library perspective, you still need to do some work to make this feature useful. The instructions at `http://www.boost.org/doc/libs/1_39_0/doc/html/boostbook/getting/started.html` describe the additional steps you need to perform.

BoostBook relies on XML to hold the content you want to place in the document. The use of XML is the reason you must install the DocBook eXtensible Stylesheet Language (XSL) (`http://docbook.sourceforge.net/`) and DocBook Document Type Definition (DTD) (`http://www.oasis-open.org/docbook/xml/4.2/`) support. You can see the XML used for BoostBook at `http://www.boost.org/doc/libs/1_39_0/doc/html/boostbook/documenting.html`. Check the main BoostBook page at `http://www.boost.org/doc/libs/1_39_0/doc/html/boostbook.html` for additional information.

After you configure BoostBook, you need to open a command prompt and test it. The instructions supplied on the Web site only partially work with BoostBook and CodeBlocks. Use these instructions to help configure the command prompt for use:

1. **Choose Start⇨Programs⇨Accessories⇨Command Prompt.**

Windows opens a command prompt.

2. **Type** `Path=C:\Program Files\CodeBlocks\boost_1_39_0\bin;C:\Program Files\CodeBlocks\MinGW\bin;%Path%` **and press Enter.**

Windows adds the MinGW executables and the Boost Jam utility to the path.

3. **Type** `\Program Files\CodeBlocks\boost_1_39_0\doc` **and press Enter.**

Windows changes directory to the Boost document directory.

4. **Type** `bjam --v2` **and press Enter.**

BoostBook generates the documentation for the Boost library and places it in the `html` subdirectory. If BoostBook passes this test, then you know you have a working setup.

Even if you choose not to use BoostBook for your project, you do need to create a common documentation format. Using BoostBook may prove complicated for the Windows developer — it seems that the originators meant this documentation format more for Unix and Linux developers. However, it's still a useful documentation format and you should consider it. If you find BoostBook lacking, you need to create a custom format or suffer the consequences of a poorly documented application.

Using QuickBook

QuickBook is an add-on for BoostBook. This utility started as someone's weekend project. Originally, QuickBook outputted simple HTML documents. However, now it outputs XML in BoostBook format so that you can quickly generate documentation that links with the rest of the documentation for your project. As described by the author at `http://www.boost.org/doc/libs/1_39_0/doc/html/quickbook.html`, QuickBook is a WikiWiki style documentation tool. It's important to note that some people simply call it a Wiki (`http://en.wikipedia.org/wiki/Wiki`) or Wiki-Wiki or even Wiki Wiki. All the terms mean the same thing.

Before you use QuickBook, you generate a documentation file. You can see an example of such a file at `http://www.boost.org/doc/libs/1_39_0/tools/quickbook/doc/quickbook.qbk`. For a complete syntax summary for QuickBook, look at `http://www.boost.org/doc/libs/1_39_0/doc/html/quickbook/syntax.html`.

At this point, you're probably wondering why you should use QuickBook at all, since you have to generate a document file for it anyway. Here are the reasons why many developers use QuickBook instead of relying on BoostBook directly:

✦ The QuickBook syntax is easier to read and use than writing XML.

✦ You can use QuickBook to generate non-Boost documentation.

✦ It's relatively easy to convert other documentation formats into QuickBook syntax.

QuickBook is a command-line utility. You find it in the `\Program Files\` `CodeBlocks\boost_1_39_0\bin.v2\tools\quickbook\gcc-mingw-` `3.4.5\release\link-static` directory after generating the Boost tools (see the "Building the Boost tools" section of the chapter for details). If you plan to use this utility, make sure you copy it to the common `bin` directory you set up as part of building the Boost tools. Here are the command-line switches you can access when working with QuickBook:

✦ **--help:** Displays a help message showing all the command-line switches, as well as the command-line syntax.

✦ **--version:** Displays version information about QuickBook.

✦ **--no-pretty-print:** Disables XML printing and uses plain text instead.

✦ **--indent** *arg*: Defines the number of spaces to use for indents (as specified by arg).

✦ **--linewidth** *arg*: Defines the number of characters in a single line.

✦ **--input-file** *arg*: Specifies the name of the input file.

✦ **--output-file** *arg*: Specifies the name of the output file.

✦ **--debug:** Places QuickBook in debug mode (useful only for developers who want to tinker with the executable).

✦ **--ms-errors:** Specifies that QuickBook should use the Microsoft Visual Studio style of errors and warnings in the output message format. This option can make QuickBook easier for Microsoft Visual Studio developers to use and understand.

Using bcp

The bcp (Boost copy) utility helps you make Boost more manageable. You can use it to

✦ Copy one or more Boost modules to another location so that you can use a subset within an application.

✦ List all the elements within a module.

✦ Create an HTML report about module content that includes:

  • License information

  • Files without licensing information

  • Files without copyright information

  • Copyright information

  • Dependency information for individual files

Theoretically, you can also use bcp to scan your application. The output report includes all the information in a standard bcp report for a Boost module. You use one of four command-line syntaxes to work with bcp as shown here:

```
bcp [options] module-list output-path
bcp --list [options] module-list
bcp --list-short [options] module-list
bcp --report [options] module-list html-file
```

Each of these command-line syntaxes performs a different task: copy, listing, short listing, and reporting. These command lines can accept a number of options, as described in the following list:

✦ **--boost=*path*:** Defines the path to the Boost library. Normally you'll have to use this option on Windows systems to ensure that bcp can find your Boost setup. Otherwise, you see the following error message:

```
**** exception(205): std::runtime_error: The Boost path appears to have
been incorrectly set: could not find boost/version.hpp in
******** errors detected; see standard output for details ********
```

✦ **--scan:** Treats the modules as a non-Boost file for the purpose of scanning file dependencies. You always use this option with your own applications.

✦ **--cvs:** Copies only files under Concurrent Versions System (CVS) version control.

✦ **--unix-lines:** Uses Unix-style line endings for the output. You won't ever use this command-line switch on a Windows system but may need it on Unix, Linux, and Macintosh systems.

Using bcp is relatively straightforward. For example, if you want a listing of files for the `regex` library, you use the following command line:

```
bcp --list --boost="C:\Program Files\CodeBlocks\boost_1_39_0" regex >> out.txt
```

The bcp utility looks in the `C:\Program Files\CodeBlocks\ boost_1_39_0` directory for Boost. Note that you must enclose the directory in quotes because it contains a space. In this case, the output appears in `out.txt`. You should always use file redirection because the output is too large to read at the command prompt.

Let's say you want a report about the `regex` module instead of a simple listing. In this case, you use the following command line (all of which should appear on a single line):

```
bcp --report --boost="C:\Program Files\CodeBlocks\boost_1_39_0" regex
 myreport.html
```

Creating a report can take a while. Eventually, you see an HTML report like the one shown in Figure 3-5. You can discover more about bcp at `http://www.boost.org/doc/libs/1_39_0/tools/bcp/bcp.html`.

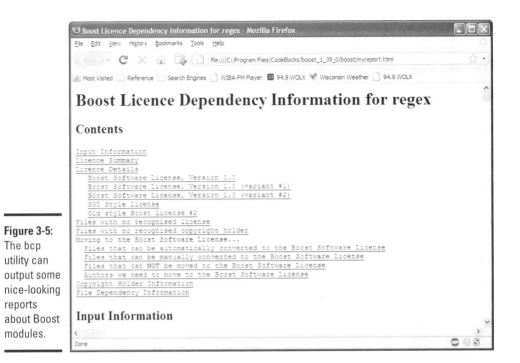

Figure 3-5:
The bcp utility can output some nice-looking reports about Boost modules.

Using Wave

The Wave utility is a preprocessor for the Boost library. Using a preprocessor can significantly speed the compilation process because a preprocessor compiles the library portion of the application. After you compile it the first time, you need not compile the library again. Theoretically, you can use Wave with any C++ compiler; however, you probably won't need it with compilers such as CodeBlocks and Microsoft Visual Studio because these products include their own preprocessor. You can find more information about the Wave utility at `http://www.boost.org/doc/libs/1_39_0/libs/wave/doc/wave_driver.html`.

There is more to the Wave utility than meets the eye, however. The Wave utility relies on the Wave library. This library ships as part of Boost and you can use it in your applications as you do any other library. The Web site at `http://www.boost.org/doc/libs/1_39_0/libs/wave/index.html` tells you more about the Wave library.

Building Your First Boost Application Using Date Time

Enough information about licensing, content, and utilities — it's time to use the Boost library for something interesting. This section shows a simple date/time example that you can't easily build without using Boost. You'll also discover some interesting setup requirements that are good to know when you work with other third-party libraries.

As normal, this example begins with a console application. The example uses the name FirstBoost. After you create the console application, perform these setup steps:

1. **Choose Project⊃Build Options and select the Search Directories tab.**

   You see the Project Build Options dialog box.

2. **Highlight FirstBoost in the left pane. Click Add.**

   CodeBlocks displays the Add Directory dialog box shown in Figure 3-6.

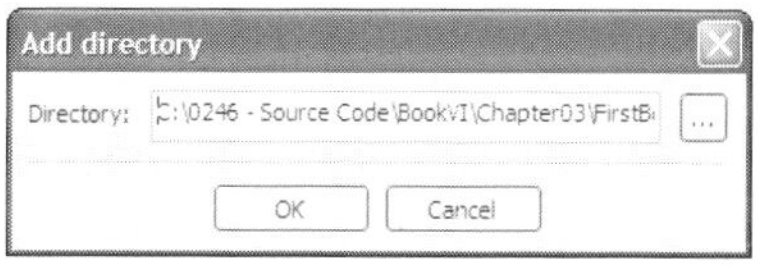

Figure 3-6:
Select
the Boost
library
directory.

3. **Click the ellipses button to display the Browse for Folder dialog box and highlight the \Program Files\CodeBlocks\boost_1_39_0 folder on your hard drive. Click OK.**

   CodeBlocks adds the folder you selected to the Add Directory dialog box.

4. **Click OK.**

   You see the folder for the Boost library as shown in Figure 3-7. Make sure you select the correct folder; otherwise the compiler won't be able to find the Boost library or the headers won't compile correctly because they point to the wrong location on the hard drive.

5. **Click OK.**

   The application environment is ready to use with the Boost library.

Now that you have the environment configured, you can begin working with Boost. Listing 3-1 shows a date/time example that displays the current time and then a modified date/time.

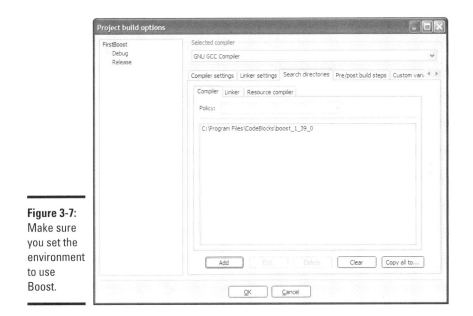

Figure 3-7:
Make sure
you set the
environment
to use
Boost.

Listing 3-1: Using Boost to Create a Simple Date/Time Example

```cpp
#include <iostream>
#include "boost/date_time/posix_time/posix_time.hpp"

using namespace std;
using namespace boost::posix_time;
using namespace boost::gregorian;

int main()
{
    // Obtain the current date and time.
    ptime Now = second_clock::local_time();
    cout << Now << endl;

    // Get the date and adjust it for tomorrow.
    date TheDate = Now.date() + days(1);

    // Get the time and adjust for an hour from now.
    time_duration TheHour = Now.time_of_day() + hours(1);

    // Create a new date/time and output it.
    ptime NewDateTime = ptime(TheDate, TheHour);
    cout << NewDateTime << endl;

    return 0;
}
```

As with any other added capability, you must include the proper library
files. Note that Boost headers use an .hpp extension, which makes it harder
to confuse them with some other header type. To define what to include as

the path to your library, simply look at the hierarchy in Windows Explorer. Locate the `.hpp` file you want to use and then copy that information from the Address bar.

Boost provides namespaces for each of the libraries. In this case, the `ptime` and `time_duration` classes appear in the `boost::posix_time` namespace and the date `class` appears in the `boost::gregorian` namespace. If you find that your application won't compile, it usually means that you've missed a namespace and need to consider where each of the classes in your application comes from.

The application code begins by creating a variable, `Now`, that contains the current time, which you obtain using the `second_clock::local_time()` method. It then displays the current time. The `ptime` class includes methods for interacting with every time element: years, months, days, hours, minutes, seconds, and so on. The example shows a few of the interactions you can perform. When you run this application, the second time you see is one day and one hour ahead of the current time.

The Boost library doesn't compile cleanly with CodeBlocks for some reason. According to CodeBlocks, there is an error in the `filetime_functions.hpp` header. You see a warning message of

```
warning: left shift count >= width of type
```

After working with Boost for a while, we haven't noticed any errors due to this issue. However, you do need to be aware of it. We hope the next version of the Boost library will fix this problem. If you find other bugs when working with Boost, make sure you report them using the process found at `http://www.boost.org/support/bugs.html`.

Chapter 4: Boosting up a Step

In This Chapter

✔ Using RegEx to parse strings

✔ Using Tokenizer to break strings into tokens

✔ Converting numbers to other data types

✔ Using Foreach to create improved loops

✔ Using Filesystem to access the operating system

*T*he Boost library is vast. It's doubtful that a typical developer will ever use everything that Boost has to offer. Of course, before you can use something, you need to know it exists. Browsing through the help file can reveal classes that you need to add to your toolkit to produce good applications. This chapter helps by taking you on a whirlwind tour of the major Boost categories. Don't expect this chapter to discuss everything — Boost is simply too large for that. If you want to see a list of what Boost has to offer, check out

✦ **All classes in alphabetical order:** `http://www.boost.org/doc/libs/1_39_0`

✦ **Categorized list:** `http://www.boost.org/doc/libs/1_39_0?view=categorized`

In addition to reviewing the examples in this chapter and looking through the help file, it also pays to browse the Boost directory for examples. For example, if you look at the `\Program Files\CodeBlocks\boost_1_39_0\libs\RegEx\example` directory, you find three examples of how to use RegEx. Every example directory contains a `Jamfile` you can use to build the examples using Boost Jam (see the "Using Boost Jam" section of Minibook VI, Chapter 3 for details). If you still haven't found the example you need, check online for more examples — Boost is extremely popular. Even Microsoft has gotten into the act by providing examples at `http://msdn.microsoft.com/library/aa288739.aspx`.

Before you begin working through the examples in this chapter, make sure you know how to configure your development environment to use Boost. The "Building Your First Boost Application Using Date Time" section of Minibook VI, Chapter 3 tells how to configure CodeBlocks to use Boost. This section also provides you with a simple example that gets you started working with Boost.

Parsing Strings Using RegEx

Regular expressions are an important part of today's computing environment. You use them to perform pattern matching. For example, if you want the user to enter values from 0 through 9 and nothing else, you can create a pattern that prevents the user from entering anything else. Using patterns in the form of regular expressions serves a number of important purposes:

✦ Ensures that your application receives precisely the right kind of input

✦ Enforces a particular data input format (such as the way you input a telephone number)

✦ Reduces security risks (for example, a user can't input a script in place of the data you wanted)

Some developers make the mistake of thinking that a regular expression can prevent every sort of data input error. However, regular expressions are only one tool in an arsenal you must build against errant input. For example, a regular expression can't perform range checking. If you want values between 101 and 250, a regular expression will ensure that the user enters three digits; however, you must use range checking to prevent the user from entering a value of 100.

Defining the pattern

The RegEx library provides a number of methods for creating a pattern. For example, if you want the user to input only lowercase letters, you can create a range by using [a-z]. The example in this chapter shows how to create a simple three-digit numeric input. However, you can create a pattern for nearly any use. For example, a telephone number pattern might appear as ([0-9] [0-9] [0-9]) [0-9] [0-9] [0-9]- [0-9] [0-9] [0-9] [0-9], where a telephone number of (555)555-5555 is acceptable, but a telephone number of 555-555-5555 isn't. The RegEx library reference appears at http:// www.boost.org/doc/libs/1_39_0/ libs/regex/doc/html/index.html.

This chapter doesn't provide you with a full explanation of all the patterns you can create.

The best place to start discovering the basics of patterns is at http://www.boost. org/doc/libs/1_34_1/libs/ regex/doc/syntax_perl.html. Boost provides a wealth of pattern types. You can see the full reference of information at http:// www.boost.org/doc/libs/1_39_0/ libs/regex/doc/html/boost_ regex/syntax.html.

How you use the pattern is just as important as how you create the pattern. For example, you can use RegEx_match to obtain a precise match. However, if you want to only search for a value, you use RegEx_search instead. The usage reference appears at http:// www.boost.org/doc/libs/1_39_0/ libs/regex/doc/html/boost_ regex/ref.html.

Defining the pattern for a regular expression can prove time consuming. However, once you create the pattern, you can use it every time you must check for a particular input pattern. The following sections describe how to work with the RegEx library.

Adding the RegEx library

Most of the Boost library works just fine by adding headers to your application code. However, a few components, such as RegEx, require a library. Before you can use a library, you must build it. The instructions for performing this task appear in the "Building the libraries" section of Minibook VI, Chapter 3. After you build the library, you must add it to your application. The following steps show you how to perform this task for any library, not just the RegEx library:

1. **Use the project wizard to create a new project.**

Nothing has changed from the beginning of this book — every application begins with a new project.

2. **Choose Project⇨Build Options.**

CodeBlocks displays the Project Build Options dialog box.

3. **Select the Linker Settings tab.**

You see a number of linker settings, including a Link Libraries list, which will be blank.

4. **Click Add.**

CodeBlocks displays the Add Library dialog box shown in Figure 4-1.

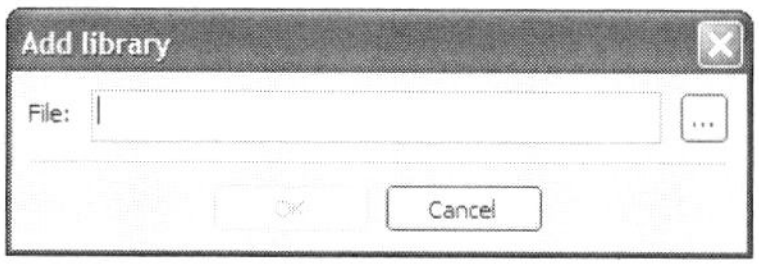

Figure 4-1:
Select the
library you
want to add.

5. **Click the ellipses.**

You see the Choose Library to Link dialog box.

6. **Locate the `libboost_regex-gcc-1_38.a` library (the release version of the library) and click OK.**

CodeBlocks adds the library to the Link Libraries list as shown in Figure 4-2.

7. **Click OK.**

The RegEx library is now ready for inclusion in your application.

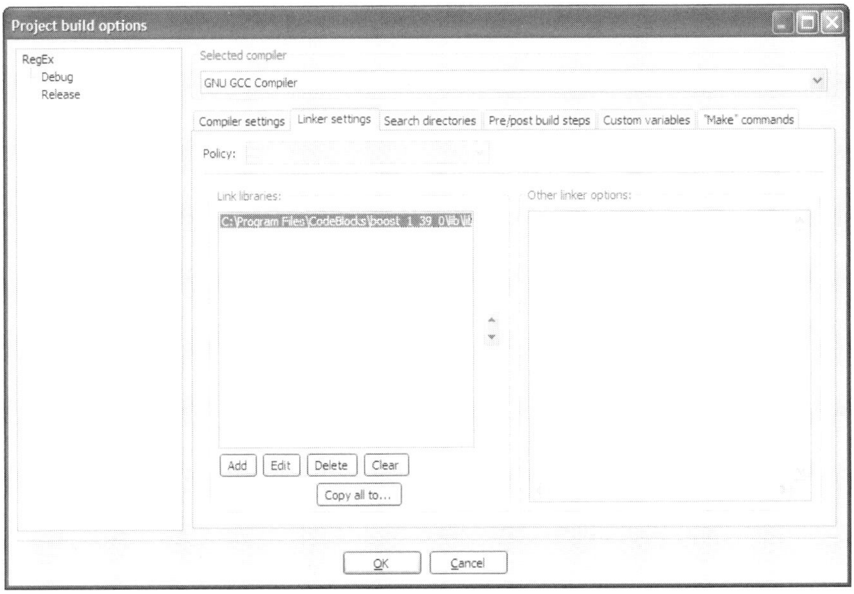

Figure 4-2:
Add the
library to the
application.

The source code CD included with this book includes a compiled version of the required RegEx library in the `Author/BookVI/Chapter04/RegEx` directory. You can use this precompiled library with the example code in this chapter. The project file may require that you change the library setting to match your system.

Creating the RegEx code

Using a regular expression is relatively straightforward. All you do is create the expression and then use it with a function to perform specific kinds of pattern matches. The function you choose is important because each function performs the pattern matching differently. The code in Listing 4-1 demonstrates how to create a regular expression and then use it in two different ways to determine whether user input is correct.

Listing 4-1:   Performing Matches and Searches Using RegEx

```
#include <iostream>
#include "boost/RegEx.hpp"

using namespace std;
using namespace boost;

int main()
{
    // Obtain an input from the user.
    char MyNumber[80];
    cout << "Type a three-digit number: ";
```

```
    cin >> MyNumber;

    // Define the regular expression.
    RegEx Expression("[0-9][0-9][0-9]");

    // Create a variable to hold the matches.
    cmatch Matches;

    // Preform a matching check.
    if (RegEx_match(MyNumber, Matches, Expression))
    {
        cout << "You typed: " << Matches << endl;
    }
    else
    {
        cout << "Not a three-digit number!" << endl;
    }

    // Perform a search check.
    if (RegEx_search(MyNumber, Matches, Expression))
    {
        cout << "Found: " << Matches << endl;
    }
    else
    {
        cout << "No three-digit number found!" << endl;
    }

    return 0;
}
```

In this case, the code begins by adding the proper header, RegEx.hpp, and the proper namespace boost. In many cases, you can get by without doing much more than performing these two steps in your code.

The first step in the code is to get some user input. Even though the prompt tells the user to enter a three-digit number, C++ doesn't enforce this requirement.

The second step is to create the regular expression. What we need for this example is a set of three ranges for numbers: [0-9][0-9][0-9]. Using ranges works well for a number of tasks, and you use them often when creating a regular expression.

The third step is to perform the pattern match. The example uses RegEx_match, which performs a precise match, and RegEx_search, which looks for the right input anywhere in the input. Both functions require three input values: the value you want to check, an output variable of type cmatch that tells where the match is found, and the regular expression.

To see how this code works, you must perform a series of three tests. First, run the application and type **0** as the input. Naturally, typing 0 means that the code will fail and you see this output:

```
Not a three-digit number!
No three-digit number found!
```

Second, let's see a success. Run the application again and type **123** as the input. This time you see

```
You typed: 123
Found: 123
```

So far, there isn't much difference between the two functions, which is why you need the third test. Run the application a third time and type ABC123XYZ as the input. Now you see the difference between a match and a search:

```
Not a three-digit number!
Found: 123
```

This final test shows that the RegEx_search function finds the three-digit value in the string. Obviously, the RegEx_search function is great when you need to locate information but not good when you need to secure it. When you need a precise pattern match, use RegEx_match instead.

Breaking Strings into Tokens Using Tokenizer

As humans, we view strings as a sentence or at least a phrase. Mixtures of words create meaning that we can see in a moment.

Computers, on the other hand, understand nothing. A computer can perform pattern matching and do math, but it can't understand Kipling (read more about this fascinating author at http://en.wikipedia.org/wiki/Rudyard_Kipling). It's because of this lack of understanding that you must tokenize text for the computer. A computer can perform comparisons on individual *tokens*, usually single words or symbols, and create output based on those comparisons.

The compiler you use relies on a *tokenizer*, an application component that breaks text into tokens, to turn the text you type into machine code the computer can execute. However, the tokenizer appears in all sorts of applications. For example, when you perform a spelling check on a document, the word processing application breaks the text into individual words using a tokenizer, and then compares those words to words in its internal dictionary.

The example in Listing 4-2 shows a method for creating tokens from strings. This basic technique works with any phrase, string, or series of strings. You'll normally process the tokens once you finish creating them.

Listing 4-2:   Creating Tokens from Strings

```
#include <iostream>
#include "boost/tokenizer.hpp"

using namespace std;
```

```
using namespace boost;

int main()
{
    // Define the test string.
    string MyString = "This is a test string!";

    // Obtain tokens from the string.
    tokenizer<> Tokens(MyString);

    // Display each token on screen.
    tokenizer<>::iterator Iterate;
    for (Iterate = Tokens.begin(); Iterate != Tokens.end(); Iterate++)
        cout << *Iterate << endl;

    return 0;
}
```

The `tokenizer` template places the tokenized form of `MyString` in `Tokens`. The application now has a set of tokens with which to work. To see the tokens, you must iterate through them by creating a `tokenizer<>::iterator`, `Iterate`. The application uses `iterator` to output the individual tokens. When you run this application, you see the following output:

```
This
is
a
test
string
```

This example shows a basic routine you can use for just about any need. However, you might need some of the extended capabilities of the `tokenizer` class. Check out the materials at `http://www.boost.org/doc/libs/1_39_0/libs/tokenizer/index.html` for more information about both the `tokenizer` and the `tokenizer<>::iterator`.

Performing Numeric Conversion

Numeric conversion isn't hard to perform — it's *accurate* numeric conversion that's hard to perform. Getting the right result as you move from one type of number to another is essential. Sure, you probably won't notice too much if your game score is off a point or two, but you'll definitely notice the missing dollars from your savings account. Worse yet, when you finally get to take that rocket into space, a rounding error can definitely ruin your day as you head off toward the sun, rather than planet earth.

The Boost library includes the `converter` template, which makes converting from one kind of number to another relatively easy. The `converter` template includes all kinds of flexibility. The example shown in Listing 4-3 presents two different levels of converter template usage, but really only scratches the surface of an infinitely more complex Boost library feature.

Why numeric conversion is necessary

Humans don't make any differentiation between one kind of number and another — seeing 1 is about the same as seeing 1.0. The computer, however, does make a differentiation between numbers at two levels:

✓ Integer versus floating point

✓ Size

The integer part of the equation comes into play because of the early processors in PCs, which could perform only integer math. For floating-point math, you had to buy a separate math coprocessor. Today, the math coprocessor comes with the processor, but integer and floating-point math still occur in different areas of the processor. When the processor performs integer math, it uses different registers and capabilities than when it performs floating-point math. So the conversion between integer and floating-point data is more than philosophical — it involves using physically different areas of the processor.

The size issue determines how large the integer or floating-point value is. Again, the difference is physical. Early processors could handle only 8 bits of data at a time, then 16 bits, and on to 32 bits, and finally the 64 bits of today. Using larger numbers in older processors required a number of additional tasks in software, so using larger numbers incurred a significant performance penalty.

Today, with memory and processor register size no longer a concern, large numbers are also no longer a concern, except that you must observe the historical reasons for using numbers of a specific size. In addition, there are sometimes benefits from a reliability, security, or speed perspective in using a smaller number. The important consideration in working with numbers is that you must observe the correct conversion techniques when you want to obtain the correct results.

Listing 4-3: Converting from double to int

```cpp
#include <iostream>
#include "boost/numeric/conversion/converter.hpp"

using namespace std;
using namespace boost;
using namespace boost::numeric;

int main()
{
    // Create the converter.
    typedef converter<int, double> Double2Int;

    // Define the variables for the example.
    double MyDouble = 2.1;
    int MyInt = Double2Int::convert(MyDouble);

    // Display the results.
    cout << "The double value is: " << MyDouble << endl;
    cout << "The int value is: " << MyInt << endl;

    // See what happens with a larger value.
    MyDouble = 3.8;
```

```
MyInt = Double2Int::convert(MyDouble);
cout << "The double value is: " << MyDouble << endl;
cout << "The int value is: " << MyInt << endl;

// We don't want truncation, so lets round.
typedef conversion_traits<int, double> Traits;
typedef converter<int, double, Traits, def_overflow_handler,
                RoundEven<double> > Double2Rounded;
MyInt = Double2Rounded::convert(MyDouble);
cout << "The int value is: " << MyInt << endl;

return 0;
}
```

The example begins by creating a `converter` object, `Double2Int`. This first object shows the minimum information you can provide — the target (`int`) and source (`double`) values. The default setting truncates floating-point values (`float` and `double` among them) to obtain an `int` value. To perform a conversion, the code relies on the `convert` method, which requires a variable of the required source type as an argument.

The `converter` template includes support for four kinds of rounding. You must use the correct kind of rounding to match your application requirements. Imagine what would happen to calculations if you used truncation when rounding is really the required operation. The following list describes all four kinds of rounding that `converter` supports:

+ `Trunc`: Removes the decimal portion of the value (rounds toward 0)

+ `RoundEven`: Rounds values up or down as needed

+ `Ceil`: Rounds the value up toward positive infinity when the decimal portion is greater than 0

+ `Floor`: Rounds the value down toward negative infinity when the decimal portion is greater than 0

The second `converter` object, `Double2Rounded`, shows the template requirements to choose the kind of rounding that the object performs. In this case, you supply five arguments to the template (the `converter` template actually accepts up to seven arguments, discover more about them at http://www.boost.org/doc/libs/1_39_0/libs/numeric/conversion/doc/html/boost_numericconversion/converter___function_object.html):

+ Target

+ Source

+ `conversion_traits`, which include the target and source types as a minimum

+ Overflow handler, which determines how the object handles conversions that result in an overflow (the default is `def_overflow_handler`)

+ Rounding template object (which includes the rounding source type)

The process for using the extended form of the `converter` template is the same as the simple form shown earlier in the example. However, you must now create a `conversions_traits` object (`Traits` in this case) and provide the required input information. (See more examples of using `conversion_traits` at `http://www.boost.org/doc/libs/1_39_0/libs/numeric/conversion/doc/html/boost_numericconversion/conversion_traits___traits_class.html`.) As before, you rely on the `convert` method to perform the conversion process. Here is the output you see when you run the application:

```
The double value is: 2.1
The int value is: 2
The double value is: 3.8
The int value is: 3
The int value is: 4
```

Note that the last two lines show the difference in rounding the value 3.8. In the first case, you see the default `Trunc`, and in the second, you see the effects of `RoundEven`. Discover more about performing numeric conversion using Boost at `http://www.boost.org/doc/libs/1_39_0/libs/numeric/conversion/doc/html/index.html`.

Creating Improved Loops Using Foreach

Writing efficient loops is a requirement if you want your application to perform optimally. Interestingly enough, many loops use a certain amount of *boilerplate* code (code that is essentially the same every time you write it, but with small nuances).

Templates and other methodologies described in this book provide a means to overcome the boredom of writing essentially the same code. However, none of the examples to date has shown a tried and true method, macros. A *macro* is essentially a substitution technique that replaces a keyword with the boilerplate code you'd normally write. Macros normally appear in uppercase, such as `BOOST_FOREACH`, which is the macro used in this section of the chapter. Instead of typing all the code associated with a macro, you simply type the macro name and the compiler does the rest of the work for you.

The magic behind the `BOOST_FOREACH` macro is that it creates all the iteration code you normally create by hand. In other words, you aren't providing any less code to the compiler, you simply let the macro write it for you. The Boost library still relies on the Standard library `for_each` algorithm; you simply avoid writing all the code you used to write when using the algorithm. You can discover more about the `BOOST_FOREACH` macro at `http://www.boost.org/doc/libs/1_35_0/doc/html/foreach.html`.

You may recognize Listing 4-4 partially from Listing 6-1 in Minibook IV, Chapter 6. However, instead of choosing specific items, the example now uses a `BOOST_FOREACH` loop to iterate through the `vector`.

Listing 4-4: Creating a BOOST_FOREACH Loop

```cpp
#include <iostream>
#include <vector>
#include "boost/foreach.hpp"

using namespace std;
using namespace boost;

int main()
{
    // Create a vector and store values in it.
    vector<string> names;

    names.push_back("Tom");
    names.push_back("Dick");
    names.push_back("Harry");
    names.push_back("April");
    names.push_back("May");
    names.push_back("June");

    // Iterate through the vector.
    BOOST_FOREACH(string Name, names)
        cout << Name << endl;

    // Iterate backward too!
    cout << endl << "Backward:" << endl;
    BOOST_REVERSE_FOREACH(string Name, names)
        cout << Name << endl;

    return 0;
}
```

This example begins by creating a vector. In fact, it's the same vector as the one used for the example in Minibook IV, Chapter 6, Listing 6-1. In this case, the example then creates a `BOOST_FOREACH` loop that iterates through `names`. Each iteration places a single value from `names` into `Name`. The code then prints the single name.

An interesting feature of the Boost library is that you can reverse the order of iteration. In this case, the code uses a `BOOST_REVERSE_FOREACH` loop to go in the opposite direction — from end to beginning. The technique is precisely the same as going forward. Here is what you see when you run this application.

```
Tom
Dick
Harry
April
May
June

Backward:
June
May
April
Harry
Dick
Tom
```

As you can see, iterating forward and backward works precisely as you expect. The `BOOST_FOREACH` and `BOOST_REVERSE_FOREACH` macros support a number of container types:

+ Any Standard Template Library (STL) container

+ Arrays

+ Null-terminated strings (`char` and `wchar_t`)

+ STL `iterator` pair (essentially a range)

+ `boost::iterator_range<>` and `boost::sub_range<>`

The macro STL container support is generalized. Any object type that supports these two requirements will work:

+ Nested `iterator` and `const_iterator` types

+ `begin()` and `end()` member functions

Accessing the Operating System Using Filesystem

Working with files and directories is an important part of any application you create. Minibook V shows some standard techniques you use to work with both files and directories. However, these methods can become cumbersome and somewhat limited. Boost augments your ability to work with the file system using the Filesystem library. Creating and deleting both files and directories becomes a single call process. You can also perform tasks such as moving and renaming both files and directories.

The most important addition that Boost makes is defining a method to obtain error information from the operating system. This feature is found in the System library, which you must include as part of your application. Among other capabilities, the System library makes it possible to convert a numeric error that the operating system returns into a human readable form. Unfortunately, the System library is still a work in progress, so this chapter doesn't demonstrate how to use it.

The source code CD included with this book has a compiled version of the required System and Filesystem libraries in the `Author/BookVI/Chapter04/OS` directory. You can use this precompiled library with the example code in this chapter. The project file may require that you change the library setting to match your system. When you set up this application properly, you should see two libraries on the Linker Settings tab of the Project Build Options dialog box shown in Figure 4-3. (See the "Adding the RegEx library" section of the chapter for additional information.)

The Filesystem library and the Standard library

The developers of the Boost library continuously add to its capabilities. Some of the additions developers make are so useful that they end up in the Standard library. The Filesystem library is one of these useful elements. You can see the proposal for adding the Filesystem library to the Standard library at `http://www.open-std.org/jtc1/sc22/wg21/docs/papers/2006/n1975.html`.

Of course, standardized libraries require discussion from multiple groups, not just the Boost developers. Consequently, the Boost library you use today may not be precisely the same library you see added to the Standard library. It's important to keep up with the proposed technical changes to the Boost library as they move to the Standard library by reviewing the documentation online.

The Boost library documentation appears at `http://www.boost.org/doc/libs/1_39_0?view=categorized`.

The movement of code from one setting to another tends to confuse developers because they suddenly find that a favorite library has seemingly disappeared. These developers also question whether they should continue using the old library or move to the new one. In all cases, you want to use the Standard library when you can because the Standard library is fully supported by a standards group, and well, standard. Consequently, when the Filesystem library finally makes the move to the Standard library, be prepared to make a change in how you work with it and update your code as needed to ensure full compliance with the code everyone else creates.

Book VI
Chapter 4

Boosting up
a Step

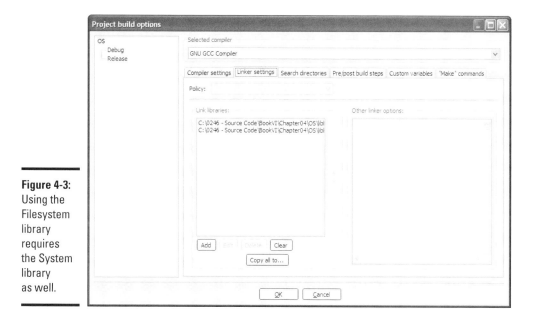

Figure 4-3:
Using the Filesystem library requires the System library as well.

The example shown in Listing 4-5 shows only a modicum of the capabilities of the Filesystem library. The big thing to remember when using this example is that it requires both Filesystem and System libraries since the System library provides error-handling support. The example begins by creating a directory and a file, adding data to the file, reading the file back in and displaying it, and then deleting both file and directory.

Listing 4-5: Interacting with the File System Using Boost

```
#include <iostream>
#include "boost/filesystem.hpp"

using namespace std;
using namespace boost::filesystem;

int main()
{
    // Check for the existence of the directory.
    if (! exists("Test"))
    {

        // Create the directory.
        create_directory(path("Test"));
        cout << "Created Directory Test" << endl;
    }
    else
        cout << "Directory Test Exists" << endl;

    // Check for the existence of the file.
    if (! exists("Test/Data.txt"))
    {
        // Create the file.
        ofstream File("Test/Data.txt");
        File << "This is a test!";
        File.close();
        cout << "Created File Data.txt" << endl;
    }
    else
        cout << "File Data.txt Exists" << endl;

    // Read the file.
    if (exists("Test/Data.txt"))
    {
        cout << "Data.txt contains " << file_size("Test/Data.txt")
             << " bytes." << endl;

        ifstream File("Test/Data.txt");
        string Data;

        while (! File.eof())
        {
            File >> Data;
            cout << Data << " ";
        }
        cout << endl;

        File.close();
    }
```

```
    else
        cout << "File Data.txt Doesn't Exist!" << endl;

    // Delete the file and directory.
    if (exists("Test/Data.txt"))
    {
        remove(path("Test/Data.txt"));
        cout << "Deleted Data.txt" << endl;
    }

    if (exists("Test"))
    {
        remove(path("Test"));
        cout << "Deleted Test" << endl;
    }
}
```

The first feature you should notice about this example is that it constantly checks to verify that the file or directory exists using the `exists` function. Your applications should follow this pattern because you can't know that a file or directory will exist when you need to work with it, even if your application created it. A user or external application can easily delete the file or directory between the time you create it and when you need to work with it again.

To create a directory, you use `create_directory`, which accepts a path as input. You create a path object using `path`. Many of the other Filesystem library calls require a path object as well. For example, when you want to remove (delete) either a file or directory, you must supply a path object to `remove`. Interestingly enough, `remove` does remove a file without creating a path object, but it won't remove a directory. The inconsistent behavior can make an application that incorrectly uses `remove` devilishly difficult to debug.

You won't throw elements of the Standard library out when working with the file system. For example, you still use `ofstream` and `ifstream` to work with file content, just as you did in Minibook V, Chapters 2 and 3. The Filesystem library only augments what you already have available. Here is what you see when you run this application:

```
Created Directory Test
Created File Data.txt
Data.txt contains 15 bytes.
This is a test!
Deleted Data.txt
Deleted Test
```

One final element to look at in this example is `file_size`, which reports the size of the file in bytes. The Filesystem library provides a number of helpful statistics you can use to make your applications robust and reliable. As previously mentioned, you want to spend time working with this library because it contains so many helpful additions to the standard capabilities that C++ provides.

Book VII

Building Applications with Microsoft MFC

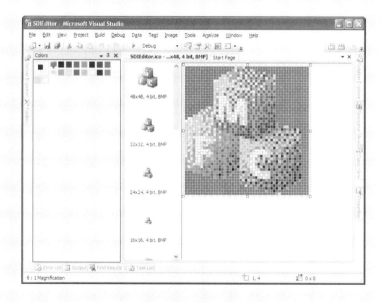

Contents at a Glance

Chapter 1: Working with the Visual C++ 2008 IDE and Projects

In This Chapter

✔ Considering the Visual C++ 2008 project types

✔ Developing a simple application

✔ Using help to write code faster

✔ Working with Solution Explorer

✔ Interacting with the standard toolbars

✔ Modifying application properties

✔ Changing the IDE appearance

Microsoft's Visual C++ 2008 is an incredibly full-featured product, and this minibook can't even begin to discuss most of the tasks you can perform using Visual C++. What you'll discover in this minibook, starting with this chapter, are the traditional options that Visual C++ 2008 offers, including Win32 console applications and Microsoft Foundation Classes (MFC) graphical applications. You won't find any coverage of Microsoft's .NET Framework and managed coding.

Visual C++ 2008 is the Microsoft view of what C++ should offer, which may or may not be the same as your view. Let's just say that Microsoft adds a wealth of features to Visual C++, some of which you'll like and others that you might want to do without. (We know of some developers who go out of their way to overcome the less-liked features in Visual C++ 2008.) For the most part, this minibook goes with the flow and shows you what Visual C++ 2008 has to offer so you can make your own decisions.

The focus of this chapter is the Integrated Development Environment (IDE). As you progress through the chapter, you discover how Visual C++ differs from the CodeBlocks IDE used for the other minibooks. In addition, you'll create your first Visual C++ application, a simple console application that shows, even in this regard, that Microsoft is a bit different.

This minibook relies on Visual Studio 2008 Service Pack 1 (SP1), Visual Studio Team System 2008 Edition. If you're using a different version, some of your screenshots will vary from those shown here. In addition, you may find that your edition requires slightly different menu commands to perform tasks or that your version has fewer capabilities. Even with these differences, the examples in this minibook should work fine with any version of Visual Studio.

Understanding the Project Types

One of the first things you'll notice is that Visual C++ offers a lot of different projects, all of which interact with Windows. To see the projects that Visual C++ has to offer, choose File⇨New⇨Project in Visual Studio. You see the New Project dialog box shown in Figure 1-1. The templates used to create new projects appear in the Visual C++ folder.

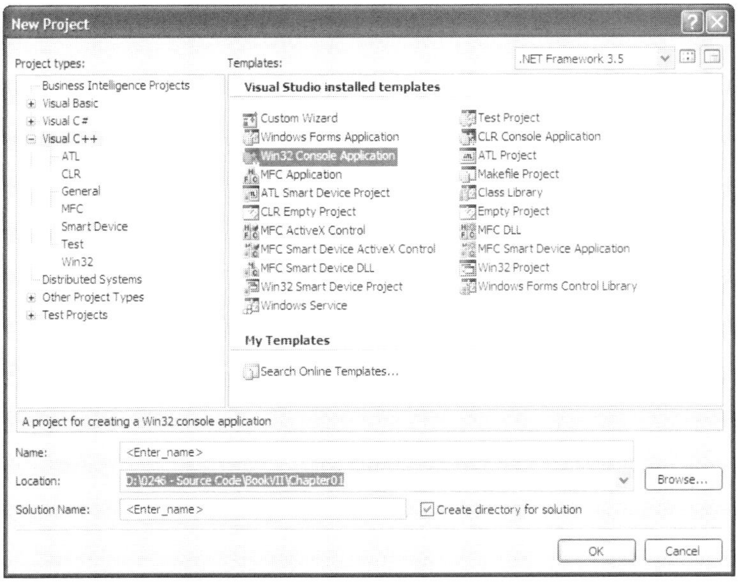

Figure 1-1:
You use the New Project dialog box to create a new empty project with nothing in it.

Figure 1-1 shows all the templates installed on the target system. Note that you can add new projects to the list by clicking Search Online Templates. It's also possible to create your own templates or to modify existing templates to meet your needs. However, creating a new template requires quite a bit of skill, so the chapter doesn't discuss this option in any detail.

The list in Figure 1-1 could be overwhelming. Microsoft categorizes these projects according to task. For example, when you select the Visual C++\ Win32 folder, you see two templates:

✦ Win32 Console Application

✦ Win32 Project

Some templates create more than one kind of application. In this case, a wizard guides you through the process of defining the application type. For example, even though you see only one MFC Application template in the Visual C++\MFC folder, this one template creates a number of application types, as you discover in Chapters 2 and 3.

Creating a New Win32 Console Application

The Win32 Console Application template shown in Figure 1-1 helps you create an application that executes at the command prompt. The application won't have any fancy Windows interface elements. In fact, the result is very much like the majority of the CodeBlocks applications created in the other minibooks. However, console applications do provide useful services and they're a good place to begin discussing Visual C++ and the Visual Studio IDE. The following sections describe how you can create your own Win32 console application.

Defining the project

Visual Studio provides two levels of application management. The top level is a solution. A *solution* is the set of executables needed to create a complete application. Every application has only one solution. The second level is the project. A *project* contains the files needed to create a single executable. A solution can contain as many projects as needed to create a complete application. This example requires only one project — the executable used to display "Hello World" at the command prompt.

Before you can begin writing code for a project, you need to define the project itself. The following steps describe how to create a Win32 Console Application project:

1. **Choose File⇨New⇨Project.**

   You see the New Project dialog box (refer to Figure 1-1).

2. **Select the `Visual C++\Win32` folder in the Project Types list. Highlight the Win32 Console Application template in the Templates list.**

3. **Type a project name in the Name field (the example uses Hello World).**

   The New Project dialog box automatically changes the Solution Name field content to match the project name. You can always type a different solution name if desired.

4. **Click Browse.**

   You see a Project Location dialog box.

5. Select a location for the project and click OK.

The Location field of the New Project dialog box contains the location you selected.

6. Click OK.

Visual Studio starts the Win32 Application Wizard. You see the Welcome page of this wizard.

7. Click Next.

You see the Application Settings page shown in Figure 1-2. The Win32 Console Application template actually provides access to four kinds of applications, including a DLL or static library. You can also add support for both the MFC and Active Template Library (ATL). The default settings work fine for the example, but it's important to know that other options exist.

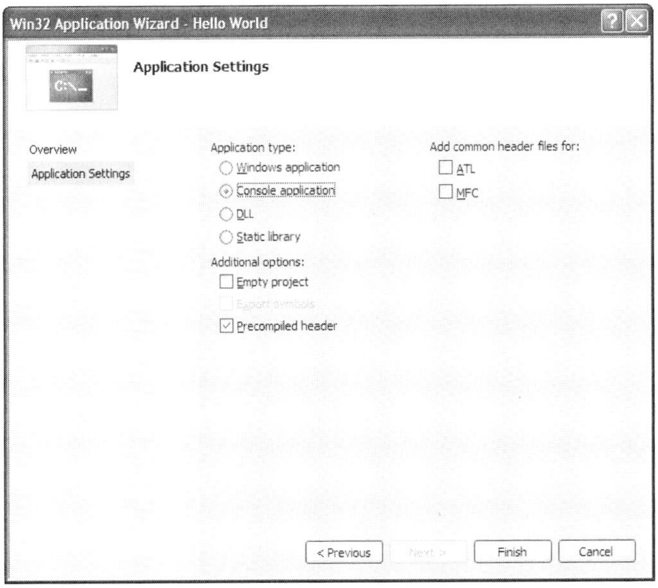

Figure 1-2:
The Application Settings page lets you choose an application type.

8. Click Finish.

The wizard creates a new solution and project that contains four files. Normally, you won't care about `stdafx.cpp`, which contains a list of standard headers for your project. You'll add any headers you need for your project to the `stdafx.h` file. The `targetver.h` file contains special code that tells the compiler which version of Windows to target for the application (you can find the acceptable values for the Windows versions at `http://msdn.microsoft.com/en-us/library/6sehtctf.aspx`). The final file, `Hello World.cpp`, contains the application source code.

Adding code

One of the first things you must decide is which version of Windows to target with your application. Open the `targetver.h` file and you'll see an explanation of its purpose. Microsoft always assumes that you'll want to target the latest version of Windows and will ignore anything older, which isn't a reasonable approach. Consequently, you normally need to change this file to match the version of Windows you want to work with. All you need to do is change the version number as shown here:

```
#ifndef _WIN32_WINNT
#define _WIN32_WINNT 0x0501
#endif
```

Using a version number of `0x0501` means that you're targeting Windows XP. If you'd wanted to target Windows 2000, you would have used a value of `0x0500`. Windows Server 2003 uses a version number value of `0x0502`.

The application will use standard input and output functionality, so you need to open the `stdafx.h` file next. You might wonder why Microsoft uses this separate file to store headers. Using a centralized location for declarations you plan to use for the entire application makes sense because you need to make changes only once. To the standard header declarations, you add `#include <iostream>` as shown here:

```
#pragma once

#include "targetver.h"

#include <stdio.h>
#include <tchar.h>

#include <iostream>
```

It's time to add the code to the `Hello World.cpp` file. Here's the simple code used for this example:

```
#include "stdafx.h"

using namespace std;


int _tmain(int argc, _TCHAR* argv[])
{
   // Display the message.
   cout << "Hello World!" << endl;

   // Pause so you can see it in the debugger.
   system("PAUSE");

   return 0;
}
```

In most respects, this code doesn't look much different from code you type in CodeBlocks. The example begins by including `stdafx.h`, which contains the list of common declarations for the example as described earlier. As with any C++ application, you must also include a namespace declaration.

The body of the example application looks similar to other examples in this book. The basic idea is to output some text to the command prompt and then pause until the user presses Enter.

The big difference is the use of `_tmain()` rather than `main()`. The `_tmain()` function declaration appears in `tchar.h`. If you look at this file, you'll see that using `_tmain()` expands to either `main()` (when working with ANSI characters) or `wmain()` (when working with Unicode characters). In short, `_tmain()` is simply a convenience that lets you compile your code for either ANSI or Unicode use as needed without having to change your application code. Microsoft provides a number of _t* declarations in the `tchar.h` file, and you may want to look at them at some point.

Running the application

At this point, your application is ready to compile and run. To compile an application using Visual C++, you choose Build⇨Build Solution. In the Output window, you see a series of build messages like the ones shown in Figure 1-3. If there are any errors when you compile your application, you see them in the Error List window (simply click the Error List tab shown in Figure 1-3 to see the errors).

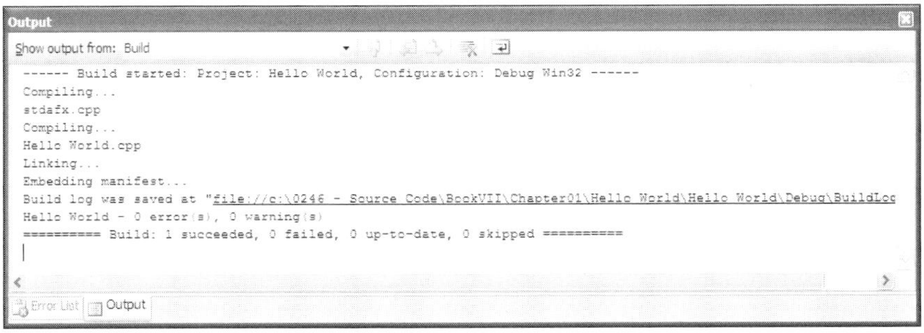

Figure 1-3:
The Output
window
shows
the steps
used to
compile the
application.

```
Output
Show output from: Build
------ Build started: Project: Hello World, Configuration: Debug Win32 ------
Compiling...
stdafx.cpp
Compiling...
Hello World.cpp
Linking...
Embedding manifest...
Build log was saved at "file://c:\0246 - Source Code\BookVII\Chapter01\Hello World\Hello World\Debug\BuildLog
Hello World - 0 error(s), 0 warning(s)
========== Build: 1 succeeded, 0 failed, 0 up-to-date, 0 skipped ==========

Error List    Output
```

To see your application in action, click Start Debugging (the green arrow) on the Standard toolbar or press F5. If you want to start your application without debugging support, choose Debug⇨Start Without Debugging or press Ctrl+F5. Figure 1-4 shows the output from this application.

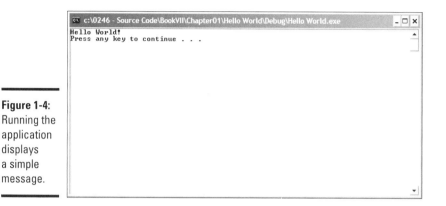

Figure 1-4:
Running the
application
displays
a simple
message.

Writing Code Faster

Microsoft provides a number of ways to obtain help in writing code faster. The two most commonly used techniques are working with the help files and relying on IntelliSense. The following sections describe how to use these two approaches.

Obtaining coding help

You have access to a wealth of help options. The first place most people look is the Help menu. The Help menu does contain a wealth of options, but the help you receive is generic. These options may open a copy of MSDN Library, but you still have to look for the topic you need help with and most developers want something faster.

Another approach is to double-click the keyword you need to understand better and press F1. Using this technique opens a copy of MSDN Library, but this time you see the help associated with the keyword. Unfortunately, you get the help that Microsoft thinks you need. MSDN Library can contain a host of entries for any given keyword. If you don't see what you want, you can always type the keyword in the Index tab or perform a search.

Visual Studio also has a feature called Dynamic Help. This window displays help based on whatever you're typing at the time. For example, Figure 1-5 shows what you see when you type **cout**. The advantage of using Dynamic Help is that you normally see multiple useful help selections, so you can click the one that looks like it will answer your question. Unfortunately, Dynamic Help can also cause problems by eating system resources and causing the IDE to work slowly. You display Dynamic Help by choosing Help⇨Dynamic Help. Simply close the window when you no longer need it.

Figure 1-5:
Dynamic
help
provides
information
about the
current task.

Working with IntelliSense

IntelliSense is a special Visual Studio feature that looks at what you're typing
and then provides suggestions on what to type next. Using this special feature means that you spend less time remembering how to spell and capitalize function names and more time coding. In many cases, IntelliSense can
direct your attention to code that you may have forgotten about. In addition
to function names, IntelliSense also tells you about function arguments and
other code you need to type.

Figure 1-6 shows an example of IntelliSense in action. In this case, the
figure shows what you see when you type the system keyword. Note
that IntelliSense shows precisely what you should type as input for the
system() function.

Figure 1-6:
IntelliSense
provides
helpful
information
about the
code you
write.

```
int _tmain(int argc, _TCHAR* argv[])
{
    // Display the message.
    cout << "Hello World!" << endl;

    // Pause so you can see it in the debugger.
    system("PAUSE");
          int system (const char *_Command)
    return 0;
}
```

You don't have to type something to see IntelliSense. To see the same display as Figure 1-6 for any function you have already typed, place the cursor within the function call and press Ctrl+Shift+Spacebar. If you want to see a list of items you can type, press Ctrl+Spacebar instead.

Viewing Your Project in Solution Explorer

Every time you create a new application in Visual Studio, you work with a solution. The solution contains one or more projects, as previously mentioned. It's helpful to see the hierarchy of solution, project, and associated files, and Solution Explorer provides this view. Figure 1-7 shows the hierarchy for the sample console application in this chapter.

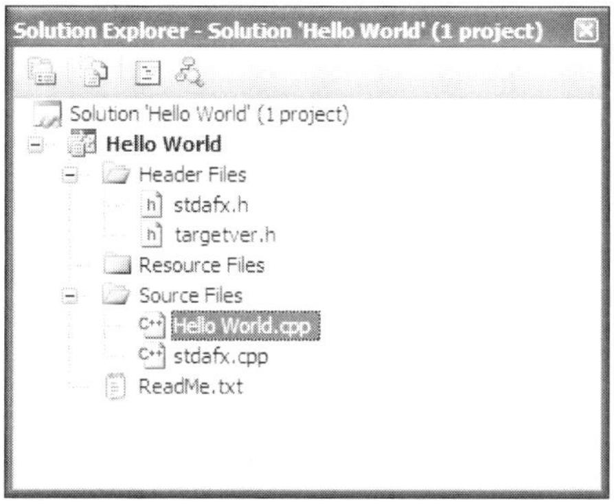

Figure 1-7:
Solution
Explorer
displays a
list of the
files in the
project.

![Solution Explorer window showing: Solution 'Hello World' (1 project), Hello World project with Header Files (stdafx.h, targetver.h), Resource Files, Source Files (Hello World.cpp, stdafx.cpp), ReadMe.txt]

Notice how Visual Studio organizes the application content for you. The solution and its name appear at the top, followed by the project, both of which are named Hello World in this case. Under the project, you see three folders containing headers, resources, and source files. In this case, the project contains two header files and two source files.

The ReadMe.txt file contains information about the project that the template creates for you. This file doesn't add anything to the application. However, it does contain useful information that can help you remember the purpose of default files in the application.

Solution Explorer can also help you interact with your project. When you right-click an object in Solution Explorer, you see a list of tasks you can perform with that object. Upcoming chapters in this minibook will point out

**Book VII
Chapter 1**

Working with the
Visual C++ 2008 IDE
and Projects

several ways to use context menus. For now, just realize that you can perform a number of tasks with each object in Solution Explorer.

Across the top of Solution Explorer, you see four buttons. These buttons provide quick access to some application features as described in the following list (not every button is enabled for every object in the Solution Explorer hierarchy):

✦ **Properties:** Displays information associated with the file or other object.

✦ **Show All Files:** By default, Solution Explorer displays only essential files to keep the display from becoming cluttered. This option displays all the files so that you can modify less-used files, such as a project file.

✦ **View Code:** Opens a source-code file for editing.

✦ **View Class Diagram:** Creates a class diagram for an application that contains classes. Although this button is always available, it produces a result only when working with an application that creates objects.

Using the Standard Toolbars

You can quickly become confused by the plethora of toolbars that Visual Studio provides. Fortunately, you work with only a few of these toolbars at any given time. In fact, the toolbar you need normally pops up in response to the task you want to perform. This minibook doesn't show you how to use every toolbar. It focuses mainly on the three toolbars described in the following list:

✦ **Build:** The Build toolbar contains just three buttons. The first builds the project you have selected in Solution Explorer. The second builds an entire solution. The third cancels a build and is disabled unless you're building a project or a solution.

✦ **Standard:** The Standard toolbar contains a number of buttons grouped into six sections. The first section contains buttons for creating new projects and saving your files. The second section contains the Cut, Copy, and Paste buttons that you see in nearly every Windows application. The third section contains buttons for undoing and redoing actions within the editors. The fourth section contains a single button containing a green arrow that lets you start debugging the application. The fifth section chooses the kind of build you'll create when you build the application (the default is a Debug build, which contains debugging information). The sixth section contains buttons that provide access to common Visual Studio windows, such as Solution Explorer and Properties.

✦ **Text Editor:** The Text Editor toolbar may not contain the buttons you'd think it would. After all, you won't format your source code, so you won't find a font selection here or the ability to add color to your text.

Instead, this toolbar contains buttons that help you interact with the text in various ways. The first section contains IntelliSense buttons that show you object members, parameter lists, and quick information about a particular function. In addition, clicking Display Word Completion automatically completes text you're typing when IntelliSense can figure it out. The second section contains buttons that change the indentation of code in your application. You can also use one of two buttons to comment or uncomment code you've written. The third section contains a series of buttons for working with bookmarks. A *bookmark* is simply a means of marking your place in the source code, much as you use a bookmark in a book.

Changing Application Properties

Visual Studio includes a Properties Window (see Figure 1-8) that you can use for a number of purposes. This chapter looks at only one use, changing application properties. However, you'll see the Properties Window in most of the chapters in this minibook.

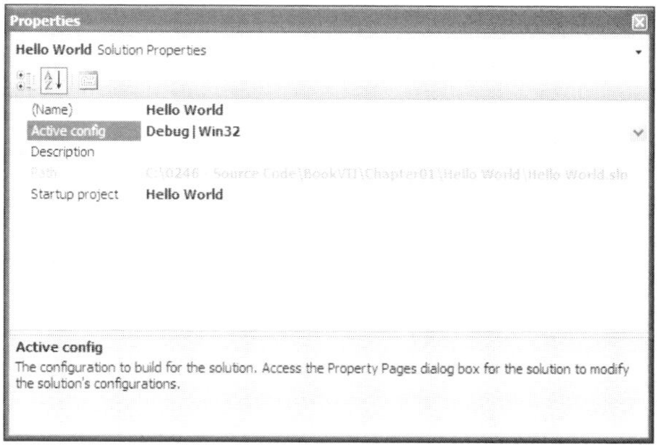

Figure 1-8:
The
Properties
Window
lets you
change the
properties
associated
with the
selected
object.

The Properties Window has two main sections. The upper section contains a list of properties and their values. You see the Active config property selected in Figure 1-8. It currently has a value of Debug|Win32. To change the active configuration, select a new value from the drop-down list box. It's possible to change any blank property value (such as Description) or a property value that appears in bold type. However, you can't change a dimmed property, such as Path.

Property names won't always tell you enough about a property to change its value. In this case, you can rely on the lower half of the Properties Window for additional information. The text description of Active config shown in

Figure 1-8 is usually enough to jog your memory. However, if you still don't understand the purpose of the property, you can press F1 for additional information. Highlighting a new property always changes the property information in the lower half of the Properties Window.

As you change selections in Solution Explorer, the content of the Properties Window changes to reflect the properties of the newly selected object. Some objects, such as the Header Files folder, won't have any properties you can modify, but it's helpful to look at the property values anyway to understand how the Solution Explorer object works.

Visual Studio normally opens the Properties Window by default. However, if you don't see the Properties Window, you can open it using any of the following techniques:

✦ Click Properties Window on the Standard toolbar

✦ Choose View➪Properties Window

✦ Press F4

Modifying the IDE Appearance

It's possible to bend Visual Studio to your will. If you don't like how Microsoft arranged the display, change it. You can add or remove menus and toolbars, create new menus or toolbars, change the position of windows, hide windows from view, or make windows disappear completely. You're the master of everything to do with the appearance of your Visual Studio setup.

Because the IDE is so flexible, your screen may not always precisely match the screenshots in this minibook. The important thing is to look for the feature or option illustrated in the figure, rather than a precise match of every figure element. The following sections describe how to work with toolbars, menus, and windows.

Changing toolbars and menus

You can modify any menu or toolbar that Visual Studio provides. In addition, you can create new menus and toolbars as needed. Most developers leave the Visual Studio menus alone and work exclusively with toolbars because toolbars are easier to use. However, you have the option of performing any kind of change you want to the IDE.

It's important to modify menus and toolbars with care. In most cases, you don't want to remove existing commands from menus or toolbars because people won't be able to help you with problems. For example, if you remove the File menu, someone won't be able to tell you how to create a new project of a specific type. Experienced developers create custom menus or toolbars to satisfy special needs and then hide the standard items from view. Using this approach makes it easy to restore the standard menu or toolbar later to interact with others.

You can change menus and toolbars in many ways. However, the easiest method is to right-click anywhere in the menu or toolbar area and choose Customize from the context menu. You see the Customize dialog box shown in Figure 1-9.

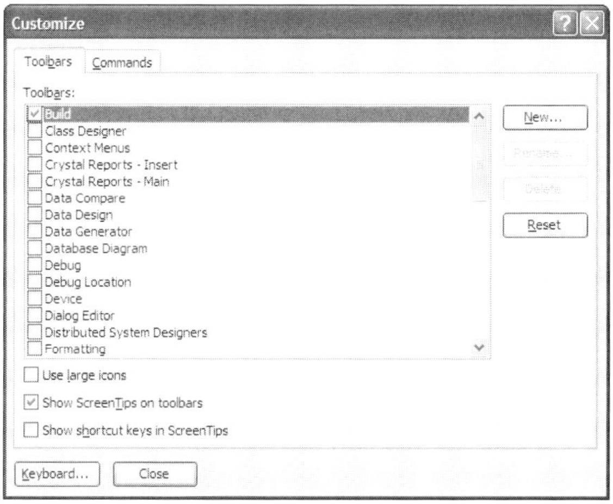

Figure 1-9:
Use the Customize dialog box to change both toolbars and menus.

The Toolbars tab shows a complete list of all the toolbars that Visual Studio supports. Place a checkmark next to any toolbar you want to display or remove the checkmark next to any toolbar you no longer need. When you don't see the toolbar you want, click New to display the New Toolbar dialog box, type a name in the Toolbar Name field, and click OK. Visual Studio automatically displays the new toolbar so that you can add commands to it. You can also use the features on this tab to rename or remove custom toolbars you create (you can't delete standard toolbars) and reset standard toolbars to their original state.

The three options at the bottom of the Toolbars tab help you control the appearance of the toolbar. The following list describes each option:

✦ **Use Large Icons:** Displays toolbar icons in a larger size to make them easier to see.

✦ **Show ScreenTips on Toolbars:** Displays the name of the icon as a tooltip when you hover the mouse cursor over the icon.

✦ **Show Shortcut Keys in ScreenTips:** Displays the shortcut for executing the command (when a shortcut is available) along with the icon name when you hover the mouse cursor over the icon.

The Commands tab displays a categorized list of commands that you can execute using either a menu entry or a toolbar icon, as shown in Figure 1-10. The Categories list helps you locate a command more quickly.

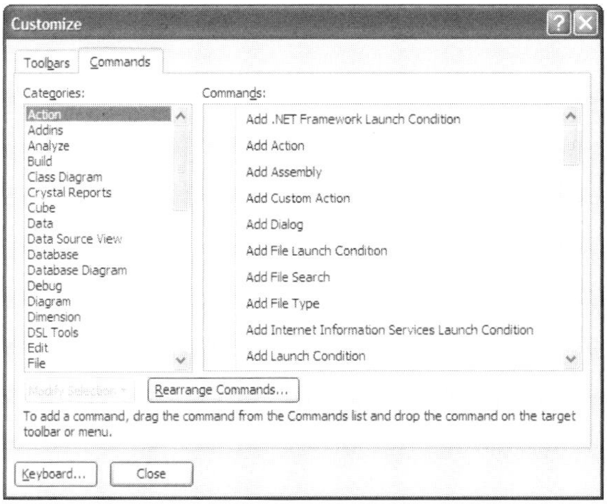

Figure 1-10:
The Commands tab shows all the commands you can execute in Visual Studio.

To use Commands tab, select an entry in the Categories list. Locate the command you want to add, drag it to a menu or toolbar, and drop it. At that point, you can right-click the command and configure it as desired.

You may wonder at this point how you add a new menu. The Categories list contains a special New Menu category. Simply drag the New Menu command to the location you want, even a top-level location, and drop it in place. Configuring your custom menu is the same as using any other command.

If you make a mistake changing a command, which includes menus, you can return the commands to their default state by right-clicking the command and choosing Reset from the context menu. Be careful about where you use Reset. If you reset a custom command, what you'll see is a blank entry, rather than an unmodified version of the command you expect because a custom command has no default state.

Modifying windows

Visual Studio provides considerable flexibility in working with windows. Windows have two states: hidden or visible. You can't hide an editing window, but you can hide any other window simply by clicking the Auto Hide button in the upper-right corner (the icon looks like a thumbtack). The window will slide out of view except for a label identifying its position. When you move the mouse over to the label, the window reappears. Hiding windows creates more space for working with editors without making the window inaccessible.

Figure 1-11 shows three kinds of windows. The editor window appears in the center. You can close it, but you can't hide it. The Server Explorer, Toolbox, Error List, and Output windows are all hidden. If you hover the mouse cursor over their labels, the windows will reappear. Solution Explorer and Properties Window are both visible. Notice the thumbtack icon in the upper-right corner of these windows. Clicking that icon will hide the window; clicking it again will make it visible.

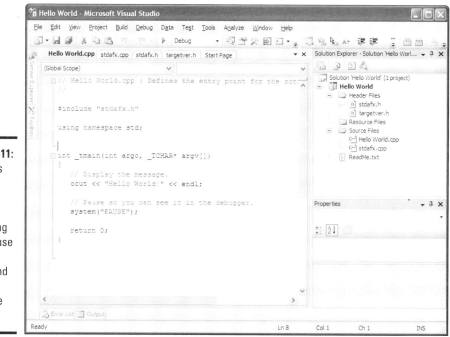

Figure 1-11: Windows have different states depending on their use in Visual Studio and how you configure them.

You can undock any visible window simply by grabbing its title bar with the mouse and dragging it anywhere you like — even outside the Visual Studio IDE window. When you drag a dockable window within the Visual Studio IDE confines, you see the docking indicators shown in Figure 1-12. Simply drag-and-drop the dockable window onto any of the docking indicators to dock it. Visual Studio shows where the window will dock by showing a highlighted area within the IDE. Windows can appear as separate areas within the IDE or as a tab with another window (where you select the window you want to see by selecting its tab).

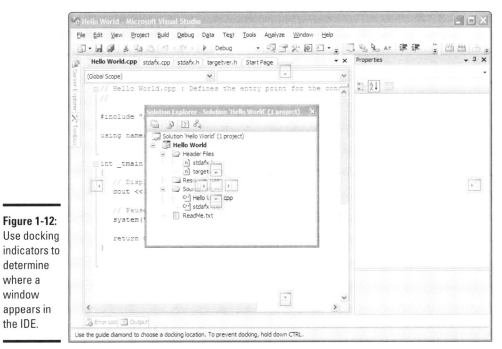

Figure 1-12:
Use docking
indicators to
determine
where a
window
appears in
the IDE.

Dockable windows need not be dockable. Right-click the title bar of the window and you can choose to make the window floating, which means it never docks, or a tabbed document in the editor.

Editor windows also provide some choices. You can right-click a document tab and choose New Horizontal Tab Group or New Vertical Tab Group from the context menu to create a new editing area. Normally, these additional editing areas simply chew up screen real estate that you could better use to edit your code. However, using multiple editing areas can be helpful when you want to compare the content of two files.

Chapter 2: Creating an MFC Dialog Box Project

In This Chapter

✔ Working with the MFC Dialog Box project template

✔ Defining a simple MFC Dialog Box application

✔ Providing a user interface for the MFC Dialog Box application

✔ Making the user interface functional

✔ Considering essential GUI application windows

S ay "dialog box" and many developers immediately think of the message boxes that appear everywhere in Windows applications. A message box is certainly a special kind of dialog box application, but it hardly scratches the surface of what you can do with dialog box applications. In fact, some applications consist solely of one or more dialog boxes. For example, most utility applications are dialog boxes. Configuration tools commonly appear as dialog box applications as well.

Dialog boxes appear just about everywhere in Windows. When you view the properties of the Windows display, you're viewing a dialog box. The icons in the notification area often display dialog boxes where you can discover more about the associated service. Even the properties pages used to con-figure some types of controls in your application are a kind of dialog box, so it's easy to see how important a dialog box application can be.

This chapter doesn't show everything you can do with the dialog box application — you'd need an entire book to do the topic justice. However, you'll see how to create and use a simple dialog box application that you can expand later as needed for your C++ development projects. In most cases, all you really do when working with a dialog box application is start with the simple project shown here and add controls and associated code as needed.

Understanding the MFC Dialog Box Project

Every Graphical User Interface (GUI) element in Windows is a window, including the dialog box background. Dialog boxes send and receive window messages and work like a window in most regards. However, dialog boxes are also containers. A dialog box can hold other controls such as command buttons and text boxes. Consequently, when you think about a dialog box project, you must consider two aspects of the dialog box:

✦ The window control that can send and receive messages that alter its appearance and how it looks

✦ The host container that can hold other controls

In some respects, a dialog box is a canvas where you draw the application you want to create. In fact, the user interface you create is a type of artistic expression in that you're free to create anything you want, yet you must communicate something to the viewer. The artistic nature of user interface design is why so many developers have a problem creating a good interface. Just following the rules may not be enough — often, you have to know when to apply artistic license to achieve the desired result.

Dialog box applications are good for short communications — a configuration task, status information, messages, or other simple tasks. You don't want to try to create a word processor as a dialog box application. In some cases, you must make a decision about the application type to use. For example, a small data entry form could fit quite easily in a dialog box application, but you wouldn't want to use a dialog box application for your order entry system.

The basic dialog box application includes a place to put new controls and two buttons: OK and Cancel. It's important not to let the appearance of the template output prejudice your use of this template. Nothing stops you from adding or removing controls, changing the initial size of the dialog box, removing the OK and Cancel buttons, or doing anything else you can think to do. The initial project simply makes some tasks faster and easier by giving you a starting point.

Creating the MFC Dialog Box Project

Visual Studio doesn't provide a specific dialog box application template. Instead, you use a generic MFC Application template and modify it to meet your needs. Of course, dialog box applications require specific settings or you end up creating another sort of application. These settings will become clearer as you create your first dialog box application project using the following steps:

1. Choose File⇨New Project.

Visual Studio displays the New Project dialog box shown in Figure 2-1.

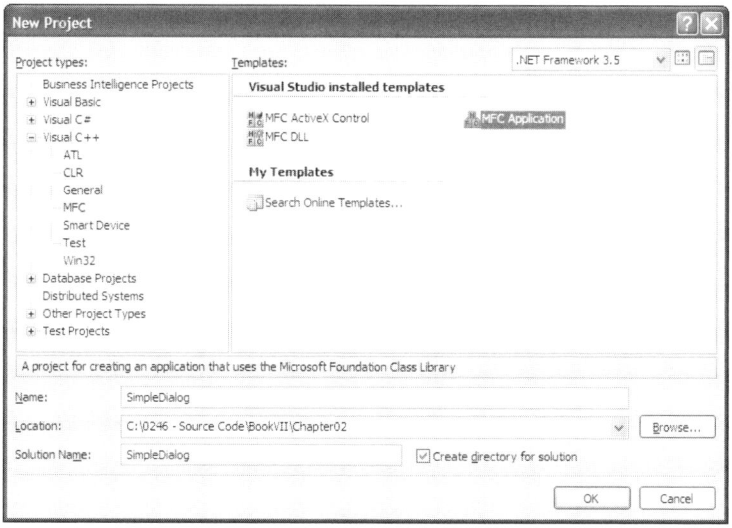

**Book VII
Chapter 2**

Figure 2-1:
Use the
New Project
dialog box
to select
a project
template.

2. **Select the Visual C++\MFC folder.**

   The New Project dialog box displays three kinds of MFC projects as shown in Figure 2-1.

3. **Highlight the MFC Application template. Type a name for the application (the example uses SimpleDialog) in the Name field.**

   Visual Studio automatically enters the application name in the Solution Name field. When working with solutions that contain multiple projects, you can choose to use a unique solution name. A simple project needs only one name. In this case, you can clear the Create Directory for Solution option to reduce the complexity of the folder layout for your application.

4. **Choose a location for the application in the Location field (click Browse if you want help in locating the parent folder for the solution). Click OK.**

   Visual Studio starts the MFC Application Wizard. You see the Welcome dialog box (see Figure 2-2) which shows the default template settings and the steps you'll follow to define a project. These steps appear on the left side of the dialog box, and you can click any step to go directly to that location in the wizard (making it faster to define your project). If you decide that the current settings will work for your project, all you need to do is click Finish at this point. However, since this chapter is about dialog box applications, you need to set the Application Type step as a minimum.

Creating an MFC
Dialog Box Project

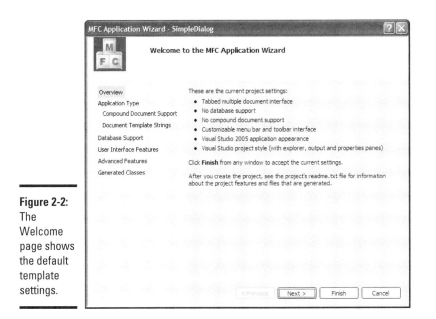

Figure 2-2:
The
Welcome
page shows
the default
template
settings.

5. **Click Next or choose the Application Type step.**

You see a list of application types and basic settings as shown in
Figure 2-3.

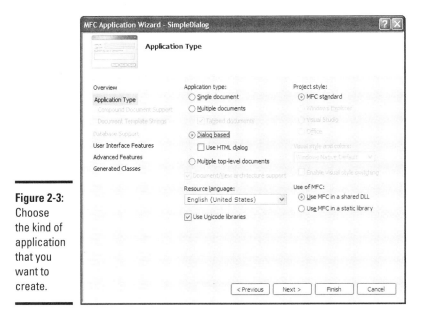

Figure 2-3:
Choose
the kind of
application
that you
want to
create.

6. Choose the Dialog Based option.

Note how the steps change — some steps are no longer available because they don't apply to a dialog box application. The number of options in the Application Type step also changes to reflect the dialog box application as shown in Figure 2-3.

7. Click Next or choose the User Interface Features step.

You see a list of available user interface options as shown in Figure 2-4. The features you choose depend on the kind of dialog box application you create. For example, a message box doesn't require a system menu or an about box. A mandatory configuration dialog box doesn't require a minimize or maximum button. However, an optional configuration or status dialog box requires these features if you want the user to work with other applications. It's also possible to define whether Windows minimizes or maximizes the application when you start it. Use a thick frame to let the user resize the dialog box as needed. As a minimum, you want to change the Dialog Title field to reflect the application purpose better.

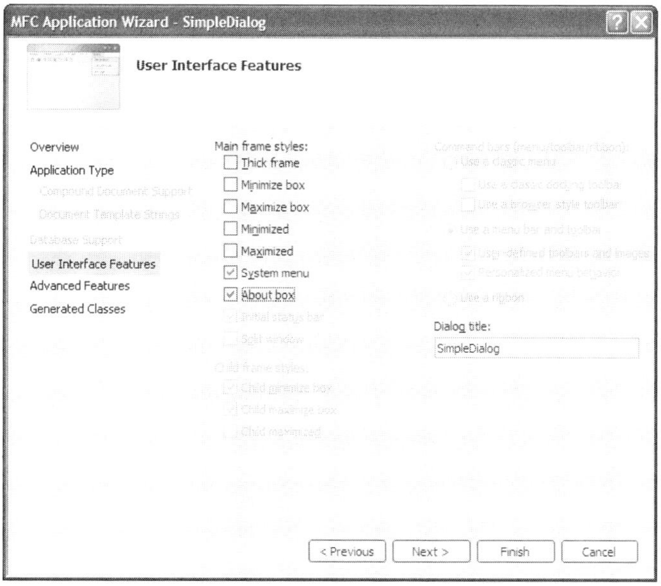

Figure 2-4:
The user interface features you choose can reduce the amount of coding you perform.

8. Type a new title in the Dialog Title field (the example uses the title "A Simple Dialog Box Example").

9. **Choose any required user interface features (the example uses the defaults).**

10. **Click Next or choose the Advanced Features step.**

You see the list of advanced features shown in Figure 2-5. In most cases, you don't need to change these settings. However, complex dialog box applications will probably require context sensitive help. It's normally a good idea to add accessibility features as well so that people with special needs can interact with your application.

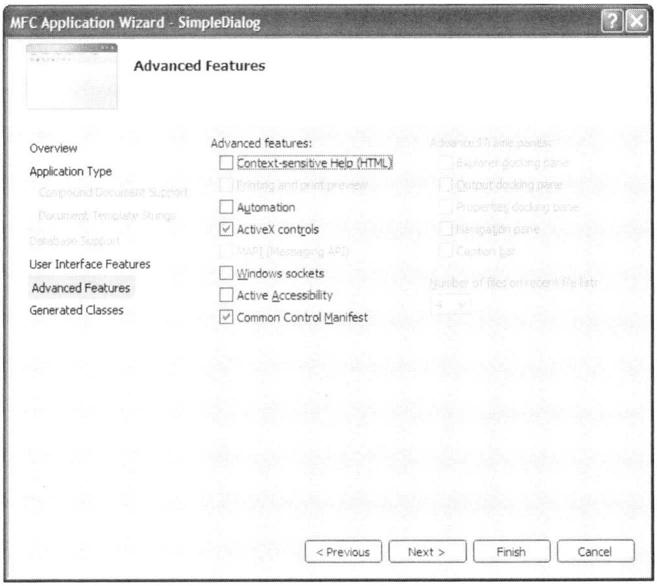

Figure 2-5:
Advanced features are useful for complex dialog box application.

11. **Choose any required advanced features (the example uses the defaults).**

12. **Click Next or choose the Generated Classes step.**

You see a list of generated classes for the application as shown in Figure 2-6. In most cases, you won't want to change these settings for a dialog box application.

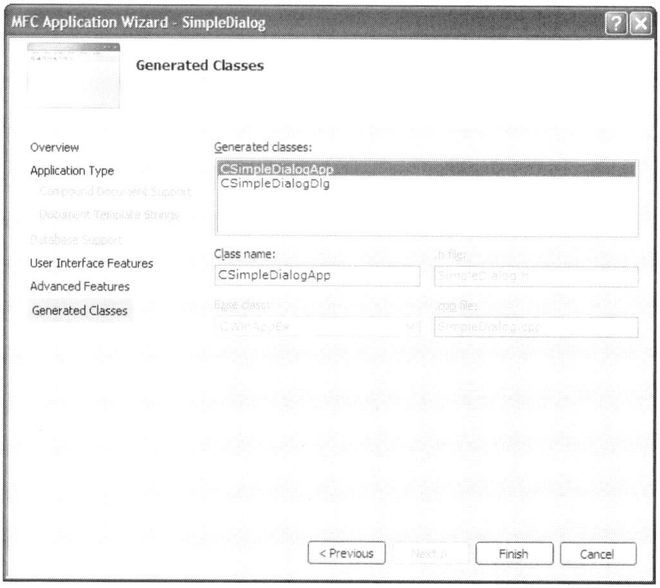

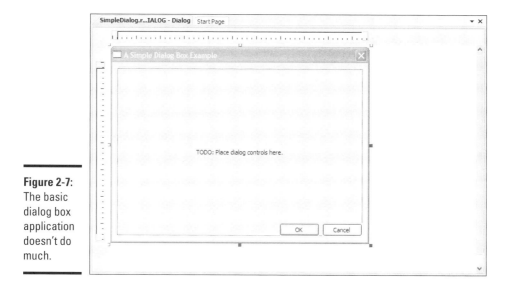

Figure 2-6:
In most cases, you won't need to change the generated class names.

13. **Click Finish.**

Visual Studio generates the application for you using the settings you provide with the template wizard. The resulting application contains some basic buttons and the title selection you provided as shown in Figure 2-7. At this point, you can begin adding controls and code to the dialog box application.

TODO: Place dialog controls here.

Figure 2-7:
The basic dialog box application doesn't do much.

Adding Components and Controls

Defining the project is only the first step in creating a dialog box application. You must also add components and controls to the application to make it useful. In addition, the components and controls must have code attached to them in the form of event handlers so the application does something when the user interacts with the application.

A *component* is an object that doesn't have a user interface. In most cases, components perform background tasks such act as a timer. A *control* is an object that does have a user interface. Controls normally appear in the foreground, such as a command button or a text box. You interact with both components and controls using special variables you create to reference the component or control. In addition, you use event handlers to perform tasks based on user interaction.

The following sections show how to add some components and controls to the example application. Although you probably won't create an application like this in real life, you do find out about the principles you need to build any dialog box application you want.

Adding the component or control

Before your application can perform useful work, you must add components or controls to it. The components and controls appear in a special window called the Toolbox that you display by choosing View➪Toolbox or by pressing Ctrl+Alt+X. The Toolbox begins by showing you a standard list of components and controls, as shown in Figure 2-8. The "Modifying the Toolbox" section of the chapter describes how to add and remove controls from the Toolbox as needed.

The example application uses three types of controls: Static Text, Edit Control, and Button. You have three options for adding controls to a dialog box form:

✦ Double-click the control in the Toolbox.

✦ Click the control in the Toolbox to select it and then click on the form where you want to place the control.

✦ Drag the control from the Toolbox and drop it onto the form.

After you add controls and components to the dialog box form, you need to set properties for each control. Highlight the control and you'll see its properties in the Properties Window shown in Figure 2-9. The upper portion of the Properties Window contains a list of properties you can change for the selected control. The lower half of the window displays a short description of the selected property.

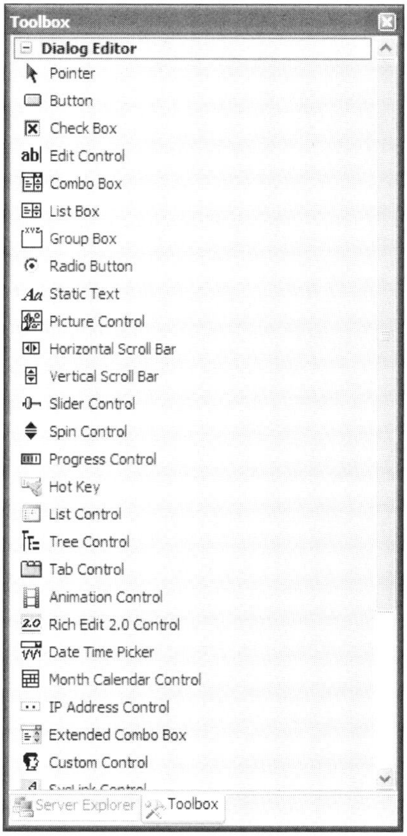

Figure 2-8:
Use the Toolbox to obtain components and controls for your application.

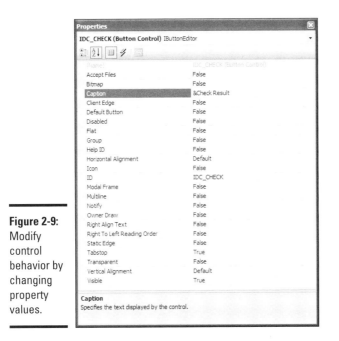

Figure 2-9:
Modify
control
behavior by
changing
property
values.

Now that you have an idea of how controls work on a form, it's time to look at the example form. Figure 2-10 shows the simple form used for the dialog box application in this example.

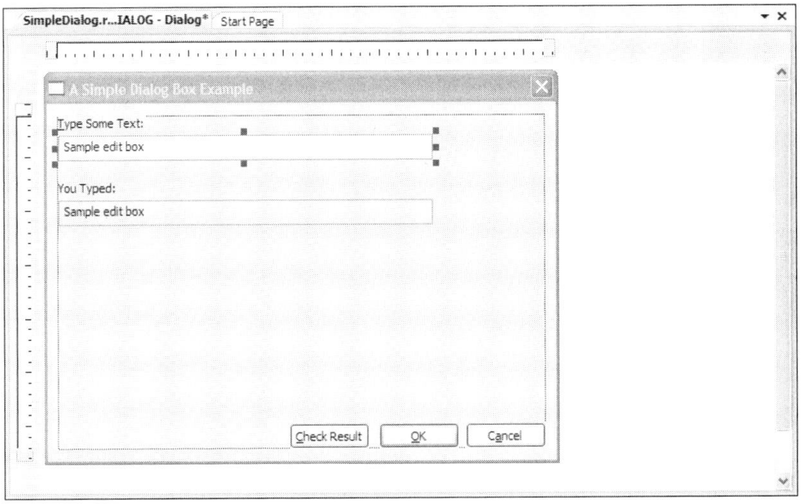

Figure 2-10:
Use
controls and
property
modifica-
tions to
create
the user
interface.

You should observe several important things about this example. The upper Edit Control, `IDC_INPUT`, has the `Tabstop` property set to `True` so that the user can select it by pressing Tab. The lower Edit Control, `IDC_OUTPUT`, doesn't because most users won't want to select it. Because `IDC_OUTPUT` is an output, it has the `Read Only` property set to `True`. You change the name of a control by modifying its `ID` property. Otherwise, Visual Studio provides unhelpful generic names that will be hard to read in your code.

At this point, you might wonder why `IDC_OUTPUT` is an Edit Control rather than a Static Text control. Users can't select a Static Text control when the application is running. They can select an Edit Control and copy its content to the clipboard. Consequently, if you want the user to interact with the text within a control, you must use an Edit Control.

The Check Result button, `IDC_CHECK`, performs tasks with both `IDC_INPUT` and `IDC_OUTPUT`. This control has an underlined letter (also called a *speed key*), which lets a user select the control by pressing Alt+C. You create the underlined letter by typing an ampersand (&) in front of the letter you want to underline. So the `Caption` property for `IDC_CHECK` is &Check Result. Edit Controls don't provide a method for adding an underlined letter. In this case, you add a Static Text control as shown in Figure 2-10 and add the underlined letter to it — pressing Alt+<Letter> selects the associated Edit Control.

Creating variables to use in your code

At this point, you have a form with some controls on it. If you compiled the application at this point, you'd see the controls. You could even type text and click the buttons. However, the controls won't do anything because you haven't written any code to perform tasks. Before you can access the controls, you have to create linkage to them. *Member variables* create the required linkage for you.

Any control can be associated with a member variable. To create a member variable, you choose Project⇨Add Variable or Ctrl+double-click the control. Visual Studio displays the Add Member Variable Wizard dialog box shown in Figure 2-11.

Visual Studio automatically fills out most of the information for you. All you need to provide is a variable name (`m_Input` in this case) and a comment so you know what the variable is for later. The example has member variables for both Edit Controls. The `IDC_OUPUT` control has a variable name of `m_Output`. After you make the changes you want to the Add Member Variable Wizard dialog box, click Finish.

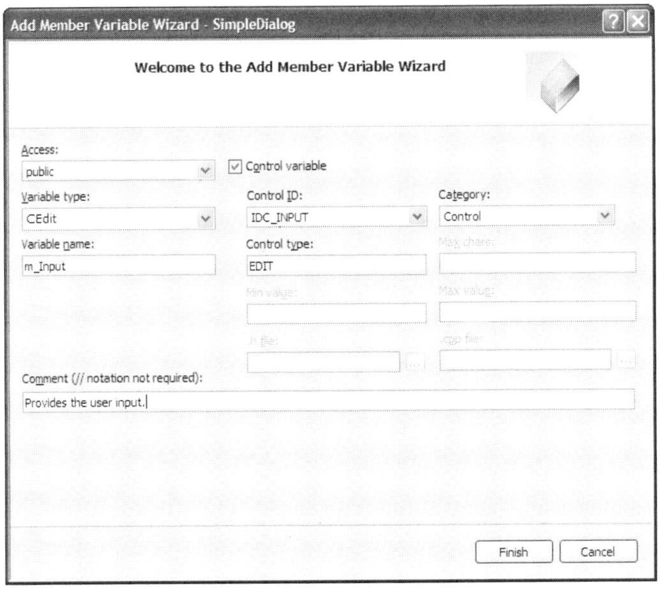

Figure 2-11:
Add member variables to access controls on a form in your code.

Defining methods to react to control events

Controls have events associated with them. An event occurs whenever a user performs specific interactions with the control, such as clicking it. The event is always present. However, nothing happens when the event occurs unless you provide an *event handler* — special code that does something when the event occurs. To create an event handler, select the control and click Control Events in the Properties Window toolbar. You see a list of events associated with the control as shown in Figure 2-12.

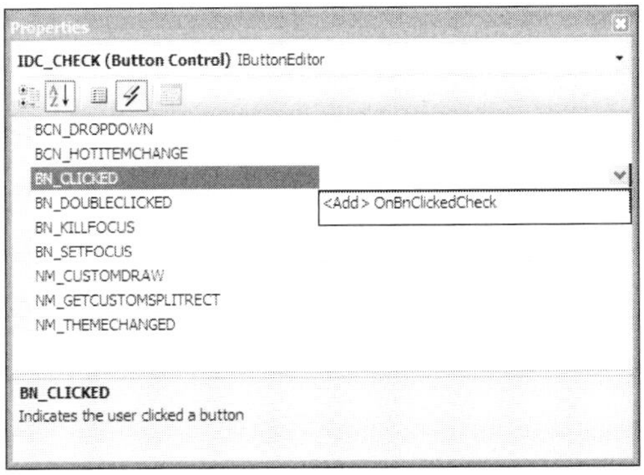

Figure 2-12:
Add event handlers to do something when the user interacts with your application.

The `IDC_CHECK` Button control has a `BN_CLICKED` event that *fires* whenever a user clicks the button. Firing an event causes the application to call the event handler. To add the event handler to this event, click the down arrow next to the event entry and choose <Add> OnBnClickedCheck from the drop-down list. Visual Studio creates the new event handler for you and takes you to that spot in the code file.

You can easily remove event handlers that you don't want. Simply find the event entry in the Properties Window and click the down arrow. Choose <Delete> OnBnClickedCheck (or any other event handler name) from the drop-down list. In addition, if you can't find a particular event handler in the code file, choose <Edit Code> from the list.

Defining the Dialog Box Code

Code is what makes an application perform tasks, as you saw in the other minibooks. In this case, the example program transfers the content of `IDC_INPUT` to `IDC_OUTPUT`. It's important to remember that you're working with a control now — a control that is actually a window on a form. Consequently, the task isn't as simple as moving the text directly from one control to another.

To move data from one control to another, you must use an intermediary variable. Listing 2-1 shows the code used in this example to move the string in `IDC_INPUT` to `IDC_OUTPUT`.

Book VII
Chapter 2

Creating an MFC
Dialog Box Project

Listing 2-1: Moving Data from One Control to Another

```
void CSimpleDialogDlg::OnBnClickedCheck()
{
    // Obtain the input string from m_Input.
    CString ThisString = _T("");
    m_Input.GetLine(0, ThisString.GetBuffer(100), 100);

    // Release the buffer created for ThisString.
    ThisString.ReleaseBuffer();

    // Place the information in m_Output.
    m_Output.SetWindowTextW(ThisString.GetBuffer());
    ThisString.ReleaseBuffer();
}
```

In this case, the example begins by creating a `CString` object, `ThisString`, to hold the string found in `IDC_INPUT`. Visual C++ provides a host of string variable types, but the `CString` is probably the easiest to use and the least likely to cause memory problems.

The GetLine() function requires that you provide the line number you want as the first argument. Because IDC_INPUT contains only one line of text, the only line available is the zero-based value of 0. The second argument is a buffer to hold the LPTSTR (long pointer to a string value). A CString isn't directly compatible as an LPTSTR. However, you obtain an LPTSTR equivalent using the GetBuffer() method as shown. In this case, you provide a specific buffer length as the only argument to GetBuffer(). The third argument to GetLine() is the buffer length. After this call executes, ThisString contains the value found in IDC_INPUT.

ThisString has allocated an LPTSTR buffer to work with GetLine(). To prevent a *memory leak* (memory that the operating system can no longer access because it thinks the memory is in use even after your application ends), you must call ReleaseBuffer() to release the memory that ThisString has allocated. Theoretically, ThisString takes care of the problem for you automatically, but it's always better to be safe when it comes to memory allocation.

Now it's time to place the data found in ThisString into IDC_OUTPUT so the user can see it. In this case, the example calls on the SetWindowTextW() method to perform the task. The SetWindowTextW() method also requires an LPTSTR as input, so you use the GetBuffer() method again. However, because the SetWindowTextW() method only reads the content of ThisString, the buffer length is unimportant. Again, you release the buffer after you use it. Figure 2-13 shows the output from this example.

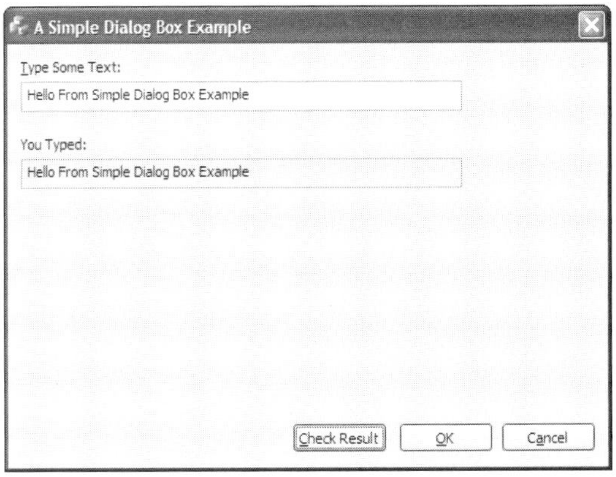

Figure 2-13: The example moves text from one window to another.

A Simple Dialog Box Example

Type Some Text:

Hello From Simple Dialog Box Example

You Typed:

Hello From Simple Dialog Box Example

Check Result   OK   Cancel

Understanding the Essential Windows

You need to know about several essential windows when working with Visual C++. One of these windows is the Properties Window that you have already worked with in the "Adding the component or control" section of the chapter. You also need to use other windows when creating complex applications or you'll spend a lot of time looking for things that you know exist, but can't find readily.

Working with Class View

Every MFC application relies on a number of classes. The dialog box application is the easiest application you create, and even it contains three classes. Each of these classes contains a number of methods, variables, and other features that you need to create the application, as shown in Figure 2-14. You reveal this window by choosing View➪Class View or by pressing Ctrl+Shift+C.

**Book VII
Chapter 2**

Creating an MFC
Dialog Box Project

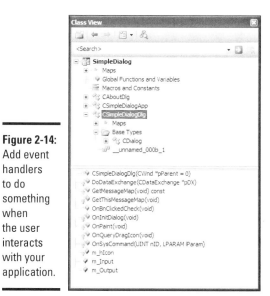

Figure 2-14:
Add event
handlers
to do
something
when
the user
interacts
with your
application.

The upper half of this window provides a hierarchical view of your application. You can drill down and see how Visual C++ puts the classes together. For example, `CSimpleDialogDlg` derives from the `CDialog` base type. Several layers down you find the base type for all Visual C++ objects, `CObject`.

The lower half of the window displays details about the entry you select in the upper half. For example, CSimpleDialogDlg defines several variables including m_Input and m_Output. It also has a number of methods, including CSimpleDialogDlg::OnBnClickedCheck(). The Class View window reveals all this information to you.

Once you locate the variable, method, event, or other element you want to work with in Class View, double-click its entry. Visual Studio will take you directly to the location of that element in the source-code file so that you can view it and possibly modify it.

Modifying the Toolbox

The "Adding the component or control" section of the chapter shows how to use the Toolbox to add components and controls to an application. However, the default Toolbox probably doesn't contain every tool you require. Fortunately, you can add and remove tools as needed: simply right-click anywhere within the Toolbox and select Choose Items from the context menu. After a few seconds (up to a minute), you see the Choose Toolbox Items dialog box shown in Figure 2-15.

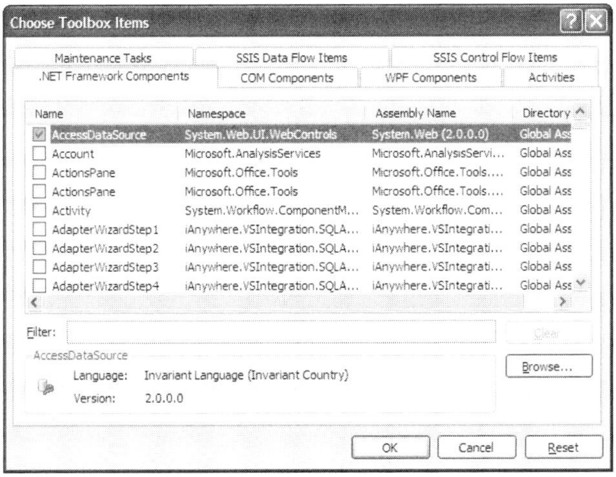

Figure 2-15:
Add or remove items in the Toolbox as needed.

To add a new component or control to the Toolbox, simply locate it in the lists shown and click to add a checkmark to its entry. When you click OK, Visual Studio adds it to the Toolbox. Likewise, you remove an item from the Toolbox by removing the checkmark next to its entry.

Not every component or control in the Choose Toolbox Items dialog box appears with every application you create. MFC applications rely on items on the COM Components tab. If you want to use items on the .NET Framework Components tab, you must create a managed application — a task that's beyond the scope of this book.

Chapter 3: Creating an MFC SDI Project

In This Chapter

✔ Working with MFC SDI projects

✔ Defining a new MFC SDK project

✔ Using the document/view architecture

✔ Creating the code for the example SDI project

✔ Using the resulting example application

*M*any applications rely on the Single Document Interface (SDI). The *SDI* is an application that opens just one document at a time and presents a single view of that document. For example, Notepad is an example of an SDI application. SDI applications are extremely useful because they can simplify user tasks and make working with the application considerably easier. However, they also have drawbacks that this chapter discusses.

The Microsoft Foundation Classes (MFC) architecture for the SDI and Multiple Document Interface (MDI) application are separate documents and views. A *document* is the data portion of the application. However, most users need to see the data contained in the document, which is where the *view* comes into play. You find a complete discussion of the document/view architecture later in this chapter.

One of the best ways to see SDI applications in action is to build one of your own. The example in this chapter is a basic text editor. After you create the example, you can augment it as desired to handle any text file on your system. The amazing thing is that there are many forms of text file out there right now that you might not quickly think about. For example, an XML file is simply a text file in disguise. Having the basic text editor in this chapter as a starting point will let you create a custom editor for any need you have.

Understanding the MFC SDI Project

As with the dialog box application described in Chapter 2, an SDI application is essentially a container. However, in this case, the application holds a special framework. The framework describes the menus and toolbars the users can interact with. In addition, the framework provides a client area in which a view presents data found in a document.

Because the framework generally gobbles up all the visible area of the application, an SDI application has a different appearance from the dialog box application presented in Minibook VII, Chapter 2. You add controls to the framework rather than to the application itself. The framework places limits on the kind and appearance of controls. An SDI application has toolbars, menus, and a status bar for you to use. The SDI application dictates the kinds of controls you see based on the type of application support you want to provide. It would be unusual to see a command button placed in the middle of an SDI application unless that application is a form.

Because SDI applications are more structured than dialog box applications, they tend to produce consistent results that help users learn the application faster. The user sees certain common constructs and can anticipate their meaning to an extent. However, SDI applications are also more complicated to write than dialog box applications and they don't offer the same level of flexibility. In short, you trade complexity and flexibility for a more powerful and consistent application approach.

Considering the MDI difference

Visual C++ lets you create either SDI or MDI applications. While an SDI application can open only one document with a single view at a time, an MDI application can open multiple documents, potentially with multiple views, at a time. An MDI application essentially uses a host application to hold zero or more forms that have a document/view combination.

Because MDI applications have multiple documents or views or both in play at a time, it also requires some form of window management, where a single window contains a document/view combination. Normally, the window management takes several forms. For example, the user may see a Window menu that contains a list of the open windows in the application. Selecting an entry opens that window for use in the application. The Window menu may also contain options for arranging the windows on screen and even creating new windows with a different view of the document.

Another form of window management lets the user minimize windows within the host application. The user can still see a window icon within the host, but the document content is hidden from view. This kind of window management lets the user move windows around. The user can then focus attention on just one or two document/view combinations at a time.

From a developer perspective, working with an MDI application is akin to working with multiple SDI applications, plus some additional code for window management. The developer still needs to open the document and then create a view of the document content. The view then appears within a window just as it would for an SDI application. The main difference is that this window appears within the host and the host provides the window management (which the project template adds automatically for the most part).

Creating the MFC SDI Project

As with dialog box applications, Visual Studio doesn't provide a specific SDI application template. Instead, you use a generic MFC Application template and modify it to meet your specific needs. The dialog box application you create in Minibook VII, Chapter 2 has limitations placed on it to allow for the requirements of being a dialog-based application. The following steps show that SDI applications have fewer limits placed on them. However, with this extra flexibility come additional requirements for creating a good application. SDI applications are inherently more complex than dialog applications.

1. **Choose File⇨New Project.**

Visual Studio displays the New Project dialog box shown in Figure 3-1.

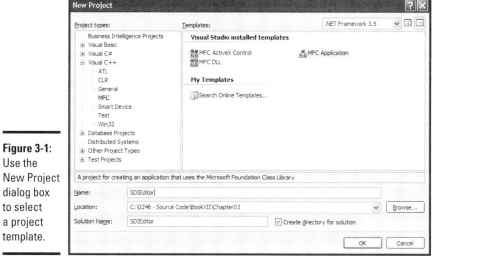

Figure 3-1: Use the New Project dialog box to select a project template.

2. **Select the Visual C++\MFC folder.**

The New Project dialog box displays three kinds of MFC projects as shown in Figure 3-1.

3. **Highlight the MFC Application template. Type a name for the application (the example uses SDIEditor) in the Name field.**

4. **Clear the Create Directory for Solution option to reduce the complexity of the folder layout for your application.**

5. **Choose a location for the application in the Location field (click Browse if you want help in locating the parent folder for the solution). Click OK.**

Visual Studio starts the MFC Application Wizard. You see the Welcome dialog box that shows the default template settings and the steps you'll follow to define a project. These steps appear on the left side of the dialog box and you can click any step to go directly to that location in the wizard (making it faster to define your project).

6. **Click Next or choose the Application Type step.**

You see a list of application types and basic settings as shown in Figure 3-2.

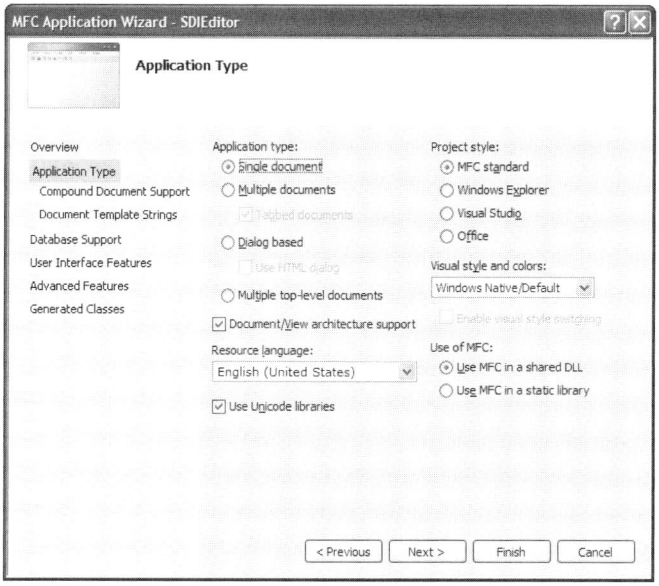

Figure 3-2: Choose the kind of application that you want to create.

7. **Choose the Single Document option.**

The picture in the upper-left corner changes as you make changes to this step. Choosing the Single Document option results in a picture that looks much like Notepad.

8. **Select a Project Style option (the example uses MFC Standard as shown in Figure 3-2).**

The picture in the upper-left changes to reflect the project style you chose. You can choose from four project styles when working with an SDI or MDI application:

• **MFC Standard:** A traditional user interface like the one found in Notepad

• **Windows Explorer:** A browser-based interface that looks sort of like Notepad but relies on Web style content

- **Visual Studio:** An interface that looks very much like the one found in Visual Studio that includes Explorer, Output, and Properties panes

- **Office:** An Office 2007 style interface that includes the Ribbon, Navigation pane, and Caption bar

9. **Choose a Visual Style and Colors option (the example uses Windows Native/Default).**

The visual style you choose determines how the user views the application. When using the Windows Native/Default option, the colors reflect those made by the user for Windows as a whole. This is the safest option if you want to ensure maximum accessibility. All other options reflect a specific Microsoft product such as Office 2007. When you choose these other options, you can also select the Enable Visual Style Switching option to allow the user to choose a different visual style and color for the application.

10. **Select the Document/View Architecture Support option.**

If you don't select this option, the application won't have any document/view support built into it, which means you'll have to add custom classes to add this support later. Unless your application has very special needs, it's usually easier to add the required support as supplied by Microsoft.

11. **Click Next.**

You see the Compound Document Support step shown in Figure 3-3. This step is important because it determines the Object Linking and Embedding (OLE) support your application provides. Microsoft divides OLE into servers and containers. A *server* provides data to a container. If a user embeds an object into the container, the container calls on the server to render and interact with the object. The *container* is a host for the embedded object. An application can have various levels of server and container support as listed here:

- **None:** The application doesn't provide any OLE support.

- **Container:** The user can embed objects into documents the application produces, but the application can't act as a server for other containers.

- **Mini Server:** The application acts only as a server. The user can't launch this application separately. The application always acts as a server for objects embedded into containers.

- **Full Server:** The application can act as a standalone application. In addition, a container can launch the server to support either linked or embedded objects.

- **Container/Full Server:** The user can embed objects into documents the application produces. In addition, the application provides full server support for both linked and embedded objects.

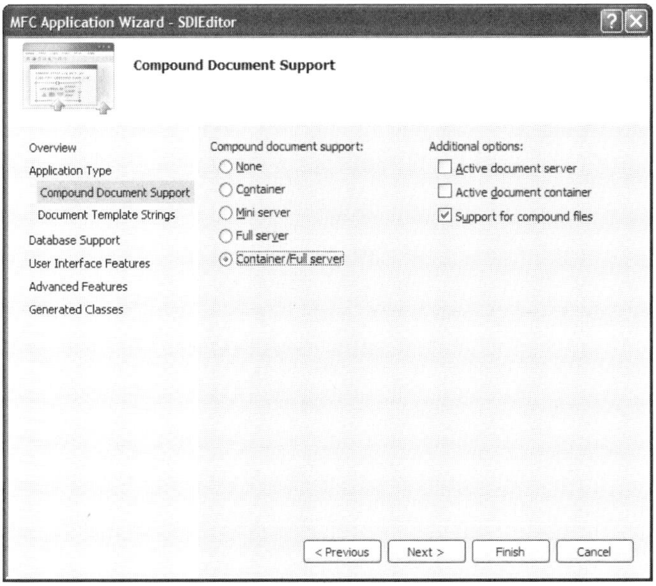

Figure 3-3:
Define the
level of OLE
support
you want to
provide.

12. **Select a Compound Document Support option (the example uses None).**

13. **(Optional) Select one or more Additional Options as described in the following list:**

- **Active Document Server (server only):** Provides the ability to manage ActiveX content using the built-in server. ActiveX is an older Microsoft object technology (albeit newer than OLE) that's still in use throughout Windows and on many Web sites. You can get an overview of ActiveX at `http://msdn.microsoft.com/en-us/library/aa261287.aspx`. You must create a file extension for your application on the Document Template Strings step (see Step 14) to use this option.

- **Active Document Container (container only):** Provides the ability to host ActiveX content within the frame of the container. ActiveX content requires that the container allow the server to add user interface features such as menus and toolbars to the container's frame when a user selects ActiveX content. For example, if you embed an Excel spreadsheet in a Word document and then select the Excel spreadsheet, the Word application features will change to reflect Excel functionality.

- **Support for Compound Files (servers and containers):** Modifies the way your application stores data to include support for embedded and lined objects. If you select OLE support, you should keep this option selected to reduce the complexity of creating your document file structure.

14. **Click Next.**

You see the Document Template Strings step shown in Figure 3-4. (The figure shows the settings for the example.)

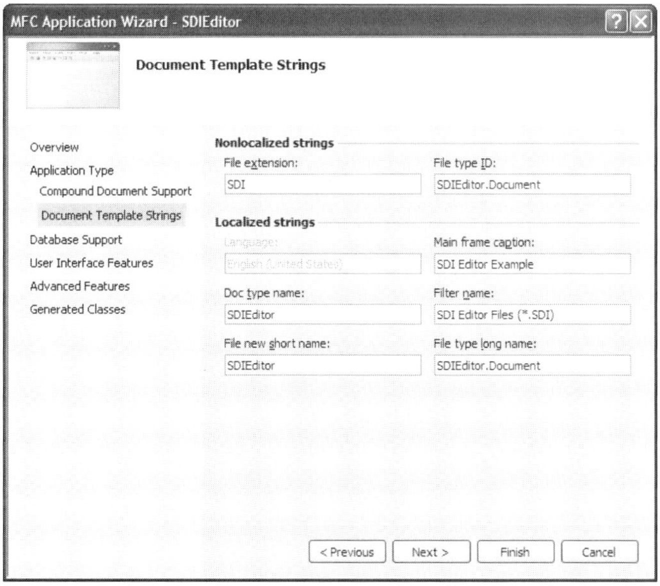

Figure 3-4:
Create a
document
template
string
for your
application.

15. **Type a file extension in the File Extension field. Optionally modify the other fields as needed for your application. Click Next.**

You see the Database Support step shown in Figure 3-5.

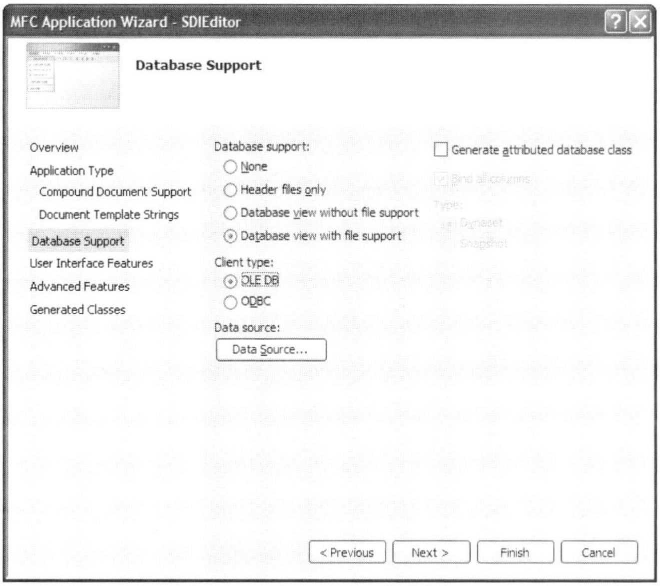

**Book VII
Chapter 3**

**Creating an MFC
SDI Project**

Figure 3-5:
Add
database
support as
needed.

16. **Choose a level of database support (the example uses None).**

Adding database support requires that you choose one of the database options, choose a client type, select a data source, and then configure any additional options. Creating a database application is outside the scope of the book, so this chapter won't discuss the requirements for creating a database application.

17. **Choose any required database option and click Next.**

You see the User Interface Features step shown in Figure 3-6. (The screenshot shows the options used for the example.)

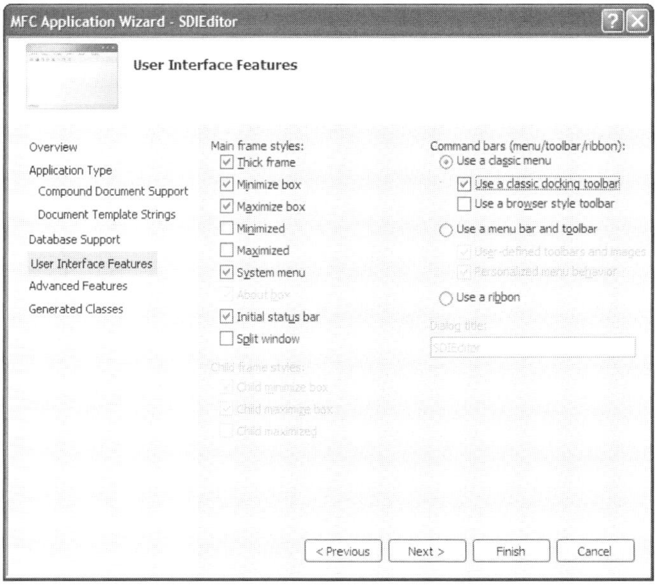

Figure 3-6: Modify the user interface as needed for your application.

18. **Choose basic user interface functionality such as the kind of border.**

Note that some of the features aren't enabled. For example, you must provide an About dialog box when creating an SDI application (this feature is optional for a dialog box application).

19. **Choose the Command Bar options you want for your application.**

The template provides you with a number of command bar options as described in the following list:

- **Use a Classic Menu:** This is the menu you've seen in Windows for many years — the kind that appears in Notepad. You can also choose either a docking toolbar (which lets the user move the toolbars around) or a browser type toolbar (which looks like the one in the older versions of Internet Explorer).

- **Use a Menu Bar and Toolbar:** This is the menu system that appears in Visual Studio. In addition, this option lets you set up the application so users can add user-defined toolbars and images. You can also let the user create personalized menus.

- **Use a Ribbon:** This is the menu system used by Office 2007 applications.

20. **Click Next.**

You see the Advanced Features step shown in Figure 3-7. In most cases, you don't need to change these settings very much. SDI applications will probably require context sensitive help. It's normally a good idea to add accessibility features as well so that people with special needs can interact with your application. The Number of Files on Recent File List setting of 4 is also too paltry for most users today — a good base setting is 10 and you may want even more.

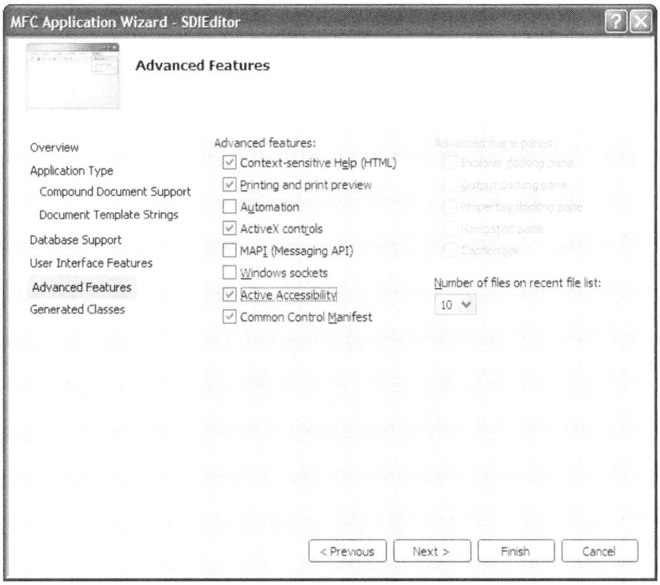

**Book VII
Chapter 3**

Creating an MFC
SDI Project

Figure 3-7:
SDI
applications
usually
require
a few
advanced
features.

21. **Choose the advanced features you want to use (Figure 3-7 shows the features for the example) and click Next.**

You see the Generated Classes step shown in Figure 3-8. This figure already has the base class changed to CRichEditView for the example. The base class you choose is extremely important. Because the example is a text editor, choosing the CRichEditView class saves considerable coding time. However, note that the figure shows a wealth of other class types. Depending on the kind of application you create, you might choose a different base class such as CFormView for a database application.

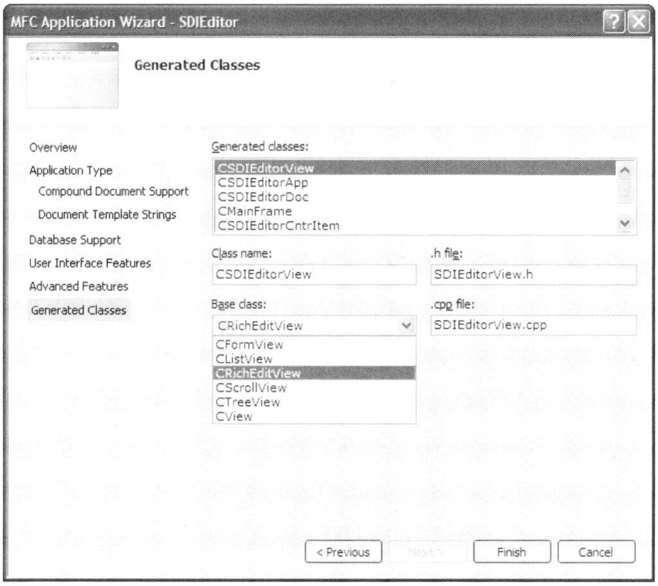

Figure 3-8:
Selecting
the right
base class
can save
you consid-
erable
coding time.

22. Choose a Base Class option and click Finish.

Visual Studio creates all the files required for your application based on the extensive list of selections you made.

If you were to compile the application right now, it would perform as a basic rich text editor. You can create new documents, save documents to disk, format document content, and even paste links to external files. Even the basic help is in place. Of course, this shell of an application is extremely generic. You still have to perform a considerable amount of customization to make it completely useable, but you do have enough elements in place to play with it a bit.

Understanding the Document/View Architecture

The document/view architecture is at the center of the vast majority of MFC applications. As the name implies, the programming technique keeps the document (the data) separated from the view (the presentation of the data). By separating the document from the view, it becomes possible to create a view of just part of the data or multiple views of the same data. For example, a spreadsheet application can present the same data in tabular and graphic form.

The base class for documents is CDocument. An application can use CDocument, but many inherit CDocument and augment its functionality.

The CDocument class does provide some essential features, such as the UpdateAllViews() method. This method makes it possible for the document to notify all views that the document has changed, no matter what the source of the change might be. The simple AddView() method lets an application add a new view of the data to a list of views.

The base class for views is CView. As with CDocument, many applications inherit CView functionality and augment it. As with CDocument, CView also implements some basic functionality you need to create a robust application. For example, CView provides the GetDocument() method which requests a copy of the current document. Many of the CView methods define what happens when the user performs a certain task, such as dropping an object on the view. Of course, many of the calls also handle rendering and determine how the user can scroll through the document when the view provides a partial presentation.

Some people think that an application needs only a document and a view to provide complete functionality. However, it's important to remember that the document/view architecture affects only the data and the user's view of that data. An application also requires some kind of framework in which to present the data and an application shell to interact with Windows.

This section provides an overview of the document/view architecture essentials. In most cases, this is all you really need to know to write MFC applications. However, you can get a more complete description of this architecture at http://msdn.microsoft.com/en-us/library/4x1xy43a.aspx.

Adding Code to Your SDI Project

Careful selection of options when you use the application template will reduce the amount of coding you must perform to create a functional application. In fact, it's quite possible to get close to a working application by using precise selections. The sample application is an example of such selections. You can use the application right now. It won't have any customization, but it will work. The following sections describe how to add code to the application shell that that template creates for you.

An overview of the essential application files

One of the major areas of confusion for anyone working with MFC is the number of files that the template creates. When you view Solution Explorer (as shown in Figure 3-9), you see a hoard of files. In fact, Figure 3-9 doesn't include the massive number of help topic files needed to create the help file associated with this application.

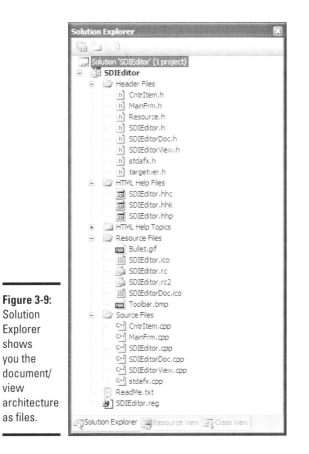

Figure 3-9:
Solution
Explorer
shows
you the
document/
view
architecture
as files.

It's important to remember the information found in the "Understanding the Document/View Architecture" section of the chapter when you look at the files. Choosing the right file is easier when you know what part of the application you want to modify. The following list describes the purpose of each of the files so that you know how they relate to the document/view architecture employed by MFC applications:

✦ **CntrItem:** Provides support for any OLE or ActiveX features in your application. The number of features found in this file depends on the options you choose through the template and the base class you choose for your application. Any form of embedding, linking, and ActiveX support depends on this part of the application. For the sample application, this part of the application implements the `CSDIEditorCntrItem` class, which provides support for the rich editing features found in the `CRichEditCntrItem` base class.

✦ **MainFrm:** Implements the application frame — the part of the application that holds the document and its view. The application frame contains the user interface features, such as toolbars and menus. For the sample application, this part of the application implements the `CMainFrame` class, which implements the `CFrameWnd` base class.

✦ **SDIEditor:** Presents the application's face to the outside world. For example, if you want to add command-line functionality to your application, you add it to this part of the application. The "Registering and unregistering the application" section of the chapter discusses the default command-line arguments that an MFC application provides. For the sample application, this part of the application implements the `CSDIEditorApp`, which implements the `CWinApp` base class.

✦ **SDIEditorDoc:** Implements the document portion of the document/view architecture. Anything that affects the data the application manipulates appears in this part of the application. For the sample application, this part of the application implements the `CSDIEditorDoc` class, which implements the `CRichEditDoc` base class.

✦ **SDIEditorView:** Implements the view portion of the document/view architecture. Anything that affects how the user sees the data that the application manipulates appears in this part of the application. For the sample application, this part of the application implements the `CSDIEditorView`, which implements the `CRichEditView` base class.

The base class you select in the template affects the base class used to create the `CntrItem`, `<AppName>Doc`, and `<AppName>View` files. Consequently, if you select a different base class from the sample application, the base classes you see used for these files will also differ.

As with any C++ application, the CPP (C++) files contain code that implements application features. The H (header) files contain declarations for the classes found in the CPP files, as well as variables used to interact with the user interface. All of the files in the Resource folder contain user interface elements — everything from menus and toolbars to strings used for versioning.

Locating Microsoft specified suggested changes

Microsoft suggests changes for the application. You need to make some of these changes to perform basic application customization. Most developers perform additional changes, so the changes described in this section are the minimum you should consider making.

None of the H files contains suggested changes. Therefore, the best way to proceed is to open the first file in the Source Files folder and go from there. To see the changes quickly, open the Task List window shown in Figure 3-10 by choosing View➪Task List or by pressing Ctrl+T, which shows the task list for the SDIEditor.CPP file.

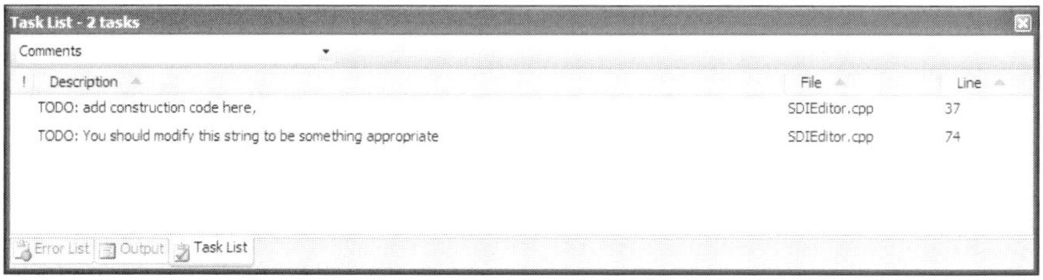

Figure 3-10:
Microsoft
makes
a list of
suggested
changes
for you.

	Description ▲	File ▲	Line ▲
	TODO: add construction code here,	SDIEditor.cpp	37
	TODO: You should modify this string to be something appropriate	SDIEditor.cpp	74

Task List - 2 tasks

Comments ▼

🔲 Error List | 🔲 Output | 📄 Task List

The task list in Figure 3-10 is typical. The first entry, "TODO: add construction code here," is optional. If you want to perform some special application-level initialization tasks, you must perform them at the location indicated. However, the second entry isn't optional. When this application starts for the first time, it looks for a registry entry that contains the application settings. These settings appear at the location indicated by this line of code:

```
SetRegistryKey(_T("Local AppWizard-Generated Applications"));
```

Normally, you change the string shown to something that reflects your company name or you as an individual. The template automatically includes an application name as part of the entry hierarchy. However, the default string is ambiguous and keeping it in place could cause problems with other applications you create. If you want to create a registration hierarchy, separate the hierarchy keys with double backslashes, such as `"MyCompany\\ TheSecondLevel"`.

When you finish making a change, remove the TODO comment from the file. Making this change reduces the number of items in the Task List window to those that you haven't completed yet. In addition, most developers find it easier to open a single file at a time and then close it when they're finished making changes. The Task List windows show all the tasks for every file you have opened, which means it can become cluttered quite quickly.

Making resource changes

The resources that come with the application template require customization. To view the resources, open the Resource folder in Solution Explorer and double-click the `SDIEditor.rc` entry. Visual Studio opens the Resource View window shown in Figure 3-11.

The Resource View window groups things by resource type. For example, the Accelerator folder contains lists of virtual keypresses — the keypresses that users can use in place of menu or toolbar selections. A typical example of a virtual keypress is Ctrl+N for the File⇨New command.

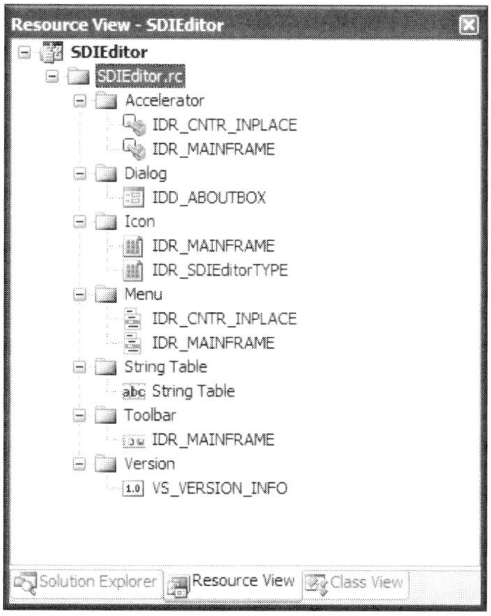

Figure 3-11: The Resource View window contains a list of all the resources for an application.

To open a particular resource for editing, double-click its entry in Resource View. One of the most commonly modified items is the About dialog box (IDD_ABOUTBOX). The About dialog box supplied with the application is extremely simple, as shown in Figure 3-12. Most companies want to add a company name, contact information, and other specifics. Some About dialog boxes include specialized features, such as a button users can click to register their application. It helps to look at what other people are doing with the About dialog box when making a decision about what to do with the About dialog box in your application.

The Icon folder contains a list of icons used with the application (typically two). The icons are generic, as shown in Figure 3-13. One mistake that many developers make is to change just the first icon. Notice that this single icon file actually includes a number of icons in different sizes. For your application to look right, you must change every one of the icons by selecting their entry in the left pane. The 4-bit icons have the fewest color choices, and the 32-bit icons have the greatest. Modifying the icons can consume quite a bit of time, so make sure you plan for this need when developing your application.

Book VII
Chapter 3

Creating an MFC SDI Project

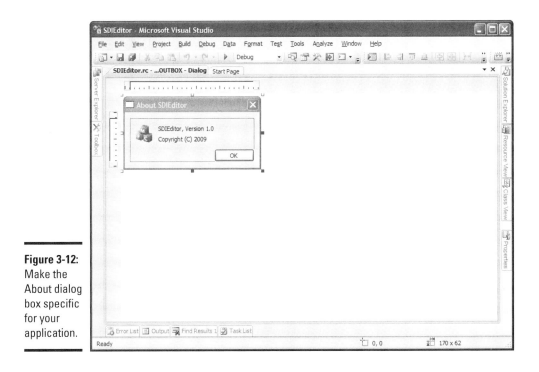

Figure 3-12:
Make the
About dialog
box specific
for your
application.

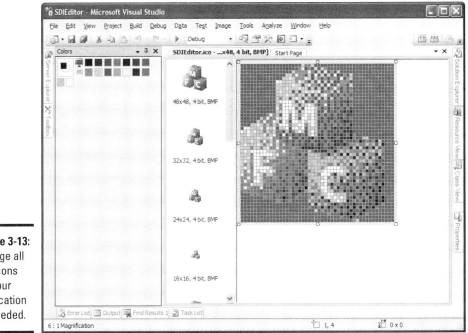

Figure 3-13:
Change all
the icons
for your
application
as needed.

The must change resource item is the version information found in the Version folder (VS_VERSION_INFO). Unlike most of the other resources, this file contains TODO items, as shown in Figure 3-14. Make sure you address needs such as your company name.

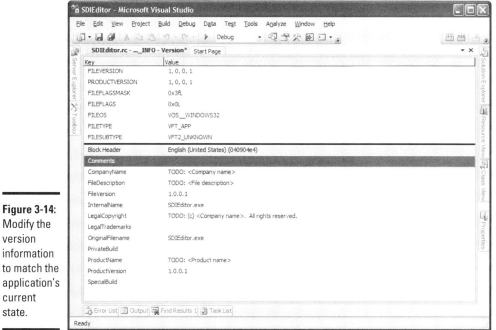

Figure 3-14: Modify the version information to match the application's current state.

Considering the help file

Depending on how you set up the template, Visual Studio can create a relatively complete help system for the application shell. Of course, this help system, like all other parts of the application, requires modification. The template doesn't customize help for your company, so you have to work on it a little.

This book doesn't provide a complete dissertation on the help system provided with Visual C++. You could very well require an entire book to obtain complete, detailed knowledge of the topic. However, you'll get a good overview and enough to get you started in this section. If you want to create a fully customized help system for a shrink-wrapped application, the information in this section probably won't provide enough information.

The help files appear in two folders in Solution Explorer: HTML Help Files and HTML Help Topics. The HTML Help Files folder contains the structural help elements, such as the help file index. The only file you need to modify in this folder is SDIEditor.hhc, which contains a few entries that don't reflect the application. For example, you must change the following entry to reflect the application name:

```
<param name="Name" value="&lt;&lt;YourApp&gt;&gt; Help Index">
```

You need to replace YourApp with the name of your application. This same file has other changes you need to make. As you add help topics, modify the functionality of the shell application, and perform other tasks, you need to make other changes to this file. For example, adding a major menu requires that you add an entry for it to the SDIEditor.hhc file.

The second folder, HTML Help Topics, contains one HTML file for each help topic in the help file. As you add features to your application, you need to add HTML files here to accommodate those features. However, at the outset, you need to worry first about the main_index.htm file, which contains a number of undefined entries such as the one shown here:

```
<TITLE>(&lt;&lt;YourApp&gt;&gt; Help Index)</TITLE>
```

As with the SDIEditor.hhc file, you must replace YourApp with the name of your application. This file also contains placeholders for any ancillary topics you want to include in your application, such as tutorials or troubleshooting information.

The YourApp entry appears frequently in the template-generated help files. It's embarrassing to have one of these entries escape notice and make it into the final product. To keep this from happening, choose Edit⇨Find and Replace⇨Find in Files to display the Find and Replace dialog box. Type **YourApp** in the Find What field and click Find All. You see a Find Results window like the one shown in Figure 3-15 that shows all the files that contain the YourApp entries you have to change. To locate a particular entry, double-click it in the Find Results window and Visual Studio will open the associated file for you.

For some reason, Visual Studio doesn't always rebuild the help file after you make changes to the content files. To ensure that your help file is updated, delete the CHM (Compiled Help Module) file in the application output folder before you perform a build. Deleting this file will force Visual Studio to rebuild the help file.

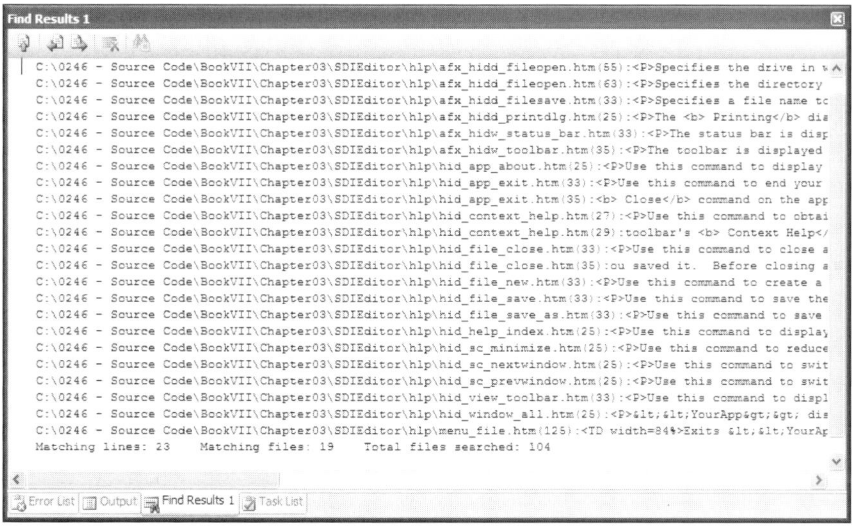

**Book VII
Chapter 3**

Creating an MFC
SDI Project

Figure 3-15:
Make sure
you find all
the YourApp
entries.

Registering and unregistering the application

Every time you start the example application, it checks the registry to ensure that it's registered. The SDI application performs two kinds of registration. First, it registers its file extension so that when you double-click a file with that extension, it opens in the appropriate application. Second, it registers the application settings. Registration is good because it helps your application to perform tasks properly.

Unfortunately, the registry entries stay in place until you tell the application to remove them. Every SDI application supports four default command-line switches. For the example application, these switches are documented in the SDIEditor.cpp file. Here's a short description of each command-line switch:

✦ **/RegServer:** Registers the application file extension support, as well as any OLE or ActiveX support it provides

✦ **/Register:** Registers the application's settings

✦ **/Unregserver:** Removes the application file extension support, as well as any OLE or ActiveX support it provides

✦ **/Unregister:** Removes the application's settings

The interesting thing about these command-line switches is that almost no one talks about them. Developer machines often end up clogged with extraneous registry entries because they don't unregister the application before making changes that affect file extension, OLE, ActiveX, or settings support. The dirty machine quickly starts to report inaccurate results and the application can go out the door with nasty bugs. To avoid this problem on your own machine, simply type **SDIEditor /Unregserver** and press Enter at the command line. Now type **SDIEditor /Unregister** and press Enter. The application registry entries are removed from your machine.

Seeing the Text Editor Project in Action

It's time to see the text editor in action. Build your project by choosing Build➪Build Solution or pressing Ctrl+Shift+B or clicking Build Solution on the Build toolbar. When the build process completes successfully, press F5 to start the application. Figure 3-16 shows what you typically see when you start the application and enter some information in it.

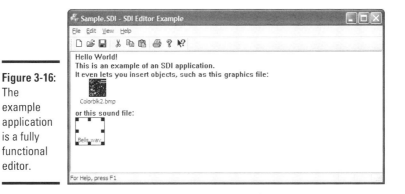

Figure 3-16:
The example application is a fully functional editor.

When you save a file, it has the extension that you've assigned to the application. The file content is standard RTF. Open it with Notepad and you'll see codes such as those shown in Figure 3-17. If you open it with an RTF-aware application such as Word, you see the document with all the formatting and objects in place.

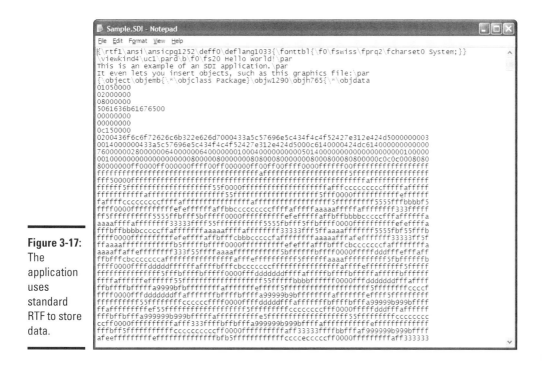

**Book VII
Chapter 3**

**Creating an MFC
SDI Project**

Figure 3-17:
The application uses standard RTF to store data.

This editor is easy to extend. You can add features such as font support. Anything you can do in RTF, you can do with this editor. It's even possible to convert the output to other formats, such as XML. In short, the example as it exists in this chapter is only the beginning.

Chapter 4: Using the Visual C++ 2008 Debugger

In This Chapter

✔ Understanding the error application

✔ Getting started with debugging

✔ Using the debugging windows

*A*s with any good programming environment, Visual C++ offers a debugger that helps you locate and squash bugs in your application. In fact, the Visual C++ debugger is one of the highlights of Visual Studio. You get a world-class debugger that can help you locate nearly any type of bug in your application and with a minimum of effort.

The Visual C++ debugger works the same as most other debuggers. You can single-step through the application or use breakpoints to stop at locations you think might contain errors. Visual C++ provides a number of debugging windows that show the application state and provide a means for watching variables as the application executes.

The thing that sets this debugger apart is that everything is well integrated so that you don't have to work quite so hard to figure things out. In addition, Visual C++ provides a number of additional windows that you won't find with other debuggers. For example, you can create more than one Watch window.

In this chapter, you discover the Visual C++ debugger. The sections split debugging into running the application and working with the debugging windows.

A debugger is a debugger

Minibook III spends considerable time discussing application debugging techniques. No matter what IDE you use, debuggers tend to work the same way and the techniques you use to debug an application are essentially the same. What differs is the number of debugger resources the IDE provides. The Visual Studio debugger works the same as the debugger for CodeBlocks but has additional functionality. For example, Visual Studio gives you four Watch windows to debug your code. It also has features such as visualizers. However, when all is said and done, the basic principles are the same, so the techniques you discover in Minibook III apply to Visual Studio as well.

Visual Studio includes many of the same windows as CodeBlocks (as do many other debuggers). For example, if you include Debug statements in your code, you still see the output in the Output window. This chapter doesn't discuss windows that have the same functionality in both IDEs.

A Quick Look at the Error Application

The example application has two errors in it. The application is supposed to obtain the value from the user, add 1 to it, and then display the result. As you can see from Figure 4-1, the application doesn't work quite right.

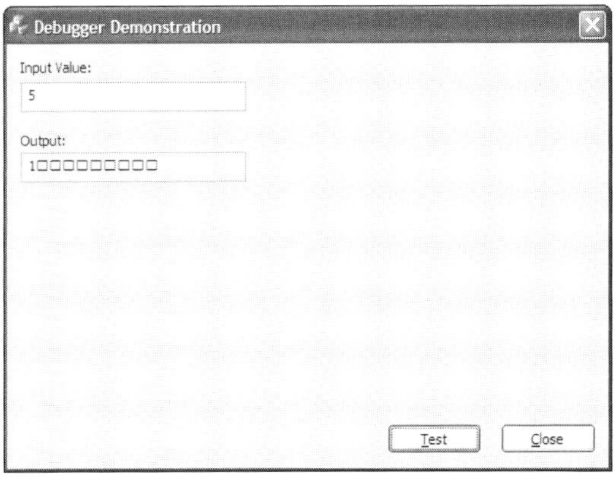

Figure 4-1: The error application is simply broken.

The purpose of this chapter isn't to keep the problems a deep hidden secret — the purpose is to show how the debugger helps you locate these problems. This application has the following two errors:

+ It relies on a variable, rather than a control, to provide access to the input value.

+ It uses the wrong function to perform a conversion.

The example code shows both the errors and the fixes required to make the application work properly. Listing 4-1 shows the target function for this example.

Listing 4-1:   Creating an Application That Contains Two Errors

```
void CErrorAppDlg::OnBnClickedTest()
{
    // Obtain and convert the value.
    int InputValue = atoi((const char *)m_Input.GetBuffer());

    // Here's the first fix.
    //CString InputString = _T("");
    //m_InputControl.GetWindowTextW(InputString);
    //int InputValue = _wtoi(InputString.GetBuffer());

    // Release the buffer.
    m_Input.ReleaseBuffer();

    // Add 1 to it.
    int OutputValue = InputValue + 1;

    // Convert the result to a string.
    CString Output = _T("0");
    _itoa_s(OutputValue, (char *)Output.GetBuffer(10), 10, 10);

    // Here's the second fix.
    //_itow_s(OutputValue, Output.GetBuffer(10), 10, 10);

    // Make sure you release the buffer.
    Output.ReleaseBuffer();

    // Output the results.
    m_Output.SetWindowTextW(Output);
}
```

The application begins by using a `CString` variable instead of a `CEdit` control for `IDC_INPUT`. As a result, `m_Input` contains a blank string instead of the value the user typed. The example fixes this error by using a `CEdit` control instead and then obtaining the value from the window. At this point, the code places the value the user typed into a `CString` variable, `InputString`.

The second error is the use of the `_itoa_s()` function to convert the integer value into a string. The error is somewhat obvious because the code has to coerce the output of the `Output.GetBuffer()` method. The fix for this problem is to use the `_itow_s()` function instead.

Starting Your Application in Debugging Mode

Debugging an application in Visual Studio requires that you first perform the right setups. These setups ensure that the application starts in the right place, stops in the right place, and has the required debugging information in the executable file. Otherwise, the debugger simply won't work. The following sections discuss all these steps.

Creating the proper build

Before you can use your application, you must ask the IDE to build it for you. Visual Studio provides two default builds for Visual C++ applications:

+ Release

+ Debug

You can create other builds as needed using Configuration Manager. To debug your application, you must select the Debug build from the Solution Configurations drop-down list located on the Standard toolbar. This same drop-down list also provides access to Configuration Manager. When you finish debugging your application, choose the Release build, and rebuild the application for distribution purposes.

Setting breakpoints

Breakpoints tell the debugger to stop in a certain location so that you can begin debugging the application. You set breakpoints wherever you think you might be able to gain information required to debug the application. For example, you might want to set a breakpoint at the location used to set an application value and again where the application uses the value to perform a task. Some global variables are initialized and used in two different methods, so setting two breakpoints isn't unusual.

To set a breakpoint, click in the margin next to the line where you want the debugger to stop. Visual Studio displays a red circle to mark the breakpoint. For example, Figure 4-2 shows a breakpoint at this line of code:

```
int InputValue = atoi((const char *)m_Input.GetBuffer());
```

After you have a breakpoint set, the debugger will stop at that location. You can also perform a number of configuration changes to breakpoints. To see the list, right-click the breakpoint and select the option you want from the context menu. Here are the standard breakpoint options:

+ **Delete Breakpoint:** Removes the breakpoint completely. You have to reset the breakpoint to stop at the location.

+ **Disable Breakpoint:** Leaves the breakpoint intact so that you can still see it in the Breakpoints window (see the "Viewing your breakpoints" section of the chapter for details) but prevents the debugger from stopping.

Figure 4-2:
Set
breakpoints
as needed
in your
application.

✦ **Enable Breakpoint:** Makes a breakpoint functional again after disabling it. To use this feature, you must right-click on the line of code or enable the breakpoint in the Breakpoints window.

✦ **Location:** Displays the File Breakpoint dialog box, where you see the path, filename, line number, and starting character of the breakpoint. This dialog box also contains an option that keeps the breakpoint functional even if the source code differs from the original.

✦ **Condition:** Displays the Breakpoint Condition dialog box, where you set a condition for the breakpoint. You may provide any expression, including variable names, and choose whether the breakpoint functions when the expression is true or has changed.

✦ **Hit Count:** Displays the Breakpoint Hit Count dialog box, where you select how often the debugger must hit a particular line of code before the breakpoint becomes functional. The default setting causes execution to stop every time. However, you can set various hit count conditions, such as when the hit count is greater than a particular number.

✦ **Filter:** Displays the Breakpoint Filter dialog box, where you define process and thread conditions for the breakpoint. For example, you can decide that the breakpoint should function for the main thread but not a child thread. You can set the following filter types:

• MachineName

• ProcessId

• ProcessName

- ThreadId
- ThreadName

✦ **When Hit:** Displays the When Breakpoint Is Hit dialog box, where you define an action to perform when the debugger encounters the breakpoint. You can Print a Message, Run a Macro, Continue Execution, or perform any combination of these tasks (you must Print a Message or Run a Macro to enable the Continue Execution option).

Viewing your breakpoints

Sometimes you want to see a list of the breakpoints you have set. Choose Debug➪Windows➪Breakpoints or press Ctrl+Alt+B to display the Breakpoints window. Figure 4-3 shows a typical example.

Figure 4-3:
The Breakpoints window shows a complete list of the breakpoints you've set.

The default breakpoint appears like the first one in this list with a red circle. When you add a condition of some sort, the red circle has a plus sign added like the second breakpoint in the list. Disabled breakpoints appear with a hollow circle, as shown for the third entry.

You can interact with the breakpoints in a number of ways. Double-clicking a breakpoint takes you to that location in the file. As an alternative, you can click Go To Source Code or press Alt+F9, then press S to go to the breakpoint location in the file.

Click Disable All Breakpoints to keep breakpoints in place but prevent the debugger from stopping at them. You can also delete individual breakpoints or all of the breakpoints at once. Right-click a breakpoint and you see a context menu where you can set conditions.

Figure 4-3 shows the default columns. The Breakpoints window provides a considerable list of additional columns. Simply choose the columns you want to see from the Columns drop-down list. The example application relies on the three breakpoints shown in Figure 4-3 without any conditions attached — all three breakpoints are active.

Starting the debugger

You can start the debugger in a number of ways. For example, you can simply click Step Over in the Debug toolbar or press F10. However, the standard method to start debugging is to set a breakpoint and then use one of these techniques:

✦ Click Start Debugging in the Debug toolbar

✦ Press F5

✦ Choose Debug➪Start Debugging

Working with the Debugging Windows

The debugging windows tell you things about your application. Precisely what the windows tell you depends on where you set breakpoints and the particular window. Most debugging windows provide some means of viewing variables and their content. Because some variables are complex, you can also drill down into the variables to see the content of objects and properties they contain. The following sections describe the debugging windows.

Viewing the focus variables using the Autos window

The most commonly used window is Autos. In fact, this window appears by default when you start the application in debugging mode. The Autos window is exceptionally useful because it helps you focus on the variables in use at a particular line of code. It shows all the variables in use, regardless of whether these variables are local or global.

The example application has a problem obtaining the value the user typed into the form. The first breakpoint takes you to the `CErrorAppDlg::DoDataExchange()` method, where the application obtains data from the form and places it in a variable at this line:

```
DDX_Text(pDX, IDC_INPUT, m_Input);
```

This line of code shows the data exchange between `IDC_INPUT` and `m_Input`. When you follow the code, you find that the `CErrorAppDlg::DoDataExchange()` method is called only when the program starts and again when you close the form. Consequently, the first problem with the application is that `m_Input` is always a blank as shown in Figure 4-4. As you discover if you look at the other debugging windows, the Autos window is the only one that provides this view and makes it possible to see the first error in this application.

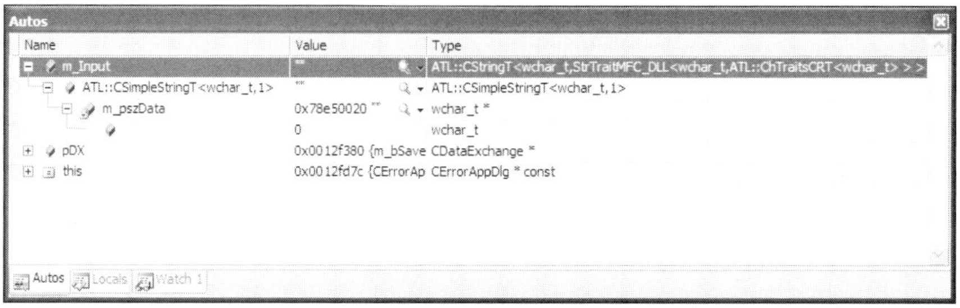

Figure 4-4:
The Autos window focuses attention on variables of interest for the current task.

The Autos window provides three columns that tell you the variable name, contents, and type. Click the plus sign next to any variable name that has one and you drill down into the object to see the elements of that variable. Note that some of the entries in the Value column have a magnifying glass next to them. Visual Studio offers visualizers for certain kinds of data, including

- ✦ Text Visualizer
- ✦ XML Visualizer
- ✦ HTML Visualizer

Select a visualizer from the drop-down list next to the magnifying glass. Click the magnifying glass to view the data using the visualizer. Figure 4-5 shows an example of the Text Visualizer for `Output` in the `CErrorAppDlg::OnBnClickedTest()` method. The Text Visualizer shows that `Output` is filled with garbage because it isn't filled using the correct function.

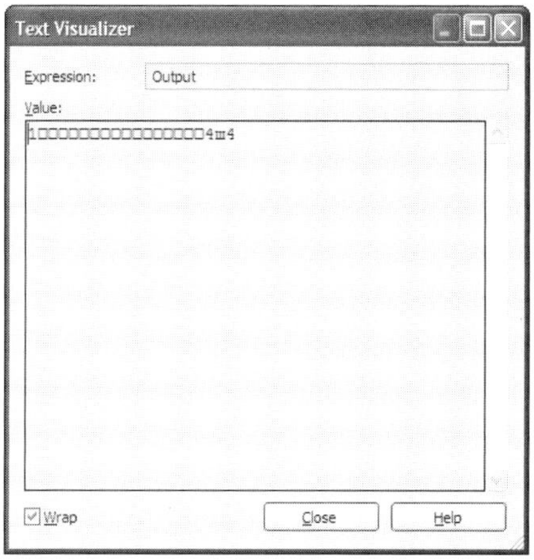

Figure 4-5:
Use visualizers to see data clearly.

Viewing all of the variables in a method using the Locals window

The Locals window focuses attention on the local method. You don't see any global variables. However, in some cases, you really do want to see just the local variables. For example, the Locals window makes the first error in the example application painfully obvious, as shown in Figure 4-6.

Figure 4-6:
The Locals window works precisely the same as Autos, only the focus differs.

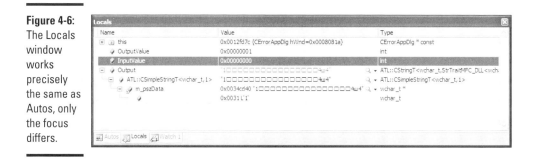

The InputValue variable in the CErrorAppDlg::OnBnClickedTest() method is 0 after the application calls int InputValue = atoi((const char *)m_Input.GetBuffer()); as shown in Listing 4-1. As a result, OutputValue contains 1 instead of the number you expect after the math calculation. The Locals window works just like the Autos window in every other way.

Screening specific variables using the Watch 1 window

In some cases, you don't want either a current line of code or a local method focus. Visual Studio supports up to four watch windows — each of which can have a different focus. The default debug setup shows Watch 1, but you can display Watch 2 through Watch 4 by choosing the corresponding option on the Debug➪Windows➪Watch menu.

The easiest way to use a Watch window is to drag a variable of interest from the Code window to the Watch window. You can also type a variable into the Watch window. If you decide that you want to monitor just part of a variable, simply edit the value in the Name column.

Even through the Watch window provides you with significant flexibility in adding the variables you want to see, it works the same as the other variable windows. In short, you can still drill down into variables and use visualizers to see variable content.

**Book VII
Chapter 4**

**Using the Visual
C++ 2008 Debugger**

Working with the Call Stack window

The Visual Studio Call Stack window is about the same as the Call Stack window found in any other debugger. However, in this case, you obtain additional information such as the name of the file that holds the code for the call, as well as the class and method name. When you double-click an entry in the Call Stack window, Visual Studio opens the required file and places the cursor at the point the call occurs so you can examine the surrounding code with ease.

Chapter 5: Analyzing Your Visual C++ 2008 Code

*H*ow fast does it work? That's the question many developers ask when the application is finally put together because it's the question that the customer will ask when the application is delivered. No one wants to spend hours waiting for an application to perform its task. In fact, people want an application that produces results as close to instantaneously as possible.

Fortunately, Visual C++ makes it possible to check the speed of your application and locate areas that don't work as quickly as they could. Of course, you must still make the changes required to produce optimal results — the tools can only point to potential sources of problems, not tell you how to correct them.

You always have to consider the consequences of actions you take. An application doesn't exist in a vacuum. When you make an application run faster, you can also cause it to perform unreliably or break security rules to get the last bit of speed. As the famous saying goes, "Speed kills." An application that goes too fast and breaks the rules in the process can kill your data, which can ultimately kill your company. Consequently, you must always consider speed improvements in light of how they affect the application environment as a whole.

Using Performance Wizard

Performance Wizard helps you check your code for potential performance issues. It's simple to use, as you see in the following steps that take you through a performance-checking session:

1. **Choose Analyze⇨Launch Performance Wizard.**

You see the dialog box shown in Figure 5-1. This first dialog box lets you choose any project in the current solution. It's also possible to select an external EXE, DLL or ASP.NET application. When you choose an external application, the wizard adds an additional step where you describe the external location to test.

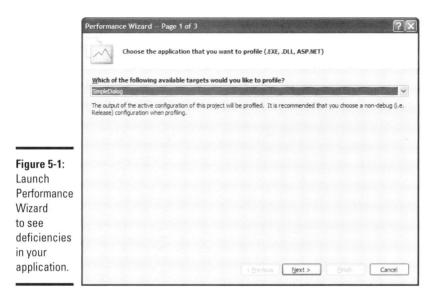

Choose the application that you want to profile (.EXE, .DLL, ASP.NET)

Which of the following available targets would you like to profile?

SimpleDialog

The output of the active configuration of this project will be profiled. It is recommended that you choose a non-debug (i.e. Release) configuration when profiling.

< Previous   Next >   Finish   Cancel

Figure 5-1:
Launch
Performance
Wizard
to see
deficiencies
in your
application.

2. **Choose a profiling option and click Next.**

   If you select a project that's part of the current solution, go directly to Step 4.

3. **Provide the external location information that the wizard requests and then click Next.**

   You see the Specify the Profiling Method dialog box shown in Figure 5-2. The profiling method you select determines the kind of statistics the wizard generates and how it generates them. The wizard offers two options as described here:

   • **Sampling:** This approach takes snapshots of your application over time. The snapshots aren't always completely accurate because you aren't performing full-time monitoring of the application. However, the snapshots do generate less data, making them ideal for processes that have to run a long time to obtain trend data. In most cases, you use sampling when you want to obtain an overall view of your application performance.

   • **Instrumentation:** This approach relies on diagnostic probes that you place in the code. The results are precise. However, instrumentation consumes considerable resources. Consequently, you normally use instrumentation to fine-tune your performance analysis after you obtain an overview using sampling.

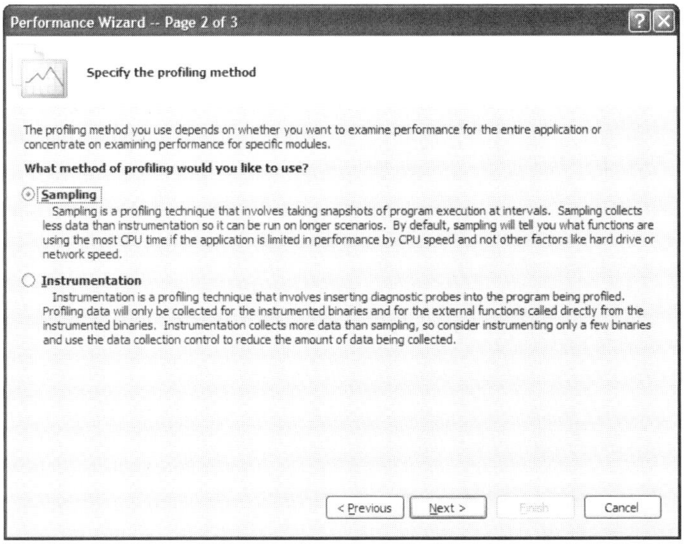

Performance Wizard -- Page 2 of 3

Specify the profiling method

The profiling method you use depends on whether you want to examine performance for the entire application or concentrate on examining performance for specific modules.

What method of profiling would you like to use?

⊙ Sampling
> Sampling is a profiling technique that involves taking snapshots of program execution at intervals. Sampling collects less data than instrumentation so it can be run on longer scenarios. By default, sampling will tell you what functions are using the most CPU time if the application is limited in performance by CPU speed and not other factors like hard drive or network speed.

○ Instrumentation
> Instrumentation is a profiling technique that involves inserting diagnostic probes into the program being profiled. Profiling data will only be collected for the instrumented binaries and for the external functions called directly from the instrumented binaries. Instrumentation collects more data than sampling, so consider instrumenting only a few binaries and use the data collection control to reduce the amount of data being collected.

[< Previous] [Next >] [Finish] [Cancel]

Figure 5-2:
Select a profiling method.

4. **Choose a profiling method and click Next.**

   You see a summary dialog box that tells you the specifics of the performance monitoring session.

5. **Click Finish.**

   Visual Studio displays Performance Explorer, which contains folders for your application elements and also a folder for reports. The Reports folder is empty when you begin the sampling or instrumentation profiling process.

Profiling the Code

Visual Studio provides a number of ways to create a profile for your application. The easiest method is to use Performance Wizard as described in the preceding section. After you create a profile for your application, you can start it and use that profile to perform your analysis. Use the following steps to begin profiling your code:

1. **Highlight the application entry in the Targets folder of Performance Explorer.**

2. **Click Launch with Profiling in the Performance Explorer toolbar.**

   Visual Studio starts your application.

**Book VII
Chapter 5**

*Analyzing Your
Visual C++
2008 Code*

3. **Work with your application as you normally do.**

   Visual Studio collects data about your application. Make sure you exercise your application using the same approach as you would normally. Using a script can help improve profiling by ensuring that you exercise the application the same way every time you test it and guaranteeing that you exercise every feature.

4. **Stop the application.**

   You see a new report added to the Reports folder of Performance Explorer similar to the one shown in Figure 5-3. Visual Studio creates a new report every time you run the profile, so you can compare reports to determine how changes in your code affect application speed.

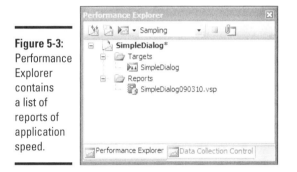

Figure 5-3: Performance Explorer contains a list of reports of application speed.

The report contains a listing of applications that cause the most work (by making calls, for example) and those that do most of the work. Figure 5-4 shows a report for the simple test application in this chapter. Most applications will generate more results, but this report gives you an idea of how the report looks.

Instrumented reports look a bit different from sampled reports. Before you begin the profile, select Instrumentation in the Method drop-down list in Performance Explorer. When you click Launch with Profiling, the Output window shows something like this:

```
Set linker /PROFILE switch (required for instrumentation) on project
   SimpleDialog.vcproj.Profiler started
Instrumenting SimpleDialog.exe in place
Info VSP3049: Small functions will be excluded from instrumentation.
Microsoft (R) VSInstr Post-Link Instrumentation 9.0.30729 x86
Copyright (C) Microsoft Corp. All rights reserved.
File to Process:
   SimpleDialog.exe --> SimpleDialog.exe
Original file backed up to SimpleDialog.exe.orig
Successfully instrumented file SimpleDialog.exe.
```

This is a normal part of the process. You test the application just as you normally do. However, the output report contains more detail, as shown in Figure 5-5.

SimpleDialog090310.vsp | Start Page | SimpleDialogDlg.cpp

Current View: Summary

Performance Report Summary

Functions Causing Most Work

Name	Samples	%
AfxWinMain(struct HINSTANCE__ *,struct HINSTANCE__ *,wchar_t *,int)	7	100.00
CSimpleDialogApp::InitInstance(void)	7	100.00
CDialog::DoModal(void)	7	100.00
_wWinMainCRTStartup	7	100.00
__tmainCRTStartup	7	100.00

Functions Doing Most Individual Work

Name	Samples	%
[kernel32.dll]	2	28.57
[ntdll.dll]	2	28.57
CWinAppEx::GetRuntimeClass(void)const	1	14.29
[UxTheme.dll]	1	14.29
AfxIsValidString(char const *,int)	1	14.29

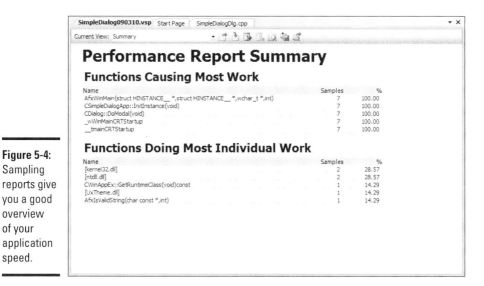

Figure 5-4: Sampling reports give you a good overview of your application speed.

SimpleDialog090310(1).vsp | SimpleDialog090310.vsp | Start Page | SimpleDialogDlg.cpp

Current View: Summary

Performance Report Summary

Most Called Functions

Name	Number of Calls	%
__RTC_CheckEsp	2,853	33.28
CSimpleDialogDlg::GetMessageMap(void)const	2,794	32.59
CSimpleDialogDlg::GetThisMessageMap(void)	2,794	32.59
CSimpleDialogApp::GetThisMessageMap(void)	15	0.17
CSimpleDialogApp::GetMessageMap(void)const	15	0.17

Functions With Most Individual Work

Name	Time (msec)	%
CSimpleDialogApp::InitInstance(void)	239,809.64	99.99
_wWinMain@16	20.38	0.01
CSimpleDialogDlg::OnInitDialog(void)	3.76	0.00
CSimpleDialogDlg::GetMessageMap(void)const	0.32	0.00
CSimpleDialogDlg::CSimpleDialogDlg(class CWnd *)	0.27	0.00

Functions Taking Longest

Name	Time (msec)	%
_wWinMainCRTStartup	239,835.24	100.00
__tmainCRTStartup	239,835.23	100.00
_wWinMain@16	239,835.02	100.00
CSimpleDialogApp::InitInstance(void)	239,814.64	99.99
CSimpleDialogDlg::OnInitDialog(void)	3.80	0.00

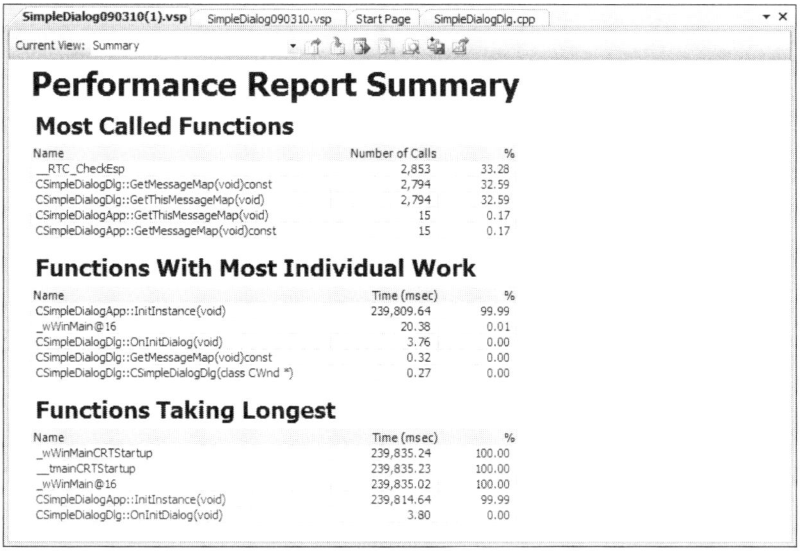

Figure 5-5: Instrumentation provides additional details.

Appendix A: Automating Your Programs with Makefiles

In This Appendix

✔ Compiling and linking your programs

✔ Automating your work

✔ Implying work with inference rules in your Makefiles

✔ Getting the most out of Makefiles

Since the beginning of time, or at least since the beginning of the Unix operating system, programmers have used a utility called make to build their programs. And it's still often used today. The make utility looks at which of your source-code files have changed and decides what needs to be compiled and built.

Development tools, such as CodeBocks and Microsoft Visual C++, don't require you to use a make utility because they have such decision-making features built in. But many free compilers use them. Fortunately, the process for creating and using make files is no longer as difficult as it once was. Third-party libraries come with make utilities (such as the Boost library's Boost Jam and Boost Build; see Minibook VI, Chapter 3) that greatly reduce the complexity of creating and using make files.

Before using make, understanding the compile and link processes is important. In this appendix, we cover the compile and link processes and advise how to use make to automate your building. Please note, however, that make itself is a complex tool, and enough information is available about it to fill an entire *For Dummies* book. Therefore, we suggest that you don't worry about mastering make and what are called Makefiles. Instead, read this appendix so you understand them. Then, if you work with Makefiles in your projects, start with an existing one. If you understand it, you can easily modify it for your project.

Compiling and Linking

When you create a program, you write your code in various source-code files. For one program, you can have many different source-code files. Some large corporate projects may have hundreds (or even thousands) of source-code files with dozens of programmers working on the different files. As you can imagine, dozens of strong-willed programmers working together makes for quite an adventure; but by using tools like make, these programmers are able to easily work together without a single disagreement ever taking place. Okay, we lied. But nevertheless, make makes their lives easier.

To transform these source-code files into a single program, you need to compile and link them.

Compiling means transforming your C++ code (or whatever language you are using) into a machine-readable language called Assembler. The Assembler language differs among types of processors. Most of you reading this book are probably working on some version of an AMD or Intel processor, so the C++ compilers you use normally translate your programs into Assembler language appropriate for the processor on your system. (You can also tell the compiler to target some other processor in many cases.) The compiler stuffs all this Assembler code into a file called an *object file* and typically names the file the same as the original source-code file but with an .obj or .o extension. For each source-code file, the compiler makes a single object file

After you have compiled all your source-code files, you run the linker. The *linker* takes the object files and combines them into a single file that you can run on your computer. This single file usually gets an .exe extension, which stands for executable. The origin of this term comes from *execution,* which refers to the running of a program and probably had something to do with what the user of the first computer program wanted to do to the programmer after using the program. But we're only guessing.

The linker can produce other kinds of output file. For example, you can create a .lib (library) or .dll (Dynamic Link Library, or DLL) file. These files contain executable code, just as the .exe file does, but you don't execute them as standalone files — an .exe file normally loads them and uses the executable code they contain.

The compiler also inserts into the object files a great deal of information in addition to the assembler code. For example, when you are still in the process of developing your program, you can instruct the compiler to put debug information in the file. (Although sometimes the debug information goes in a separate file; it depends on the compiler.) Debug information includes the names of your variables and the line numbers of the source code. When you use a debugger tool, that tool knows about your code by looking at the debug information.

The compiler also puts information about the code, such as the names of items that occur, in other source-code files. For example, if you are writing code that calls code in another source-code file, the compiler includes the name of that code in the object file. That way, the linker can connect the two.

Understanding external linkage

An example of where you may encounter external linkage is when code in one source-code file calls a function in another source-code file. When the compiler compiles the first source-code file, it doesn't know where in the compiled assembler code the routine will be when it compiles the second source-code file. And even if the second source-code file is already compiled, the compiler isn't particularly interested in digging around the other object file to figure out where it is. So instead, the compiler simply creates a *reference* to the routine. It places this reference inside the first object file.

Later, the linker replaces the reference with the address of the call, and that address is what will end up in the final executable. This address, however, is just temporary and serves as a placeholder until the final program is loaded into memory. When you run the executable

and the program gets loaded into memory, a special application called the *loader* replaces the address with the actual memory address where the routine is located. Whew!

Your code may also call code that lives outside your program, such as a routine in a DLL. In that case, the compiler still puts the name of the routine inside the object file. But at link time, the linker includes a placeholder that notes the name of the item (or perhaps a unique number) and the name of the DLL file. The linker puts that information inside the executable file. When you run the executable file and the program gets loaded into memory, the computer first makes sure that the DLL is loaded (following the same steps here that it's using to load the executable! Oh my!) and then replaces the information with the real live address of the DLL's routine. Again, Whew!

Finally, a compiler can add resources to the object files, such as graphics and sounds that your application requires. These resources appear as data that the application accesses later. Data appears in separate areas from executable code within the file, but you don't need to worry about the object file organization — the compiler takes care of managing both code and data for you.

Automating Your Work

When you're developing a program and working with, say, ten different source-code files and you're ready to compile and link your work, you could compile each source-code file separately and then link them all together. However, it would be nice if you had to compile only the source files that have changed since the last time you compiled. After all, if one of the source-code files was compiled to an object file earlier and hasn't changed since the last compile, why bother compiling it again?

The solution is to use some kind of special program that checks to find out which source files have changed and compiles only those. Or if none of the source files have changed, the special program checks only to see whether any external libraries have changed and, if necessary, does only a link. Or if nothing has changed at all, do nothing and call the program up to date.

That is exactly what the make utility does. Using make, you can be sure that only the object files and executables that are out of date get updated. How does make do this? It just compares the dates on the files, that's all. It looks at a source-code file and its associated object file. If no object file is associated with the source code, it definitely compiles the source-code files. If an object file is available, and the object file is newer than the source-code file, make knows that the source-code file hasn't changed since the last compile, and therefore there's no reason to recompile it. But if the source-code file is newer than the object file, it must have changed since the last compile, and thus the make utility compiles it.

To build your program by using make, you just type this at the console (that is, either the Unix prompt on Unix computers or the DOS window on Windows computers):

```
make
```

Note that different make applications have different names. For example, Microsoft provides the nmake utility that you can read about at http://msdn.microsoft.com/en-us/library/dd9y37ha.aspx. When using these other kinds of make utilities, simply type its name instead of make.

If anything in your project needs building, make will do it. Otherwise, it prints the simple but sweet little message:

```
make: `myprogram' is up to date.
```

Well, this is all fine and dandy, except for one little catch: the make utility needs something called a Makefile. The Makefile lists information about what exactly it's supposed to make. Unfortunately, Makefiles aren't exactly simple. The make utility and its Makefile concept was, after all, invented something like 30 years ago, back in the dark ages when computers were made of stone and cars had square wheels. But that's okay. Today's computers still handle Makefiles, and you can find out how to use them. The next section covers what exactly goes inside these animals. The things in the files are themselves interesting little animals called *inference rules*.

Implying with Inference Rules

Everybody loves rules, and so does the make utility. Before make knows what to make, you need to supply it with a set of rules. Programmers have decided to call these rules *inference rules* for lack of a better term. Well, actually, tons of better terms that take up less space are available. But they chose *inference* because the make utility will infer what it's supposed to do based on the rules implied by the Makefile.

In general, an inference rule specifies the file you want to create (such as an object file) and the file or files it depends on (such as its associated source-code file). Next the rule states how exactly to create that file. For example, if you have an object file that depends on a source-code file, the way to create it is by running the compiler command.

A typical inference rule looks like this. The first line specifies the name of the file you want to create, then it has a colon, and then the files it *depends* on are listed. The next line starts with a tab and then lists the commands to run to create that new file, with one command per line. The following example is a rule for creating a text file:

```
test.out: test.txt
    cp test.txt test.out
    echo WORKED >> test.out
```

The first line means that we want to create a file called test.out, and it depends on the file called test.txt. If test.txt is newer than test.out (meaning it has changed since the last time this rule was run), make executes the two commands that follow. In this case, the first one copies test.txt into the test.out file, and the second one appends the word WORKED at the end of test.out.

You may notice something interesting about the preceding inference rule. Instead of using the usual Windows/DOS command copy, here we used the command cp, which is the equivalent under Unix. Many of the free make utilities on the market, such as Cygwin, rely on Unix-style commands. If you prefer to work with the MinGW compiler or the Borland compiler, you can use the DOS copy command instead.

If you want to try out this Makefile, create a text file called Makefile, and put the following in it:

```
test.out: test.txt
    cp test.txt test.out
    echo WORKED >> test.out
```

(Note that the second and third lines begin with a single tab; do not start the first line with any tabs.) Next, make a text file in the same directory and call the file test.txt. Finally, while in the same directory, type the following command:

```
make
```

Note that you will need to have a `make` command installed. For example, you can obtain Cygwin at `http://www.cygwin.com/`. Minibook VI, Chapter 3 describes the Boost Jam and Boost Build compilers. You can also obtain the Borland compiler from `http://www.codegear.com/downloads/free/cppbuilder`.

If you do some exploring, you are likely to discover that you can optionally name your `Makefile` something other than `Makefile` and then specify your filename in the `make` command. For most versions of `make`, you do this by typing

```
make -f filename
```

However, we do not recommend doing this. Most programmers always use the filename `Makefile`, and if you call yours something different, you are likely to rattle their chains a little. Computer people are not known for their flexibility; and if you do this, your coworkers probably won't pay for your pizza this Friday.

Using rules that depend on other rules

Some special situations arise when working with inference rules. For example, `test.out` may not exist at all. In that case, the commands will definitely run because the idea is that this rule tells how to create a `test.out` file.

Another special situation deals with `test.txt` itself in the previous examples. Does *it* depend on anything? For example, another rule may say this:

```
test.txt: originalfile.txt
    cp originalfile.txt test.txt
```

This rule states that `test.txt` depends on `originalfile.txt`. If `originalfile.txt` has changed, `make` creates `test.txt` based on the command, which is a `cp` command.

As it turns out, `make` is surprisingly smart for such an old computer tool. Before it ventures into the rule to create `test.txt`, it sees that `test.txt` depends on `originalfile.txt`, and checks if `originalfile.txt` has any rules. If so, `make` keeps tracing backwards until it gets to a rule with no prior dependencies.

So these two rules would all be lumped together into a single `Makefile`:

```
test.out: test.txt
    cp test.txt test.out
    echo WORKED >> test.out
test.txt: originalfile.txt
    cp originalfile.txt test.txt
```

You can have multiple rules in your `Makefile`, and they don't all have to depend on each other. If you have multiple rules without such interdependencies in your file, however, `make` starts by running the first rule that it encounters.

Making specific items

When you have a `Makefile` filled with all sorts of rules, you may possibly want to build only one particular item inside it. For example, if you have dozens of source-code files, you may just want to compile the source-code file you're working on, without building the whole shebang all the way to the final executable.

To specify exactly *what* you want to build, just throw in the name of the item after the word `make`:

```
make test.txt
```

If you are working with the `Makefile` with rules for both `test.out` and `test.txt`, then when you issue this command, you create only `test.txt`; you will not create `test.out`. However, if `make` requires other rules to be built before this rule can run, it will run those rules.

So with the example we gave regarding multiple source-code files, if you want to compile only the one called `NiftyFeature.cpp`, you would type

```
make NiftyFeature.o
```

Note that the file extension in this line is `.o`. The reason is that, although you're compiling the source file (`NiftyFeature.cpp`), you are *making* the object file (`NiftyFeature.o`). Therefore, you specify the name of the object file in the `make` command when you want to compile a particular source file.

Depending on multiple files

Not only can you have multiple rules in your `Makefiles`, but you can have one rule that depends on multiple files. This is common when building files, particularly in the link step. For example, the final program itself, such as `myprogram.exe`, is going to depend on many files, including all the object files in your project, as well as any libraries.

To list multiple dependencies, you create your `Makefile` rule, listing all the dependencies on the right of the colon, separated by spaces, as in the following example. (Don't use commas or semicolons to separate them.)

```
test.out: test1.txt test2.txt
    echo hello > test.out
```

Here, `test.out` depends on both `test1.txt` and `test2.txt`. When you run `make`, if either of these two latter files has changed since the last time you ran `make`, the echo line executes.

If you have lots of files to the right of the colon, you can put them on multiple lines if you prefer by ending each line except the final one with a backslash (`\`), as in the following example.

```
test.out: test1.txt \
 test2.txt
    echo hello > test.out
```

Often, people indent the following lines with a single space, as we did there, primarily for readability. Although using a tab here is okay, we don't recommend doing that because the tabbed line makes it harder for us mere humans to read because the tabbed line will be aligned with the commands that follow.

If a header file changes and your source-code file uses it, you will want your source-code file to be rebuilt the next time you run `make`. Therefore, including header files in your list of dependencies is a good idea. But it can be difficult to figure out what header files your source file depends on. It turns out that there's a nifty little trick that can help you do this. Compilers such as Cygwin and MinGW can build such a list for you. To do this, you use the `-M` option, as in the following example:

```
g++ -M main.cpp
```

When we ran this on one of our source-code files, we saw the following appear on the screen:

```
main.o: main.cpp /usr/include/g++-3/iostream.h \
 /usr/include/g++-3/streambuf.h /usr/include/g++-3/libio.h \
 /usr/include/_G_config.h \
 /usr/lib/gcc-lib/i686-pc-cygwin/2.95.3-5/include/stddef.h \
 /usr/include/sys/cdefs.h main.h
```

Notice the left of the colon is the object file, `main.o`. To the right are the files it depends on, starting with our source-code file (`main.cpp`). The several include files follow, including their paths. To use these, you would then paste them into your `Makefile`; they represent the first line of the rule.

If you want to use the `-M` option to generate your dependencies (but only want to list the header files in your project and not all those other bizarre ones that live inside the main include directory), you can throw an extra *M* in, as follows.

```
g++ -MM main.cpp
```

When we run this, we see only the header files in our project. Here's the output we get:

```
main.o: main.cpp main.h
```

Often, this is more useful because it's rare that the system header files change.

Compiling and linking with make

To really use `make` in your projects, you need rules that tell `make` to run the compiler. For each of your source-code files, you want to build an object file; and from there, you want to link the object files into a single executable. You can write a `Makefile` that specifies these rules, such as the following:

```
mystuff.o: mystuff.cpp
    g++ -c mystuff.cpp -o mystuff.o
```

The first line says that our object file depends on the source file. The second line is the command to run to create the object file.

Linking is a bit more complex because to successfully link a program, you need to include several libraries. Which libraries you include depends on which compiler you use.

The beauty of using `Makefile`, however, is that after the information for compiling and linking is there, you don't need to do anything else. When it's time to build your program, you simply type

```
make
```

Certainly, you will be compiling and linking. Remember that with `Makefiles`, the best way to use them is to simply understand them. That way, you can take an existing one and fix them up so they work with your particular project. Writing one from scratch requires a strong knowledge of the intricate workings of the inference rules. Toward the end of this appendix (in the "Discovering more about `make`" sidebar), we tell you where you can find that information if you really want to study it.

Cleaning up and making it all

When you have a `Makefile` and a huge project, you may want to periodically start over fresh, cleaning out all your object files and the final executable, before you do a build. For example, you may be working on a project, and so much has changed that you would prefer to start out fresh with your next build. To do this, you can include a `clean` section in your `Makefile` that looks like this, if you're using Cygwin:

```
clean :
    rm -f *.o
    rm -f *.obj
    rm -f myprogram.exe
```

Note that no files are listed after the colon. Thus, when you type

```
make clean
```

the `rm` commands (which delete the files) will always run.

If you're using either the MinGW or Borland compilers, you want your `clean` section to look like this:

```
clean :
    del *.o *.obj myprogramexe
```

Using macros

Environment variables can include macros. A *macro* is basically a word that represents something else that is probably more complicated. For example, you may have something like this:

```
MYFILES = one.cpp two.cpp three.cpp four.cpp
```

Then, any place in your `Makefile` where you want to refer to the four files `one.cpp`, `two.cpp`, `three.cpp`, and `four.cpp`, you can instead simply write

```
$(MYFILES)
```

When you access a macro, you precede it with a dollar sign ($), and you put the name inside parentheses. The `make` utility then knows that this is a macro and needs to be expanded.

Discovering more about make

If you want to be a serious, diehard, late-into-the-night, big-time maker, you can read its online manual. You can do tons and tons of things with `make`, and you could easily stay up all night playing with it all — or, at least, trying to learn it all. You may not ever have a need for all the things you learn, but you never know. Here's the site: `www.gnu.org/manual/`.

Scroll down to find the entry on `make`. (make will be followed by a hyphen and some numbers representing the version number.) When you click it, you will see an enormous page filled with the wonders of `make`. Trust us: It's long and boring.

Getting the most out of Makefiles

Here are some other features you can use when working with `Makefiles`:

✦ If your lines run long and you want to continue them on the next line without confusing poor old `make`, you can end a line with a backslash (`\`), and then continue it on the next line.

✦ Your best bet when working with `Makefiles` is to start with one you know works and then change it so it applies to your current project. The truth is, almost no programmer creates a `Makefile` from scratch. They don't like to work that hard on auxiliary projects like messing with `Makefiles`. They'd rather get to their programming. So if you need a starting point, you can find a sample in this appendix.

✦ Most `Makefiles` will have a rule called `all`. The idea behind this rule is that it encompasses all the other rules. When you type **make all**, you can build your whole project.

✦ You can include comments in your `Makefiles` by starting them with a `#` character. These comments are not used by the `Makefile`.

✦ Makefiles can include what are called *implicit rules,* which are rules that pertain to a whole set of files with the same file extension (such as `.cpp`). These comments can help you understand the `Makefiles` when working with them.

✦ If you don't like `Makefiles`, you don't have to use them. Development environments such as CodeBlocks and Microsoft Visual C++ make it possible to create great applications without ever touching a `Makefile`.

Appendix B: About the CD

In This Appendix

✔ System requirements

✔ Using the CD with Windows, Linux, and Mac

✔ What you'll find on the CD

✔ Troubleshooting

*E*veryone likes free stuff. Well, that's what the CD is all about. All that code you thought you were going to have to type is included on the CD, so now you don't have to type it. Likewise, you get the CodeBlocks compiler. Just install it and start reading. Of course, you do need to know a bit more about the CD before you use it. The following sections tell you all about the CD to ensure that you have the most pleasant computing experience possible.

System Requirements

Make sure that your computer meets the minimum system requirements shown in the following list. If your computer doesn't match up to most of these requirements, you may have problems using the software and files on the CD. For the latest and greatest information, please refer to the ReadMe file located at the root of the CD-ROM.

✦ A PC running Microsoft Windows or Linux with kernel 2.4 or later or a Macintosh running Apple OS X or later (the screen shots in the book show the Microsoft Windows version of CodeBlocks).

✦ At least 512MB of RAM.

✦ The disk space you need depends on packages you install. The configuration used in this book requires 538MB, not including the source code. The fully compiled source code uses an additional 430MB of hard drive space.

✦ An Internet connection.

✦ A CD-ROM drive.

If you need more information on the basics, check out these books published by Wiley Publishing, Inc.: *PCs For Dummies*, 11th Edition by Dan Gookin; *Macs For Dummies*, 9th Edition by Edward C. Baig; *iMacs For Dummies*, 5th Edition by Mark L. Chambers; *Windows XP For Dummies*, 2nd Edition and *Windows Vista For Dummies*, both by Andy Rathbone.

Using the CD

To install the items from the CD to your hard drive, follow these steps.

1. **Insert the CD into your computer's CD-ROM drive.**

    The license agreement appears.

    Note to Windows users: The interface won't launch if you have autorun disabled. In that case, choose Start⇨Run. (For Windows Vista, choose Start⇨All Programs⇨Accessories⇨Run.) In the dialog box that appears, type ***D*:\Start.exe**. (Replace *D* with the proper letter if your CD drive uses a different letter. If you don't know the letter, see how your CD drive is listed under My Computer.) Click OK.

    Note for Mac users: When the CD icon appears on your desktop, double-click the icon to open the CD and double-click the Start icon.

    Note for Linux users: The specifics of mounting and using CDs vary greatly between different versions of Linux. Please see the manual or help information for your specific system if you experience trouble using this CD.

2. **Read through the license agreement and then click the Accept button if you want to use the CD.**

    The CD interface appears. The interface allows you to browse the contents and install the programs with just a click of a button (or two).

What You'll Find on the CD

The following sections are arranged by category and provide a summary of the software and other goodies you'll find on the CD. If you need help with installing the items provided on the CD, refer to the installation instructions in the preceding section.

This CD includes the source code found in the book, plus the CodeBlocks compiler. The source code works fine with Windows, Linux, and the Macintosh. You must have a special version of CodeBlocks for your platform of choice.

The programs fall into one of the following categories:

✦ *Shareware programs* are fully functional, free, trial versions of copyrighted programs. If you like particular programs, register with their authors for a nominal fee and receive licenses, enhanced versions, and technical support.

✦ *Freeware programs* are free, copyrighted games, applications, and utilities. You can copy them to as many computers as you like — for free — but they offer no technical support.

✦ *GNU software* is governed by its own license, which is included inside the folder of the GNU software. There are no restrictions on distribution of GNU software. See the GNU license at the root of the CD for more details.

✦ *Trial, demo,* or *evaluation* versions of software are usually limited either by time or functionality (such as not letting you save a project after you create it).

CodeBlocks Compiler
Freeware version.

For Windows, Linux, and Mac. CodeBlocks is a free compiler you can download at `http://www.codeblocks.org/downloads/5`. (You can send a donation for CodeBlocks if you desire, but you are under no obligation to do so.) This CD includes the 8.02 version of CodeBlocks, which was used to create the examples in this book. CodeBlocks is distributed under the GPL v3.0 license, which you can read about at `http://www.codeblocks.org/license/3`.

Author-created material
For Windows, Linux, and Mac. All the examples provided in this book are located in the Author directory on the CD and work with Windows, Linux, and Macintosh computers. These files contain all the sample code from the book.

During the writing of this book, a few of our beta readers reported some odd behavior from their anti-virus programs. It seems that some anti-virus programs don't like a few of the source-code files. Just what the anti-virus programs dislike about the source-code files is unclear, but we assure you that the source-code files are clean. In fact, you can view the content of most of these files using a simple text editor and see that there isn't anything to warrant concern.

The structure of the directory that holds the examples is `Author/BookX/ChapterYY`, where X is the book or chapter number.

Troubleshooting

We tried our best to compile programs that work on most computers with the minimum system requirements. Alas, your computer may differ, and some programs may not work properly for some reason.

The two likeliest problems are that your system doesn't have enough memory (RAM) for the programs you want to use, or you have other programs running that are affecting installation or running of a program. If you get an error message such as `Not enough memory` or `Setup cannot` continue, try one or more of the following suggestions and then try using the software again:

✦ **Turn off any anti-virus software running on your computer.** Installation programs sometimes mimic virus activity and may make your computer incorrectly believe that it's being infected by a virus.

✦ **Close all running programs.** The more programs you have running, the less memory is available to other programs. Installation programs typically update files and programs; so if you keep other programs running, installation may not work properly.

✦ **Have your local computer store add more RAM to your computer.** This is, admittedly, a drastic and somewhat expensive step. However, adding more memory can really help the speed of your computer and allow more programs to run at the same time.

Customer Care

If you have trouble with the CD-ROM, please call Wiley Product Technical Support at 800-762-2974. Outside the United States, call 317-572-3993. You can contact Wiley Product Technical Support also at http://support.wiley.com. Wiley Publishing will provide technical support only for installation and other general quality-control items. For technical support on the applications themselves, consult the program's vendor or author.

To place additional orders or to request information about other Wiley products, please call 877-762-2974.

Index

• E •

• *I* •

• *M* •

• U •

• *V* •

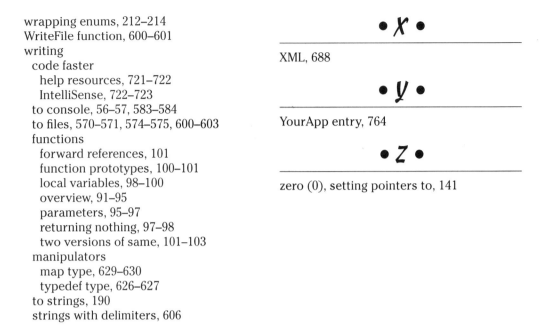

Wiley Publishing, Inc.
End-User License Agreement

READ THIS. You should carefully read these terms and conditions before opening the software packet(s) included with this book "Book". This is a license agreement "Agreement" between you and Wiley Publishing, Inc. "WPI". By opening the accompanying software packet(s), you acknowledge that you have read and accept the following terms and conditions. If you do not agree and do not want to be bound by such terms and conditions, promptly return the Book and the unopened software packet(s) to the place you obtained them for a full refund.

1. **License Grant.** WPI grants to you (either an individual or entity) a nonexclusive license to use one copy of the enclosed software program(s) (collectively, the "Software") solely for your own personal or business purposes on a single computer (whether a standard computer or a workstation component of a multi-user network). The Software is in use on a computer when it is loaded into temporary memory (RAM) or installed into permanent memory (hard disk, CD-ROM, or other storage device). WPI reserves all rights not expressly granted herein.

2. **Ownership.** WPI is the owner of all right, title, and interest, including copyright, in and to the compilation of the Software recorded on the physical packet included with this Book "Software Media". Copyright to the individual programs recorded on the Software Media is owned by the author or other authorized copyright owner of each program. Ownership of the Software and all proprietary rights relating thereto remain with WPI and its licensers.

3. **Restrictions on Use and Transfer.**

    a) You may only (i) make one copy of the Software for backup or archival purposes, or (ii) transfer the Software to a single hard disk, provided that you keep the original for backup or archival purposes. You may not (i) rent or lease the Software, (ii) copy or reproduce the Software through a LAN or other network system or through any computer subscriber system or bulletin-board system, or (iii) modify, adapt, or create derivative works based on the Software.

    (b) You may not reverse engineer, decompile, or disassemble the Software. You may transfer the Software and user documentation on a permanent basis, provided that the transferee agrees to accept the terms and conditions of this Agreement and you retain no copies. If the Software is an update or has been updated, any transfer must include the most recent update and all prior versions.

4. **Restrictions on Use of Individual Programs.** You must follow the individual requirements and restrictions detailed for each individual program in the "About the CD" appendix of this Book or on the Software Media. These limitations are also contained in the individual license agreements recorded on the Software Media. These limitations may include a requirement that after using the program for a specified period of time, the user must pay a registration fee or discontinue use. By opening the Software packet(s), you agree to abide by the licenses and restrictions for these individual programs that are detailed in the "About the CD" appendix and/or on the Software Media. None of the material on this Software Media or listed in this Book may ever be redistributed, in original or modified form, for commercial purposes.

5. **Limited Warranty.**

   (a) WPI warrants that the Software and Software Media are free from defects in materials and workmanship under normal use for a period of sixty (60) days from the date of purchase of this Book. If WPI receives notification within the warranty period of defects in materials or workmanship, WPI will replace the defective Software Media.

   (b) WPI AND THE AUTHOR(S) OF THE BOOK DISCLAIM ALL OTHER WARRANTIES, EXPRESS OR IMPLIED, INCLUDING WITHOUT LIMITATION IMPLIED WARRANTIES OF MERCHANTABILITY AND FITNESS FOR A PARTICULAR PURPOSE, WITH RESPECT TO THE SOFTWARE, THE PROGRAMS, THE SOURCE CODE CONTAINED THEREIN, AND/OR THE TECHNIQUES DESCRIBED IN THIS BOOK. WPI DOES NOT WARRANT THAT THE FUNCTIONS CONTAINED IN THE SOFTWARE WILL MEET YOUR REQUIREMENTS OR THAT THE OPERATION OF THE SOFTWARE WILL BE ERROR FREE.

   (c) This limited warranty gives you specific legal rights, and you may have other rights that vary from jurisdiction to jurisdiction.

6. **Remedies.**

   (a) WPI's entire liability and your exclusive remedy for defects in materials and workmanship shall be limited to replacement of the Software Media, which may be returned to WPI with a copy of your receipt at the following address: Software Media Fulfillment Department, Attn.: *C++ All-in-One,* 2nd Edition, Wiley Publishing, Inc., 10475 Crosspoint Blvd., Indianapolis, IN 46256, or call 1-800-762-2974. Please allow four to six weeks for delivery. This Limited Warranty is void if failure of the Software Media has resulted from accident, abuse, or misapplication. Any replacement Software Media will be warranted for the remainder of the original warranty period or thirty (30) days, whichever is longer.

   (b) In no event shall WPI or the author be liable for any damages whatsoever (including without limitation damages for loss of business profits, business interruption, loss of business information, or any other pecuniary loss) arising from the use of or inability to use the Book or the Software, even if WPI has been advised of the possibility of such damages.

   (c) Because some jurisdictions do not allow the exclusion or limitation of liability for consequential or incidental damages, the above limitation or exclusion may not apply to you.

7.U.S. Government Restricted Rights. Use, duplication, or disclosure of the Software for or on behalf of the United States of America, its agencies and/or instrumentalities "U.S. Government" is subject to restrictions as stated in paragraph (c)(1)(ii) of the Rights in Technical Data and Computer Software clause of DFARS 252.227-7013, or subparagraphs (c)(1) and (2) of the Commercial Computer Software - Restricted Rights clause at FAR 52.227-19, and in similar clauses in the NASA FAR supplement, as applicable.

8.General. This Agreement constitutes the entire understanding of the parties and revokes and supersedes all prior agreements, oral or written, between them and may not be modified or amended except in a writing signed by both parties hereto that specifically refers to this Agreement. This Agreement shall take precedence over any other documents that may be in conflict herewith. If any one or more provisions contained in this Agreement are held by any court or tribunal to be invalid, illegal, or otherwise unenforceable, each and every other provision shall remain in full force and effect.

GNU General Public License

Version 3, 29 June 2007

Copyright © 2007 Free Software Foundation, Inc. <http://fsf.org/>

Preamble

The GNU General Public License is a free, copyleft license for software and other kinds of works.

The licenses for most software and other practical works are designed to take away your freedom to share and change the works. By contrast, the GNU General Public License is intended to guarantee your freedom to share and change all versions of a program—to make sure it remains free software for all its users. We, the Free Software Foundation, use the GNU General Public License for most of our software; it applies also to any other work released this way by its authors. You can apply it to your programs, too.

When we speak of free software, we are referring to freedom, not price. Our General Public Licenses are designed to make sure that you have the freedom to distribute copies of free software (and charge for them if you wish), that you receive source code or can get it if you want it, that you can change the software or use pieces of it in new free programs, and that you know you can do these things.

To protect your rights, we need to prevent others from denying you these rights or asking you to surrender the rights. Therefore, you have certain responsibilities if you distribute copies of the software, or if you modify it: responsibilities to respect the freedom of others.

For example, if you distribute copies of such a program, whether gratis or for a fee, you must pass on to the recipients the same freedoms that you received. You must make sure that they, too, receive or can get the source code. And you must show them these terms so they know their rights.

Developers that use the GNU GPL protect your rights with two steps: (1) assert copyright on the software, and (2) offer you this License giving you legal permission to copy, distribute and/or modify it.

For the developers' and authors' protection, the GPL clearly explains that there is no warranty for this free software. For both users' and authors' sake, the GPL requires that modified versions be marked as changed, so that their problems will not be attributed erroneously to authors of previous versions.

Some devices are designed to deny users access to install or run modified versions of the software inside them, although the manufacturer can do so. This is fundamentally incompatible with the aim of protecting users' freedom to change the software. The systematic pattern of such abuse occurs in the area of products for individuals to use, which is precisely where it is most unacceptable. Therefore, we have designed this version of the GPL to prohibit the practice for those products. If such problems arise substantially in other domains, we stand ready to extend this provision to those domains in future versions of the GPL, as needed to protect the freedom of users.

Finally, every program is threatened constantly by software patents. States should not allow patents to restrict development and use of software on general-purpose computers, but in those that do, we wish to avoid the special danger that patents applied to a free program could make it effectively proprietary. To prevent this, the GPL assures that patents cannot be used to render the program non-free.

The precise terms and conditions for copying, distribution and modification follow.

Terms and Conditions

0. **Definitions.** "This License" refers to version 3 of the GNU General Public License. "Copyright" also means copyright-like laws that apply to other kinds of works, such as semiconductor masks. "The Program" refers to any copyrightable work licensed under this License. Each licensee is addressed as "you". "Licensees" and "recipients" may be individuals or organizations. To "modify" a work means to copy from or adapt all or part of the work in a fashion requiring copyright permission, other than the making of an exact copy. The resulting work is called a "modified version" of the earlier work or a work "based on" the earlier work. A "covered work" means either the unmodified Program or a work based on the Program.

   To "propagate" a work means to do anything with it that, without permission, would make you directly or secondarily liable for infringement under applicable copyright law, except executing it on a computer or modifying a private copy. Propagation includes copying, distribution (with or without modification), making available to the public, and in some countries other activities as well.

   To "convey" a work means any kind of propagation that enables other parties to make or receive copies. Mere interaction with a user through a computer network, with no transfer of a copy, is not conveying.

   An interactive user interface displays "Appropriate Legal Notices" to the extent that it includes a convenient and prominently visible feature that (1) displays an appropriate copyright notice, and (2) tells the user that there is no warranty for the work (except to the extent that warranties are provided), that licensees may convey the work under this License, and how to view a copy of this License. If the interface presents a list of user commands or options, such as a menu, a prominent item in the list meets this criterion.

1. **Source Code.** The "source code" for a work means the preferred form of the work for making modifications to it. "Object code" means any non-source form of a work. A "Standard Interface" means an interface that either is an official standard defined by a recognized standards body, or, in the case of interfaces specified for a particular programming language, one that is widely used among developers working in that language.

   The "System Libraries" of an executable work include anything, other than the work as a whole, that (a) is included in the normal form of packaging a Major Component, but which is not part of that Major Component, and (b) serves only to enable use of the work with that Major Component, or to implement a Standard Interface for which an implementation is available to the public in source code form. A "Major Component", in this context, means a major essential component (kernel, window system, and so on) of the specific operating system (if any) on which the executable work runs, or a compiler used to produce the work, or an object code interpreter used to run it.

   The "Corresponding Source" for a work in object code form means all the source code needed to generate, install, and (for an executable work) run the object code and to modify the work, including scripts to control those activities. However, it does not include the work's System

Libraries, or general-purpose tools or generally available free programs which are used unmodified in performing those activities but which are not part of the work. For example, Corresponding Source includes interface definition files associated with source files for the work, and the source code for shared libraries and dynamically linked subprograms that the work is specifically designed to require, such as by intimate data communication or control flow between those subprograms and other parts of the work.

The Corresponding Source need not include anything that users can regenerate automatically from other parts of the Corresponding Source.

The Corresponding Source for a work in source code form is that same work.

2. **Basic Permissions.** All rights granted under this License are granted for the term of copyright on the Program, and are irrevocable provided the stated conditions are met. This License explicitly affirms your unlimited permission to run the unmodified Program. The output from running a covered work is covered by this License only if the output, given its content, constitutes a covered work. This License acknowledges your rights of fair use or other equivalent, as provided by copyright law.

You may make, run and propagate covered works that you do not convey, without conditions so long as your license otherwise remains in force. You may convey covered works to others for the sole purpose of having them make modifications exclusively for you, or provide you with facilities for running those works, provided that you comply with the terms of this License in conveying all material for which you do not control copyright. Those thus making or running the covered works for you must do so exclusively on your behalf, under your direction and control, on terms that prohibit them from making any copies of your copyrighted material outside their relationship with you.

Conveying under any other circumstances is permitted solely under the conditions stated below. Sublicensing is not allowed; section 10 makes it unnecessary.

3. **Protecting Users' Legal Rights From Anti-Circumvention Law.** No covered work shall be deemed part of an effective technological measure under any applicable law fulfilling obligations under article 11 of the WIPO copyright treaty adopted on 20 December 1996, or similar laws prohibiting or restricting circumvention of such measures.

When you convey a covered work, you waive any legal power to forbid circumvention of technological measures to the extent such circumvention is effected by exercising rights under this License with respect to the covered work, and you disclaim any intention to limit operation or modification of the work as a means of enforcing, against the work's users, your or third parties' legal rights to forbid circumvention of technological measures.

4. **Conveying Verbatim Copies.** You may convey verbatim copies of the Program's source code as you receive it, in any medium, provided that you conspicuously and appropriately publish on each copy an appropriate copyright notice; keep intact all notices stating that this License and any non-permissive terms added in accord with section 7 apply to the code; keep intact all notices of the absence of any warranty; and give all recipients a copy of this License along with the Program.

You may charge any price or no price for each copy that you convey, and you may offer support or warranty protection for a fee.

5. **Conveying Modified Source Versions.** You may convey a work based on the Program, or the modifications to produce it from the Program, in the form of source code under the terms of section 4, provided that you also meet all of these conditions:

a) The work must carry prominent notices stating that you modified it, and giving a relevant date.

b) The work must carry prominent notices stating that it is released under this License and any conditions added under section 7. This requirement modifies the requirement in section 4 to "keep intact all notices".

c) You must license the entire work, as a whole, under this License to anyone who comes into possession of a copy. This License will therefore apply, along with any applicable section 7 additional terms, to the whole of the work, and all its parts, regardless of how they are packaged. This License gives no permission to license the work in any other way, but it does not invalidate such permission if you have separately received it.

d) If the work has interactive user interfaces, each must display Appropriate Legal Notices; however, if the Program has interactive interfaces that do not display Appropriate Legal Notices, your work need not make them do so.

A compilation of a covered work with other separate and independent works, which are not by their nature extensions of the covered work, and which are not combined with it such as to form a larger program, in or on a volume of a storage or distribution medium, is called an "aggregate" if the compilation and its resulting copyright are not used to limit the access or legal rights of the compilation's users beyond what the individual works permit. Inclusion of a covered work in an aggregate does not cause this License to apply to the other parts of the aggregate.

6. **Conveying Non-Source Forms.** You may convey a covered work in object code form under the terms of sections 4 and 5, provided that you also convey the machine-readable Corresponding Source under the terms of this License, in one of these ways:

a) Convey the object code in, or embodied in, a physical product (including a physical distribution medium), accompanied by the Corresponding Source fixed on a durable physical medium customarily used for software interchange.

b) Convey the object code in, or embodied in, a physical product (including a physical distribution medium), accompanied by a written offer, valid for at least three years and valid for as long as you offer spare parts or customer support for that product model, to give anyone who possesses the object code either (1) a copy of the Corresponding Source for all the software in the product that is covered by this License, on a durable physical medium customarily used for software interchange, for a price no more than your reasonable cost of physically performing this conveying of source, or (2) access to copy the Corresponding Source from a network server at no charge.

c) Convey individual copies of the object code with a copy of the written offer to provide the Corresponding Source. This alternative is allowed only occasionally and noncommercially, and only if you received the object code with such an offer, in accord with subsection 6b.

d) Convey the object code by offering access from a designated place (gratis or for a charge), and offer equivalent access to the Corresponding Source in the same way through the same place at no further charge. You need not require recipients to copy the Corresponding Source along with the object code. If the place to copy the object code is a network server, the Corresponding Source may be on a different server (operated by you or a third party) that supports equivalent copying facilities, provided you maintain clear directions next to the object code saying where to find the Corresponding Source. Regardless of what server hosts the Corresponding Source, you remain obligated to ensure that it is available for as long as needed to satisfy these requirements.

e) Convey the object code using peer-to-peer transmission, provided you inform other peers where the object code and Corresponding Source of the work are being offered to the general public at no charge under subsection 6d.

A separable portion of the object code, whose source code is excluded from the Corresponding Source as a System Library, need not be included in conveying the object code work.

A "User Product" is either (1) a "consumer product", which means any tangible personal property which is normally used for personal, family, or household purposes, or (2) anything designed or sold for incorporation into a dwelling. In determining whether a product is a consumer product, doubtful cases shall be resolved in favor of coverage. For a particular product received by a particular user, "normally used" refers to a typical or common use of that class of product, regardless of the status of the particular user or of the way in which the particular user actually uses, or expects or is expected to use, the product. A product is a consumer product regardless of whether the product has substantial commercial, industrial or non-consumer uses, unless such uses represent the only significant mode of use of the product.

"Installation Information" for a User Product means any methods, procedures, authorization keys, or other information required to install and execute modified versions of a covered work in that User Product from a modified version of its Corresponding Source. The information must suffice to ensure that the continued functioning of the modified object code is in no case prevented or interfered with solely because modification has been made.

If you convey an object code work under this section in, or with, or specifically for use in, a User Product, and the conveying occurs as part of a transaction in which the right of possession and use of the User Product is transferred to the recipient in perpetuity or for a fixed term (regardless of how the transaction is characterized), the Corresponding Source conveyed under this section must be accompanied by the Installation Information. But this requirement does not apply if neither you nor any third party retains the ability to install modified object code on the User Product (for example, the work has been installed in ROM).

The requirement to provide Installation Information does not include a requirement to continue to provide support service, warranty, or updates for a work that has been modified or installed by the recipient, or for the User Product in which it has been modified or installed. Access to a network may be denied when the modification itself materially and adversely affects the operation of the network or violates the rules and protocols for communication across the network.

Corresponding Source conveyed, and Installation Information provided, in accord with this section must be in a format that is publicly documented (and with an implementation available to the public in source code form), and must require no special password or key for unpacking, reading or copying.

7. **Additional Terms.** "Additional permissions" are terms that supplement the terms of this License by making exceptions from one or more of its conditions. Additional permissions that are applicable to the entire Program shall be treated as though they were included in this License, to the extent that they are valid under applicable law. If additional permissions apply only to part of the Program, that part may be used separately under those permissions, but the entire Program remains governed by this License without regard to the additional permissions.

When you convey a copy of a covered work, you may at your option remove any additional permissions from that copy, or from any part of it. (Additional permissions may be written to require their own removal in certain cases when you modify the work.) You may place additional permissions on material, added by you to a covered work, for which you have or can give appropriate copyright permission.

Notwithstanding any other provision of this License, for material you add to a covered work, you may (if authorized by the copyright holders of that material) supplement the terms of this License with terms:

a) Disclaiming warranty or limiting liability differently from the terms of sections 15 and 16 of this License; or

b) Requiring preservation of specified reasonable legal notices or author attributions in that material or in the Appropriate Legal Notices displayed by works containing it; or

c) Prohibiting misrepresentation of the origin of that material, or requiring that modified versions of such material be marked in reasonable ways as different from the original version; or

d) Limiting the use for publicity purposes of names of licensors or authors of the material; or

e) Declining to grant rights under trademark law for use of some trade names, trademarks, or service marks; or

f) Requiring indemnification of licensors and authors of that material by anyone who conveys the material (or modified versions of it) with contractual assumptions of liability to the recipient, for any liability that these contractual assumptions directly impose on those licensors and authors.

All other non-permissive additional terms are considered "further restrictions" within the meaning of section 10. If the Program as you received it, or any part of it, contains a notice stating that it is governed by this License along with a term that is a further restriction, you may remove that term. If a license document contains a further restriction but permits relicensing or conveying under this License, you may add to a covered work material governed by the terms of that license document, provided that the further restriction does not survive such relicensing or conveying.

If you add terms to a covered work in accord with this section, you must place, in the relevant source files, a statement of the additional terms that apply to those files, or a notice indicating where to find the applicable terms.

Additional terms, permissive or non-permissive, may be stated in the form of a separately written license, or stated as exceptions; the above requirements apply either way.

8. **Termination.** You may not propagate or modify a covered work except as expressly provided under this License. Any attempt otherwise to propagate or modify it is void, and will automatically terminate your rights under this License (including any patent licenses granted under the third paragraph of section 11).

However, if you cease all violation of this License, then your license from a particular copyright holder is reinstated (a) provisionally, unless and until the copyright holder explicitly and finally terminates your license, and (b) permanently, if the copyright holder fails to notify you of the violation by some reasonable means prior to 60 days after the cessation.

Moreover, your license from a particular copyright holder is reinstated permanently if the copyright holder notifies you of the violation by some reasonable means, this is the first time you have received notice of violation of this License (for any work) from that copyright holder, and you cure the violation prior to 30 days after your receipt of the notice.

Termination of your rights under this section does not terminate the licenses of parties who have received copies or rights from you under this License. If your rights have been terminated and not permanently reinstated, you do not qualify to receive new licenses for the same material under section 10.

9. **Acceptance Not Required for Having Copies.** You are not required to accept this License in order to receive or run a copy of the Program. Ancillary propagation of a covered work occurring solely as a consequence of using peer-to-peer transmission to receive a copy likewise does not require acceptance. However, nothing other than this License grants you permission to propagate or modify any covered work. These actions infringe copyright if you do not accept this License. Therefore, by modifying or propagating a covered work, you indicate your acceptance of this License to do so.

10. **Automatic Licensing of Downstream Recipients.** Each time you convey a covered work, the recipient automatically receives a license from the original licensors, to run, modify and propagate that work, subject to this License. You are not responsible for enforcing compliance by third parties with this License.

An "entity transaction" is a transaction transferring control of an organization, or substantially all assets of one, or subdividing an organization, or merging organizations. If propagation of a covered work results from an entity transaction, each party to that transaction who receives a copy of the work also receives whatever licenses to the work the party's predecessor in interest had or could give under the previous paragraph, plus a right to possession of the Corresponding Source of the work from the predecessor in interest, if the predecessor has it or can get it with reasonable efforts.

You may not impose any further restrictions on the exercise of the rights granted or affirmed under this License. For example, you may not impose a license fee, royalty, or other charge for exercise of rights granted under this License, and you may not initiate litigation (including a cross-claim or counterclaim in a lawsuit) alleging that any patent claim is infringed by making, using, selling, offering for sale, or importing the Program or any portion of it.

11. **Patents.** A "contributor" is a copyright holder who authorizes use under this License of the Program or a work on which the Program is based. The work thus licensed is called the contributor's "contributor version".

A contributor's "essential patent claims" are all patent claims owned or controlled by the contributor, whether already acquired or hereafter acquired, that would be infringed by some manner, permitted by this License, of making, using, or selling its contributor version, but do not include claims that would be infringed only as a consequence of further modification of the contributor version. For purposes of this definition, "control" includes the right to grant patent sublicenses in a manner consistent with the requirements of this License.

Each contributor grants you a non-exclusive, worldwide, royalty-free patent license under the contributor's essential patent claims, to make, use, sell, offer for sale, import and otherwise run, modify and propagate the contents of its contributor version.

In the following three paragraphs, a "patent license" is any express agreement or commitment, however denominated, not to enforce a patent (such as an express permission to practice a patent or covenant not to sue for patent infringement). To "grant" such a patent license to a party means to make such an agreement or commitment not to enforce a patent against the party.

If you convey a covered work, knowingly relying on a patent license, and the Corresponding Source of the work is not available for anyone to copy, free of charge and under the terms of this License, through a publicly available network server or other readily accessible means, then you must either (1) cause the Corresponding Source to be so available, or (2) arrange to deprive yourself of the benefit of the patent license for this particular work, or (3) arrange, in a manner consistent with the requirements of this License, to extend the patent license to downstream recipients. "Knowingly relying" means you have actual knowledge that, but for the patent license, your conveying the covered work in a country, or your recipient's use of the covered work in a country, would infringe one or more identifiable patents in that country that you have reason to believe are valid.

If, pursuant to or in connection with a single transaction or arrangement, you convey, or propagate by procuring conveyance of, a covered work, and grant a patent license to some of the parties receiving the covered work authorizing them to use, propagate, modify or convey a specific copy of the covered work, then the patent license you grant is automatically extended to all recipients of the covered work and works based on it.

A patent license is "discriminatory" if it does not include within the scope of its coverage, prohibits the exercise of, or is conditioned on the non-exercise of one or more of the rights that are specifically granted under this License. You may not convey a covered work if you are a party to an arrangement with a third party that is in the business of distributing software, under which you make payment to the third party based on the extent of your activity of conveying the work, and under which the third party grants, to any of the parties who would receive the covered work from you, a discriminatory patent license (a) in connection with copies of the covered work conveyed by you (or copies made from those copies), or (b) primarily for and in connection with specific products or compilations that contain the covered work, unless you entered into that arrangement, or that patent license was granted, prior to 28 March 2007.

Nothing in this License shall be construed as excluding or limiting any implied license or other defenses to infringement that may otherwise be available to you under applicable patent law.

12. **No Surrender of Others' Freedom.** If conditions are imposed on you (whether by court order, agreement or otherwise) that contradict the conditions of this License, they do not excuse you from the conditions of this License. If you cannot convey a covered work so as to satisfy simultaneously your obligations under this License and any other pertinent obligations, then as a consequence you may not convey it at all. For example, if you agree to terms that obligate you to collect a royalty for further conveying from those to whom you convey the Program, the only way you could satisfy both those terms and this License would be to refrain entirely from conveying the Program.

13. **Use with the GNU Affero General Public License.** Notwithstanding any other provision of this License, you have permission to link or combine any covered work with a work licensed under version 3 of the GNU Affero General Public License into a single combined work, and to convey the resulting work. The terms of this License will continue to apply to the part which is the covered work, but the special requirements of the GNU Affero General Public License, section 13, concerning interaction through a network will apply to the combination as such.

14. **Revised Versions of this License.** The Free Software Foundation may publish revised and/or new versions of the GNU General Public License from time to time. Such new versions will be similar in spirit to the present version, but may differ in detail to address new problems or concerns.

    Each version is given a distinguishing version number. If the Program specifies that a certain numbered version of the GNU General Public License "or any later version" applies to it, you have the option of following the terms and conditions either of that numbered version or of any later version published by the Free Software Foundation. If the Program does not specify a version number of the GNU General Public License, you may choose any version ever published by the Free Software Foundation.

    If the Program specifies that a proxy can decide which future versions of the GNU General Public License can be used, that proxy's public statement of acceptance of a version permanently authorizes you to choose that version for the Program.

    Later license versions may give you additional or different permissions. However, no additional obligations are imposed on any author or copyright holder as a result of your choosing to follow a later version.

15. **Disclaimer of Warranty.** THERE IS NO WARRANTY FOR THE PROGRAM, TO THE EXTENT PERMITTED BY APPLICABLE LAW. EXCEPT WHEN OTHERWISE STATED IN WRITING THE COPYRIGHT HOLDERS AND/OR OTHER PARTIES PROVIDE THE PROGRAM "AS IS" WITHOUT WARRANTY OF ANY KIND, EITHER EXPRESSED OR IMPLIED, INCLUDING, BUT NOT LIMITED TO, THE IMPLIED WARRANTIES OF MERCHANTABILITY AND FITNESS FOR A PARTICULAR PURPOSE. THE ENTIRE RISK AS TO THE QUALITY AND PERFORMANCE OF THE PROGRAM IS WITH YOU. SHOULD THE PROGRAM PROVE DEFECTIVE, YOU ASSUME THE COST OF ALL NECESSARY SERVICING, REPAIR OR CORRECTION.

16. **Limitation of Liability.** IN NO EVENT UNLESS REQUIRED BY APPLICABLE LAW OR AGREED TO IN WRITING WILL ANY COPYRIGHT HOLDER, OR ANY OTHER PARTY WHO MODIFIES AND/OR CONVEYS THE PROGRAM AS PERMITTED ABOVE, BE LIABLE TO YOU FOR DAMAGES, INCLUDING ANY GENERAL, SPECIAL, INCIDENTAL OR CONSEQUENTIAL DAMAGES ARISING OUT OF THE USE OR INABILITY TO USE THE PROGRAM (INCLUDING BUT NOT LIMITED TO LOSS OF DATA OR DATA BEING RENDERED INACCURATE OR LOSSES SUSTAINED BY YOU OR THIRD PARTIES OR A FAILURE OF THE PROGRAM TO OPERATE WITH ANY OTHER PROGRAMS), EVEN IF SUCH HOLDER OR OTHER PARTY HAS BEEN ADVISED OF THE POSSIBILITY OF SUCH DAMAGES.

17. **Interpretation of Sections 15 and 16.** If the disclaimer of warranty and limitation of liability provided above cannot be given local legal effect according to their terms, reviewing courts shall apply local law that most closely approximates an absolute waiver of all civil liability in connection with the Program, unless a warranty or assumption of liability accompanies a copy of the Program in return for a fee.

 END OF TERMS AND CONDITIONS